INNER ASIAN FRONTIERS
OF CHINA

BY

OWEN LATTIMORE

BEACON PRESS   BOSTON

To
My Father
DAVID LATTIMORE

PART I. THE HISTORICAL GEOGRAPHY OF THE GREAT WALL

CONTENTS

CONTENTS

CONTENTS

CONTENTS

PART III. THE AGE OF NATIONAL STATES

CONTENTS

PART IV. THE IMPERIAL AGE

CONTENTS

CONTENTS

LIST OF MAPS

LIST OF MAPS

INTRODUCTION TO SECOND EDITION OF
INNER ASIAN FRONTIERS OF CHINA

It is now eleven years since this book was first published. The continued demand for it, especially from younger scholars working in the same field, justifies a new edition—even though it is naturally, after eleven years, no longer the book that I should like to publish if I could assemble all the material afresh and rewrite it from the beginning. For one thing, the resources that can be drawn on now are much richer than those available to me eleven years ago.

Even so, however, and even without the revision of faults and the filling in of gaps, the republication of *Inner Asian Frontiers of China* at this time may be of help especially to the younger scholars whose systematic training is far superior to mine but who, owing to the conditions of the time, are unable to travel widely and freely as I did when gathering so much of the material that went to the making of this book. The late Ellis H. Minns, speaking of *Scythians and Greeks* (Cambridge, 1913), his great pioneer study of a frontier between an urban and agricultural society and its fringing steppe tribes, once said, "Yes, that was a good book—badly out of date now, which proves that it was a good book." He meant that he did not regret not having written the last word on his subject, but was content instead that by what he had written he had helped others to make his own work out of date.

It is my hope that the republication of *Inner Asian Frontiers of China,* with all its imperfections, may still be useful in some such way as this. The time has perhaps not yet come to attempt a new book on Inner Asia as a whole. On the other hand, there is a present need to survey some of the directions in which new work could profitably be pushed. For more than a decade of war and cold war, communication between scholars in different countries has been slowed down and at times almost completely suspended. Even in Western countries there is often a delay of some years before scholars begin to make free use of each other's materials,[1] and the lag in Western countries, in making use of materials published in Chinese, Japanese, and Russian is much greater.

This unevenness in the pushing forward of Inner Asian studies will be largely overcome in the next few years. On the one hand, there has been a very rapid increase—especially in the United States—in the number of scholars qualified to work with Chinese, Japanese, and Russian materials; though unfortunately there has not been a similarly rapid increase in Mongol, Turkish, and Iranian studies, or in the study of the Inner Asian frontiers of India, Pakistan, and Afghanistan. On the other hand, the political consequences of the Second World War have enlarged and sharply defined the geographical frame within which Inner Asia should be studied, making clear both the problems that should be taken up and the manner in which research in the different sectors of the geographical area should be coordinated.

In first publishing this book I emphasized an alternation between periods of continental and maritime development in the world history of the Old World (pages 4 and 5). Prior to the Age of Columbus the most important activities in the long and slow evolution of civilized man were within the great land masses of the Old World. It is true that the movement of people, the spread of trade, and the interaction of cultures by sea began in very ancient times; but all this, as I then described it, was no more than a "fringe of maritime activity." The main process of history was continental, and its phases in Asia, Africa, and Europe were not so sharply differentiated from each other as they have since come to seem in retrospect.

The Age of Columbus was revolutionary in the changes that it brought about. The maritime activity of mankind began to deflect and even subordinate developments within the great land masses. Old World and New World were combined in a manner overwhelmingly more significant than anything that had resulted from primitive migrations from Asia into North and South America and Stone Age navigation in the Pacific. Before Columbus, an Alexander could thrust from the Mediterranean into India; an Attila could fight his way from the South Russian steppe into France; the Mongol armies could range from China to Poland and the Adriatic—but while these military activities could change the rule of kingdoms, the scope of economic activity was much more constricted. There was no form of ancient conquest that could truly integrate Asia and Europe. After Columbus, the reach of economic integration began to rival and even exceed that of military integration. Even a small sailing ship could in one voyage carry from Canton to London more cargo, in a shorter time and at a higher profit, than could be moved by a succession of caravans plodding from ancient or medieval China to the markets of the Mediterranean. Caravan trade, moreover, dealt in treasures and rarities which contributed to the ostentation of courts but did not alter the character of societies. With oceanic navigation there began the bulk transportation of raw materials, the processing of which transformed the economic activities and the social and political structure of whole nations.

This transformation was a multiple process. It included the building of "accumulative" colonial empires, separated by oceans from the countries ruling them, of which the British Empire was the type; the growth of "incorporative" empires, by the acquisition of contiguous territories within the same land mass, of which the Tsarist Russian Empire was the major exemplar[2] and the rise of new states, especially in North and South America, characterized by large territory, surplus food-producing capacity, wide margin for population growth, and varied raw materials for industrial development.

By the opening of the twentieth century these post-Columbian developments had gone so far that they provided the conditions for a new period of world history. One way of describing the new conditions is to say that the ability of a few states in the nineteenth century to dominate the world in power politics by the exploitation of steam-driven oceanic shipping, backed up by navies representing an immense investment of capital (subject, moreover, to rapid obsolescence), but only a small commitment of manpower, was beginning to be balanced by the growth of vast continental states. There were differences among the great continental states, but also resemblances. The United States, to take one example, was a great continental state with a great navy; Russia, to take another, was a comparable continental state, but with a navy of only minor importance; but the two types resembled each other in that they were both immune to the type of naval coercion, backed up by only small land forces, that had dominated the power-calculations of the nineteenth century.

When the First World War ended, these new conditions were foreshadowed. West of the Pacific and east of Europe "Great Britain, the United States, and Japan were left deadlocked in an uneasy balance; but at the same time from under the feet of the Western world and Japan there came the rumbling of an earthquake, as the Soviet Union shook itself out of the ruins of the Russian Empire. As a result of that landslip, the center of gravity of the land mass lying between the Atlantic and Pacific shifted from somewhere near the Rhine to somewhere near the Urals." (See below, Chapter I, p. 7.)

With the end of the Second World War the center of gravity in this vast area shifted again, from the Urals toward the Inner Asian frontier. The importance of naval power has further declined. This decline has been mitigated by the rapid rise of air power, which can be used in association with naval power; but, on the other hand, air power can also be used in association with land power. In the Second World War neither unchallenged supremacy in local naval power nor overwhelming superiority in local air power enabled Japan to subdue China, and with the end of the war it should have become plain that China—like India, Indonesia, Pakistan, Argentina, and Brazil—has been added to the countries which, combining large area, large population, and great diversified natural resources for internal industrial development, can no longer be dominated by across-the-ocean projection of either naval or naval-and-air power.

American long-range thinking on the problems of the new and still-changing distribution of world power is still dangerously clouded by a lingering tradition of across-the-ocean thinking, a tradition that struck deep roots in the nineteenth century. America's ability either to fight or to trade by a combination of mobility across the oceans and in the air is a factor of major and continuing importance, but American policy should not be concentrated on the oceans and the air to an extent that involves the neglect of other factors of rising importance. To assume that the security of Alaska can be guaranteed by a policy of nondevelopment and remote control by air and sea is as illusory as to assume that the structure of government or the methods of economic development in China can be manipulated from offshore positions in Japan, Okinawa, and Formosa.

To a certain extent it may be possible to "contain" China from the seaward side—but that is all. "Air and naval bases on Formosa would menace the coast of China even if they did not control it; but even the most strongly fortified bases on Formosa would in fact rest on the control of the sea necessary for planes and warships. A self-contained aviation industry could never be developed on Formosa because control of the sea would still be necessary to bring to the factories most of the metal and other necessary war materials. In the long run—and here it does not matter whether we speak in terms of one decade or several decades—China's own aviation industry will develop deep in the western hinterland, where all or most of the resources for a complete aviation industry are available, including oil. In the long run, it would be impossible for sea-supported air power, based on Formosa and projected toward China, to challenge the land-supported air power of China, based on secure industries and communications in the deep hinterland and projected toward the coast and Formosa."[3] In the same way, the ultimate balance of power between Russia and Japan "is not a question of the exposed position of Vladivostok. It is a question of the deep Siberian bases from which Soviet power could defy any such challenge, and project a far more formidable counter-challenge."[4]

Mere mention of the changing distribution of major centers of power and development in the world and the changing relationships between them is enough to establish the enhanced significance of the Inner Asian frontier—not only that between Russia and China, but those between Russia and Korea, Russia and Afghanistan (closely approaching the India-Pakistan frontier in the Pamirs), Russia and Iran, and Russia and Turkey. On one side of this linked frontier from the Black Sea to the Yellow Sea, from Turkey to Korea, there is only one sovereignty, the collective sovereignty of the Soviet Union. Strategic policy, political directives, and programs of economic development can easily be coordinated. Even in research, the Russians can easily organize an integrated approach.[5] On the other side of the frontier there are a number of separate sovereignties, and the several countries concerned are either hostile to each other or have little to do with each other.

In view of the increased and still rapidly increasing importance of the Inner Asian frontiers, it can be said that in a way we have returned to the age of Marco Polo, when Inner Asia was a pivotal area of military power and when communication by land between the Mediterranean and China (or, as in the journeys of William of Rubruck and Pian de Carpini, between South Russia and China) was more important than the coast-hugging trade between Arabia and China. We have not, however, returned to the age of Marco Polo in the sense that we have turned our backs on the age that opened with Columbus. The true problem of our time is to reach, as quickly as we can, an accurate understanding of the relation to each other of the "Columbus" and the "Marco Polo" factors that by their interaction shape the conditions under which we live. To do so, it is important to push forward our studies of Inner Asia until they match in depth and maturity our studies of the Asian countries and regions that we reach by ocean routes and enter through seaports.

During the war years, and the years of continuing dislocation since the war, work on these problems has suffered, as I have already pointed out, from lack of communication between scholars in different countries. Nevertheless, much important work has been done.

Work either in the field or in the library was especially difficult for Chinese scholars. As an indication of the rate of output (for Mongolia alone, not for the whole of the Chinese sector of the Inner Asian frontier), Mr. Chang Chih-yi includes in his selective and critical list only some seventeen books and articles by Chinese authors for the war and civil war years from 1937 to 1950.[6] The quality of these Chinese studies varies a great deal. Some are valuable, some worth little. Perhaps the thing most worth noting about them, however, from the point of view of the future development of American studies dealing with Mongolia, is that nothing or practically nothing has even been translated from them into English or any other Western language.

The output of "ideological" literature, as might be expected, did not cease during these years. Discussion and controversy dealt principally with relations between the Chinese and the minority peoples of China, and ranged from extreme theories of the desirability of the most rapid absorption and sinization of the non-Chinese by the Chinese to theories of cultural and territorial autonomy, combined with stringent political controls and safeguards, modeled on Soviet theories and practices.[7] It is worth comment in passing that Chiang Kai-shek, though strongly associated with the policy of identifying non-Chinese minorities as mere subdivisions of the Chinese people (see his *China's Destiny,* authorized version, New York, 1947), went so far in his speech of August 24, 1945, recognizing the independence of Outer Mongolia, as to recognize also the theoretical right of secession of other non-Chinese minorities.[8]

Work in the field, though difficult in Free China, did not entirely cease, but most of it dealt with Southwest China, including the Burma frontier and the Tibetan border province of Sikang, on the frontiers of Ssuchuan and Yunnan[9] Outstanding work both in the field and in the library was done by Li An-che and his wife, Yü Shih-yü, much of whose work was based at the Tibetan frontier monastery of Labrang.[10] The devoted attempts of Dr. and Mrs. Li to promote better relations between the Chinese and their non-Chinese frontier minorities, especially the Tibetans, illustrate the tragedy of the non-Marxist Chinese liberals in the years of the decline and fall of the Kuomintang. During the war years their work was seriously hampered by the authoritarian "thought control" of the Kuomintang. After the war they visited the United States and Britain to study the work of their Western colleagues in anthropology and sociology. They then returned to the West China Frontier Research Institute, connected with West China Union University at Chengtu, one of the great internationally supported Christian centers of education in China. There they remained when Ssuchuan province fell to the Chinese Communists—and it has since been reported that the political and cultural part of the program by which the Chinese Communists have been trying to win over the Tibetans is based on the approach worked out by Dr. Li, but rejected by the Kuomintang.[11]

Some important work was also done by Chinese who remained in Japanese-occupied China during the war, including, in studies in the field of frontier history, the publishing of two collections of Chinese books that had been prohibited or expurgated under Manchu rule in the eighteenth century because of the manner in which they discussed the Manchus and other "barbarians."[12] This recovered material, from long-hidden manuscripts or from copies that had been preserved in Japan includes maps. It is ironic to think that it also includes such material as a treatise on "ninety-nine schemes" for destroying the Manchus, and that such expressions of the Chinese hatred of earlier invaders should have been made available again to scholars under the auspices of the temporary conquerors of the coastal provinces in the twentieth century.

Foreigners resident in Peking continued to publish throughout this period contributions of great value to frontier studies. The list is headed by the great Belgian Mongolist, Father Antoine Mostaert, whose dictionaries of the Monguor dialect (with Father A. de Smedt), and of Ordos Mongol, exactly transcribed and magnificently edited collections of folklore, and contributions to history, sociology, and bibliography have enhanced our ability to understand the whole southern, Chinese frontier side of the Mongol area to an extent that cannot be described, and certainly cannot be adequately praised, in a short notice.[13] Among other Belgian missionary scholars, Father Paul Serruys has published comparative notes on the Ordos folklore collected by Father Mostaert;[14] Father Henry Serruys has worked in both the Chinese and the Mongol regions of the provinces of Suiyuan and Chahar, and Father Grootaers initiated studies for a linguistic atlas of China which, in the regions of ancient "barbarian" penetration and acculturation in North China, should have great historical significance in revealing traces of "tidemarks" of invasion.[15]

For the period of the Ming dynasty (1368-1643), for which Western studies of Chinese-Mongol relations are weak, Dr. Rudolf Loewenthal translated Pokotilov's Russian work of 1893, and Dr. Wolfgang Franke added a valuable supplement.[16] Dr. Walther Heissig was able to make field trips in southern and eastern Inner Mongolia, and published an important study of the *Bolur Erike,* the Mongol chronicle by Rasipungsug (1774-75), including the tenth book, which is missing in the printed Mongol edition (Kalgan, 1941).[17] Heissig's study throws light on the tampering with Mongol documents that accompanied the Ch'ien Lung "inquisition" which expurgated the Chinese historical material dealing with "barbarian" history.[18] Dr. Heissig is now at work on Mongol material dealing with the spread of Lamaism and the persecution of shamanism in eastern Mongolia. Mention should also be made of the work of Walter Fuchs, a leading scholar in Manchu and Chinese, especially his publications on the Jesuit Atlas and the "Mongol Atlas" of China.[19]

By far the most important historical activity in China recently, however, has been a wide-ranging process, among Chinese scholars, of re-examining every aspect of Chinese history and re-evaluating the entire record of the evolution of society and the state in China. The frontier aspects of Chinese history form only a part of the whole process of examination and criticism, and it is too early to attempt to assess current historical controversies and new theories in terms of their significance for Western scholarship; but of the importance of this overhauling of history and historiography by Chinese historians there can be no doubt.

The process began after the Chinese Revolution of 1911, when the fall of the Manchu dynasty left Chinese scholars free to re-examine and to discuss with impunity the history not only of the Manchus but of all their previous "barbarian" invaders and conquerors. It was speeded up by a new generation of historians of whom Hu Shih, later Ambassador to the United States, may be taken as an example; men who knew the old Chinese methodology of criticism of texts and comparison of sources, and had added to this the methodology of Western history. It gained still further momentum, and took a sharper tone of controversy, with the rapid spread of Marxist ideas and techniques in the 1920's. Ideas like historical materialsm and class conflict were often taken over in a superficial way and not really absorbed into the thinking of those who used them; but new ideas, even if they are used as mere catchwords, frequently have a stimulating effect in promoting a fresh examination of old facts. Certainly in China, especially during the 1930's, Marxist influences of this secondary kind could be found in the writing of men who did not think of themselves as Marxists, were not classed as Marxists by others, and had no difficulty in publishing their work under the Kuomintang regime.

Yet another impetus was added by the discovery of new archaeological material throwing light on the early history of China at a stage that many had called legendary.[20] The revelation of the firm outlines of reality in what had been considered dim and mythical ages gave added enthusiasm to the search for old facts, especially those bearing on social and economic history, that had been embedded for centuries in the traditional historical sources but had long been treated in a strictly conventional way; these old facts were now subjected to fresh examination and new treatment, with results often giving the effect of original and surprising discovery. There was an extreme contrast between this

sense of discovery and the growing stagnation of the Kuomintang and the intellectual regimentation that it imposed
on universities and intellectuals. In combined response to
the conditions of wartime China, which invited bold and
novel thinking, and reaction against increasing repression
by unthinking bureaucrats and party zealots, men of robust
mind tended either to invent their own individual "radical"
interpretations of China's historical and contemporary
problems, thus defying the unimaginative orthodoxy of the
Kuomintang but at the same time baffling its "thought
police" by not identifying themselves with the Marxist
opposition on the suppression of which the authoritarian
controls were concentrated ; or else, as a gesture of defiance
against the orthodoxy that the government and the Kuomintang sought to impose on them by mandate, they declared themselves volunteer adherents of the Marxist dogma
and the political party that was bent on winning enough
power to enforce it as an authoritarian rule of thought.

These developments, which rapidly evolved toward a
climax in war and civil war China, account for an "intellectual climate" in the early years of Communist rule that
would otherwise be puzzling. The first historian to be recognized by the new regime as worthy of setting standards
of historical interpretation for colleges and universities
throughout China is Fan Wen-lan, a scholar who instead
of coming up through Communist Party ranks declared
himself a convert to Marxism only rather late in life, after
he had won recognition as an historian along orthodox lines.
He is the chief author of a work which is the nearest
approach to an "official'" history under the new government, being published under the auspices of the Chinese
Historical Research Association under the double title of
General History of China and Modern History of China.[21]
Of him and his work Professor Teng Ssu-yü has written
that he "has received too much training to be very radical,"
and that in his treatment of ancient history (in which

Marxist orthodoxy is normally apt to assert itself with a special severity), "he is much more conservative than Professor Ku Chieh-kang"[22]—Professor Ku being an un-Marxist scholar of orthodox training, formerly professor at the great Christian University of Yenching, an authority on early Chinese history, founder of *Yu Kung*, a journal of historical geography which attained a deserved preeminence in the 1930's, and a man conservative in his cast of mind but at the same time a bold explorer of new kinds of historical evidence, especially in the form of archaeological material.[23]

Considerations of this kind suggest that the time has not yet come to attempt a definition of "the" Chinese view of Chinese history; but they also suggest that this is a time when Western historians should follow more closely than they have in the past contemporary Chinese discussions of history, including Chinese views of historical geography and frontier history. The historians whose views are proclaimed to be authoritative in the early years of a rapidly developing revolutionary movement are more likely to lose their eminence in a few years than to retain it; but for this very reason the study of the successive stages of a revolutionary interpretation of history may offer an especially revealing insight into the character of the revolution itself.

In Japan, during the years of imperialistic control over Manchuria after 1931 and all-out invasion of China after 1937, Inner Asian frontier studies had a readily understandable importance. The western, Mongol margin of Manchuria and the Inner Mongolian frontier of North China were flank positions of great strategic significance. The Japanese work of these years often shows high competence in the fields of geography, history, sociology, economics, and the analysis of religious institutions, yoked to thoroughly practical purposes of imperialistic expansion.[24] Detailed research was done on the historical derivation and present distribution of the Mongol tribal groups; on the relation of the administration unit to the territorial unit; on the modification of the society by the combination of administrative practice, territorial division, the nature of economic activity (pastoralism or farming), and trade; on the Lama Buddhist religion, monastic organization, and monastic administration over territorial units of jurisdiction; on the history and impact of Chinese colonization; on the history of Mongol, Manchu, and pre-Manchu relations with China, and later with the Manchu Empire, Russia, and Japan; and finally on modern Mongol nationalism. The studies of nationalism are of great but limited value; studies of this kind could not offend the prevailing policy of Japanese expansionism, and consequently could not be done from within the Mongol society, but had to aim at fostering Japanese-approved forms of nationalism.

As I am unable to consult Japanese sources myself, my colleague, Professor Arthur F. Wright of Stanford has kindly drawn my attention to two important publications which review Japanese work of the war years and discuss the present state of Japanese studies in the Inner Asian field. The first of these is the *Annual of historical studies* for 1949, in which Yamada Nobuo (pp. 152-161) discusses Inner Asia and Kanda Nobuo (pp. 161-166) Manchuria and Korea. According to this review vast numbers of collectanea and reference works were put out and a great quantity of Western work translated, giving a considerable stimulus to Japanese scholarship. Various specialized research organizations brought out their own publications, among which the field investigations of the South Manchuria Railway Inquiry Section are considered outstanding, notably its report on the society and the economy of Inner Mongolia. The three major research trends of the post-war years are listed as problems of relationships between herdsmen and farmers on the Mongolian-Chinese frontier; problems of Yuan Dynasty history; and studies of oasis areas in Inner Asia.

The second reference is to the *Journal of historical Science,* 59, No. 5, May, 1950, in which there is a survey article on "Retrospects and prospects" of historical studies in Japan in 1949. The Chinese and Japanese sections of this survey are to be summarized by Mr. Philip Yampolsky in a forthcoming issue of *Far Eastern quarterly.*[25]

Japanese work dealing with Outer Mongolia and with Inner Mongolia west of the area of penetration by Japanese arms and agents is of less value; but one interesting example of the Japanese treatment of the subject of Outer Mongolia is readily accessible, indicating the amount and kind of information available and the political approach.[26] An item to be noted in connection with the period of Japanese activity in Mongolia is a pamphlet or small book that appeared in Russian, printed in Japanese-occupied Shanghai, under the title *Red Hand Over Mongolia,* by a Captain Bimba.[27] It told the story of an officer of the Outer Mongolian Army who deserted to the Japanese in 1938. In terms of psychological warfare, the pamphlet exactly fitted the Japanese specifications for Mongol Nationalism, being even more anti-Russian than anti-Soviet. It was later reported among Mongols that this "deserter" was shot by the Japanese as a spy who had been sent over to the Japanese side under pretense of being a deserter. But according to the pamphlet he was killed in action on the Japanese side in the course of fighting on the Manchurian-Mongolian frontier in 1939.

Western work on the frontier regions of China during the long period from the late 1930's to the present has inevitably been based more on research in the library than in the field. During the earlier part of the period, however, the Germans were able to work in Japanese-controlled Manchuria and Japanese-occupied North China.[28] One product of these conditions was a serviceable one-volume geography of Manchuria. As might be expected, it is "geopolitical" in conception — a geography designed for use under the "strong" government of a conquering power; but it is the most inclusive geography of Manchuria in any Western language, based on extensive field observation and a thorough use of library resources.[29]

In the main, however, the Western work of this period is historical and philological. Of special value is Eberhard's *History of China*,[30] the work of a scholar with unusual qualifications, primarily a sociologist, with excellent command of Chinese sources and field experience in China, followed by years of residence in Turkey. Eberhard's sociological interest, reinforced by looking back to China while working in Turkey, has resulted in the only one-volume history of China that is strongly sociological in its review of each successive historical period. It also devotes much more attention to frontier history than most compendious histories of China, which normally gravitate toward the "Chinese" rather than toward the "barbarian" factors in Chinese history. It is a great misfortune that the author makes a number of mistakes, especially in his later chapters, which will distract attention from the really solid merits of his work— especially his fascinating treatment of the interpenetration of Turks and "barbarized" Chinese in the early Middle Ages, comparable to the barbarization of the later Roman Empire from its continental frontiers. His more specialized volume, *Das Toba-Reich Nordchinas, Eine Soziologischen Untersuchung* (Leiden, 1949) is a masterly study of a dual barbarian-Chinese social order.

Modern French work has also advanced the study of the Inner Asian aspect of Chinese history. In the French encyclopaedic tradition, René Grousset has written both on the history of China, on the Mongols, and on the Inner Asian frontier as a whole.[31] On the history of the Manchurian and eastern Mongolian sector of the Chinese frontier, Rolf Stein made an outstanding contribution in his study of the Liao (Khitan) dynasty, translating and copiously annotating one of the important Chinese sources. His work is

especially valuable in showing the deep penetration of a
frontier tribal society by Chinese cultural influences even
before the later period of sinization when Khitan rule over
North China was solidly established.[32] Wittfogel and Feng
further opened up the study of the Liao period with their
volume of more than 700 pages devoted to the history of
the Liao and comment on its Chinese and frontier aspects.[33]
This work is the combined product of the leading Chinese
authority in the field, whose knowledge of the Chinese literature of the period is masterly, and a Western theorist
in the methodology of Chinese history whose theories have,
in the most unfortunate tradition of German scholarship,
grown more doctrinaire and less original with the passage
of the years. The result is that much of the extraordinarily
valuable and rich raw material presented, although subjected
to repetitive and even redundant processing, still remains
raw.[34]

On the Mongolian sector of the frontier, Martin has
provided a new narrative of the campaigns of Chingis Khan,
especially the Mongol campaigns in North China,[35] Friters
has treated the modern history of the international relations
of Outer Mongolia,[36] while De Francis has translated the
observations of a conservative Chinese revolutionary on the
more radical revolution among the Mongols.[37] Looking from
the other side of Mongolia, Spuler in Germany has written
both on the Golden Horde in Russia and on the Mongols
in the Middle and Near East, following the conquests under
Chingis.[38]

On the Sinkiang side of the frontier, Pelliot, whose death
before he could complete a number of major publications
was an untimely loss to international scholarship in the field
of China and Inner Asia, threw new light on the border relations with Ming China (1368-1643)—at the same time,
in the Pelliot manner, dealing with a vast range of other
topics, including relations with the Portuguese and the use
by the Ming Chinese of cannon acquired from them.[39] A

wartime account of Sinkiang was given by Norins,[40] and after the end of the war a group of colleagues and I at Johns Hopkins published an "area study" of that province.[41]

West of Sinkiang, in the Soviet republics of Central Asia, Western scholarship is just beginning to take up the study of a new problem—the significance of Soviet industrialization. Soviet planning in this region has long anticipated the Point Four concept of the use of the industrial resources of advanced countries for speeding up the development of pre-industrial countries. From the evidence supplied in an interesting article by Wilhelm,[42] it can be seen that the control of the rate of development, which must be an essential in the thinking that goes into any Pour Four program, should take into consideration the rate at which development is being pushed forward by the Russians in Inner Asia. Western thinking has emphasized the traditional assumption that industrialization of underdeveloped countries will be a rather long and slow process of catching up. But the essence of the Soviet concept seems to be that while the people of an underdeveloped area have to catch up, the kinds of industrial enterprise planted among them can represent not the surplus of Soviet equipment, but the most advanced equipment and technique available. This difference of concept foreshadows the possibility that while industrialization and modernization may spread slowly inland at a leisurely catching-up pace from the "front doors" along the coasts of Asia, they may forge ahead more rapidly along the "back door" corridor of the Inner Asian frontier—in which case Asia might come to look, as it never has before, inland toward Russia for the highest standards of efficiency and "progress," and not, as it traditionally has, outward across the seas.

There is, of course, one essential difference between development programs in Soviet Inner Asia and any Point Four program that could be undertaken by the United States anywhere in Asia. The United States has to operate by agreement with sovereign nations whose governments it can influence but which it cannot control. The Soviet program is carried out within territories that are under a common sovereignty and a system of centralized government planning. The point remains, however, that American Point Four economic thinking should be broadened to take in not only the needs of any country whose development the United States is assisting, and the capital and resources that the United States is able to allocate, but also a study of the characteristics of the Soviet programs of development with which the United States is, in fact, competing for influence and prestige.

Among the non-Chinese peoples of the Inner Asian frontiers of China there are the beginnings of a modern, nationalistic literature among the Uighurs of Sinkiang, but it is almost inaccessible and consequently almost unknown in the Western world. Much more advanced stages of development have been reached in both Inner and Outer Mongolia. During the Japanese occupation of Inner Mongolia there was great publishing activity at two centers, Kalgan and K'ailu.[43] Old manuscripts were collected and put into print, and there was also a considerable output of new nationalist literature. The tone of the nationalist output from K'ailu was closely supervised by the Japanese. At Kalgan, where the Japanese control was less stringent, the inspiring influence was that of Prince Te (Demchukdongrub of West Sunid; in the Chinese form, Te Wang) and it was possible to maintain a tone that was subtly independent of official Japanese aims. Unfortunately, no general account of the Mongol publishing of this period has yet appeared, and to my regret I have not even completely catalogued my own collection, which represents but a fraction of the total output.

In many ways, the publishing output of Outer Mongolia is even more significant, but little of it is available to the Western world. The few titles known to me include an

official history of the Mongol Revolution and official biographies of Suke Batur, the first Mongol revolutionary
leader, and Maksorjab (known by the honorary title of
Khatan Batur), one of the early military leaders. These
titles I have translated, and am now annotating for publication. In addition, unique material is being prepared for publication by my colleague the Dilowa Hutukhtu, formerly of
Narobanchin Sume, in western Outer Mongolia, who fled
from that country in 1931 as a political refugee. As one of
the important "Living Buddhas"[44] of the Outer Mongolia, he
held also a number of secular administrative positions, and
his experience covers a long period from before the Revolution of 1911 until after the Communists assumed control,
at first indirectly and then more and more directly in the
middle and late 1920's. He has dictated his autobiography,
and in addition has written his political reminiscences,
which I have translated; working with my colleagues, Dr.
David Aberle and Mr. Harold Vreeland, he has also provided the material for an institutional and social description
and analysis of the position of the Lama Buddhist Church
in the pre-revolutionary Mongol society.

The information on Outer Mongolia provided by the
Dilowa Hutukhtu is being linked up with Inner Mongolia
by two other Mongol colleagues of mine at Johns Hopkins,
Mr. John Hangin, a Chahar Mongol of Taibas Banner in
the center of southern Inner Mongolia, and Mr. Peter Onon,
a Butkha Daghor Mongol from the Nonni valley in northwestern Manchuria. With Dr. William Austin they have
worked on the linguistic description and grammar of Chahar
and Daghor Mongol, and with Mrs. Hangin and Mrs. Onon,
both of whom come from Jehol Province, they have provided material for sociological and cultural analysis. This
group research, the first of its kind ever undertaken in the
Western world with the aid of Mongol participants, will
throw new light on the processes of change in modern
Mongol society associated with the intensified influence of

China, Japan, and Russia. In association with the same research group, Father Louis Schram is completing for publication his description of the sociology of the "Monguor"
Mongols of western Kansu, where the Russian and Japanese factors are not involved, but where Moslem and
Tibetan influences are important, in addition to the Chinese
influence.

At this point it is logical to turn to the Russian work on
the Inner Asian frontiers of China because it, in turn, is
the logical link between the Chinese frontier and the Inner
Asian frontier as a whole. The Russian work is the greatest
in quantity of all studies of these frontiers, and much of
it is excellent in quality. No attempt will be made here at a
detailed review; but it is worth drawing attention to several
characteristics of Russian scholarship.

In the first place, an excellent foundation was laid in the
nineteenth century, and even earlier, by the Russians themselves and by foreigners, especially Germans, in the Russian
Imperial service. The Siberian tribes were probably better
described in detail, at the period of very early contact with
the Russians, than were the Indians of North America in
the earliest period of European penetration and contact.
Following this the geographical, geological, and botanical
exploration of Inner Asia and its Siberian fringes was
carried out in the nineteenth century by scientists who in
addition to being competent in their fields were also often
industrious in acquiring ethnological and linguistic information; and for more than a century the Russians have had
Mongol and Turkish specialists of a high order. One of
the most valuable recent activities of Soviet publishing
has been the reprinting of the narratives of Prjeval'skii,
Potanin, Obruchev (who, at a great age, is still an active
scholar), Semenov-Tian-Shanskii, Kozlov, and others;
their works, exceedingly difficult to obtain in the original
editions, contain much that is still of great contemporary

value, and much that has never yet been fully absorbed into
the body of world scholarship dealing with Inner Asia.

Building on these strong foundations, the Soviet work
has continued to show great competence in the gathering
and organizing of material. Murzaev's geographical work
on Mongolia, for instance, compares well both with the
"German thoroughness" of Fochler-Hauke's survey of
Manchuria, cited above, and with the classic French clarity
of Grenard's geographical description of Mongolia (which,
in turn, draws much more heavily on the Russian field work
of Tsarist times than do most Western geographical references to Mongolia).[45]

In dealing with Inner Asia, however, Soviet scholarship
has two weaknesses that need to be watched carefully by
those who deal with Russian sources. One is an old weakness that existed previously in Tsarist times: the failure in
the social sciences, especially in history, to integrate the
use of Mongol and Turkish sources with the use of Chinese
sources. To an amazing extent the Soviet Inner Asian
specialists continue to rely, for Chinese citations, on Bichurin (Hyacinth), and this dependency is underlined by the
recent appearance of an excellent new edition of Bichurin,[46]
(1777-1853) while translations of new material on anything like the same scale appear to be lacking. Bichurin was
one of the great pioneers; but in dealing with the history
of Inner Asia, international scholarship should no longer
act as if it were still in the pioneer stage. To rely on even
the great translators encourages the dangerous assumption,
especially in comparative historical analysis, that the significant material is that which has been translated—whereas
much of the material most relevant for "tribal" history
has never been translated. It is true that sources in many
languages are clustered around the Inner Asian field of
study; but this problem can be dealt with by group research. Contemporary Russian scholarship lags behind in
this respect.

The second great weakness of Soviet scholarship is the ebb and flow of the doctrinal tide, which not only makes it difficult to determine when theories are being modified by fresh facts and when facts are subject to doctrinal selection in order not to disturb accepted theory, but also makes it necessary to try to discover, when the work of one decade differs from the work of a previous decade, how far the difference is due to the accumulation of new knowledge and how far to mandatory changes in thinking as the result of arbitrary doctrinal directives.

These are impediments that make it more difficult to use the contemporary Russian sources; but they do not mean that we can dispense with these sources any more than we can afford to dispense with the Japanese and German contributions to Inner Asian studies made during a period when political controls over research and interpretation were equally harsh. The Russian work is in fact indispensable, because vast areas of Inner Asia are inaccessible for field work in geography, archaeology, sociology, economics, and linguistic study except to Russians and other Soviet citizens.

Recent Russian work has both widened the field of Inner Asia geographically and deepened it historically. Okladnikov, through his studies of the historical origins and migrations of the Yakuts, has made it clear that we can no longer assume that we have a rounded view of Inner Asia if, in concentrating on the southern margin of contact between "barbarian" tribes and the great civilizations from China to the Mediterranean, we neglect the northern margin of expansion from Inner Asia toward the sub-Arctic and Arctic.[47] From Okladnikov's material it is strongly arguable that while the pressure of tribal wars was one cause of migration toward the north, another factor was the attraction of the north in proportion to the acquistion of techniques for living in the north.

Another phase of Soviet research is represented by

Bernshtam, who after publishing on the Orkhon Turks in northern Mongolia has become an expert on Kirghizia and adjacent regions.[48] He has worked in archaeology, history, and historical sociology. Almost a Lysenko of the social sciences, he pushes his evidence to extremes in the effort to validate a preconceived scheme of social evolution—the orthodox Marxist scheme of primitive communism, followed by clan societies, matriarchal and patriarchal, followed by slavery and then by feudalism—a stage that is held to have continued into modern times in Inner Asia and indeed Asia generally.

The rigidity of this scheme does not allow for one of the major phenomena of Inner Asian history—the constant alternation of evolution and devolution of the structure of "tribal" and "barbarian" societies in contact with the high agricultural and urban societies to the south of them. Because of this contact a frontier people that was in an ascendant phase in its military and other contacts with a civilized state or states could, as it were, climb on an already established framework of the organization of property, revenue, administration, and status, and could thus evolve very rapidly a feudal and even imperial organization of its own. When this kind of overlord rule by a frontier people broke down, however, devolution back to a war-band or tribal level of organization could be even more rapid. Failure to deal adequately with this phenomenon is almost a common characteristic of recent and contemporary Russian work.

The phenomenon of alternating evolution and devolution is one that can best be dealt with in a regional framework. Many of the Russians are excellent regionalists in that their training in languages, archaeology and the use of historical sources is well adapted to specialization in a region; but an adequate concept of the function of historical geography seems to be lacking. The kind of concept that is needed was, however, sketched out a good many years ago by one of the great exile Russian scholars, Rostovtzeff, in the introductory pages of his work on the Iranians and Greeks in South Russia. His aim, he says, is

". . . to give *a history of the South Russian lands* in the prehistoric, the protohistoric, and the classic periods. . . . By history I mean not a repetition of the scanty evidence preserved by the classical writers and illustrated by the archaeological material but an attempt to define the part played by South Russia in the history of the world in general. . . . (p. vii)

". . . Much has been written about South Russia, but the writings are always dissertations on the Greek towns, commentaries on the fourth book of Herodotus, or studies of one or two isolated objects. Even the great work of Minns, an extremely useful and an extremely learned book, is but a repertory, although as a repertory almost faultless: what he gives us is a juxtaposition of Scythians and Greeks, two separate parts, copiously illustrated, and no more. . . .

". . . My own point of view in all these questions of South Russian history is a different one. I take as my starting-point the unity of the region which we call South Russia; the intersection of influences in that vast tract of country—Oriental and southern influences arriving by way of the Caucasus and the Black Sea, Greek influences spreading along the sea routes, and Western influences passing down the great Danubian route; and the consequent formation, from time to time, of mixed civilizations, very curious and very interesting, influencing in their turn Central Russia on the one hand, by way of the great Russian rivers, and on the other central Europe, especially the region of the Danube. (p. 7)⁴⁹

I have quoted these words at length because they have such value, it seems to me, for those who work in any of the regional "compartments" of the Inner Asian frontier. Rostovtzeff, it will be noted, speaks of the forming of mixed civilizations "from time to time," which allows for the phenomenon of alternating evolution and devolution, or relapse.

An attempt can now be made, I believe, to put together an inclusive view of the Inner Asian frontier as a whole. The feeling that such a view is needed is not new. In 1934, in the third volume of his *Study of History,* which I have already cited, Toynbee attempted an inclusive review of the history of pastoral nomadism. His interpretation is marred by the conception that the natural environment is a kind of impersonal machine, grinding out the destinies of peoples who live within a certain range of aridity of climate; but his approach is nevertheless bold and constructive in making it clear that we need not and should not limit ourselves to the separate histories of Mongols, Turks, Arabs, and so forth, but should attempt to grasp the significance of a kind of society in which the basic similarity of the way of life is more important than diversities of language and religion.

In 1939, Teggart, propounding a theory of "historical correlations," discussed wars on the barbarian frontiers of the Romans and the Chinese in the period between B.C. 58 and A.D. 107, and came to the conclusion that there was a causal relationship between these wars, and that one of the most important causes was the interruption of trade from time to time, such as trade along the Silk Route from China[50] Teggart's theory, and the data he assembles in support of it, are a valuable contribution to the formation of an inclusive view of frontier history. The point on which his treatment needs to be refined is the conception of trade. Doubtless the interruption of trade was often a proximate cause of frontier disturbance; but what led to the interruption of trade? There is danger in assuming that trade in the times with which he deals can be defined in the same way as trade after the rise of machine industry, capitalism, and modern banking. It was often in part a form of tribute, in part an exchange of luxuries rather than necessities, among ruling princes and great nobles, and in part, in transport and sale of grain from agricultural regions to pastoral nomads, it contributed to the symbiosis, in times of peace, between the two kinds of society. Behind the "interruption of trade," therefore, it is necessary to look for and examine relations of power and tribute, and the relative ascendancy, in the period being examined, of barbarians over the civilized states or of the frontier administrators of the great states over the neighboring barbarians.

In 1948 the study of parallel or equivalent phenomena on the Roman and Chinese frontiers was further advanced by Thompson's valuable study of Attila and the Huns.[51] His Aetius, who learned the Hun manner of warfare while a hostage among the Huns; his Romans in the Hun service and Huns in the Roman service; his Greek merchant who had been captured by the Huns, had served in their ranks (as prisoners often did), had bought his freedom with his share of warrior's loot, and now preferred the kind of "peace and order" available to him under Hun rule to the harsh taxation, arbitrary exactions, and corrupt courts under Roman rule; above all, his description of how Aetius, after his great victory over Attila in Gaul deliberately chose not to follow up the victory because on the one hand he did not want a victory that would give too much strength to his own Gothic and Frankish allies, and on the other hand he had it in mind that he himself might yet, at some future turn, want to hire Hun mercenaries, as he had in the past— all these, both the events and the personalities, can be matched in the records of Chinese frontier history.

With these explorations in the Western literature may be compared an interesting Russian essay by Yushkov, comparing the Kievan state of the ninth and tenth centuries, the Mongols before the rise of Chingis Khan, and the Anglo-Saxon kingdoms of the sixth to ninth centuries as functionally equivalent "barbarian" societies, "contemporary" in the sense that each represented the same process of partial breakdown of an old order, combined with the emergence of new forms of organization, out of which feudalism arose.[52] This is the only passage known to me in the Soviet literature that uses this concept of "contemporaneity" as set forth by Toynbee in his *Study of History*. There is no doubt whatever that by the use of this approach, which is also akin to Teggart's "correlations," new advances can be made in the building up of our understanding of the Inner Asian frontier as a whole. And to its westward continuation in Europe, the northern, forested frontier of Mediterranean civilization.

We should next, I think, consider what may have been the major processes that led to the evolution of a single frontier, or a chain of linked, functionally equivalent frontiers from the Black Sea to the Yellow Sea. In the main I believe that the ideas I put forward, in first publishing this book, about the evolution of a frontier society and a frontier style of politics, within a recognizable geographical zone adjacent to the great civilizations, will be found valid and can be supported by the literature of the subject since published. These ideas, moreover, can probably be usefully applied not only to the Chinese frontier but to the comparable frontiers of Asia and Europe as a whole.

Probably a major key to the complex historical problems involved is the phenomenon of the fortification of their northerly frontiers by the great civilized empires that were based on agriculture, cities, and internal trade. Between the Roman *limes*, the fortified Rhine-Danube frontier, and the Great Wall of China there were many other "great wall" systems. Though I had not had access to this passage in his writings when I wrote before, this common factor was pointed out long ago by Barthold, in a series of lectures given in Turkey in 1926. Referring to the fact that walls against barbarian invasion had been built from Britain to China and Manchuria, he said that the first wall of this kind in the region of the Amu Darya, Zarafshan and Syr Darya—the middle sector of the whole frontier line—could be dated to the fourth century B.C. to protect the oasis of Merv against nomads who were probably of other than Turkish origin.[53]

Barthold can be supported by many other citations. As long ago as 1896, de Morgan referred to a "double line" of fortifications in northern Iran.[54] Since then, Masson has mentioned a "wall of Sogd" between Mavrannakhar (the "Mesopotamia" between the Amu Darya and Syr Darya) and Turkistan.[55] Bernshtam has a map that appears to show local "great walls" in Ferghana, but they are not explained in his text.[56] Finally, Tolstov deals on a great scale with fortified cities and oases east of the Caspian and north of the Amu Darya.[57] There were even local "great walls" defending the Crimea and, apparently, the agricultural part of the Kuban steppe.[58] Other citations could be made, but these are enough to show that the scheme of fortification can be filled in between the Roman Empire and the Great Wall of China, especially if fortified oases be taken as an equivalent of "great walls," in regions where the lack of population between oases would have made difficult the manning of a continuous fortified line.

Although walls were also built as far south as mid-China (see below, Chap. XIV, especially p. 436), it is clear that the really important walls of the great empires were on their northern or northerly frontiers. These walls can be summarily described, I believe, as marking the end of a great period—the long growth of farming, the increase of population, and the rise of great cities, and the development of relatively cheap bulk transportation, especially the transport of grain by waterways. This development reached the stage of "great wall" building several centuries before the beginning of our era, the exact date varying along different sectors of the frontier.

What had taken place in this period was a process of differentiation among the thinly scattered neolithic populations of the Old World. Around the Mediterranean, in Mesopotamia, in those parts of Iran and Central Asia where a natural oasis structure favored agriculture, in India, and in China, there was a steadily increasing exploitation of the inherent advantages of agriculture. When the use of the plow was added to the use of the hoe (the hoe not being displaced, or not entirely displaced, in irrigated agriculture), a wide belt of rainfall farming was added, extending to the northward until expansion was slowed down in Europe by heavy forests, and in South Russia to a certain extent, and Inner Asia more decisively, by a low rainfall that made conditions good for pasture but hazardous for agriculture.

Nor was the growing of food and agricultural raw materials the only factor. Economic transportation, making large urban concentrations possible, was most favorable around the Mediterranean and, in Asia, where rivers and canals could be used. The great ancient civilizations that arose out of this period of growth needed certain minimum conditions of cheap transportation toward their urban centers (*not thr* outthrust of trade in search of new markets) in order to arrive at an optimum combination of their organizational and administrative ability and the use of the large but slow-moving armies that they could mobilize from their large populations. Where they ceased to find these minimum conditions—notably on their northerly frontiers—the wise policy of empire was to cease to annex new territory and to refuse to include within civilization the peoples of the unwanted territory.

I need not here refer in redundant detail to many of the points dealt with in this book—the fact that where optimum conditions of pasturage adjoined minimum conditions of agriculture, the poor farmer could become a prosperous nomad by abandoning his underprivileged share of civilization and taking to the steppe; the fact that while empires reached a line of demarcation at which it was to their interest to cease to grow, it was profitable for many individual subjects of the empire to cross this line of demarcation and to throw in their lot with the barbarians; the fact that "great walls," therefore, had a function in keeping in the subjects of the empires as well as in keeping out the barbarians.

The new point that needs to be made—it is implicit in the argumentation of this book, but it can be made explicitly, and with reference not only to China but to all the great empires and all the barbarians—is that it was a period of south-to-north growth of agriculture and urban civilization that preceded and stimulated the great historical period of east-west and west-east barbarian migrations, and the southward-striking invasions from this east-west line of movement. For when empires ceased to grow, they could be blackmailed. What fed their economic life was centripetal tribute, not centrifugal export trade. A wide trade in small quantities of luxury goods never ceased, because the rulers of civilization wanted luxuries and were willing to pay for them; what they did not want was the bulk export of grain and other commodities which formed the most important part of their system of taxation and tribute within their own empires.

But the barbarians whom each great empire wished to exclude from its *orbis terrarum* could demand a price for staying in outer darkness.[59] They could demand as a privilege the trade, especially in grain, cloth, and metal wares, which was useful to them though not profitable to the exchequer of the civilized state. Their power of blackmail was their mobility and the ease with which they could raid; they could make the frontier proconsul choose which was less expensive—to allow trade to leak out (for, from the proconsul's point of view, it was an expensive leakage, not a profitable expansion), or to pay the cost of levying and maintaining troops to prevent the raids.

The double process of raids on civilization and wars between barbarian tribes constantly threatened to harden the tribal armies into forces capable of shifting from local raids to deep invasions. The alternative evils of stagnation through cessation of growth or drainage of resources through pushing their frontiers too far into barbarian territory constantly threatened to undermine the civilized empires. It was the interaction of the conditions that favored the barbarians— both those of forested Europe and those of the Eurasian steppe—with the conditions that favored the great civilized empires; it was this interaction, and not fluctuations of climate, that for a whole age of history set the rhythm of the pulse of Asia and Europe. There are modern analogues to these historical combinations of social and geographical factors, but to discuss them in the detail they deserve would require another book.

August, 1951.

NOTES

[1] As an unimportant but illustrative example, René Grousset, *L'Empire Mongol (Ire phase)*, Paris, 1941, p. 339, devotes a page to refuting, on quite sufficient grounds, the idea that "the periodicity of the Turco-Mongol invasions of China" was due to "the rhythm of the periods of drought in Mongolian territory." In so doing he cites me (without precise identification of source) as if I were the originator of the theory of climatic "pulsation"; but the reference can only be to early work of mine when I had read and been influenced by Huntington, but had not yet read the Chinese chronicle material, or learned Mongol and traveled in the Mongol manner among Mongols. Probably Grousset's reference is to my article "Caravan routes of Inner Asia," *Geographical Journal*, LXXII, 6, London, Dec. 1928, where Huntington is quoted on p. 519 for the theory of "climatic pulsation"; but Grousset does not himself cite either Huntington, whose *Pulse of Asia* was published in 1907, or A. J. Toynbee, in the third volume of whose *Study of History*, published in 1934, the Huntingtonian interpretation is subjected to the most learned (but untenable) elaboration it has yet received. Nor was Grousset aware, in citing apparently an article of mine published in 1928, that in an article published in the same journal in 1938 I had criticized in great detail the rigidly mechanical concepts of geographical determination. (Lattimore, "The Geographical Factor in Mongol History," *Geographical Journal*, XCI, 1, London, Jan. 1938, especially pp. 2-3; see also the section of *Inner Asian Frontiers of China* beginning on p. 328, with footnote reference to Toynbee on p. 329.) It is all too likely that well-informed readers will find that I myself have been guilty of more incomplete citations of this kind than the learned and industrious M. Grousset.

[2] Lattimore, *The Situation in Asia*, Boston, 1949, pp. 15-17. In the same discussion, originally read as a paper before the December 1948 meeting of the American Historical Society at Washington, D. C., I described the traditional Chinese state as an "absorptive" empire, making the distinction that while the Russians "incorporated" new subjects, by a process in which "ordinary people were held in subjection, but a part of the ruling class of each people was assimilated to the status of the Russian ruling class," the Chinese showed a "willingness throughout their history to accept as Chinese any barbarian who would drop his language and learn Chinese, wear Chinese clothes, farm like the Chinese, and accept the other conventions of being a Chinese."

[3] Lattimore, "The Inland Crossroads of Asia," in *Compass of the World*, ed. Hans W. Weigert and Vilhjalmur Stefansson, New York, 1944, p. 379 (quoted by permission of Macmillan Co.). This passage was written before (quoted by permission of the Macmillan Co.). This passage was written before the atom bomb was known, but the long-range view of the trend of development that it expresses is not invalidated by the existence of the atom bomb.

[4] *Ibid.* p. 380.

[5] While the Russians have not yet taken full advantage of their opportunity to organize research, they have recently taken an important step by organizing a "trustified" institute for research in the social sciences dealing with Asia. "Vertically," they are now organized so that they can coordinate studies deal-

ing with a selected area, such as Iran, from Stone Age to oil age. "Horizon-
tally," a Russian working on problems in Korea can, if he thinks it relevant,
turn for comparative data to a colleague working on problems in Turkey, in the
same institute. In the United States, there is extreme unevenness in the development of studies dealing with Asia. Chinese and Japanese studies are comparatively well advanced; studies of Inner Asia are poorly developed, and so
are studies of Burma, Afghanistan, and a number of other countries. There is,
moreover, excessive compartmentation of studies dealing with countries that
have a common frontier with Russia, and almost no communication between
compartments. For the reorganization of Russian research on Asia, see *Current
Digest of the Soviet Press*, II, 33, pp. 3-4; also *Vestnik Akademii Nauk*,
1950, 9, Moscow (in Russian).

⁶ Chang Chih-yi, "A Bibliography of Books and Articles on Mongolia,"
Journal of the Royal Central Asian Society, Parts 2 and 3 of Vol. XXXVII,
London, 1950. Also distributed as a reprint by the American Institute of Pacific
Relations, New York. (Includes only titles in Chinese, Japanese, and Russian,
and is a selective, not an inclusive, bibliography, with a short notice of each
item included.)

⁷ Owen Lattimore, "Some recent Inner Asian studies," *Pacific Affairs*, XX,
3, New York, 1947); also Owen Lattimore and others, *Pivot of Asia*, Boston,
1950, especially pp. 107-118; also John De Francis, "National and Minority
Policies," in *Annals* of the American Academy of Political and Social Science,
special issue on People's Republic of China, ed. H. Arthur Steiner, Philadelphia,
Sept. 1951.

⁸ For citations, see *Pivot of Asia,* as above, pp. 108 and 115, note 15.

⁹ See, for example, Chen Han-seng, *Frontier land systems in southernmost
China,* a comparative study of agrarian problems and social organization among
the Pai Yi people of Yunnan and the Kamba people of Sikang, New York,
Institute of Pacific Relations, 1949 (mimeographed).

¹⁰ For a brief notice of the work of Dr. and Mrs. Li see Lattimore, "Some
Recent Inner Asian Studies," cited above. This notice does not nearly exhaust
the list of their printed work.

¹¹ For the last statement of Dr. Li's liberal philosophy as expressed in terms
of frontier studies and made in an environment free both of Kuomintang
authoritarianism and Communist dogma, see his "China: a fundamental approach, *Pacific Affairs*, XXI, 1, New York, March 1949.

¹² For a brief notice, with reference to other notices, see L. Carrington
Goodrich, "Some publications in 'occupied' China," *Pacific Affairs*, XX, 4,
New York, Dec. 1947; for the suppression of books, see L. C. Goodrich, *The
literary inquisition of Ch'ien Lung,* Baltimore, 1935.

¹³ For a major bibliographical article on recent Mongol studies, listing in
detail the contributions of such leading European Mongolists as Mostaert,
Pelliot, Haenisch, and many others, see N. N. Poppe, "Stand und Aufgabe der
Mongolistik," *Zeitschrift der deutschen Morganländischen Gessellschaft*, 100
(25), pp. 52-89, Wiesbaden, 1950.

¹⁴ Notes marginales sur le folklore des Mongols Ordos," *Han-hiue,* III, 1-2,
Peking, 1948.

¹⁵ Fr. Willem A. Grootaers, "Problems of a linguistic atlas of China," presented by the Bureau of Linguistic Geography, Catholic University, Peiping,

¹⁶ *History of the Eastern Mongols during the Ming dynasty from 1368 to
1634,* by D. Pokotilov, Part I, translation by Rudolf Loewenthal, *Studia Serica,*
Monograph series A, 1; Part II, Addenda and Corrigenda, by Wolfgang
Leuvense Bijdragen, XXXVIII, Leuven (Belgium), 1948.

Franke, same series, No. 3, Chengtu 1947 and Chengtu and Peiping, 1948.

[17] For brief notice, see Lattimore, "Some recent Inner Asian studies," as cited above.

[18] Walther Heissig, *Bolur Erike, Monumenta Serica*, Monograph X, Peiping, 1946. Other contributions by Dr. Heissig include "Beobachtungen ueber Sesshaftigkeit und Kulturwandel bei den Mongolen des Jouda Chigulgan," *Folklore Studies*, Catholic University of Peking, II, 1943; "Ueber Mongolische Landkarten," *Monumenta Serica*, IX, 1944; "Zum Umfang der Mongolischen Geschichtsliteratur," ibid., X, 1945.

[19] Walter Fuchs, *Der Jesuiten Atlas der Kanghst Zeit: China und die Aussenlaender*, Peiping, 1941, with a further volume in 1943, containing index of place names for Manchuria, Mongolia, Sinkiang, and Tibet (the place names, especially for Manchuria, are important for the identification of "tidemarks" of Mongol, Manchu, and Chinese population distribution); also *The "Mongol Atlas" of China by Chu Ssu-pen and the Kuang-Yu T'u* (with 48 facsimile reproductions of maps), Monograph VIII, *Monumenta Serica*, Peiping, 1946. For notices, see Lattimore, "Some recent Inner Asian studies," cited above;. also *Geographical Review*, XXXVIII, 4, New York, Oct. 1948.

[20] The most vivid account of these finds from the second millennium B.C. is still H. G. Creel's *The Birth of China;* this and other works by Creel are frequently cited, below, in the chapters dealing with ancient history.

[21] In order to provide Western scholars with an insight into this transitional period of Chinese historical interpretation by making available a comprehensive Chinese history of China (and no such history has ever yet been translated), a translation of the Fan Wen-lan history is now being undertaken at the Johns Hopkins, under the general supervision of my colleague, Dr. John De Francis.

[22] Teng Ssu-yü, "Chinese Historiography in the Last Fifty Years." *Far Eastern Quarterly*, VIII, 2, Ithaca, Feb. 1949, p. 147.

[23] For Ku Chieh-kang see Arthur W. Hummel, trans., *Ku Chieh-kang: The autobiography of a Chinese historian*, Leyden, 1931.

[24] For a selective list of Japanese publications in these years, see Chang Chih-yi, "A bibliography of books and articles on Mongolia," as cited above.

[25] Japanese references: *Rekishigaku nempo*, 1949, Tokyo, 1950, and *Shigaku zasshi*, 59, 5, Tokyo, 1950.

[26] Andrew J. Grajdanzev, *A Japanese view of Outer Mongolia*, condensed translation of *The Outer Mongolian People's Republic*, by Yasuo Misshima and Tomio Goto (Tokyo, 1939), New York, Institute of Pacific Relations, 1942 (mimeographed).

[27] Shanghai, N. D., about 1940. Being in Russian, and printed in the old Tsarist orthography, the pamphlet may have been intended primarily for the anti-Soviet exile Russian community in Shanghai.

[28] Hence such publications as those bv Fuchs and Heissig, already noted above.

[29] Gustav Fochler-Hauke, *Die Mandschurei*, Heidelberg-Berlin-Magdeburg, 1941.

[30] Wolfram Eberhard, *A History of China*, London 1950 (first published in Switzerland, in German, as *Chinas Geschichte*.)

[31] René Grousset, *L'empire de steppes, Attila, Gengis-Khan, Tamerlan*, Paris 1939; *L'empire mongol, lre phase*, Paris 1941; *Histoire de la Chine*, Paris 1942; *Le conquerant du monde* (vie de Gengis-Khan), Paris 1944. In his

Empire mongol he has made an especially interesting effort to support his text with material from the *Secret History* of the Mongols.

[32] Rolf Stein, "Leao-Tche", *T'oung Pao*, XXXV, pp. 1-154, Leyden, 1939.

[33] Karl A. Wittfogel and Feng Chia-sheng, *History of Chinese Society, Liao (907-1125)*, Philadelphia--New York 1949.

[34] The narrow obscurity of Wittfogel's dogmatic approach is well exemplified by the astonishing statement, in a review of the German edition of Eberhard's *History of China (Artibus Asiae*, XIII, 1-2, Ascona, 1950, p. 105), that "In contrast to the West where power followed wealth, in the Orient wealth followed power." It should be obvious that wealth-and-power, like chicken-and-egg, is a compound or reciprocating phenomenon; the question is not "which came first?" but how the joint phenomenon evolved.

[35] H. Desmond Martin, *The rise of Chingis Khan and his conquest of North China* (introduction by Owen Lattimore, edited by Eleanor Lattimore), Baltimore 1950.

[36] Gerard M. Friters, *Outer Mongolia and its international position* (introduction by Owen Lattimore, edited by Eleanor Lattimore), Baltimore 1949.

[37] *Chinese agent in Mongolia*, by Ma Ho-t'ien, translated by John De Francis, (introduction by Owen Lattimore), Baltimore 1949.

[38] Berthold Spuler, *Die goldene Horde, die Mongolen in Russland 1223-1502*, Leipzig 1943, and *Die Mongolenzeit*, Berlin 1948. See also the excellent *La horde d'or*, by B. Grekorv and A. Yakubovskii, translated from the Russian by François Thuret, Paris 1939.

[39] Paul Pelliot, "Le Hoja et le Sayyid Husain de l'historei des Ming," *T'oung Pao*, XXXVIII, Leyden, 1948. The material on the use of "frankish" cannon goes far beyond the meager information previously known to me (see below, Chap. I, p. 6). Later, the Chinese used for cannon the term *p'ao*, which must be connected with the Mongol *bo* and, perhaps, the Russian *pushka*. The Russians, in turn, became acquainted with cannon through the Germans, toward the end of the fourteenth century and, a few years earlier, through the Kazan Turks (see V. Mavrodin, "On the appearance of firearms in Russia," *Voprosy Istorii (Questions of History)*, Moscow, 1946, 8-9). Thus when Russians and Manchus encountered each other in the area between Siberia and China about the beginning of the seventeenth century, both had firearms which, technically, were undoubtedly of joint Eastern and Western lines of descent. For other publications by Pelliot see the article by Poppe already cited above. Pelliot's posthumous works are in course of publication, and his influence continues strong in French scholarship, through his pupil Hambis and others.

[40] Martin R. Norins, *Gateway to Asia: Sinkiang, frontier of the Chinese far west* (introduction by Owen Lattimore), New York 1944.

[41] Owen Lattimore (with C. Y. Chang, H. S. Chen, J. De Francis, E. Lattimore, K. H. Menges, D. Thorner, and with an appendix on "Ancient art and modern archaeology" by Alice Thorner), *Pivot of Asia: Sinkiang and the Inner Asian frontiers of China and Russia*, Boston 1950.

[42] Warren Wilhelm, 'Soviet Central Asia: Development of a backward area." *Foreign Policy Reports*, XXV, 18, N. Y., Feb. 1, 1950.

[43] The K'ailu Mongol press was at first under the direction of my old friend and teacher Bugegesik, who was later put to death by the Japanese on suspicion of a not-sufficiently collaborationist form of nationalism; to my sorrow, I have been told that one of the counts against him was that pictures of me and my family were found in his possession.

[44] I use the term in quotation marks because it has no equivalent in Mongol

usage; it has passed into the Western languages through translation of a Chinese term.

[45] E. M. Murzaev, *Mongolian people's republic, a physical geographical description*, Moscow, 1948 (in Russian); the same author's volume on the political geography of Mongolia does not appear to be available outside the Soviet union; F. Grenard, "Haute Asie," in *Géographie universelle*, ed. P. Vidal de la Blache et L. Gallois, VIII, Paris 1929.

[46] N. Ya Bichurin (the monk Hyacinth), *Collection of notices of the people inhabiting Central Asia in ancient times*, Moscow-Leningrad 1950, reprint of the original edition of 1851 with introductory notices by A. N. Bernshtam and N. V. Kiuner (in Russian).

[47] A. P. Okladnikov, *Essays in the history of the western Buryat Mongols*, (17th-18th centuries), Leningrad 1937; *Historical course of the peoples of Yakutia*, Yakutsk 1943; also many articles in journals (all in Russian). See also Owen Lattimore, "Yakutia and the future of the north," in *New compass of the world*, ed. Hans W. Weigert, Vilhjalmur Stefansson, and Richard Edes Harrison, New York 1949; originally published in *American Quarterly on the Soviet Union*, New York, Feb. 1945.

[48] A. Bernshtam, *Social-economic structure of the Orkhon-Yenisei Turks of the 6th-8th centuries. The eastern Turkish Khaghanate and the Kirghiz*, Moscow-Leningrad 1946; also many articles in journals (all in Russian).

[49] M. Rostovtzeff, *Iranians and Greeks in South Russia*, Oxford, 1922.

[50] Frederick J. Teggart, *Rome and China*, Berkeley 1939. See also below, Chap. XVI, p. 529.

[51] E. A. Thompson, *A History of Attila and the Huns*, Oxford, 1948.

[52] S. Yushkov, "On the question of the pre-feudal ('barbarian') state," *Questions of history*, pp. 45-65, 1946,7, Moscow (in Russian). See also Owen Lattimore, "Inner Asian Frontiers," in *New compass of the world*, as cited above. For a Russian commentary on the views of Yushkov, approving them in general but criticizing some of the details, see K. Vasilevich, "A Sketch of the Periodization of the History of the U.S.S.R. in the Feudal Period," *Questions of History*, 1949,11, pp. 65-90, Moscow (in Russian).

[53] W. Barthold, *Historie des Turcs d'Asie centrale*, French translation by M. Donskis, Paris, 1945. Unfortunately this edition does not give the footnote references to sources of the original.

[54] J. de Morgan, *Mission scientifique en Perse*, Vol. IV, p. 128, Paris, 1896; cited in T. J. Arne, "La steppe turcomane et ses antiquités," in *Hyllningskrift tillägnad Sven Hedin*, Stockholm 1935.

[55] M. E. Masson, "On the periodization of the ancient history of Samarkand," *Journal of Ancient History*, 1950, 4, Moscow (in Russian).

[56] A. N. Bernshtam, "Ancient Ferghana," *Journal of Ancient History*, 1949, 1, Moscow (in Russian).

[57] S. P. Tolstov, *Ancient Khorezm*, Moscow, 1948 (in Russian). See also V. F. Gaidukevich, "On the History of Ancient, Agriculture in Central Asia," *Journal of Ancient History*, 3 (25), Moscow, 1948, pp. 193-204 (in Russian), discussing antiquity of agriculture and irrigation and their reaction to nomadism, and stressing small-scale origins, before improvement of technique made major irrigation works possible.

[58] See, for example, K. Grinevitch, "Defense of the Cimmerian Bosporus," *Journal of Ancient History*, 2 (16), Moscow, 1946, pp. 160-164 (in Russian); also Restovtzeff, *Iranians and Greeks in South Russia*, as already cited.

[59] My colleague, Professor Eberhard of Berkeley calls my attention to a book which contains a discussion of this topic: J. Wentersse, *Paysans de Syrie*, Paris, 1946.

INTRODUCTION

Ten years ago I planned to write this book and several years later began a first draft, in which were embodied mainly ideas formed or partly formed in the course of travel beyond the Great Wall of China. This attempt to outline the scope of the subject showed that it was necessary to go on traveling, studying, and reading for several more years. The book as it now appears is therefore the product of a long growth, and so can only be described and explained in terms of the experience that went into the making of it.

In 1925 I first visited the Inner Mongolian Frontier of China. Talking there with men engaged in the caravan trade with Mongolia and Chinese Turkistan, I determined to resign from the business firm in which I was employed and to travel into Inner Asia. A year later my wife and I began a journey that took us, partly by separate ways, from China through Chinese Turkistan (Sinkiang) into India. Our interest at the time, growing naturally out of my previous employment in China, was chiefly in caravan routes and caravan trade. We traveled so modestly that the heaviest part of our baggage was the books we took with us. Out of Stein's *Ruins of Desert Cathay,* Huntington's *Pulse of Asia,* Carruthers' *Unknown Mongolia,* Yule's *Marco Polo,* Shaw's *Visits to High Tartary, Yârkand and Kâshghar,* Hedin's *Trans-Himalaya,* and other books consulted and studied and compared along the way, there grew a continually wider interest in history and geography and the many different ways of life of the peoples of Inner Asia. As we could see for ourselves, and prove by comparison of the books, a great deal of the information concerning these problems was uncertain, the opinions of "the authorities" did not always agree. There was much to be learned and much to be discovered.

We wanted to go on and learn more. Returning to America we obtained support from the Social Science Research Council, which sent me first to the Division of Anthropology at Harvard University for eight months. Then, in 1929, with additional support from the American Geographical Society—out of which grew the planning of this book—we went to Manchuria. Here we spent nearly a year, rounding out our knowledge, through travel, of the whole Great Wall Frontier of China, from Manchuria through Inner Mongolia to Chinese Turkistan.

Although the ground for a general study of the Inner Asian Frontiers of China had thus been roughly covered, it was obvious that a great deal of preparatory work had still to be done. The first necessity was a study of written Chinese, for though I spoke the language well I could not read freely. Much that I had seen I could not yet fully understand; and though my head was full of folklore and "folk history" I did not know how far documents and chronicles would support the unwritten traditions of even so history-permeated a people as the Chinese. Besides this I also wished to study the Mongol language, for until this time my wife and I had traveled among the Mongols only with Chinese caravan men, traders, or soldiers.

Going from Manchuria to Peiping in 1930, we settled down for several years, first under a fellowship from the Harvard-Yenching Institute, then for two years under the John Simon Guggenheim Memorial Foundation. A grant from the Royal Geographical Society in 1930 contributed to a first attempt at traveling in Mongolia in the Mongol style, with only a Mongol companion and nothing but Mongol equipment. Similar journeys were made almost yearly from that time on.

In 1933 we returned to America, and that winter I was offered the editorship of *Pacific Affairs,* under an arrangement that was to include spending all available spare time on the continued preparation of this book, under the auspices of the International Secretariat of the Institute of Pacific Relations. To this association, and to the flexible working routine supervised by Mr. E. C. Carter, the Secretary General of the Institute, my wife and I owe six happy years. The number of articles quoted from *Pacific Affairs* is in itself enough to show how closely it has been possible to combine editorial work with continued research. In the winter of 1936-37, also, without taking leave from the Institute, I studied Russian in London, and thus gained access to another rich literature on Inner Asia. During these years we were able not only to live about half the time in Peiping, but to continue to travel frequently in North China and Inner Mongolia.

Finally, at the end of 1937, after the first six months of the disastrous Japanese attempt to conquer China, we returned again to America and the writing of this book was begun. The first half, after revision, was again rewritten and considerably improved at the suggestion of my colleague Mr. W. L. Holland, the Research Secretary of the Institute of Pacific Relations. The book itself thus constitutes a report in the International Research Series of the Institute. The second half was completed after my appointment to the Page School of International Relations at The Johns Hopkins University. This was possible only because Dr. Isaiah Bowman, President of The Johns Hopkins University, who has encouraged me and supported my projects ever since 1928, when he was Director of the American Geographical Society, generously allowed me time for the writing during the first year of my appointment.

This account is enough to explain the growth of the book and the relation between text and footnotes. In part, what I have learned in traveling has led me to books, and in part what I have learned from books has taught me to see a little better when traveling. The literature of Inner Asia ranges into a number of languages. To acquire all of them is nearly impossible; three of them I did not have at my command before beginning to work, but had to study while working. For this reason the sources that are cited in the footnotes, while they give samples of the literature, do not pretend to be exhaustive. In this connection the large number of references to my own previous writings may be mentioned. Naturally, in the course of years my ideas have grown and altered, and it seemed only fair to provide some way of referring back to statements and ideas that have been changed or amplified in this book.

Fortunately for me my friends are generous. The first of them is my wife, who besides other kinds of help has always sacrificed her share of our joint interest, especially in the last two years of double and sometimes treble work. My father, David Lattimore, Professor of History at Dartmouth College, who read and criticized the first draft, the final manuscript, and intermediate versions of several chapters, has given me the support of nearly forty years that he has spent in the study of Chinese culture and history. He has been both the first and the final critic of the whole text.

When it became evident that I should have to come well within the Inner Asian Frontier and for the first time attempt to study certain ancient aspects of Chinese history in order to understand some of the origins of nomad history, I was especially fortunate. C. W. Bishop, who during a friendship of many years in Peiping had often let me draw on his wide comparative knowledge of Asia, read the whole manuscript. His unrelenting but always patient criticism helped me to find my way step by step into the Stone Age, and at least part way out of it.

K. A. Wittfogel, to whom I have been able to turn with arguments and questions ever since we walked over the Shansi hills and rode across the plains of Shensi together in 1936, also read the whole manuscript. He has given me countless references and suggestions when new problems, or new aspects of old problems, have come up. Above all, he has allowed me to draw on the written material he has gathered for his book on the "Economic and Social History of China" which he is now finishing. The footnotes do not by any means reveal all that I owe to him and to Mr. Bishop.

H. G. Creel has read and criticized the chapters in which I have quoted him most frequently; but I owe him more than that. It was when I was most nearly in despair over the labyrinthine obscurities of the second millennium B.C. that his "Studies in Early Chinese Culture" gave me a clue.

To Ch'ao-ting Chi, whose "Key Economic Areas in Chinese History" first impressed me with the importance of irrigation and canal transport in Chinese history, I owe a special debt. In spite of the great pressure of his own work he has laboriously checked all the Chinese references and has given me additional references. Feng Chiasheng, one of the most widely read of the younger Chinese authorities on frontier history, who several years ago labored to help me with the reading of Chinese sources, has also given me a number of references.

To Dr. John K. Wright and Miss Mabel H. Ward of the American Geographical Society the book owes a great many editorial improvements. The diagrammatic maps are also the work of the Society's draftsmen.

To name all who have helped me would make the list too long; but some I must mention, however inadequately. Mr. and Mrs. R. LeM. Barrett, whose travels link them with the great era of Central Asian explorations, have for ten years encouraged, helped, criticized and stimulated everything that my wife and I have done. I should like to mention at least the names of my Mongol teachers, Bughegesik and Gombojab. There have been many others who have been teachers and also friends, friends and also teachers—Chinese, Mongols, Americans and Europeans. One of them, Arash, the companion of all my journeys in the Mongol style, taught me a great deal about what it is like to be a Mongol. Only a few days ago the news of his death came to me in a letter from a friend, together with a little gift he had made ready for me a short time before. "Moses" Li Pao-shu, who traveled with us in Turkistan and Manchuria, has been a trusted friend not only to my wife and myself but to my father before me and to my son. Besides these there are two men who taught me much about the Mongol-Chinese border that cannot be learned in any book—Georg Söderbom and Torgny Öberg.

Because of the series of scholarships and fellowships already mentioned, which enabled my wife and me to travel and study for four years, I am especially glad to be able to acknowledge recognition of a similar generosity as the work neared completion. At the beginning of this year Grinnell College honored me with an invitation to deliver the Rose F. Rosenfield Lectures on International Relations, and at the end of the year Northwestern University invited me to present the substance of this book in the Norman Wait Harris Lectures. The preparation of these two series of lectures enabled me to review and clarify the main body of my work, and to test it by applying to the Japanese war against China and to American interest in a free and victorious China the theories developed out of a study of history. The chapters that were drawn on most heavily for the two series of lectures were those on China, Mongolia, Manchuria, and Chinese Turkistan, in the first half of the book, and the final chapter; but all parts of the book, including the study of ancient history, were also reviewed and used in composing the lectures. To the Norman Wait Harris Foundation and the founder of the Rose F. Rosenfield Lectures I offer here, in print, what I hope will prove to be an adequate substantiation of the ideas they so hospitably invited me to discuss.

OWEN LATTIMORE

The Walter Hines Page School of International Relations, The Johns Hopkins University, November 20, 1939.

Part I

THE HISTORICAL GEOGRAPHY OF THE GREAT WALL

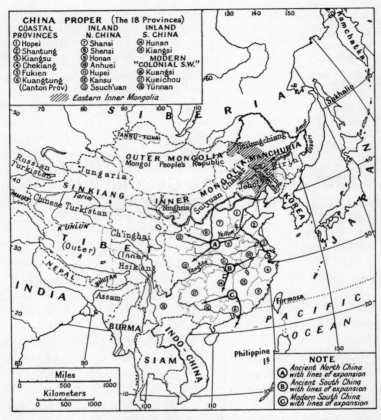

MAP I—China and neighboring regions: early lines of expansion; the eighteen provinces of China proper.

CHAPTER I
CHINA AND ITS MARGINAL TERRITORIES

Between the Pacific Ocean and the Pamirs, and from the Pamirs curving southward into the bleak highlands that divide China from India, lie the lands of Manchuria, Mongolia, Chinese Turkistan, and Tibet. These are the Inner Asian barrier lands, one of the least-known frontiers in the world, which limit the geography and history of China on one side as the sea limits them on the other. There have been periods when the landward edge of China was abruptly set off by a linear demarcation. The Great Wall, holding for a score of centuries as the most colossal tide mark of the human race, stands as the symbol of this aspect of Chinese history. In recurrent periods, however, the inland border of China has not been a sharp edge, defined by the Great Wall, but a series of frontier zones, varying in depth from south to north (and in Tibet from east to west) and stretching away indefinitely into the plains and mountains and forests of Siberia, the vague depths of Central Asia, and the wastes of Tibet.

Although it was in these territories that some of the most important conquests and migrations in history originated, they acted on the whole as insulating bands which allowed only irregular and usually feeble communication and interaction between China, the Middle and Near East, and Europe. In spite of the fact that the largest continuous land mass in the world lies between the southern coast of China, the Indian Ocean, the Mediterranean, the Atlantic coast of Europe, and the Arctic Ocean, the processes of history were never uniform in the East and the West. It is only now, in our own time, that the full potentialities of a new age are beginning to express themselves. Contemporary history no longer respects the isolation of China or any other country, by land or sea. The supersession of the old historical modes by new forces works in two ways. On the one hand, the regions and subregions of China and the major and minor zones of its frontier territories are being more and more sharply defined and differentiated. On the other hand, new general forces are asserting their supremacy, in the Far East as in the rest of the world, over every kind of geographical, national, and cultural particularism.

Continental and Maritime Periods of History

Within limits—but only within limits—this new phase in the relations between China and its Inner Asian frontier zones, and between Greater China and the rest of the world, can be made clearer by reference to the alternating "continental" and "maritime" periods in the world's history. From immemorial times until only about four centuries ago the major movements that went to form the Chinese nation, culture, and civilization originated on the landward, Inner Asian side of China. Maritime factors in Chinese history, acting often over remarkably great distances, are recognizable from a very early period and there is no need to discount their importance, but it is clear that this importance was of a secondary order. This holds true not only for the movement of peoples but for the early growth of political states and the evolution of the economic system and social structure that formed the core of the dynastic Chinese Empire, the "Center of the World."

In the Old World of Europe, and in the Near and Middle East also, "continental" modes of history were dominant. The fringe of maritime activity off the Atlantic coast, in the Red Sea and Indian Ocean, and especially in the Mediterranean, was deeper than off the coast of China and contributed more to the interaction of peoples and cultures. Nevertheless, it was true of both West and East that the forces generated within human society could act at a greater range by land than by sea, while even by land no social effort was yet capable of universal application.

The Age of Columbus was therefore as revolutionary for Europe as it was for Asia and the Americas. It is not enough to say that with the opening of the sixteenth century a maritime age of sea power succeeded the continental age of land power, making it possible for Europe to reach out both east and west. The significant historical phenomenon lies deeper: the older processes of society had accumulated a momentum that carried them to a higher level of development, one of the manifestations of which was a startling increase in range of action and force of impact. It was a new society which opened the new age of geography. The reasons that account for the Western European origin of the new age of maritime power cannot be dissociated from the origins, rise, and triumph of modern capitalism. Social evolution in Western Europe had reached a point that opened up certain new potentialities unknown to the feudal past, and when it reached this point the material resources necessary to animate first mercantile capitalism, and then industrial and finance capitalism, were available within the geographical environment of Western Europe itself.[1]

The new forces at work in society at once identified themselves with the expansion of sea power—partly because the older social structure above which they were struggling to rise was fortified with vested interests identified with the older standards of land power. This, and the political rise of England through its control of sea power, long tended to obscure the fact that there was no inherent reason for identifying the new standard of sea power with the new categories of commercial, industrial, and financial power. Politically, these new kinds of power could be based as effectively on control of land routes as

[1] For the difference between post-feudal evolution in Europe and in China compare Chapter XII, below.

on sea routes; they were, in their own nature, universally applicable. The advantages of an early start and accumulation of resources made Western Europe the center of gravity of the new age and kept England, in particular, at the controlling point of balance, until the twentieth century. The maturing of North America and the evident possibility of raising to the same or even higher levels of development huge regions like South America, Africa, Russia, and Asia, which hitherto have lagged at different stages of backwardness, now promises first to displace the center of gravity and then to do away with it altogether, making possible an evenly spread world balance.

EFFECTS OF LAND AND SEA POWER ON CHINESE HISTORY

It is not hard to apply these considerations to the history of China, where the truly effective impact of the West began quite early in the age inaugurated by Columbus. Until then the "foreign affairs" of China had been concerned primarily with the Great Wall Frontier. Overseas foreign relations had been of minor importance. Then, under the last imperial dynasty of Chinese origin—that of the Ming (1368-1643)—began the penetration of Jesuit missionaries and of Portuguese and other traders. European guns and gunnery even held back, for a little, the Manchu conquest.[2] Sea power for the first time challenged land power in the control of China; it was not yet successful, but already European trade was more important than it had been when Marco Polo was rated a liar in the thirteenth century, or when Pegolotti in the fourteenth century listed the Central Asian trade routes and the merchandise to be carried along them.[3]

The Manchu conquest of China in the seventeenth cen-

[2] Morse and McNair, Far Eastern International Relations, 1931, p. 26; Giles, China and the Manchus, 1912, pp. 17-18; Hauer, K'ai-kuo Fang-lüeh, 1926, p. 140.
[3] Yule, The Book of Ser Marco Polo, edit. Cordier, Vol. I, 1921, pp. 54, 115. Yule, Cathay and the Way Thither, Vol. III, pp. 137 et sqq.

tury was the last rush of the tide whose ebb and flow along the Great Wall Frontier had been so important in working the mechanism of Chinese history ever since the remote centuries in which that mechanism had been set up in its first crude forms. By the nineteenth century the momentum of the powers that were breaking their way into China from the sea had become irresistible. The strength of the lands beyond the Great Wall, from which Manchus, Mongols, and Turks had once issued, seemed to have withered away. In the deeper land masses behind them the inchoate strength of Imperial Russia died away in vague preliminary heavings—in the overrunning of an inert Central Asia, in asserting a sluggish acquisitive interest in Outer Mongolia, in seizing the Russian Far East (then almost empty) north of the Amur and east of the Ussuri, and in floundering defeat in Manchuria. In the Far East as a whole the paramount sea-power nations of Western Europe and America imposed their own standards at their own discretion.

In the war of 1914-18 this period reached its apex, and toppled. Great Britain, the United States, and Japan were left deadlocked in an uneasy naval balance; but at the same time from under the feet of the Western world and Japan there came the rumbling of an earthquake, as the Soviet Union shook itself out of the ruins of the Russian Empire. As a result of that landslip, the center of gravity of the land mass lying between the Atlantic and Pacific shifted from somewhere near the Rhine to somewhere near the Urals. Fascist Italy and Nazi Germany have thrust and threatened savagely to make an opening for Danubian conquests in order to prevent the shift from being made permanent, and British policy has wavered between fear of Italian and Japanese encroachments on its power at sea and in the Far East and reluctance to abandon to Germany its control of the balance of power in Europe; but with the growth of the Chinese Revolu-

tion the new distribution of weight between Europe and
Asia appears to be settling into place.

It is true that the Japanese invasion of Manchuria and
attempted conquest of China has in some ways the appearance of a head-on collision between land power and sea
power. It is unmistakably an attempt to subject the Inner
Asian land frontier of China to control from the sea. To
this extent it is true that the issue which failed to come
to a head in the nineteenth century—the issue as between
control of China from the Great Wall Frontier and Inner
Asia, and control from the sea—has now come to a head.
The "Open Door" policy, which John Hay's friend, Henry
Adams, conceived as a device for holding Imperial Russia
in check and guarding access to China from the sea, was in
large part responsible.[4]

THE WESTERNIZING OF CHINESE CIVILIZATION

At their best, however, these concepts of land power and
sea power make possible an analysis of "power politics"
only. The real roots of history lie deeper. The new age
of Columbus is now old and a still newer age is taking
shape. Such new ages grow up from within their predecessors, not to one side of them and independently of them.
In part they destroy and in part they merely reshape and
reanimate the forms that they supersede; they must break
up old vested interests in order to establish new paramount
interests. The Age of Columbus was not inherently "maritime" in its characteristics, but from the beginning took
on a maritime appearance partly because of its reaction
against vested interests based on a "continental" distribution and structure of power. In the same way, the new
age in which we live assumes a "continental" aspect in its
reaction against vested interests that inherited the nine-

[4] Adams, The Education of Henry Adams, 1918, pp. 423, 439. Compare
Lattimore, Open Door or Great Wall? 1934; The Land Power of the Japanese
Navy, 1934; Land and Sea in the Destiny of Japan, 1936.

teenth century empires established and linked together so largely by naval power. The determining consideration, however, is not the political factor alone but the working out in combination of all the complex potentialities of the new age. A crude isolation of political arguments is untenable; the next chapter of China's history will have more in it than a record of struggle for geographical expansion between automata marked "Russian communism" and "Japanese imperialism." It is the Westernizing of China's own ancient civilization that will in fact be decisive. Can that be done more effectively by Japanese conquest, or by European and American loans to a China that is also able to draw on the resources already accumulated by the Russian Revolution? How much of the ancient fabric will have to be destroyed? How stable a modern structure can be set up on the ancient foundations?

In order to answer these questions it is necessary to examine the geography of the whole of this field of history, determining the differences between the areas into which it can be divided. The relation of primitive society to geographical environment in each of these regions must also be considered in order to distinguish any early difference of bias toward alternative lines of social and political evolution in each region. The gradual gathering of momentum of the different contributory forces of Chinese and Great Wall history can then be assessed.

AREAS AND POPULATION

An attempt to estimate the geographical balance of the areas and populations of China within the Great Wall and the frontier regions of Manchuria, Mongolia, and Chinese Turkistan reveals at once the uncertainty and inadequacy of the figures available, but the following make possible a comparison of relative orders of magnitude:

AREAS IN SQUARE MILES

China within the Great Wall[a].........................   1,532,795

Manchukuo:[b]

   Manchuria (Liaoning or Fengt'ien; Kirin;

     Heilungchiang)   348,038

   Jehol..................................   52,126

   "Eastern Inner Mongolia" (Hsingan Prov-

     ince)   148,034   548,198

Outer or Northern Mongolia:

   Mongol People's Republic[e].......................   580,000

   Tannu-Tuva People's Republic (formerly Urianghai)[d]   58,000

Inner Mongolia (Frontier provinces of Chahar, Suiyüan,

   Ninghsia)[e]...   334,100

Chinese Turkistan (Hsinchiang or Sinkiang)[f] *of the order of*   600,000

Tibet proper[g].......................................   349,419

Tibetan-Chinese frontier provinces of Ch'inghai (Koko-

   nor) and Hsik'ang[h]...............................   463,666

POPULATION STATISTICS

China within the Great Wall[i].........*of the order of*   450,000,000

Manchukuo:[j]

   The three Manchurian provinces: main-

   ly Chinese but including 657,430 Ko-

   reans and an indeterminable number of

   Mongols. Japanese, Russians and other

   foreigners excluded..................   29,025,049

   Jehol: mainly Chinese, but presumably

   including some Mongols..............   2,606,472

   "Eastern Inner Mongolia" Hsingan:

   mainly Mongols, but presumably in-

   cluding an indeterminable number of

   Chinese...........................   1,078,128   32,709,649

Outer Mongolia:

   Mongol People's Republic[k].........*of the order of*   1,000,000

   Tannu-Tuva People's Republic (ex-

   cluding Russians)[l]................*not more than*   60,000

Inner Mongolia (Chahar, Suiyüan, Ninghsia): Chinese

   now outnumber the Mongol population, which I esti-

   mate to be of the order of one million; total, Mongol

   and Chinese[m].......................*of the order of*   5,000,000

Chinese Turkistan: includes, in approximate order of
numbers, Central Asian Turks (settled and nomadic),
Moslem Chinese, non-Moslem Chinese, Mongols,
Manchus, other lesser minorities[n]. . . . *of the order of*   3,500,000
Tibet proper[o]. . . . .*of the order of*   1,500,000
Tibetan-Chinese frontier provinces (Ch'inghai or Koko-
nor; Hsik'ang)[p]. . . .*no reliable figures; rough estimate*   3,000,000

[a] *China Year Book*, 1935, p. 1. An alternative figure of approximately 1.4
million sq. m. can be arrived at from the table of statistics of area given by
Warren H. Chen, An Estimate of the Population of China, 1930.

[b] Computed from the statistics in Fourth Report on Progress in Manchuria
to 1934, p. 13.

[c] Equivalent to 1.5 million sq. km., the round figure given by Viktorov and
Khalkhin, The Mongol People's Republic, 1936, p. 3 (in Russian).

[d] Equivalent to 150,000 sq. km., the round figure given by Kabo, Studies in
the History and Economics of Tuva, 1934, Vol. I, p. 8 (in Russian). On
Chinese maps Tuva is considered a part of Outer Mongolia. The total of the
figures I have here given for the Republics of Mongolia and Tuva is 638,000
sq. m. In *China Year Book*, 1935, p. 4, Mr. Tsen Shih-ying gives 622,744
sq. m. for the combined regions.

[e] Tsen Shih-ying, *loc cit.* W. H. Chen, *op. cit.*, gives 307,218 sq. m.

[f] *China Year Book*, 1935, gives both 550,579 sq. m. (p. 1), and 633,802
sq. m. (Tsen Shih-ying's figures, p. 4). W. H. Chen gives 703,562 sq. m.

[g] Tsen Shih-ying. W. H. Chen gives 703,562 sq. m.

[h] Tsen Shih-ying. W. H. Chen gives 440,000 sq. m.

[i] Estimates vary from about 350 million to about 500 million. W. H. Chen
(*op. cit.*, p. 6) estimates about 445 million.

[j] Computed from the statistics in Fifth Report on Progress in Manchuria to
1936, p. 151. It is especially difficult to estimate the number of the Mongols
in Manchuria. At one time I suggested a round figure of two million (The
Mongols of Manchuria, 1934). This estimate was attacked in an unsigned
article in the *People's Tribune* (Shanghai, No. 24, Aug. 1, 1935), citing a
Rengo dispatch from Ch'angch'un (Hsinking) of July 13, 1935, giving Japanese census figures of "something over" 470,000 Mongols in Hsingan and
113,258 in other parts of Manchuria. The same report gave 604,601 Chinese
in Hsingan—more than the Mongols. I do not know how reliable these
figures are. Nomad Mongols usually understate their numbers for fear of
taxation, while many of the numerous agricultural Mongols in Manchuria
(including a great part of Hsingan) may have registered as Chinese.

[k] The conventional Russian estimate appears to be 600,000. See, *e. g.*, A.
Rish, Mongolia Guards Its Independence, 1935, p. 107 (in Russian). Higher
Russian figures are also given, however; *e.g.*, 900,000 on p. 5 of Viktorov
and Khalkhin, cited above. In *China Year Book*, 1935 (article "Mongolia"),
I estimated 800,000; in The Mongols of Manchuria I estimated (roughly) one
million.

[l] Figures of 1914-15, cited by Kabo, *op. cit.*, p. 65. Of these, at least
40,000 may be taken as pastoral nomads and less than 20,000 as forest
nomads (hunters and reindeer breeders). The same author (p. 173) lists
nearly 12,000 Russian colonists in 340 settlements, as of 1918.

[m] Includes 1,997,234 in Chahar and 2,123,914 in Suiyüan (W. H. Chen,
op. cit.). For Ninghsia, Cressey (China's Geographic Foundations, 1934, p.
55) cites the Chinese Post Office estimate (1926) of 812,066, noting that it
deals only with the parts of Ninghsia formerly included in Kansu. For my

From these figures it appears that China within the Great Wall, or China proper, comprising the Eighteen Provinces[5] of the last imperial period under the Manchu dynasty, has an area of about one and a half million square miles with a population of between 400 and 500 millions, while the regions beyond the Great Wall, together with Tibet, have an area of something like three million square miles and a population of the order of 45 millions. That is to say, they have an area of twice but a population of the order of only one tenth of that of China within the Great Wall. Furthermore, well over two thirds of the population beyond the Great Wall (approximately thirty millions in Manchuria alone) is Chinese. The various tribes and peoples in this immense region who do not speak Chinese and are conspicuously different from the Chinese in their ways of living cannot possibly number more than five or six millions—very little more than one per cent of the total number of the Chinese people.

The historical questions raised by these figures are startling. Tne population of China 2500 or even 2000

---

estimate of the Mongol population of this part of Inner Mongolia, which is very rough, see The Mongols of Manchuria, p. 25.

    [n] W. H. Chen, op. cit., gives 2,567,640 (Chinese figures of 1928). Chinese official estimates of non-Chinese populations are, I think, usually too low.

    [o] China Year Book, 1935, p. 1; also, on p. 2, a Chinese estimate of 6.5 million (census of 1910). The latter figures must include Hsik'ang, then considered a border area of Ssuch'uan, and may have been a guess.

    [p] This figure is frankly a guess.

---

    [5] Three of these provinces—Yünnan, Kueichou, and Kuangsi—are "colonial" according to Wittfogel's definition (Wirtschaft und Gesellschaft Chinas, 1931, pp. 219 et sqq.). They are not part of the ancient core of China and have never been fully assimilated to the normal Chinese intensive agriculture and the social order based on it. The spread of the Chinese into these regions dates from not long before and not long after the Mongol conquest of the thirteenth century. The area of these three provinces is approximately 300,000 sq. m. and their population according to the China Year·Book, 1935 (pp. 2 and 4) is not more than 34 or 35 millions. There are also other regions to the south of the Yangtze that cannot be included in the earliest beginnings of Chinese history. The Chinese Year Book, 1938-39, gives the following figures of "tribal," non-Chinese population: in Yünnan, 8.6 millions out of 11.8 millions; in Kueichou, 4.3 millions out of 7 millions; in Kuangsi, 4.47 millions out of 13.3 millions. Kuangtung also has over half a million "aborigines," and Sanch'uan three quarters of a million.

years ago must have been relatively small. As it increased it filled up the Yellow River and Yangtze valleys, attaining eventually an average density of thirty to the square mile (taking the approximate figures of one and a half million square miles and 450 million people). A better idea of the real conditions is given by such figures as 554 to the square mile in a typical rice-growing region of the lower Yangtze valley[6] and 183 to the square mile in a typical North China region growing wheat, millet (including kaoliang), and cotton.[7] In spite of this crowding within an area roughly comparable to that of the United States east of the Mississippi, and in spite of direct access by land to territories rather larger than that of the United States west of the Mississippi, the Chinese never established themselves permanently and effectively beyond the Great Wall. Why?

CHINESE FRONTIER EXPANSIONISM

Within living memory, it is true, there have been phenomenal migrations of the Chinese into Inner Mongolia and especially into Manchuria, where the population increased from an estimated fifteen millions in 1910[8] to approximately thirty millions in 1931, the year of the Japanese invasion. The maximum rate of population movement was in the years 1927, 1928, and 1929, in each of which more than a million people entered Manchuria. The

[6] This is the average for the whole province of Chekiang (W. H. Chen, op. cit., p. 3.). The province of Kiangsu has the much higher average of 813 to the square mile, but I have not taken this as the example because the province contains the great cities of Shanghai and Nanking.
[7] This is the average for the whole province of Shansi (Chen, loc. cit.). The northern province of Hopei has 583 to the square mile, but it includes the large cities of Tientsin and Peiping. The larger part of Shansi is mountainous and thinly inhabited, which makes the average of 183 remarkably high. It is regrettable that there are no figures of population to the square mile of cultivated land illustrating different regions and their crops.
[8] China Year Book, 1935, p. 1. The population of Manchuria may not even have been so large as this in 1910; the Chinese estimate on which the figures are based arbitrarily calculated the population of Fengt'ien (Liaoning, the most thickly inhabited region) at the rate of 8.38 persons to a family, while for the rest of China the rate of 5.5 to a family was taken.

average net settlement figure for each of these years, after the return to China of seasonal migrants (harvest workers and so forth), was more than 600,000 persons.[9] It is important to note these figures in order to make it clear that they are not typical of the older processes of Chinese history. They belong exclusively to the modern period of railway-stimulated migration.

American history here offers a useful comparison. Westward expansion was a factor in American life even before the Revolution. Land-grant policies designed to increase the rate of expansion became a part of the federal and state organization from the time independence was achieved, and private enterprise was also bound up with the advance westward. Heavy immigration from Europe had something to do with the speed with which the Pacific coast was reached and linked organically with the Atlantic. Even without this immigration, however, it is clear that the process of filling up the American continent would have been essentially the same and the speed with which it was accomplished only relatively slower. The resulting society would also have been generically of the same structure and temperament. The original colonies on the Atlantic coast had acquired the essentials of the industrial revolution before the opening of the nineteenth century, and it was the industrial revolution, rather than any particular stream of migration, that fulfilled itself in the peopling of America in the course of the nineteenth century.

This comparison makes it clear that the special problems and characteristics that have to be sought out and studied in Chinese history belong to the period before Western industrialization, and the political. action that went with it, began to take effect in China. In the older processes of Chinese history the trend of migration and also the trend of conquest (expressing the political mo-

* Fifth Report on Progress in Manchuria to 1936, p. 121.

bility of power but not necessarily of whole populations) was predominantly from north to south and from west to east. No "population pressure" generated by the thick peopling of China ever produced a drive outward for permanent occupation of the forests of Manchuria, the steppes of Mongolia, the oases of Central Asia, comparable to the nineteenth century drive through the forests and across the prairies of America.

China's modern Frontier expansionism has in fact meant a considerable deflection of the lines of movement of both people and power established during earlier history. The most important factor in causing this deflection has been the force of industrialization, introduced from abroad and exerted by the industrial, commercial, financial, and at times the political and military activity of the Western nations and Japan, bearing down on China from the sea and working from the coast inland. By the time forces of this kind had reached as far as the ancient line of the Chinese inland Frontier (partly through their own momentum and partly because of being taken up and passed on by Chinese hands), they had been considerably modified. To a certain extent they destroyed or weakened old Chinese institutions and modes of action, but to a certain extent they were also themselves tempered and changed by the Chinese and Frontier environments in which they had been set to work. For this reason the Western influence along the inland Frontier may be called secondary as compared with the primary influences at work along the coast.[10]

As a result of all this it is now impossible to estimate the character of contemporary history in any zone of Chinese colonization, from Manchuria to Tibet, without discriminating between the relative degree of energy of "old" and "new" factors. Railways and modern arma-

---

[10] Lattimore, China and the Barbarians, *in* Empire in the East, 1934. Also end-paper map of same volume, showing periods of invasion and depths of penetration.

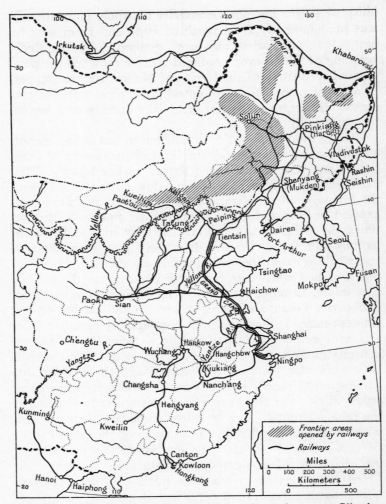

MAP 2—China, Manchuria, Korea, and southeastern Siberia: railways and frontier areas opened by railways.

ments are among the most potent of the "new" factors. The functional importance of each railway opening up a zone of colonization varies according to the degree of direct or indirect alien pressure exerted through it. In Manchuria before 1931 the power of Japan radiated from a corridor of direct control in the Kuantung Leased Territory and along the South Manchuria Railway into a much larger "sphere of influence" held tributary by indirect control. Beyond this there was a further margin within which operated both "modern" Chinese agencies—railways, modern banks, and so forth—and such "old" forms of activity as agricultural settlement; but the range of spread of the apparently old-style colonization was in fact greatly extended by the new railways and other new agencies. And both old and new Chinese agencies extended the scope of the agencies introduced by Japan while at the same time reacting against and competing with the expansion of Japan's interests. By undertaking the outright conquest of Manchuria in 1931, Japan attempted to enlarge the area of its control and to convert all of its activities to a higher pitch of intensity; but it has never yet succeeded in overcoming the resistance that springs both from the newer elements implanted in Chinese life and from the old, pre-Western, unmodified society.

By going back to the years immediately preceding the Japanese invasion of Manchuria, when the Chinese were flooding to the north of the Great Wall, it can be seen that the interactions between pre-Western and post-Western factors were highly complex. In certain aspects this Chinese colonization, although unprecedented in scale, appeared to exhibit the operation of "natural," "inevitable" forces which had been extant or latent in the relationship between China and Manchuria for centuries. Yet it was clear that the effective *range* of these "inevitable" forces had been expanded by something new; for in all the foregoing centuries during which China and Manchuria had interacted on each other, Chinese population pressure, statesmanship, economic power, and military action had never been able to master Manchuria and make it Chinese beyond certain recognizable zones in the extreme south. It was the use of railways, modern arms, and new financial, industrial, and commercial enterprises, different from those evolved in the previous history of China, that lifted the Chinese apparently once and for all out of the lower Liao valley and into the ancient Tungus forests of North Manchuria and the Mongol plains of West Manchuria.

Farther to the west the Great Wall had fronted against Inner Mongolia for centuries. Here the processes of recent history reflect the Manchurian scene; but the reflection is a little dim. The processes have been of the same kind but less intense in degree. This can immediately be referred to the fact that railway activity along this edge of the Frontier zone was far less vigorous than in Manchuria. Moreover, the only railway was Chinese, there was no direct foreign enterprise, and the degree of compromise between the introduced Western-style activities and the older style of dealing between Chinese and non-Chinese was much greater. Still farther to the west, where there are no railways, this fading intensity becomes even more noticeable. There has been a certain degree of penetration by motor routes, a certain livening of communication by post and telegraph, a certain stirring of new educational influences, and a yeasty working of new trade activities, in spite of weak financial and industrial development; but on the whole, in the Moslem Northwest (parts of Ninghsia and Kansu), in Chinese Turkistan (Sinkiang), and in Tibet it can be said that Chinese Frontier relationships have remained closer to the style of the T'ang dynasty (618-906) than to that of the twentieth century.

HISTORICAL PROBLEMS OF THE INNER ASIAN FRONTIER

To understand the obvious as well as the more subtle

aspects of what is now taking place along the Great Wall Frontier, it is necessary to return to the older history of the Chinese and their barbarian frontagers. In the society of China and the societies of its inland Frontier region, which characteristics and peculiarities are of major importance and which are subordinate? Which of them are destroyed when the modern world breaks in on them and overrides them? Which of them are able to survive? In order to survive must they compromise and modify themselves, and, if so, in what way? Which, again, of the characteristics of what we call "modern civilization" are primary and indispensable and which are secondary or unessential? Which of them, as the twentieth century invades the older civilization of China, are shed or mutilated; through which of them does "modern civilization" establish its ascendance; and do they, even in triumph, have to concede and compromise and submit to modification?

All of these questions must be answered if our judgment of the issues that are being worked out on the continent of Asia in our own time is to penetrate below the surface and cope with the real processes of history. In order to answer them it is necessary to go back to the most remote accessible origins of these historical processes. Unless the origins have been identified and the processes of development analyzed, it is impossible to describe accurately the behavior of the mature organisms of Chinese and Inner Asian society in the arena of contemporary history. Examination of the type of behavior reveals at once innumerable overlapping phases, for the relative importance of which it is necessary to establish standards.

My purpose in the study here undertaken is to cover only certain sectors of the historical field and only the earlier span of the total time range in order to establish, if possible, first principles whose later development and application can be followed out in future work. The major problems, as I see them, are the following: What are the earliest social forms and continuous historical processes that we can detect in China within the Great Wall? What was the landscape—the setting of environment—in which they began and pursued their development? Similarly, what are the basic landscape and environmental characteristics of the Great Wall Frontier and trans-Frontier regions—Manchuria, Mongolia, Chinese Turkistan, and Tibet—and what are the original forms and historical processes out of which developed their later societies? What is the type and style of interaction between the history of China and that of the different sectors of the Frontier and the Frontier as a whole?

I shall not here attempt to carry beyond A.D. 220 (the end of the Han dynasty) the record of early history and the analysis of its different regional aspects, though freely casting forward into later history when it is necessary to illustrate the processes of development, and at times working back from mature periods to the analysis of rudimentary phases. By A.D. 220 the main characteristics of the history of China and its Great Wall Frontier were settling into a pattern of interacting forces. In its later working out this pattern became first more rich and then more stereotyped; but a judicious estimate of the prime characteristics that had been established at the level of A.D. 220 makes it possible to discriminate, in subsequent periods and in the Chinese and Frontier societies of today, between ancient origins and later accretions. It is for this reason that I have tried, in the foregoing remarks, to set out a style and spirit of approach that will not isolate the remote past from the present but will make it possible to give historical depth and a well-rounded perspective to the scrutiny of the present.

CHAPTER II
THE FRAMEWORK OF THE GREAT WALL FRONTIER

Before attempting to discuss the origins of Great Wall history I shall set down, one by one, a summary characterization of the major regions that have to be considered: China, Mongolia, Manchuria, Chinese Turkistan, and Tibet. I shall try to describe the landscape in each of these regions, the society that has evolved in each landscape, and the lives that people lead; and I shall have something to say about the past history from which the present society has evolved and about the main problems that the people of each society face in our own time and in the immediate future. This will show, I hope, how each region of the Great Wall Frontier differs from all the others, and how closely, at the same time, all are linked with each other. My intention is to make easier the approach to remote origins by providing points of reference from which to work back into the past and a horizon to work towards from the past. In this way, I think, it is possible to show how the differences between the peoples of the Great Wall Frontier have emphasized each other by interaction, and how important a vivid sense of continuity is to the understanding of history.

In appearance, the general line of the Great Wall of China marks one of the most absolute frontiers in the world. To the south of it, from Tibet to the sea, innumerable rivers flow to the great arteries of the Yellow River and the Yangtze. Even those drainage networks that are not directly tributary to the arterial rivers are subsidiary to them. All water here reaches the sea. To the north of the Wall the rivers weaken and most of them die, either

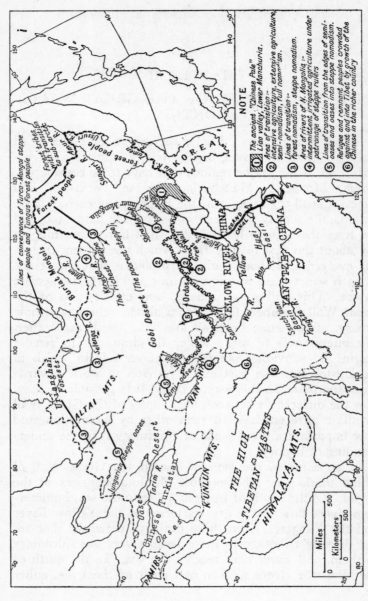

MAP 3—The Great Wall Frontier as a zone of differentiation between environments.

NOTE

☐ The ancient "Chinese Pale".
① Liao valley, Lower Manchuria.
   Area of transition : extensive agriculture,
② intensive agriculture, cattle-breeding,
   semi-nomadism, full nomadism.
   Lines of transition :-
③ forest nomadism, steppe nomadism.
   Area of rivers of N. Mongolia :-
④ intermittent, irrigated agriculture under
   patronage of steppe rulers.
   Lines of transition from the edges of semi-
⑤ oases and oases into steppe nomadism.
   Refugee and remnant peoples crowded
⑥ against and into Tibet by growth of the
   Chinese in the richer country.

KOREA
CHINA
GRAND CANAL
Hual basin
Han R.
Wei R.
Yellow R.
Szechuan Basin
YANGTZE
Yangtze R.
YELLOW RIVER
Semi-oases
Ordos
Great Wall
Shara Muren
Eastern Inner Mongolia
Amur R.
Ussuri R.
Sungari R.
Nonni R.
Forest people
Forest tribes
Forest transition
with wub-arctic
to tundra
Lines of convergence of Turco-Mongol steppe
people and Tungus forest people
Buriat Mongols
Onon R.
Kerulen R.
Selenga R.
The richest steppe
Gobi Desert (The poorest steppe)
NAN-SHAN
Semi-oases
Tarim R.
Oases
Chinese Turkistan Desert
KUNLUN MTS.
THE HIGH
TIBETAN WASTES
HIMALAYA MTS.
PAMIRS
Oases
Jungarian Steppe oases
ALTAI MTS.
Uriankhai Forests

Miles
0   500
Kilometers
0   500

vanishing in their shallow valleys or discharging into lakes and marshes with no outlets, many of them saline. Water here does not reach the sea.[1] In China regular rains feed the rivers; the climate is related to the monsoons of South-eastern Asia, but this relationship weakens as the rain-bearing winds move from south to north.[2] At the edge of the steppe the rain begins to fail, and in the heart of Mongolia and Chinese Central Asia there is an "outlaw" climate, not ruled either by the weather system of China or that of Siberia, though in the north of both Mongolia and Chinese Turkistan there are rich pastures at altitudes well above the central deserts, and forests on the northern slopes of the mountains, that acknowledge the moisture of Siberia.

Agriculture teems in China, and mankind swarms. Beyond the Great Wall men are fewer and more widely scattered. It is true that water can be found in sufficient quantity in some places, especially along the skirts of certain mountains, to offset the lack of regular rain and make possible an oasis agriculture that is quite as intensive as the farming of the Chinese; but such oases are isolated from each other by deserts and vast reaches of arid and sub-arid steppe.[3] Over thousands of miles of territory men neglect agriculture altogether; they do not live directly off the vegetation of the earth but interpose a special mechanism between it and themselves. The secret of the nomadic life is the control of animals by men: sheep, camels, cows, horses, and wild animals eat the vegetation, and

[1] With the exception of such marginal streams as the Shira Muren (upper course of the Liao), flowing into Manchuria; the Kerulen, which is part of the headwater system of the Amur; and the streams flowing into Siberia. The Tibetan streams flowing to India and Burma belong in a separate category. For the hydrography and orography of Mongolia, Chinese Turkistan, and Tibet, see the section "Haute Asie," by F. Grenard, in Vol. VIII of *Géographie universelle,* 1929.

[2] Coching Chu, The Aridity of North China, 1935, p. 212: "the moisture-bearing southeast monsoon blows against the coast in South China, but along the coast in North China."

[3] Lattimore, The Geographical Factor in Mongol History, 1938.

thus by managing domestic herds and hunting wild animals men provide themselves with food, clothing, tents made of felted wool, and dry dung for fuel.

Many other differences—including race, nationality, language, religion, and form of political organization—can be referred to the Great Wall line of cleavage. In China, for instance, in spite of wide variations of dialect (which reach an extreme on the southeastern coast), all men speak the Chinese language. There are still non-Chinese aborigines with aboriginal languages, but they are not strong enough to change the structure of society, though they modify its appearance. They are the survivors of ancient peoples, most of whom have been absorbed by the Chinese, and they are themselves peoples who are not yet Chinese rather than rivals of the Chinese. North of the Wall such languages as Manchu, Mongol, and Central Asian Turkish (all of which are related to each other) are not "dialects" of Chinese; they belong to an entirely separate linguistic family.

In all such differences the working of a powerful influence can be detected: the effect on the individual of the way in which the group lives. The wider the divergence of the way of life, the sharper the differences of race, language, religion, political loyalty, and so forth. Yet in fact the physical appearance of a camel-riding nomad in the most arid part of Mongolia, the language he speaks, the religion he honors, are all governed to a very important extent by the fact that he is a camel rider and not a farmer in the Yangtze delta alternately draining and flooding rice-paddies. Even "race," the absolute original differences of which it is impossible to isolate, is modified by diet and every other practice of the ordinary routine of living, and "national" characteristics of all kinds are even more plastically subject to social influences. The facial appearance of "pure" Manchus has considerably changed in the last thirty years and become more "Chinese" because Manchu children now grow up as Chinese children do; they are no longer strapped in cradles when small, with a hard pillow stuffed with grain, which flattens the back of the head— an artificial moulding of the head shape contributing to the facial cast that used to be considered "typically" Manchu.[4]

The Great Wall only approximates to an absolute frontier. It is the product of social emphasis continuously applied along a line of cleavage between environments. The difference of environment is not equally sharp along every sector of the Great Wall, and this corresponds historically to the fact that there are many loops and variations and alternative lines of "the" Great Wall. Indeed, Ch'in Shih-huang-ti, who "built" the wall in the third century B.C., did so by linking together different sectors that had already been built by several Chinese border states before his time. It is necessary therefore to discriminate between the natural environment and the social emphasis added to the environment in the course of history. In early phases the influence of environment on society is relatively powerful; but as the society matures it begins to assert control over the environment and choice between alternative uses of the environment. Study of the historical geography of the Great Wall of China therefore demands acute appreciation of the influence of environment on society, the adjustment of society to the environment, and the way in which different forms of society, as they mature, function and develop within their environments and attempt to control them.

[4] Lattimore, The Gold Tribe, 1933.

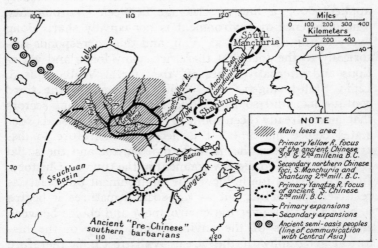

MAP 4—Foci and expansion of the northern and southern Chinese in the third and second millennia B.C.

CHAPTER III

THE LOESS REGION AND THE ORIGINS OF CHINESE SOCIETY

Beginnings of Chinese Culture in the Loess Region

When we approach the problems of the most ancient history of China the first thing that becomes obvious is a severe narrowing of the geographical area. The history of the Chinese did not begin at a number of points widely scattered over what is now China, spreading from these points until the initial areas merged with each other and a general culture became possible which represented the sum of many contributions. There are only two focal areas for the origins of Chinese history: a primary focus in the middle Yellow River valley and a secondary focus in the middle Yangtze valley.[1] In time the processes of diffusion from each of these foci began to overlap and interact. This raised the question whether the North or the South was to be dominant. In the upshot the North prevailed, partly because it had certain inherent advantages at the early level of development and partly because, as the general interplay of historical forces became more complex, it developed into the area in which equilibrium was to be sought between the history of agricultural China and the history of the Inner Asian steppes, with their marginal oasis, mountain, and forest zones.

When the sum of the forces at work had once taken this bias the geographical spread of the Chinese became uneven. Toward the south their expansion was immense. The ancient South China, lying between the middle Yangtze and the Huai and lower Han basins, became mid-

[1] Bishop, The Beginnings of North and South in China, 1934, and The Rise of Civilization in China, 1932.

China, as one primitive barbarian tract after another was occupied and incorporated beyond the Yangtze to form the new South China. On the north expansion was not only unequal but irregular and fluctuating. Periods of advance alternated with periods of retreat. The line of the Great Wall came to represent the mean of these fluctuations. Analysis of the reasons for this unequal development makes it possible to define the pattern of Chinese history and the type of historical movement animating the pattern.

Neolithic man probably was widely, though thinly, scattered over all the geographical and climatic regions of what is now China. Neolithic "history," however, was almost static. Weakness of social organization made it possible to transmit acquired knowledge and improved ways of doing things only clumsily and with much waste. This weakness lingered even after the slowly accumulating knowledge of how to do things, and how to make things for doing things, and how to take advantage of things done by others, had made possible a slightly greater assertion of human initiative. It was because of this weakness that the relatively sudden acceleration of human history toward the end of the neolithic period, and the leap forward from the use of stone and wood to the use of metals, was possible only in certain kinds of environment.

The lower Yellow River, flowing across the Great Plain of northern and middle China, frequently flooded and changed its course, creating wide marshes. The clearing, draining, and protective diking of such country required a level of organized social effort altogether beyond primitive mankind. The region very likely had a neolithic population of fen people, who hunted, fished, and gathered wild fruits and plants; but it cannot have been the homeland of "the" original Chinese, as maintained by Maspero.[2] As for the middle Yangtze, its heavier rainfall

[2] Maspero, Les origines de la civilisation chinoise, 1926; Chine et Asie cen-

meant not only marshes but rank jungle. It was an elaborate technique of irrigated rice-growing that eventually made settled agriculture possible and profitable for large populations along the middle and lower Yangtze.[3] To assume the working out of such a technique at the earliest stages of cultural and social development implies the ability to take a second major step forward at a time when the first tentative step had barely become possible.

Therefore it was the loess region that became the primary focus of Chinese history. So far as I know, it is always taken for granted in the older scholarship of the Chinese that the heart of the most ancient Chinese culture was in the general region of the great bend where the Yellow River, after running from north to south between what are now the provinces of Shansi and Shensi, turns to the east and enters the Great Plain. Modern Chinese commentators of major importance, like the late V. K. Ting, definitely hold this opinion.[4] Europeans like the great Richthofen[5] and Legge,[6] and more recently Conrady,[7] have tried to specify more exactly the Wei basin in Shensi or the southernmost part of Shansi and the part of Honan adjacent to it, across the Yellow River—near the edge, that is, of the Great Plain, but still within the loess highlands.

Wittfogel, however, has clearly established standards for determining the geographical area of the earliest Chinese history. The proto-Chinese must have made their first significant advances in the loess terrain of the Yellow

trale, 1927; La Chine antique, 1927. For comment on Maspero's theory, see Wittfogel, Wirtschaft und Gesellschaft Chinas, 1931, pp. 40-41.

[3] Bishop, Beginnings of North and South, 1934, pp. 316 and 319.
[4] Ting, Professor Granet's "La Civilisation chinoise," 1931, p. 268.
[5] Richthofen (China, Vol. I, 1877, pp. 340 et sqq.) considered that the Chinese came into Shensi from Central Asia.
[6] Legge (The Chinese Classics, preface dated 1865, Vol. III, p. 189) believed that the Chinese migrated to the middle Yellow River from as far away as the Black Sea.
[7] Conrady (China, 1910, p. 482) emphasized the development of the Chinese culture in China.

River bend, not because it was the richest land within their reach, but because it was the easiest land to work. The loess soil never carried a primeval forest of heavy timber difficult to clear away, and it was a soil in which a poor and crude agriculture could be started with the inefficient tools and weak social organization of a neolithic people. This mattered more than the fact that millet (of several varieties) and wheat, the major crops of the loess region, have never been so rich as the crops of the alluvial soils of the Great Plain, and not nearly so rich as the rice harvests of mid-China and the South.[8]

A number of tributary streams discharge into the Yellow River both above and below its final turn to the east. In their valleys water was available, but parts at least of the valley floors were not ordinarily subject to flood. Here the crucial transition could be made from the gathering of wild crops to a tentative agriculture, while the old wild crops still remained accessible. There was also an auxiliary supply of food, skin clothing, and bone utensils from the trapping or hunting of deer, pheasants, and partridges. Even the tiger still survives in North Shensi[9]; and leopards and wild boar, together with deer and almost unbelievable numbers of pheasants and partridges, are to be found in both Shensi and Shansi. Wilderness tracts in both provinces, covered with brush and small trees but without heavy timber (except where no thick deposit of loess hides the core of the underlying mountain structure), still preserve something of what must have been the appearance of the most ancient China.

[8] Wittfogel, *op. cit.*, p. 42. He notes that the culture of Egypt did not originate in the Delta of the Nile (the richest terrain), but far upstream in the region of Memphis. Sauer, in his American Agricultural Origins (1936, pp. 282, 295, 297) emphasizes the importance of a soil "amenable to few and weak tools," and states that American Indians first cultivated inferior soils because they were easier to work. He believes, however, that there may have been forests on loess soils which were destroyed by primitive man. Ting, a good geologist says positively (*op. cit.*, p. 269) that the Chinese loess was always of a semi-steppe character.
[9] Snow, Red Star Over China, 1938, p. 390.

RELATION OF EARLY CHINESE CULTURE TO SOIL AND CLIMATE OF THE LOESS REGION

The characteristics of soil and climate in this region were of special significance for the emerging Chinese culture. Thick loess deposits are notable for being free of stones and easily worked with primitive instruments. The vertical cleavage of the soil makes it easy to hollow out large caves in loess cliffs which are cool in summer and easily kept warm in winter.[10] Well-placed caves are still used at times for refuge from bandits, and in primitive times the ability to hold such refuges against raiding enemies must have been important.

The exceptional porosity of loess enables it to absorb water rapidly. The moisture is then drawn to the surface again to nourish the roots of plants. The natural cover of a loess region is grass, with brush and small trees in the valleys. There is a slow accumulation, which increases the depth of the soil and causes the grasses to flourish on successive surfaces. As the old surfaces are buried the roots of the old grasses decay, adding to the vertical porosity of the soil and also enriching it chemically. As rain or irrigation water sinks into loess and returns to the surface again, it brings with it, in solution, plant food in the form of natural chemical fertilizer. Consequently, the fertility of loess fields is never exhausted even when they are not manured—if only there is enough water.[11]

This characteristic is of special importance when the climatic factor is considered. Within the whole expanse of agricultural China it is this very region that has the maximum variability of rainfall. Drought years are never severe enough to kill off the natural vegetation, so that a

---

[10] Modern loess caves are dug into the faces of cliffs or banks, but the primitive method was to dig vertically into the soil (Bishop, *op. cit.*, p. 301).

[11] The classical description of the Chinese loess is by Richthofen, *op. cit.* Wittfogel (*op. cit.*, pp. 23-61) emphasizes the agricultural importance of loess in comparison with other soils. For technical discussion see also Barbour, *Recent Observations on the Loess of North China*, 1935.

primitive people that was beginning to develop agriculture and still relied in part on hunting and the collection of berries, fruits, roots, and so forth, would not be driven away. On the contrary, it would be encouraged to apply water from the streams to its crude, small fields wherever the water was available. The soft soil was so easy to work that there is no reason to suppose that irrigation on a small scale, by means of channels from one point on a stream to fields a few hundred yards below on the floor of the same valley, could not have been practiced in neolithic times— though it is hardly likely that this can ever be proved. Some of the simplest irrigation channels in Shansi and Shensi today, though actually dug with iron implements, could with very little extra difficulty be scratched with tools of bone, wood, or stone.

The society, however primitive, that first attempted such enterprises was predestined to a certain evolutionary bias. This first affected the way in which it was differentiated from other primitive forms of society that could have survived in the same landscape, and later influenced its whole course of growth—the tendencies it avoided, the tendencies it found congenial, and the mature form it eventually attained. The initial problems of differentiation are all-important. The question of the ethnic identity of the early Chinese and the barbarian tribes with which they were in contact need not yet be discussed. It would be interesting to know whether two or more races, or a mixture of peoples, took part in the founding of China; but the matter is not of decisive importance, because the major interest at this level of history is not the blood that ran in people's veins but rather the question of the way of life and the flexibility of that way of life—its capacity for elaboration within the original landscape and its adaptability to a wider range of territory.

Conclusions drawn from the geological, geographical, and climatic data all converge on one point: farming could not be made secure, capable of supporting a larger number of people and of releasing them from dependence on such auxiliary practices as hunting and the gathering of wild plant food, without control over water. The first clumsy efforts toward bringing water to the soil that needed it could be made by one man and his woman and children. Beyond that, the control of soil and water in combination lay only within the reach of groups of people, helping each other to dig larger channels and perhaps to build embankments that would keep flood water out of the bottom lands. Communal labor probably required, at this primitive level, communal ownership.

Whatever the original form of landownership—family or clan or "public"—progress in land utilization made collective action unavoidable. It is thus convincingly evident that within the original landscape the power of social institutions, irrespective of such classifications as "chief," "clan council," "king," or "state," could be applied more directly and emphatically through the control of collective labor than it could even through the ownership of land. If a man or group was able to decide how many people should go to a given point to bring new land and water under control, that man or group held the essential power to rule the community.

Early Expansion from the Loess Region

Expansion into new territory, moreover, followed water rather than land. The technique of building embankments is not essentially different from that of digging channels. The Great Plain of North China, therefore, lay open to settlement as soon as it had become possible to marshal really large numbers of men and to direct their operations. This is the chief point to be considered when inquiring into the historicity of the semi-mythical labors of Yü, according to legend the founder of the Hsia dynasty (at about the beginning of the second millennium B.C.) and the first ruler to undertake conservancy works on a large scale. The sources that deal with Yü have been examined to see whether places, persons, and dates can be determined, what parts of China are concerned, whether a number of legends have been gathered into one, whether a truly historical period is indicated. Yet the most important inference is relative: the whole account tends to show that when the Chinese passed from the primitive working out of their agricultural technique to the wider territorial application of it, "history" became necessary. A hero was created, and legends gravitated to his name.[12]

When they began to expand into the Great Plain the Chinese found the lower Yellow River a formidable opponent. After its long, straight run from north to south between the highlands of Shensi on the west and the mountains of Shansi on the east, the river discharges an enormous volume of water into the low plain. In passing through the soft loess lands it accumulates a heavy charge of silt. Checked by the abrupt eastward turn the water slackens, running across the plain. The silt is dropped and the bed of the river builds up. The highly variable rainfall over the whole of the river's upper catchment area means that in some years the volume of water coming into the plain is much greater than normal or average. When this happens after years of silt accumulation, the river easily floods its low banks and the low plain, forming great marshes and frequently changing its main channel. Permanent agriculture was therefore possible only when the primitive society of China had become mature enough to organize embankment and drainage work on a really large scale.

[12] For the Yü legend see Richthofen, *op. cit.*, pp. 277-364; also Herrmann, Die Westländer, etc. (in Hedin, Southern Tibet, Vol. VIII, 1921). In recent years the Yü legend, its dating and significance, have been much discussed by Chinese scholars; notably, Ku· Chieh-kang and his colleagues. For a review of the whole problem see Wittfogel's Economic and Social History of China, to be published in 1940. For Ku Chieh-kang, see Hummel, trans., Ku Chieh-kang's Autobiography, 1931.

Once this was possible, there was nothing to prevent the incorporation of the Great Plain into "China." The fen people who already lived there may have been ethnically the same as the Chinese of Shansi and Shensi, or ethnically different,[13] but organization of the first forms of the Chinese agriculture was impossible for them because of the difficulty of the environment. When the Chinese forms had become workable on a larger scale, however, both the land and its tribes could be brought within the scope of the expanding Chinese culture and made Chinese.

Transition was equally possible by a route across from Shensi to the enclosed basin of Ssuch'uan, on the upper Yangtze, and by a quite separate route from the Great Plain to the middle Yangtze, the lower Yangtze, and later the barbarian wilderness beyond the Yangtze. It may be granted that the rice culture of mid-China (then the South, the modern South China being a distant, barbarian, jungle wilderness) originated separately from the millet and wheat culture of the North. Apparently the easier physical conditions in the more open North made possible an earlier advance to a relatively large scale of economic enterprise, social integration, and political unity. It is probable that some of the methods of the North—methods which the peoples of the Yangtze were advanced enough to adopt though they had not been advanced enough to originate them—reached the South before the "true Chinese" were able to integrate the Yangtze politically with the North. It is quite possible that the spread was accomplished partly by small war bands of Northerners who established themselves as rulers in the South,[14] carrying with them their superior technical ability but becoming detached socially and politically from their old homes.

Certainly it is clear that the South became and for a long

[13] For the barbarians with whom the early historical Chinese states of this region contended, see Fu Ssu-nien, East and West Theory of the I and Hsia, 1936 (in Chinese).

[14] Bishop, *op. cit.*, pp. 318, 320.

time remained a separate cultural focus. It was even doubtful for a time, when in each focus the social and political
ability to organize larger units and operate at longer range
had become important, which would prove to be the primary and which the secondary focus. I believe that certain
characteristics developed along the steppe frontier of the
North eventually determined this decision,[15] but this aspect
of Chinese history may be left until later.

In any case, the Northern and Southern streams of Chinese history eventually converged. The result was an agricultural society of manifold activities. Its wide range of
local variation was offset by one dominant characteristic:
it was everywhere an intensive agriculture. Wittfogel,
surveying the relevant material, makes the point that there
have been considerable misconceptions, especially among
Western observers and students, regarding a supposedly
more intensive Southern agriculture and more extensive
Northern agriculture. There are undoubtedly differences
in the degree of intensiveness as between the rice paddies
of the South and mid-China and the millet and wheat and
beans of the North. In kind, however, they are not different. The agricultural economy of the North is as intensive
as the social organization of the Chinese can make it.
Where irrigation channels to take water from the streams
to the plains are not practicable, North China is a land of
wells, and the limited amount of water from each well
supports in the aggregate a vast agricultural activity which
is so intensive that it resembles gardening.[16]

Even on the terraced hillsides of the North and those of
the loess highlands to which water cannot be brought,
"dry farming" is only marginal to the intensive cultivation
that forms the core of the economy, dictates the social
structure and the classification of landownership, and is in
turn so exclusively the object of all organized activity as

[15] Lattimore, Origins of the Great Wall of China, 1937.
[16] Wittfogel, Wirtschaft, etc., pp. 189-223.

to hamper forms of development that a different balance of society and economy might make profitable. In the North, as in the South, the determining consideration is the farming of the best land, the concentration of the most people on the most productive land, and multiple cropping in order to keep the land and the people busy.

This has created in both the North and the South a farming landscape strongly marked by large and frequent walled cities. On the edges of these areas of concentration the people and the farming thin out rapidly.[17] Good farming has its fringe of poor farming, but beyond the poor farming there is practically no significant activity at all. The exploitation of mountainous country by methods alternative to agriculture is astonishingly weak in comparison with the mature development of specialized agriculture in the areas of concentration.

WEAKNESS OF NORTHWARD EXPANSION

On turning to the northern, steppe margins of the Chinese field of history a strikingly different aspect becomes evident. North of the main line of what eventually became the Great Wall the geography of Asia changes more rapidly than its climate. There are no rivers with a volume of water sufficient for irrigation. Over a large part of Inner Mongolia agriculture is possible, it is true, but only if a change is made from intensive to markedly extensive forms of cultivation and preferably to "mixed farming," with considerable dependence on livestock. In the modern phase this has already been done on a large scale, and colonization is still going forward; but this is only because railroads have totally changed the ancient balance of social and economic factors. From the earliest beginnings of Chinese history until the end of the nineteenth century there was never any such decisive spread, either by colonization or by the assimilation of the steppe peoples. The Chinese

[17] Thorp, Geography of the Soils of China, 1938, pp. 430-432.

did advance beyond the Great Wall repeatedly, it is true; but haltingly and indecisively. Periods of expansion were followed by periods of retreat. In the same way the tribes of the steppe invaded China time and again; but south of the Great Wall they never established permanently the steppe economy and the society of pastoral nomadism.

This contrast between a margin of differentiation and limitation on the north[18] and a margin of indefinite expansion on the south makes it possible to determine which of the processes of Chinese history, within China proper, were of decisive importance. Stated briefly, the main linkage appears to be as follows. Any one of the major regions of China is capable of supporting an advanced civilization. The region in which the first significant growth can be traced was not the richest of these, but the one that offered the least impediment to the weak initial stages of cultural growth and at the same time the powerful stimulus of rich rewards for even the crudest attempts at irrigation. The bias toward intensive agriculture thus imparted at the very beginning continued to develop because the regions into which the Chinese expanded, though somewhat different in geography and climate, and some of them naturally more fertile than the original center of diffusion at the Yellow River bend, also responded favorably to an intensive agriculture based on irrigation. Some of them might have developed successfully under a different economic and social order, but the special Chinese trend had the advantage of being the first to assert itself, and thereafter it was easier to develop toward uniformity than toward multiformity.

Only in the north did sharp differentiation take the place of convergent evolution toward uniformity. This was because the early Chinese were already committed to

    [18] Lattimore, *op. cit.*; also The Geographical Factor in Mongol History, 1938; and China and the Barbarians, 1934, for the difference between South Manchuria and other regions beyond the Great Wall.

agriculture. It was impossible for them to evolve toward an increasingly elaborate intensive agriculture and at the same time to devolve toward extensive and mixed agriculture.[19] In fact, there appeared in this region an altogether different order, that of the nomadic pastoralism of the steppe. Out of this there developed a perpetual antagonism, which demanded a decisive choice of every people and state that in the course of history overlapped the Great Wall Frontier, whether its founders were Chinese or non-Chinese—the choice between agriculture of a notably intensive form and nomadism of an especially dispersed form. Of the repeated attempts to create societies or states that could integrate both orders not one succeeded.

THE STYLE OF CHINESE HISTORY

At this point it is possible to describe broadly the *style* of Chinese history without, for the moment, going into such problems as the question of an early matriarchal system, feudalism, or the exact structure and functioning of the unified imperial state in its mature form.

In the landscape of China the irrigated fields were the best fields. The conservancy works necessary for establishing and maintaining irrigation were too great for the private enterprise of even the richest landowners.[20] State administration was unavoidable, and therefore the ability to influence this part of the activity of the state was even more the mainspring of political power than ownership of the land itself. The state also held large surpluses of grain, because land taxes were paid partly in kind. The storage of this grain demanded a community center, and one that could be defended—a walled city. This made for a regional structure of "compartments," each with a walled

---

[19] Lattimore, Origins of the Great Wall of China, 1937.
[20] Bishop, The Rise of Civilization in China, 1932, p. 627, for the importance of forced labor in forming the type of Chinese intensive agriculture; Wittfogel, Wirtschaft und Gesellschaft Chinas, 1931, *passim;* also Foundations and Stages of Chinese Economic History, 1935.

city and enough adjacent farmland to make a convenient unit of local trade, exchange, and administration. Part of the grain surplus of each "compartment" was concentrated in granaries at a smaller number of metropolitan points, at the disposal of the government for feeding the garrisons which represented the extension of the central, dynastic power into the provinces.[21]

Accumulated grain meant more than wealth. In time of war granaries made it possible to support garrisons; for irrigated lands, much more than the farms of extensive agriculture, predicate a slow, positional warfare of garrisoned cities and siege operations. More important still, in the normal activities of the state and its people stored grain made it possible to assemble large numbers of men to carry on further work. either in the maintenance of existing irrigation systems or in new enterprises. A surplus of grain and a surplus of manpower were in fact complementary; each made it possible to produce the other.

This was especially important because intensive agriculture demands intensive labor. Although landlords might own very big holdings, the working unit of land farmed by a tenant or hired laborer was very small. In order to keep rentals up and wages down the social system demanded not merely enough people but too many people, a demand that was met by family and social institutions favoring rapid population increase. This in turn must have contributed to the low development of machinery in China: those whose vested interest lay in the control of manpower discouraged the development of alternatives to manpower. Since it was these interests that were also most closely bound up with agriculture, they discouraged at the same time the development of mining, industry (except local handicraft industry), and all other activities that might threaten the supremacy of the irrigation-controlling, land-controlling, manpower-controlling classes who were

[21] Ch'ao-ting Chi, Key Economic Areas in Chinese History, 1936, *passim.*

the real rulers of China at each successive stage of its history.

The same considerations explain the Chinese inability to spread permanently beyond the Great Wall, except in limited zones and usually for short periods. Change from intensive agriculture meant a relatively wide dispersal of the population and a loosening of the methods of administration that had become standard. Moreover, the lack of irrigation activity meant the dropping out of what early became and always remained an essential link in the chain of economic, social, and political control.

The filling of China by the Chinese was therefore accomplished by the adding together of innumerable units, which in spite of local differences were essentially homogeneous, each consisting of a rural landscape watched over by a walled city—never, in the more fertile parts of the country, more distant than a day's walk from the next city. Yet in spite of this homogeneity China as a whole rarely acted in unison, because each "compartment" was as nearly as possible self-contained. The grouping together of series of these units resulted first in the formation of separate kingdoms and then in a unified imperial state. Political agglomeration of this kind had little effect on the scale of agriculture, but it did increase the scope of state-administered water-conservancy enterprise. It also made necessary the concentration at metropolitan points of part of the local grain surplus of each urban-rural unit.[22] This was accomplished by the use of rivers and canals, which were made to serve as cheap transport routes and at the same time as arterial irrigation conduits.

The extraordinary way in which all social forces converged on a more and more elaborate development of this line of evolution is illustrated in a quite peculiar and startling way by the Grand Canal, which runs from north to

[22] This analysis of the relation between city and country is, I think, clearer than that which I gave in Manchuria: Cradle of Conflict, 1932, Ch. XI.

south, roughly parallel to the seacoast. So long as the dynastic state power was vigorous enough to maintain the upkeep of the Grand Canal (which was not simple, because it ran at right angles to the flow of the rivers), the shipment of goods along it altogether overshadowed in importance any shipments along the coast. This can only have been because the society of China as a whole favored the manpower standard of barges towed along canals and discouraged the centrifugal tendency of sea-borne trade. Moreover, canal traffic passed through the cultivated area, and could be organized in such a way that it interlocked with the rural administration. Sea traffic was an independent and therefore to some extent competitive activity. Probably navigation was also affected by the way in which the monsoon winds, as described by Coching Chu, blow to and from the southern coast but *along* the northern coast.[23]

The Grand Canal was also an "artificial Nile,"[24] the control of which brought to its most mature form the balance of key economic area and key political area which has been acutely expounded by Ch'ao-ting Chi. The control of China by the dynastic imperial state came to mean the simultaneous control of a political and military capital in the North, watching the unassimilable Frontier, and a region of optimum surplus agricultural production to feed the capital. The position of both capital and key economic area varied in different historical periods.[25]

COMMERCE, MINING, AND THE MANDARINS

Until the time when China was invaded from the sea in the nineteenth century, most of its people and most of its trade did not have to move far between urban market and rural market. Only special commodities and special people circulated more widely. Salt, iron, tea, and silk

[23] Chu, The Aridity of North China, 1935, p. 212.
[24] Wittfogel, Foundations and Stages, 1935, p. 52.
[25] Chi, *op. cit.*

were not everywhere produced but were widely distributed. Tea and silk, being special commodity products of the main food-supplying agricultural activity, could be handed on from local trader to local trader; but salt and all metals, especially iron, invited special regulation because the agricultural society of China could not get on without them and did not produce them as part of its normal farming enterprise. Therefore from very early times it was profitable to limit the refining and distribution of salt and the mining of metals under monopolistic licenses granted by the state.

The results were curious. It is a commonplace in China that the worst salt is sold in the immediate vicinity in which it is produced and at relatively high prices, because of monopolistic control. The better salt, being more concentrated, can stand the price of transport. It is despatched to more distant markets—but it can be adulterated again before being sold, to increase the profit. The public is forced to pay the price because the peasants, who consume the greatest quantity, live almost entirely on grain and vegetables and salt is chemically necessary to their diet. A contemporary example of the importance of salt is the fact that lack of salt, which had been denied them by blockade and was having a debilitating effect on the people, slowly became as important as the military campaigns of the Nanking Government in forcing the Chinese Communists to abandon in 1936 the areas south of the Yangtze that they had held since 1928.[26]

As for mining, it has always been crippled by methods of taxation that approximate to blackmail. The major apparatus of the state in China was occupied with the closely developed areas of cultivation. Mining was an activity

[26] Snow, *op. cit.*, p. 174. The debilitation of the peasants in these long-blockaded regions, through lack of salt, was vividly described to me by a Nanking officer who had campaigned against the Chinese Soviets. He said with conviction that had they not been so weakened the Red Army could never have been driven out of this region.

apart, in the hills, usually out of reach of this apparatus.[27] Officials, busy promoting their own careers by attention to the main business of the state, were indifferent to the promotion of mining and treated mining licenses merely as a source of profit. If a mine turned out to be rich, the charge to the individual or private association working it was at once raised. Improved methods of extraction were thereby retarded, because the extra investment needed to make them possible was an indication of wealth which immediately brought demands for extra fees and the appointment of officials as "inspectors" or "administrators." Nor was there any penalty for not developing mineral resources, because lack of metal was accepted as normal. This accounts for the fact that in China the state and the culture of the people were in some respects able to develop an extraordinary maturity and sophistication, while mineral resources within close reach were exploited only on a scale that made available the small supplies needed by an artisan style of manufacture, and while people burned grass roots within a few miles of easily accessible coal.

A special class of people, the mandarins, presided over the interests of the state in these and other matters. Unlike the peasants, the townsfolk, and even most of the merchants, they were not confined to one of the "compartments" of China, but circulated freely. Since they also conducted the business of the state within each compartment and graduated from local service to general service, they were the most important link between the life of each homogeneous but largely isolated unit and the life and affairs of the nation as a whole. Their position in this respect being a kind of monopoly, they were naturally inclined to preserve it by favoring repetition and routine and discouraging variation and experiment of every kind.

---

[27] Lattimore, *op. cit.*, p. 120. At this time, however, I had not yet worked out clearly in my own mind why the state in China had developed its peculiar attitude toward such activities as mining.

Recurrent Cycles in Chinese History

Repetition, accordingly, ruled the course of events in China, with evolution checked in every direction except that of further specialization of the already dominant peculiarities. The rise and fall of dynasty after dynasty is a calendar of recurrent phases. First, increasing returns as the result of concentrating people in favorable areas in order to organize them for water-conservancy works on a large scale and for the practice of agriculture. Second, apparent stability as production reached its peak by means of these activities, and those who controlled the order of the state settled down to maintain the working of the order and to discourage all initiative that trended away from it. Third, diminishing returns, because the social system emphasized large families, while the economic system resisted new kinds of activity to employ the surplus manpower. An oversupply of human labor was a condition of the prosperity of those who lived by the control of law, order, and tradition. Out of this was bred agrarian depression and collapse, a more and more intolerable contrast between the few who were literate, sophisticated, well-to-do, and ordained to rule, and the illiterate many who were ordained to live by their muscle but who were denied the right to work and life if the market was oversupplied with muscle. Fourth, agrarian risings which destroyed the state but did not open up a way to build a new kind of state.[28]

The time and the people were then ready for a new strong-man dynasty. Order could be restored by force, but not the flow of taxes. Therefore the strong man, when his power had been acknowledged, protected those who repaired the water-conservancy works and called out the survivors of the scholar-bureaucrats to organize the infinite activities of listing and checking the men at work and filing the returns of grain transport and grain tribute.

[28] Compare Chapter XVII, below.

With a new margin of profit to be eaten up, after the famines and depopulation that were characteristic of such rebellions and wars, the new dynasty began the ascendent phase of the new cycle. But neither in the tearing down of the structure nor in the rebuilding of it was the foundation touched. The society as a whole remained centripetal and the old way of life the only one that was understood. No large bodies broke away to found a new order in the steppes that were contiguous to China but had never been considered proper to the landscape of China.

THE NINETEENTH CENTURY: WESTERN INTRUSION INTO THE CHINESE CYCLE

From these points of reference it is possible to draw out the lines that make a diagram of China at any phase of the repeated historical cycle. In the beginning of the nineteenth century, for instance, the Manchu dynasty, founded by barbarian conquerors but long since ruling in the Chinese manner, had outlived its vigor. The society as a whole was mellow, but rotten patches were beginning to spread. The terrible devastation of the T'aip'ing Rebellion (1850-65), though predictable, had not yet begun. What was the appearance of China then to a stranger approaching from the sea, and who were the typical Chinese?

The ports along the coast were busy with trade; a significant foreign trade was developing, but this was chiefly at the instance of the foreign merchants. Although a new class of Chinese merchants rose and flourished with the foreign trade, the interchange of commodities essential to the carrying on of the Chinese way of life was not dependent on what could be sold overseas or brought in from other countries. The Chinese trade of the Chinese ports was, in fact, with other parts of China; coastal trade was only an alternative to inland trade by road, river, and canal. Each coastal port had its own hinterland of agricultural production and its exchange at short range with this hinterland and at long range with other parts of China, which did not differ in kind or function from the short-range and long-range trade of far inland cities like Sian in Shensi and Ch'engtu in Ssuch'uan.

Inland, the geographical setting of the working machinery of Chinese life was plain to see. Each expanse of intensively cultivated land was broken up into small units marked by walled cities. Where this kind of land ran into poorer land or hilly country there was a rapid falling off of agriculture and population, not adequately compensated for even where compensation was possible by the development of mining, industrial manufacture for wide distribution, or even mixed farming. In the southern provinces of Yünnan, Kueichou, and Kuangsi, it is true, there was a mixed economy of livestock and farming; but this did not represent a trend away from the prevailing Chinese usages. The Chinese had spread to these regions only in comparatively recent centuries[29] and were still engaged in assimilating the aborigines and the local practices to their own standards.

The great and profitable activity of trade, especially at short range, and the distribution of commodities made on a handicraft scale in every city were the business of a merchant class who were essentially middlemen and agents. It was difficult to free capital for independent investment in production and distribution. The general rule was that the longer the range at which trade was carried on the more it was limited to luxuries and tended to exclude necessities. Because essentials were dealt in at short range there was no special emphasis on speed, ease, and distance of communication—except for collecting the grain surplus, for which purpose the Grand Canal outranked the imperial highways in importance.

Grain, accumulated and stored, was beyond question the standard of real wealth in essentials. The development of

[29] Wittfogel, Wirtschaft, etc., 1931, pp. 222-223.

money wealth in an easily invested, transferable, circulating form was weak. Money had never been freed, in China, from the crude custom of storing bullion and jewels. This meant that the merchant, however wealthy, could not easily rise above the status of an agent. The landlords were the class for which he acted and the landlord, accordingly, had more power in the state than the merchant. Even in money lending the capital of the landlord had better access than that of the merchant to the borrowing peasant, and it had better security, because the landlord actually controlled agriculture while the merchant did not.

The landlords were none other than the mandarins, the "special people" who have already been mentioned—the "scholar-gentry." [30] The landlord, as mandarin, was his own rival, for there was a constant struggle between the authority of the state and the power of the ruling class. The state held the upper hand in so far as it could enforce the rule that no mandarin could hold office in his native province, where his family might be strong. The gentry held the upper hand in so far as they dealt, in matters of state, only with "their own class of people." Consequently, tax demands were pressed more lightly against the gentry and the deficiency was made up by exactions from the peasantry and from trade. The wealthy merchant, it is

[30] Travel in Manchuria first impressed on me the identity of landlords and bureaucrats and the significance of the written language as a bureaucratic code. Since then, in editing *Pacific Affairs,* I have been able to learn a good deal more about the subject. See particularly, in *Pacific Affairs,* The Rise of Land Tax and the Fall of Dynasties in Chinese History, by Wang Yü-ch'üan, June 1936; The Good Earth of China's Model Province, by Chen Han-seng, Sept. 1936; The Dragnet of Local Government in China, by N. D. Hanwell, March 1937; A Large-Scale Investigation of China's Socio-Economic Structure, by K. A. Wittfogel, March 1938. Without experience of the unwieldiness of a non-alphabetic writing it is difficult to realize the gulf between the man of letters and the illiterate peasant in China. A man must have money to live and time to work for years in order to master the written symbols without which it is impossible to rule and administer. The tradition has always been to preserve the Egyptian obscurity of writing, and advocacy of a simplification has by no means yet broken down the traditional resistance of the elect. For this one reason it is much harder to be a "self-made man" in China than in Western countries.

true, could make a place for himself among the elect by using his wealth to convert himself into a combined landlord-trader, which meant a discreet subordination of his trade enterprises to his landed interests.

Literacy was the link that made the scholar-gentry–landlord mandarins a ruling class of Siamese twins: a recondite literacy, which fostered difficulty and mystery in the written language and consciously resisted simplification and wide dissemination among the people. It "separated social classes but united regions." [31] It required a long apprenticeship, which could only be afforded by families of leisure, so that the nominal equality of all men in the public examination halls was in fact an equality of opportunity only for those who already monopolized the power of the state. Only those who had passed the tests could approach the mysteries of measuring and taxing land, assessing grain tribute, apportioning water from the main irrigation systems, and levying and organizing forced labor for the maintenance of canals. It was easy for them to insure that they and their families should own the best lands and have access to the most water. They did not even need to organize themselves as a military caste, for no soldier, however able in the field, could make the apparatus of production and revenue work unless he commanded the highly codified written language and a corps of scribes to manipulate it for him. Even alien conquest, therefore, could not destroy the Chinese literati, for no matter who ruled in name, they ruled in practice.

The "typical" Chinese, therefore, was two quite different people—a peasant whose functions were little higher than those of a draught animal, and a scholar whose long fingernails were the proof that he did no hard work. "Culture" was the monopoly of a class that combined the grossest corruption (above all in the peculation of state revenue) with the most delicate artistic refinement and the most

<hr>

[31] Wittfogel, Foundations and Stages, p. 54, n. 3.

subtle training of the intellect (though only in certain directions). The peasants also had their traditions; for though their world was cramped, centuries of work in highly specialized agricultural practices and coördination of the muscular effort of large numbers of men working together to accomplish what would otherwise have been impossible without machinery had developed in them also a heritable social instinct. They had the ability to reduce theory to the essentials of practice, to work in combination with little apparent leadership, and to climb rapidly from lower to higher levels of organization and the use of resources when free of pressure from above.

It can be seen that as the mounting insistence of the Western nations forced China open in the nineteenth century, especially after dynastic stability had been weakened by the T'aip'ing Rebellion, a new process began which meant the destruction rather than the conversion of the old Chinese way of life. The West introduced many new kinds of wealth and power but these were welcomed least by those who already had the most power and the most wealth under the old order. The mandarinate, accordingly, turned the whole country against the West as long as it could. The first signs of conversion came not from them, but from the middlemen-merchants, who were able to serve the foreigners as brokers if that offered them more profit than their old function as the agents of the scholar-gentry.

Since, however, some of these merchants also had a footing among the scholar-gentry, the process of conversion spread in time among the families that for centuries had provided China's landlords and mandarins. The solidity of the old form of rule was undermined. Some families and individuals rose, in proportion as they mastered the new ways of doing things, while others began to sink, in proportion as they clung exclusively to the old ways.

In the contemporary phase, China has been dominated

by the families that have diversified their activities; they continue to hold large landed properties, but at the same time are active in trade, industry, and banking.[32] The artisan class is being rapidly converted into an industrial proletariat, divorced from the villages and the peasant family standard. The last to be affected have been the peasants. This makes the fate of the peasant decisive for the nation. If he is to be held down to the old way of life while the rest of the nation changes, then China will become a vast Japan, with an industrial development high in certain activities but uneven as a whole, and with a disastrous and widening gap, as in Japan, between the mechanical progress of the factories and the human-labor standard of the farm.[33] Either the peasant must be liberated and granted equal rights to progress with the rest of the nation or else the overproduction of human labor on the farm, under serf-like conditions, will drag down the wages and standards of factory labor and undermine the whole national economy—again, as in Japan.

[32] Chen Han-seng, The Present Agrarian Problem in China, 1933; also Landlord and Peasant in Southernmost China, 1937.
[33] Utley, Japan's Feet of Clay, 1936.

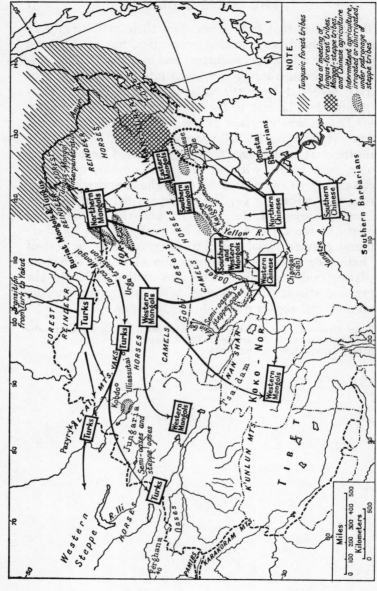

MAP 5—Steppe and forest tribes and economy in relation to China and the Great Wall Frontier.

CHAPTER IV

THE STEPPES OF MONGOLIA AND THE CHARACTERISTICS OF STEPPE NOMADISM

Rather than undertake the survey of the Great Wall Frontier in arbitrary geographical order, from Manchuria on the east through Mongolia and Chinese Turkistan to Tibet on the west, it is better to examine at once the steppe region of Mongolia. This is the *locus classicus* of all Frontier history. From the mixed geography of Manchuria on the east, and from the oases and deserts of Chinese Turkistan and the high, cold plains of Tibet on the west, there originated societies whose historical cast is best regarded as a series of variations on the history of the Mongolian steppe. These variant forms were powerfully modified by what happened in Mongolia and also by the influence of China, an influence differing locally in each region but of the same general order.

There is evidence that the neolithic people of Inner Mongolia tended to concentrate around marshy areas, that they were hunters who also had stone implements with which they may have grubbed up edible roots, and that they may also have practiced a "hoe agriculture." Stone implements and fragments of pottery are especially frequent in wide, shallow depressions now filled with sand dunes, some of them bare and some covered with vegetation.[1] In such areas the subsoil water is usually very near the surface.

[1] I write here from what I have seen in Inner Mongolia and heard from Mongols. For the literature of the subject, see the wide references in the writings of Bishop and Wittfogel, already quoted; also Creel, Studies in Early Chinese Culture, 1937, and Menghin, Weltgeschichte der Steinzeit, 1931. There was also a neolithic culture of mixed hunting, fishing, food gathering, and herding—the herding must at first have been very weakly developed—as far north as Buriat Mongolia (Pomus, Buriat-Mongolian ASSR, 1937, p. 96, in Russian).

While there may have been a general increase of aridity all over Mongolia since neolithic times, there is no reason to suppose that desiccation was drastic or sudden enough to give a sharp bias to the course of evolution from the neolithic life to the later steppe nomadism. It is clear that it was not a change from moist to arid climate that prevented the evolution of an agriculture comparable to that of China. On the contrary, dunes of sand came right up to the edges of some of these ancient marshes, and even at that time there was no network of streams that would have encouraged intensive agriculture over large areas.

EARLY CULTURAL DIFFERENTIATION BETWEEN NORTH CHINA AND MONGOLIA

The decisive difference between China and the steppes of Mongolia is this: the neolithic hoe culture of the steppe did not develop even into an "extensive" farming of the open plains or into a mixed economy of farming combined with livestock breeding. It was pastoral nomadism that eventually became the ruling order, though not the sole order. There is a range of economic variation to be considered here. Irrigated agriculture makes possible the maximum (in pre-industrial societies) of intensive economy and concentrated population. Unirrigated farming, especially when the rainfall is light or irregular, and the combination of agriculture with pastured livestock predicate a more extensive economy and a thinner concentration of people. Pastoral nomadism is notably an extensive economy, forcing a wide dispersal of society. In the north of Mongolia and Manchuria, where the steppe gives way to the Siberian forests, there must be taken into account a still more extensive economy and still wider scattering of humanity among the forest hunting tribes, some of which are also breeders of reindeer or drivers of dogs. Beyond these tribes the ultimate transition is to the sub-Arctic and Arctic societies. Within the possible scale of variation, it

THE STEPPES OF MONGOLIA

is to be noted that the steppe did not come to be ruled by "dry" or mixed farming, which would have been one degree removed from the intensive agriculture of China, but by an emphatic pastoral nomadism which was two degrees removed from the economy of China and in the upshot proved to be irreconcilable with it, until the rise of industrialism.

Working back from this, it seems probable that what took place during the later neolithic and the Bronze Age, from perhaps 3000 B.C. to about 500 B.C., was a broad but very slowly accelerating process of differentiation. This went on over an extremely wide and vague area, overlapping both the steppe, in which it was too difficult to advance beyond hoe agriculture even in favored spots, and the loess regions, where experiment was relatively easy and was repaid with immediate profit. In the heart of the loess region, at the Yellow River bend, the rate of change became conspicuous in the second millennium B.C. Near the edge of the steppe, it was only in the second half of the first millennium B.C. that it became rapid enough to force a sharp increase in the social importance of geographical and climatic differences between regions. In the much longer antecedent period the same kinds of men could live at much the same cultural level in all kinds of regions that were potentially, but not in actual use, much richer or poorer than each other. The importance of the process of economic differentiation here suggested supports, I think, Maspero's theory that the "northern barbarians" were ethnically of the same general stock as the northern Chinese, being descended from groups that had been "left behind" by the proto-Chinese who developed a higher agriculture in North China.[2]

On the whole, however, it does not greatly matter whether the savages scattered from the Yangtze valley to Mongolia were of the same general ethnic stock or be-

[2] Maspero, La Chine antique, 1927, p. 11.

longed to different "races." Nor does it matter a great
deal whether bands of them drifted from one region to
another, or whether changes in climate poured a little more
rain over the Yangtze valley or dried up a few marshes
in Mongolia. Geographical contrast, cultural borrowing,
social interchange, and migration were still fortuitous considerations that had no creative value until much later,
after the processes of evolution had begun in specific regions. The deciding impetus resided in the improved
usages that men began to practice, probably haphazard, in
key regions where the natural balance of limiting and
favorable factors made possible the momentous change
from the repetition of primitive acts to the development
of slightly less primitive habits. Once this kind of change
had begun advances could be made either through local
discovery or as the result of importation, migration, or
cultural borrowing.

Whether or not the proto-Chinese had originally migrated inward to the great bend of the Yellow River, the
important historical phenomenon was their advance near
this point beyond the crudest stage of hoe agriculture.
There followed a spread outward from this core to the
loess region as a whole and the Great Plain of North
China. This was at first a process of assimilation and convergence, in which the Chinese encountered "barbarians"
on every front. On the whole, these barbarians are not
described even at later periods as different "races," but as
people who had not yet adopted the complex of economic
practices and social organization that the Chinese were
carrying with them.[3] In any case, the environment itself,
except on the steppe Frontier, permitted the Chinese to

    [3] Maspero, *op. cit.*, Ch. I; also Wittfogel's review of the question of racial
relationship between Chinese and barbarians (Wirtschaft und Gesellschaft
Chinas, pp. 11-16). For a modern Chinese review of barbarians within
North China, see Fu Ssu-nien, East and West Theory of the I and Hsia,
1936 (in Chinese).

take over each terrain and absorb each people they encountered, and the question of "barbarism" thereupon became of secondary importance and tended to disappear.

As they approached the steppe, however, the environment increasingly retarded the Chinese. It enabled the "barbarians," whoever they were, to resist with increasing effectiveness; and therefore the "barbarism" of these barbarians, instead of being overcome, was increasingly emphasized. The decision between nascent culture and recalcitrant barbarism had, moreover, to be separately fought out over each foot of terrain, because the change from loess to steppe, although relatively rapid, is nowhere determined by a hard and fast line of cleavage. The gradation is from irrigable land through less irrigable land to nonirrigable land; and the land that is in the category of being not non-irrigable but less irrigable is unmistakably cultivable. This in turn shades off into land that, though not non-cultivable, is less cultivable. In all such territory, especially at a time when the Chinese way of life, though on the way to becoming highly specialized, had not yet become set in its peculiarities, the relative balance of the factors that favored the Chinese and those that opposed them could only be determined by experiment.[4]

It is no surprise, therefore, to find in the early Chinese chronicles that the peoples of the northwest and north, and later the northeast, though apparently considered barbarian and hostile, are not described in any way that makes their un-Chineseness decisively apparent. A clear differentiation between Chinese cultivators and barbarian herdsmen had yet to be established. The Chinese themselves were still hunters on a large scale, and also herders of cattle, and therefore all that can prudently be said of their northwestern tribal contemporaries is that the tribesmen did more herding and less farming while the Chinese

[4] Compare Chapters XII and XIII, below.

did more farming and less herding. Certainly the shepherd tribes were not yet mounted steppe-nomads.[5]

RISE OF PASTORAL NOMADISM IN THE STEPPES

The essential problem is to determine when and why differentiation became so acute that categorically different and hostile forms of society emerged, whose relations with each other were thenceforward determined more by the degree of divergence than by the still surviving degree to which they overlapped each other. This extraordinarily important phase of history seems to be clearly associated with the technical differentiation between the use of stall-fed horses for chariots and carts and the use of pasture-fed horses in war and for travel and food (horseflesh and mare's milk) ; in other words, between harnessed horses and ridden horses. Pasture-fed horses can do less work than stall-fed horses, which have their hay and grain brought to them. Therefore a larger number of horses is needed, which in turn makes wide pastures necessary and a social organization that enables people to move with their livestock from pasture to pasture.

Much has been written about the domestication of the horse and about the later technical specialization of chariot driving, horse riding, the invention of the stirrup (which appears to have been remarkably late as well as extraordinarily important in war), and so forth.[6] The discussion has turned too much, it seems to me, on whether these technical uses were imported or locally discovered and whether importation meant the arrival of "invading races" or "conquering peoples" in the Chinese field of history.

This has allowed a more important consideration to drop

[5] Creel (*op. cit.*, p. 184) describes wars over grazing rights in the second millennium B.C. These, however must have been wars between peoples who were cultivators and also had livestock, not between cultivators and nomad herdsmen. See also his p. 243, n. 31.

[6] See Menghin, *op. cit.*, for references to the literature, and compare also Chapter VI, below.

out of sight: that what is historically significant is that certain peoples were increasingly being excluded by the trend of development within China from adhering to "Chinese civilization" on a footing satisfactory to themselves —because their environment, although it overlapped that of the peoples who were coming to be Chinese, did not contain so many natural "Chinese" factors as the terrain nearer the kernel-region of Chinese history. For this reason they were constrained increasingly to neglect the use of agricultural resources and to develop as an alternative the use of pastoral resources. It was only when this diverging specialization had been carried to a certain point that the marginal steppe society ceased to be marginal and committed itself definitely to the steppe. Having reached that point it was ready to take advantage of a steppe technique of horse usage in order to increase the efficiency of life within the steppe environment.[7]

Whether the required technique was locally developed or imported or borrowed or imposed by conquerors is therefore a subordinate problem (to which I shall return in discussing the oasis world of Central Asia). What is here important is the fact that the technique was of no use until there was a society ready to use it. The time level at which this degree of readiness was attained can be only approximately determined; but certain major facts are clear. In the first place, the primitive Chinese continued to raise cattle, sheep, and goats, and also to hunt, long after the technique of irrigation had given a special bias to their agriculture. In fact, the exploitation of these resources always remained important in China, though not important enough to challenge the supremacy of agriculture. In the second place, it is clear that from neolithic times onward the society of the steppe and the steppe margin was never exclusively pastoral. On the margins of

[7] For this "retreat" of marginal groups away from agriculture and into the steppe, see Chapter XIII, below.

the steppe and in specially favored regions within the steppe agriculture survived either continuously or intermittently. The historical search must therefore be narrowed down to the attempt to establish the time level at which irrigated agriculture became the determinant within China and nomadic pastoralism the determinant within the steppe.

It can be said at once that the bias in China was established much earlier than the bias in the steppe. What gave the Shang-Yin people of the Honan-Shansi region their distinctive character in the second millennium B.C. was not the "primitive" hunting and herding that they still retained, but the concentration which they had already achieved of well developed agriculture around great cities.[8]

In the next millennium, as the evidence of Chinese history becomes clearer and firmer, the details of "barbarian" wars are more and more plentiful. The various barbarians, though listed under separate names, are not specially differentiated from each other according to their habits of life. None of them are described as horse-riding nomads until a late period. The impression that is conveyed concerning all of them is merely that they were less civilized than the Chinese.

It is in the second half of this millennium that references to the horseman begin to be recorded; and the moment that the horseman appears it is plain that he is to be taken as an index of a way of life that is different not in degree but in kind. The references do not by any means imply a sudden "discovery" of the horse. Indeed the Chinese long before this had war chariots; but whereas they had once used these chariots against barbarians who fought on foot, the barbarians now raided the Chinese borders as horsemen. Moreover, the tribal names of these mounted barbarians overlap to a certain extent with the names of the bar-

---

[8] For this period generally see Creel, *op. cit.;* also Wittfogel, Economic and Social History of China, with very full Chinese documentation.

barians formerly described as fighting on foot. It is evident that we have to deal with the rapid rise of a society of mounted nomads, especially on the north and northwest, who were of a different order altogether from the merely "inferior" barbarians who had until then been encountered on the fringes of the Chinese expansions, although these "new" barbarians were probably the same people, for the most part, as the old barbarians.

So far as I can determine, the period of definitive change was in the fourth and third centuries B.C.—the date being set by full accounts in the Chinese chronicles of two men who were not barbarians but important figures in the then rapidly developing Frontier statesmanship of China.[9] They were Chinese who actually adopted the mounted archery of the nomads and based their political power on it. The phenomenon is of interest because it shows that the Chinese and the barbarian ways of life by this time had become alternative and were becoming mutually exclusive. The difference was no longer in the stage of development but in the kind of society. Moreover, the status of this new kind of "barbarism" was high enough to induce important Chinese to go over to it in certain circumstances.

FUNCTIONAL EXPLANATION OF THE RISE OF STEPPE SOCIETY

This new high status, which resulted from the creation of a new kind of society partly recruited from tribes already known to the Chinese, can only be explained functionally by close analysis of the way in which the people lived. It is unmistakable that the critical environment was the extreme periphery of China, along the margin of the steppe. The Chinese chronicles do not directly explain the problem. Nor has it been discussed, so far as I know, in the modern Chinese literature of Frontier history. Perhaps

[9] Lattimore, Origins of the Great Wall, 1937.

one reason why the functional explanation has been neglected and scholars have concentrated instead on the attempt to find out who the people were, by studies of their
names, etc., is the fact that there is no "culture hero" of
steppe nomadism comparable to mythical and semi-mythical
heroes of agriculture, drainage, and so forth in ancient
China at a very remote period. This in itself carries the
inference that the technique of intensive, irrigated agriculture originated early in China and always remained at the
heart of the developing Chinese culture. Therefore its
early legends are among the oldest surviving material.
The technique of horse-using nomadism originated a good
deal later, in a peripheral region, and always remained
irreconcilable with the Chinese culture. Therefore no
reverent accounts of its beginnings were preserved by the
Chinese. The nomads themselves had no written records
until much later, and accordingly no old accounts are available from any source.

Naturally, I do not mean to imply that the steppe society
was a sudden discovery or creation or that the use of cavalry was an abrupt invention of the fourth and third centuries B.C. There must have been an antecedent period in
which rudimentary forms of the steppe society—perhaps a
whole series of them—had been developing. Nevertheless,
the importance of the period I have selected for the *conclusive* differentiation between Chinese society and steppe
society cannot be disputed. Before this time the chronicle
material does not make it possible to identify a specific
and unmistakable steppe society. During this time a series
of rapid changes gathered headway in China itself, ending
in the disappearance of the old state form, a radical alteration of the social structure, and the creation of a new, centralized imperial state. This was completed under the
brief Ch'in dynasty in the third century B.C. At the same
time, the Frontier defenses of several states were united to
mark out the main line of "the" Great Wall. The creation

of a Hsiungnu empire of the steppe lagged only a little behind these changes. The two-thousand-year history of the recognized Steppe Frontier had begun.[10]

The functional explanation to which I have referred concerns the way in which the most extensive of several cognate modes of economy came to be the determinant of steppe society and history, just as the most intensive practices of agriculture determined the character of society as a whole in China. As the primitive Chinese culture of the Yellow River bend has spread eastward and southward it has prospered through increasing returns. As it has moved toward the steppe it has encountered diminishing returns. In about the fourth and third centuries B.C. the spread up to the land of no running water had made the degree of diminishing returns critical. Tribes along the margin of the steppe, which until this time had been neither exclusively agricultural nor exclusively pastoral, began to take up "for good" an unmistakable pastoral steppe nomadism. They established a sphere of activity of their own, eccentric to the sphere of "civilized" society in China.

The use of horses, accordingly, became of paramount importance. Though it certainly was known before—the Chinese for centuries had used chariots and somewhat later had developed cavalry—what now occurred in the steppe was different. It was the rapid working out of a specialized technique of horse usage, which gave emphasis, range, and speed to the mobility that had become necessary in proportion to the decreasing practice of agriculture and increasing concentration on pastured livestock. Once it had been recognized by the people who were diverging from the Chinese way of life that the standard of wealth, importance, and power was henceforth to be determined by the exploitation of steppe resources, the ability to move with ease from a used pasture to a new pasture took on a

[10] *Ibid.*

special value, and the importance of ability to control a wide range of alternative pastures was emphasized.

Mounted movement was functionally important because it heightened the characteristics and the efficiency of the symbiosis of steppe-fed herds and herd-fed society. The probable order of progression was: 1) abandonment of marginal culture and transition to a culture of clearly steppe character; 2) complete dependence of all livestock on grazing, without stored grain or even hay; 3) greater need of movement, in order not to stay in exhausted pastures; 4) the particular need for a higher degree of skill in the control of horses—because the average farmer who has always tethered or stabled his horses and fed them with grain and hay has difficulty in recapturing them if he turns them loose on open grassy plains; 5) the acquisition, consequently, of marked skill in riding and in the control of loose herds of horses.

These are the steps in order of social adaptation to economic needs. There is a further series in the evolution of a military technique appropriate to the society. The steppe was treeless, and warriors who formerly fought on foot were now mounted. This meant economy of wood in the making of bows, combined with the effort to make a bow not too unwieldy for a horseman to carry. These two things probably account for the nomad use of the compound bow, which is notably short for its great power and is made of horn—a steppe material—and short pieces of wood spliced double.[11] The art of shooting from horseback is clearly an advance over merely carrying the bow while riding. It is this, finally, that accounts for the invention of the stirrup, known to be a late refinement even in steppe

[11] Creel (Studies, pp. 246-47) shows that the compound reflex bow is much older in China (second millennium B.C.) than true nomadism in the steppe. He also shows that it is a link between ancient China and the circumpolar culture areas. The bow itself may therefore have spread into the steppe either from China or from Siberia, or from both; but the steppe use of the bow as peculiarly fitted to mounted archery must have been evolved in the steppe itself.

society. The stirrup gave the last touch of effectiveness to the mounted archer because it made possible a steady shot while galloping away from an attacker—the "Parthian shot" which was the deadliest tactical maneuver of the steppe warrior.[12]

I have here simplified the functional explanation to an extreme. Obviously some steps may have been made in a different order by particular groups, and some groups could acquire the whole of the technique, or part of it, by borrowing—if it suited their order of society. The Chinese, for instance, took over the whole of the technique of mounted archery, but without subordinating their agricultural economy to the nomadic economy. This meant that both their horses and their archers were inferior to those of the nomads, except in abnormal periods when years of consecutive campaigning at ruinous cost to their settled economy produced a professional cavalry that could match the "natural" cavalry of the steppe.

The main purpose of this digression into the economy and warfare of nomadism is to establish the principle that technical practices are significant only when they suit the needs of a society. To explain the rise of the nomads on the Chinese Frontier entirely by "invasions" of new peoples or the "borrowing" of the compound bow from some distant place is no explanation at all. "Invaders" could not have maintained themselves in the steppe without a technique for living there, however irresistible they were as warriors. The compound bow was worth neither "borrowing" nor inventing except by a society that had already arrived at a point that made the special qualities of the compound bow advantageous. The question of historical interest, therefore, is the interaction of society and tech-

[12] I am indebted to C. W. Bishop (personal letter of March 16, 1938) for a number of valuable suggestions on the domestication and use of the horse, and particularly for drawing my attention to the importance of the compound bow and its use. I had always read the Chinese term *ch'i-she* as "riding and archery," and had not seen that it specifically means "mounted archery"—an important technical distinction.

nique rather than the creation of societies by technical devices alone or the invention of devices merely *pour épater les chinois.*

SOCIAL AND ECONOMIC CONTRASTS BETWEEN THE STEPPES AND CHINA

Inability of the Chinese and the peoples of the steppe to coalesce is implied by the diverging line of development of steppe society. It is not only probable but certain that the steppe society was not ruled by a standard of land-ownership comparable to that of China. No single pasture could have any value unless the people using it were free to move to some other pasture, because no single pasture could be grazed continuously. The right to move prevailed over the right to camp. "Ownership" meant, in effect, the title to a cycle of migration.[13]

In the late centuries people like the Mongols have been restricted within territorial boundaries. The title to such territories belongs to the tribe as a whole, not to the chief or prince of a tribe. There is, accordingly, no individual property in land, though in practice the common, tribally-owned land is administered by the prince, who has the final decision in allotting the use of pastures to different families. The result, of course, is that the noble families, in spite of having no outright ownership, have direct use of the best pastures, in addition to exacting both services and tribute in kind from the non-noble families, which use the poorer land.[14] Even in this late and stagnant form of the steppe society, however, it is possible to see indications

[13] Lattimore, Manchuria: Cradle of Conflict, 1932, pp. 48-49. It seems to me that the Mongol word *nutuk,* the land or "country" where a man "belongs," may perhaps be related to the verb *neghuku,* "to move," "to migrate"; whence *neghutel,* vernacular form *nutel,* as in *nutel ulus,* "nomad people" as distinguished from "settled people."

[14] I doubt whether this represents a true evolution from the steppe-tribal society toward feudalism. It is more probably a recurrent or intermittent phase of stagnation, a phenomenon of periods when steppe and settled land were under the same rule—as when the Manchu sovereign was both emperor of China and emperor of the Mongols.

of the original standard: that individual or family which can dictate the movement of dependents or retainers is dominant, and that tribe is dominant which controls a major cycle of migration and can allot subordinate cycles to other tribes. Consequently, the phases of steppe nomadic history are to be traced by the rise and fall of greater and lesser lords who are "protectors" of the right of movement of lesser men, from whom in return they demand services in peace and war and a variety of tribute in kind.[15]

Even the technique of pastoral economy is affected by the sovereign importance of movement, just as the crucial, privileged importance of the control of human labor in China limited the development of labor-saving devices and atrophied such enterprises as mining and mechanical industry. In parts of the steppe the grass is long enough to cut for hay; in parts it is not. The use of hay produces better cattle and is potentially of special value in the early spring, the season when the new grass has not yet grown, the season when the cattle are weakest, the season of calving and lambing, and also the season of the worst storms. Yet hay-cutting was never widely or continuously practiced, because prescriptive claims to hay meadows would have led to fixed landownership and the restriction of movement. The individual was reluctant to attempt to establish private ownership of this kind, because it would have left him naked of social protection when the rest of the tribe moved; and at the same time the chiefs, whose power was organized according to the mechanism of a mobile society, would not permit the individual to escape in this manner from their close control.

The more extensive economy of the poorer parts of the steppe, where movement was imperative, thus dictated more movement than was strictly necessary to the people in the richer part of the steppe, where a less extensive

[15] Lattimore, review of Grenard's Genghis-Khan, 1937.

economy would have been feasible. Similarly, there are wide prairies that carry almost no stock even in good seasons because relatively deep and expensive wells would have to be dug. The digging of easy, shallow wells in areas where any number of wells can be dug and the water is accessible to everyone was always as permissible as it was necessary; but "special" wells would have created special values and claims to fixed local ownership that did not suit the general interests of the society.

It is not surprising therefore that the situation has entirely changed in Outer Mongolia today, where the Mongol People's Republic has abolished the control of society by princes (and the later-developed class of monastic "princes of the church"), has instituted a new form of social control, and is beginning to splice together the productive resources of the old pastoral economy and the processing functions of a new industrialism created to serve it. Mobility is no longer sovereign; the economy remains basically pastoral but the society need no longer be nomadic. The storage of hay is accordingly becoming a general practice and pastures formerly unused are being opened up by the digging of wells.[16] The result is a simultaneous increase in the number of cattle and improvement in the quality of the stock.

Clear economic demarcation did not result in political isolation of China from the steppe. The Frontier, in spite of mighty and successive efforts at Great Wall building, never became an absolute line of cleavage. Geographically, economically, and politically it was a marginal terrain, which varied in depth. This was because the average and the determining degree of extensivity and intensivity were never identical in either the steppe or China. Neither society was permanently uniform. There was a range of variation in China from the more intensive to the less inten-

[16] Viktorov and Khalkhin, The Mongol People's Republic, 1936, p. 36 (in Russian).

sive, with concurrent political vacillations. In the steppe, the variation was from the more extensive to the less extensive, also accompanied by political alternations.

It is important to note, further, that the steppe was even less uniform than China; not only did it enclose oasis-like areas and permit on its fringes interpenetration of forest tribes and steppe tribes, of agricultural economy and pastoral economy, but it produced less natural internal trade and exchange than China. The steppe economy is a good deal more self-sufficient than that of settled societies. Its herds produce food, clothing, housing and fuel, and also transport. Lack of economic pressure creating internal trade is, however, offset by social demand for external trade. The steppe demand for trade with China (or the oases of Turkistan or Persia) was more insistent than the demand of settled agricultural communities for trade with the steppe. This was because the universal spread of essentials within the steppe society encouraged a demand for luxuries from outside the range of the society itself as a sure way of distinguishing between the greater and the lesser people, the rulers and the followers.

In a country like China, on the other hand, differences in natural resources made internal exchange a necessity. Communities that did not have salt or iron (commodities of prime importance, marking even sharper differences between undeveloped communities than between highly developed communities) could not move periodically as whole communities to the source of supply. Traders were necessary to act as representatives and intermediaries. As a by-product of this difference it was easy for the professional traders of China to control the internal trade of the steppe as well as its external trade.

It may be noted in passing that handicrafts and the beginnings of industry, as well as internal exchange of commodities, were much more weakly developed in the steppe than in China. The Mongol smith, for instance, could move easily to the supply of ore and easily carry away with him enough to keep him employed on a very small scale. He could not, however, settle down at the source of supply of his raw material to develop his craft on a larger scale without detaching himself from his society. Nor could he, without settling near the supply of raw materials, employ apprentices or workmen for production on a larger scale. He never even became an itinerant professional artisan, but remained an owner of livestock and a normal member of a pastoral society. This holds true in spite of the fact that smiths in early periods appear to have held a specially favored position in their society. (The Mongol word *darkhan,* a smith, came later to mean also a privileged man, a man exempted from tribal taxes and services. It may also be connected, I suppose, with the word *darogha,* a leader or chief.) The same general considerations applied to work in wood, textiles, and so forth; no artisan activity could be developed on a large scale because it impaired mobility. Beyond a certain point, therefore, the steppe society as a whole encouraged the acquisition by trade of metal implements and wares and manufactured commodities generally. It inhibited the maturing of all occupations tending to break down the "nomadicness" of nomadism. Spontaneous evolution of industrialism was therefore checked in the steppe as in China, but for different reasons and at an even lower level.

CHARACTERISTIC PHASES OF STEPPE HISTORY

By taking into account the fact that the least typical, marginal territories of China and the steppe overlapped along the line of the Great Wall, an attempt can be made to describe the characteristic phases of steppe history. These phases can be related to the stratification of marginal steppe, poor pasture, rich pasture, valleys (like some of those in Northern Mongolia) where even irrigated agriculture was possible, the transition zones between Northern Mongolia and the Siberian forests, and so on. The need for mobility, which approximated to a law of survival in the steppe, produced a norm of steppe-tribal society as unmistakable as the manpower norm of society in China, though departures from the norm were more extreme in the steppe than in China. The demand for freedom to move gave extraordinary power to the tribal lords who regulated the allotment of pastures and orbits of migration. This led to tribal wars, but it also made possible periods of relative stability based paradoxically on the smooth adjustment of claims to mobility.

In such periods, the superfluity of livestock, which the chief drew in tribute from the followers whose claims he upheld and who in return served as his men-at-arms, tended to become so great as to blot out its own meaning. The great chiefs, accordingly, were prompted either to take advantage of their mobile following in order to raid China if China were then weak, or to patronize trade if China were strong, and even to experiment with agriculture in their own domains—thus accentuating the differences in the scale of luxury as between the great and the humble. (It was typical in such periods to import Chinese or Central Asian oasis people to do the work of farming, not merely because they were more skillful but because the exploiting of such a subject population left the fabric of the steppe society itself as far as possible intact.)[17]

In time, these departures from the steppe norm, whether they were based on conquest beyond the steppe or diversification within the steppe, brought up the issue of the

[17] Ta Ch'ing Huitien, edition of 1818, under Li Fan Yüan, 17, Ch. 742; Lattimore, The Mongols of Manchuria, 1934, pp. 79-82; also Mongols of the Chinese Border, 1938. William of Rubruck (thirteenth century), gives a general description of nomad society and customs when he first enters the area of the Mongol conquests in South Russia. He says: "The great lords have villages in the south, from which millet and flour are brought to them for the winter. The poor procure [these things] by trading sheep and pelts." (Rockhill, William of Rubruck, 1900, p. 68).

inability of the steppe society and the agricultural society to coalesce. When he had become committed to the rule of a mixed society the steppe lord found it impossible to adjust his acquired functions to his traditional functions. This was equally true of Chinese border potentates in periods of Chinese expansion into the steppe. Under the ruler, whether nomad or border Chinese, those whose vested interests were in the extensive economy began to pull against those whose interests were vested in the intensive economy.[18] This pull eventually broke up the mixed state, which in its fall caused confusion but made possible a return once more to relative stability, as farmer and herdsman gravitated back to the geographical environment that permanently favored each of them.

In such processes of cracking up and sorting out, the leading new political figures were likely to be men from the lower strata of the ruling class. Such men, while they understood the working of politics and war and the handling of the society and economy whose control they now set out to capture, had not been destroyed by the fall of their own vested interests, as had the upper strata of the same class.[19] Thus the decisive political agent was the man of the lesser nobility (like Chingghis Khan) ; but the geographical determinant, in such phases, was not the marginal terrain but the unmistakable steppe terrain, because in the poorer steppe nomadic society had been least affected during the period of temporary and illusory coalescence. There the technique of steppe nomadism, based on the most extensive economy and the extreme of social mobility, had been conserved.[20] From it, accordingly, steppe nomadism reasserted its ascendancy over that part of the marginal terrain in which the balance of factors favored the pastoral economy, while the Chinese culture

[18] Lattimore, The Geographical Factor in Mongol History, 1938.
[19] Compare Chapter XVII, below.
[20] Lattimore, op. cit.

returned to power along the river valleys to the south of the Great Wall, within that part of the marginal terrain where the balance of natural factors favored the walled city and its circumjacent fields.

VARIETIES OF NOMAD ECONOMY. IMPORTANCE OF SHEEP

In Mongolia, therefore, the course of history veered away persistently from the Chinese kind of concentration. The movement of people was all important: mankind had to keep up with its moving cattle. The ruler was the man who directed this movement and prevented people, other than those under his own control, from getting in the way.

This does not mean that the scope of nomadic movement is always infinite.[21] Within the world of the steppe there are many types of migration cycle, governed partly by geography and partly by social specialization in the use of different animals. There are groups that move over considerable distances and others that move only a few miles in the course of a year. Some nomads have a pastoral range which includes both rich and poor grazing, while some never leave the sub-arid steppe or remain entirely in good meadow country. There is an intricate relationship between the kind of pasture that predominates, the frequency of moving camp, the distance traveled from one grazing ground to the next, and the climate and soil. Sheep and camels do not do well on wet pastures; a lime soil is best for horses and a saline soil for camels. Goats and sheep crop the pasture more closely than other animals,

[21] Ralph Fox, Genghis Khan, 1936, p. 9: "The longest migration in the yearly cycle is well under 300 kilometers. The average is about 150." Fox's source appears to be A. Simukov, Mongol Migrations, in *Contemporary Mongolia*, No. 4 (7), Ulan Bator, · 1934 (in Russian). My own observation indicates that Inner Mongolian migrations can rarely reach 150 kilometers. As I have elsewhere pointed out, the ability of steppe nomads to move over very great distances when necessary is not due to a habit of distant travel but to the fact that the mobile organization of their life can be converted from short-range movement to long-range movement (see Caravan Routes of Inner Asia, 1928).

therefore they can graze where cattle and horses have already passed; but cattle and horses cannot feed on a pasture where sheep and goats have recently been feeding. All these details of technique affect the degree of specialization in sheep, camels, horned cattle, yaks, and the hunting of wild game, which in turn modifies the degree of military aptitude of different tribes, especially under the bow-and-arrow standard of warfare.

Moreover, the tendency to specialization and the tendency to standardization have always reacted against each other in the nomadic economy. Horses are of special value in war. Skill in the use of camels gives freedom of movement in the most arid steppe and access to the widely scattered spots within arid regions where water and grass are relatively good. Cattle and yaks, on meadow and alpine pasture, give a higher output of milk and meat per acre than other livestock. Oxen drag heavy, primitive carts with more economy of power than either horses or camels, if they can feed well enough.

None of these animals, however, equals the sheep in all-around economic value to the steppe nomad.[22] For the Mongol of today, as of the past, the sheep provides wool for the felts with which the tents are covered, skins (tanned with the wool on them) for clothing, milk in summer and a surplus of cheese and butter to be stored for winter, meat in winter, and dung for fuel. (Sheep can be penned at night so that the dung which they drop is trampled hard within the enclosure; this eventually forms

[22] Lattimore, The Geographical Factor in Mongol History, 1938. In the decadent pastoral economy of Inner Mongolia, where the Mongols have been forced into the poorest pastures by Chinese colonization, goats are becoming more common than sheep, leading to a further vicious impoverishing of the environment and a more acute degeneration of the Mongol economy and society. This is aggravated by the fact that goats are more subject to fatal epizootic diseases than sheep. Goats are able to live on poorer pasture than sheep and give much the same products, though of poorer quality. Both sheep and goats, especially goats, destroy pasture land when grazed too closely and too long because their sharp hoofs cut the turf. This exposes the topsoil, which is blown away by the wind, with results that are often mistaken for climatic desiccation.

a thick deposit which is dug out in "bricks" for burning.) Sheep, therefore, more than any other kind of livestock, establish the basic economic standards of food, housing, clothing, and fuel.[23]

At the same time, a strictly shepherd economy has two weaknesses. The sheep move slowly and do not provide transport (although they are used in some parts of Tibet to carry small packages of salt and borax). Transport, accordingly, is what really distinguishes the Mongols from the Chinese of many marginal areas, who practice an "extensive" agriculture of "dry farming" and at the same time pasture sheep and goats. It was probably the development of skill in the pasturing of transport animals in addition to food animals that enabled some of the "barbarians" of early Chinese history to abandon alternative kinds of economy and commit themselves to the steppe, while others relinquished animal husbandry in proportion as they prospered by farming and were eventually assimilated to the economy and society of China.

Certainly the technique of steppe life in Mongolia has always depended on combining the transport uses of horses, camels, and cattle, and the basic standard of wealth in sheep in different proportions according to the way in which the local environment varies from the edge of the Siberian forests to the depths of the Gobi. Even the military ascendancy of tribes with the best horse pastures was of no permanent use unless it was applied to the protection of sheep and sheep pasture; and the ability of the camel-using Mongols to resort to the poorest part of the Gobi in order to escape war never developed, so far as I know, to the point of a pure camel nomadism without reliance on sheep,[24] though camel-riding Mongols of the Western

[23] Lattimore, The Eclipse of Inner Mongolian Nationalism, 1936.
[24] Vladimirtsov (Social Structure of the Mongols, 1934, p. 39, in Russian) points out that the terrain in Northern Mongolia where Chingghis founded his tribal power was not suitable for camels. On p. 36 he states that the Northern Mongols did not have many camels until after the conquest of the

Gobi relieve their dependence on sheep to some degree by hunting gazelles and wild asses.

It was the self-sufficiency of the shepherd economy, with its variations, that restricted the growth and prevented the permanent survival in Mongolia of any true mixed economy. The social law of movement governing the dominant pastoralism never permitted agriculture, the working of metal, or the making of things to rise above subordinate importance. In *potential* resources, a country like Mongolia ranks with that part of the United States lying west of the Mississippi, east of the Rocky Mountains, and north of Texas. It can combine the exploitation of agriculture, livestock, mining, and industry. The necessary methods, however, could not be evolved by a society that grew out of the use of only such resources as could be exploited at a primitive level. By restraining more advanced enterprise, except when carried on by subject people, nomadism committed itself to a "vested interest" in mobility.

WEALTH VERSUS MOBILITY

Both stability and instability were inherent in steppe nomadism, the stability of self-sufficient economic resources and the instability resulting from the way in which access to and use of the various kinds of resources were combined in different proportions. In every possible combination the emphasis had to be either on wealth or on mobility. There was no ideal balance equally suitable to every region. The extreme of mobility was the mounted war-

---

Tanggot or Hsi Hsia kingdom (modern Ninghsia). He refers to a passage in the edition of the "Secret History of the Mongols" used by him; presumably this is the passage to be found on p. 68 of the Russian translation of the "Secret History" by Palladius. Here the Tanggot are described as a settled people (they were in fact a semi-oasis people) with quantities of camels. It is entirely probable that camels were first domesticated not on the northern side of the Gobi, but on the southern side, or in the Turkistan oases, by people who were at most semi-nomadic. Though I have found several references to camels in the Chinese chronicles for the first two centuries B.C., all these references point to the oasis routes. not to the steppe. See, *e.g.*, Ch'ien-Han Shu, Ch. 94, second part, on the Hsiungnu.

rior; the extreme of invulnerability or inaccessibility was the camel rider of the Gobi; the extreme of wealth was the patch of intensively cultivated land in a watered valley, isolated in the general expanse of the steppe and exploited by nomad overlords. Yet the mounted warrior lost mobility in proportion as he accumulated plunder; the camel rider could not rise above a low level of wealth in the poor environment of the Gobi; the protected oasis immobilized its protectors and, if it became too wealthy and its protectors insufficiently mobile in the warfare of the steppe, it was always overwhelmed by raiders.[25]

Nevertheless, the rulers of the nomads never tired of working out new combinations of mobility and wealth. For this reason, although the steppe as a whole stood apart from China as a whole, the two never ceased to interact. The maximum control of mobility over wealth was achieved when nomad invaders conquered China, but this in itself led to the undermining of mobility by wealth, and to the dependence of the conquerors on the swarming bureaucracy needed to collect revenue and to allot patronage. After the nomadic rulers had moved into China they became detached from the sources of their power and identified with the clumsy and vulnerable apparatus of agriculture, so that when their exploitation of the settled civilization had reached its point of diminishing returns they were overwhelmed, either by the same kind of rebellion that destroyed Chinese dynasties or by fresh nomad invaders. The maximum control of wealth over mobility was when strong dynasties in China reduced the nomads of the steppe to vassalage, but this in itself led to the undermining of wealth by mobility. Those who were appointed to rule the Frontier began to dissociate themselves from the Chinese sources of wealth and associate themselves with the steppe sources of power. The vassal began to demand a higher price for his loyalty, resorting to his mobility in order to

[25] Lattimore, Caravan Routes, 1928; also The Geographical Factor, 1938.

escape punishment; and thus the exploitation of wealth by mobility began again.

The last of these historical cycles was under the Manchu dynasty, from 1644 to 1911.[26] The Manchus made good use of Mongol auxiliaries to turn the flank of the Chinese positions guarding the direct route from Manchuria to China. These were Eastern Mongols, of the tribes occupying most of what is now Jehol and the western part of what is now Manchuria. The loot of China enabled the Manchus to subsidize these tribes, thus projecting the Manchu influence into the steppe and establishing a barrier between the new empire in China and the outlying, unconquered Mongol tribes. The result was a "sphere of influence" extending from the western plains of the modern provinces of Heilungchiang, Kirin, and Liaoning, across Jehol, Chahar, and Suiyuan to the deserts of Ninghsia. This is the historical Inner Mongolia, including "Eastern Inner Mongolia," which lies in Jehol and the Manchurian provinces.

To the west of Manchuria and the north of North China the good pasture of Inner Mongolia thins out into the Gobi. This at first made a convenient limit to the influence of the Manchus. It would have required expensive major campaigns, not compensated for by the acquisition of new sources of revenue, to bring the rest of Mongolia under control. Within a hundred years, however, the Manchus were able to intervene at much less cost in wars between the Khalkhas or Northern Mongols, holding most of what is now Outer Mongolia, and the Western Mongols or Ölöts, holding the Altai region of Outer Mongolia, the northern part of Chinese Turkistan (Jungaria), and the Tsaidam region in the northeast of Tibet. (Western Mongol tribes later settled in the Alashan and Edsingol regions of what is now Ninghsia province; these territories, ac-

[26] Lattimore, The Historical Setting of Inner Mongolian Nationalism, 1936; Where Outer and Inner Mongolia Meet, 1938; also, for listing of tribes of Manchurian Mongolia ("Eastern Inner Mongolia"), with dates at which they came over to the Manchus, The Mongols of Manchuria, 1934.

cordingly, form a geographical extension westward of Inner Mongolia but belong tribally to Western Mongolia.) By this intervention the Manchus in the end became overlords of both the Khalkhas and the Western Mongols.

Virtually all of the Mongols thus became vassals of the Manchus. The ascendancy of wealth over mobility under this arrangement reached its peak in the eighteenth century. Nominally, the Mongols were obliged to raise military contingents for the Manchus whenever required, and such contingents were actually raised for service against the T'aip'ings and against the French and British in the middle of the nineteenth century.[27] Although this military vassal relationship never worked very effectively, it has had other important results. The idea of nomad vassals of a settled state requires interference with the fluidity of the nomadic migration cycle and the substitution of a more rigid territorial system. The overlord must know not only how many troops can be summoned from each tribe, but where they can be found. He must also prevent tribal war between his different vassals by insisting that claims to pastures and right of movement be referred to him. Under the true steppe-tribal system, claims to territory were asserted through the control of mobile tribes. Vassalage converted this into the quite different system of granting titles to territory, which carried with them the right to rule over tribes.

The significance of this change needs to be emphasized. In the tribal society two processes alternated with each other. The tribes were never static. Claims to pasture and the right of movement either led to the splitting up of tribes and the formation of separate clan-like groups, or to the coalescence of small groups under the more and more formidable leadership of great khans. The system of territorial vassalage prevented the process of agglomera-

---

[27] Lattimore, The Mongols of Manchuria, 1934, p. 205, career of Senggerinchin, or Sankolinsin.

tion (because it threatened the overlord power) and left only the process of parcelling and repartitioning territorial units, thus automatically subdividing the tribal formations. The princes drew subsidies from the Manchu court but had to acknowledge in return that the Manchu emperor had the right of confirming them in their hereditary succession. This right was used in order to split up territorial and tribal units under a gradually increasing number of princes. Disputes over boundaries and jurisdictions that the tribal society itself would have settled by the special tribal form of war (which consisted of summoning extra followers in order to claim a wider cycle of migration and more pastures), were now settled by compromise, and the sovereign, instead of permitting one claimant to defeat the other and take over his following, made both of them equal princes with diminished territories.

Two other processes confirmed the ascendancy of wealth over mobility. For reasons already described it was easy for Chinese merchants to control both the external and the internal trade of Mongolia. It was also natural for the Mongol princes to act as patrons of this trade, sharing in the profits. By insisting on the tribal duties of each of their subjects they prevented the rise of a separate Mongol trading class, because it would have tended to become independent of them. By guaranteeing the safe-conduct of merchants, the extension of credit, and the collection of debts, they stood between merchant and customer, taking a toll on all transactions.

MONGOL UNITY UNDER CHINGGHIS KHAN AND ITS LATER DECAY

The second process was the spread of the Lama-Buddhist religion. Lamaism had originally been taken up by the Mongols when they held empire in China in the thirteenth and fourteenth centuries. There is no doubt that the Mongol rulers interested themselves in this for

the purpose of creating a national unity that would consolidate the Mongols and at the same time differentiate
them from the Chinese. They wanted to make the Mongols
a permanent ruling class, with a code of its own sanctioned
by an organized religion. Chingghis Khan had brought the
Mongols together after a series of tribal wars that had
placed each tribal unit under a chief personally responsible
to the supreme khagan. He needed, further, a common
standard that would offset the dangerously great individual
power of each of these chiefs. He was also aware, like
other great nomad leaders who had dealt with settled
peoples, of the way in which the mobile power of a nomad
empire could be undermined by attachment to the immobile, agricultural sources of "civilized" wealth.

Chingghis therefore chose Uighur Turks from the oases
of Chinese Turkistan to create a Mongol written language
and the beginnings of a civil service. The use of Uighurs
who were largely Nestorian Christians and of Moslems
who spoke Turkish, Persian, and Arabic enabled his successors to administer China without immediate surrender
to the Chinese scholar-gentry, who until then had smoth-
ered all barbarian conquerors by making them dependent
for their revenues on the services of a bureaucracy which
had almost the sole access to a written language so difficult
that it was virtually a professional secret.

Khobilai Sechin, or Kublai Khan, the grandson of
Chingghis and the first Mongol to rule the whole of China,
continued this policy. He asked the father and uncle of
Marco Polo to bring him Catholic priests from Europe in
large numbers, presumably in order to promote a Mongol
national culture separate from that of the Chinese.[28] These
priests did not arrive; but others, like John of Montecorvino,[29] preached the Catholic cause under the patronage
of the Mongol court. The Mongols never succeeded in

[28] Yule, Marco Polo, 1921, Vol. I, Ch. VII.
[29] Yule, Cathay and the Way Thither, 1914, Vol. III.

identifying their power in China with any of the non-Chinese religions—probably because none of these religions, when transplanted, was culturally vigorous enough to hold out against the tough code of the Chinese mandarinate.

Nevertheless it is remarkable how an unschooled people like the Mongols evaded the Chinese bureaucracy for as long as they did, until their connections with Central Asia and Persia weakened in the fourteenth century. Up to that time the Mongols in China "salted" their administration with accomplished Uighur Turks and Persians. Neither Mongol, Turkish, nor Persian became the sole administrative language of China, but it is noteworthy that none of the texts of Marco Polo have preserved any mention of the Chinese written language. Indeed, the general character of Marco Polo's narrative suggests that he had little or no knowledge of either written or spoken Chinese and must have been able to get along with Mongol or Persian, or perhaps both, during his 27 years in China, in the course of which he held important official appointments.[30] Furthermore, we have evidence from the Chinese side that the "scholarly" Chinese language was actually broken down, during this period, to such an extent

---

[30] Polo claimed to have mastered four languages and four scripts. The four scripts may well have been two scripts, each used in two ways—one for Persian and Arabic, one for Uighur Turkish and Mongol. Yule and Cordier, Polo's editors, are not in full agreement on the question of his possible knowledge of Chinese. Very likely during his long residence he picked up a smattering of the spoken language; on the other hand his mention of a few words and names shows that he cannot have known the language well and therefore cannot have been able to read and write it. No foreigner ever learned to read and write Chinese without boasting about it. (Yule, Marco Polo, 1921, Vol. I, Ch. XIV and notes.) William of Rubruck, however, a little earlier than Polo, described Chinese writing very well: "They write with a brush such as painters paint with, and they make in one figure the several letters containing a whole word" (Rockhill, Rubruck, 1900, pp. 201-2). Rashideddin, writing in Persia at the beginning of the fourteenth century, shows a detailed knowledge of the numbers of Persians, Uighurs, and Nestorian Christians in the Mongol service in China (Yule, Cathay, 1914, Vol. III, pp. 117 et sqq.). Bretschneider (Mediaeval Researches, 1888, Vol. I, p. 189), in a brief notice of the Chinese dynastic history of the Mongols in China, also calls attention to the many foreigners in Mongol service.

that even documents of all kinds were frequently written in an unscholarly, vernacular, and even partially "Mongolized" Chinese.[31]

REINTRODUCTION OF LAMAISM (SIXTEENTH CENTURY)

The Mongols also experimented with Tibetan Lamaism, a syncretic religion which is nominally Buddhist but almost certainly includes borrowings from Nestorian Christianity and Manichaeism. Although by the crude standards of the Mongols this was a religion of culture, it was also quite incapable of maintaining itself against the superior learning of the Chinese mandarins. On the expulsion of the last Mongol emperor from China, Lamaism vanished from both Mongolia and China because the Mongols were thrown back on their old steppe standards and there was no longer any need for a special cultural device to integrate the dominant steppe territory of the state with the subject territory of agriculture and cities.

Accordingly, when Lamaism reappeared among the Mongols in the sixteenth century the first converts were not the Mongols of the outer steppe but the border Mongols who had clung to the edge of China. When the Ming dynasty reëstablished Chinese rule in China in 1368 it profited by a great cleavage between the Mongols of the north, who had always looked at China from afar, and those of what is now Inner Mongolia, who had been closely

[31] See the interesting remarks by Palladius on pp. 8 and 9 of the preface to his translation of the "Secret History"; also Laufer, A Sketch of Mongol Literature, Russian edit., 1927, pp. 10-11; and Chavannes, Inscriptions et pièces de chancellerie, 1904, p. 11, where the style of the Chinese written by scribes in the Mongol service is commented on as *fort bizarre*. It may be added that one reason for the textual difficulties of the "Old" and "New" official Chinese histories of the Yüan or Mongol dynasty is presumably the barbarisms in the documents used by the compilers. By the courtesy of K. A. Wittfogel I have been able to go over the sections from the Mongol period in an important study on which he is engaged, with the aid of Chinese collaborators—a series of selections from the Chinese dynastic histories to serve as an index to material on administration and political and economic development. For a preliminary account, see his A Large-Scale Investigation of China's Socio-Economic Structure, 1938.

associated with the apparatus of Mongol rule in China. Even as early as 1260, the choice of Kublai Khan by the dynastic council to be supreme Khagan had displeased the northern Mongols, who considered that he was too Chinese and too little in sympathy with the military steppe tradition.

On the fall of the Mongol dynasty many of the southern Mongols actually went over to the service of the new Chinese dynasty, and it was largely because of this that the first Ming emperors were able to campaign at a great distance in the north of Mongolia. These campaigns blunted the military power of the steppe Mongols enough to remove the immediate danger of a renewed Mongol invasion of China, but did not result in subjecting the outer steppe to Chinese rule. Thereafter the Chinese turned back to organize the traditional machinery of agriculture, taxation, and state granary accumulation within China. The maintenance of the Great Wall Frontier was turned over to vassal Mongols of the Inner Mongolian fringe, who were not—for the time being—strong enough to be a danger to China but were willing, for the sake of conserving their own local privileges, to refuse coalition with the tribes of the steppe beyond the Gobi.

The most important Mongol vassal state lay along the great northern loop of the Yellow River, in what is now Suiyüan province. By the sixteenth century these Mongols, gathered in a federation of which the modern remnants are the Tumets and the Ordos tribes, were powerful enough to begin anew the process of making mobility ascendant over wealth. From about 1530 until his death in 1583 their chief, Altan Khan (Anda), harried Shensi, Shansi, and the metropolitan region of Peking. Westward he was overlord as far as Tibet and defeated the Western Mongols. The success with which he practiced the blackmail code of loyalty was rewarded by the Chinese with the title of Shun-i Wang—Obedient and Loyal Prince. At the same time the Chinese name of Kueihua (Return to Civilization) was conferred on Kuku-khota (Gughe-khota, the Blue City), which he had built.[32] His most important demand on the Chinese was the privilege of holding fairs for trade. The inference is that without the revenue of these fairs he could not forego the profits brought in by his raiding wars.

It was under this prince that Lamaism was again introduced among the Mongols; the conditions I have described explain why. Altan Khan was a city-building prince. The territory he ruled was not in the heart of the steppe; its economy was of a mixed character. In order to attain stability the ruler wanted to convert accumulation by war into exchange by trade. Undoubtedly the state included agricultural and artisan subjects as well as pastoral people.[33] Such a following and such a state needed a unifying agency. Like the great Chingghis, Altan Khan wished to avoid the adoption of Chinese culture because it would not unify his marginal state but assimilate and subordinate it to China. Lamaism was just what he needed.

Above all, a celibate church with monastic property made possible a better management of the most important working problem of all such border states of mixed economy and society. The church's corporative, impersonal title to property achieved a higher degree of integration between mobile pastoral property and fixed landed property than the society of the time could manage in any other way. It both stood between and linked together the families that were attached to the tribal structure of power and those whose power was based on landed estates, tenantry, and city activities. Had not the non-family organization of the

[32] Mengku Yumu Chi (preface dated 1859), 1, 2, 21b. Lattimore, The Mongols of Manchuria, 1934, p. 48. See also the many references in Baddeley, Russia, Mongolia, China, 2 vols., 1919. Also Howorth, History of the Mongols, Vol. I, 1876, p. 418, citing De Mailla, Histoire générale de la Chine, Vol. X, 1779, p. 319.

[33] Lattimore, A Ruined Nestorian City in Inner Mongolia, 1934. At this site there was later discovered, by Mongols, a stone inscribed with Altan Khan's invitation to the Dalai Lama to reintroduce Lamaism into Mongolia.

church offered this neutral economic standard, rivalry between the two kinds of noble families would have split the
state internally. It is hardly probable that Altan Khan
thought this all out for himself in advance; what he probably did was merely to grasp and promote the function of
the church in practice, in the course of the administrative
routine of adjustment and compensation of forces that
must necessarily have preoccupied the ruler of such a state.

LAMAISM AND THE RISE OF MANCHU POWER IN MONGOLIA (SEVENTEENTH AND EIGHTEENTH CENTURIES)

When its origins have thus been stated it becomes much
easier to follow and understand the subsequent history of
Lamaism in Mongolia. Among other things, the fable of
the fostering of Lamaism as a method of pacifying the
turbulent Mongols is disposed of completely. After the
death of Altan Khan the control of Mongol power along
the Great Wall Frontier passed from the Tumets to the
Chahars; [34] but at the same time the Chahars were being
overtaken and passed by a new mixed power, that of the
Manchus. By alliance with the Eastern Mongols the
Manchus prevented the Chahars from consolidating a new
and greater Chahar-Tumet state and forestalled the possibility of a new, direct Mongol conquest of China. They
had still, however, to round off the conquest of China,
beginning with the occupation of Peking in 1644, by dealing
with the Great Wall Frontier as a whole.

Inner Mongolia quickly went over to the Manchus because it was easier to accept the position of subordinate
allies, entitled to some of the benefits of conquest, than to
challenge the Manchus in direct control of China. This
made it possible to set up an "inner" Frontier structure
that included Southern and Western Manchuria, Inner
Mongolia, and the territory of the predominantly Chinese-

---

[34] For this period generally, see Baddeley, *op. cit.*

speaking Moslems in what are now the provinces of Ninghsia and Kansu. To this was added under the greatest of the Manchu emperors, K'ang Hsi (1662-1722), an "outer" Frontier or trans-Frontier of tribes and peoples who were under control but not under direct rule, in North Manchuria, Outer and Western Mongolia, the territory of the predominantly Turkish-speaking Moslems of Chinese Turkistan, and Tibet. The Manchu position in these outer territories was not based on direct conquest. It was achieved by a policy of waiting for the Western Mongols to exhaust themselves in a series of attempts, beginning before the Manchu invasion of China in the seventeenth century and ending in the eighteenth century, to create a new empire pivoted on the Altai region and the steppes of Northern Chinese Turkistan and extending westward into Tibet and eastward across Outer Mongolia.

The Western Mongols (first the Ölöts and then the Jungar or "Eastern Wing" of the Ölöts) failed partly because their pressure drove the Inner Mongolian tribes under closer Manchu control. Then the Khalkha or Northern Mongol princes began to ask for Manchu support. Finally the Manchus found allies also in Tibet and among the Moslem rulers of several oases in Chinese Turkistan, and the empire of the Western Mongols fell apart before it could be consolidated. Under Ch'ien Lung (1736-96) the outermost limits of Manchu control were defined. Some of the Western Wing of the Ölöts, who had broken away from the Jungar or Eastern Wing in 1686 and migrated across the southern Siberian steppes to the Volga, were invited back to Chinese Turkistan in 1771 (those who remained in Russia becoming the Kalmuks). This marked the end of Western Mongol power.[35]

It was in the course of these wars that control of the

[35] Duman, Agrarian Policy of the Ch'ing Government in Sinkiang at the End of the XVIIIth Century, 1936 (in Russian); review by Lattimore, 1939; Courant, L'Asie centrale aux XVII° et XVIII° siècles: empire kalmouk ou empire mantchou? 1912 (mainly based on Tunghua Lu).

Lama church came to be identified with control of the Mongols. When the Western Mongols invaded Tibet they raised the "princes of the church" to be their vassals and gave them ascendancy in temporal rule. They thus gave the Lama church a new political importance. Turning back to the steppe, they then attempted to combine control of the church with their claim to supra-tribal empire and to make the church the symbol of Mongol unity and Mongol control over Tibet and the territories of mixed character adjacent to the Great Wall of China.

In this period, therefore, the favorite device of Mongol aspirants to power was to nominate their own relatives to high ecclesiastical positions in order to bracket control of the church and of the state. The fourth Dalai Lama of Tibet (1589-1616) was a Mongol and the only Dalai Lama not of Tibetan birth and nationality. In fact, this title (which is Mongol, not Tibetan) was granted by the Altan Khan of the Tumets who has already been mentioned.[36] Under the fifth Dalai Lama (1617-82) ascendancy in Tibet passed from the Southern Mongols to the Western Mongols.[37] A little later the Jebtsundamba "incarnation," was established among the Khalkha tribes, the first incumbent being a son of one of their greatest princes.[38] In this way the Dalai Lama came to be associated to a certain extent with the Western Mongol claim to Mongol hegemony and the Jebtsundamba Khotokhto, or "Urga Living Buddha," with the cause of the northern Mongols.[39]

The Manchus in maneuvering for control did not miss the significance of this half-completed combination of church power and state power. In taking advantage of the

[36] Compare Baddeley's account, *op. cit.*, Vol. I, p. lxxvi; also that given by Sanang Setsen (a member of the Tumet princely house), in Ch. IX of Schmidt's edition of 1829; also Schmidt's note 27.

[37] See Baddeley's account of this very confused period (*op. cit.*, Vol. I, p. lxxxi).

[38] Baddeley, *op. cit.*, Vol. II, pp. 232-234.

[39] *Ibid.*

wars between Western and Northern Mongols they negotiated with Living Buddhas as well as with hereditary
princes. In the upshot they were able to perpetuate a Mongol church that was independent of the princes, thus creating a permanent dyarchy in Mongol affairs, with a
church that looked toward Tibet (whose pontiffs were
granted Manchu patronage) and princes that looked directly to the Manchu court in Peking. In order to maintain this dyarchy they made it a definite administrative rule
that the sons and nephews of ruling princes might not be
selected in infancy as Living Buddhas.[40] The heirs of
temporal princes had to be confirmed in their succession by
imperial consent, and under a quite separate system the
Manchus also asserted a kind of right of censorship in the
selection of as many as possible of the Living Buddhas,[41]
who became, so to speak, Bishops and Archbishops Pala-
tine, with both spiritual authority and temporal power—
vassals of the empire with a separate standing.

MONGOLIA UNDER THE MANCHUS: ESTABLISHMENT OF FIXED TERRITORIAL BOUNDARIES

Mongolia thus became a pastoral country of a new kind.
Nomadism was restricted within boundaries that were both
tribal and territorial. Fixed property became an institution through the building of temples and monasteries.
Numbers of monasteries had territory of their own and
stood entirely apart from the tribal system. The lay families in such territory were subjects of a Living Buddha
and not of a prince. Other monasteries were built on tribal
land and maintained at tribal expense. This helped to an-
chor the tribe to a fixed territory. The old nomadic cycle
was broken up. Migration from pasture to pasture no
longer led to conflict over the right of movement and to an

---

[40] Ta Ch'ing Huitien, Li Fan Yüan 13, Ch. 738; also Wei Tsang T'ungchih,
1896, Ch. 5. Compare Lattimore, The Mongols of Manchuria, 1934, p. 255.
[41] Ta Ch'ing Huitien, Li Fan Yüan 12, Ch. 737.

alternating process of tribal integration under great chiefs and disintegration under minor chiefs. Movement was restricted within the territory that belonged to each tribe as a whole. Within this publicly owned territory the hereditary prince and his council of nobles allotted pastures to clans and families. In theory the land belonged to the tribe; in practice, because each family "belonged" to the tribe and the tribe "belonged" to the prince, the land also belonged to the prince.

In earlier history the prince had been a "protector" as well as a leader. The individual or family, if dissatisfied with the "protector," fled to a new one. This method of gathering a following and at the same time depleting the tribes of rivals was part of the mechanism of the cycle of integration and disintegration.[42] The new allocation of fixed boundaries, held fast by temple property in addition to the overlord's decree, brought the old transfer of allegiance under a new ruling and made of it a new crime— not desertion from the tribal lord but flight from the tribal territory. The migrant who thus left his lawful territory became a vagrant and as such was returnable on demand by the tribe into whose territory he had entered.[43] Princes were no longer ready to fight each other for new subjects and followers, because their relation to the Manchu overlord was now not determined by the number of their followers but by the size and position of their territory.[44]

Not that the stability thus attained was new in every re-

[42] The record of the early years of Chingghis provides examples of such transfers of allegiance, affecting various individuals and tribes. Chingghis— and this marked him as an able chief—was adept at condemning such transfers when they were against his interest and justifying them when they suited him.

[43] It was also forbidden for lamaseries to accept novices to whom they were not entitled, and to run away from a lamasery. A man who ran away from the territory to which he belonged was liable to the death penalty, or to 100 lashes if he returned of his own free will (Riasanovsky, Fundamental Principles of Mongol Law, 1937, p. 135).

[44] Hence it is characteristic of the Mengku Yumu Chi (1859), as a nineteenth century Chinese document on the Mongols, that its chief aim is territorial identification.

spect. The administrative ideal of the Great Wall Frontier, whether it were ruled from the steppe or from within China, always worked toward the allocation of a fixed territory for each tribe and regular duties and prescribed honors for each tribal lord. The theoretical permanence of such periods was part of the legal assumption that the dynasty that had instituted the arrangements would go on forever. Wealth prevailed once more over mobility. Lamaism and the institution of fixed monastic property had become instruments for dividing and ruling the Mongols instead of uniting them, because the tribes themselves had veered toward a fixed relation to the Manchu emperors, who were both suzerains of the Mongols and rulers of the Chinese.

Yet the continued working of historical change, under the appearance of a permanently fixed order, produced in time a severe distortion. This was due chiefly to the fact that while the upper levels of the Mongol society—the old aristocracy of the tribes and the new aristocracy of the church—had committed themselves to new standards of power and methods of rule, the lower levels were still governed under the sanctions of the steppe-nomadic life. Yet in fact the decrease in mobility had altered the technique of steppe nomadism. The economy had changed and so had the inner structure of society. The people who pastured the herds had lost some of the real advantages of nomadism but none of their theoretical obligations and duties as nomads, while those who ruled the people who pastured the herds retained most of their old tribal authority and had now added to it new forms of authority created by the new conditions.

For instance, when a prince demanded the return to his territory of a tribesman who had moved into other territory, he invoked the new law of territorial identification and at the same time was backed by the old tribal sanction that gave authority to a chief over a follower; while the follower had lost the protection of that other canon of nomadic tribal life which had once permitted him to offer allegiance to another chief and claim protection in return for service. Thus the privileges of those in authority had been enhanced, while the duties of those whom they ruled had been added to because they were held answerable to two kinds of power and law.

MONGOLIA UNDER THE MANCHUS: INCREASE OF TRADE AND ITS EFFECTS

Economically, the chief effect of this was in the development of trade. The tribal standard which prevented the formation of a Mongol trading class (because internal trade was not essential to the steppe-nomadic order and would have weakened the authority of the chiefs), remained in force. Consequently, trade between Mongols and Mongols, as well as trade between Mongols and Chinese, was handled almost exclusively by a special class of Chinese traders. These men were different from the merchants who carried on the internal exchange of commodities in China itself. Most of them were controlled by a few great firms which operated like Hudson's Bay companies. Even individual small traders, who were nominally independent, actually got their goods on credit from these great firms and so in practice were tributary to them.

Artisans of all kinds, most of them financed at usurious rates by the same firms, carried further the destruction of the self-sufficient nomadic economy. Chinese itinerant smiths did metal work for the Mongols, driving out of business the herd-owning Mongol smiths who could not work continuously at their craft. Other smiths and artisans of all kinds worked permanently in the few towns, like Urga, Uliassutai, and Kobdo, or in border cities like Kalgan and Kueihua. Chinese carpenters made carts and water butts and even parts of the wooden framework of Mongol tents. Chinese wool clippers and felt makers, traveling with the buyers who collected wool from the Mongols at iniquitous purchase rates against goods advanced to them on credit, even made for the Mongols the felts with which they covered their tents. Chinese-owned caravans carried trade goods about the country and carried back wool, hides, fur, and salt. A certain number of Mongols were hired by the Chinese to work with their caravans or drive back to the markets of China the sheep, cattle, horses, and camels collected against trading debts; but the business and the profits belonged to the Chinese.[45]

Thus the Mongols were made economically tributary to Chinese trade while remaining tribally subject to their own princes and monasteries, whose old canons of authority had been reinforced by new sanctions. The surplus of idle men created by the taking over by Chinese of almost all productive activity, except herding, was absorbed by the monasteries. By the end of this period of distorted social and economic values, from forty to sixty per cent of the male population were lamas.[46] Boys were presented to the monasteries at the age of seven or eight and grew up under lama tutelage. Few of them became literate beyond the point of being able to read Tibetan prayers (without understanding them). Even this was literacy in a foreign language which had no creative social value among the Mongols. It was possible to bring such enormous numbers of men under the control of the church because women and children could do most of the work about camp and the work of herding, except in periods of seasonal activity. For

[45] In parts of Inner Mongolia the ruin of Mongol society has gone so far that Chinese even work for the Mongols as shepherds and are hired to substitute for Mongols in compulsory tribal military service (Lattimore, Mongols of the Chinese Border, 1938).

[46] Viktorov and Khalkhin (op. cit., p. 30) give 40 per cent of the adult male population, or 120,000 lamas, as the figure for Outer Mongolia before the Mongol People's Republic. The proportion in Inner Mongolia is probably higher, the Manchu control there having been more direct and the abuses of the system accordingly more pronounced—more temples and monasteries, more Living Buddhas. Viktorov and Khalkhin state that in 1921 the monasteries owned about 20 per cent of the livestock in Outer Mongolia.

these seasons many lamas returned from their monasteries to their families. Moreover, the great increase in the number of lamas was not a direct expense to the church because most of them continued to be fed and supported by gifts from their own families.

Most of the lamas were idle parasites, but the higher lamas—Living Buddhas, abbots, and ecclesiastical administrators—together with the ruling princes and those of the aristocracy who administered tribal affairs under the princes, were active parasites. They accumulated more and more visible wealth in return for less and less necessary functions in the ordering of society. Their real functions were in fact largely transferred from the working processes of Mongol life to participation in the profits of Chinese trade. They lent their authority to the Chinese and drew dividends on it. At first they were the patrons of the traders, from whom they demanded tribute in return for the permission to trade. Then many of them became actual partners in trade, investing capital in Chinese firms.

To this they added the active use of their tribal authority in two ways: the enforcement of collective responsibility and the enforcement of corvée services. The tribe as a whole endorsed and was responsible for the debts contracted by individuals. If cattle plague or storm reduced a man's livestock so that he could not pay his debts, the trader could collect from the tribal treasury, and the tribal authorities in due course collected from the individual, with interest.

As a matter of fact, the collective debts of whole Banners (tribal-territorial units) became funded bookkeeping accounts, which enabled the traders to take over year by year the entire surplus production of the tribe or monastic foundation. Against this they issued at a higher book value just enough materials for clothing, utensils, commodities, and grain or flour for winter provision to keep the community going. The compounded bookkeeping debt grew yearly at usurious rates and became the symbol of the legal status and power of the trader within the community. The account-book debts of the Mongols were so important for this reason that even if a Banner offered to pay off the debt entirely the Chinese firms refused to accept payment, preferring to let the account run. Interest was paid at the rate of as much as 500 per cent per annum. The total Chinese trading debt of Outer Mongolia alone, in 1911 (when the Manchu dynasty fell), stood at about fifteen million *taels* (ounces of silver), an average of about 500 taels per household. One firm alone, the famous Ta Sheng K'uei of Kueihua, drove away into China every year 70,000 horses and 500,000 sheep, collected against interest on debts.[47]

The use of corvée labor illustrates the invoking of old tribal sanctions for new non-tribal purposes. Besides tribute in kind, the tribesman was called on for stated personal services to his immediate lord, to the prince above his lord, and to the tribal organization (*hoshigo* or *hoshio,* the "Banner"). In the old steppe-nomadic order these had been essential services, distributing duties that were really functional and social, though they also provided a garnishing of privilege for the aristocracy. Under the later perversion the prince either personally or on behalf of the tribe could summon tribesmen with camels or carts to carry loads for a trader—often the "official" trader of the tribe, with whom part of the tribal funds or the prince's own funds were invested. For this they might be paid nothing at all, or given their food, or even paid a small wage, according to the nature and duration of the *alba* or service; but in any case the prince could collect a private fee for each animal and man furnished by this use of his social power.

[47] Doksom, Report (to the Party Committee of the Mongol Government), 1936 (in Russian). For casual mention of the firm of Ta Sheng K'uei, see Lattimore, Desert Road to Turkestan, 1928, pp. 64-65.

Mongolia at the End of the Nineteenth Century

Western travelers in the second half of the nineteenth century were attracted by the free spaces of the open steppe, the hospitality and noble manners of the aristocracy, the strange and mostly incomprehensible rites of the monastic religion.[48] Abundant herds gave the impression of great wealth. Only the sharper observers noted that the common herdsmen consumed very little of the mutton and beef and milk that walked about the pastures under their charge and that the poorer people were bitterly poor, although it is true that the degradation of the Mongol economy had not yet gone so far as that of the Chinese economy.[49] Even when it is in decay, a pastoral order of life does not destroy its livestock so readily as a degenerating agriculture exhausts and destroys its fields. Nor does even a tyrannical chief in a pastoral society keep his people at so low a level that they cannot reproduce—as recurrently happens in agricultural societies in phases of retrogression. He looks on his people as a breeder looks on livestock.

The poor Mongol, in spite of conditions that were becoming unbearably distorted, was therefore better fed, better housed, and better clothed than the poor Chinese. Yet few travelers were interested in deducing from the comparison of poor people and rich herds that the "free" life of the nomad was restricted even in freedom of movement, and that ownership had passed from the herdsman to princes and ecclesiastical dignitaries and was in process of passing again from them into the hands of Chinese trading firms. A pastoral equivalent of tenantry was in fact widely spread and especially practiced by the monasteries, which gave herds out to the care of individuals, reclaiming the natural increase on terms that brought them in more

[48] The English classic, notable for clear perception of detail and an intimate participation in Mongol life, which the author's very honest and simple Christian bias does not spoil, is Gilmour, Among the Mongols, n.d. See also Huc and Gabet, Travels in Tartary, Thibet and China, edit. Pelliot, 1928.
[49] Lattimore, Prince, Priest and Herdsman in Mongolia, 1935.

than their "investment" and progressively impoverished the herdsman.[50]

Most travelers noted, however, that the Mongols were no longer warlike, and this was unfailingly attributed to the teaching of Lamaism. The official Chinese writings produced under the Manchu Empire confirmed this.[51] Neither Westerners nor Chinese nor even the Manchu statesmen who fostered the Lama church perceived that it was not the teaching but the function of the church that mattered. They slid over the fact that the church had been at the center of the bloodiest tribal wars between the Western and Northern Mongols. What had really come to pass was that church property in buildings and land reinforced the secular policy of assigning fixed territories to tribes and their princes, thus defeating the mobility inherent in steppe pastoralism, which had formerly compensated for the abuse of power by chieftains through the degree of choice in allegiance allowed to commoners. In this way war had been eliminated, but at the price of economic degradation and social enslavement.

MONGOLIA IN THE TWENTIETH CENTURY

At the turn of the twentieth century new conditions arose which confused still further both the Western and the Chinese understanding of Mongol life. Already, along the southern borders of Inner Mongolia and on the east in Manchurian Mongolia, subordination of the Mongol extensive economy to the Chinese trading economy had passed over into replacement of Mongol pastoralism by Chinese agriculture, through colonization. This economy was much more intensive than that of the Mongols, though not nearly

[50] Viktorov and Khalkhin, *op. cit.*, p. 30, where it is stated that in some Banners the monasteries owned from 50 to 60 per cent and even from 70 to 90 per cent of the total livestock.

[51] It is a set convention of the edicts and official documents of the Manchu dynasty that lamaism had converted the Mongols from a warlike people into a peaceful people.

so intensive as the agriculture of China within the Great Wall, because even at the margin of the steppe there was not enough water from either streams or wells to make irrigation a general practice.

Moreover, while agriculture in some respects effected an extension of the Chinese economy, in other respects it was not linked directly with the economy of interior China. Cumbrous transport made it unprofitable to send grain cargoes from the steppe into China. As the cart animals hauling the grain passed through cultivated country they had to be stall-fed. This meant that they ate up the value of a cartload of grain in a few days. It was more profitable to export the grain farther into the steppe either in carts or on pack camels. Traveling into the steppe, the transport animals fed freely and their owners were charged only a small pasture fee by each Mongol tribal-territorial government. In this way grain could be sent to a great distance; it was traded to the Mongols as food, and the traders got in exchange either commodities like salt (easily gathered from salt lakes) or livestock which could be driven to China and sold for much higher prices than grain would fetch, or wool and hides.

In times past this kind of thing had happened recurrently and had caused Frontier adjustments of the highest importance. Some of the Chinese border colonizers passed from extensive agriculture to the still more extensive economy of mixed agriculture and pastoralism, and some of them broke away from agriculture altogether and became nomads. At the same time, some nomads modified their pastoralism by the ancillary practice of agriculture, and some in time transferred altogether from pastoralism to agriculture, and became Chinese. Whether the predominant movement was toward extensive economy and nomadism or toward intensive economy and fixed agriculture depended on the general complex of Frontier relations—on

THE STEPPES OF MONGOLIA 99

the alternating increase or diminution in importance of the
factor of mobility in the historical cycle.

What happened at the turn of the century was that
Mongolia came within the range of altogether new forces.
The Trans-Siberian Railway skirted its northern horizon.
Railways in Manchuria altered the status of Eastern Inner
Mongolia. The Peiping-Suiyüan Railway reached up
toward the southern edge of Inner Mongolia. Railways
entirely altered the cruder adjustments between extensive
and intensive economy that had existed before.[52] From the
north the railway sent Russian traders from its flanks into
Outer Mongolia. Russian colonists followed, at least as far
as Buriat Mongolia and the Tannu-Tuva or Urianghai
regions, adjacent to Outer Mongolia.[53] From the east and
south the railways despatched into Inner Mongolia even
more Chinese colonists than Chinese traders, because rail
transport reversed the direction of grain export, making the
Chinese market more profitable than the steppe market.

Firearms emphasized the change by altering in their own
way the ratio between nomad mobility and agricultural
immobility. The old method of adjustment, by which border communities tended to break away from China and
gravitate to the steppe when changes from intensive to extensive economy had created a suitable degree of mobility,
was now impossible. Although colonization, as it pushed
into the steppe, distorted more and more severely the Chinese economy and with it the Chinese family and social
system (leading, for instance, to the development of special
forms of banditry and Frontier-provincial war-lordism),
this new extensive-economy China remained linked uncom-
fortably to the old intensive-economy China by the alien
devices of steel rails and firearms.

[52] Lattimore, Chinese Colonization in Inner Mongolia, 1932; Where Outer
and Inner Mongolia Meet, 1938; On The Wickedness of Being Nomads, 1935.
[53] Kabo, Studies in the Economy and History of Tuva, 1934 (in Russian);
see review by Lattimore, 1937.

It is interesting to speculate on what would have happened at the fall of the Manchu dynasty if it had not been for these factors and others related to them. Undoubtedly Mongolia and China would have tended to cleave apart along the Great Wall Frontier. The distortions brought about by slow change and encroachment under Manchu rule would have broken up sharply as the old underlying values of mobility and immobility, extensive economy and intensive economy, reasserted themselves and gravitated toward their natural geographical environments and social forms.

In Mongolia there would certainly have been a great struggle between the church and the princes, for the old traditions still vested in the princes would have responded to the reasserted need for mobility, while the church's great privileges would have been hard to dissociate from its territorial property because both privileges and property had been acquired in the process of subordinating Mongolia as a whole to the Manchu Empire.

In the end, the princes and steppe tribalism would have won, and the lamas would have disappeared as they did when the Mongols first went back into the steppe after losing their empire in China in the fourteenth century; or perhaps they and their church would have been subordinated to nomad forms as they were during the seventeenth century wars between Western and Northern Mongols. The principle of nomadism had not been entirely exterminated even in the church; in the regions most remote from China—in Northwest Outer Mongolia and among the Mongols of Chinese Turkistan—it was still customary for lamas to leave their monasteries in the summer and live in tents around portable "tent-temples."[54] Incidentally, the root difference between princes and church explains why in Outer Mongolia under the Mongol People's Republic the church has resisted revolution more stubbornly than the

[54] See Haslund, Men and Gods in Mongolia, 1935, pp. 282-286.

aristocracy. The Republic's principle of grafting suitable forms of industry on to the existing pastoral economy preserved pastoralism but destroyed the nomadic or tribal structure of society. The church, on the other hand, was already non-nomadic in its political structure; it therefore preserved, in part, an alternative method of basing a non-pastoral organization on a pastoral economy and so could keep up the struggle longer.

Actually a return to the past was inhibited by the new forces that had penetrated both Mongolia and China. Instead, Outer Mongolia was first made a victim of Tsarist Russian imperialism and then set free by the non-exploitative policy of the Soviet Union toward the Mongol People's Republic, the granting of loans without interest, economic aid, technical help, and the creation of an army trained and equipped by the Soviet Union but not officered by the Soviet Union or under its orders.

In the meantime China, itself laboring under the imperialistic pressure of the Western nations, was able by the use of railways and firearms to pass on a kind of second-degree imperialistic pressure against the Mongols. In the greater part of Inner Mongolia this has been replaced since the invasion of Manchuria by Japan in 1931 by direct Japanese imperialism, which is bearing so heavily on both Mongols and Chinese that it is fast creating the possibility of a new relationship between the two peoples of mutual aid and coöperation in the common interest—approximating to the relationship between the Soviet Union and Outer Mongolia.[55] If this is carried to fulfillment there is the possibility of entering into still another historical period. The economy of Mongolia and that of China are not necessarily antagonistic to each other. Under modern conditions they can be complementary. What was lacking in the past was an adequate method of coördinating them. Industrialism

[55] Lattimore, The Lines of Cleavage in Inner Mongolia, 1937; Where Outer and Inner Mongolia Meet, 1938.

and machinery can now link the steppe and the plough-land, the mine and the city, and link them in amity and without social subordination of one people to the other, if the social antagonisms derived from the past are prevented from carrying over into the future.

NOTE: While in this chapter I have described the changes in Outer Mongolia as a rather gradual process (especially if compared with the results of the invasion of Manchuria), it is obvious that there has been a great acceleration in the past year. This chapter is a preparatory account, as good as I have been able to make it; but it cannot be read as a complete description of what Outer Mongolia is like today.

Probably the principal event of 1939, for the Mongols, was the arrival of Russian troops on the Mongolian-Man-churian border to fight against the Japanese. This event must have been accompanied by many significant changes, as Outer Mongolia necessarily went on to a full war foot-ing. The result may well have been to increase Soviet in-fluence, and even Soviet control; but this must be attrib-uted more to Japanese aggression than to Soviet policy, as can be seen from the past record. There still remains another political and military move that could be made—a reconciliation between Outer Mongolia and China lead-ing to an alliance against Japan.

CHAPTER V

AGRICULTURE, FOREST, AND STEPPE IN MANCHURIA

The Historical Disunity of Manchuria

Southern Manchuria has been part of China ever since the beginning, in the third century B.C., of the succession of imperial dynasties that lasted into the twentieth century.[1] Long before then, as the neolithic evidence establishes, its people were not dissimilar in physical type from the people of North China, and their culture was one that overlapped into North China.[2] It was one of the proto-Chinese elements out of which the historical Chinese culture was formed. Yet this was true only of Southern Manchuria—the lower valley of the River Liao and the coast that looks across the Gulf of Peichihli to the Shantung Peninsula. The open western plains were linked more closely with Mongolia than with China,[3] the forested mountains of the east continued for centuries to belong to what is now Korea,[4] and the mountain and forest wilderness of the north was not distinguishable from what is now Siberia until as late as the seventeenth century.

It is therefore of prime importance to distinguish be-

[1] The Great Wall of Ch'in Shih-huang-ti, in the third century B.C., ran to the north of the hilly part of the province of Jehol instead of to the south, as does the present main line of the Great Wall, which is for the most part the work of the Ming dynasty (1368-1643) (Li Chi, Manchuria in History, 1932, p. 236, n. 8).

[2] Davidson Black, The Human Skeletal Remains from the Sha Kuo T'un Cave Deposit, 1923, pp. 96-98; Andersson, The Cave-Deposit at Sha Kuo T'un in Fengtien, 1923, pp. 40-43; Japanese archeologist cited by Li Chi, op. cit., pp. 229-231.

[3] Davidson Black, et al., Fossil Man in China, 1933, p. 139.

[4] The political frontier between the present Manchuria and Korea is determined by rivers, which do not form a natural frontier; on the contrary, the wooded hills on the Manchurian side form an extension of the environment of Korea.

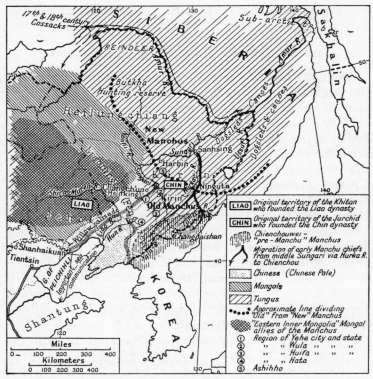

MAP 6—Early Manchuria: historical reference map.

tween the historical geography of ancient Manchuria and the political geography of modern Manchuria. The essential distinction is between three kinds of terrain: the farming lands of the lower Liao in the south, the western steppe, and the forests of the east and north. Each terrain is unmistakable, but the natural frontiers between the three are not sharp. They merge into each other, so that the edges of each area are less distinct than the main sweep of its terrain. The region of Ch'angch'un, which under the name of Hsinking (Hsinching, New Capital) has been made the capital of Manchukuo, is the focal point of all modern Manchuria not only because it commands the railway network of the country but because it is approximately the meeting point of the three geographical areas, which have interacted on each other all through Manchurian history.

Ch'angch'un or Hsinching, however, is a modern city. The ancient capitals of the land are not to be sought in this region but nearer to the core of each main geographical area, for in the past the different parts of Manchuria were never thoroughly or permanently assimilated to each other. Political centers changed according to the ascendancy of peoples of the steppe, the forest, or the agricultural "Chinese Manchuria" of the south. For this reason the records of Chinese history do not deal with Manchuria as a whole but with a succession of peoples and states based on different regions within Manchuria at different times.

There is not even an inclusive Chinese term for Manchuria that holds good for all periods.[5] In fact, the name "Manchuria" is of foreign origin and has no proper Chinese translation. It derives from the fact that foreign political rivalry for the control of China in the later nineteenth century first made Manchuria a region to be dealt with as a whole. A new kind of unity was then imposed upon it by the building, first through foreign insistence and enterprise and then through the activity of the Chinese themselves, of

[5] Lattimore, Manchuria: Cradle of Conflict, 1932, p. 7.

railways which affected Manchuria earlier and more rapidly and thoroughly than China itself was affected. They
bound together the different territories and their peoples
in a way that had not been known before, and it was out
of this change in status that a new political concept of Manchuria arose. "Manchukuo," it need hardly be added, is an
even more artificial term than "Manchuria." It is composed of two Chinese words meaning "country of the Manchus"; but this is neither an expression that was ever in
Chinese use nor the translation of a term that was ever in
Manchu use. It is nothing but the ultimate insult of a name
invented by conquerors; the contemptuous evasion of a
truth that cannot be hidden. "Manchuria" was originally
a geographical expression; "Manchukuo" was invented as a
political expression, forcing the people of Manchuria to
admit conquest.

Historically, then, the problem is to show the linkage
between the adventitious unity of modern Manchuria and
the past record of shifting states and peoples grouped in
varying combinations. Though based on regions that have
always been distinct, these groups have always tended to
overlap at the edges but have never been wholly amalgamated until quite recent times. The approach is not too difficult because the considerations of agricultural society and
history in China and of steppe society and history in Mongolia have already been discussed. The new factors to be
examined are the world of the forest and the way of life
of its people.

LOWER MANCHURIA IN RELATION TO CHINA

Agricultural Manchuria centered on the Liao, a river
whose headwaters run eastward across what is now Jehol
province. Its lower course, from the point where it turns
to the southward, has always been the artery of Chinese,
agricultural Manchuria.[6] Its valley here is wide and shal-

---

[6] Lattimore, China and the Barbarians, 1934, p. 28.

low, the lowest part of an open plain. Barges can carry grain cargoes to the sea from far up in the plain, and from the river's mouth it is a short and easy sea crossing either to the Shantung peninsula or to the neighborhood of the present city of Tientsin, from which again inland water communication reaches back into the metropolitan region of the North China plain. The climate of lower Manchuria does not differ from that of North China; the crops and agricultural conditions are the same. Everything favors intensive cultivation, an accumulated grain surplus, cheap transport by water. Consequently the land, the society, and the state have always been a homogeneous extension of China.

But it is a homogeneity with minor peculiarities, especially a partial isolation that makes it possible politically to cut off lower Manchuria from China. Land communication with China included several routes that could be used by armies but only one that was profitable for trade— the narrow coastal plain running to Shanhaikuan, a corridor that could easily be closed. The routes of invasion across the hills of Jehol made cart haulage too difficult and expensive. To the east, again, the plain of the lower Liao rose to the hills of eastern Manchuria. Into these hills the Chinese could penetrate, but not rapidly; the greater the distance from the sea and the inland waterway of the Liao the less profitable it was to haul back the surplus produce of a Chinese type of agriculture. Consequently this region remained more Korean than Chinese until very late times.

To the north, the lower Liao valley gives access to a still greater plain, the center of the Manchuria of today; but here the rainfall becomes lighter, the rivers smaller, and the environment as a whole less and less like that of North China and more and more like that of the steppes of Mongolia. Into this plain, therefore, the Chinese could not expand unless they consented to alter the mode of their economy, making it less intensive. This in turn meant altering some of the important structural details of their society and made impossible an enlarged Manchurian-Chinese state homogeneous with the rest of China.

It is true that beyond the difficulties and impediments of the eastern forested hills and the steppe-like central Manchurian plain that immediately bordered the ancient "Chinese Pale"[7] of lower Manchuria, there lay terrain that favored in a marked way the Chinese mode of agriculture and style of society. The valleys of the Nonni, the middle and lower Sungari, and to a lesser extent the Tumen, the Ussuri, and the Yalu, were potentially capable of intensive agriculture assisted by cheap water transport. For many centuries, however, the state in China did not acquire sufficient range of political action to reach out beyond the impeding territory and assert itself in the more favorable territory. Even when it did there was an economic difficulty that could not be overcome. Of the eastern and northern rivers of Manchuria only the Yalu runs to the south, and it runs between high mountains with only narrow arable stretches beside the stream. The Tumen, the Ussuri, and the Sungari all run to the north, away from China; the Nonni runs toward China only until it discharges into the Sungari, which carries its waters away to the north. Moreover, all of these valleys together did not provide an area large enough to support an independent and vigorous agricultural society. Their arable lands were widely dispersed, and each promising stretch of land lay open to forest peoples or steppe peoples who from time to time patronized and exploited agricultural settlements but always prevented the rise of independent agricultural states. Nor could the Chinese improve and expand their general

[7] I use the term "Chinese Pale" by analogy with the old "English Pale" in Ireland and also because the Chinese defined the territory permanently held by them by enclosing it within the Willow Palisade. See Gibert, Dictionnaire historique et géographique de la Mandchourie, 1934, under Liou-t'iao-pien.

position in Manchuria by a flank approach through Jehol. The southern half of Jehol is mountainous, with valleys opening southward toward the North China plain. This has created a "debatable land," in which for centuries peoples of the steppe, moving down through some of the valleys, and peoples of the plain, moving up through other valleys, have interpenetrated each other.[8] Throughout the older history of China the issue was never settled. Furthermore, the Chinese, if they pushed all the way through the hills, came out into the high steppe of northern Jehol, a territory belonging geographically and climatically to Inner Mongolia, not to North China. Here, quite as much as in the Central Manchurian plain, necessary adaptations to the environment undermined their economy and society.

The Chinese Pale of lower Manchuria therefore remained isolated. Even its land communication with China through the Shanhaikuan gap could be threatened from the flanking Jehol hills. This partly accounts for the close maritime connection between Manchuria and Shantung, and for the fact that Shantung Chinese have always been numerous in Manchuria.[9] At the same time, because the transit by sea was not a very serious enterprise the Chinese of Manchuria never developed special ships of long-distance navigation. Their little territory remained an advanced provincial outpost of North China; their important frontiers faced the forest and the steppe; their political history was warped by an infinite series of combinations of the kinds of power that could be based on intensive agriculture, on the pastoralism of the steppe, and on the peculiar economy of the forest peoples.[10]

[8] Lattimore, Chinese Colonization, 1932, p. 296.
[9] Lattimore, Manchuria: Cradle of Conflict, 1932, pp. 21, 198.
[10] T. C. Lin (Manchuria in the Ming Empire, 1935, pp. 1 and 2) unduly minimizes the importance of sea communications with Manchuria, at the same time emphasizing the importance of access through Jehol. He fails to distinguish between military access and economic access; although he notes (p. 29) that under the Ming dynasty Liaotung (the Chinese Pale) was affiliated administratively to Shantung, which means that communication was more effective by sea than by land.

Environment and Economic Circumstances of Northern and Eastern Manchuria

The forests of Northern and Eastern Manchuria create an environment homogeneous in some respects but not in others. They cover a zone of transition that reaches from Siberia all the way to the edge of the "Chinese" environment of lower Manchuria, and also far into Korea. The distribution of the resources that could be used by primitive peoples is not even. These resources include fish, game, edible plants, nuts and berries, animals to be domesticated, the possibility of agriculture. Consequently, the primitive horizon of Manchurian forest society reveals very early trends of specialization.

On the southern, Chinese edge (the slope of the hills looking toward the lower Liao plain) and on the eastern, Korean edge (valleys of the Yalu and the Tumen) it is probable that agriculture was the most important focus of activity even in neolithic times, but not the sole activity. Climate, relief, and other natural factors suggest a hoe agriculture in clearings in valley bottoms, combined with the gathering of berries, hazelnuts, and so forth. The pig could be domesticated, and was;[11] but it was attached to the household, not herded in the forest glades as in Northern Europe, because Manchuria lacked the heavy growth of beech and oak that made it profitable in Northern Europe to herd swine under the trees, feeding on beech-mast and acorns. In Manchuria, as in China generally, the pig was not a herded but a captive animal, feeding on refuse.[12]

[11] The pig is the primary domestic sacrifice animal of the Manchus (offerings of game, grain, and wine are also made), as the sheep is of the Mongols. Its importance was conserved in the shaman rituals at the K'un Ning Tien, in the Forbidden City in Peking, where were the marriage bed and kitchen for the marriage feast of the Manchu emperors. A shaman pole still stands outside this hall, with a pig-bone impaled on it in the traditional way. De Harlez, La Religion nationale des Tartares orientaux, 1887, especially p. 87 (ritual of sacrifice); Shirokogoroff, Social Organization of the Manchus, 1924, pp. 105, 133 (care of pigs as the business of the women).

[12] Wittfogel, Wirtschaft, etc., 1931, p. 463; Lattimore, The Gold Tribe, 1933.

In these primitive communities the men hunted in the forests and fished in such rivers as the Yalu and the Tumen; their activities were markedly seasonal. Hoe agriculture alternated seasonally with hunting. It is probable that the men helped to clear brush away for the patches of tillage, but parallels all over the world suggest that the women did the cultivating and also stored, handled, and prepared for use what they had cultivated; they also fed and "owned" the pigs. This gave their work a continuity all through the year that the work of the men did not have, made them the most stable element in the community, and prompted an organization of society that centered on the functions of the women. Therefore traces of a matrilineal order in the society of the Manchus and also in that of the Chinese are not surprising.[13] This, of course, does not mean that the women actually ruled. The men merely identified themselves and their children with the women who worked for them. Transition to a patrilineal order followed naturally when the environment encouraged increasing emphasis on agriculture, with steady work in the fields for the men and consequently identification of the land with the men instead of with the women.

In the upper valleys of the Sungari and the Hurka or Mutan, in the regions now marked by Kirin City and Ninguta, conditions were similar but not identical. The climate was a little more severe, the winter snow lay deeper, the timber growth was heavier, which made it more difficult to clear land for tillage, and the emphasis on agriculture was lighter. It is true that here also the cultivation of millet and the domestication of the pig are very ancient,[14] but the change from women's agriculture to men's agriculture

[13] For the Manchus, see Shirokogoroff, *op. cit.*, 1924, Ch. III; the degree of significance that should be attached to matrilineal organization in ancient China is to be dealt with in some detail by Wittfogel in his forthcoming Economic and Social History of China.

[14] Millet is the grain used in the Manchu sacrifices. A special millet was sent from Wulakai (about 25 miles from Kirin City) to the court at Peking, as I was informed when living there in the winter of 1929-30.

was undoubtedly slower. The men could here be more continuously engaged in activities other than agriculture. The upper Sungari is wide enough and yet slow-running enough to encourage the use of canoes. Fish are plentiful and some of them are very large. In addition to hunting, therefore, the technique of fishing is conspicuous, in both summer and winter, from the shore, from canoes, through the ice, and with lines, harpoons, and nets. This is also the southernmost limit of the use of dogsleds and skis.[15] The region as a whole is plainly a zone of transition in which the alternatives to agriculture are stronger and more numerous than on the Chinese and Korean edges of the forest.

Still farther north the transition becomes even more marked. Right up to modern times the lower Sungari and the Ussuri, both discharging into the Amur, have been the habitat of tribes of a marked river-and-forest culture. On the lower Sungari and the Ussuri women's agriculture and the domestication of the pig are clearly weaker than on the upper Sungari and the Hurka; on the lower Amur, Sakhalin Island, and the Kamchatka peninsula they disappear entirely. The traces of matrilineal organization also become fainter. On the other hand, the techniques of hunting and fishing become more and more developed, with the use of canoes, dogsleds, skis, and snowshoes. The men's activities are decidedly dominant over those of the women.

Along the Amur, which runs around the "top" of Manchuria and receives the Sungari and Ussuri from the south and a number of small, narrow, rapid streams from both north and south, still further transitions take place. Small groups of river-and-forest people hold many of the streams that fall into the Amur, but at the same time the technique of dog domestication begins to give way to the technique of reindeer domestication. The forest use of the reindeer

[15] Lattimore, The Gold Tribe, 1933.

marks a very strong tendency to withdraw from the rivers and to rely on nothing but the resources of the forest. It combines a minor use of reindeer milk with a major use of the reindeer for transport,[16] making possible the peculiar nomadism of an almost unmodified hunting economy, which is even more "extensive" than the pastoral nomadism of the steppe.

As the forests of Siberia give way, far to the north, to the tundra of the sub-Arctic, forest use of reindeer in small herds, primarily for transport, gives way to the tundra use of reindeer—a quite different economy, in which the emphasis is on large herds and hunting is only a minor activity. For the nomad of the tundra the reindeer combines the uses of both the sheep and the horse in steppe nomadism.[17] The Arctic and the sub-Arctic lie almost beyond the horizon of Chinese history, but not quite, for tribes like the Yakuts and the Tungus link these regions, in a series of economic gradations and social variations, with the Manchus, the Mongols, and the Turks of Central Asia. From the reindeer herders of the tundra there is a transition to the reindeer-using hunters of the forest, and from these reindeer users there is a further transition to the use of horses.[18] This can be traced in the past and even at the present day in the mountain enclave of Tannu-Tuva (Urianghai)[19] and also in the northwest of Manchuria.[20] Here the Nonni rises not far from the Amur, but flows away from it, to the south. It then turns to the east and reaches the Sungari, which returns its waters to the north. By the opening of the Nonni valley the steppe interpenetrates the forest, bringing horse users and reindeer users

[16] Lindgren, North-Western Manchuria and the Reindeer Tungus, 1930, pp. 532-533.

[17] Hatt, Notes on Reindeer Nomadism, 1919. Hatt, however, believes that reindeer were not domesticated first as transport animals but as decoys by hunters following migrating reindeer herds.

[18] Lattimore, Geographical Factor, 1938; Griaznov, The Pazirik Burial of Altai, 1933.

[19] Carruthers, Unknown Mongolia, 1913, Vol. I, pp. 209-211.

[20] Lattimore, Mongols of Manchuria, 1934, p. 184.

into contact with each other. Through the Daghor tribe
there has been communication even in modern times between the two ways of life; and undoubtedly in the past
there have been both southward migrations, with change
from the reindeer-using, forest-hunting technique to use
of the horse and the technique of steppe pastoralism, and
migrations from south to north, in which horses and herds
have been left behind and reindeer and the hunting techniques taken over.[21]

It can be seen, then, that historical processes of real importance are possible within the forest, river, and mountain world that overlaps from Manchuria into Siberia and
Korea and sweeps to the edges both of the Mongol steppe
and the Chinese Pale of lower Manchuria. General homogeneity is offset by particular disparities; but changes are
not abrupt and the degree of homogeneity that prevails
therefore serves as a flux, making it possible to change
from one to another of the more specialized forms or to
merge them into each other. It is this that explains the
interpenetration or overlapping of Tungus and Korean
characteristics (both physical and social) in East Manchuria and North Korea;[22] of Tungus-Manchu and Chinese characteristics at the southern fringe of the forest;[23]
of Tungus and Mongol characteristics in Central and
Northwestern Manchuria.[24]

The working of these processes can be established by a
study of Manchu history and applied by inference to the
history of the earlier peoples and states of Manchuria:
the Sushen of antiquity (supposedly from the second millennium B.C. to the fifth century after Christ), the Tunghu

[21] Lattimore, loc. cit.
[22] Lattimore, The Gold Tribe, 1933; for Korean activity on the Yalu-Tumen
frontier in the fourteenth and fifteenth centuries, see T. C. Lin, op. cit., pp.
15-19.
[23] Lattimore, Manchuria: Cradle of Conflict, 1932, p. 61 (rapid spread of
Chinese among the Manchus).
[24] Lattimore, Mongols of Manchuria, 1934; see index under Daghor, Solon,
Yehonala, etc.

(third century B.C. to third century after Christ), the Kaochüli or Kokuri, astride the Yalu in both Manchuria and Korea (from the first to the seventh century after Christ), the Hsienpi or Hsienpei (third and fourth centuries), the Hsi (fourth to seventh centuries), the Moho (sixth and seventh centuries) who founded the state of Pohai (eighth and ninth centuries), the Khitan (fourth to ninth centuries) who founded the Liao dynasty (tenth to twelfth centuries), the Juchen or Jurchid (seventh to eleventh centuries) who founded the Chin dynasty (twelfth and thirteenth centuries), and a number of other tribes.[25]

NURHACHI, FOUNDER OF THE MANCHU DYNASTY

Manchu history begins nominally in the sixteenth century, with the wars of a number of petty states overlooking the Chinese Pale of the lower Liao from the north and northeast. The clan line of Nurhachi, the founder of the Manchu Empire, can, however, be traced back to the beginning of the fifteenth century, when his ancestors were established at Sanhsing (Ilan Hala, "Three Clans" in Manchu) on the middle Sungari.[26] They derived from outlying tribal followers of the Juchen or Jurchid of the Chin dynasty (twelfth and thirteenth centuries), who had lost their position of special privilege when the Mongols conquered both Manchuria and China in the thirteenth century. They called themselves Aisin Gioro, the Golden Tribe—an echo of the name Chin, "Gold," which the Jurchid had taken as their dynastic style.[27] Nurhachi, in his

[25] See Gibert, *op. cit.*, under Sou-chen, Tong-hou, Kao-keou-li, Sien-pi (also Mou-jong, and the various individuals of that clan), Hi, Mouo-ho, Pouo-hai, K'i-tan (also the numerous individuals listed under the clan name of Ye-liu), Joutchen (also under the clan name of Wan-yen), and many other entries. This admirable handbook (see review by Lattimore, 1935) facilitates access to both the Chinese and the "tribal" aspects of Manchurian history. Unfortunately, it does not give specific references to the Chinese materials on which it is based, though the main sources are listed in the introduction.

[26] Gibert, *op. cit.*, under Nourhats'i, Ilan Hala, etc.

[27] Gibert, *op. cit.*, under Aisin Kioro.

first period of successful conquest, set up his new ruling house as the Hou Chin, meaning "Later" or "Restored Chin," and it was only under his successor that the Manchus adopted the wholly new dynastic style of Ch'ing, "Pure," by which they are known in Chinese history: Another of their aristocratic clans was known as Irgen Gioro, a name meaning both "Subject Tribe" and "Chinese Tribe," claiming descent from two Chinese emperors of the Sung dynasty who had been held as hostage prisoners in Manchuria by the Chin dynasty.[28]

These clans of the middle Sungari were not yet known as Manchus, for the name Manchu was only invented at about the time that the dynastic style of Ch'ing was proclaimed. They were known to the Chinese as the people of Chienchou, a name which, as written in Chinese, has every appearance of being regional and not tribal at all.[29]

[28] Gibert, *op. cit.*, under Irgen Kioro. As for the term *Manchu* itself, the most plausible explanation is that given by Hauer, K'ai-kuo Fang-Lüeh, 1926, p. 592. An early ancestor of Nurhachi was named Manjusri—Mongol names being common among the Manchu tribes, and Manjusri (itself a name of Sanskrit origin) being common among the Mongols, having traveled to them from Tibet along with Lamaism. As a petty chief in contact with the Chinese, this Manjusri acquired the Chinese name of Li Man-chu (the Man-chu representing Manjusri). When the Manchus later wanted a dynastic and national name that would be ancient but not identical with such historical names as Chin or Jurchid, they turned to this ancestor or founder of the house of Aisin Gioro. If this explanation is correct the connection between Manchu and the Manjusri of Lamaism is accidental and not primarily religious. Gorski, however (On the Ancestor of the Ch'ing Dynasty, 1852, p. 139 [in Russian]), claimed that *Manchu* is an old tribal term for "chief," going back to the fifth and sixth centuries.

[29] Gibert, *op. cit.*, under Kien-tcheou-wei. It is to be noted that this "regional" name migrated with the Chienchou Manchus from the middle Sungari to Southeastern Manchuria. This suggests—I cannot carry it beyond a suggestion—that the name was not in the first place regional, though it came to be used regionally, but a re-transcription into Chinese of a Tungusic corruption of the Chinese Chin-tsu—"tribe of the Chin," or Jurchid. Compare Gorski (*op. cit.*, p. 125), who identifies Chienchou as a branch of the Chin. Many parallels could be adduced. Thus the Mongol word *taiji*, "a prince of the blood," is a corruption of the Chinese *t'ai-tze*, "heir apparent"; but it is re-transcribed into Chinese as *t'ai-chi*, even the syllable *t'ai* being written with a different symbol, and the Chinese do not generally recognize that this "Mongol" word is really Chinese—though Mongols who know Chinese frequently detect it. Franke (Beschreibung des Jehol-Gebietes, 1902, p. 30, n. 1) identified the Chinese and Mongol terms. Laufer (Sketch of Mongol Literature, Russian edit., 1927, p. 43) failed to do so. Note also,

In the course of the fifteenth century they migrated up the valley of the Hurka from the middle Sungari to the region where later the city of Ninguta was built (and where earlier cities had stood). They then crossed over to the valley of the Tumen, which now forms part of the frontier between Manchuria and Korea. This brought them to the easterly side of the Ch'angpaishan, the highest part of the mountains of Eastern Manchuria. Some of their chieftains continued to hold territories along the Korean-Manchurian border, but one line moved on around the easterly side of the mountains until it reached the southerly side, and established itself at the headwaters of the Hun River, which flowed into the Chinese Pale as the largest northern affluent of the lower Liao.

It was here, on the edge of the Chinese Pale, that Nurhachi began his career. His original status was almost unbelievably petty, although he ranked as an aristocrat. The private annals of the Manchu imperial house, under the year 1583, describe two night attacks on him, which reveal that he kept no state, had no bodyguard, and posted no sentries. Thus he woke once at night, hearing steps outside. First he armed himself and hid his children. Then he made his wife go outside, pretending that she needed to relieve herself. He kept close behind her, so that the assassin did not see him. Then he slipped into shelter behind the chimney [30] and from this hiding place attacked the would-be attacker and captured him. On the

---

and particularly, that the Mongol word *taiji* became a clan and tribal name (the Taijigat of the time of Chingghis). This again suggests that Chin-tsu, corrupted into Chienchou, may also have been used as a clan and later as a tribal and regional name.

[30] The old "Manchu" style of house, probably in part at least, adapted from the Korean style (Lattimore, The Gold Tribe), commonly had a chimney made of wood, or even of coiled, mud-impregnated straw rope (*laha*). The roof of the house was thatched, and since both roof and chimney were inflammable the risk of fire was diminished by placing the chimney outside of the house at a distance of a few feet, the smoke being conducted from inside the house to the chimney by an underground flue. This explains how a man could come outside the house to hide behind the chimney in the night.

second occasion he captured another man in much the
same way. When urged to kill the marauder, he said:

> If I kill him, his master will make a pretext of the affair and
> will raise troops and come and steal our grain. If our grain is
> stolen, our tribesmen will be short of food and will certainly re-
> volt and scatter, and we shall be left alone. Our enemies would
> certainly take advantage of this. Without enough arms, how
> could we resist? I also fear that others would consider that we,
> having killed a man, were the guilty party. We had better let
> him go.[31]

Even in these early years, it is true, Nurhachi is described as leading bodies of 400 and 500 men in war; but
these were the combined forces of several chiefs and not
all his own followers. He was as yet only a minor swash-
buckler, who had to expose himself to prove his valor—
climbing on one occasion to the roof of a house, where he
sat astride a roof-ridge and shot down into the village
that his men were attacking, until he was dangerously
wounded in the throat by an arrow. Probably the true
scale of his personal importance is given in the account of
a raid which he led in 1584, in which he had only 50 followers of whom only 25 had defensive armor. The raid
failed and his band was waylaid by other enemies as it
was returning. Nurhachi killed two men but extricated
his little force more by stratagem than by valor, one of
his devices being to have his men take off their helmets
and expose them so that it looked as if extra men were
lying in ambush.[32]

Like Chingghis, the great Mongol conqueror, Nurhachi

[31] The only edition that I have seen is that entitled "Manchou Shihlu,"
photolithographically reproduced in one t'ao from the Chinese text only, of
a Chinese-Manchu-Mongol MS taken from the imperial palace at Mukden
and published about 1930. The illustrations (one of which, depicting the
enthronement of Nurhachi, is reproduced in Gibert, op. cit., facing p. 680)
are titled in Manchu, Chinese, and Mongol. For these annals and their
archival sources, see Fuchs, The Personal Chronicle of the First Manchu
Emperor, 1936; also Beiträge zur Mandjurischen Bibliographie und Literatur, 1936, Ch. V.
[32] Manchou Shihlu.

rose from very small beginnings. Like Chingghis also, he spent his youth attempting to revenge his father, who had been killed in a treacherous border war.[33] Revenge was not simply a matter of honor for either Nurhachi or Chingghis. It was an essential step in their political careers. Both were very young; both were of aristocratic descent; but both were threatened with loss of status and loss of their followers when deprived, so young, of the protection of their fathers. Both would have sunk permanently to the status of common warriors, vassals of some other chief, if they had not, through the appeal to the blood feud and the clan war, proved themselves as leaders and won their way to a gradually increasing power.

From ratifying their titular claims each of the two men went on to astonishing conquests, which are probably explained by the fact that in the time of each of these men major adjustments were already beginning all along the Great Wall Frontier between the interests of settled empire in China and the tribal power of the outer Frontier "barbarians." In such times both those who controlled the dynastic powers of empire and those who held the most privileged positions on the Frontier (the Tumet Mongols, in the time of Nurhachi) were paralyzed by their own vested interests. They stood to lose more than they had to win. It was the petty chiefs, like Chingghis at the turn of the thirteenth century and Nurhachi at the turn of the seventeenth, who were free to act; who knew how to act, because as vassals of vassals they were familiar with different kinds of power and understood how to carry themselves both in the tribal world and in the dynastic world; and who were spurred to action by the prospect of winning far more than they stood to lose.[34]

[33] Gibert, *op. cit.*, under Nourhats'i, Nikan Wailan, and Li Tch'eng-liang —the last being a Chinese border administrator of Korean origin. See also the "official" version as translated and annotated by Hauer, *op. cit.*
[34] Compare Chapter XVII, below.

Manchurian Politics at the End of the Sixteenth Century

From this approach the politics of the petty states of Manchuria, at the end of the sixteenth century, become less confusing. When compared with their legends, the known migrations of the early Manchus, from the middle Sungari to the east and south of Manchuria, indicate a remarkable instability. The Manchu legends, and also those of the Gold or Heje tribe, describe a southerly point of origin and a northward, *downstream* early migration. The legends of the Heje and the historical records of the Manchus then reverse this first phase by describing a southward, *upstream* migration (as when the Manchus moved from Sanhsing up the Hurka southward to the Ninguta region).[85] From this I infer that two processes were constantly at work, either in alternation or simultaneously. While some tribes moved in from the rivers and forests toward the orbit of dynastic and imperial politics in lower Manchuria and North China, modifying their way of life as they moved, others fell back into the forest, losing the characteristics they had acquired in contact with the Chinese and reverting to forest-and-river tribalism.

The Manchus were of the general stock from which had issued the Jurchid who founded the Chin dynasty of the twelfth and thirteenth centuries. Some of their clans may have been of true Jurchid descent, while others derived from auxiliary tribes that the Jurchids had cantoned in Manchuria when the main body of their own people invaded and conquered North China in the twelfth century. When the Chin dynasty fell some of their non-Chinese adherents in Manchuria went over to the Mongol Empire. Others retreated down the Sungari and the Ussuri. The Ming dynasty of the Chinese, established in the fourteenth century, was less powerful in Manchuria than

[85] Lattimore, The Gold Tribe, 1933.

the Yuan dynasty of the Mongols. Accordingly, some of the northern groups began to move upstream again toward the south, along the Sungari and the Ussuri, and from the Sungari across by the Hurka valley toward the eastern mountains of Manchuria, the Ch'angpaishan range, into territories that they regarded as ancestrally theirs—territories from which the Mongol garrisons had been withdrawn and which the Chinese were unable to occupy with fresh garrisons.

Those who came within reach of Chinese trade and political negotiations changed their way of life considerably, just as their direct or collateral ancestors or tribal congeners had often done in past centuries. This was easy because their tribal culture was not rigidly identified with any one activity but had several aspects. They were not faced with an abrupt conversion to a totally different order of life; they had merely to emphasize particular aspects of their economic occupations and social organization and to neglect others—a process by which their chiefs, having the initial advantage of authority, were able to increase their power very considerably. In this they were favored by the circumstance that it was easier for them to gravitate toward the edge of the Chinese Pale than it was for the Chinese to expand beyond the favorable environment of lower Manchuria. Expansion into either the steppe or the forest meant, for the Chinese, a decrease in the intensivity of their agriculture, the cohesiveness of their society, and the political centralization of their state. It was consequently easier to create "barbarian" satellite communities than Chinese satellite communities at the edge of the main Chinese orbit.

The nature of the changes taking place in forest-tribal society can accordingly be defined. The tendency of forest peoples on the middle and lower Sungari and on the Ussuri was to live in small groups. This enabled hunting parties to range through and take advantage of the whole forest

domain. Because the men specialized in hunting and fishing, agriculture was mostly in the hands of the women.
Although all of these peoples were kin to each other in
race and speech, wide dispersal encouraged an organization in clans rather than tribes. There was a vague tendency toward tribal groupings larger than the clan, but it
did not take a firm political shape. It was related, rather,
to categories of occupation and region because of degrees
of differentiation between those who practiced valley agriculture in addition to hunting and fishing, those who lived
in the valleys and fished in addition to hunting but had no
agriculture, those who extended their range of forest
movement by using reindeer for transport and accordingly
did less fishing or no fishing, and so forth.

When people of this kind came within closer range of
the Chinese, considerations of trade and politics modified
their scale of values. It paid the chiefs to make themselves
intermediaries between the Chinese and the more distant
forest people. The supervision of new kinds of trade and
an increased total trade activity enhanced their authority.
In order to take advantage of this, however, they had to
decrease their mobility. This in itself put them to a certain extent in the hands of the Chinese, though not under
direct Chinese rule. They had to accept a kind of vassal
standing. Fixed territorial position and official regulations
governing the duties and privileges of chiefs in their dealings with the Chinese authorities created something quite
new—a feudal structure. This feudalism had several peculiarities. In the first place, it did not evolve directly out
of the forest clans but resulted from the contact between
the clans and the Chinese administrative system. In the
second place, the "aristocrats" of the forest people, though
raised from the status of clan chiefs to that of tribal princes
with fairly well defined territories, were not important
enough to be personal vassals of the Chinese emperor. Instead of standing in this personal relationship, which is

essential to a true feudalism, they were the impersonal vassals of the Chinese Frontier administrators.

Beneath the political innovations, moreover, other changes have to be considered. Both proximity to the Chinese and permanent territorial fixation meant a decrease in the amount of game and consequently increased emphasis on the practice of agriculture, involving cardinal changes in the order of society. Instead of the old broad distinction between women's business in small fields and men's business in the wide forest, it became necessary to increase agricultural production and make it much more "professional." This could not be done unless men worked in the fields. From this an entirely new classification resulted, distinguishing between farming men and hunting men. Since in any gradually changing society it is always those who rule that hang on to the best of what is left of the old order and at the same time take the best of what is offered by the new, a considerable diversification was in time produced. Hunting became clearly an aristocratic privilege. At the head of the border society stood princes who owned land but did no field work whatever. Ruling was their profession and hunting their diversion—none the less a diversion because it was also economically a source of food and revenue and a training for war. Under them were rich freemen who owned land and cultivated it, but who could afford to own slaves or hire laborers or rent land to tenants who did most of the work. Under them again were poor freemen who had to work as laborers or tenants, slaves, Chinese whom rich "barbarians" hired as laborers or employed as artisans,[36] and others.

[36] Hence the fact that both *Khitat*, the Mongol name for the Chinese, and *Nikan*, the Manchu name, have the vernacular connotation of "slave," which in neither case is justified by the etymology. Zakharov, in his Manchu-Russian Dictionary, 1875, does not give the meaning "slave," but does give "peasant," "villager," in addition to the primary meaning "Chinese." He derives *Nikan* from the Chinese *Han*, in the sense of "Chinese." If this is true, which is not self-evident, then the syllable Ni- may be from a Chinese word meaning "rebellious"; in which case the term *Nikan* would originally mean "renegade Chinese" living among the Manchus.

Manchuria differed from Mongolia in that this kind of overlapping did not concern only the Chinese and one type of border society. Besides the people of forest origin to the north and northeast of the Chinese Pale there were steppe Mongols to the north and northwest. Furthermore, steppe people and forest people overlapped with each other [37] as well as with the Chinese, producing petty states like Yehe, not far from the modern Ch'angch'un (Hsinching), which has already been pointed out as the focus of closest approximation between the three main environments of Manchuria and their societies. In Yehe the aristocracy was of partly Mongol origin,[38] the people were mainly of Tungus-Manchu stock, and the culture, with its walled cities and well-developed farmlands and marginal herding and hunting activities, was Frontier Chinese.

ADMINISTRATIVE DECAY IN CHINA IN RELATION TO THE MANCHURIAN FRONTIER

Stability in political relationships was not necessarily threatened by this kind of historical change and elaboration. Conquest of the Chinese was far beyond the horizon of such petty border chiefs as the immediate ancestors of Nurhachi. Their greatest ambition was to be received at the Chinese court at Peking, an honor which gave them something of an idea of being personal vassals of the emperor and something more than administrative subordinates of the provincial Frontier officials.[39] Even such promo-

[37] Lattimore, Mongols of Manchuria, under Solon, Daghor.
[38] Gibert, op. cit., under Yehe; Lattimore, Mongols of Manchuria, 1934, under Yehonala (Mongol *yeghe nere,* "great name," "great clan").
[39] Li Chi, op. cit., 1932, with reproduction of an interesting document concerning one of Nurhachi's ancestors. Also Lin, op. cit., pp. 33-41. I think that my analysis of the "de-tribalizing" of forest peoples under these conditions is an advance over Lin's more purely political analysis. In the period of Ming decline the "tribute missions" received at court became a method of taking advantage of the Chinese. The "tribute bearers" came with retinues running into hundreds, at the expense of the Chinese authorities, which inflated their political importance. At the same time they brought "non-tribute" goods for trade, which cut the profit of the Chinese Frontier traders. See Lin, Manchurian Trade and Tribute in the Ming Dynasty, 1937. By

tion did not lead to any real danger of encroachment. The frame within which they moved specified for such princes an ambition of being important only as parasites. For their revenue they depended largely on extending the range of Chinese trade and quasi-Chinese farming farther than they could conveniently be spread by direct Chinese conquest and administration. For their social prestige they depended on their ability to reach back into the wilderness and enforce tribute demands for furs and other marketable hunting products on tribes that were akin to them but more "barbarous" and politically unorganized.[40]

Stability, therefore, was determined in the main by the soundness of the dynasty and its imperial administration within China proper, including the Chinese Pale of lower Manchuria. Chinese dynasties did not normally weaken along the Frontier until they had first decayed at the core. Imperial revenues dwindled in proportion as the power of the central government was weakened in the provinces by the overdevelopment of the "scholar-gentry," the landholding families from which the civil service or bureaucratic administration was staffed. When these families became powerful enough to put their private interest before their professional duty, they connived with each other in evading taxes on their own lands. The imperial revenue immediately fell. To keep it from falling too fast extra

exaggerating the "benevolence" and political acumen of Chinese rule beyond the Great Wall, he fails to extract the full significance of his rich source material.

[40] The fur tribute survived under the Manchu Empire almost until our own times, in the Butkha (Pu-t'e-ha) Hunting Reserve in the Hsingan range, west of the upper Nonni. "Hunting tribute," under the Manchus and under various overlords of other forest tribes, was an important device for the exploitation of forest tribes whose economy, being self-sufficient, did not especially prompt them to trade of their own accord. Military peoples like the Mongols and the settled Manchus therefore sought to compel such tribes to produce a surplus. Kabo, Studies in the History and Economy of Tuva, 1934, pp. 79-80 (in Russian; review by Lattimore, 1937); Koz'min, On the Question of Turco-Mongol Feudalism, 1934, pp. 29 *et sqq.* (in Russian); Baddeley, Russia, Mongolia, China, 1919, various references, especially Vol. II, pp. 443-445; Lattimore, Mongols of Manchuria, 1934, under Buteha.

revenues were collected from the poorer landholders and farmers, who had no political power. This produced an increase in mortgages, foreclosures, landlessness, and peasant unrest at the same time that the imperial revenue decreased and the power of the central government declined, and at the same time that the scholar-gentry-bureaucracy developed their privileges and immunities more and more arbitrarily beyond the reach of the law.[41]

The decay of government and law concurrently with the growth of private wealth meant, however, that wealth became more vulnerable in proportion as it grew more bloated. The ground was thus prepared simultaneously for internal rebellion and for Frontier unrest and barbarian incursions. Up to this point, and even beyond, it was not the magnates of the Frontier who most seriously threatened the Chinese. Anda, the Altan Khan of the Tumets, might convert "loyalty" into blackmail and begin to improve his Inner Mongolian Frontier position at the expense of the Ming dynasty instead of in partnership with it, but even in so doing he was only building up his vested interest in a particular kind of power of limited range. He could not aim at general conquest, which would have meant reaching out for a new kind of power, without staking his valuable vested interest on the ability to master China and to hold off rivals along the Frontier and in the depths of the outer Frontier while doing so. The rise of the Chahar Mongols at the end of Altan Khan's reign, displacing in power the Tumets whom Altan Khan had led, shows how difficult this was.[42]

In fact, the non-Chinese border magnate was in this respect on the same footing as the Chinese magnate in the heart of China. The instinct to defend what he already had limited the scope of his political outlook and activity. This goes far to explain why new dynasties in China and

[41] Wang Yü-ch'üan, The Rise of Land Tax and the Fall of Dynasties, 1936.
[42] See Chapters IV, above, and XVII, below.

dynasties of Frontier origin were normally founded by men of intermediate or hanger-on status who had little to lose, but were high enough to know the working of authority and low enough to understand and lead the discontented. The difference between China and the Frontier in this respect is that there were in fact two kinds of Frontier people: those who had been modified by close contact with China and those of the outlying tribes who had not been so modified.[43] A commoner of one of these kinds of people was not likely to have a subtle understanding of the social and political mechanism of the other kind. At the same time, the great men of both the "inner" Frontier and the "outer" Frontier were trying to maintain equilibrium and protect the established order, since it favored their special positions. This left only one kind of man free to take advantage of the rising forces of disequilibrium— the minor aristocrat with more to gain than to lose and with a working knowledge of both the "inner" and the "outer" Frontier.[44]

CAREER OF NURHACHI AND ESTABLISHMENT OF THE MANCHU DYNASTY

Nurhachi, like Chingghis Khan, was a man of this class. He came of a line of minor importance. The decay of law and order late in the Ming dynasty allowed his father's interests to be encroached on by more important men who had the "benevolent neutrality" of corrupt Chinese Frontier officials on their side.[45] The death of his father weakened his position among those whom he would otherwise

[43] See Chapter VIII, below.
[44] Lattimore, review of Grenard's Genghis-Khan, 1937.
[45] Gibert, op. cit., under Nourhats'i, Nikan Wailan, and Li Tch'eng-liang; also the "official" account in Hauer, op. cit. Nikan Wailan represented that part of the Frontier aristocracy that wished to continue to serve Chinese interests to its own advantage, Nurhachi the lesser aristocrats who saw a chance to improve their position. Even the name Nikan Wailan shows mixed origin: Nikan, the Manchu name for Chinese; Wailan, from a Chinese title (Hauer, op. cit., p. 614).

have considered his equals. It forced him to develop his talent for organizing, leading, and protecting men still less important than himself and to rise on their shoulders by gratifying their demands until he was able to recover his old position and reach out still further. Exactly like Chingghis Khan, he made his first reputation by giving power and rewards to his followers and even to men who had been loyal followers of his old enemies. By the act of doing so he created a new aristocracy which had to consolidate its gains against the old aristocracy. They could not then stop, but had to go on to complete conquest and the establishment of a new order dominated by themselves.

Dynasties founded in Manchuria could not succeed in really wide conquest unless the period of decay of the dynasty at whose expense they rose was both protracted and disorderly. This was true of the Khitan-Liao (eleventh and twelfth centuries), the Jurchid-Juchen Chin (twelfth and thirteenth centuries), and the Manchu Ch'ing (1644-1911). Before they could make any major effort to penetrate south of the Great Wall, close juxtaposition of the steppe, the forest, and the agricultural Chinese Pale made it necessary for them first to determine whether their Frontier center of gravity lay in the steppe or the forest, and then to gear their combined Frontier power to the control of the Chinese Pale, which although homogeneous with North China was considerably detached from it and very provincial in character.

At the turn of the sixteenth century the rotting of the Ming dynasty and the inability of the Mongols to break into China along the main sweep of the Great Wall Frontier gave the Manchus the time that they needed to learn the uses of power. The most threatening Mongol movements were in the south (the Chahars) and west (the Ölöts). This prevented the Khalkhas of the north from acting and at the same time pressed the Eastern Mongols inward on Manchuria. It is a matter of record that the

Manchu conquest of the Eastern Mongols was not thoroughgoing and that the most important tribes joined the Manchus in alliance in order to protect themselves from the Chahars.

A little earlier than this, Nurhachi had first made himself important by the blood-feud wars in which he avenged his father and recovered his tribal standing. This gave him command of a strategic position on the edge of the Chinese Pale, with forest tribes to the north and northeast and tribes of the steppe fringe to the northwest and west. That this was the key to his political ascent is proved by the fact that the lords of the steppe fringe attempted to enlist the forest tribes of Eastern Manchuria in a coalition against him.[46] They failed partly because Nurhachi's position enabled him to strike at the steppe and at the forest alternately, but even more, I think, because the forest derivation of Nurhachi's Manchus endowed him with the social knowledge of how to handle the forest people, while the Chinese influences that had interpenetrated the Manchus revealed to him the tribal, social, and political peculiarities of the people of the steppe fringe, who had been similarly modified. He was better prepared than any other man of his time to handle Chinese, forest, and steppe problems in combination.

Control of the Chinese Pale, in turn, gave access to China proper. Control of the nearer forest tribes made it easy almost at once to convert even the most remote forest and river-valley groups politically into "Manchus." Their languages, for one thing, were much more closely related to that of the Manchus than to that of the Mongols. Control of the part-Mongol, part-Tungusic, part-Chinese groups of the steppe fringe, like the Hulun federation of Wula, Yehe, Huifa, and Hata,[47] grouped to the northeast, east, and south of the present Ch'angch'un (Hsinching), opened up

---

[46] Gibert, *op. cit.*, under Neyen, Mandchou, etc.
[47] *Ibid.*, under Ou-la, Yehe, Houifa, and Hata.

the farther steppe. The forces necessary for a Frontier invasion of China were then geared together and ready for action.

Nurhachi's career as an invader and as the greatest lord of the Manchurian Frontier began formally in 1616, when he took the style of Khan of the Chin.[48] This revival of the dynastic name of the Jurchid or Juchen asserted a claim to tribal hegemony. In 1618 he published a famous manifesto against the Ming dynasty; this was in the nature of a declaration of independence and was also the equivalent of announcing an intention to dispossess the Ming dynasty of its empire in China.[49] By 1626, the year in which he died at the age of 68, Nurhachi had conquered most of the Chinese Pale; but it was only in the course of the next ten years that the Manchus began to cross the Great Wall and raid at a considerable distance within China. Finally, in 1636, the son and successor of Nurhachi changed the Manchu "national" style from Chin to Ch'ing ("Pure").[50] The new name, which had no tribal connotation, set up for the first time a claim to general empire over the whole of China and the whole of the Great Wall Frontier—the *t'ien hsia,* the "all under heaven," or "universe," which is the equivalent in Chinese history of the Roman *orbis terrarum.* This new claim was not made good until 1644, the year conventionally taken as the beginning of the Manchu dynasty; but Manchu official usage always dated the establishment of the dynasty from 1636.

MILITARY AND POLITICAL ORGANIZATION OF THE MANCHU CONQUEST

One of the most important phenomena in the turn from Frontier ascendancy to inclusive conquest was the enlist-

[48] *Ibid.,* under Nourhats'i, etc.; also the "official," chronological account in Hauer, *op. cit.;* also Gorski, *op. cit.,* p. 133.

[49] Hauer, *op. cit.*

[50] Gibert, *op. cit.,* under Ts'ing, Nourhats'i, and Houang-t'ai-ki; Hauer, *op. cit.*

ment of Chinese followers. Crude subjugation of the Chinese Pale of lower Manchuria would not have been enough. Its agricultural economy and political structure had to be integrated with the power of the Manchus, which involved important modifications of the character of both Manchu society and the society of the Manchurian Chinese. This is a question, however, that has been almost ignored by Western students and evaded as far as possible by Chinese historians because of national and cultural pride. The essential point is that, at a certain stage in the increase of tribal pressure coincident with failure of support from within China, the local, regional interests of Chinese communities along the Frontier tended to turn away from China and to identify themselves with the political power of non-Chinese invaders.

Nurhachi thoroughly understood this variability of the Frontier Chinese. The petty Manchu "states" represented a hesitant compromise between the clan cohesion of the old forest tribes in which personal leadership was all-important, and a new territorial solidity in which the identification of the tribe with its leader was being converted into identification of the leader himself with the possession of a fortified town and the rule of the land surrounding it. Was the next step to be a reversion toward tribal standards by the agglomeration of tribal units into an increasingly powerful horde, or an advance toward an enlarged and centralized territorial state?

Nurhachi dealt with the problem by creating the Manchu "Banners," which converted both the territorial levies of the petty states and the tribal followers of outlying chiefs into a professional standing army. As a nucleus he took the Manchu *niru* (or arrow), a levy of an approximately feudal kind, service in which appears to have been partly hereditary (members of the same clan or tribe) and partly a condition of the holding of land (a natural development among those of the Manchus who had attached themselves

to the different "states"). In 1606 these were reorganized
into four Banners. Because none of the Banners had any
specific territorial identification this at once converted a
loose group of states with feudal levies into a nation with a
professional army. Each Banner kept up its complement
by recruiting from families hereditarily attached to it;
but not all of these families came from the same clan
groups, nor were they grouped according to the former
states.

In 1615 the four Banners were increased to eight. The
next step was to brigade Chinese and Mongols with the
Manchu Banners, leading eventually to the formation of
separate Mongol and Chinese cadres. (These Mongol Banners were quite different from the Mongol tribal-territorial
Banners, for which the same terminology was used. The
Mongols who entered them were detached from their
tribes and the authority of their hereditary chiefs, and
became hereditary professional soldiers of the "national"
army.) The status of Chinese Bannermen was the same.
Eventually several complete brigades of eight Banners
were formed—in Manchuria, at Peking, in the Chinese
provinces—but this territorial identification was not of a
"feudal" kind and could not lead to the formation of semi-
independent military satrapies because all Bannermen were
liable to universal service.[51]

In this way conquest of the Chinese Pale was converted
into the participation of selected and privileged Chinese
in the profits of Manchu conquest, which gave the Manchus control of both the economic and the political resources of the Chinese Pale by enlistment instead of by
the feudal kind of conquest that the Normans effected in
Saxon England. The story of Wu San-kuei,[52] who let the
Manchus through the Great Wall at Shanhaikuan in 1643

[51] Gibert, op. cit., under Pa-k'i; also Tunghua Lu, under the years mentioned.
[52] Ibid., under Ou San-kouei; Lattimore, Mongols of Manchuria, 1934, pp.
67-68; Hauer, General Wu San-kuei, 1927, p. 564.

and opened the way to Peking, illustrates this phase of Manchurian history. The accepted explanation of Wu San-kuei's action is entirely romantic. He is supposed to have turned to the Manchus because his favorite concubine had been captured by a Chinese rebel who was attacking Peking from the west. He is also supposed to have had some idea of using the Manchus to defeat this rebel (who had sacked Peking, causing the last Ming emperor to commit suicide), in order later to restore the Ming dynasty.

All of this ignores the fact that Wu San-kuei was a native of the Chinese Pale in Manchuria. As a high military official he must have had important holdings and family connections there, and many former colleagues who were already serving with the Manchus. At the moment of maximum confusion, therefore, when Peking had already fallen, his obvious move was to join the Manchus, who had long since given an honorable color to such transactions by treating them as enlistments rather than as surrenders. This explanation is not in the least weakened by the fact that Wu San-kuei later turned against the Manchus, for in doing so all that he attempted was to "capture" the Manchu-Chinese coalition from the Manchus and bring it under the control of the Chinese of the Chinese Pale, who were already so important within it.

Chinese Influences in Manchuria During the Early Period of the Manchu Dynasty

Manchuria in the first 150 years of Manchu rule differed from Manchuria under the Ming dynasty in certain significant ways.[53] Under a dynasty based within China the

---

[53] I omit here a separate discussion of the Mongol steppe of Western Manchuria, for which see "Mongols of Manchuria." I have developed a good deal differently—as can be seen from the context—the ideas that I held at that time (1934) about the political significance of the Manchurian Mongols; but this does not affect such questions as their present and past geographical distribution which are there discussed, with maps.

Chinese could expand rapidly and effectively up to the limits of the Chinese Pale. The interest of the state was to hold them back from venturing beyond this frontier, because within it the environment favored both the Chinese people and the Chinese state, while beyond it the modification of intensive agriculture led to social changes and a political tendency to break away from control. The dominant economic interest of a system of grain marketing, grain collection, and grain transport, oriented toward China, coincided with this political interest.

When the political and military center of gravity shifted into Manchuria itself these considerations lost force. The greatest wealth and power accrued to those Manchu, Chinese, and Mongol chiefs and generals and administrators who moved into China. Not all could go, however, for the conquest of China had been undertaken before the Manchus had made their hold secure along the Great Wall Frontier as a whole. Important and trusted men had to be left behind to maintain the Frontier balance of power, and especially the coalition between the original federated Manchu clans and the Mongols of the western steppes of Manchuria. These men could not be refused the privilege of a provincial imitation of the metropolitan glories of Peking.

Consequently, one of the first results of the Manchu conquest was to draw Chinese agriculture, city building, and artisan manufacture far deeper into Manchuria than they had ever penetrated in the Ming period.[54] Manchu

---

[54] Compare Gibert, *op. cit.*, under Lin-houang-fou (near modern Lintung, in old Mongol territory in North Jehol), for similar Chinese expansion under the non-Chinese rule of the Liao, in the tenth century; under Houei-ning-fou (modern Paich'eng, near Ashihho or Ach'eng, southeast of Harbin), for the same phenomenon under the Chin, in the twelfth century. For the manner in which Chinese tenant-colonists were brought in by the Mongol princes, especially in Jehol, against the Manchu regulations, with the result of converting Mongol rulers into landlords and Mongol tribesmen into peasants, see Lattimore, Mongols of Manchuria, 1934, pp. 79-82 (Kharchin Mongols), and 83-85 (Khorchin and Gorlos Mongols). See also Chapter XVII, below.

nobles and Mongol princes developed landed estates cultivated for them by Chinese tenants. The surplus grain they traded out farther into the forest and the steppe. This greatly extended the range of Chinese commercial activity also; but the result was not decentralization and a political tendency to break away from China, as it would have been under Chinese rule, because the political ambition of those who patronized it was not independence but promotion to office within China.

EFFECT ON THE STEPPE AND FOREST PEOPLES

At the same time, the drawing of the Chinese and Chinese influences deeper into Manchuria was accompanied by a closer approach of the steppe and forest peoples to the Chinese Pale in the south of Manchuria. The Manchus especially needed to recruit their own numbers by drawing on the forest and river-valley tribes that spoke Tungus dialects related to Manchu in order to avoid being swamped by the Chinese they had enlisted in the Chinese Pale. This was done by giving outlying tribes the status of "New Manchus" (Iche Manju) under a system corresponding to that of the Manchu Banners, though necessarily looser.[55] Equilibrium between the Manchu and Mongol interests in Eastern and Western Manchuria was maintained by a different method—through marriage alliances which made the princes of the Mongols, rather than the Mongol people, allies of the Manchu imperial house.[56]

[55] Lattimore, *op. cit.*, p. 174; also The Gold Tribe, 1933; Gibert, *op. cit.*, under I-tch'e Man-tcheou.

[56] Many princely families of the Eastern Mongols became, as a result of these marriages, almost more Manchu than Mongol. The way in which the upper classes, but not the Mongol people as a whole, were associated with the Manchus is also shown by the administrative use of the Manchu language. Until a generation ago the officials of the Chahar Mongols wrote documents in Manchu, not Mongol—which made law and government a mystery to the common people. The same practice has survived to the present time in the Barga region, Northwest Manchuria. When traveling there in 1930, my "Mongol passport" was made out in Manchu. My friend, Mr. B. Pankratov, now of the Far Eastern Institute of the Academy

Manchu history, in short, makes it possible to identify the separate links of a chain that reaches from the Chinese Pale into the remote wilderness of Siberia. The earliest materials in the history of "the" Manchus refer to the middle Sungari and the northern part of the border between Manchuria and Korea. In proportion as these Manchus developed away from the forest-tribal society and settled in vassal states on the edge of the Chinese part of Manchuria, the field covered by the records of their history narrowed down to a small region in the south of Kirin, with a sketchy tribal background in the north and avenues of approach to the Mongol-inhabited plains of the Nonni and upper Liao (Shira Muren) in the west, the Chinese Pale in the south, and Korea in the east. This narrowing is only apparent, however, and is due to the concentration of the records on the line of historical development that proved most significant. Once a decisive method of further growth had been determined, the nuclear area expanded rapidly to take in regions that until then had been marginal.[57]

Conquest and stabilization finally revealed that there was an uninterrupted line of communication from the Siberian Tungus to the Manchus, but that movement of the forest and river Tungus along this line, gravitating toward the Manchus, was much more free than reflex movement of the Manchus back toward the deep forest. It is necessary to keep clear of the usual phraseology, which deals with barbarians "pressing inward" in time of conquest and being "thrown back" by reflex movements. What really took place at a time like the rise of the Manchus was a process of recruiting; and what took place when a dynasty like that of the Manchus fell was not a series of migrations back to the north but simply a disbandment of the outlying

---

of Sciences in Leningrad, told me that once when he was traveling in a car with some Barga officials he observed that when they had something to say that they wished to keep private from the driver they spoke in Manchu.

[57] Lattimore, The Gold Tribe, 1933.

adherents of the dynasty. Much the same things happened at the beginning of the twelfth century, when the Jurchid or Juchen had created out of their tribal society a dynastic empire that ruled the whole of Manchuria and conquered the north of China, and at the fall of the dynasty, when its outlying tribal affiliates broke up into small clans without political cohesion.

The significance of this kind of movement from forest barbarism to agriculturally-supported empire can best be brought out by comparison with the conditions of today. There is not a great deal of absolute difference between the reindeer-riding or dogsled-driving Tungus of the present day and the Tungus of the beginning of the seventeenth century, or even of the twelfth century. It is a relative difference that is important. Most of the system to which the Siberian Tungus once belonged has been destroyed. He is now a living relic, without functional adjustments outside of his limited society and economy. He has a tradition but it no longer connects with anything that works. On the other hand, the Tungus of the time of Akuta, who founded the Chin dynasty, or of the time of Nurhachi, who founded the Manchu dynasty, was in communication through a well-recognized system of satisfactorily functioning gradations with a tide of conquest that was gathering headway on the edge of the Manchurian forests. He could go south to take service with a somewhat more sophisticated people whose language was related to his own and whose social forms were easy to acquire. He could in his own lifetime become a great captain and might well live to see his son a great mandarin in Peking. The transition from reindeer-herding or canoe-paddling or dogsled-driving to the court of a great empire did not take more than fifty years.

The range of this transition was as great as that accomplished by the Siberian Tungus of today who learns to drive a tractor, but there was no break. The whole change took place within a graduated series of social forms that were well understood and for which there were traditional precedents. For the Siberian Tungus of today the situation is different; there is a break, and a violent one. There is no continuity between reindeer and tractor. Such tribes in the world of today are faced with two sharp alternatives: revolution, which really means abrupt transposition—not transition—from one world into another and totally unconnected world, or victimization—like that of the American Indians—through being subjected to a civilization whose history does not gear into that of their own society.

MANCHURIA IN THE NINETEENTH CENTURY

Contemporary Manchuria and its problems cannot be accurately appraised if this complex background is ignored. By the beginning of the nineteenth century the Manchu dynasty had converted itself from a Frontier dynasty ruling over China into a Chinese dynasty whose chief concern with the Frontier was to maintain the vassal stability of both the Manchurian Manchus and the Mongols. It had already passed through a phase of attempting to limit expansion in Manchuria in the typically Chinese manner. Regulations forbade the Chinese to settle beyond the Chinese Pale, and repeated edicts exhorted the Manchus not to become soft and urbanized and Chinese but to practice their ancestral accomplishments of archery and hunting.[58]

[58] Some of these edicts are quoted in the Chilin T'ungchih. The gradual change in attitude is interesting. In Ch. 1, 54th year of Ch'ien Lung (1789), and in Ch. 2, 25th year of Chia Ch'ing (1820), guns are not forbidden, but there is a fear that the use of them will lead to the neglect of archery, which true Manchus ought to cherish. In Ch. 3, 2nd and 7th years of Tao Kuang (1822 and 1827), it is taken for granted that Manchus use guns and that they ought to hunt in order to keep up their prowess; but there is worry because *Chinese* are making and using guns. The reluctance to let archery die out is interesting. Archery requires constant practice. As long as the Manchus were a privileged class with the time to keep up their bowmanship they were, in spite of their small numbers, superior to great numbers of unarmed and unskilled Chinese. The musket was socially dangerous because anyone could use it, and because it might get into the wrong hands. It was a weapon that could destroy the special military ascendancy on which the Manchu rule had been based. In Europe also the first muskets were inferior

This policy had failed because highly placed Manchus and Mongols wanted Chinese colonists and tenants, and were able to evade the law.

The advance of Russia through Siberia then made it seem politically advisable to fill up Manchuria with Chinese in order to prevent Russian penetration. Relations between the Manchus and the Russians underwent an important transformation. Small bands of Cossacks were opening up the region of the Amur just at the time the Manchus were conquering China. So far as the Manchus were concerned these Cossacks were nothing but quasi-Mongol tribesmen, except for the fact that their firearms gave them a relatively high striking power because both Mongols and Manchus were as yet using the bow more than the musket.

In the nineteenth century this quasi-tribal pressure of the Russians developed into something new. In proportion as Russia proper became Europeanized and Russian capital and industry set up new standards of trade and a demand for an export market, Siberia took on a colonial character. The Cossacks, who had laid on the Siberian tribes a tribute of furs (whose high value and small bulk and weight made it profitable to send them all the way back to Russia and Europe), now became subject themselves to a colonial pressure. Westernized Russia demanded a colonial market for its manufactured commodities and therefore increased agricultural settlement. This pressure was passed on in such a manner that the overland approach of Russia to Mongolia and Manchuria became roughly equivalent to the overseas approach of Western Europe and America to the shores of China.[59]

---

in range, accuracy, and rapidity of fire to the bow; but they grew in importance with the struggle against feudalism because the use of them did not require years of habit, and consequently they destroyed the old superiority of the feudal lords and their specially trained followers.

[59] For the early Russian advance to the Amur, see the accounts of the various Cossack bands in Baddeley, *op. cit.*, 1919. For the later change from demand for tribute to commercial exploitation, see Kabo, *op. cit.*, 1934 (in Russian).

Russian expansion was different from that of the West, however, in one very important respect. It represented a transformation of existing relations. The activity of the Western nations along the coast of China, beginning with the Treaty Port era (Treaty of Nanking, 1842), had the effect of a much more sudden impact. It is true that the beginning of Western imperialism in China also superseded an older style of trade connection. There was, however, a difference between the graduated approach by land and the abrupt confrontation of strangers who had crossed the sea. The change of phases in the activity of the maritime nations therefore exerted a much more jerky and disturbing effect on China than did the transformation of Russian pressure. Manchuria assumed a peculiar importance because it was the corner at which the overland advance of Russia met the invasion from overseas of the other nations, among which Japan was to become the most important.

By this time international usage no longer dealt with "the Manchus" but with "the Chinese Empire." It seemed advisable to the Chinese Empire to meet the change in character of colonial Siberia with a change in the character of colonization in Manchuria and Mongolia in order to forestall a possible Russian attempt to come in and settle. This policy failed because the Chinese could not take their economy with them and flourish at more than a certain distance beyond the territory already solidly occupied in a Chinese manner. The result, accordingly, was that the Chinese increased enough in the south and middle of Manchuria to swamp the Manchus and the easternmost Mongols, to draw most of the Chinese Bannermen in Manchuria away from the Manchus and make them once more homogeneous with ordinary Chinese, and to make the Chinese Pale in lower Manchuria much less like a special Frontier domain and more like a part of China proper. That was all. The Chinese economy and society did not have enough inherent vigor to occupy North Manchuria in strength,[60] and the Chinese colonies in North Mongolia, having no economic link to bind them effectively to China, became subordinate to the pastoral economy of the Mongols.

THE INFLUENCE OF RAILWAYS

Then, with the approach of the twentieth century, came railways.[61] These were the product of economic and political forces alien to the whole structure of China. Moreover, they marked an advance from the penetration of Western trade in commodities to the actual investment of alien money, which brought with it not only economic intervention but indirect and sometimes direct political interference. This was especially important in Manchuria, which from the beginning had a much greater railway mileage in proportion to territory than the rest of China. While this enormously increased the Chinese interest in Manchuria it did not proportionately increase Chinese control. The economic working of colonization now took on a

[60] North Manchuria and the Chinese Eastern Railway (edit. I. A. Mihailoff, 1924, pp. 67-68) points out that the Russian colonization which reached out across Siberia to Manchuria was highly extensive: "It rapidly, though superficially, conquered enormous territories." Chinese colonization, on the other hand, stubbornly retained as much of the intensive character of the Chinese economy as it could. It grew in connection with the growth of cities (except, as I have pointed out, where subordinated to non-Chinese interests), and spread only as "the constant increase in population necessitated a certain surplus . . . drop by drop, to flow over the edge." The Russian peasant "could carry on his general farming wherever he pleased"; for the Chinese it was "an economic absurdity" to farm intensively when out of contact with the city that was a normal part of his economic setting—unless he were farming for a tribal "patron."

[61] In 1931 the total track of Chinese railways, exclusive of Manchuria, was 10,157,397 kilometers (the figure includes sidings and all extras), according to *China Year Book*, 1934, p. 571. Total track in Manchuria was 6,141 kilometers. Of this, 1,287 kilometers had been built by the Chinese with their own capital, 1,723 belonged to the Chinese Eastern Railway (Russo-Chinese), 1,110 to the South Manchuria Railway (Japanese). The remainder was operated by the Chinese, independently or with British or Japanese participation, but had been built with Japanese and British loans. (These figures from Third Report on Progress in Manchuria to 1932, p. 87; original figures in miles.) This means that Manchuria, in terms of railways, was proportionately far more "modern" and "westernized" than China proper.

character different from anything in past history. First and foremost, it effected a great and annually increasing extraction from Manchuria of agricultural and other unprocessed materials, the ultimate conversion of which into money through foreign-financed and foreign-controlled trade paid the dividends on the foreign railway investments. Although the increasing number of Chinese in Manchuria in some respects made the connection between China and Manchuria closer than ever before, in other respects Manchuria began once more to grow away from China. Nor was this like the old tendency for outlying Chinese to break away into the political field of control of pastoral nomads or forest tribes. China now had to contend with the drag of political power from beyond its old geographical horizon, power based on the economic forms of industrialism and capitalism, which could not be countered by the methods of the old Frontier tradition.

A new regional separatism therefore troubled China from the fall of the Manchu dynasty and the beginning of the civil war period under the new Chinese Republic. It partly coincided with and partly differed from the old regionalism that had always made the structure of China cellular—an agglomeration of relatively self-contained units. Each railway, particularly when it was associated with new industries and commercial enterprises developed by foreign capital, imposed a sphere of domination over part of the old geographical area of China, distorting within that area the old economic units of territory and political units of administration. The society of China, as a whole, was brought under alien control. Within the general subjugation, however, a number of groups began to differentiate themselves. A class of agents or go-betweens, the compradores, working in the service of foreign trade, industry, and finance, became clearly established. With the profits it accumulated this class eventually widened its activities, becoming engaged in enterprises of its own in addition to the business activities of different kinds in which it was directly employed by foreigners.

From this there arose the phenomenon of a "secondary" imperialism, through the encroachment of some Chinese on other Chinese and on the Frontier.[62] The old society of China resisted foreign control as best it could, the resistance naturally being led by the scholar-gentry, which was recruited among the landlords and therefore dominated China's agricultural economy. From it again was recruited the civil service which dominated politics and administration. The scholar-gentry now found that, while it was being subjected to external pressure by the foreign nations, it was also being undermined from within by the new class which had grown wealthy in association with the foreigners. The importance of this broad distinction was modified but not eliminated by the overlapping that took place when scholar-gentry families bought their way into the new kinds of enterprise and when new, upstart families bought their way into the landholding scholar-gentry class.

This provided the background for the period of civil wars, especially from the death of Yuan Shih-k'ai in 1916 to the beginning of the new or Great Revolution in 1925. Although the doctrine of the "Open Door" largely prevented the defining of spheres of influence controlled by separate foreign powers, it did not succeed entirely. The civil wars accordingly reflected in part the relation between individual war lords and individual foreign powers, in part the struggle between the old and new powerful classes in China, and in part the distortion of old economic regions by new economic forces. The latter aspect came to be expressed largely in civil wars for railway control. All railways in China proper were nominally government rail-

[62] Lattimore, The Historical Setting of Inner Mongolian Nationalism, 1936. See also Boeke, The Recoil of Westernization in the East, 1936, in which a whole range of phenomena of this order is discussed.

ways, even those that had been built by foreign capital in the form of loans; but in practice the war lord who controlled a line of railway and the country economically tributary to it could set himself above the central government within a kind of principality.

In Manchuria this interlacing of the old and new included compromises and conflicts between old and new Frontier processes. Railway politics were of special importance. They gave the Chinese a greatly extended reach outwards, as has been described; but the two main railway systems, one in the north and one in the south, not only represented investment of foreign capital but were owned outright and directly administered by Russia and Japan. Chang Tso-lin, who was the chief war lord of Manchuria from the Revolution of 1911 to the Great Revolution of 1925-27, was a man whose bandit origins identified him with the older strata of Frontier history. Nevertheless, though he achieved a quasi-independence he could not operate it in the old manner because the field of action was no longer bounded by China, the forest, and the steppe, but by Russia and Japan. These foreign countries not only dealt with him across his frontiers but penetrated the heart of his domain with their railways and other industrial, financial, and commercial activities.

All that prevented foreign imperialism from mastering China outright was rivalry between the imperial powers. The same rivalry was all that prevented Russia and Japan from seizing Manchuria and turning it inward against China, until the Russian Revolution and the rise of the Soviet Union left Japan with a free hand. British interest in the Peiping-Mukden Railway and other enterprises in Manchuria was not enough to offset the much greater and more directly exercised means of control that the Japanese had at their disposal. "Open Door" principles had never been so emphatically upheld in Manchuria as in China proper, because the maritime nations as a group had made special allowances for Japan at this "corner" in order that it might uphold the general interest in the maritime approach to China against the special interest of Russia in the overland approach.[63] Consequently, with Russia eliminated as a competitor in imperialism,[64] Japan moved a long way nearer to monopoly in the control of Manchuria. Without losing any of its importance as a strategic gateway to both China and Mongolia, Manchuria therefore sank to a status much more colonial than that of the rest of China, which remained under multiple instead of single foreign super-vision—a form of control not strong enough to force on China everything that the foreign powers wanted but strong enough to prevent anything that they did not want.

Unable to play off the other foreign powers against Japan except to a very weak degree, the Chinese in Manchuria faced a grave problem of defense. One of the chief measures undertaken after the surrender by the Soviet Union of the old Russian monopoly control of the Chinese Eastern Railway was the creation of a Chinese net of railways to prevent deeper Japanese penetration and to link Manchuria more intimately with China. This was an enterprise in "secondary imperialism" in so far as it increased Chinese control over the western, Mongol plains of Manchuria and made possible a greater oppression of the Mongols through the expropriation of their lands. It also offered the financially strong and newly privileged Chinese who manipulated the power of the railways new opportunities to exploit the financially weak and unprivileged Chinese colonists.[65] At the same time, from the broad point of view of China's resistance to Japanese monopolization of Manchuria it was an effort at defense against imperialism.

[63] Lattimore, Open Door or Great Wall? 1934.
[64] For the altered significance of the Soviet Union in China's Frontier relations, see the next chapter.
[65] Lattimore, Manchuria: Cradle of Conflict, 1932, p. 283.

Japan's Position in Relation to Manchuria and China

It is often said that conflict between Japan and China was inherent in the situation, but it is more correct to say that conditions within Japan itself made enhanced imperialistic pressure in Manchuria inevitable. It is necessary to consider this point closely, because on it turns the question whether Japan can make itself the heir, in Manchuria and Inner Mongolia, of the Great Wall type of historical process, enlisting the Manchurian Chinese and the Mongols in a conquest of China in the way that the Manchus did.

Japan's expansion springs from within Japan itself, not from "rivalry" within Manchuria. When the Treaty Port era began in 1842 China was under the decaying rule of an alien dynasty and its own ruling class, the scholar-gentry, was also corrupt. No one in the country was able to cope vigorously with the forces introduced from outside. It was therefore the foreigners themselves who remained in control of the changes that they introduced. When, on the contrary, Perry opened Japan in 1853, Japan was under the strong if turbulent rule of its own aristocracy. Seeing that it had to deal with new developments that could be manipulated but not resisted, this aristocracy proceeded to take control. It modified the form of the government by doing away with the Shogun and elevating the Emperor to a new importance; but this did not mean control by the Emperor. Control remained in the hands of the old aristocracy which by manipulation of the Emperor merely pooled and centralized the power that it already held.[66]

Japan was then "westernized" by acquisition of all that its rulers felt it was necessary to have to prevent conquest by foreigners and eventually to make Japan itself one of

[66] Lattimore, Rising Sun—Falling Profits, 1938.

the great powers. In the process these rulers acquired new industrial and financial power without surrendering or greatly modifying their old power as the lords of Japan's agricultural economy.[67] The low rural standard of living, in fact, provided extremely cheap labor for the new industries. As a result, Japan was able to sell its products abroad as fast as it could increase its manufacturing capacity; but it was not able to develop an internal market because changes in rural economy and society did not— as in England, for instance—accompany the development of capitalism and an export economy. Such changes were, in fact, deliberately prevented by the ruling aristocracy, which was accordingly able to impose capitalism by government control while itself controlling the government, thus making itself both a feudal and a capital-owning aristocracy instead of being undermined and largely replaced—as in England—by a new capital-owning aristocracy.

Since the aristocracy that dominates the state, finance, and industry also dominates the army and the navy, the fighting services in Japan are much more a part of the state and much less a separate instrument of the state than in other countries. This gives a peculiar emphasis to another aspect of Japan—the lack of industrial raw materials. The importance of the army and the navy enhances the demand for control of raw materials rather than mere commercial access to them. The expansion of Japanese rule therefore presses as closely as it can on the heels of the expansion of Japanese trade. Japan's complaints as a "have-not" nation (like the complaints of Germany and Italy) do not arise from the inability to buy raw materials but from insistence on their strategic control; and this, in turn, is not necessary for peaceful expansion but is necessary for aggressive expansion by conquest.

Japan's position in Manchuria, therefore, as in Korea

[67] Utley, Japan's Feet of Clay, 1936.

and Formosa, has aspects that make Japan totally alien to the Great Wall tradition of Chinese history and unable to take it over. Japan in Manchuria is geographically the heir of the Manchus, but not historically. It is unable to enlist the Manchurian Chinese and Mongols in a participative conquest of China, as the Manchus did. The reasons for this are Japanese, not Manchurian. By the control of Manchuria Japan increases its raw-material resources and adds to its export-trade expansion, but it is unable to create a satisfactory Manchurian market for its manufactures for the same reason that it is unable to create a satisfactory internal market in Japan. Manchuria's ability to consume depends on its standard of living. Japan is forced to keep the standard of living in Manchuria even lower than in Japan, because to raise the standard of living of the conquered people without raising that of rural Japan would create uncontrollable discontent among the peasants from whom the Japanese army is recruited and at the same time make impossible the only methods of exploiting Manchuria's resources that Japan's social organization allows.

Obstinate refusal to liberate its own peasantry from feudal subjection therefore drives Japan from one conquest to the next; nor can Japan enlist the willing service of conquered peoples like the Koreans and the Manchurian Chinese, because it cannot offer them a share in the profits of further conquest but forces them to pay the cost instead. The Manchu method of conquest built ladders, so to speak, that reached from the Mongols of Western Manchuria, the Chinese of lower Manchuria, and the remote forest tribes of the north into the armies that conquered China. Japan is prevented by its policy in Japan, and consequently by its policy in Manchuria, from using this device, and therefore its methods of conquest are necessarily additive and increasingly difficult instead of cumulative and increasingly easy.

The Great Wall Frontier can never be stabilized so long

as Manchuria is controlled from overseas by an aggressive foreign power. China is bound to recover Manchuria because the Japanese method of conquest runs much earlier into disastrous diminishing returns than the old Manchu method. A new type of stabilization of the Great Wall Frontier will then be possible, because Japan in invading China has thrust aside the other nations (especially Britain and America), and these, in failing to restrain Japan, have forfeited the whole system of joint foreign supervision over China and will never be able to resume it. Since victory over Japan will carry with it a new freedom from these indirect foreign forms of control, China will for the first time be in a position to dispense with the vicious phenomenon of internal or "secondary" imperialism. It will then become possible to coördinate the economics of agriculture, railways, and industries, instead of subordinating agriculture and the subject population that it supports to the new forms of industry and finance and the ruling class that they create, as in the period of civil wars. By an extension of the same process it will be possible to link together and integrate farmland, steppe, and forest by the use of industrial techniques, which were lacking in China's past, and thus to eliminate for the first time in Asiatic history the old processes by which different environments have generated different economies, which in turn have nourished mutually hostile societies.

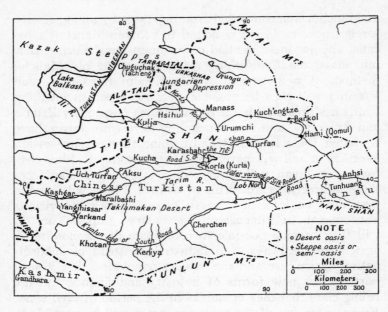

Map 7—Chinese Central Asia: locational map.
Map 8—Tibet, Ch'inghai, and Hsik'ang: locational map.

CHAPTER VI
OASES AND DESERTS OF CENTRAL ASIA
THE WIDE RANGE OF TERRAIN IN CENTRAL ASIA

Chinese Turkistan lies at the western end of the Mongolian steppes, as Manchuria lies at the eastern end. Like Manchuria, it has time after time deflected movements of the steppe nomads, converting the record of their migrations and conquests into something rather different from the tribal history of North Mongolia, and a good deal more complicated. As one goes northwestward from the ancient China of the Yellow River there is a marked transition from the uniform landscape of Chinese intensive agriculture to the oasis agriculture of Central Asia—equally intensive and sometimes even more so, but broken up into relatively small patches whose isolation promotes a stubborn separatism.[1] Into Central Asia the Chinese have merely penetrated, whereas in Manchuria they have expanded. If today Chinese Turkistan appears to be an area where the influences of both Mongolia and China fade out or become transformed, this should not obscure an earlier phase, which I believe to be of great importance, in which the influence of the Central Asian oases radiated into both the nomadic steppe and agricultural China.

Geographically, the key to Chinese Turkistan is the T'ien Shan, or Heavenly Mountains, a range whose northerly slopes look toward the climate of Siberia and are well forested, like the northerly slopes of the Outer Mongolian mountain systems. The southerly slopes of the Outer Mongolian mountains, however, overlook a steppe that fades gradually into the Gobi, whereas the southerly slopes of

[1] Lattimore, The Kimono and the Turban, 1938, p. 274.

the T'ien Shan look out over the Taklamakan, a desert of extreme aridity with almost no rainfall and no true pasture.

The major peaks of the T'ien Shan rise to heights of over 20,000 feet.[2] From the ice and snow that they conserve rivers flow down toward the desert on the south. Each of these rivers has to cut through a barren foothill range in order to reach the flat, open desert. This provides a series of points, from east to west, at which the river water can be taken off in channels and spread out fanwise for irrigation. Across the rain-starved Taklamakan,[3] still farther to the south, the land rises again to the huge mass that divides China and its outlying regions from India. From the K'unlun, the frontal range of this mass, rivers run north into the Taklamakan, repeating the orographical and hydrographical structure of the T'ien Shan rim of the Taklamakan. Westward the K'unlun and the T'ien Shan trend toward each other and meet in the heights of the Pamirs. The complete framework, therefore, is an oval enclosed by mountains on the south, west, and north, but open on the east. This oval is an area of inland drainage; none of the waters that flow into it escape by the eastern opening. All of the rivers coming from north, west, and south either reach or attempt to reach[4] the Tarim, the main river in the heart of the Taklamakan. The Tarim itself, a stream of many shifting channels especially in its lower course, finally discharges a part of its waters into Lob Nor.[5]

[2] The highest is Khan Tengri (7200 meters) according to Grenard (Haute Asie, 1929, p. 295, map); for the region in general, see also Merzbacher, The Central Thian Shan Mountains, 1905.

[3] Although rain is undependable, "rare but really heavy rains do occur in the Lop desert. Both in April 1928 and now in June 1934 I experienced a torrential downpour." (Bergman, Newly Discovered Graves in the Lop-Nor Desert, 1935, p. 51, n. 1).

[4] This is a simplified, schematic statement. For an excellent account of the hydrography and orography of Chinese Turkistan, see Grenard, op. cit.

[5] For changes in the course of the Tarim and the position of Lob Nor, especially between the visit of Prjevalski in 1876-77, the visit of Hedin in 1900 and 1901, and the discovery in 1928 by Hedin himself that another change had taken place, which he had predicted in 1903, see Hörner and Chen, Alternating Lakes, 1935, with full citations of the literature.

North of the T'ien Shan the structure is repeated but with important differences. The rivers of the northerly slopes do not combine in one system like those of the Tarim. Some of them vanish in the desert of Jungaria; others discharge into separate lakes and meres. The main difference is that the desert regime of Jungaria is not so rigid as that of the Taklamakan. The summer rainfall is greater, more regular, and supports a more or less continuous belt of pasture along the skirts of the mountains. Then again, on the northern side of the depression the land rises to the Altai range, beyond which lie the lake basins of Northwest Mongolia and the great expanses of the open steppe.[6] On the southerly side of the Altai many small streams lead down into the Jungarian depression but do not flow very far out into it. The depression, furthermore, is partly closed off at its western end by a series of mountain masses: the Ala Tau, Maili Tau, Jair, Urkashar, and Tarbagatai.

In short, the desert of Jungaria is like that of Taklamakan but its conditions are milder. It is also an oval, open at the east but not abruptly closed at the west, where a number of gaps lead through into the steppes of Russian Turkistan. An important belt of grazing land follows along the northern edge of the T'ien Shan and a much richer skirt of steppe borders the southern edge of the Altai. These pastures make continuous nomadic movement possible from east to west and west to east.[7] The rivers on the northern side of the T'ien Shan, like those on the south, can support a series of irrigated oases, but historically these oases have been dominated by the wide movement of pastoral nomads.

This describes briefly the kinds of terrain within the political frontiers of what is now Chinese Turkistan. The political frontiers must not, however, be allowed to restrict

[6] For general descriptions of both Jungaria and Northwest Mongolia, see Carruthers, Unknown Mongolia, 1913.
[7] Lattimore, Caravan Routes of Inner Asia, 1929.

the historical field of reference. To the west, around the southern and western rim of Russian Turkistan, communicating thence with Persia and reaching right into the Near East, a similar geographical pattern is repeated in varying combinations of mountains, mountain-fed streams, deserts, and steppes; and also to the east, in Kansu and Ninghsia, which stand to Chinese Turkistan much as Inner Mongolia stands to Outer Mongolia.[8] Within Chinese Turkistan it is around the rim of the Taklamakan that each of the special characteristics of oasis geography can be studied in its most developed form and at the same time in balance with all the other features. The pronounced and unmistakable oasis must also be studied in comparison with regions which, though presenting only some of the features of the oasis, carry far outward the radiating influences of the kinds of economy and society that function most naturally in the typical oasis.

OASIS GEOGRAPHY AND AGRICULTURE

The fact that some, but not all, of the distinctive features of oasis geography are to be found well within China and also in Persia, Mesopotamia, and even Egypt accounts, I think, for certain prime characteristics of the economy of each of these regions and of the society nourished by each economy. These prime characteristics have been molded differently in each of the regions by features that the regions do not have in common. We have therefore to deal with several historical groupings and historical modes. Distinct though these are, they retain from their remote origins a haunting resemblance to each other which cannot be so well accounted for by migration and cultural borrowing as by the earliest habits that a society acquires in the process of adjusting itself to its environment.

An oasis, as here defined, is an area isolated from other similar areas by desert in extreme instances or by steppe

[8] Lattimore, Chinese Turkistan, 1933, p. 98.

in less extreme instances. Within an oasis water must be easily accessible in order to be artificially applied to the land for the support of regular agriculture. In the typical Central Asian oasis water is more easily accessible than in many oases of Arabia and North Africa where it can only be obtained from deep wells, difficult to dig and maintain. Oases of the latter type cannot be occupied at a really early and primitive level of society; they are meeting points, established at much later periods, of the settled life and the nomadic life.

In a typical oasis on the rim of the Taklamakan the conditions that encourage a very early practice of agriculture are unmistakable. A river comes down from high mountains that store ice and snow. It breaks through a lower, desert barrier range and enters flat country. Here it tends naturally to break up into several channels and in the season of high water it spills over into lakes and marshes. In the lowland there is practically no rainfall—certainly no rainfall regular enough to support agriculture. The difference between the vegetation nourished by the water from the highlands and the desert vegetation dependent on rare rainfall is pronounced.

Game is plentiful in the hills behind the desert barrier range, and even more plentiful and more easily taken along the stream channels and the edges of the lakes and meres in the lowland. Wild fowl swarm and are especially easy to catch with snares; fish also can be trapped by the crudest methods in the shallow, marshy waters. The life of the Lopliks, or people of Lob Nor, as described by travelers in the last century, shows how a folk with very feeble technical equipment can live in those parts of the Taklamakan that are reached by water.[9] The natural en-

[9] The culture of the Lopliks indicates that marshes, when too wet, prevent the rise of agriculture; the Lopliks depend not only on fishing and hunting but on reeds, which furnish them with edible shoots as well as with fuel and with the material for their huts. Grenard, *op. cit.*, p. 330; see also Prince Henry of Orleans, in Bonvalot, Across Tibet, 1892, Ch. IV.

vironment, in short, permits the survival of a society based on hunting, fishing, and the gathering of wild edible plants, fruits, and berries. These are the essential conditions antecedent to a deliberate practice of cultivation.

The conditions essential to a transition to agriculture are also present. The natural growth within reach of water is profuse and even "jungly," but not too heavy to be readily cleared by fire and even by hacking and grubbing with rough tools. The soil itself is easily worked, so easily that a very crude form of hoe has always remained the characteristic tool of the Taklamakan oases; it is used not only for cultivation but for making irrigation channels and for all kinds of excavation work, and with a skill that has drawn the comment of travelers and archeologists.[10] Finally, the rewards of applying the water that can be so easily led from the stream channels are even more obvious than in the loess country of the Yellow River bend. In the loess country the irregularity of rainfall encourages irrigation in a soil in which channels can be dug without difficulty. This is true also of oases of the less pronounced type (oases in the steppe), but in the oases of more pronounced type (oases in the desert) the even greater deficiency of rainfall makes irrigation actually imperative.

In this there is a significant resemblance between the irrigation problems of Egypt and of the extreme type of oasis. The water must come from a river, and it so happens that the water is most plentiful at precisely the time when it is most needed. Each advance in technique, bringing more land under irrigation and cultivation, is rewarded at once with increased crops and wealth. In Chinese Turkistan this is because in the increasing heat of summer the fields need more water, which is automatically provided by the melting of snow and ice in the high mountains.[11]

[10] Shaw, Visits to High Tartary, 1871, pp. 469-470; Stein, Ruins of Desert Cathay, 1912, Vol. II, p. 71.
[11] Lattimore, op. cit., p. 100.

At the same time the crops are almost completely free of the danger of damage by unseasonal, unwanted rain. In both Egypt and the Taklamakan oases, consequently, the society that eventually established itself was almost exclusively devoted to a limited range of activities, which were so all-sufficient that other forms of development were inhibited. There are also important differences as between either Nile irrigation or Yellow River irrigation and oasis irrigation, largely attributable to differences in scale of territory, scale of public works, and multitude of population.[12]

Midway in character between the Yellow River and the oasis-in-the-desert stands the oasis-in-the-steppe. Because of this middle position, the steppe oasis is of special importance in the early differentiation of main types of economic activity and social organization. Fortunately, there is available for the study of this type of oasis the extensive material collected in the archeological investigation of Anau and other sites in Russian Turkistan.[13] The foremost conclusion suggested by this material is that while desert oases favored an early concentration on agriculture, developing into irrigated agriculture as soon as technical accomplishment became adequate, the history of steppe oases wavered between alternative kinds of development. The evidence is clear that in this part of the Central Asian terrain agriculture (apparently associated with and evolving out of mixed activities in collecting wild plants and hunting) actually preceded pastoralism. This was probably in the third millennium B.C.[14] In later periods oasis

[12] Estimated area of the Kashgar oasis, the largest in Chinese Turkistan, 2650 sq. km., with a city population of 35,000; Yarkand, 2100 sq. km., city population 60,000; Khotan, 1600 sq. km., city population 26,000; combined oasis of Aksu and Uch Turfan, 1500 sq. km., city population of Aksu about 20,000. Grenard estimates the density of population in these oases at 116 per sq. km. and believes that they account for 88 per cent of the Taklamakan oasis population. He counts only 30 more oases of more than 50 sq. km. (Grenard, *op. cit.*, pp. 319, 321).

[13] Pumpelly, Explorations in Turkestan, 1908, 2 vols.; with discussion of the characteristics of oases.

[14] Pumpelly and some of his associates believed that the change from oasis life to pastoralism began in the eighth millennium B.C. The later and more

agriculture alternated with steppe pastoralism, cultivation being reëstablished at intervals only to be overwhelmed intermittently by pastoralism.

The original investigators were strongly biased in favor of theories of climatic change. They believed that the disappearance of agriculture was likely to be caused by recurring periods of drought, which gave an advantage to the mobile people of the steppe, who were able to migrate to more favorable pastures, while the return of cycles of good rainfall permitted the reëstablishment of agriculture. I have elsewhere argued that exclusive reliance on climatic theories is unnecessary.[15] Fluctuations in climate may have coincided with and assisted social changes, but a more fundamental cause of change lies in the ability of any given human society itself, as it changes either through growth or because of the effect on it of other societies, to choose alternative uses of the marginal environments that permit more than one kind of activity.

THE SEDENTARY ORIGINS OF NOMADISM

The oasis, and especially the steppe oasis, favors the domestication of animals. It has been argued that captive animals were first used in "hunting magic" to promote the plentifulness of game and that true domestication then

---

probable date is suggested by Hubert Schmidt, in Pumpelly, *op. cit.*, Vol. I, p. 186. Stratification makes it incontestable that the culture had wheat, barley, spinning, painted pottery, and some knowledge of lead and copper (but not of tin, and therefore not of bronze) before the domestication of the ox, horse, pig, and two breeds of sheep; and all of these animals were domesticated before the dog (Vol. I, pp. 38-42, 67). Duerst (Vol. II, pp. 437-438, of the same work), discussing the animal remains, points out that it was necessary first to domesticate animals before the stage of driving herds to seek new pastures could be considered.

[15] Lattimore, The Geographical Factor, 1938. Pumpelly himself points out (*op. cit.*, Vol. I, pp. 33-34) that in the periods of irrigation silts were deposited to depths of 12 to 15 feet, and even to a depth of 22 feet. This must have meant changes in the level at which water had to be distributed, and possibly increased flood hazards. The hydraulic problems may have become too great for the technique of the society. For the various ways in which human society, by its own activities, can produce imitations of "change in climate," see Lowdermilk, Man-Made Deserts, 1935.

followed as a second stage.[16] I suggest that the use of captured wild animals as decoys may have been even more important and may have been involved in the origins of "hunting magic" itself. In any case, the "hunting magic" explanation does not go far enough, for it fails to deal with the practical details of domestication. Here the question that has to be answered is: What kind of society, living in what kind of environment, is best able to undertake the domestication of wide-ranging animals like horses, cattle, and sheep?

The answer is: An oasis society—the oasis here probably being not of the desert type, but a patch of relatively high fertility with open, running water, in a wider landscape of general steppe character. Men who do not already have domestic animals find it difficult to move rapidly and freely enough in the open steppe. Even if such men, venturing into the open steppe, should succeed in catching wild animals—which is easy when the animals are very young —how are they to keep them until they have become domesticated? The difficulties are so great that only one conclusion is possible: the domestication of pastoral animals did not grow out of life in the steppe, but, on the contrary, life in the steppe became safe only after the domestication of animals.

The chances of early domestication are greater when a society, though attached by agriculture to some point on the margin of the steppe, also engages actively in auxiliary hunting. The man who lives in one place is better able to keep a captive animal and tame it than the wandering hunter—or even the pastoral nomad. Wild sheep can easily

[16] Bishop (Origin and Diffusion of the Traction-Plow, 1938) points out the great importance of the technique of castration as a means of making the larger animals tractable. He suggests that the effect of castration may first have been discovered through fertility sacrifices of the sex organs. In this connection, what are we to make of the technique of gelding reindeer by biting (crushing the testicles or severing the ducts, without removing the organs)? Can this be referred to some extremely primitive notion of magic? Hatt, Notes on Reindeer Nomadism, 1919, pp. 110-111, refers to the problem, without explaining it.

be tamed if kept in an enclosure.[17] Captive wild asses (*kulan*) are more likely to be kept by outlying oasis settlers[18] in Chinese Turkistan than by pastoral Mongols or Tibetans. Russians have successfully kept Asiatic wapiti in captivity in order to cut off their antlers when "in velvet" and sell them to the Chinese for medicine. This is done in both the Altai and Ussuri regions of Siberia,[19] but has never been done by the native hunting peoples, who might be expected to profit by the practice. I have also seen a captive wapiti kept by Kazaks in Chinese Turkistan but although the household was of nomad-pastoral origin, it was noticeably Russianized. On the other hand, although nomad Mongols occasionally succeed in catching a wild camel they rarely succeed in keeping it permanently.[20]

Domestication may well be associated with the fact that game is noticeably plentiful near the edge of an oasis in or near steppe country, especially if the oasis (like many of those in the northern part of Chinese Turkistan) has not been fully exploited by agriculture. The wild animals tend to draw in towards the oasis for grazing, going back into the steppe when they have eaten enough. In the centuries before firearms were known this is likely to have suggested the use of captive animals as decoys to attract wild game. The keeping of decoy animals, furthermore, is likely to be connected with the practice of castration, which makes half-tame animals more tractable, and undoubtedly

[17] My friend Mr. Torgny Öberg kept one for several years in Kueihua, a city just below the edge of the Inner Mongolian plateau. It was so tame that it would follow him through city streets and also out into the open country, and never ran away. Duerst (in Pumpelly, *op. cit.*, p. 437) cites Mucke, Urgeschichte des Ackerbaues, 1898, on the point that enclosures are essential to the breeding of animals. This is true, until the more complex technique of nomadism has been evolved.

[18] Carruthers, *op. cit.*, Vol. II, pp. 602, 603, and photograph; Grenard, *op. cit.*, photograph opp. p. 312.

[19] Graham, Through Russian Central Asia, 1916; Lattimore, High Tartary, 1930; Dmitrenko, When Horns Were in the Velvet, 1933.

[20] Lattimore, Desert Road to Turkestan, 1928, pp. 195-196, 219-220, for the easternmost areas in which wild camels are now found. On the difficulty of domesticating wild camels my information is from Mongols, and refers chiefly to the Edsin Gol region.

the knowledge of castration is essential to the technique of steppe pastoralism.[21] Otherwise the unnecessarily large number of male animals, fighting each other and attempting to lead away bands of females, would make it impossible to keep stock in large, tractable herds on unfenced pasture.

Given the gradual acquisition of domestic animals and the gradually increasing knowledge of how to pasture them and to use products like milk and wool without slaughtering the animals, it can be seen how groups originally attached to an oasis and engaged in several kinds of activity would be encouraged to place their whole reliance on their herds, detaching themselves from the oasis and risking themselves permanently in the open steppe. It is at this point, I conjecture, that the special steppe technique of horse herding and horse riding became of real importance. Prior to this, at the edge of the steppe but not exactly in the steppe, the horse could be first hunted for food and then kept in small numbers in enclosures and trained first to haul and then to be ridden. (It seems reasonable to suppose that it was easier first to teach a led horse to draw weights than it was to develop the art of riding; but this is not a question of prime importance.)

To recapitulate: the general domestication of sheep, goats, cattle, and horses in this part of Asia (like the domestication of the pig in neolithic China and Manchuria) appears not to have been the work of wandering, hunting groups, and certainly not the work of a primitive herding society, but is probably to be associated with groups already stabilized to at least a certain extent by the partial practice of agriculture. In the next phase, in the general region in which China, Central Asia, and Mongolia approach each other there appears to have been an increasing differentiation of societies according to choice

[21] For forest nomadism (hunting, with the use of reindeer for transport) as one of the origins of steppe nomadism, see Chapter XIV, below.

in the use of the environment. Choice was open because a large part of the terrain was marginal and could be used in several ways. As differentiation proceeded the societies of agricultural China and the pastoral steppe became more and more irreconcilable with each other. On the flank of both of them stood the Central Asian oases. Of these, the desert oases, because of their intensive agriculture, had more affinity with China but could not easily communicate with China on account of the difficulty of desert transport; while the steppe oases, being set in a less absolute terrain, wavered between agriculture with a Chinese orientation and pastoralism with a steppe orientation.

In this review of the probable development of pastoralism I have not yet dealt with the problem of migration. Is it to be assumed that the first appearance of pastoral nomadism within the horizon of Chinese history was the result of a migration from Western Asia? I do not think so. As soon as horse nomadism is mentioned in the fourth and third centuries B.C. we have accounts of Chinese going over to the new way of life.[22] The general impression, however, is not one of the "conversion" of Chinese by strangers who have suddenly appeared, but one of the rapid rise, on the fringe of the environment favorable to the Chinese, of a new local way of life divergent from that of the Chinese.

In any case, "migration" settles nothing, for the original evolution, somewhere, of the pastoral way of life has still to be accounted for. The important thing is this: a complex of techniques, like that necessary to pastoral nomadism, cannot either be evolved locally or acquired by borrowing until the society supposed to be affected has already arrived at a level that permits it to take advantage of the new techniques and "convert" itself. We know there

[22] Lattimore, Origins of the Great Wall, 1937. Berthelot (L'Asie ancienne, 1930, pp. 19, 22) believes that horses were used in harness (in Central Asia) in the third millennium B.C., but that the mounted war horse was not used until five or six centuries before Christ.

were steppe-like societies on the edges of the oasis-like societies in both Egypt[23] and Mesopotamia[24] long before they became active on the Great Wall Frontier of China. We do not, however, have any clear evidence of the sudden impact against China of peoples of distant steppe origin. In view of this, and in view of the wide distribution of oases and oasis-like geography, it seems more reasonable to assume, in the first place, the independent breaking away of separate pastoral groups in different marginal regions, and in the second place, migration, conquest, culture borrowing,[25] and so forth, after the different pastoral peoples had begun to move freely in the steppe and to come in contact with each other.

THE SUB-OASIS GEOGRAPHY INTERMEDIATE BETWEEN CHINA AND CENTRAL ASIA

Thenceforward the relations between the different types of society were determined largely by the scale of activity and the range of operations. It was very likely by this growth in scale and range that the transition from prehistory took place. Herrmann[26] has incontestably established that the links between China and Central Asia, and even between China and the outer parts of the provinces of Ninghsia and Kansu, were almost insignificant until as late as the third century B.C. The importance of this had not

[23] For example, the Hyksos, or so-called "Shepherd Kings," beginning in the seventeenth century B.C. See Breasted, History of Egypt, 1912, pp. 214 et sqq.; but it should be noted that these may have been by origin as much an oasis people as a nomad people, judging from Breasted's account.

[24] For example, the Hittites of the second millennium. From the article "Hittites," by Hrozny, 1930, it appears doubtful whether the early Hittites, though they were able to migrate from one oasis region to another, can be called true pastoral nomads.

[25] Such as that which spread the "Scythian" or "animal style" bronze technique over the steppes between South Russia and Outer and Inner Mongolia.

[26] For example, in his discussion of the name K'unlun, in Hedin, Southern Tibet, Vol. VIII, pp. 131 et sqq. The validity of Herrmann's argument in this respect is not affected by his acceptance of very ancient and doubtful dates.

before been realized because the Chinese themselves, as they penetrated into the west, carried with them certain names and legends from their own already remote past and identified them with the new lands. In this way an impression was created and later accepted as historical fact that a large part of Central Asia, which really had newly been brought within the scope of Chinese history, had been intimately associated with China from extremely ancient times. These traditions were easily accepted by Western scholars, who were predisposed by their own training to theories of migration and culture borrowing and were also all too eager to accept "evidence" that would associate the origins of Chinese culture with lines of ethnic and cultural migration running through Central Asia.[27]

Herrmann's analysis is closely argued from a study of place names and tribal names, and from the ancient geographical ideas of the Chinese: their search for the sources of the Yellow River, for instance, and the mistaken but tenaciously held identification of the Tarim, far away in Chinese Turkistan, with the Yellow River.[28] Confusions of this kind inevitably followed the naïve practice of identifying ancient names with new regions. Herrmann demonstrates, to take one important example, that the name K'unlun, now universally accepted as the inclusive, general name of the mountain system overlooking the southern edge of the Taklamakan depression from the massive heights of Tibet, was originally not a geographical name at all but a tribal name, and that it was not at first associated with the far west but with the edge of the Ordos region.[29] As it was transported into more and more remote

[27] Naturally, I do not mean by this to deny culture borrowing as a factor, and often an important factor, in cultural growth, but merely to emphasize that in Chinese history the main process was growth outward, eventually resulting in close contact with Central Asia, rather than growth inward from Central Asia.

[28] Hedin, *op. cit.*, map opp. p. 238, etc.

[29] *Ibid.*, pp. 131 *et sqq.*

regions of the west, its meaning and the legends of which it was a part could not but become increasingly garbled.

All of this does not mean that there was an uncrossed chasm between Central Asia and the nuclear area of Chinese cultural development at the Yellow River bend. What it does mean, I think, is that there was a broad field of primitive habitation which included both the oases of Chinese Turkistan and the valley sites of the proto-Chinese at and near the Yellow River bend. Within this field slow cultural exchange and population movement may have taken place.[30] In the eastern part the valley sites were easily accessible to each other. Far to the west, around the rim of the Taklamakan, the river-fed oases were sharply marked off from each other by desert intervals. In between there lay a region of what may be called sub-oases, especially in Western Kansu, from where Lanchow now stands westward along the northern foot of the Nan Shan to Anhsi, where begin the difficult desert traverses northwestward to Hami (Qomul) and westward to Lob Nor. This geographical zone was enlarged by the Edsin Gol, running far into Mongolia, and by that part of the Yellow River which runs from Lanchow past the city of Ninghsia, in Ninghsia province. The characteristic of what I have here called the sub-oases (a characteristic found again in the oases of Jungaria or Northern Chinese Turkistan) was that they were less accessible to each other than the valley sites of the Yellow River bend but more accessible to each other than the oases around the rim of the Taklamakan.

Over the whole of this great field the practices by which the most primitive men sustained life need not have differed greatly. The geographical environment, in other words, was not the sole determinant; the significance of the graduated range of geographical characteristics could

[30] Compare Andersson, Der Weg über die Steppen, 1929.

only be brought out later by the differing uses that evolving societies made of one or another characteristic of the environment.

When the primitive agriculture of the Yellow River bend began to gather historical momentum, subordinating the importance of hunting and herding, the homogeneity of the region permitted a spread outward from each point where agriculture had become permanently established and had been improved by the first attempts at irrigation. Even in this part of China there was probably something similar to the oasis structure so long as agriculture was limited to the most easily cultivated patches of land. Increasing skill in irrigation, enlarging the areas to which water was brought artificially, then raised an increasing quantity of what had been marginal land to the level of the naturally best land. The spread outwards from innumerable oasis-like centers resulted in a coalescence, creating a broad terrain within which the technical practices of agriculture could be developed and improved on a really large scale.

This was responsible for an abrupt contraction of the early Chinese historical horizon, hiding Central Asia from view. Chinese agriculture, and the society and state based on it, first turned inward on themselves. They then had to become very much *more* mature—and centuries were required for the necessary development—before they could reach out and attach to themselves the sub-oasis areas of Ninghsia and Western Kansu. It is not to be doubted that the peoples of the sub-oases practiced primitive agriculture as early as did the Chinese of the Yellow River bend; but here the natural conditions did not allow the spread outwards from each favorable point to create a large and continuous terrain occupied by intensive agriculture. This is borne out by the fact that even today, after many centuries of the maximum application of the Chinese methods of canal digging, the greater part of Ninghsia and Kansu remains noticeably oasis-like, the patches of intensive irrigated agriculture, though some of them very large, being separated from each other by stretches of much poorer land in which extensive agriculture or dry farming and even the herding of livestock on a large scale are much more important than along the middle and lower Yellow River.

The result was that these peoples became more and more noticeably different from the Chinese and necessarily came to be treated as increasingly hostile and "barbarian." In time the steady evolution of culture and civilization among the Chinese made the situation of the sub-oasis peoples acute. They began to waver in their own evolution. Unable to widen the geographical scale of their agriculture beyond certain limits, groups of them turned to the exploiting of alternative resources of their environment. The technique of domesticating animals and pasturing them on land that could not be cultivated proved to be the most important alternative employment. This led, further, to detachment from the oases and complete reliance on the steppe, aided by a special technique in the control of horses pastured at large, diverging from the horse usage of the agricultural oasis peoples and the Chinese, which continued to resemble more closely the original practice of keeping captive animals.

It is to be noted that we cannot assign a definite importance to race in any of these processes of evolution and differentiation. We know that the "Alpine" stock which is important in Chinese Turkistan has been there from very ancient times and that there are strong traces of it also in Kansu, especially in the Nan Shan regions of most oasis-like character.[31] We have very strong reasons for believing that most of the stock in Kansu and Ninghsia, west of the nuclear area of Chinese cultural development,

[31] Dixon, Racial History of Man, 1923, pp. 284, 300, and his bibliographical reference to Stein, Serindia, Vol. III, 1921, pp. 1351-1389. Shaw (op. cit. p. 21) long ago noticed the "Aryan" appearance of the oasis people of Chinese Turkistan.

was of the same general physical character as the Chinese themselves, and for believing that there was little if any racial difference between the Chinese proper and most of the "barbarians" with whom they were in immediate contact on the west before the relatively sudden appearance of horse nomads hostile to the agricultural Chinese between the fifth and third centuries B.C. We cannot, however, mark off any sharp racial frontiers, although we know that for later times the general rule is that the greater the distance beyond the Great Wall the clearer the physical distinctions between the Chinese and such peoples as the Turks and Mongols. The conclusion to be drawn from the total weight of all kinds of evidence, therefore, is that migration, economic system, and social organization in this part of the world have no convincing association with race, but must be studied chiefly by interpreting the evidence drawn from cultural differentiation, checked by constant reference to geographical environment.

With the clear separation of horse-using pastoral nomadism from the herding of sheep, cattle, and horses as activities marginal to agriculture, the rate of historical development begins to accelerate. This phase can be dated approximately to the period between the fifth and third centuries B.C. It corresponds, therefore, with the decline of the Chou, or "ancient" or "feudal" society in China (using these terms with caution and in only a general way), and with the rise of the dynastic-imperial state whose later evolution can be traced uninterruptedly from the third century B.C.[32] The chief political phenomena of this phase, serving as convenient indices to other questions of historical evolution, are the sharp and increasingly important conflicts between the Chinese and the horse-using nomads of the steppe, the linking up of a number of local defenses to create a unified and grandiose Great Wall, and the notably increasing outward reach of the Chinese to assert con-

[32] Lattimore, *op. cit.*

trol over the oases of the Taklamakan. This political rivalry as a whole, moreover, is clearly to be interpreted as the result of an external Chinese imperialism.[33]

CHINESE PENETRATION INTO CENTRAL ASIA

An important criterion for the study of Chinese penetration into Central Asia is thus established. The steps, as far as I can distinguish them, were as follows. As the Chinese filled up the natural environment of the Yellow River bend, which favored the type of agriculture that they had made their own, they created a major focus of historical activity. This reduced to minor importance the "sub-oases" of Ninghsia and Kansu, where the natural limits of agricultural expansion prevented a form of development fully integrated with that of the Yellow River bend. This resulted in a kind of frustration that led part of the sub-oasis people to develop, as an alternative, the possibilities of true steppe nomadism, which rapidly became so important that a new major focus of historical activity was created.[34] There then arose the question whether the sub-oases, which could not themselves be independently developed on a sufficiently large scale, were to be dominated from the steppe or from China.

In the long run the Chinese prevailed, because they could dominate better than the steppe people the oasis-like regions that were marginal to China proper. They could dominate them but they could never fully integrate them with the main expanse of China proper, because the "cellular" structure of contiguous regions which was charac-

[33] For an excellent recapitulation of Chinese activity, especially in the Han period (B.C. 206 to A.D. 220), under the minor dynasties following it, and in the T'ang period (618-906), see Fuchs, Das Turfangebiet, 1926. This has wide references to the source material in Chinese and to the subsequent literature of the subject in several languages.

[34] Compare the sketch of a theory of Arabian history—groups moving out from the southern oases, turning nomad in the desert, moving across to Syria or Mesopotamia, and settling again, combined with movements in the reverse directions—in Lawrence, Seven Pillars of Wisdom, 1935 edit., pp. 34-37.

teristic of China was here distorted by special problems of distance and communications and above all by intervals of arid, "un-Chinese" terrain, which made it impossible ever to draw the oasis-like "cells" into complete contiguity either with each other or with the main bulk of China. Consequently, in Ninghsia and Kansu there have survived right into modern times many strong characteristics of regional, social, and political separatism under the surface of a general assimilation to China in culture.

The mere fact that these regions could be dominated and assimilated but not fully integrated gave a certain instability to this flank of the Chinese Empire. This led to a search, intermittently abandoned but as often renewed, for a further flank position that would provide more solid support. To deal with the threat that this flank position might be turned by the people of the steppe, the Chinese had to experiment themselves with the possibility of turning the flank of the steppe. It was this that led them into the Taklamakan and Jungarian basins of Chinese Turkistan. In the course of centuries of alternating political control these two regions became differentiated from each other as follows: Around the rim of the Taklamakan the highly intensive character of oasis agriculture created a fundamental affinity to the society and culture of China, while the lack of continuous pasture in the desert intervals between oases hindered pastoral migration. Along both the southern and the northern edges of the trough-like Jungarian depression, on the other hand, continuous pasture reached from stream to stream and from oasis to oasis. Here, in consequence, the people of the steppe had direct access to the oases, which they accordingly dominated because the Chinese were kept at a distance by the difficulty of the desert crossing from northwestern Kansu to the eastern end of the T'ien Shan, the range that divides Jungaria from the Taklamakan.

The history of the Chinese in Central Asia, therefore, is

a history of imperialism, of conquest. The Chinese could not here expand, adding contiguous region to contiguous region as they did in their advance toward the Yangtze and beyond, but had to subjugate and dominate from afar. They had, moreover, to compete with the imperialism of the steppe, which also attempted to assert its control over the oasis world. The record of the Chinese in Central Asia is therefore by no means continuous; in fact, their effective control has been estimated at only about 425 out of about 2,000 years, divided into a number of periods, of which the present Chinese rule in the province of Sinkiang is the fifth major period.[35]

Given the discontinuity of independent rule within the oases and of both Chinese and steppe-nomad rule over the oases, and given the special qualities of oasis isolation together with the ever-present possibility of communication with both China and the steppe, it is not difficult to define the general historical style of this Central Asian world. It stood apart, yet not altogether apart.

While the oases of the Taklamakan had a strong generic resemblance to each other, they remained invincibly separate from each other. The valley that led back from each oasis through a barren barrier-range into the high mountains gave access at a relatively short distance to several different kinds of territory, with different kinds of resources, but without large populations to threaten the concentration of people in the oasis. From the mountains timber could be fetched, though not in large sizes or great quantities because of the difficulty of transport. Metal (and in the K'unlun, jade) could also be worked in the mountains, and fur-bearing animals could be hunted. There was a certain amount of trade also in livestock. Thus a few necessities and a few luxuries that the highly

[35] Skrine, Chinese Central Asia, 1926, p. 58. This reckoning was made for Kashgar. For Chinese Turkistan as a whole the estimate can be considerably varied according to the allowance made for minor dynasties, periods of partial control, and so on.

developed agriculture of each oasis did not provide could
be obtained in the immediate mountain hinterland. There
was no compulsion whatever toward trade between oases.
For this reason the people of the various oases could be
homogeneous in race, language, and culture and yet almost
totally indifferent to each other. The relatively small scale
of oasis territory even choked political development. The
surplus of men, food, equipment, and money that could
be raised in one oasis made it possible now and then to attack and conquer one or two other oases, but there was
nothing organic or functional to hold such a conquest together; it could not be integrated into the form of a new
and larger state, and therefore it tended to fall apart into
its original components. Both effective general trade and
effective general conquest, in fact, had to be projected into
the oasis region from a base outside, in either China or
the steppe.

Caravan Routes and Trade

Eventually all of the oases were linked up by a road system that ran around the rim of the Taklamakan like a loop
of string, on which the oases hung like beads. Historically
the first line of communication is that known as the Silk
Road. It ran from the western point of Kansu toward
Lob Nor and then along the foot of the K'unlun all the
way to Khotan, Yarkand, and Kashgar. Later the Chinese began to open up communication with the oases north
of the Taklamakan.[36] There were two main lines of approach, each with a number of variants. The eastern traverse went from Kansu to Hami (Qomul). It avoided
the most desert part of the Taklamakan but lay open to attack from the steppe. The western traverse went from
Tunhuang, in Kansu, a little westward in the direction
of Lob Nor and then right across the Taklamakan to the
Turfan group of oases. The desert which made this route

[36] For the separate historical steps, see Fuchs, *op. cit.*

difficult also masked it from steppe nomad attack, and consequently control of access by this route to the northern edge of the Taklamakan was for centuries the strategic key to Chinese imperial policy among the Turkistan oases as a whole, both north and south of the Taklamakan. Undoubtedly this consideration was more important than any postulated change in climate (increased aridity) in causing this route to supersede in importance the earlier Silk Road.

The main line of communication attained by crossing to the north of the Taklamakan ran east and west the whole length of the southern foot of the T'ien Shan, from Hami (Qomul) to Kashgar, and was accordingly known to the Chinese as the T'ien Shan Nan Lu, the Road South of the T'ien Shan. At Kashgar it converged with the Silk Road, thus closing the loop around the Taklamakan. From Kashgar a pass traversed the mountains westward to the oasis region of Ferghana, Khokand, and Samarkand, in the south of Russian Turkistan of today, and thence in turn roads led to Persia and the whole Near East. The importance of this route as a whole was that it enabled caravans to pass all the way from the Near East to China, moving from oasis to oasis with the minimum exposure to the open steppe and to the demands or interference of the steppe tribes.[37]

It seems to be generally accepted that the policy of China in keeping open these roads to the west was governed by the desire for distant trade and the export of silk, a commodity of high value for small bulk and weight, which could be profitably exchanged for other luxury goods not produced in China. This I think is incorrect.[38] I suggest that the first westward expansion of China was a consequence of the filling up of the middle Yellow River coun-

[37] Later, especially in periods of general empire, trade as well as migration moved chiefly on the north side of the T'ien Shan (Grenard, op. cit., p. 326; map on p. 327). Caravan costs are lowest when camels can move over relatively good steppe, grazing daily.

[38] Compare Chapter XV, below.

try, which led naturally to an effort to occupy the marginal, semi-oasis country lying in Ninghsia and Kansu. Since the topography of this region prevented it from becoming as compactly Chinese as the area from which the Chinese had expanded, it could never be freed of a certain political instability and a tendency to gravitate toward the tribal power of the steppe. It was necessary, therefore, to maintain still more distant outposts, whenever possible, in order to turn the flank of the steppe.

Trade must have been originally a result rather than the cause of this kind of imperial policy; though naturally trade interests that prospered and grew strong could later become a secondary influence favoring the continuance of the original policy. I suggest, therefore, that trade arose in the course of an adjustment of the activities of the Chinese to an environment akin to that of China in some respects but different in other important respects. The maintenance of Chinese imperial policy was expensive. The cost could not be met simply by imposing a grain levy, the major source of revenue in China proper. The cost of transporting grain back to China was prohibitive. Grain revenue could be used for the maintenance of local garrisons, it was true; but at the same time it was not practical simply to subjugate the oases and extract wealth from them. Revolt was too easy. The oases had to be encouraged to look toward Chinese overlords instead of toward steppe overlords.

Forms of trade that would bring profit to the oases as well as to the Chinese must therefore have evolved both spontaneously and as the result of policy. Most of the oases, however, produced almost exactly the same things. Gold came from certain regions and jade from others, but there was a minimum demand for the exchange of necessities. Long-range trade was accordingly a matter of exchanging luxuries. Silk (and, later, tea and porcelain) were the exports from China. Gold, jade, horses of fine breed, metal wares from west of Kashgar, delicacies like raisins, and slaves, girls, and musicians were imported into China.

Naturally trade of this kind had very little to do with the subject peoples of the oases. It was an affair of their rulers and the overlords of their rulers, but it suited Chinese imperial policy because it gave the native rulers of the oases an interest in political affiliation to China. All of this partly explains why the interchange of commodities, which is normally called trade, was carried on largely by "embassies," which brought "tribute" to the Chinese court and carried back "gifts" from the imperial court to its "loyal subjects." This to a certain extent disguises what was really going on ; but it can hardly be doubted that one of the results was the accumulation of great private wealth by individuals.

At the eastern end of the Road South of the T'ien Shan passes led over the mountains from Hami (Qomul) to Barkol and from Turfan to Urumchi (Tihua). Here, along the southern rim of the Jungarian trough from Barkol in the east through Kuch'engtze, Urumchi, and Manass to Hsihu, ran the Road North of the T'ien Shan. At Hsihu it forked, one branch running northwest to Chuguchak (T'ach'eng) at one of the important gaps opening from Jungaria into the Kazak steppes of Russian Turkistan, and the other branch running west to the Ili valley which opens into the same steppes.

The oasis structure of the North Road is similar to that of the South Road, with the difference that the northern oases lie much more open to the steppe. For this reason steppe conquerors could move right along the line of the northern oases, whose history is therefore much more catastrophic than that of the Taklamakan oases.[39] Large displacements of population are known to have taken place, and pastoral occupation of the oases themselves alter-

[39] Lattimore, Chinese Turkistan, 1933, p. 104.

nated with agricultural occupation. In contrast to this, each oasis of the south was a "pocket" in which agriculture was permanent and the population relatively stable. In periods of Chinese ascendancy the Chinese advanced their administration from oasis to oasis. In periods of steppe ascendancy the nomads could sweep along the line of oases north of the mountains, but had to strike back over the mountains at each individual southern oasis. Both forms of domination affected the rulers of the separate oases much more than they did the subject population.

SOCIAL AND POLITICAL INFLUENCE OF RELIGIONS

Such, in outline, was the political superstructure rising from the geographical structure of the northern and southern divisions of Chinese Turkistan. One special characteristic of oasis history, the peculiar importance of religion, remains to be considered.

Buddhism became ascendant in the Taklamakan oases about the first century of the Christian Era, after the first large-scale Chinese imperial activity in the last two centuries B.C. Much learned work has been devoted to the penetration of Buddhism from India through Kashmir and Ladakh into Central Asia, to its further spread into China, and to its religious history and cultural influence; the languages and scripts that it introduced; the Hellenistic influences, especially in sculpture, that it carried from Gandhara into Turkistan and far away east to the cave sculptures of Yunkang (near Tat'ung, on the border between Shansi and Inner Mongolia), executed under the Wei dynasty (of steppe nomad origin) in the fifth century; the translations of the scriptures; and the pilgrimages of Chinese monks through Central Asia to India, from the Han period to the T'ang dynasty, ending at the turn of the tenth century.[40]

[40] General references: Stein, Serindia, 1921; Von Le Coq, Auf Hellas Spuren in Ostturkistan, 1926.

Nothing like the same attention has been paid to the social and political importance of Central Asian Buddhism. Without laboring the details, I suggest that Buddhism took hold rapidly and firmly in Chinese Turkistan because it offered something that the oasis communities had not been able to evolve themselves: a method of enhancing an economic and cultural homogeneity that they had no way of expressing in political unity. Monastic foundations provided a device for the unified ownership of property and wealth in politically separate oases. At the same time, the power and prestige of the church did not threaten the position of the secular princes, because the activities of the church compensated for the lack of political unity but did not threaten to substitute a new form of political rule superseding that of the princes. On the contrary, the higher ranks of the church offered a link to join the ruling families of the separate oases.

This view of the function of Buddhism in Chinese Turkistan is borne out by its comparative failure in China, where it several times rose to importance but always fell again to the low status of a cult without political significance. This, I think, was because the small scale of the oasis communities did not permit the rise of a bureaucracy intervening between the hereditary rulers and real power. In China, on the other hand, the imperial power was repeatedly, and even normally, mastered and exercised by a professional bureaucracy, which was identified with the landholding classes and carried out on a national scale the policies favored locally and regionally by the landholders (though not, of course, without an alternating ascendancy as between regional interest and national interest, private interest and state interest).

In the fabric of society in China there was no lack for which Buddhism could compensate. On the contrary, its corporative, impersonal, landholding interests conflicted with those of the scholar-gentry, and its command of a

mystery of learning rivalled the carefully guarded difficulties of scholastic and documentary Chinese. The
scholar-gentry bureaucracy had not only a corporative interest of their own but a well-nourished professional code,
Confucianism. It is therefore no surprise to find that
when Buddhism acquired a dangerously great influence—
as, for instance, in the reign of the Emperor Hsuan Tsung
(713-765) of the T'ang dynasty and again in the reign of
the Emperor Wu Tsung (841-847) of the same dynasty—
it was viciously persecuted.[41] Such attacks might be conducted under the color of favoring Taoism or under some
other excuse, but they could not be made effective unless
heartily supported by the scholar-gentry. It is also to be
noted that when it attained special prosperity as well as
when it underwent special adversity Chinese Buddhism was
closely associated with the person and policy of the emperor, which suggests the inference that it was not only
the church that was concerned but the question whether
the emperor or the bureaucracy was to dominate the state.

The later importance in Chinese Turkistan of religions
like Manichaeism, Nestorian Christianity, Islam, and Maz-
daism, which flourished especially in the seventh, eighth
and ninth centuries (T'ang period), confirms the views
that I have here advanced. All of them penetrated also
into China but never became widely spread, with the exception of Islam. Nestorian Christianity had a notable
effect in the Mongolian steppe, where it survived until
about the fourteenth century; but it cannot be said that it
became truly a religion of the steppe for it was associated
particularly with the courts of princes who, though they
ruled over steppe nomads, lived an urban or semi-urban
life.

All of these religions belong to the landscape of oases
and oasis-like regions lying between the Near East and

---

[41] Encyclopaedia Sinica, 1917, under Buddhism in China; Franke, Geschichte
des chinesischen Reiches, esp. Vol. II, 1936, pp. 203 *et sqq.*

Central Asia. Produced by the cultures of peoples living in towns, with fields about them but with deserts or steppes intervening between them and the next similar community, they met the need for expressing and strengthening the common interests, common way of life, and common outlook of peoples living in dissevered groups. In the period in which they flourished in Chinese Turkistan these religions were largely patronized by resident alien traders who lived in quarters of their own in each of the prosperous trading towns on the main caravan route, which by then crossed from Kansu to Turfan, from Turfan traversed to the north side of the T'ien Shan, and thence ran westward along the line of the steppe oases. Such traders were also to be found along the route of the desert oases from Turfan to Kashgar, which continued to form a subsidiary line of communication. Their quarters—the communities were probably more permanent than the individuals—recall in some ways the Treaty Ports of the China coast in the nineteenth century, Turfan being the Shanghai of the overland approach to China, and Sian (in Shensi), which was the Hankow of that time, being the advanced post of the foreign penetration into China. The difference was that these aliens were not as yet the agents of political as well as of commercial encroachment. They were simply middlemen, and in the oasis towns of Turkistan they displaced nothing and altered nothing—merely added to what was already there. The religions that they brought with them served, therefore, merely to link them with their kindred communities to the east and west and challenged neither the Buddhism nor the political forms that were locally dominant.

ISLAM IN CHINESE TURKISTAN

Finally Islam in Chinese Turkistan was raised to a new political significance in the tenth century by Turks of the steppes of Russian Turkistan, who had moved into and

mastered the Samarkand-Khokand-Ferghana belt of oases
and from there had crossed to the Taklamakan oases, just
as peoples of the Mongolian and Jungarian steppe occasionally took control of the oases along the Road North of
the T'ien Shan and from there crossed the mountains to
reach Turfan, Karashahr, and Kucha.[42] Islam did not,
however, finally displace Buddhism and the other faiths
until the fourteenth century, when the Mongol Empire fell
apart. The Mongols of the appanage of Jagatai, ruling
both Eastern and Western Turkistan but centering politically on Western Turkistan, had by then become Turkish in language and Moslem in religion and had transferred their social emphasis from the steppe to the oases.
The decay and fall of the Mongol empires, and concurrently the weakening of political power among the steppe
peoples, thereupon gave Islam an opportunity to dominate the oasis world.

Islam, like Judaism, Christianity, Nestorian Christianity, and Manichaeism, sprang from a culture that attempted
to coördinate the society of pastoralism and that of the
oasis and to create a community of outlook in town and
tent and field, between trader and peasant and herdsman.
Akin to these other religions culturally and historically, it
was younger than they, and within the group of religions
to which it was related it functioned partly as a reform
movement. It is not too fanciful to call the Moslems the
Protestants of the oasis world of North Africa, the Near
East, and Central Asia.

This reforming impulse made Islam, when it became ascendant in Turkistan, more political than was Buddhism;
it reintegrated the religions, politics, and society of the
oases, converting the Buddhists by force and reforming the

---

[42] It was in this manner that Turkish became the language of the oases
from the ninth century, through the Karluk Turks who conquered Kashgar,
Aksu, Yarkand, and Khotan, and the Uighur Turks who ruled the "Five
Cities" at the eastern end of both North Road and South Road (Grenard,
op. cit., p. 317).

Near Eastern sects that still lingered. Although Islam
was not able to set up a new political structure including
all the far scattered oases under one united rule, it created
a community of outlook somewhat approximating national
feeling among all the oases of Turkistan, made the Turkish
language paramount, and drove on far into the sub-oasis
regions of Ninghsia and Kansu. There it planted strong
colonies of both invaders and converts, who, helped by the
topography, held aloof from the Chinese as a quasi-national
minority—a minority impatient of control and one that
the Chinese have never been able to assimilate fully or
reduce to innocuous subordination.

THE MANCHUS AND THE MOSLEMS OF CENTRAL ASIA

The final conquest of Islam in Turkistan coincided with
the political retraction of the Chinese under the Ming
dynasty (1368-1643) all along the Great Wall Frontier.
China did not again engage in imperial politics in Central
Asia until after the Manchu conquest. When the Manchus
ventured into Turkistan it was once more to turn the flank
of the steppe and complete the breaking up of the Jungar
or Olöt confederation of the Western Mongols.[43] They
therefore appeared as allies of those Moslem rulers (notably in Qomul and the Turfan group of oases) who had
been subject to the Mongols. Thereafter, Manchu imperial rule was the power most to be feared by the Moslems. The Moslems in the northwestern territory, where
they were strongly represented, had been ascendant over
the Chinese under the Ming dynasty, but under the
Manchus their prestige was threatened and consequently
Moslem "rebellions" disturbed the whole of the nineteenth
century—1818, 1826, 1834, 1855 (in Yünnan), 1862-77
(Kansu and Turkistan), and 1895 (Kansu).

During the greatest of these wars, from 1862 to 1877,
the transition toward the modern aspect of Chinese Turkis-

[43] Duman, Agrarian Policy of the Ch'ing Government, 1936 (in Russian).

tan was prepared. This war partly overlapped with the rebellion of the Moslems of Yünnan province, which began in 1855, but the action of the northwestern and southwestern Moslems was not concerted, for there was little communication between them.[44] Since it also overlapped with the non-Moslem T'aip'ing Rebellion in the Yangtze valley, a peasant war that lasted from 1851 to 1865, this war of the northwestern Moslems in Kansu and Chinese Turkistan may be described as one of a series of centrifugal movements that would have broken up the Manchu Empire in the second half of the nineteenth century had it not already been the general policy of the Western powers in China to bolster up the Manchu dynasty—a policy that preserved the empire as the master of the Chinese and the servant of the foreigners until 1911.

The Moslems of Kansu are mainly Chinese in blood, language, and culture, with a few communities that remain Turkish in language and predominantly Central Asian by blood.[45] They are the landholding majority in some of the scattered, irrigated, relatively highly cultivated, oasis-like regions. In other similar regions, where the Chinese are the landholding majority, the Moslems are town-dwelling, trading minorities. Over the province as a whole the weight of numbers is heavily in favor of the Chinese, at the present time about two thirds.[46] The Moslem religion

[44] The Yünnan Moslems may have derived originally from the maritime spread of the Arabs to Southeast Asia, rather than from the penetration of Islam through Central Asia. They were well established by the time of Marco Polo. See Yule, Marco Polo, 1921, Vol. II, p. 66. Rashideddin also knew of the Moslems in this part of China (Yule, Cathay and the Way Thither, 1914, Vol. III, p. 127).

[45] General references: Broomhall, Islam in China, 1910; Andrew, The Crescent in North-West China, 1921; Bales, Tso Tsungt'ang, 1937, which contains a good deal of incidental reference to the oasis and semi-oasis isolation of the Moslems in Ninghsia and Kansu.

[46] The Chinese Year Book, 1938-39, p. 63, lists 48,104,240 Moslems for the whole of China, including the surprisingly high figures of 7,533,680 for Manchuria and 4,129,090 for Shensi. Comparing p. 63 with p. 34, it gives for Kansu a total population of 6,080,559, including 3,518,920 Moslems; for Ninghsia, a total of 666,890, including 753,400 Moslems (an indication of

and social organization, however, as an organic development of oasis life, gave to their scattered communities a greater cohesion than the Chinese drew from their social and administrative organization, which was not native to the oasis environment but had been transplanted into it from the areas of continuous, unisolated Chinese agriculture. Considered apart from the particular quarrels in which it originated, therefore, the Kansu Moslem rebellion may be described as an attempt to take advantage of the weakening of central dynastic authority in China in order to assert the superior Moslem unity and maneuverability over the loosely organized Chinese of Kansu.

Chinese Turkistan was not only cut off from the Empire by the rising in Kansu but was also the scene of rebellions, one of which took place among the T'ungkan, who form the majority of the oasis population in northern Chinese Turkistan, especially from Urumchi to Manass and Hsihu. The T'ungkan are descended from Turkish-speaking Moslems who settled in Kansu and parts of Shensi and Ninghsia principally in the fourteenth and fifteenth centuries and, like the majority of the Kansu Moslems, were there outnumbered by their converts—the chief method of "conversion" being the adoption of children—and consequently became Chinese in language, in many cultural characteristics, and in appearance. In the seventeenth and eighteenth centuries, at the end of the wars with the Jungar Mongols, contingents of these Kansu Moslems were brought back to northern Chinese Turkistan by the Manchus to settle the oases there and restore the ascendancy of settled government, based on the oases, over the tribes of the steppe.[47] The T'ungkan rebellion,

how untrustworthy even the latest official figures are!); for Ch'inghai (formerly part of Kansu), 1,195,054, including 1,186,590 Moslems. Andrew, op. cit., gives about 10 million for Kansu (apparently including Ch'inghai), with about 3 million Moslems.

[47] Some of them spread as far west as Russian Turkistan. For a very interesting account of the whole war or rebellion, together with its historical

in short, was comparable to that of the Kansu Moslems.

The Taklamakan oases formed the third main area of this period of war. Here the Moslem military and religious conquest of the fourteenth century had left a heritage of family politics, linking the oases of Eastern Turkistan with those of Western or Russian Turkistan. Princes of the Jagatai line of descent from Chingghis—who by this time were Moslems and quite distinct from the Mongols—were giving way in power to the religious clan of the Khojas.[48] This clan, founded in the sixteenth century by a religious teacher from Bokhara, was both religious and political in its activity. The phenomenon is appropriate to the character of Islam as a movement growing out of an effort to integrate under religious sanctions a political unity difficult to maintain by strictly political methods in a world of scattered oases.

In the eighteenth century when the Manchus had finished dealing with the Jungar Mongols they set up an imperial colonial administration over the whole of Chinese Turkistan. The major oases of the Road South of the T'ien Shan were placed partly under survivors of the Khoja family and partly under other noble families which had gone over to the Manchus. The affairs of the separate oases were coördinated by resident imperial officials.[49] The question of overlord and vassals was not definitely settled, however, because the Manchus did not go on to a conquest of the oases of Western Turkistan. The still independent Khojas of these western oases, therefore, continued intermittently to attempt to reassert themselves in Eastern Turkistan, especially at Kashgar,[50] where the great

background, based evidently in part on the tradition of the westernmost T'ungkans, see Shakhmatov, Studies in the History of the Uighur-T'ungkan National Liberation Movement, 1935 (in Russian).

[48] Duman, *op. cit.*, p. 62, etc.
[49] Details in Duman, *op. cit.*
[50] Shakhmatov, *op. cit.*

family shrine of Hazrat Apak was a source of immense wealth from pilgrim offerings.

When Manchu imperial access from China was cut off by the risings of the Chinese-speaking Moslems, these attempts were renewed; but in the upshot the Khojas themselves were thrust aside by Yakub Beg, a military adventurer and ex-dancing boy in their service. Yakub Beg set himself up at Kashgar as head of both church and state in the typical manner of oasis Islam, brought Yarkand and Khotan under control, and set out to extend his authority eastward all along the Road South of the T'ien Shan.[51]

At this point the relative cohesion and superiority of Islam prevailed over the society and dynastic state of the Chinese within the oasis environment, in part of Shensi and Ninghsia, most of Kansu, and the whole of Chinese Turkistan. From this point onward, however, the apparent Moslem success in northwest China and colonial Chinese Central Asia was followed by rapid disintegration. The maximum of cohesion had been attained in the effort made against the infidel. Thereafter separate economic and regional interests began to assert themselves. Political success against the Chinese in Kansu did not relieve the Kansu Moslems of dependence on China for their external trade. Different religio-political families—in the name, characteristically, of different sects of Islam—began to struggle against each other both for hegemony as between Moslems and for control of external relations as between Moslems and Chinese. The T'ungkan of the North Road in Chinese Turkistan had no reason to gravitate toward the oases of the South Road, and Yakub Beg's attempt to acquire hegemony over them involved far heavier fighting than had been necessary to get rid of the Manchu-Chinese colonial administration. The Turkish-speaking nomad Moslems of the Jungarian steppe and the mountain pas-

[51] For the period of Yakub Beg, see Shaw, *op. cit.*

tures of the T'ien Shan and the Pamirs wavered between raiding the oases and drawing aloof from them altogether.[52]

In the meantime, the Manchus, aided by direct and indirect foreign intervention, had put down the T'aip'ing Rebellion. They could now send westward large numbers of Chinese troops, partly trained and equipped in the Western style. These troops, under the famous Tso Tsungt'ang,[53] are supposed to have succeeded in a phenomenal march of conquest right across Kansu and into Turkistan. The truth is that Tso Tsung-t'ang was first defeated by the Moslems,[54] which made him move cautiously in regaining the initiative. The pacification of Kansu was thus based on the acknowledgment, tacit in definition but real in practice, of the local power of the leading Moslem families in the more important centers of Moslem concentration. It was understood that the Chinese were to be allowed to present reports of victory at the imperial court but were not to tax or administer the Moslems except through the Moslem chiefs, untitled though these chiefs remained. This has been the practical working rule as between Chinese and Moslems in Kansu ever since.

Moving on into Chinese Turkistan, the Chinese armies of the Manchus varied their policy. It was essential to prevent a coalition of the Chinese-speaking T'ungkans of the North Road and the Turkish-speaking oases of the South Road. This was done by treating the T'ungkans as defiant rebels, while offering to compound with the Turkish-speaking Moslems as the unwilling victims of a foreign usurper, Yakub Beg. This was all the easier because representatives of the Khoja families remained in several of the oases and were more afraid of Yakub Beg than of the imperial administration. This policy was rewarded by the surrender

---

[52] At the same time, T'ungkan raiders crossed the Altai into Northwest Outer Mongolia (Elias, Narrative of a Journey Through Western Mongolia, 1873, p. 127, etc.).

[53] Bales, op. cit.

[54] Shakhmatov, op. cit.; Andrew, op. cit., p. 84.

of oasis after oasis along the South Road, until Yakub Beg, his followers dwindling, either committed suicide or was poisoned.[55] The T'ungkans, at the same time, having made the steppe hostile to them by their treatment of the Mongols,[56] were penned in their North Road oases and slaughtered in great numbers.

The Chinese armies then restored the Manchu imperial colonial administration, which resumed outwardly its old form but was thenceforward controlled by a group of Chinese families who took office in the administration and were able, as the central dynastic power of the Empire declined, to convert themselves in fact, though never in name, into a hereditary civil and military administrative service.[57]

POLITICAL AND ECONOMIC CONDITIONS IN CHINESE TURKISTAN, 1911-1928

Thus was created the Chinese Turkistan of the present day. It went through the Revolution of 1911 with scarcely a change, the real power being seized immediately by an experienced official of the civil service, who flew the flag of the Republic but ruled the province for himself until his assassination in 1928.

During this period Sinkiang (Hsin-chiang, the New Dominion), comprising Eastern Turkistan proper and Jungaria, differed greatly from the Mongolian and Manchurian sectors of the Frontier beyond the Great Wall. The "secondary imperialism" of the Chinese war lords, which radiated from the new railway systems into Inner Mongolia and into Manchuria far beyond the ancient Chinese Pale, could not operate in Turkistan, which was out of reach of the economic influence of railways. Nor was the direct imperialism of foreign pressure so strong in

[55] Sykes, Through Deserts and Oases of Central Asia, 1920, p. 291.
[56] However, Elias, op. cit., gives the impression that the Mongols can hardly have been reliable allies of the imperial troops in putting down the T'ungkans, of whom they were much afraid.
[57] Lattimore, Chinese Turkistan, 1933, p. 99.

Chinese Turkistan as in China proper. Inter-imperial rivalry was confined to the British and the Russians, whose chief preoccupation was to find out whether their own frontiers in Russian Turkistan and India were vulnerable to each other.[58] When exploration had proved that there were no easy routes of invasion either across the Pamirs or through Tibet, both nations were content to let Sinkiang stagnate.

The Chinese therefore continued to rule in the old manner, under the remarkable fiction that they were conquerors, able to defend all their frontiers and to put down internal disaffection by force. As a matter of fact, they had no real power of any kind—economic, political, or military —but ruled on sufferance as the least obnoxious people in sight, insulating the oases from the steppes, the mountains from the plains, the townsmen from the peasants and tribesmen, the Moslems from the infidels, and supervising whatever circulation of trade was convenient.

With the opening of the civil-war period that lasted in China from the death of Yuan Shih-k'ai in 1916 to the Great Revolution and the establishment of a National Government in 1928, this fiction became essential to both rulers and subjects. The "conquerors" were poorly armed and had no modern training for their few troops. They could not obtain arms from either Russia or Great Britain without opening the way to foreign penetration and control. Nor could arms reach them from China, because they would have been seized on the way by one of the war lords through whose territory they would have had to pass. Consequently, the only way in which to rule was to hold a balance, as just as possible according to the conservative ideas and vested interests of the most important people among the subject races, between the different economic regions and population groups.

Lack of compulsory import and export trade assisted

[58] Younghusband, The Heart of a Continent, 1896.

in keeping the province stable. Distance from China proper and poor communications,[59] making the exchange of luxuries the only profitable trade, encouraged a special form of alliance between Chinese officials and Chinese traders. It was necessary to promote the traditional forms of prosperity in order to obviate resentment against Chinese rule, which the Chinese would not have been able to deal with by force. Therefore, the great men of the oases must be allowed to accumulate land and the great men of the nomads to accumulate herds; but food, clothing, and other necessities must remain cheap, and the Chinese officials themselves must not directly "squeeze" the people.[60]

This was an extremely important consideration. In China the traditional method of acquiring private fortune and capital for investment was through maladministration—a necessary consequence of the supremacy of the scholar-gentry, whose sanctions were neither military nor economic but vested in the moral code of Confucianism. This code worked in practice in such a way that a few model officials retired from service poor but a great many competent officials retired wealthy. Because they preyed directly on the people, both as administrators and as private landholders, the officials resented the profits of independent trade in removing from their reach a certain amount of wealth, and therefore the tendency was to overtax any trade enterprise that threatened to grow beyond the local control of local landholders.

In Turkistan, as in Mongolia and other parts of the outer Frontier, it was regarded as dangerous to tax the non-Chinese people directly in such a way as to focus dislike against Chinese political representatives. Therefore

---

[59] It was to the interest of the Chinese in Sinkiang to keep up steady trade, in order to avoid discontent among the subject peoples, but to keep the rate of movement along lines of communication slow so as to hinder both invasion from the outside and the spread of insurrection within the province. Lattimore, *op. cit.*, p. 109.

[60] *Ibid.*, p. 110.

the official kept his hands off the people and let the traders rob them, and instead of plundering the traders he himself went into partnership with them, as did also the Mongol princes and Living Buddhas and the Turkish Begs and Bais. The special variation of this general form in Turkistan was due to the fact that external trade in luxuries and internal trade in necessities did not supply profits in the negotiable currency that was needed. Throughout the period of warlordism and secondary imperialism in China there was an enormous concentration of Chinese-owned wealth under foreign protection in foreign banks in the Treaty Ports. There was also an abnormal Chinese investment in land in the Treaty Port concessions and in territories under foreign jurisdiction, like Dairen and Hongkong, creating false and inflated values. With the concentration under foreign flags of the wealth extracted from the interior, paper currencies in the interior depreciated. This was true also in Turkistan, where several paper currencies [61] circulated without backing and with an almost purely fictitious value. In Turkistan, however, owing to the distance and lack of banks it was difficult to remit to the coast. Therefore the only way in which officials could hoard wealth was to go into partnership with merchants, who went into partnership with the rich men of the subject races. The colonials retained their profits locally; the officials and their merchant partners invested their profits in local raw produce (especially wool and cotton, which was one reason for keeping taxes and prices low, in order that such goods could stand the price of caravan transport). When these products were sent by caravan to railhead in China and thence to the Treaty Ports to be sold for export, the proceeds could be finally banked in a safe place.

---

[61] *Ibid.* The use of several currencies, each restricted to a region, made it possible to detect at once any effort to accumulate a reserve fund for political purposes in any one place.

The end result would have been to impoverish and exhaust the country, though gradually, had it not been possible to increase productivity. Freedom from war and banditry, however, and also from crop failure and famine —because the irrigation water from the snows of the high mountains never failed to increase in quantity as the weather grew hotter—made for a steady growth in population. Under Asiatic conditions this meant an increase in productivity, because manpower could be commandeered for public labor on irrigation works, thus increasing the cultivated area.

Gradually, however, the stability of Chinese rule worked toward its own destruction. In order to explain this paradox it is necessary to go into some detail. The societies of both China and the oasis world set automatic limits to the development of their own technical skill, and, if technical ability be regarded as a constant, then there is a maximum beyond which the irrigation of each river-fed oasis cannot be expanded. As the land becomes flatter silting increases; also, the accumulation of salts, inevitable in a desertic climate, makes it necessary to let a large part of the marginal land lie fallow for long periods. (Silting and salting, and also the damage done by water continuing to run at flood pressure through irrigation works damaged in war, account for many of the abandoned and sand-smothered oases that have sometimes been explained as the result of desiccation or climatic pulsation.[62])

Attainment of the maximum oasis prosperity completes one of the phases in the interacting historical cycles of the steppe and the oasis. The people of the oases at this point must begin to encroach on the steppe. Some of the land accessible to them, if they or the overlord power are strong enough to take it from the nomads, is marginal and can be

[62] On the climatic factor, compare Huntington's theory of alternating moist and dry periods (The Pulse of Asia, 1907) with Stein's theory of the gradual decrease of the reserves of snow and ice in the high mountains (Innermost Asia, Its Geography as a Factor in History, 1925, pp. 474-475, 490).

cultivated for only a few years before it is exhausted, or only in years of good rainfall. Some of it can be permanently cultivated, but only with the changes in technical practices that have already been discussed in connection with agriculture in Mongolia, involving extensive farming or mixed farming and livestock herding, and consequently a gravitation away from the structure of oasis society.

Chinese Turkistan went through a change of phase of this kind in recent years. It led to an increasing movement of Turkish-speaking cultivators to the northern side of the T'ien Shan.[63] Some of these were assigned lands in North Road oases that had been depopulated or underpopulated ever since the T'ungkans had been reduced by slaughter at the end of their rebellion. Others, however, began to move into the most cultivable pastures of the nomads, which had an immediate economic effect, and caused political tension. In these and many other regions the most cultivable pastures of the nomads are their sheltered winter pastures, and owing to the severity of the climate good winter pastures are much more difficult to find than good summer pastures.[64]

THE HIGH POINT OF CHINESE FRONTIER EXPANSIONISM

In Sinkiang, as in the whole expanse of the outer Frontier, 1929 marked the high point [65] of Chinese "secondary imperialism." In that year the Central Government probably attained its maximum control over the still partly independent governors of the provinces along the Great Wall. Colonization was pushed ruthlessly in Inner Mongolia and the western, Mongol plains of Manchuria. Chinese railways, especially in Manchuria,[66] were used to counter the penetration of foreign-controlled railways, as

[63] Schuyler, Turkestan, 1876, Vol. II.
[64] Lattimore, op. cit., pp. 113-115.
[65] This was the year in which the Chinese provincial government in Manchuria attempted to seize the Russian interest in the Chinese Eastern Railway.
[66] Lattimore, Manchuria: Cradle of Conflict, 1932, especially p. 30.

a counter fire is used to prevent the spread of a forest fire. The prevailing policy was that of the Kuomintang, which had dropped some of the most vital principles of Sun Yat-sen after the split with the Communists in 1927. Essentially the new policy, which I have called secondary imperialism,[67] meant the abandoning of the attempt that had been made during the Great Revolution of 1925-27 to throw off all forms of foreign control. Instead there was an attempt, under an alliance of the new (Western-model) industrialists and bankers and the old landlords, to *anticipate* the wider spread of foreign control over China by subjugating the whole interior and hinterland under a Chinese conquest, led and controlled by the most highly organized Chinese groups. In Frontier questions this meant treating all non-Chinese peoples beyond the Great Wall as conquered subjects in order to provide China with a margin of imperial expansion compensating for the privileges surrendered, in the coastal provinces, to foreign imperialism.

In 1929 this policy risked and lost a gamble in North Manchuria in attempting to bluff the Soviet Union, which had already surrendered the political privileges acquired by Tsarist Russia, into giving up its financial interest in the Chinese Eastern Railway without adequate compensation. This attempt the Soviet Union defeated by prompt military action. One result of this was to demonstrate that the foreign nations as a group would no longer intervene to prevent military action against China by any one nation. The Soviet Union withdrew its troops without making a single "imperialistic" demand, after successfully defending itself against a high-handed attempt to repudiate by force treaty arrangements amicably entered into with-

[67] The term is not wholly satisfactory, for it may be misconstrued as implying an imperialism of the whole Chinese nation. In actual fact, only a few classes of the Chinese were concerned, and their interests were conspicuously not those of the nation as a whole. In Sinkiang also something besides imperialism was involved. Growing antagonisms between groups and interests had a good deal to do with the diminishing returns of local prosperity.

out the use or threat of undue pressure. Internationally, however, this aspect of the Soviet-Chinese settlement was ignored; instead, Japan converted the precedent of the Soviet defensive measures of 1929-30 into a precedent for the open invasion and conquest of Manchuria in 1931.

This digression is important because the Japanese invasion had further consequences. In the next few years, after bitter struggles within China the Kuomintang policy of secondary or internal imperialism, having been proved inadequate because it failed to protect China against direct or primary imperialism, was first modified and then abandoned.[68] The "united front" in China proper against foreign conquest is making possible a new orientation toward each other of China and the Frontier domains and a defensive alliance between the Chinese and minority peoples like the Mongols and Moslems—a return to one of the most important principles of Sun Yat-sen.[69]

The working of these changes can be followed out in Chinese Turkistan. Distance from China, and the presence of independent and semi-independent war lords between them and the Central Government, had made the ruling Chinese minority in Sinkiang keep carefully clear of China's politics and civil wars. It was as if the British minority in India were attempting to carry on its imperial rule when cut off from all communication with Great Britain.[70]

The Kuomintang had never been able to extend direct control over the province. Nevertheless, the cast of thought represented by the Kuomintang had been spread-

[68] General references: Snow, Red Star Over China, 1937; Bertram, First Act in China, 1937, also Unconquered, 1938; Lattimore, Where Outer and Inner Mongolia Meet, 1938, also Kimono and Turban, 1938.
[69] Sun Yat-sen, San Min Chu I, trans. Price, 1929. The attitude toward national minorities is implied, though not expressly stated, in the remarks about "rescuing the weak and lifting up the fallen" (p. 147). On the other hand, Sun Yat-sen regarded Mongolia and Tibet as territories to which China succeeded when the Chinese Revolution overthrew the Manchus (pp. 256, 258).
[70] Lattimore, Chinese Turkistan, 1933, p. 99.

ing among the Chinese rulers of Sinkiang. At the same time the general harmony between the different subject peoples ruled by the Chinese had been gradually changing to tension and hostility as the paradoxical result of a long period of peace and stability, in the course of which migration from the South Road to the North Road, the encroachment of agriculture on the steppe, and the concentration of landownership in the hands of rich town dwellers in the oases had altered the economic and political balance between regions and peoples. The growing acuteness of such antagonisms made it insufficient to rely, as in the past, on practically untrained and poorly armed levies raised in one part of the province and garrisoned in another, using region against region and race against race.[71] It seemed necessary to display an overriding Chinese force, and accordingly the administration for the first time began to buy arms. The details have never become generally known, but it seems that the Chinese, themselves fearing the economic domination of the Soviet Union [72] and playing on the British fear of "Soviet-fomented" risings, obtained arms from the British in India.[73] The "show of force" made with these arms brought disaster because the first tests revealed the weakness that the arms were intended to disguise.

Already, during the long period of firm, or at least firm-appearing, Chinese rule, the privileges and direct subsidies

---

[71] *Ibid.*, pp. 116-117.

[72] Lattimore, Chinese Turkestan or Sinkiang (Hsinchiang), 1935, p. 40, etc.

[73] Lack of published information makes it extremely difficult to piece together the record of this political phase. According to one report—carried by word of mouth and impossible to verify—the arms supplied by the British consisted partly of rifles which had been issued to British-led Persian levies about 1918-19. These rifles had been called in; to get rid of them they were dumped in the Persian Gulf. Pearl divers, however, began to recover them and sell them, and some of them got into the hands of tribesmen hostile to the British on the Northwest Frontier of India. The rifles were therefore dredged up, then reconditioned and sold to the Chinese. Some of them had originally been bought by the British from Japan; for this reason, when they were captured from the Chinese by the Moslem rebels reports of Japanese attempts to intrigue in Central Asia were strengthened.

of Mongol princes, Kazak and Kirghiz chiefs, and the Khoja and other noble families of the Turkish-speaking oases had been much cut down, although the people affected continued to prosper in association with Chinese traders and officials. Only one important "native state" survived among the oases of the South Road—that of Qomul or Hami. About 1929 the prince of Hami died. It was decided to discontinue the "native-state" administration and substitute direct Chinese rule. The real reason for this was the need for increased revenue to pay for such things as the arms that were intended to assure Chinese rule, but the formal reason given was that hereditary princes ought to be gradually displaced within the territory of the Chinese Republic. The people of Hami were assured that under direct administration their taxes would not be increased; but when lands were remeasured and it became apparent that, although the rate of taxation was not changed, units of measurement were being decreased in order to provide an increase of tax-revenue, rebellion began.[74]

At the first encounter the new Chinese "show of force" collapsed. The troops fled and the rebels captured their arms. The danger of rebellion spread. The Mongols, with the best "native troops" in the province, refused to march against the Moslems because their most able leader had already been assassinated by the Chinese, who feared his political power.[75] In the meantime a Moslem war had also begun in Kansu and Ninghsia—partly a factional war between Moslem leaders and partly a war between Moslems and Chinese—and Ma Ch'ung-ying, a leader from Kansu, invaded the Hami oasis. The Chinese, in desperation, impressed "White" Russians—most of them refugees who had fled into Chinese Turkistan after fighting against the Russian Revolution; but these men, who had lived in des-

[74] Lattimore, op. cit., p. 43; also Chinese Turkistan, p. 117.
[75] Haslund, Men and Gods in Mongolia, 1935, especially p. 325.

perate poverty for years, were no sooner armed than they also began to make demands in their own interest. Then, with the entry of Chinese troops who had been driven out of Manchuria by the Japanese in 1931 and 1932 and had first been interned in Siberia and then repatriated to Sinkiang,[76] still another factor became operative.

RECENT INFLUENCE OF THE SOVIET UNION

From this time on the details are both meager and confused; but it also becomes imperative to discuss the position of the Soviet Union as the power whose frontiers march with all the territories beyond the Great Wall. Chinese Turkistan provides the best approach to the study of these questions, in spite of the lack of detailed information. On the Manchurian frontier the Soviet Union stands defensively against the plain threat of a Japanese invasion. Outer Mongolia was forced into close alliance with the Soviet Union first by a Chinese war-lord attempt at "reconquest" of the Mongols, backed by Japan,[77] and then by the necessity of getting rid of the "White" Russian bands which used Outer Mongolia as a base against the Russian Revolution. Since then the danger of Japanese invasion has kept the Khalkhas of Outer Mongolia pressed to the side of the Soviet Union. In Chinese Turkistan, however, there is no apparent need for a Soviet "forward policy." It is necessary, therefore, to examine the character of Soviet influence in Chinese Turkistan, both in order to determine what kind of addition it has made to the ancient pattern of Chinese history and in order to determine whether there is a Soviet counter penetration of China from the remote hinterland challenging the Japanese in-

[76] Hedin, The Flight of "Big Horse," 1936, especially pp. 1-17.

[77] "Little" Hsü, the Chinese general who attempted a reconquest of Outer Mongolia in 1920, belonged to a clique of corrupt war lords and politicians who intrigued with the Japanese; the "Mad Baron" Ungern-Sternberg, who was also active in Outer Mongolia, was associated with Semenov, another agent of the Japanese.

vasion from the coast. Is there, in short, a Soviet policy of "capturing" the history of the outer Frontier equivalent to the Japanese attempt in Manchuria that has already been discussed?

The Soviet Union claims to have an economic system that relieves it of all necessity to compete in export markets and consequently of the need to exert political influence beyond its own borders. At the same time, what the Soviet Union has done within its own borders has gravely changed the economic position of Chinese Turkistan. From 1917 to 1930 civil war and competitive taxation between regional governments in China proper had withered the flow of trade along the routes leading through China and Inner Mongolia toward Chinese Turkistan. Outer Mongolian independence and the refusal to recognize Mongol debts to Chinese traders had closed the routes through Mongolia. Trade with India could not be increased because of the physical difficulty of transport over the K'unlun, Karakoram, and Himalayas.[78]

The Five Year Plans, by completing the Turksib Railway, altered the whole question of transport into and out of Sinkiang. The richest parts of the province lie in the northwest and west. The shortest caravan route from Hami through Inner Mongolia to railhead at Pao-t'ou is about 1,200 miles, taking caravans about ninety days if all goes well. Motor cars have made the run in an average of not less than twelve days, but only intermittently and at an expense that prohibits anything but passenger and luxury goods traffic. From either Chuguchak (T'ach'eng) or Kulja, however, it is less than 200 miles to the Turksib, and good motor roads make it possible to carry bulk merchandise cheaply. Even from Kashgar, over mountain roads, it takes caravans only about twelve days to reach Soviet railhead, whereas from Kashgar to railhead in China it is at least 2,500 miles.

[78] Lattimore, Chinese Turkestan or Sinkiang, pp. 39-40.

Since foreign trade is a necessity to the officials as well as to the traders of Chinese Turkistan, and since trade with China has declined and trade with India cannot be increased, Sinkiang, like Outer Mongolia, has inevitably become economically a province of the Soviet Union.[79]

In Outer Mongolia Soviet policy has indisputably used the power thus accruing to it in the interests of the Mongol people as a whole. Political changes inherent in the condition of Outer Mongolia itself and the structure of its society began the overthrow of the princes and high lamas who ruled the country; economic changes, assisted by the Soviet policy, have confirmed these political changes. As a result the Khalkha Mongols now have, under the Mongol People's Republic, the most popular and representative government they have ever had and a rising standard of living shared equally throughout the country.[80]

In Sinkiang the situation is not different in kind though much more confused in detail, because there are several main types of economy, a number of linguistic, religious, and ethnic or national groups, and over all an alien ruling caste. When political disorder became general in Chinese Turkistan as a result of the inherent conditions that I have already described in Chinese Turkistan itself, what appears to have happened is roughly as follows.

The Soviet Union did not close its frontiers, leaving the various factions in Chinese territory to kill each other off. There was, however, no longer a single Chinese colonial government with which the Soviet authorities could deal. Several factions had formed even among the governing Chinese. Different factions had formed also among the subject races. It appears that a number of these factions, among both the rulers and the ruled,[81] appealed for

---

[79] *Ibid.*

[80] Lattimore, Where Outer and Inner Mongolia Meet, 1938.

[81] There is not, so far as I know, any account of this period that fits together all the pieces of the puzzle; but Hedin, *op. cit.*, vividly describes T'ungkans, Chinese, Turkis, Mongols, and Red and White Russians engaged

Soviet support for their interest and intervention "to restore order." The Soviet Union, answering these appeals in its own way, did in fact assist "to restore order," since it was to its own interest not to have war along its frontiers.

The form of order that was of interest to the Soviet Union was not, however, one which could be achieved simply by ejecting the invaders from Kansu, crushing the various risings, and restoring exactly the conditions that had existed before and had made an outbreak inevitable. Nor was it to the interest of the Soviet Union to aid, for instance, the Kansu invaders to establish by conquest a rule of Chinese-speaking (T'ungkan) Moslems over all the peoples of the province, in place of the rule of the non-Moslem Chinese. Restoration of order, to be permanent and constructive, must allow scope for development and progress and must remove as many as possible of the inequalities that had previously built up, although slowly, an increasing tension that was bound to break down in disorder. If it were merely to substitute Russian overlordship for Chinese rule the causes of disorder would remain.

Consequently, the Soviet interest lay in assisting a form of settlement that would eliminate as far as possible the subjection by force of one people, religion, culture, or economic activity to another, and set up at least the beginnings of an equal and proportional representation of the different interests within the province. It is clear that on the whole it was the Chinese who were assisted to restore order, for the province is now peaceful and the administration remains Chinese. Among the Chinese, however, it is not clear what faction gained the ascendency or how it is composed, but it appears to have been a coalition group representing partly the old administration and the repatriated Manchurian troops, as well as a number of pro-

in the tumultuous events which in the nature of things he could report only disconnectedly.

vincial interests not previously prominent in governing activities.[82]

As for the methods by which order was restored, it is known that Soviet arms and even airplanes were furnished.[83] Moreover, Russian troops entered the province not officially as Russian troops but under the name of the Altai Army.[84] At the same time, the "White" Russian forces raised in the province by the Chinese themselves continued to serve; [85] and, as these were not the kind of men likely to become "Bolshevized" in a hurry, it is to be inferred that the military operations were also a coalition measure and were not aimed at immediate and fundamental revolution.[86]

Finally, Soviet military aid or intervention was withdrawn immediately when order began to appear. No Soviet forces remained in the country to effect a conquest in the Japanese manner. This also meant something more. The coalition, mainly Chinese, which restored order could not have done so by reliance on main force. Order, which had been restored, could only be maintained by the removal of serious grievances; otherwise disorder would have begun again.

One of the chief changes thus brought about appears to be greater equality of all races.[87] Government office, to be held by merit and ability, is now open to the subject races equally with the Chinese.[88] In order to assist

[82] Sheng Shih-ts'ai, who established the coalition, is a Manchurian officer, but did not enter the province with the troops who had retreated into Siberia from Manchuria. He had been for a number of years in the service of the Nanking Government and had been sent to Sinkiang as an expert to advise on the training of the provincial troops.

[83] Hedin, op. cit.

[84] Ibid.; Goldman, Red Road Through Asia, 1934.

[85] Hedin, op. cit.

[86] Ibid., p. 184: "When we asked how it was possible for Reds and Whites to work together, a powerfully built, fair-haired fellow replied: 'Why, when we've got a common object we get on all right.'"

[87] Ibid., p. 246.

[88] Information from Moslem pilgrims, mostly from Turfan, who had traveled through Russia on their way to Mecca, and whom I met on an Italian steamer going from Greece to Egypt early in 1937.

them to take their part in public life education is being widely promoted,[89] whereas formerly the native education of both Moslems and Mongols was almost entirely religious and the Chinese were interested only in training interpreters to transmit the orders of the administration.[90] Since the subjection of the native races—not only to the Chinese but to their own princes, chiefs, Living Buddhas, Begs, Bais, Mollahs, landlords, and so forth—was made inescapable by their own ignorance, it is plain that a broad and rapid democratization is now to be expected.

Again, since these changes are visibly progressive, since they have been expedited by active Soviet policy, since the Soviet Union has not taken advantage of its power to fasten an "imperial" control on the province, and since Soviet trade remains important in keeping up the progress that has been begun, the total result has not been to fasten Soviet control on the province but to set up in the province itself a drift toward the Soviet Union. This, which I have elsewhere described as the phenomenon of "negative accretion," [91] results in a wide expansion of the influence of the Soviet Union beyond its own borders, not by a process of acquisition and control but by the action of the peoples who come within reach of Soviet policy. Finding that they are not subordinated either economically or politically to the Soviet Union but are helped to help themselves, these peoples continue of their own accord to seek a closer association.

If this drift toward the Soviet Union had been accompanied, as in the case of Outer Mongolia, by Chinese attempts to reconquer Turkistan, the province would have been driven into a close and open Soviet alliance and its condition would have come to resemble that of Outer Mongolia very closely. The invasion of China by Japan, how-

[89] Cable, The New "New Dominion," 1938; an account of conditions in 1936, apparently, though the date is not given in the text.
[90] Lattimore, Chinese Turkistan, 1933, p. 112.
[91] Lattimore, Russo-Japanese Relations, 1936, p. 534.

ever, has prevented any such development. Instead, Chinese "secondary imperialism" has been abandoned and the Chinese themselves have begun a movement of "accretion" toward the Soviet Union, which, largely by the transport of munitions through Chinese Turkistan, is aiding them to defend their national independence. With this vital line of transport depending largely on good relations between the Chinese and the Moslems (in Kansu as well as in Sinkiang), a renewal of Chinese attempts to subjugate the Moslems is impossible.[92]

In a broad way these contemporary changes can be related to the past history of Chinese Central Asia. The cycles of steppe ascendancy, alternating with Chinese overlordship combined with oasis ascendancy, were associated with an inability to integrate the life of the steppe and the oasis. "Mixed" and extensive farming stood midway between the extensive economy of the steppe and the intensive economy of Chinese and oasis agriculture. Neither the steppe peoples, the Chinese, nor the oasis peoples could *evolve* toward this mixed economy, because it meant a *devolution* from the social structure based on each existing economy. For cognate reasons, inhibitions inherent within these different forms of society prevented the emergence of mechanized industry from any of them. Yet industrialism alone can integrate these different economic forms into one broad base on which to erect a higher social structure.

It can be said, therefore, that the phase of Chinese rule in Central Asia that has just closed represented the completion of a cycle of oasis ascendancy of very much the old type. Instead of a countercycle of the old type of steppe ascendancy, however, there is beginning an entirely new phenomenon of integration, on a scale greater than that of any previous historical cycle, affecting the steppe, the oasis world, and China itself. In this new phase the

[92] Lattimore, Kimono and Turban, 1938.

inrush of ideas and influences from the Soviet Union could be crudely compared with an ancient invasion of barbarians from the western steppe—but only crudely,[93] for the Soviet influences are not being thrust into Mongolia, Chinese Turkistan, or China by force, but drawn in by the increasing demand of the affected peoples themselves.

NOTE: As in the chapter on Mongolia, I have here attempted to bring the record of history up to the threshold of the present. It has been impossible, however, to bring completely up to date the account of Soviet policy. This is partly because during the year 1939 Soviet policy has changed in answer to the spread of war conditions from Asia to Europe. This much is obvious, but the details are obscure.

A dispatch from F. Tillman Durdin to the *New York Times* of January 2, 1940, states that "Hand in hand with the large measure of Russian control [in Sinkiang] has gone notable material progress and political modernization . . . A provincial assembly advises the government, the large number of different races send delegates to province-wide conferences."

An anonymous German article entitled "Durchdringungs-politik in Zentralasien," in *Berichte des Asien Arbeitskreises* (No. 1, February, 1939; published in Vienna and Peiping) cited in "The Russian Domination of Sinkiang," *Journal of the Royal Central Asian Society* (October, 1939), bitterly describes how "Russia stepped in and worked with all her craft and power." Since, however, it also mentions Moslem "prophets" sent into Sinkiang by the Japanese, and names three of them, there would seem to be some justification for the "Anti-Imperialist Party" which Mr. Durdin describes as dominant in Sinkiang.

The situation in Sinkiang, at the same time, is by no means exactly like that in Mongolia. In both regions the

[93] Lattimore, Chinese Turkistan, p. 119.

actual advance and growing threat of Japan alarms and weakens the social groups and political tendencies which in themselves would otherwise be most resistant to the idea of closer association with Russia. Both regions are in this way "pushed" into a closer association with Russia than could be effected by the "pull" of Soviet ideas or propaganda.

In Mongolia, however, contact with Russia spreads the effect of Soviet ideas and policies in a relatively even and general way through a homogeneous population and over a uniform economy. In Chinese Turkistan the people affected speak a number of different languages, are grouped according to more than one religious creed, and live under several economic systems. The impact of Russian influences and Soviet ideas must therefore be relatively uneven. Both China and Russia must accommodate themselves in more than one way to more than one kind of people. Since for both China and the Soviet Union the immediately urgent problem is the transport of munitions over a long and difficult route, it is to be expected that both the maintenance of Chinese rule and the penetration of Soviet influence must accommodate themselves primarily to the need for conciliating and winning the support of as many as possible of the national minorities and regional and political groups.

CHAPTER VII

THE HIGH WASTES OF TIBET *

GEOGRAPHICAL FACTORS

Along the Great Wall Frontier China for centuries attempted not only to hold back invasion but to limit the spread of its own people because from early times the Chinese, when they penetrated too deeply into the steppe environment, were likely to break away from the main body of the nation. In the far south, on the contrary, however deeply they penetrated, the Chinese never broke away from China but added to it new territories, whose peoples they recruited and converted gradually into Chinese.[1] This process has never come to an end, as is witnessed by the fact that in provinces like Yünnan and Kueichou the Chinese are still outnumbered by aborigines, whose economy and society present for study a number of stages in evolution toward the Chinese standard but who have not yet lost their own languages nor the whole of their tribal independence. The South, accordingly, is an open frontier of indefinite depth, while the North is a frontier artificially closed but never quite successfully closed. Tibet, overlooking the main bulk of China from the west, is a frontier region of a third kind. Its history is governed by its dominant geographical characteristics: it is almost impassable and almost impenetrable.

The massive heights of Tibet, dividing China from India, also nourish the sources of the Yangtze and the Yel-

---

* For map see p. 150.

[1] V. K. Ting, How China Acquired Her Civilisation, 1931, pp. 10-11: in the Chou period the true Chinese "did not go much beyond the Yangtze." They began to spread farther under the Ch'in (B.C. 255-209). Ssuch'uan was "sinized" under the Han (B.C. 206—A.D. 220); Kuangtung (Canton province) under the T'ang (618-906); Fukien and Kiangsi under the Sung (960-1278, including the Southern Sung); Kuangsi, Yünnan, and Kueichou under the Ming (1368-1643).

low River flowing into China, the Indus and the Brahma-
putra flowing into India, the Mekong flowing into Siam,
and the Salween flowing into Burma.[2] The upper courses
of these major rivers reach far back into the interior of
Tibet. A number of minor streams begin nearer the rim
of the high country. Like the great rivers, they cut down
through gorges from the highlands to lower levels. It is
not easy to travel up and down these gorges, but here and
there they open out giving room for cultivation, which in
some sectors of the mountain periphery can be supported
by the natural rainfall while in other sectors artificial irrigation is imperative.[3]

As an area of human habitation Tibet may therefore be
defined as follows. The center of the country is a land of
great height, in parts mountainous and in parts level or
undulating. It varies in climate from the arid to the sub-
arid, because rainfall is caught by the mountains near the
edge, overlooking the lower country. Around the periphery
of the central mass, where streams break down from the
upper levels—and the streams are most numerous in the
east and southeast—agriculture is possible. Nowhere is
agriculture continuous over a large area, however; on the
contrary, it is confined to "pockets" strung out in an irregular cordon around the edge of an immense mass of inhospitable terrain. Five sixths of the settled area is distributed
over an arc running from west of Lhasa, in the Tsangpo
valley, around by the east and northeast to the Kansu frontier.[4] Communication is difficult, either between neighboring valleys or across the central highlands between distant
valleys.

In the high central plains there are stretches of grazing
land that can support pastoral nomadism, but in few of
them is the grazing so good as in the more favored parts

[2] For a general survey of hydrography and orography, see Grenard, Haute
Asie, 1929.
[3] Ibid., p. 366.
[4] Ibid., p. 364.

of Mongolia.[5] There is access to each of these grazing regions from one or more of the valleys that cut the rim of Tibet. Consequently, in addition to contact between nomad groups there is a range of social contact from the main social conglomerations of China and India up to the valley dwellers of the outer periphery of Tibet and then into the deep interior. These converging lines of cultural, economic, and social intercourse make the center of Tibet a meeting ground of influences drawn remotely from a number of geographical regions and differing societies.

Most if not all of the valley populations around the rim of Tibet are to be regarded as Tibetan in a secondary and derived sense—politically, linguistically, and so forth. In a more primary sense they are to be regarded as "pocketed" communities; that is, peoples of a distant origin in Central Asia, India, North China, the trans-Yangtze jungles of Southwest China, and the fringes of Burma, who now look down from their niches in the escarpment of Tibet on the countries and racial congeners of their past. They live in what may be described as oases, isolated by mountains instead of by deserts; and they have affiliations, however tenuous and ancient, with societies based on the economy of irrigated agriculture in India, Central Asia, and North China. In the valleys that lead down to Ssuch'uan and Yünnan they also have affiliations with the ancient trans-Yangtze peoples—the T'ai and a few minor groups [6]— whose descendants continue to live by a mixed economy of forest or jungle agriculture (much more "extensive" than that of the true Chinese) together with hunting and meth-

[5] *Ibid.*, p. 365.

[6] An account of the Yünnan frontier of Tibet, on which Dr. Joseph Rock has been working for some years and which may be published within the year, should advance the knowledge of this region very greatly. Other general references for the Chinese approaches to Tibet: Rockhill, The Land of the Lamas, 1891; Gregory, To the Alps of Chinese Tibet, 1923; Stevenson, The Chinese-Tibetan Borderland, 1927-28; also Human Geography of the Chinese-Tibetan Borderland, 1932.

ods of livestock breeding that are to be clearly distinguished from steppe nomadism.

SOCIAL ORIGINS OF THE TIBETAN POPULATION

In order to detect and describe the historical character of a people so dispersed and of such disparate origins as the Tibetans, it is plain that a functional method must be applied. Why and how did people originally become "pocketed" in the valleys that give access to Tibet? Why and how did they penetrate from these valleys to the open heights of the interior and develop there the necessary technique of pastoralism? In the process of social adaptation to environment what secondary trends of social and political evolution were generated?

Mountain people, especially when they are broken up in small communities, are frequently described as refugees "pushed" into these remote valleys by stronger tribes. This is not wholly or universally true. In order to determine the degree to which it is true the social texture must be examined.

In marginal steppe countries, for instance, when an advance of agriculture displaces a nomad society a certain number of the nomads are likely to remain behind and be "converted" to agriculture and assimilated by the agricultural society. These individuals are not usually, however, the chiefs of the nomads, eagerly seeking to "raise themselves to a higher standard." On the contrary, they are normally the weakest and poorest of the nomads, who have little or no vested interest in the working of nomad economy or the structure of nomad society. Those among the rich and powerful who own the most herds and control poorer men who do the actual work for them tend to withdraw into the more distant steppe out of the reach of the rival rulers of the agricultural society,[7] taking their

[7] Lattimore, Chinese Turkistan, 1933, p. 115.

dependents and subjects with them. When nomad chiefs patronize agriculture it is a subject agriculture that they prefer, exploited under their military protection and practiced by imported peasants, between whom and the dominant nomads there is an emphatic social distinction.[8]

This provides an analogy by which the nature of the "retreat" of fragmentary peoples into mountain fastnesses may be tested. It is to be conjectured that the original society, at the foot of the mountains, became affected by marked changes, which may have been the result of local evolution or may have been caused by invasion. In either case, resistance to the new order must have been strongest among those whose interests were identified with the old order in such a way that they stood to lose more than they might gain by going over to the new order. These are the individuals or classes who are most likely to have led the "retreat" into the mountains, taking with them the dependents whose subordination gave them the relatively high status that they wanted to preserve. In other words, the "retreat" was in fact a retreat to the extent that it represented the retirement of an old people or an old order before a new people or a new order; but at the same time it represented a victory for those who ruled the groups that were taking refuge. They preserved their particular status and interests regardless of the general changes in the society from which they departed.

That this was in fact the general character of the early, peripheral valley populations of Tibet is indicated strongly by survivals of old social forms (like polyandry and traces of matriarchy or matrilineal succession) known to have existed formerly outside of Tibet, and also by the universally robust control of the local rulers of Tibetan communities, whether secular nobles or ecclesiastical dignitaries, over their subjects and clients.

What I have here said is necessarily a simplification,

[8] Compare Chapters IV and V, above.

difficult to elaborate for lack of early historical material and specific economic and social studies made over a wide range of Tibetan communities. Speaking in general, however, one type of historical process may be confidently assumed: those who withdrew into the mountains with their followers in order to escape one or another kind of change to which they were hostile became subject nevertheless to many different and complicated changes arising both out of necessary adaptation to environment and out of the effort to maintain their ascendancy as the social structure changed. From these changes were generated at different points on the periphery the lines of development that eventually fused into a general history of Tibet.

TIBETAN AGRICULTURE AND NOMADISM

Tibetan agriculture cannot be considered original. It represents, rather, the successful establishment in a difficult and harsh terrain of methods developed elsewhere. Its "primitive" aspect is attributable largely to crude tools and perhaps to a certain degeneration, because of meager returns and the poverty of the people, of practices that once were more developed.

In the same way, the climate and vegetation of the central highlands of Tibet do not provide the setting in which to look for a spontaneous discovery of the technique of pastoral nomadism. The herdsmen of Tibet derive partly from the valley dwellers, as is shown by their frequent political and social subordination, especially in the east and south, to valley-dwelling nobles or to ecclesiastical establishments.[9] They also readily turn, or return, to agriculture if they have the opportunity.[10] Moreover, the form of the Tibetan nomad tent, taken together with the kind of

[9] Grenard, op. cit., pp. 367-368. The fact that many Tibetan nomads are partly yak herders and partly hunters of the wild yak recalls the theory that reindeer nomadism originated from the hunting of the wild reindeer (Hatt, Notes on Reindeer Nomadism, 1919).

[10] Grenard, op. cit., p. 364.

fireplace used in it, suggests an improvised shelter pitched over exactly the kind of fireplace that the settled people use.[11] In part, the nomads of Tibet derive also from a true steppe nomadism, which penetrated from the north and was able to maintain itself in an environment worse than that of the Mongolian steppe and of the extensive semi-steppe of Kansu, because it had already mastered the technical practices of pastoral economy. The mingling of true steppe nomadism with the extemporary nomadism that has not developed far beyond the pasturing of outlying herds belonging to village proprietors can be seen at the present time among partly Tibetanized Mongol nomads in the north of Tibet.[12]

While the relation between nomadism and settled agriculture in Tibet suggests the relation between oasis and steppe in Central Asia and Mongolia, there are significant differences. Most of the valley settlements of Tibet are easier to defend against nomad attack than the open, vulnerable oases of Central Asia. They have therefore been the centers of power as well as of wealth, and the southern and eastern nomad groups have accordingly not been able to break away from them but have remained herders of livestock belonging to the settlements instead of becoming the subjects of independent steppe lords. Only the Goloks ("Rebels") of the basin of the Ma Chu or upper Yellow River have attained to an independence of this kind; their independence within Tibet they maintain partly by a trading alliance with the Salar Moslems of Kansu.[13] The Salars, being Turkish by origin and language,[14] have a separatism of their own to defend against the Chinese-speaking Moslems as well as against the Chinese proper.

[11] *Ibid.*, p. 365.
[12] General reference: Roerich, Trails to Inmost Asia, 1931. For a complicated series of shifts from Mongol-Turkish nomadism to sedentary life, and thence partly toward sinization, partly toward Tibetanization, see Schram, Le Mariage chez les T'ou-jen, 1932.
[13] Grenard, *op. cit.*, p. 376. See also additional note on p. 237, below.
[14] Andrew, The Crescent in North-West China, 1921, pp. 15-18.

Farther to the north the Det Mongols [15] of the Tsaidam region, though descended from sixteenth-century conquerors of Tibet and still ruled by true steppe lords, are of a declining importance. The poverty of the environment does not allow them to develop the steppe forms of wealth on a sufficiently large scale, and they do not have suitable access to oases with which to associate themselves as do the Tibetan nomads.

On the whole, therefore, the pastoral economy in Tibet has remained ancillary to the agricultural economy, and the nomads have remained subordinate to the settled people. The pastoral fringe helps both to diversify the economy of the major valley concentrations and to maintain communication between them without dominating them politically. It is partly for this reason that the oasis-like valley communities of Tibet fall short of the extreme "compartmentation" of the Turkistan oases. The depressed heart of Chinese Turkistan, with its ring of oases around the circumference, is comparable diagrammatically with the raised heart of Tibet and its peripheral valley settlements; but the Taklamakan lacks the linking, mobile, subordinate pastoral groups of the central Tibetan uplands. This is important in spite of the slow rate of movement along the lines of communication crossing Tibet—three and a half months for yak caravans, for instance, from Lhasa by way of Batang to Tatsienlu, and 120 days from Lhasa to Leh in Ladakh.[16]

Nor are the separate communities of Tibet so homogeneous in internal structure as the oases of Central Asia. In addition to the diversification accounted for by the pastoral fringe of agriculture, there is a range of difference within agriculture itself between irrigated and unirrigated

[15] The term *det* means "upper"—Mongols of the plateau.

[16] Grenard, *op. cit.*, p. 370. For a description of the caravan route from Sining in the north to Lhasa, see Huc and Gabet, Travels in Tartary, 1928 edit.

methods of farming. Topographically the zones of the two kinds of agriculture overlap in the region of Lhasa. As this region was relatively accessible from a number of other agricultural regions and also stood midway between the most concentrated agriculture and the outlying pastures, and was, over and above all this, a convenient transfer point between the distant Chinese frontier on the northeast, the Indian frontier on the south, and the Ladakh frontier on the west, it eventually became the center of gravity of the whole country.

It is interesting to note, however, that the political knitting together of the loose communities of Tibet probably did not begin at Lhasa but in Ladakh,[17] which is now not even thought of as a part of Tibet proper because it lies far to the west and is politically subordinate to Kashmir, which in turn is an outer ward of the Indian Empire. Yet it seems more likely than not that the establishment of a kingdom at Lhasa claiming authority over all Tibet was the work of a conqueror coming from Ladakh. I suggest that this was because the people of Ladakh, where irrigation is conspicuously important, arrived at a compact social unity before the rest of Tibet. This gave to their rulers a high degree of local authority, carrying with it the ability to maneuver externally and conquer the larger but more loosely organized region to the east. However, while Ladakh was the the base from which the unifying conquest was projected, Lhasa thereafter became a better seat of government because it lay nearer the natural center of gravity whereas Ladakh lay far out on the periphery. There is here a close analogy with the process of unification of China, which began with the conquests of the peripheral northwestern state of Ch'in in the third century B.C. but was followed in later centuries by a recurrent tendency to shift the capital either toward the east or toward

[17] Francke, The Kingdom of gNya khri btsampo, 1910.

the south.[18] This vacillation was far greater in China than in Tibet, however, because in China the domestic reasons for making the capital more central were offset by the military necessities of the Great Wall Frontier, which demanded a northern capital so situated as to be able to coordinate defense against invasion from the steppe.

EARLY TIBETAN CONTACTS WITH CHINA

The chronicles of Tibet become continuous only after the establishment of the Lhasa kingdom. It is noteworthy that this is unmistakably associated with the introduction of a late and already corrupt syncretic form of Buddhism[19] in the seventh century after Christ. The specific Tibetan Lama church was not evolved from this for some time, but nevertheless Buddhism was from the first an affair of state. Its later evolution was chiefly concerned with the working out of detail and method.

Tibetan history, therefore, is notably a history of late maturity—far later than that of China and later even than that of Chinese Central Asia. Not only are the high wastes of Tibet an extension rather than an integral part of the Great Wall Frontier of China, but they did not enter into the history of the Great Wall Frontier until after such regions as Manchuria, Mongolia, and Chinese Turkistan had already become important and had begun the development of their own historical "style."

The term *Ch'iang* or *Chiang*, written in a way that indicates the meaning "shepherd," is an old generic designation for non-Chinese tribes of the Kansu-Tibetan border. It appears probable that out of the early barbarians of this region, who were not yet true mounted nomads and probably had a mixed economy of herding, hunting, farming, and the gathering of wild plants, some were incorporated and

[18] Chi, Key Economic Areas, etc., 1936.
[19] Waddell, The Buddhism of Tibet, 2nd edit., 1934, pp. 13-14, 19-20.

"converted" into Chinese and some were crowded over to the north and northwest, up to the Kansu-Tibetan border. The general term *Ch'iang* was applied to those who withdrew to the uplands of Tibet, where some of them kept up at least a partial practice of agriculture in the border valleys, while others took to a pastoral nomadism comparable to that of the steppe.[20]

Later, in the first great period of their Central Asian activity in the second century B.C., the Chinese had frequently to deal with Ch'iang tribes distributed from the Ma Chu (headwaters of the Yellow River) across the Kokonor and Tsaidam uplands of Tibet to the Nan Shan, overlooking the Kansu "corridor" to Central Asia; but owing to the poverty of the environment these tribes could never muster the numbers or attain the importance of the steppe tribes. In handling them, accordingly, the major objective was to prevent them from affiliating themselves with the steppe tribes. As long as this could be done their "attacks" on the Chinese were of the order of brigandage rather than war.[21] In all of this period there is as yet no question of Tibet as a whole but only of northeastern Tibet.

POLITICAL UNIFICATION OF TIBET

Three original regions of Tibet may be discerned: the northeast, whose peoples and history are linked with the ancient sub-oasis and sub-steppe terrain of Kansu; the east, where there is a similar link with the ancient trans-Yangtze T'ai peoples ("Mantze" aborigines), and with the Tibeto-Burmans; and the south and southwest, where the affinities are with Bhutan, Nepal, Ladakh, and Bal-

[20] Andersson (Children of the Yellow Earth, 1934, pp. 242-243) suggests that the scarcity of pigs' bones and the large number of bones of game ruminants and tame cattle at a site excavated by him on the Kansu-Tibetan border indicates a late neolithic population of "hunters and cattle-raising nomads." These, however, were probably a migrant people of mixed culture, rather than a true, specialized, steppe nomad people.
[21] Compare Chapter XV, below.

tistan. The significance of the rise of the Lhasa kingdom is that it sets the maturing of Tibetan history, through the integration of these disparate regions, at the relatively late level of the seventh century. The inference is that the difficult environment in each and every part of Tibet had a retarding effect; only after long, slow development could the political requisites of unification be worked out in one of the constituent areas and imposed on the others. Consequently, the political unity of Tibet was not only late in appearing but had from the time of its appearance an artificial character because for the east and north of the country it was not a unity that had been evolved but one that had been imposed.

From these considerations the historical function of Tibetan Lamaism becomes unmistakably evident. The traditional "explanation" is that Srongtsan Gampo, King of Lhasa in the seventh century (it is he who may have moved the capital from Ladakh to Lhasa [22]), took one wife from Nepal (thus bringing in Buddhist and Indian influences) and one from China.[23] This indicates that at the time "royalty" was attained the culture was syncretic.

The tradition oversimplifies but does not contradict the historical convergence on a common center of national life that I have been trying to delineate as a multiple process. It was a process to which each community clinging to the broken edge of Tibet contributed by trying to reach out into the central plains and highlands or to come into closer touch with the comparable communities on either side of it. The effective joining together of this net of influences was necessarily delayed until some at least of the many centers from which the spread was attempted had reached relatively high levels of development; it was not the kind of thing that could be carried out by really

[22] Francke, *op. cit.*
[23] Waddell, *op. cit.*, pp. 19-20.

primitive groups, weak in social cohesion and limited in range of action by inability to conserve and organize their economic resources.

Consequently, by the time these isolated communities were mature enough to overcome the difficulties of the environment in keeping in touch with each other and co-ordinating the interests that they had in common, they were paradoxically hampered by the fact that they had each developed a pronounced particularism—a by-product of their local self-sufficiency. This particularism could never be eliminated entirely, for geographical reasons. It was necessary to create a superstructure that would admit the necessary degree of continuing isolation but at the same time compensate for it. The society whose needs had to be satisfied was not as homogeneous as that of China, since it had to allow for an important minority of pastoral nomads; nor were its agricultural regions contiguous or closely juxtaposed, as in China. Therefore the evolution of a national bureaucracy, like that of China, superimposed on a local regionalism, was inhibited. The multiple separatism of the Tibetan communities was more like that of the Turkistan oases, but even more extreme; and Tibet accordingly developed in an even more extreme form than Chinese Turkistan the ecclesiastical symbol of unity and common interest.

POLITICAL FUNCTION OF LAMA-BUDDHISM

Hence the functional importance of Tibetan Lama-Buddhism. It was at first the instrument of the secular kings, who used it to circumvent the feudal power of local nobles. The church was corporate; its institutions could be established in every locality and could penetrate both the settled and the nomad societies, yet in so doing it did not succumb to particularism but retained its corporate, centralized interest and character. It successfully eliminated the danger and difficulty of imposing the rule of one

great family or one locality over other families and localities, for the hierarchical succession to power is relatively
impersonal. In the Lama church, as in the Catholic church
of the Middle Ages, the general aim of religious rule is
to supersede the feudal method of dividing power between
a number of hereditary great families. Even when this
aim is not completely achieved personal or family control
of power is disguised and weakened, for the church, once
established, is powerful enough to maintain the principle
(without which it cannot survive) of preventing father-to-
son succession. Even a family which temporarily controls the church must limit itself to appointing a junior
member to the supreme ecclesiastical position. Furthermore, a hierarchical personage of such origin does not
control the interests of his own family for he is not the
head of it; he therefore combines family *influence* with
church *rule*. Accordingly, while in some circumstances his
family interest may override his church interest, in other
circumstances his individual church interest may decide
him to break with or subordinate his family interest.

Because its corporate interest was always continuous
and at the same time resistant to both local and family
bias, the Lama church eventually superseded the secular
kings of whom it had originally been the instrument. In
Mongolia at a much later period, as has already been
pointed out, the issue of ecclesiastical supremacy over
hereditary temporal rule was raised but never settled. The
Manchu Empire, intervening in the affairs of the Mongols,
"froze" the development of the Lama church and effected
a permanent cleavage between the Mongol state (divided between many princes) and the Mongol church (unified and powerful but not supreme), thus preventing a
national unity of all the Mongols. In Europe the Catholic
church first succeeded in limiting and to a large extent
subordinating the feudal succession of family power; but
thereafter the uniform control of all Europe at which it

aimed was broken up by the rise of new national structures of a cohesion superior to the previous feudally ruled nations and empires, which continuously encroached both on what remained of feudalism and on the political power of the church.

In Tibet the church advanced further than it did in Mongolia. First, in alliance with the kings of Lhasa it assisted in creating a Tibetan state, incorporating widely scattered communities that until then had almost certainly been ruled by powerful families but could hardly be called states. Thereafter it superseded the kings themselves by subordinating the state and incorporating it within the church. No new form of state arose, however, to displace, in turn, the church. This was partly for internal reasons—the extreme dispersion of the Tibetan communities, the small scale of local organization, and the difficulty of communication and concerted action—and partly for an external reason. In Tibet as in Mongolia the processes of history ceased to develop and became stagnant, though at a different stage of development; and as in Mongolia this was because of considerations of imperial and Frontier politics in China. The church maintained at a dead, unchanging level the supremacy that it had acquired within Tibet because it allied itself, externally, with the dynastic interests of the Manchu Empire in China and its corona of stabilized Frontier societies.

This is a summary statement which telescopes the separate stages of growth of the church in Tibet. In fact, I do not believe it is yet possible to isolate entirely each period in the history of the Tibetan church and analyze it in detail. There are a number of problems that can be stated but cannot as yet be fully answered. This is not only because precise knowledge of the growth and maturing of certain functions and aspects of the Lama church is insufficient, but because we do not yet know nearly enough about the structure of Tibetan society as a whole and the way it works. In order to provide the specific information that is needed studies have yet to be made in the variations of Tibetan economy, the range of difference between individual Tibetan communities, and especially those peculiarities that do not contribute to the general homogeneity of Tibetan society but have been subdued by it. Studies of these kinds are particularly necessary for Tibet because of the poverty of the written records.

TIBETAN CONQUESTS IN WESTERN CHINA AND TURKISTAN (EIGHTH CENTURY)

The first problem, which can be stated more easily than it can be answered, is that of the period of rapid expansion that followed the establishment of the seventh-century Lhasa kingdom. In the eighth century the Tibetans were strong enough to encroach on western China and on Chinese Turkistan, and still farther west they came into contact with the Arab empire based on Baghdad.[24] What caused this extraordinary widening of the Tibetan horizon, and why was the expansion directed to the north and west? The concentration of political power had been effected in the extreme southeast, where the environment permitted the largest and closest grouping of population; but instead of moving southward from this base, against India, the Tibetans reached out over the vast distances of the most empty and difficult part of their own terrain, toward western China and Central Asia.

The answer can be given only conjecturally, but it may be supposed that the reasons were Tibetan rather than Chinese or Central Asian. The moves that had made Lhasa a capital had integrated the affairs of the most important Tibetan communities and had raised them from oasis-like isolation to at least a crude national level. The new state could not be stabilized at this level, however. Any attempt

[24] General references: Stein, Serindia, 1921; also Ruins of Desert Cathay, 1912; Francke, op. cit., pp. 110-111.

to stabilize without further development would necessarily have taken the form of internal conquest and the harsh domination of one region over others. The resentment arising out of this, working together with the obdurate geographical isolation of the various regions, would have resulted in breaking apart the new state and dislodging the king from his new position of superiority over the families that ruled the separate localities of the kingdom. It was necessary to compensate the interests that had been subordinated by extending the range and activity of conquest so that they too could benefit.

The required movement of conquest could not be directed southward into India or the foothills of the Himalayas; for although even a small military kingdom could strike with advantage across the Himalayas from a base in the Lhasa region, and withdraw again behind the protecting mountains, it could not do so with safety while itself exposed to attack from the inner expanses of Tibet. Although the peoples of the north and northeast of Tibet were too few and too scattered to set up for themselves the nucleus of a united Tibet, they had the advantage of terrain in attacking the otherwise better-situated Tibetans under the control of Lhasa should the ruler of Lhasa take his eyes off the outlying parts of Tibet. This meant that the degree of centralization already achieved by Lhasa could only be safeguarded by drawing into the new confederation the outlying Tibetans of the north and northwest, and simultaneously turning them outward against Central Asia and western China. Only in this way, by making them participants in external conquests, was it possible to compensate those who had been subordinated to Lhasa.

This explains, I think, why the rise of Lhasa was accompanied by an expansion radiating not from Lhasa itself but from the side of Tibet most distant and most inaccessible from Lhasa. These outlying Tibetans could only be "conquered" by converting them into conquerors; it was impossible to humble them within a closed "kingdom of Tibet" because of the difficulties of terrain and communication. These difficulties, however, did not prevent the Tibetans of the north and northeast from encroaching on the oases of Chinese Turkistan and the semi-oasis regions of northwest China, in spite of their small numbers, once they had the backing of the greater wealth and numbers of the Lhasa region. Each oasis was small enough in scale and vulnerable enough in position to be conquered by small expeditions, and the Tibetans themselves had the advantage of a position in which it was difficult to counterattack them. Accordingly, by the end of the eighth century the Tibetans held Turfan and were dominant in all the southern part of Chinese Turkistan; they also were overlords of the oases and sub-oases of Kansu, and had even taken Ch'angan, the great classical city of Shensi province, though they were not powerful enough to hold it permanently.[25]

It was in this period that the early syncretic Buddhism already known in Tibet was fashioned into the beginnings of the Lama church by Padma Sambhava.[26] The fact that Padma Sambhava came into Tibet from Kashmir, and therefore presumably through Ladakh, reinforces the supposition that the Lhasa kingdom was created by a conquest based on Ladakh and resulting in the transfer of the royal capital from Ladakh to Lhasa. The Buddhist influences of this period, moreover, being drawn from the Turkistan oases as well as India, were well adapted to the trend of Tibetan political development. Monastic Buddhism probably served to unite, in a community of religion and outlook, social groups isolated territorially, and to keep them in touch with each other through the ministra-

[25] Fuchs, Das Turfangebiet, 1926; Herrmann, Die Westländer, etc. (in Hedin, Southern Tibet, Vol. VIII, 1922), p. 271 (based on Chavannes, Les deux plus anciens spécimens de la cartographie chinoise, 1903).
[26] Schlagintweit, Lebensbeschreibung von Padma Sambhava, Part I, 1899, p. 422; Part II, 1903 (his life in India); Waddell, op. cit., p. 24.

tions of a church that was identified with each locality by property holdings.

EARLY ASCENDANCY OF THE LAMA CHURCH

In the ninth, tenth, and eleventh centuries there followed a period of retraction, in which the Tibetans were dislodged from their conquests in Turkistan [27]—chiefly as the result of a new phase of nomad ascendancy under the Uighurs and other Turks, who were better able to dominate the oases from the open steppe than the Tibetans were from their bleak highlands. This was accompanied by political changes in Tibet, as was to be expected. The expansion of the northern Tibetans, backed by those of the south, had forced these two divisions of the Tibetan people to maintain contact with each other across the empty middle spaces of Tibet, but now a tendency to separatism ensued. The Lhasa Tibetans readjusted themselves to the limits of their own domains, while the smaller aggregation of northern tribes—loosely called Tanggot (Tangut) by the Mongols, and Tang (which is the same word), or Tang-hsiang, or Hsia, by the Chinese—dealt as best they could with the Chinese to the east of them and the steppe nomads to the north. They succeeded in holding on to some of their positions in northwest China, which was not for several centuries brought under full control by either China or the nomads of the steppe.

For the social and political history of Tibet this period was clearly of great importance, though the changes that occurred cannot be traced in detail. For one thing, the withdrawal from Turkistan had brought into the church an increased number of borrowings from the other oasis religions, adding to the heterogeneity of the syncretic compound of Lamaism. At the same time, the growth of church property and power increased until it threatened the secu-

---

[27] See various references in Stein, Serindia; Fuchs, *op. cit.*

lar authority. In the tenth century there was an anti-ecclesiastical reaction under the king Langdharma [28]— known ever since in Lama tradition as the incarnation of wickedness. The persecution failed and the church was not destroyed. On the contrary, it was the kingdom that fell, giving way to a constellation of minor principalities—the breakup that had been deferred in the eighth century by the conquest or enlistment of north Tibet and by expansion into Central Asia and western China.

From this time on the church was ascendant in Tibet over the divided state; but though its interests were more generally spread throughout the Tibetan population than the influence of any principality or noble family, the church itself was not yet centralized under a "papal" hierarchy. The scattered monasteries were better able to act in common than the rival principalities. Probably the growth of a centralized religious state was not entirely a matter of internal Tibetan evolution. Here it must be borne in mind that while the chronology of Tibet had already come to be marked chiefly by the succession of ecclesiastical events, the real processes of history lay deeper. The period was one of great formative importance throughout Inner Asia. Generally speaking, the nomads of the steppe were in the ascendant; but they were not able to subdue completely the oases and other marginal regions. Consequently, the "professional" history of the exponents of religions like Islam and Lamaism, based on these marginal regions, reflected changes, adaptations, and attempts to achieve political unity in a number of marginal societies that were homogeneous with each other in some respects but acutely different in others.

In the eleventh century there was a great reforming activity in Tibetan Buddhism, or Lamaism. The formal tradition of the church refers this to saints coming from

[28] Waddell, *op. cit.*, p. 35.

India and Kashmir, like Atisa, who founded the Kadampa reformed sect.[29] The tendency to split up into rival sects led to the formation of rival hierarchies associated with rival secular principalities. These particular tendencies were offset by the effort to create a supreme ecclesiastical authority.

This was the period in which Islam was penetrating the oases of Turkistan and the marginal regions of northwest China. The discrepancies between the steppe society and that of the oases prevented a general conversion of the steppe peoples and a permanent amalgamation of the oases and steppes of Central Asia under Islam. The success of Islam among the nomads was limited to that part of the Turkistan and Jungarian steppe most under the influence of the western and eastern oases of Turkistan; it did not spread into the wide Mongolian steppe. In the oases, however, it displaced and destroyed Buddhism, Manichaeism, and Nestorian Christianity by asserting in a stronger and more militant form a concept which they also professed— that of a religious community inclusive of local communities.

The religions that were submerged in this way were also represented in the "secondary" oasis region of Kansu and Ninghsia, and likewise in trading communities in the heart of China proper. Some of the followers of these religions, it is well known, were eventually converted to Islam; but, given the earlier political importance of the Tibetans in Turkistan and their continuing importance in Kansu, it cannot be doubted that a number of different religious bodies took shelter under Tibetan protection. This means that they contributed, eventually, to the tenets, ritual, and speculative philosophy on which the Indian reformers of Lamaism worked. It also very strongly suggests that the "reformation" of Lamaism was in part a counter reformation against Islam. A ragged frontier was thus formed.

[29] *Ibid.*

The oases of Turkistan were Islamic. The true steppe of Mongolia and the harsher upland pastures of Tibet were non-Islamic. Between them, and not fully controlled by either of them, lay Kansu, Ninghsia, and western and northern Shensi, where some localities resembled oases and others resembled the steppe.

PERIOD OF MONGOL INFLUENCE (1206—CA. 1700 A.D.)

In this way there was prepared the next stage in the history of Tibet, under Mongol influence. Chingghis in 1206 and again in 1226-27 campaigned against and conquered the Tanggots or northern Tibetans, who by this time were the rulers of an extraordinary conglomerate state based on both agriculture and pasture. It extended from northeastern Tibet to Ninghsia and the mountains of Alashan, and included peoples of several races, languages, and religions. Then, in 1270, Khobilai Sechin (Kublai Khan), the grandson of Chingghis, who had become Emperor of all China and overlord in title of the several Mongol empires, settled the tributary or feudatory status of Tibet by recognizing the head of the Sakya sect as primate of the Lama church and concurrently the supreme secular authority in Tibet.[30]

Politically, the supreme pontiffs of Tibet have from the beginning acted as the agents of one or another alien overlord. This converted regional politics into sect politics. The rise of a new sect normally reflected an increase in the relative importance of a region; if the increase went far enough the sect could assert control over the whole church. Thereupon, however, the pontiff in whom this control was vested had to attempt to arrest the native Tibetan processes that tended to make different regions and the sects representative of them vary in importance and influence. This could be most simply managed by leaning on a power external to Tibet. The supreme pontiff, in

[30] *Ibid.*, p. 38.

other words, is to be understood as the symbol of stagnation within Tibet and of alien imperial power over Tibet.

Although this system was already foreshadowed in the time of Kublai Khan, it could not yet become rigid because from the fourteenth to the seventeenth century no one empire succeeded in controlling both China within the Great Wall and the steppes beyond the Great Wall. Consequently the fall of the Mongol (Yüan) dynasty in 1368 was followed by schism in the Tibetan church. Different sects claimed either independence or primacy, each of them being headed by one of the notable monasteries and each monastery being, in fact, the political "capital" of a region.[31] Certain of these church parties, moreover, negotiated for the patronage of the Ming dynasty in China, while others gravitated toward the successive Mongol coalitions that attempted to win supremacy over the steppe.

Under the Ming dynasty (1368-1643) the political power of the Chinese receded almost entirely from the Ninghsia-Kansu-north Tibetan border region, and their access to Tibet and especially to the Lhasa region must have been entirely by the routes leading from Ssuch'uan and Yünnan. As for the Mongols, they had fallen into Western (Ölöt), Northern (Khalkha), Southern (Ordos-Tumet-Chahar), and Eastern (Manchurian) tribal federations. This gave a special importance to the region of north Tibet (Amdo), Kansu, and Ninghsia. It included high Tibetan pastures and the sub-oases and sub-steppe of Kansu and Ninghsia. Its people were Tibetan, Moslem, Chinese, and Mongol. They had neither the homogeneity nor the re-

---

[31] These changes can be faintly traced in Waddell's account of Tibetan ecclesiastical history; but Waddell makes no attempt at the analytical and comparative method which I have here roughly employed. My attempt to condense this complicated aspect of Tibetan history is necessarily speculative; but see also Hilarion, Sketch of the History of the Relation Between China and Tibet (reprint of 1910), pp. 262-264 (in Russian), whose account suggests that at the beginning of the Ming dynasty the Chinese policy was to favor numerous individual potentates of the Red sect, at the same time that Mongol influence favored supremacy of the Yellow sect, under the Dalai Lama, following the reforms of Tsongkapa.

sources needed for a strong independent kingdom; but theirs was a debatable land, a key to general empire over Tibet, Chinese Central Asia, the Mongolian steppe, and China itself.

Tsongkapa,[32] the great religious reformer, came from this region. At the beginning of the fifteenth century he founded the Gelugpa sect, from which have issued the two main lines of pontifical succession in modern Tibet—that of the Panchan or Banchin Lama of Tashilhumpo and that of the Dalai Lama of Lhasa. The church tradition does not make the land of Tsongkapa's nativity the chief scene of his work but associates him with the three great monasteries of Galdan, Drepung, and Sera, grouped around Lhasa. Nevertheless, it may well be that the result of his reforms was to subordinate the southern influences of Buddhism coming from India and to emphasize those northern influences derived from the Buddhism, Manichaeism, and Nestorian Christianity that flourished in Chinese Central Asia from the seventh century onward. It is more than likely that these northern influences had been passed on or at least assisted by the syncretistic rituals patronized or tolerated by the Hsia or Tanggot kingdom after the tenth century and had lingered until the time of Tsongkapa himself. All of this very strongly suggests that the ecclesiastical triumphs of Tsongkapa were not the result of a simple "borrowing" by Lhasa from northern Tibet, but were the reflection in Lhasa and the part of Tibet dependent on it of a new, northern, regional ascendancy.

What is known of the Mongol history of the sixteenth and seventeenth centuries confirms this. The Mongol patronage of Lama Buddhism had lapsed with the fall of the Mongol (Yüan) dynasty in 1367. The "second flowering" of Lamaism in Mongolia began under Gegen Altan Khan of the Tumets in the Suiyüan-Ordos region in the sixteenth century. This was not the result of simple

[32] Waddell, *op. cit.*, pp. 38-39.

proselytism. The Ordos-Tumet Mongols and the West-
ern Mongols (the Oirat, later the Ölöt, and still later the
Jungar or East Wing of the Ölöt) were political rivals.
The Ordos-Tumet tribes, by expanding into what is now
Ninghsia and toward Kansu and Tibet, attempted to turn
the flank of the Western Mongols, and in the process began
to take up Lamaism once more and to exalt it politically.
Thus Tibet and especially the northeastern borderlands of
Tibet rose in importance.[33]

In the course of these tribal wars the hegemony passed
first from the Ordos-Tumet tribes to the Chahars, who
held the central position in Inner Mongolia, and then to
the Western Mongols.[34] Then, in the eighteenth century,
in the course of the wars between the Western Mongols
and the Khalkhas or Northern Mongols, the balance of
power came into the hands of the Manchus. From the
beginning of the eighteenth century, therefore, the Manchus were extending to Northern and Western Mongolia
the control that they already held in China and Inner
Mongolia. This carried with it the overlordship of Tibet.
The Manchu dominions were finally rounded out by the
conquest of Chinese Turkistan in the eighteenth century.[35]

POSITION OF THE DALAI AND PANCHAN LAMAS UNDER THE MANCHUS

Under the fifth Dalai Lama, when the Western Mongols
dominated Tibet, the internal structure of Tibet took on
the final shape that was confirmed and regulated under the

[33] This part of the account can be followed in Sanang Setsen's chronicle.
Sanang Setsen has been criticized for his inaccuracies, and Schmidt's translation, though remarkable for its day (1829), is not perfect—as when he
fails to render as alliterative verse the lament of Toghon Temur at the
beginning of the sixth book. Yet Sanang Setsen has a special value; he
expresses perfectly the romanticism of the somewhat decadent steppe aristocracy of his time and makes it possible to understand the manner and style
of his age.

[34] Compare Chapter IV, above.

[35] Courant, L'Asie centrale aux XVII⁰ et XVIII⁰ siècles, 1912; Duman,
Agrarian Policy of the Manchu Government in Sinkiang, 1936 (in Russian).

Manchus. The fifth Dalai Lama was in fact the first Dalai Lama of full pontifical status, for it was only after his status had been defined that his four predecessors were posthumously raised to the same dignity.[36]

Briefly, then, the rule of the Dalai Lamas may be defined as follows. It does not represent the extension of the power of Lhasa over the country. On the contrary, it was founded on the projection toward Lhasa, and the areas of greater Tibetan population, of the power of the numerically weaker but strategically stronger Tibetans of the north, allied first with Mongols and then with the Manchu conquerors of China. The status of the Dalai Lama as the supreme pontiff is, moreover, modified in certain important respects by the status of the Panchan Lama of Tashilhumpo as a secondary pontiff. There is a recondite and typically ecclesiastical explanation of the high position of the Panchan Lama, who is regarded as "holier" in certain strictly limited respects than the Dalai Lama.[37] Probably the true explanation is that in the fifteenth century, when the power of the north was beginning to penetrate into southern Tibet, the monastic potentates of the Tashilhumpo region allied themselves with the northerners and thus acquired a position of relatively high privilege. In short, there is a rough analogy between the way in which the Manchus allied themselves with certain of the northern Chinese, conquered the whole of China, and set up their capital at Peking, and the way in which the northern Tibetans allied themselves with the Tashilhumpo Tibetans and took over the capital at Lhasa. The analogy may even be pursued further, for just as the Manchu-Chinese capital at Peking eventually reduced Manchuria to provincial status, so also the ecclesiastical capital at Lhasa eventually

---

[36] Waddell, *op. cit.*, pp. 229-232.

[37] *Ibid.* Grenard, on the other hand (*op. cit.*, p. 376) realistically points out that the Panchan Lama is important because he controls a separate territorial enclave and is temporally inferior to the Dalai Lama "only because his principality is smaller."

made provincials out of the once dominant northern Tibetans.

At this point it is possible to set out the chief characteristics of the combined mechanism of the internal and imperial rule of Tibet through the Lama church. The pontifical succession through "reincarnation" is far less divine than political. The "doctrine of reincarnation," as applied to the Dalai and Panchan Lamas and other minor "Living Buddhas," was invented as a justification for the fact that those who controlled the political power found it convenient to select and appoint the incumbents of church office. Native Tibetan control of the internal affairs of Tibet therefore tended to produce nepotism so as to keep the mechanism of the church in the hands of powerful families. Foreign imperial control, on the other hand, especially under the Manchus, manipulated the apparently impersonal apparatus of the church in a different way, selecting as pontiffs not merely minor children but children of insignificant families which would be unable to use their fortuitous new connection in forming new regional or aristocratic factions.[38]

Naturally, a procedure of this kind does not usually appear in history as a sudden invention but is more likely to be a product of growth and evolution. Preliminary and anticipatory forms of the Tibetan pontifical succession can be detected long before the modern functions of the Dalai and Panchan Lamas became standardized.[39] There are also early variant forms that have managed to survive. In certain monasteries the hierarchic succession has remained

[38] The Wei-Tsang T'ungchih (1896 edit., Ch. 5) and the Ta Ch'ing Huitien (Li Fan Yuan 13, Ch. 738) give the Manchu regulations forbidding the selection of sons of princely families as Living Buddhas, and also the regulations governing the "selection" of the reincarnations of the Dalai Lama, Panchan Lama, and other leading Living Buddhas by drawing lots from an urn. The drawing of lots was preceded by the selection of a panel of candidates by the church authorities; the subterfuge of drawing lots enabled the imperial authorities to make sure of an innocuous choice.

[39] Kublai Khan's nominee as the supreme pontiff of Tibet was succeeded by a nephew (Waddell, op. cit., p. 38).

the perquisite of secular families, thus perpetuating secular aristocratic rule through the apparatus of the church.[40] Instances of this exist in Mongolia[41] as well as Tibet. Generally speaking, however, it can be said that the Manchu Empire succeeded in both Mongolia and Tibet in arresting the processes of tribal and regional alternation and variation, thus maintaining a dead level of stagnation. This was watched over within the outer-Frontier societies by privileged groups, which the imperial power both regulated and supported. The political object was to keep up a balance that would neither lead to Frontier pressure on China nor disturb the poise of empire within China itself by drawing out of China and into the orbit of Frontier affairs any groups, interests, or functions that might lead to an unsettling expansion of the Chinese beyond what had come to be recognized as their proper geographical and environmental limits.

MODERN CONFLICT OF CHINESE AND BRITISH INTERESTS IN TIBET

Stagnation of this kind could endure indefinitely, although in Tibet as in Mongolia the induced artificial rigidity was not absolutely complete. The operation of trade, for instance, encroached on and distorted the officially protected economic and social order. What eventually produced a new situation, however, was the intrusion of Western imperialism into Chinese affairs, deflecting the "natural" changes inherent in the decay of the Manchu dynasty and thus creating a kind of history new to China.

The "secondary imperialism," which was one of these innovations, has already been discussed. War-lord politicians, unable to keep up a frontal resistance against the penetration of Western political and economic imperialism

---

[40] *Ibid.*, p. 233.
[41] Lattimore, Mongols of Manchuria, p. 256, citing Ta Ch'ing Huitien, Li Fan Yuan 13, Ch. 738.

from the Treaty Ports of the coast and the Yangtze, eased the pressure to a certain extent by transmitting some of it to their inland frontiers.[42] By taking over some of the methods of the West they acquired kinds of strength that the Chinese of earlier centuries did not have, and so were able to practice on relatively weaker peoples some of the imperialistic measures from which they themselves were suffering. Thus the conversion of the old Manchu and Mongol domains in Manchuria, together with the Chinese Pale of the lower Liao, into the Chinese provinces of Liaoning (Fengt'ien), Kirin, and Heilungchiang, and the conversion of Inner Mongolia into the provinces of Jehol, Chahar, Suiyuan, and Ninghsia, was matched in Tibet by the formation of the provinces of Ch'inghai (Kokonor), marginal to Kansu, and Hsik'ang (part of it formerly known as Ch'uanpien), marginal to Ssuch'uan and Yünnan. These two provinces define an "Inner Tibet" adjacent to China and analogous to Inner Mongolia, leaving the regions that are still administered directly by Lhasa as an "Outer Tibet" analogous to Outer Mongolia.

In Manchuria and Mongolia the new Chinese expansionism had to contend with the active imperialism of Japan and Tsarist Russia. In Tibet the active Chinese imperialism which aimed at bringing "Inner Tibet" under direct Chinese administration, partly driving out the native tribes and partly forcing them to "become Chinese," and at the same time promoting Chinese colonization, was countered in "Outer Tibet" by the "stationary" imperialism of the British in India—a phenomenon that deserves separate examination.

India, in spite of its extreme diversity of races, languages, religions, climates, methods of agriculture, and types of direct and indirect administration, forms a recognizable entity under British rule. In conquering and occupying it the British moved stage by stage up to an arc

[42] Lattimore, China and the Barbarians, 1934.

of natural inland frontiers. Until they reached these limits every political and territorial acquisition was a profitable accretion, enlarging an empire with a natural center of gravity of its own. Beyond these limits it was unprofitable to expand because expansion became converted into a drag away from the center. The inland frontier of India is to this extent analogous to the Great Wall Frontier of China.[43] It must, however, be divided into two distinct sectors, the Northwest Frontier and the Northeast Frontier.

Of these the Northwest Frontier is closely comparable to the Chinese Great Wall Frontier, with its "Inner Mongolia" of tribal districts and states—divided into two categories, the more and the less closely administered and supervised—running up to the "Durand Line." [44] Beyond the Durand Line is the "Outer Mongolia" of Afghanistan, with Baluchistan lying on the flank as Manchuria lies on the flank of both Inner and Outer Mongolia. The British policy of preventing the coalescence of "inner" and "outer" tribes, by favoring different tribes in different degrees, while evading the unprofitable expense of outright conquest and administration, is cousin german to the ancient Chinese Great Wall policy. The insoluble difficulty is also the same: in dealing with the "inner" tribes the British select and patronize the chieftains because of their tribal functions; but the very fact that these functions are patronized and protected by an overlord power transforms and distorts them,[45] with the result that the planned stability breaks down into an alternating policy of advance into the tribal regions—in order to correct abuses that have become

[43] Lattimore, Origins of the Great Wall, 1937, p. 548.

[44] The Durand Line is the political frontier of India, lying beyond the zone within which the British actually enforce their administration. The zone between the "administrative border" and the Durand Line is known as the "trans-border."

[45] See the interesting anonymous article Tribal Problems of Today (a notice of the career of Sir John Sandeman), 1930; Coatman, The North-West Frontier Province, 1931; Barton, Problems of Law and Order . . . in the North-West Frontier, 1932. See also note 2, p. 244, below.

intolerable under the patronized chiefs—and withdrawal from them in order to evade the expense of permanent occupation.

Along the Northeast Frontier the situation is different. The passages for the invasion of India by land lie along the Northwest Frontier. On the northeast the mountain barriers dividing India from Central Asia and Tibet are so high and wide that military invasion need not be feared. One of the chief incentives for the exploration of the Pamirs, the Karakoram, and Tibet that was conducted at the end of the nineteenth century was the fear that there might exist a route that could be used by artillery and wheeled transport.[46] Once this fear was laid the Northeast Frontier could be considered dead, and the only necessity was to keep it dead. So long as the prestige of both Russia and China could be kept out of these regions the British could also remain quiescent,[47] saving themselves a yearly expenditure of millions of pounds; for it is obvious that the Indian Empire would be financially ruined if it had to provide along the Tibetan frontier fortifications and garrisons like those that hold down the Northwest Frontier Province.

In essence this means that the Tibetan frontier is now for the British a frontier against ideas. Even in 1904, when the Younghusband expedition was sent to Lhasa, its mission was not to prevent a Russian military threat but to put an end to the spread of the prestige of the Tsarist empire. The prestige indispensable to the rule of the British over India demands that their subjects shall not be allowed to see on any horizon the rise of a power even remotely comparable to that of the British. This governs British policy in Tibet. Chinese rule over the whole of Tibet would not greatly threaten India in a military way, but the idea that "native" peoples can gravitate away from

[46] Younghusband, The Heart of a Continent, 1896.
[47] Bell, The North-Eastern Frontier of India, 1930, p. 221.

the British orbit and into the orbit of an Asiatic country like China must be kept out of Indian minds. Consequently, British policy in Tibet aims not even at extensive exploration or the exploitation of possible mineral wealth but simply at keeping Tibet inert under the unchanging rule of native potentates who will look to the British for support against any encroachment by the Chinese or others.

Until quite recently the policy of the Chinese arose out of directly opposite considerations. They were able to exploit Tibet less profitably than either Manchuria or Inner Mongolia; but the prestige value in China itself of an expanding frontier in Tibet was immense, and, in addition, control over the holy places of Lamaism in Tibet had a political value in Mongolia. It is this, rather than contest over natural wealth, that accounts for British support of the Dalai Lama in recent years against Chinese backing of the Panchan Lama. The character of the problem has now changed, partly because the deaths of the Dalai Lama in 1933 and of the Panchan Lama in 1938 have raised acute questions of internal politics and external patronage in the appointment of successors, but much more because China in the course of its war of national liberation against Japan has necessarily been abandoning the "secondary imperialism" of inland expansion. In Tibet as along the Great Wall Frontier proper the question of the day is not how to escape from the reach of China, but how to move inward on China as allies, not subjects, in the struggle for immediate political freedom and for ultimate release from the oppressive bondage inherited from the past. The frontier against the spread of ideas, still patrolled by the British on the Indian side of Tibet, has been thrown open on the Chinese side.

Additional note to note 13, p. 212, above: A valuable study by Robert B. Ekvall (Cultural Relations on the Kansu-Tibetan Border, Chicago, 1939) now clearly proves that among some of the Northeastern Tibetans the valley people are "inferior" and the nomads "superior."

CHAPTER VIII

THE "RESERVOIR" AND THE MARGINAL ZONE

DISTINCTION BETWEEN FRONTIERS AND BOUNDARIES

In discussing each sector of the Inner Asian Frontiers of China it is necessary to distinguish between the terms "boundary" and "frontier." This is because the geographical and historical boundaries conventionally set down as lines on a map represent in fact the edges of zones—or "frontiers." The Great Wall of China itself is evidence of a prodigious political effort kept up for century after century to maintain a linear boundary sharply distinguishing the terrain that it was proper to include in the Chinese *t'ien hsia* or *orbis terrarum* from the barbarian "outer darkness." Yet the fact that there are many variant, alternative, and supplementary lines of Great Wall fortification, which may be studied as the tidemarks of different historical periods, proves that the concept of a linear boundary could never be established as an absolute geographical fact. That which was politically conceived as a sharp edge was persistently spread by the ebb and flow of history into a relatively broad and vague margin.

Nor is this a phenomenon peculiar to Chinese history. The Roman Empire, when it had attained the convenient workable maximum of expansion, attempted to set limits (*limites*) designed to separate that part of Europe which was focused cohesively on Rome from the inchoate Germanic and trans-Danubian "outer darkness," which it was thought better to exclude from the Roman *orbis terrarum*. In modern times the British, after rounding out the convenient limits of their Indian Empire, have attempted to make its political boundaries absolute and permanent. In this they have been favored on the northeast by the abrupt and absolute character of the Tibetan mountain border, where geography comes to the aid of politics; but on the northwest the politically plotted line of sharp demarcation has worn away into something different—a marginal zone. The "Durand Line" of the Indian Northwest Frontier has been transformed in practice into zones of "administered" and "unadministered" tribal territory which are strikingly similar to the Inner and Outer Mongolia of Chinese history.

It is the regular practice, whether dealing with the Roman, the Chinese, or the British-Indian imperial boundaries, to state the historical problem in a one-sided manner. It is assumed that an imperial border policy is concerned solely with keeping out the barbarians—Germans and Slavs in Roman history; Huns, Turks, Mongols, Manchus, and so forth in Chinese history; and Pathans and other tribesmen in contemporary British-Indian policy. This obscures the fact that such a boundary is equally important in another respect: it represents the limit of growth of an imperial system. It is natural to delimit a boundary in geographical terms by including certain kinds of terrain and excluding others, and to justify this by disparagingly characterizing the peoples who inhabit the unwanted terrain as alien and barbarian in language, religion, customs, and "race." The empire that is responsible for defining a boundary takes it for granted that what has been established is a line that is not to be crossed. Yet the very fact that the "barbarians" of the excluded territory are always described as aggressive raiders, attackers, and invaders shows that geographical limits that appear "natural" and inevitable to one society are not necessarily regarded as geographical obstacles by other societies, which may in fact treat them as merely political obstacles.

In short, a major imperial boundary of the kind here considered is not merely a line dividing geographical regions and human societies. It also represents the optimum limit of growth of one particular society. In other words, an imperial boundary that is described as defensive, being supposedly designed to keep out unwanted barbarians, has in fact a double function : it serves not only to keep the outsiders from getting in but to prevent the insiders from getting out.

For the Great Wall Frontier of China I think this has been sufficiently established in the preceding chapters. While the statesmen of China were consciously concerned with the necessity of preventing barbarian attacks from beyond the Great Wall, they were less consciously but nevertheless very seriously engaged in preventing the spread of Chinese and Chinese interests beyond the Great Wall. Even when Chinese administration was pushed out into the outer-Frontier and supported by garrisons, the aim was not expansion but preventive occupation in order to close gaps through which the boundary line itself might be attacked. In order to make this kind of policy effective it was necessary to restrict Chinese enterprise beyond the Great Wall. This was because Chinese who ventured too far beyond the Great Wall became a liability to the state; the business in which they engaged, whether farming or trade, contributed more to the barbarian community than it did to the Chinese community. They passed out of the Chinese orbit. Therefore, in order to prevent Chinese from engaging in activities that contributed more to the strength of the barbarians than to that of China it was necessary to keep the Chinese in China as well as to keep the barbarians out of China.[1]

This aspect of Great Wall history may also be defined in other terms. The society and state of the Chinese were based on an agricultural technique that could be practiced within certain limits of geographical environment. At

---

[1] Chinese statesmen of the first century B.C. gave reasons for keeping the Frontier situation "in hand" which had even more to do with the necessity of controlling the Chinese than with the desirability of guarding against invasion. Compare Chapter XV, below.

first these limits were relatively vague. As technical practice improved, however, it was adapted more and more closely to a more and more limited range of environment. The most conspicuous requirement was water for irrigation. Step for step, moreover, as the dominant economy attached itself to certain primary requirements, the society and the state based on these requirements became limited in their adaptability and flexibility. When the combined economy, society, and state, interacting on each other, had finally worked out the range of practices most profitable and satisfactory to them, they thereby defined also the geographical and environmental limits within which they could prosper. Within these limits "China" could expand and prosper. Economically the process was one of accretion, because each new territory acquired made it possible to employ the recognized agricultural practices on a larger scale. Socially the process was one of increasing returns, because it supported a larger number of families holding the kinds of wealth and power that were already recognized, while at the same time it meant more wealth and more power for the families that were already wealthy and powerful. Politically the process was one of centripetal growth, because to the state the profit of expansion was far greater than the cost.

Toward the south the range of Chinese expansion proved to be more or less unlimited, but not toward the north and northwest. The steppes of Mongolia and western Manchuria and the high wastes of Tibet denied the primary Chinese economic requirement of intensive, irrigated agriculture. The forest wilderness of eastern and northern Manchuria and the scattered oases of Chinese Turkistan denied the social and political requirements of dense population in contiguous areas. In these outer Frontier regions, therefore, the process of accretion was converted into one of dispersion, because in entering "un-Chinese" terrain the Chinese had to modify or abandon their Chinese economy, thus weakening their attachment to other Chinese. Increasing returns were converted into diminishing returns, because those who ruled and prospered in the Chinese order of society could not hold their advantage when the environment favored the already established barbarian societies. Centripetal gain, accordingly, was converted into centrifugal loss; for Chinese who left the Chinese orbit and accommodated themselves to an unChinese economic and social order inevitably began either to adhere to barbarian rulers or to practice barbarian forms of rule themselves—to the disadvantage of China.

FRONTIER CONDITIONS AND POLICIES AS ILLUSTRATED BY THE NORTHWEST FRONTIER OF INDIA

Considerations that are similar, though not identical, clearly apply to the Roman Empire and even to the British-Indian Empire, which is the result of alien conquest and not of native growth. India is imperially profitable because its large, dense population and cheap labor, and the differential between the backward economy of India as a whole and the highly developed economy of Great Britain give British capital the advantages it needs. Capital, it is true, knows no patriotism, and it is conceivable that some British enterprises could make money in the marginal regions of the Northwest Frontier, which the British do not wish to bring under direct administration. Here the governing consideration appears to be the rate of profit rather than the bare possibility of profit. Within India the costs of administration and profits of exploitation have necessarily to be averaged over poor and rich regions, but on the outer margin of the Northwest Frontier it is plain that the possible profit to individuals would not compensate the state for the cost of enlarging the conquered, garrisoned, policed, and administered area. Consequently, a British investor can place his capital profitably either in India, under imperial rule, or in countries like China and

Persia if he is willing to operate as a concessionaire; but the marginal territories of the Northwest Frontier are neither one thing nor the other. The encouragement there of British enterprise would only draw away from the imperial center of gravity in India more strength than it could contribute. Imperially and economically the line of the Northwest Frontier marks the limit of diminishing returns.

Frontiers of this kind form and tend to harden as the result both of conscious policy and of the less conscious trend of ordinary administrative working practice. The line that marks an imperial boundary on a map is a diagram of the limit of outward spread from a center of imperial growth, but such a diagram can only be approximate. Both by conscious methods and unconscious trends an imperial state can slow down its own outward spread, but this does not take into account the processes of growth and rate of development of the excluded peoples. It is at this point that absolute concepts break down into practical compromise. The needs and motives of the cis-frontier society and state must make concessions to those of the trans-frontier peoples. The very act of drawing a boundary is an acknowledgment that the peoples excluded are not under control and cannot be ruled by command. They must be dealt with by negotiation.

The form of negotiation and compromise does not depend only on the imperial state, though it appears to be the positive agent in establishing the boundary. It also depends on the excluded peoples, who are nominally, as the objects of exclusion, in a negative or passive position. They may in fact be meek and acquiescent. In this case they attract the enterprise, particularly the trading enterprise, of individuals and groups within the imperial state. There thus arises a conflict between minority interest and majority interest within the imperial state. While the general policy of the state seeks to establish the limit at which its interests can remain centripetal, and to prevent excessive expansion from passing over into centrifugal dispersion, this policy is resisted and evaded by the particular interests of traders, would-be colonizers, ambitious political and military careerists, and so forth, who see opportunities for themselves across the border. Thus there grows up a nexus of border interests which resents and works against the central interest. This phenomenon of the border society, differing in orientation from the bulk of the nation, recurs in history at all times and in many places.

Or the emphasis may be across the border rather than within it, if the excluded "barbarians" feel strong enough to attempt conquest, to raid sporadically over the boundary, or to insist on the kinds of trade that they themselves want. In such cases the frontier-maintaining empire may adopt a policy ranging anywhere from steadfast patrol of the border and negotiation only with representatives who come in from the trans-border, to active intervention with insistence on the right of supervising and controlling trans-border affairs. The first alternative is known to the British in India as the "close border policy"; it amounts to an attempt to make absolute in practice the concept of a frontier that both restrains and excludes. The second in British terminology is known as the "forward policy"; it amounts to the negation, in practice, of the concept of a linear boundary. The result is to create a situation in which:

strictly speaking, there are two frontiers. . . . There is the so-called administrative border, which divides the five regularly administered districts . . . from the tribal territory. . . . Now, the hills again are divided from Afghanistan by what we call the Durand Line . . . the tribal territory, although not administered by us as we administer the ordinary districts of the Frontier Province, is nevertheless part of the greater India.[2]

[2] Coatman, The North-West Frontier Province, 1931, p. 336. Compare also the other references in note 45, p. 235, above. All of these articles are in the *Royal Central Asian Journal* (until the end of 1930, *Journal of the Central Asian Society*). They have the special value of being quasi-professional discussions of the problems with which members of the services

Within this anomalous territory, the frontier zone beyond the boundary proper, methods may vary from the "Sandeman system" of consultation and arbitration (together with giving subsidy) [3] to the system of "non-intervention tempered by punitive expeditions," [4] which again is akin to the "close border policy."

However erratically a border policy may swing between the possible extremes, the result averages out over a long period of time as a negation of both the containing and the excluding functions of the boundary in question. Inevitably the boundary-maintaining state becomes involved beyond the boundary in the affairs of the peoples whom the boundary was designed to exclude. A phenomenon of great importance then becomes apparent. Gradually the idea of negation—of a limit or an end—inherent in the concept of a linear boundary is modified to one of neutralization and transferred from the physical boundary itself to the peoples in the frontier beyond. Outer-frontier policy develops into a search for methods by which the "outer barbarians" can be neutralized, so that they neither press inward against the boundary nor draw out beyond it the interventionist activity of the boundary-maintaining state.

Naturally, the exact character of the neutralizing policy varies according to expediency, being modified by such questions as terrain, the cost of military intervention, the relative stage of development of both the boundary-maintaining empire and the outer-frontier tribes, the risks and profits of trade, and many other things. In general terms, however, it can be said of the Roman, Chinese, and British-Indian empires alike that the method that worked best was

responsible for administering British imperial policy in Asia have to deal year in and year out. See also in the same *Journal* the following references, which have not been separately cited: Wigram, Defence in the North-West Frontier, 1937; Cunningham, Reforms in the North-West Frontier, 1937; Brock, Air Operations on the N.W.F., 1930, 1932.

[3] Bruce, The Sandeman Policy . . . Today, 1932.
[4] Tribal Problems of Today (anonymous), 1930.

one of enlisting the services of the very tribes that were supposedly excluded by the boundary, thus turning them about so that they faced away from the boundary instead of toward it. In this way the abstract concept of an absolute boundary was transformed administratively and politically into a system of zones: the boundary itself, with a more or less differentiated population adhering to it even on the hither side; the "auxiliary" tribes in the frontier zone adjacent to the boundary, the outer edge of whose territory was treated as an outer-frontier zone; and beyond that, again, unregenerate barbarism. The policy worked as well as it did because it was a compromise between the interests of the boundary-maintaining state, the interests of particular groups within the state, and the interests of border tribal groups. Nevertheless, it was a method that haunted the imperial state responsible for it, because it created a sword of two edges capable of striking outward when held in a strong hand but of cutting inward when the hand weakened.

From border societies of this kind, linked with boundary-maintaining empires, were drawn the "barbarian auxiliaries" of Rome and the "tributary barbarians" of China; from a similar society the British Empire in India recruits both regular troops and tribal levies. From the same societies came invaders and conquerors of both Rome and China; and the people of the same kind with whom the British now deal are as dangerous as they are useful:

. . . the North-West Frontier, as it happens, is one of the few spots on the earth's surface where we, the British, if I may use a homely metaphor, can take a knockout blow. It is like the solar plexus or point of the jaw in a boxer: if he gets a blow there he is knocked out. The question of the North-West Frontier . . . is thus bound to be not only of interest, but of painful and vital interest to us.[5]

[5] Coatman, op. cit., p. 335.

Since the historical phenomena concerned can be traced through such a long course of time and such a great range of territory, any inferences that can be drawn from them must be widely applicable.

THE INNER ASIAN "RESERVOIR" OF TRIBAL INVASIONS

Thus far I have referred chiefly to the Northwest Frontier of India in order to show how broad is the subject of interest. From what has been said in earlier chapters, though, the pertinence to the geographical structure and historical processes of China's Great Wall Frontier is unmistakable. The physical structure of the boundary proper, the inner Frontier zone, and the outer Frontier zone is clearest in the relationship between the Great Wall and Inner and Outer Mongolia, but it exists also in Manchuria (Great Wall, Chinese Pale, Willow Palisade; with Mongols on the west and northwest and Manchus on the east and northeast); in Chinese Turkistan (taken together with the Moslem Pale of Kansu and Ninghsia); [6] and in a vaguer form in Tibet, where the mountain escarpment takes the place of the Great Wall.

Some years ago, in attempting to analyze the Inner Mongolian type of differentiated Frontier tribes and to relate their historical function to their geographical position, I used the term "reservoir" or "reservoir of tribal invasions." [7] The argument ran as follows. For more than two thousand years China has been recurrently attacked by northern invaders. Frequently the invaders founded kingdoms occupying part of China and sometimes empires ruling the whole of China. At such times part of the invading people entered China, but a part was left behind in the territory adjacent to the Great Wall on the north. This rear guard of the invaders defended the conquered terri-

[6] Lattimore, Chinese Turkistan, 1933, p. 98.
[7] Lattimore, Manchuria: Cradle of Conflict, 1932, especially pp. 36-42.

tory from any rival tribes that might come down from the still remoter north; but it also served as the "reservoir" from which were drawn officials and garrison troops for the rule of China. North of the "reservoir" lay the "lands of the unregenerate," the tribes that had not participated in the conquest made by the lords of the reservoir. Because of this, Inner Mongolia (taken as the type of all such border zones) had a regional importance transcending both its tribal and its cultural importance: it was the key to the sovereignty of North China and sometimes of all China. In periods of Chinese ascendancy, it is true, it was the area in which the outward spread of Chinese political control and cultural influence had the maximum effect; but even more important was the way in which it served as the line of departure for invading conquerors of China.

As far as it goes I do not believe there is anything wrong in this approach, but it does not go far enough. The historical problems are not limited to the alternating "imperial expansion" of the Chinese (political conquest of nomad territory) and the "invasion" or "conquest" of China, where the environment favors agriculture, by nomads whose steppe environment favored a pastoral economy. The tendency generated within China itself to check Chinese expansion at the line of the Great Wall must also be considered. This tendency, in turn, raised up its own òpposition by emphasizing the difference between the majority interest, which held back from any attempt to integrate politically the irrigated agriculture of China and the pastoralism of the steppe, and the minority interest of border Chinese whose activities were bound up with political as well as economic exchanges between the ploughed lands and the unploughed steppe.

Similarly, in the steppe itself a homogeneous nomad pastoralism prevailed most of the time in the outer Frontier, but the inner Frontier was held by border nomads who looked part of the time toward their kindred of the steppes and part of the time toward the agriculture and cities of China. The tendency, not always equally strong, for the border Chinese to cleave apart from the main body of China was thus matched by the tendency of border nomads to differentiate themselves from outlying nomads.

The problem as a whole therefore needs to be restated. Primary societies formed within the primary environments. Of these the most important were the river lands of China and the steppe of Mongolia. There were also other environments that were primary in the sense that they nourished distinct societies, like the forests of Manchuria and the oases and deserts of Central Asia; but these were not of a major order historically. The primary societies produced marginal, secondary societies partly by interaction and partly also from within themselves, because each had its limit of profitable spread and was consequently subject to the law of diminishing returns. In this way the simple action and reaction of nomads and farmers became an extremely complicated multiple process, the secondary phenomena subdividing into tertiary and quaternary levels of development, and so forth.

An infinite series of types of political state can accordingly be distinguished. In the fourth and third centuries B.C. the states of Ch'in in Shensi and Chao in Shansi drew part of their strength from the ascendancy of border Chinese over border nomads.[8] The Han Empire at its height, in the first century after Christ, made China as a whole stronger than the steppe and Central Asia as a whole. From the fourth to the sixth century the Northern Wei asserted the domination of the most important inner part of the trans-Frontier over the most important part of North China. Under the Mongols in the thirteenth century the outermost or "unregenerate" barbarians

[8] Lattimore, Origins of the Great Wall, 1937.

flooded this "inner" trans-Frontier or "reservoir" and combined the primary and secondary peoples of the steppe in a general conquest of all China.[9]

Moreover, each gradation of society, whether in the main the product of its own environment or partly influenced by the interaction of other societies, reacted toward its environment in an effort to stabilize its prevailing social order within the geographical area that it occupied. Mixed societies, trying to adjust themselves, were likely either to extend or change their territory or to alter the components and proportions of their economic and political systems. Chinese of the border, either on their own initiative or backed by the power of the whole state, tried at times to push agriculture farther into the steppe; but on the other hand, instead of being pushed agriculture was also at times drawn into the steppe by rulers of steppe origin. Nor was it a question only of the spread of agriculture. Under the Orkhon Turks an intensive irrigated agriculture was patronized far in the north of the steppe, in Outer Mongolia, in the eighth century of the Christian Era;[10] but there is also the tradition that Chingghis Khan proposed to exterminate the agricultural population of North China and replace it with herdsmen.[11] Steppe rulers, again, who forced their way into China regularly converted themselves into rulers of a Chinese type; but border Chinese, venturing into the steppe, were equally

[9] For a summary list of barbarian conquest-states in China from the fourth to the fourteenth centuries, see Lattimore, Manchuria: Cradle of Conflict, 1932, p. 37.

[10] Radlov (Die alttürkischen Inschriften der Mongolei, 1894) and Thomsen (Inscriptions de l'Orkhon déchiffrés, 1896) have restored the text of the Orkhon Turkish inscriptions. These reveal vividly the fluctuation between forest tribalism and sinization, but do not mention agriculture. However, this is only to be expected, as the language used is "traditional" and exalted, and derives from the tribal history of the Turks more than from their later cultural borrowings, in spite of the evident Chinese influence. Thomsen (op. cit , pp. 67-68) cites a translation from the Chinese which mentions the sending of seed-millet and agricultural implements to the Turks.

[11] Fox, Genghis Khan, 1936, pp. 244-245. The tradition is that Yehlü Ch'uts'ai, a Chinese of Khitan descent, persuaded him that it would be more profitable to rule and tax a subject race. See Yüan Shih, Ch. 146.

likely to graft their political power onto a steppe-tribal organization.

Where, in all this welter of simple and complex economic practices, ways of living, and social orders, are the prime impulses of historical change to be sought? Given the broad classification of geographical regions and environments, we can assign to them the crude categories of agricultural, pastoral, and forest peoples. We can also assume a spread of the major orders of society until they met and overlapped along the general line of the Great Wall, and infer from this the appearance of intermediate societies. From this point onward, however, where is the center of gravity of Great Wall history to be placed—in China, in the steppe, or in the marginal Frontier lands? These are the proper subjects of the remainder of this book.

PART II

THE LEGENDARY AND EARLIEST
HISTORICAL AGES

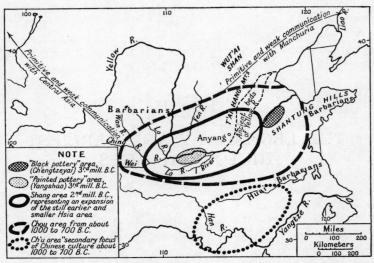

MAP 9—Centers of Chinese culture in the Yellow River and Yangtze River valleys, 3rd millennium B.C. to 700 B.C.

CHAPTER IX

DIFFERENTIATION OF CHINESE AND BARBARIANS

On turning from the combined geographical and historical survey of the Great Wall Frontier, sector by sector, to a study of the historical origins of the Frontier as a whole, we are at once confronted by difficult problems. In its main lines the Great Wall emphasizes politically a geographical demarcation. To the south lie the lands of Chinese agriculture, to the north the lands of the steppe nomadic societies, to the northwest the oases of Chinese Central Asia. Beyond the western end of the Wall are the high wastes of Tibet; beyond the eastern end are southern Manchuria—repeatedly tending, because of its geographical character, to become a "little China"—and the forests of eastern and northern Manchuria.

It by no means follows, however, that we can deal *ab initio* with the histories of separate primitive steppe, forest, oasis, and Tibetan societies, each developing and spreading until the whole group met the developing and spreading Chinese and made it necessary for them to mark off the Great Wall Frontier. Though we have definite knowledge of neolithic and even earlier cultures that overlapped both into North China and into Manchuria, Mongolia, Central Asia, and probably Tibet, these are all general primitive cultures, not specialized "Chinese" or "steppe" cultures.[1]

Historically, therefore, we must deal first with the wide distribution of a primitive society so undifferentiated that

[1] Bishop (Origin and Development of the Traction-Plow, 1936) puts the first appearance of pastoral nomadism in Mongolia at about "the middle of the first millennium B.C." Before that, in neolithic times, the culture of Mongolia was of a "sedentary 'peasant' type."

it could make use of both the Chinese environment and the steppe environment and its adjacent regions. Thus the problem of origins is a problem of differentiation. The first historical movements and changes concern the manner in which peoples of a roughly equal primitiveness began to diverge from each other, not only following different trends of evolution but following them at different rates of speed. Since the earliest Chinese historical and quasi-historical material is much richer than that of the other societies, it is necessary to make at least a survey of the origins of Chinese history as a whole before approaching the particular history of the Great Wall Frontier. For the Chinese, at a certain stage in their own evolution and along the line of the Great Wall, did not merely encounter societies different from their own; to a significant extent the evolution of China itself created these inimical fringing societies.

GENERAL CHARACTER OF NEOLITHIC CULTURE IN CHINA

The Chinese are the bearers of the most important living culture that can be traced back in unbroken derivation to the Stone Age. A few objects of daily use, like knives and spinning whorls and pottery vessels, preserve shapes that were once used in the same geographical regions by men who did not yet know the working of metal.[2] More than that, the oldest historical documents of the Chinese, going back to the beginning of the first millennium B.C. and incorporating still older material, can be linked up with inscriptions on bone and tortoise shell of about the fourteenth century B.C. These inscriptions, in a writing so elaborate that it predicates a long anterior development, carry the edge of Chinese history back into culture strata which prove that the use of stone survived into the Age of Bronze and even the Iron Age. Certain characteristics

[2] Creel, Studies in Early Chinese Culture, 1937, pp. 173-174; Andersson, Children of the Yellow Earth, 1934, pp. 204-223.

of these strata link up with even earlier sites occupied by people who left behind them no metal of any kind.

It is true that this continuity is lacking in many details. There is even yet not a great deal that can be said of neolithic China, but then there is not really much that it is absolutely essential to know. What we do know is enough to establish a few general principles. The "China" to which these principles apply means the middle Yellow River valley. It was only gradually, as will be seen from the later discussion, that the Yangtze region came within the horizon of ancient China.

Physically, some at least of the neolithic people of North China were of the same stock as the North Chinese of today; moreover, these people overlapped into Manchuria, Mongolia, and the northwestern corridor leading through Kansu to Central Asia.[3] How far toward the Yangtze and South China they spread it is impossible to say; but it is reasonable to suppose that then, as in later times, there was a transition toward different but kindred physical types. In point of remoter ancestry, the "Peking Man" discoveries open up the possibility that the neolithic men of North China, or some of them, were descended from a paleolithic stock native to the same region.[4]

Culturally, even the little that can be put together about neolithic hunting, fishing, and agriculture makes it possible to distinguish between primitive and mature levels. At the primitive level there was a general uniformity which was more important than local specialization. Fish were caught and birds and animals hunted (and presumably also trapped) wherever they could be found. Edible grasses, plants, and fruits were also gathered, and it is probable that this was the level at which agriculture originated in a desultory encouragement of the spread and reproduction

[3] Creel, *op. cit.*, pp. 153-155; Black, Human Skeletal Remains from Sha Kuo T'un, 1925; also The Prehistoric Kansu Race, in Andersson, Preliminary Report, 1925.
[4] Creel, *loc. cit.*

of wild plants already known. This was also the level at which first the dog and then the pig were rather widely domesticated.[5]

In other words, this was a level at which human society was as yet so crude that it did not make specialized use of different environments. It was able to survive within a rather wide range of environment, but it tended to make the same kind of use of every environment that it penetrated. One group was differentiated from another only by such obvious and accidental usages as greater reliance on game where game was most plentiful or on fishing where fish were easily to be caught.

Nomadism did not yet exist even in the steppe in the sense of deliberate movement from pasture to pasture with controlled herds. Migration must be reckoned on, however, for groups must have moved away from places where they had exhausted the game or even the soil. Movement of this kind undoubtedly increased the scope of war, trade, and the borrowing of techniques. Movement in rather small groups was probably the norm. It is easy to imagine the perils that would deter a solitary wanderer. The migration of whole "races" would be even more difficult, in a different way. A low level of culture means lack of ability to organize and to store up or transport the accumulated resources necessary for the movement of large bodies of people. Even for a relatively advanced neolithic society the movement of a thousand people for a hundred miles must have been more than ten times as difficult as the movement of a hundred people for ten miles. It is likely to have been at least a hundred times as difficult.

For estimating the critical phases of change in a long and for the most part slow process of evolution it is necessary to form some conception of the manner in which the gradual increment of individual and family experience

[5] Bishop, Neolithic Age in Northern China, 1933, pp. 394, 396: "There is no trace whatever of a pastoral form of life."

is accumulated as a social fund, storing up the energy for evolutionary momentum. It is necessary to see, at least in the mind's eye, a world in which no man knew how to work metal, in which all culture was neolithic in kind, and yet in which some stone-using men were so much more advanced and some so much more backward that the range of difference between them very nearly approached a difference in quality or kind. At the lower end of this range the social accumulation of experience is possible—the acquisition of knowledge that can be transferred from one individual to another but does not necessarily result in immediate and significant social change. At the upper end this fund of experience has been drawn on and put to use. The society as a whole has gone forward; it has more or less done everything possible within one stage of evolution, and further progress is likely to precipitate it rather suddenly into a newer and higher stage.

Two Zones of Neolithic Culture

At least the rough outlines of a chart of this kind can be filled in from the knowledge of neolithic China that is already available. Two major zones of Chinese neolithic culture can be recognized. In the western part of North China there was a relatively crude "painted pottery" culture. Towns and even solidly built dwellings were rare—though G. D. Wu has recently described a "big" city in this culture area, on a site "continuously occupied throughout the whole period" up to the Shang.[6] In the eastern part there was a "black pottery" culture, which was more advanced. Walled towns were built. One, which has been excavated, measured about 450 by 390 meters.[7] The zones of the two cultures approached each other in the region of the great bend of the Yellow River. At the Hou Kang site, near Anyang (the center of the bronze culture of the

[6] Wu, Prehistoric Pottery in China, 1938, p. 77; Creel, *op. cit.*, p. 179.
[7] Creel, *loc. cit.*

Shang period), there is a pre-bronze "painted pottery" stratum overlain by a "black pottery" stratum, also pre-bronze; but there is no continuity between the two levels, for apparently the site was left unoccupied for a period.[8]

In comparing these two neolithic cultures we may say that the "painted pottery" was "early" in the sense of being less evolved, while the "black pottery" was "late" and more highly evolved. Does this mean that there was an evolution from "painted pottery" to "black pottery," combined with migration and expansion from the eastern edge of the "painted pottery" area, or does it mean that the two cultures were on the whole independent of each other and existed side by side until the more advanced "black pottery" people began to encroach westward on the "painted pottery" people? Wu holds that there was a definite chronological—and therefore evolutionary—progression from the cruder "painted pottery" to the more advanced "black pottery." This involves the assumption that when a "black pottery" site is found without an underlying "painted pottery" stratum, the site must have been occupied after the age of the "painted pottery" had closed—at least in that region.[9]

Wu may prove to be correct; but this does not remove the possibility—in fact, the probability—that even if the "black pottery" culture originated as an evolutionary advance at the eastern edge of the "painted pottery" area and then expanded farther to the east, the more backward "painted pottery" survived for a considerable time in the western area. Either under the hypothesis of two culture areas independent of each other, or of two areas one of which evolved from and separated from the other, the possibility of a focus of higher culture contemporary with a focus of lower culture must be admitted.

Geographical environment should here be taken into

8 *Ibid.*, p. 171.
9 Wu, *op. cit.*

account as the setting within which social evolution took place. For a stone-using people the environment is of immense importance. It is not the potential resources that matter but those that can be put to use by the most weakly developed and organized people. If these immediate resources are limited the people may remain virtually timeless and unchanging, like the Eskimos or the primitive Australians. Even in potentially rich environments a stone-using people may be held back indefinitely by the fact that the first steps are too difficult to take. The social reasons for this are even more important than the technical reasons. The people of a thinly scattered, weakly organized jungle society, for instance, may acquire metal implements by trade and yet not be transformed rapidly into a new kind of society. The mere fact that they can now cut down trees and clear land which previously they would have had to leave alone, or clear by fire, is not enough. They may still be slow to change their methods unless their habits of thought have been conditioned to make use of the advantages of metal by the social organization and individual desires already developed out of their previous way of life. These considerations are especially important in establishing the difference between primitive society in the relatively open country of North China and in the trans-Yangtze jungles of ancient South China.

On the other hand, a people with no knowledge of metal whatever can progress to a remarkable maturity of culture and complexity of social organization if the environment makes easy the all-important first steps. In North China, and particularly in the region about the great bend of the Yellow River, precisely the right conditions existed. Here game abounded, and also seed-bearing grasses, probably including millet; hemp provided a textile fiber.[10] The soft

---

[10] Wittfogel, Foundations and Stages of Chinese Economic History, 1935, p. 37.

loess earth,[11] easily worked with stone tools, favored the transition from the gathering of wild plants to early agriculture. Farther to the east the lower Yellow River undoubtedly changed its main course often, overflowing into marshes that had to be drained before agriculture was possible[12] except at the edge of the Shantung hills,[13] which accordingly are among the important known centers of neolithic life in China. Farther to the west the climate became steppe-like, even well on the hither side of the true steppe. The rainfall was probably then as now more uncertain than in the east, so that the profits of agriculture were not so regular.

About the great bend, however, and in Shantung, agriculture could become predominant even in a neolithic society, making possible a relatively dense population and opening the way to a political organization of settlements and even towns, ruled perhaps by chiefs of a warrior class (the forerunners of the feudal nobility) and fed and maintained by peasants who were enslaved either as individuals or as a class (the depressed ancestors of the feudal serfs). This was the region in all of North China where men could best get ready for the use of metal. Once they were ready it was more or less an accident whether they discovered metal for themselves or acquired it by borrowing.

THE PROBLEM OF THE INTRODUCTION OF BRONZE-AGE CULTURE

Bronze is the undoubted link between neolithic China and the China of the Shang age, but the way in which the link was welded into the chain of evolution has yet to be clarified by historical methods. Bronze work of superb

[11] Wittfogel, Wirtschaft und Gesellschaft Chinas, 1931, p. 35.
[12] Ibid., p. 36.
[13] Creel, op. cit. p. 176; Bishop, op. cit., p. 392: "As in Europe, so in China, settlement in neolithic times sought the drier and more open lands, since these could more easily be brought under cultivation by people having no effective means of clearing forests or draining marshes."

quality is associated with the Shang culture of Anyang, in Honan, going back to about the fourteenth century B.C.[14] This was a well developed culture with a sophisticated writing (an ancestral form of Chinese, most of which can be read). Historically it presents two problems: that of its evolution from neolithic cultures, and the problem of bronze itself—whether this technique was evolved out of the antecedent Chinese neolithic or introduced from outside the field of Chinese neolithic history.

It is beyond dispute that the Shang culture had strong roots going down into the "black pottery" neolithic culture [15] and somewhat weaker roots going down into the "painted pottery" culture.[16] Creel mentions a "black pottery" level that is "without doubt a Shang cultural deposit" [17] but contains no bronze. About thirty "black pottery" sites are now known in the several districts around Anyang.[18] "In view, then, of such evidence as is now available," Creel concludes, "it is distinctly possible that Shang culture was a branch of this same black pottery culture upon which was grafted the technique of making bronze and certain other culture traits." [19] Moreover, he mentions a "painted pottery" level underlying the two "black pottery" levels.[20] There is thus a fairly complete time scale reaching from neolithic to bronze, but it is without a complementary evolution scale. There is a gap between the "painted pottery" and "black pottery" levels, one being sometimes superimposed on the other but with-

[14] The best general reference is Creel's Studies in Early Chinese Culture, on which I have already drawn so freely. Later and more ambitious in its classification of pottery is G. D. Wu's book, cited above, note 6. The whole discussion will be carried further in Wittfogel's Economic and Social History of China, which is to appear in 1940, and will be based on archeological material, ancient inscriptions, and the modern Chinese scientific literature.

[15] Creel, op. cit., pp. 191, 194.
[16] Ibid., p. 173.
[17] Ibid., p. 172.
[18] Ibid., p. 193.
[19] Ibid., p. 194.
[20] Ibid., p. 171.

out continuity. Above all, there is no continuity between the "black pottery" site described as "without doubt a Shang cultural deposit" [21] but without bronze, and the Shang sites that do have bronze.

Although linkage with the "painted pottery" neolithic is weaker, it can also be traced. "Even in this culture," according to Creel, "we find types of artifacts which are also found in Shang culture and which are not found in Europe or the Near East." [22]

While the evolutionary process cannot be traced in full, it can be held that the Shang culture did in certain respects evolve out of the main neolithic cultures in North China. The separate problem of bronze must next be considered. Was the use of bronze technique imported into China? If so, was it acquired by trade and imitation, or was it part of the superior equipment of invaders who were able with their bronze weapons to conquer the neolithic people of China? Or was the technique independently discovered in China? These have always been considered the main aspects of the problem.

Each aspect has its difficulties. Not only is the bronze work of the Shang period of high quality, but it has usually been considered axiomatic that the earlier a Chinese bronze can be dated the better it is both artistically and in technical workmanship.[23] This is held to be a strong reason for believing that the use of bronze was brought to China suddenly, in a form already highly developed, and probably by invaders. It is also agreed that the most likely line of penetration for invaders is that running from the oases of Central Asia into northwest China.[24] On the other hand, no neolithic sites lying between the Shang cultural

[21] *Ibid.*, p. 172.

[22] *Ibid.*, p. 173.

[23] *Ibid.*, p. 233: "Chinese bronze vessels are equal to the finest objects of the sort ever produced anywhere by man. Shang bronze vessels, as a group, are probably the finest of Chinese bronzes."

[24] V. K. Ting, How China Acquired Her Civilisation, 1931, p. 3; Bishop, Beginnings of North and South in China, 1934, p. 307.

focus at Anyang and northwest China, or between Anyang and any other part of China, have revealed clear evidence of a line of invasion, or of stages of conquest, or even stages of cultural infiltration. It is to be noted, however, that Andersson's finds in Kansu, on the line of supposed cultural penetration, do include very *crude* copper and bronze.[25]

Against the possibility that the use of bronze was evolved independently in China the argument is brief but has always been considered crushing. No evidence of evolution has been recognized.[26]

Here the problem is usually allowed to rest, but I think the attempt to solve it can be carried a little further. The main argument against the introduction of bronze from the northwest *in a high form* is that it predicates invaders, or at least carriers, of a superior order of culture. If these hypothetical invaders or carriers moved so rapidly from the Near East or Central Asia that they left no traces in northwest China, they must have been culturally very superior indeed. If they were not able to move with this rapidity it is astonishing that no traces have been found either of their own intermediate settlements or of their influence on the neolithic culture of northwest China, by either conquest or trade. Nor is there evidence, in the area that includes both "black pottery" and Shang sites, of a suddenness of conquest matching the suddenness of the appearance of bronze.

[25] Andersson (Preliminary Report, 1925, p. 30) speaks of his bronze finds in Kansu as "small and plain." See also Creel, *op. cit.*, pp. 232-234, with further reference to Andersson, Der Weg über die Steppen, 1929.

[26] V. K. Ting, *op. cit.*, p. 11. Bishop (*loc. cit.*) believes that "the Bronze Age civilization, as an integrated complex, reached China by way of the Central Asiatic steppe belt." On the other hand, Bergman in his Archaeological Researches in Sinkiang, 1939, a valuable report of the findings of the Sven Hedin expedition of 1928-31 in comparison with previous material, shows the weakness of the links as yet discovered between Kansu and Western Central Asia (pp. 22-25). Turfan is the most likely locality for further finds, but Bergman seems inclined to believe that cultural discoveries traveled not so much by the migration of bodies of people as by filtration through a number of already established agricultural settlements.

Therefore it seems to me necessary to work on the compromise hypothesis that bronze was introduced into China at a crude, not high, level of technical development, and not by superior conquerors but by the processes of cultural "drift" and borrowing. This involves the important assumption that the knowledge of how to work in bronze filtered past the settlements of neolithic people in the western part of North China, whose cultural development was too low to enable them to make any advance in the use of it, until it reached settlements about the great bend of the Yellow River, where a distinctly higher level of neolithic culture had been evolved.[27] The people of this higher level were not only able to make use of bronze as soon as they acquired the knowledge of it, but were already so far advanced in their general culture that they were able in a relatively short time so to perfect a technique that had been introduced to them in a crude form that archeologists, working on the evidence that now survives, have formed the impression that the technique must have been already highly developed when it was introduced into China.

Although admittedly speculative, this reasoning respects what seem to me to be major considerations: the fact that the neolithic level of culture was distinctly lower in the western part of North China than in the eastern part, and the fact that what we know of the neolithic period generally allows us to imagine a good deal of trading and culture borrowing and also a rather wide movement of small groups of people. The reasoning I have here urged also allows for differences in the nature of evolution under varying conditions. If either copper or bronze had been

[27] This reasoning is not contradicted, and in fact on the whole is confirmed, by the account that Andersson gives in Der Weg über die Steppen, of a poor and primitive use of copper and bronze in Northwest China. Andersson's account may be held to suggest that a primitive bronze technique was transmitted into China but that it had to penetrate through a "cultural desert" before it reached more advanced neolithic centers farther to the east.

independently discovered by the "black pottery" people we might well look for signs of an early, experimental stage. Knowing, however, that without the knowledge of any metal whatever these people had already progressed as far as the building of small towns, it is not conceding too much to suppose that they were able to take over a new technique in a crude form and develop it very rapidly to a level that better suited their already high neolithic culture—a phenomenon that would stimulate a rapid advance toward the Shang civilization as it is known from the Anyang finds.

SOCIAL AND ECONOMIC EFFECTS OF THE "DISCOVERY" OF BRONZE

The probable social atmosphere of the time must also be considered. What would be the effect on a neolithic society of the "discovery" of copper and bronze—whether the discovery was local, or acquired by trade and imitation, or imposed by conquerors? What factors would govern the further development of the technique, once it had been acquired?

It can be predicated that the knowledge of working in metal did not spread at an equal rate through any primitive society. If it were discovered locally, access to the supply of ore gave some groups an advantage over other groups. Where the knowledge was diffused by trade and borrowing there was again an advantage for those who were near the routes of trade or migration. Where metal weapons were carried by war bands the invaders had an advantage over any stone-using peoples they encountered. In every case there would be a social advantage of the same general type: as between two primitive groups of men of approximately equal wealth, strength, tribal standing, and cultural development it might be more or less accidental which one first became the maker or owner of metal; but those who first acquired metal, no matter how they acquired it, became superior to the others.

If, on the other hand, the two groups were not equal to begin with, then it can be taken for granted that the stronger would seize the metal. From this it follows that, whether or not any given primitive society had begun to develop separate classes of chiefs and subjects before acquiring the knowledge of metal, the mere acquisition of metal would be enough to confirm this kind of social differentiation where it existed already, or to create it if it did not already exist. Whether a metal-using people conquered a stone-using people or whether a metal-using group arose from the midst of a stone-using society, the result would be the same. Either a new structure of society would be created, with a subjugated or tributary lower stratum still restricted largely or wholly to the use of stone, and an upper stratum of rulers armed with metal; or, if the society was already well differentiated as between rulers and ruled, the new knowledge of metal would be controlled by the rulers, who would thereby probably rather rapidly advance and improve their superior status.

In the particular case of China, the framework of history includes a relatively "low" and a relatively "high" neolithic society. The oldest use of bronze can be traced to the area occupied by the "higher" society. Therefore the lack, or apparent lack, of a crude and "early" bronze technique in the area with which the later and higher technique is identified is the critical point of doubt.

In this connection Creel has noted something that may prove to be of the greatest significance. Dated bronze work of the Chou period, centuries later than the Shang culture, is inferior to Shang bronze. Han bronze, again, is inferior to Chou bronze, which is earlier. There is thus an indisputable process of devolution in the technique of bronze from the work of artists to the work of artisans— a process parallel to the steady and undoubted evolution among the Chinese of higher forms of economy and a more sophisticated society. The necessary anterior evolution from a crude bronze technique to the high technique of the Shang culture has been left a mystery. Against the assumption that the oldest bronzes are technically the most perfect, however, Creel reasons cogently:

> The argument that crude bronzes, showing earlier stages in the technique of casting, have not been found in China, is not necessarily very telling. Very few indeed are the places in China where bronzes have been "excavated" rather than merely dug up surreptitiously. . . . If we should find bronzes from a period much earlier than that represented by Anyang, there is good reason to believe that they would be uninscribed. . . . More primitive bronzes would probably be undecorated—not a few plain, undecorated pieces were made even by the Shang people. If early, crude, undecorated pieces were dug up at random by peasants and sold to antique dealers they would probably be set down as late pieces—possibly Han—of poor quality . . . late in 1934 the National Research Institute excavated just such a vessel from a Shang grave along with many other typical Shang bronzes and artifacts. . . .
> As a matter of fact I have seen a large number of Shang bronzes which were very crude as compared with the finest work of the Shang craftsmen. . . . It would seem that a great many centuries must have been required to make the transition from the technique which produced the poorest to that evidenced by the best even of the Shang bronzes we know. Yet there is some reason to suppose that the exquisite and the crude were produced side by side at Anyang, for people of varying prestige or economic status.[28]

Creel's conclusion is that "the craft of bronze manufacturers and casting was raised to a pitch of excellence which can hardly have been known to those who brought or transmitted the bronze technique to Northeast China."[29] If this is true, then what were the factors governing first the evolution and then the devolution or vulgarizing of the technique of working in bronze?

Perhaps the most important evidence as to the kind of forces at work is the fact that bronze was used only for

[28] Creel, *op. cit.*, pp. 222-224.
[29] *Ibid.*, p. 252.

weapons and ceremonial objects. A bronze knife may be regarded both as a weapon and as a kind of tool, but except for knives there is no evidence that the Chinese made much use, if any, of metal tools until the second half of the last millennium B.C. The Chinese peasantry (as distinct from the feudal aristocracy) seem never to have had a Bronze Age at all, but to have gone directly from the neolithic into the Iron Age, just as most peoples have done.[30] The bronze weapons, chariot fittings, and ceremonial vessels of the Shang culture belonged to a ruling class. The agriculture and other work of the people whom they ruled was carried on with implements of bone, stone, and wood. Agricultural implements, in particular, were probably of wood and have therefore disappeared.[31] The ox-drawn plough was not used, the primary implement being a "foot-plough." [32]

Therefore it seems to me a clear and legitimate inference, taking all the factors into consideration, that in the area of the Shang culture the technique of working in bronze was taken over in a rather undeveloped form by a people who had already evolved a relatively high general culture. It must have been agriculture—an agriculture sufficiently specialized and intensive to support in at least a few places a population concentrated in small walled towns—that gave the economic "leverage" for the attainment of this cultural level. These little towns were the centers of the rule and defense of areas, also proportionately small, in which agriculture was more advanced than in the rest of North China, and society in them must have been distinctly more specialized and articulated than the cruder kinds of hunting, fishing, food-gathering, and at the same time agricultural

[30] Bishop, Neolithic Age, 1933, p. 404.
[31] Eberhard, Early Chinese Cultures, 1936, p. 524.
[32] Ibid., p. 525. Bishop (Origin and Early Diffusion of the Traction-Plow, 1936) dates the introduction of the ox-drawn plough into China "about the middle of the Epoch of the Warring States (403-255 B.C.)." For an account of the foot plough in early China see Hsü Chung-shu, On Some Agricultural Implements of the Ancient Chinese, 1930 (in Chinese).

neolithic society. Many of the people who lived in the shelter of the walls—perhaps most of them—may have been employed in cultivating fields near at hand, so that they were rural in their occupation and townsmen by residence. Nevertheless, the mere building of such strong places must have created new social functions and defined the beginnings of social differentiation between those who cultivated the fields and those who had the responsibility of defending the walled town and the area of cultivation of which it was the center. It is a fair assumption that this latter class either "owned" the fields and those who worked them, or soon came to own them.

Granting this probable and reasonable differentiation —or beginning of a differentiation—between rulers and ruled, holders of the town and workers in the field, and without being in any way dogmatic or insistent, I find it no longer difficult to imagine how a primitive technique of working in bronze could have been rapidly brought to a high point of sophistication. In a culture still wholly neolithic walled towns predicate an agriculture already dominant in importance over hunting and raiding—not a migrant agriculture of patches of land sown haphazard for a year or two, but orderly cultivation of permanent fields. This in turn predicates comparatively heavy crops per acre, yielding a surplus to be stored in the towns. While the question whether irrigation was already practiced at this early historical level may be left open, under the conditions of climate and soil prevailing in North China,[33] it is at least not impossible that even with stone tools irrigation runnels on a small scale were grubbed out to bring water to the fields. This may have been attempted first in bad years, when the rain failed, and then adopted as a regular technique because of its proved effect in yielding a heavier crop.

Would the introduction of bronze into such a society be

[33] Wittfogel, Foundations and Stages, 1935, p. 38, n. 3.

primarily social in its effects, or primarily economic? The uses to which bronze was put would seem to indicate that its effect was primarily social. It was not made into improved tools to increase the output of the farming worker or to lighten his labor, but into weapons with which the rulers increased their range and efficiency as rulers: with better weapons they could lay wider lands and more people under tribute and assemble a greater following of men-at-arms. Thus the essential standard of use for metal was in weapons, with a second standard of luxury use in ornaments and heavy ceremonial vessels, representing a reserve accumulation or treasure of metal that it was not necessary to convert at once into weapons. Treasure of this kind was a sort of currency of the nobles who hoarded it, a symbol of their military and aristocratic scale of values.

Therefore the fabrication of metal also, though it had an applied economic value in the acquisition and safeguarding of revenue, must have been governed in the first instance by social standards of a non-economic kind. Since it was not "usefully" employed, none of the costs of extracting and transporting the ores and none of the processing costs for time and labor were determined by ordinary market considerations of supply and demand. Everything depended on the level of development of the society. Where the level was low and every man did more or less every kind of thing that every other man could do, technical improvement was bound to be haphazard. But where the level was higher and the society had already been differentiated into rulers and ruled, the ruler who lived in the security of a walled town and had a reserve of stored grain to feed those through whom he exercised his rule could set a few retainers or slaves to work at the newly learned technique of making things in metal. Since their time and their labor were not reckoned by cost and profit, the only standard they had to meet was one of effective weapons and satisfactory ornaments. They were thus free to progress technically, and as their work was consecutive and specialized their progress was cumulative and could be amazingly rapid.

Moreover, by distinguishing in this way between the social and the economic factors, it is possible to account both for a first phase of technical progress and a later degeneration. First, an economic factor, the special development of agriculture in certain localities, produced a differentiated society. Second, this differentiated society, although it did not independently discover the use of metal but acquired a crude technique from elsewhere, was able to make rapid and cumulative improvements in the technique because it could set certain members of the society to work exclusively with metal under social rather than economic sanctions. In the meantime, the same technique remained weak and crude in the hands of the "backward" neolithic groups through which it had filtered to the "advanced" neolithic groups.

Third, the small nuclei that were able to carry forward the technique of metal-working in this way—nuclei probably all rather closely grouped in terrain favorable to early agricultural specialization—were themselves reacted on by the powerful political agent that they had thus created. Craftsmen protected by warriors turned out better weapons, the superior weapons made the warriors éven more powerful, and the social grouping and ranking of the warriors became more and more elaborate and distinct and more like a nobility. How far the most significant development was "vertical," in the setting apart of kings, nobles, free warriors, and so on, and how far it was "horizontal," in establishing the rule of metal users over stone users within a much enlarged territorial horizon, is not altogether clear.

Fourth, improvement in technique under the patronage of a military aristocracy gradually gave way to increased quantity of production and the production of things other than weapons and objects of luxury. Eventually, when the Iron Age succeeded the Bronze Age in China,[34] even the subject classes emerged from the Stone Age and acquired metal implements. This may have been because iron was available in greater quantity than copper and the alloys used in making bronze. It may also have been influenced by the fact that the structure of society as a pyramid of royalty and nobility resting on a base of labor employed in agriculture had become so stable that it was not threatened by the wider diffusion of the knowledge of how to make things out of metal.

Fifth, wider diffusion of technical knowledge was accompanied by a decline in artistic finish and technical skill. The best Chou and Han bronzes are inferior to the best Shang bronzes. This is because there was again a shift from a social to an economic emphasis. The skilled men who fabricated the bronze of the Shang age were artists rather than artisans. They could maintain a superlative standard because they worked under patronage—were not dependent on the sale of their product on the market.[35] With the diffusion of technique and with the new noble classes relying more on their control of the social structure as a whole and less on their mere monopoly of weapons, the artist lost the economic shield of patronage and became an artisan, a producer for the open market, who had to calculate time and cost, supply and demand. There is an obvious parallel between this and the level of skill and beauty attained by Renaissance metal artificers in Europe under noble patronage. With the development of the European commercial economy their status and the quality of their work also declined from artistry to artisanship.

---

[34] V. K. Ting, op. cit., p. 4, supposed that iron was introduced into China "not much earlier than the sixth century B.C., which date is several hundred years later than the beginning of the iron age in Egypt or Mesopotamia, and perhaps more than a thousand years later than in India."

[35] Cruder work was of course done at the same time. Compare Creel, op. cit., p. 224.

ORIGINS OF THE DIFFERENTIATION OF CHINESE AND BARBARIANS

Wider conclusions are also suggested though not proved by this line of reasoning. On the one hand, there is no need to deny the importance of migration, invasion, trade, and other agencies of culture diffusion even at the lower and feebler levels of neolithic social organization. There is, in fact, good reason to believe that all of these human activities contributed to the gradual building up of an evolutionary momentum. On the other hand, it is not necessary to assume that any of these factors, or any other single factor, was the main causative agent in creating the origins of Chinese history. Without "proving" the exact significance or even the exact chronological sequence of each aspect of neolithic culture in China that is known to us, it is possible to allow for multiple processes of historical growth.

One of these processes was a gradually accelerating differentiation between "backward" and "advanced" groups within the territorial field of Chinese history, a differentiation largely focused on local ranges of variation within the same general geographical environment. Two tendencies, at first rather vague but in the end emphatic, developed out of this process: the more backward areas and social formations began to group themselves in an orbit of slowly changing primitives, while the more active areas and social formations began to split off and group themselves in a new orbit of more rapid evolution. One became, in time, the orbit of "the barbarians," the other the orbit of "the Chinese."

By this I do not mean to imply a total stagnation and lack of evolution among "the barbarians." Far from it. The question is rather one of different rates of change in the two main groupings. Both the simple "early barbarians" and "early Chinese" in due course regrouped themselves; more than one kind of barbarian came to be distinguishable, while among the Chinese not only the geographical focus but the cultural or social or political focus moved from one position and one process to another in answer to the complicating influence of many factors.

For one thing, it is quite certain that the two orbits did not remain separate from each other. The more active history of "the Chinese" inevitably generated expansionism. As a result, group after group of the barbarians was brought under Chinese influence in an ever widening area. In some cases this meant that communities which had not themselves developed a significant evolutionary momentum acquired that momentum from the Chinese and were thus converted into Chinese. In other cases it meant that groups which in the beginning could have been better described as "un-Chinese" than as "non-Chinese" were affected in such a way that they were not converted into Chinese but transformed into new kinds of barbarians. Of these, again, some eventually did become Chinese, while others tended to shift from the vague category of being "un-Chinese" into a strongly "non-Chinese" category.

Geographical environment, moreover, continued to exert a long-term molding influence. As proto-Chinese tendencies and characteristics became more recognizably and typically Chinese they worked out for themselves, like all strong cultures, a collective affinity for their own optimum kind of environment. The Chinese, consequently, from the moment they become distinguishable as a historical force, can be followed in an unending search for a wider "Chinese environment." In some areas they found an environment of this kind ready and waiting for their expansion; in some areas they were able to modify the environment to suit their needs by applying the methods of irrigation and drainage that went with the Chinese intensive agriculture.[36] In other areas, however, they were able

[36] See Chapter III, above.

to achieve only a poor approximation to their own optimum standard; and, finally, certain kinds of region resisted altogether, or almost altogether, the penetration of the Chinese way of life.

By keeping always in view both the sum of the factors of the geographical setting and the sum and proportions of the elements out of which the most typical Chinese culture of any historical period was compounded, and by allowing always for the interaction of environment and society, we may identify, at least in a broad way, the center of gravity and the periphery of the Chinese field of history at any level of historical development. In each period "typical" Chinese evolution is focused at the historical center of gravity (which does not necessarily coincide with the exact geographical center); around the periphery are clustered groups not wholly Chinese but subordinate to the influence of China; beyond these again are the groups that resist being drawn into the Chinese orbit and gravitate, simultaneously, toward the terrain that resists the Chinese way of life. Even this power of resistance, however, must not be considered a total immunity; it will be found, on examination, that the effect of the process of resistance is to stimulate a kind of evolution different from the "natural" evolution that the resistant society might otherwise have followed.

The major environment that resisted Chinese penetration was the steppe, and the steppe society was the most obdurate in setting itself against the society of China. Together with the steppe must be taken the other regions of the Inner Asian Frontier, which were more open to the influence of the steppe than to that of China. True steppe society and history are later in evolution and even in origin than the society and history of China. They were in fact partly a by-product of Chinese history. Not all steppe nomadism is peripheral to China; but the first true steppe nomads with whom the Chinese dealt—beginning about the fifth century B.C.—were largely the descendants of "barbarian" tribes whom the expansion of the Chinese pushed toward the steppe from the poorer parts of northern and northwestern China. For this reason the remote origins of the steppe nomadism with which the Chinese had to deal in later centuries may be traced to the changes that took place in China within a limited but specially favored environment near the great bend of the Yellow River, when certain "progressive" neolithic groups acquired metal and began by the use of it to expand at the cost of other, more "backward" neolithic groups. In doing this they opened up an immense historical horizon: the creation of "the Chinese" and the creation of "the barbarians."

CHAPTER X

AGRICULTURAL EVOLUTION AND NOMAD REPETITION

MODERN SCHOLARSHIP AND CHINESE HISTORICAL TRADITIONS

Can a true line of connection be traced between the early documented history of China and the remote neolithic foreshadowing of history that has just been discussed? A few of the oldest Chinese documentary materials go back to the "Western" or earlier Chou period—B.C. 1122 (according to the traditional chronology) or B.C. 1050 (according to Bishop's chronology) to B.C. 770.[1] Certain books, or portions of books, have also been assigned by Chinese tradition to the Shang period in the second millennium B.C. and even to the still earlier Hsia period, at the opening of the second millennium B.C.[2] The problems involved need only the briefest discussion in a book like this.

"Orthodox" Chinese tradition includes a whole canon of very ancient history.[3] At the end of the nineteenth century a notable school of Chinese critics began to shake this tradition. They proved by comparative textual study

[1] For dating, see Bishop, The Chronology of Ancient China, 1932; especially the statement on p. 237 that the lists of succession of the rulers of the separate states of China "became continuous and reliable during the middle of the ninth century B.C." See also Creel, Studies in Early Chinese Culture, 1937, pp. xvi-xxii.

[2] Creel, *op. cit.*, pp. 49-95, 96-100.

[3] For the following very brief summary of schools of Chinese thought I am especially indebted to K. A. Wittfogel, who has let me study the first draft of his forthcoming Economic and Social History of China. See also Wang Yü-ch'üan, Development of Modern Social Science in China, 1938, with table of leading Chinese theories about ancient society; Hummel, trans. of the Autobiography of Ku Chieh-kang, 1931; and Pelliot, L'Edition collective des oeuvres de Wang Kouo-wei, 1929.

that one after another of the ancient sources was not of the age or origin that had been attributed to it. In this kind of work, which went a long way toward clearing the ground for fresh appraisal of the sources, the names of K'ang Yu-wei, Hu Shih, and Ku Chieh-kang, stand out.

A strong skepticism naturally resulted—a tendency to assume that when the authenticity of a document had been called in doubt in any way none of the material it contained could be trusted. This tendency was later corrected. New materials and criteria began to be recognized, among them the extraordinary Bronze Age and neolithic finds at Anyang and elsewhere, especially those that had been scientifically excavated under the patronage of the Chinese government. The traditionally preserved names of the rulers of the Shang period were on the whole substantiated by the oracle-bones of Anyang. Even the order of succession was confirmed.

Accordingly, there is once more a tendency to use the legendary material in the written sources. The validity of the work that has been done in textual criticism is not questioned, but other methods are also being applied on the principle that even though a document is not what it had at one time been supposed to be it may still contain references of real worth. It is largely a question of the method of analysis and comparison. The value of folklore especially is being emphasized. As it is not authentic record, folklore cannot be employed in reconstructing the events of history; but it can serve to present an idea of the kind of society that once existed even when the political events of that society cannot be restored.

Among the leading Chinese authorities there is now a wide range of outlook and method, corresponding to the different tendencies that have been at work in the last few decades. The late Wang Kuo-wei, one of the very greatest in establishing the "texts" of the oracle-bone inscriptions, is to be bracketed with the critics who so largely revised the traditional written sources; they scrutinized texts that had already been established, while he has helped to establish a new kind of text. Lo Chen-yü is another great decipherer. Among those who have won distinction in field archeology there are many, like Tung Tso-pin, Hsü Chung-shu, Ting Shan, and others, who have not only helped to classify the new material but have attempted to set up and test a number of working theories.

Still more theoretical in their approach are men like Fu Ssu-nien, T'ao Hsi-sheng, and above all Kuo Mo-jo. It is the theorists, naturally, who have been boldest in attempting to convert protohistory into history. Because they have been bold not all of their work has met with equal assent; but their theories, though modified from time to time by new facts, are of the greatest value in the work of assessing these new facts.

Western scholarship still follows the Chinese textual scholars more closely than the Chinese theoreticians. Franke, confronted by the "fictitious" character of the old legends,[4] hesitates to apply to them the methods of anthropology and folklore. Creel, the most deeply versed in the current work of the Chinese archeologists, deals more with the results of their work in classification than he does with their essays in speculation.[5] Bishop, however, cautiously but persistently accumulates and applies economic and sociological data;[6] while Eberhard has recently published a "working hypothesis" of ancient China focused not on historical periods but on kinds of culture.[7] Finally, Wittfogel is engaged in a comprehensive study of source material and of both Chinese and Western theories of Chinese origins.[8]

[4] Franke, Geschichte des chinesischen Reiches, Vol. III, 1937, p. 53.
[5] Creel, op. cit.
[6] See Bibliography for articles by Bishop quoted in this book.
[7] Eberhard, Early Chinese Cultures, 1936.
[8] See his forthcoming Economic and Social History, mentioned above, note 3.

Early Legendary "Emperors"

A number of shadowy figures appear, or seem to appear, at the farthest edges of Chinese history. There is a "creation legend" of P'an Ku, a "pastoral age" of Fu Hsi (B.C. 2953), and an "agricultural age" of Shen Nung, the "Divine Cultivator" (B.C. 2838). The terms "pastoral" and "agricultural" are of course conventional. Then come Huang Ti, the "Yellow Emperor" (B.C. 2698), Shao Hao (B.C. 2598), Chuan Hsü (B.C. 2514), Ti K'u (B.C. 2436), and Ti Chih (B.C. 2366).[9] This leads up to China's Golden Age, under Yao (B.C. 2357) and Shun (B.C. 2255). Shun then delivered the "empire" to his "virtuous minister," Yü, who founded the Hsia "dynasty," the dates of which according to the conventional chronology are B.C. 2205-1766, while Bishop's chronology gives B.C. 1989-1559. The Hsia eventually gave way to the Shang (conventional chronology, B.C. 1765-1123; Bishop's chronology, 1558-1051). The Shang in turn were succeeded by the Chou (conventional chronology, B.C. 1122-256; Bishop's chronology, B.C. 1050-256). For the Shang period a relative chronology exists, in the order of the Shang rulers; but the first absolute date in Chinese history is the year 841 B.C.,[10] thirty years after the division between the "western" or earlier phase of the Chou period and its "eastern" or later phase.

V. K. Ting argued that most of the Chinese legends about very ancient "emperors" originated in writings that are later than the fourth century B.C.[11] In fact, it may be

---

[9] Chih (Ti Chih) is listed as one of several sons of K'u (Ti K'u), and is important only as the brother, supposedly, and worthless predecessor of Yao.

[10] Bishop, Chronology, etc., 1932, p. 235; Franke, *op. cit.*, Vol. III, 1937, p. 71, gives the year 842 as an alternative. This is a note on his Vol. I, 1930, p. 101.

[11] V. K. Ting, How China Acquired Her Civilisation, p. 2. Ting belonged to the most skeptical school of Chinese criticism. Since the publication of his article, in 1931, the trend of research has been toward the belief that legends written down late preserve a good deal of genuinely early material.

said that the more ancient the period to which a figure of legend is assigned, the later the first actual mention of him is likely to be. Moreover, some of the legends do not belong to the focal area of the earliest reliable Chinese history but derive from its periphery or from even farther away.

P'an Ku is mentioned in Chinese literature in the sixth century after Christ, but he is also found in the legends of the non-Chinese Yao aborigines,[12] in the far south. The legend may therefore be "barbarian" in origin.

Fu Hsi is a figure transferred to Chinese legend from the legends of the I barbarians of the Huai basin, intermediate between Yellow River China and Yangtze China, and there is no mention of him in the earlier Chinese writings.[13] Shen Nung, again, is not mentioned in the Chinese writings until the time of Mencius (fourth century B.C.).[14] The agricultural deity of the main Chinese historical focus in the middle Yellow River region was Hou Chi, who was claimed by the Chou Chinese as a kind of ethnic ancestor. The date at which Shen Nung appears in the Chinese documents indicates that his cult was adopted after there had been a good deal of interaction between the true Chinese focal area of the Yellow River and the secondary, not quite so Chinese, focal area of the middle Yangtze. Huang Ti, the "Yellow Emperor," though given by convention a date of great antiquity, does not appear in Chinese historical writing until the third century B.C.[15] His "tomb," which may of course have been a sacred place before his legend became attached to it, is in the modern Shensi province, in the valley of a stream tributary to the Yellow River, near the "center of gravity" of the oldest Chinese history.

---

[12] Ku Chieh-kang, Notes on Ancient History, Vol. I, 1926, p. 121 (in Chinese). The older source from which he quotes also indicates a "southern barbarian" connection. See also Yen Fu-li and Shang Ch'eng-tsu, Report on an Investigation of the Yao, 1929, pp. 21-22 (in Chinese).

[13] C. W. Bishop, personal letter of July 12, 1938.

[14] Ibid.

[15] Ibid.

Such legends are, however, not without their value. The fact that descendants of the most ancient Chinese have borrowed the legends of descendants of the most ancient barbarians leads naturally to the suggestion that the same kind of borrowing may have been important in very ancient times. Moreover, if it can be said that both "Chinese" and "barbarians" derive ultimately from the same prehistoric stock, or group of primitive stocks, as has already been suggested, then even the most genuinely Chinese body of ancient legend may contain details that sound more characteristic of a "primitive barbarian" culture than of a "primitive Chinese" culture.

It is from this point of view that the next group of legendary figures must be considered. Several of the Chinese authorities on ancient history have attempted to elucidate the lists of the ancestors of the Shang rulers.[16] Wang Kuo-wei combined his analysis of genealogy with an essay on the ancient geography of China. He believed that the earliest geographical focus of Chinese cultural origins was in the eastern part of North China. This was followed by a shift toward the northwest (Shansi) in the period with which he identifies Yao, Shun, and Yü (the legendary founder of the Hsia "dynasty"). In the Hsia period there began a move back toward the lower Yellow River, followed in the Shang period by a definite concentration in the Anyang (North Honan) region. In his geographical argument he even uses traditional material concerning T'ai Hao (another name for Fu Hsi), whom I have briefly described above as taken probably from the legends of the barbarians intermediate between Yellow

[16] My reading of the modern Chinese literature on this ancient period has been limited, as can be seen from the direct references given. My ideas have been formed largely by correspondence and discussion with C. W. Bishop and K. A. Wittfogel, whose field of special research this is. Where no direct references are given I have drawn on Wittfogel's preliminary material; but this should not be allowed to prejudice his discussion of the modern Chinese authorities in his forthcoming Economic and Social History of China.

River China and Yangtze China (east of what is now the line of the Peiping-Hankow railway).

In his genealogical analysis Wang Kuo-wei traces back the line of the Shang rulers as far as Ti K'u and one of his sons, Ch'i or Hsieh. (Ti Chih, whose name I gave in the short "orthodox chronology" above, was also supposedly a son of Ti K'u, as was Yao.) Tung Tso-pin has followed up this part of the work of Wang Kuo-wei, and so has Chu Fang-p'u in his historical study of the Shang based on the oracle-bones. Kuo Mo-jo, whose list is in general similar to that of Wang Kuo-wei, suggests that there was a legendary "prime ancestor" or founder of the Shang line of rulers. This personage was later differentiated or multiplied into three people: K'u (Ti K'u), Chün (a name which appears in the "orthodox" account as the "personal" name of K'u), and Shun—the "virtuous minister" who supposedly succeeded Yao.

A linkage, however indefinite and puzzling, is thus established between the earliest connected and reliable Chinese history, in the last millennium B.C., and neolithic times. The first date that is absolutely as well as relatively determined is B.C. 841. The early writings of the Chou Chinese preserve, however, lists of the rulers of the Shang period. The Anyang excavations have confirmed at least the later kings of these lists. The Anyang culture goes back to about the middle of the second millennium B.C. Its exact chronology has not been fixed but its relative chronology is dependable, inasmuch as the order of succession of the rulers according to the oracle-bones confirms in the main the order given in the written lists. Although the Shang bronze culture as revealed at Anyang was highly developed, there survived in it many elements of the older neolithic culture. If, therefore, any legitimate use can be made at all of the legends dealing with the earlier Shang rulers, with the Hsia people who are supposed to have preceded them, and with the still more ancient and more vague "emperors" before the Hsia, then it must be conceded that these legends go far back toward truly neolithic time, and perhaps all the way back.

It is true that there is one most important difference between the "protohistorical" Shang and the "prehistorical" Hsia. The writings of the Chou Chinese refer to their Shang predecessors; but in the Shang inscriptions there has been found no reference at all to their supposed predecessors, the Hsia. This is not enough to dismiss the Hsia from history, however. Even V. K. Ting, a strong skeptic as regards the early dating of Chinese origins, conceded that the confirmation of the Shang "legends" by the Shang oracle-bones was enough to establish the possibility that the Hsia "legends" might yet be confirmed in a similar way.[17] Kuo Mo-jo deals with the Hsia legends not as pure myth but as a legendary account of a discernible early period. So do Ting Shan, Hsü Chung-shu, and Tseng Chien.[18]

Geographical Evidence in the Early Legends

The legends themselves contain two kinds of evidence which, with due caution, can be used—the geographical and the sociological.

P'an Ku, in view of the probability that he is a rather late borrowing from the "southern barbarians," need not be further considered.

Fu Hsi (T'ai Hao) I have listed above as probably borrowed from the Huai I or barbarians of the Huai basin. This low-lying, marshy area has always been a barrier to strategic movements down the coast of China from the lower Yellow River to the lower Yangtze. Its barbarian inhabitants were not subdued until the age of the Warring States, which prepared the way for the founding of the first unified empire under Ch'in Shih-huang-ti in the

[17] V. K. Ting, op. cit., p. 10.
[18] For elaboration in detail, see Wittfogel, op. cit.

third century B.C.; and even then the conquest was not the work of the Northern Chinese but a triumph of the Yangtze state of Ch'u.[19] Nevertheless, Wang Kuo-wei, who places the origin of China's earliest culture well to the east of the great bend of the Yellow River, used the identification of this legendary figure with the Huai region as evidence in favor of his theory. Wang Kuo-wei, however, did not fully take into account the importance of environment in conditioning the economic life, social grouping, and evolution of primitive people.

Shen Nung has been listed above as a borrowing from the Yangtze region; he therefore belongs to a focus of Chinese history that is relatively late and secondary though of great importance. There is always the possibility, however, that his legend became merged with original legends from the generally accepted primary focus in the middle and lower Yellow River valley.

Huang Ti, the Yellow Emperor, is a rather late figure, as far as the written record can be cited, but the tradition that his tomb is at a place in Shensi which is undoubtedly an ancient site suggests that an old and genuine tradition has been confused with late and unreliable legends. At any rate, T'ao Hsi-sheng believes that there is a kernel of historical truth in the Huang Ti story. Kuo Mo-jo is more specific; he identifies the figure concealed by the Huang Ti legend with the "prime ancestor" of the Shang line of rulers, and believes that this ancestral personage, and his sons and grandsons, may have been multiplied and given new names in later legends. It is in this way that he identifies K'u (Ti K'u) with Shun, and so forth.[20]

I think, therefore, that these names need not be taken one by one, except for K'u, who is of special importance. According to later tradition, the Chou line of rulers in the last millennium B.C. was descended from the son of K'u's

[19] Bishop, Beginnings of North and South in China, 1934, pp. 318-319.
[20] Wittfogel, op. cit.

first wife, while the Shang rulers descended from the son of his second wife. The son of his third wife was Yao and the son of his fourth wife Chih (Ti Chih).

Next comes the Hsia period, represented as the history of a dynasty founded by Yü. The name of Yü serves to join up the tradition or legends of the Hsia period with the group of names to which an even greater antiquity is ascribed. Both Yü and these other names figure in the remoter genealogy—or genealogical cult, perhaps it would be better to say—of the Shang rulers as a number of workers in China have attempted to reconstruct it. A hypothetical connection between the Hsia and Shang periods is thus provided, despite the lack of specific reference to a Hsia period or even to the name of Hsia in the Shang inscriptions. Here the question of chronological or strictly historical veracity may be left, for the moment.

Some of the geographical references in these legends are perfectly reasonable, given the very general assumption that the origins of Chinese culture and history are to be sought somewhere near the great bend of the Yellow River. Other references are of interest because they mention the natural barrier areas and transit areas between the Yangtze and both the loess region west of the great bend of the Yellow River and the Great Plain east of the great bend. These areas must have been just as important in the earliest expansion from the nuclear "Chinese" territory as they have been throughout later history. Finally, there are the references that are inherently improbable because they are obviously far outside the horizon of primitive China. It cannot be argued, however, that the improbable references entirely discredit the reasonable references. It would have been natural for the Chinese in their later spread to carry with them old legends and to add new place names to them in order to make them seem more real; natural, also, to transfer place names from the legends of conquered or assimilated barbarians to the legends of the dominating Chinese.

Leaving out of consideration the inherently improbable references, the following names of places and regions may be listed:

Fu Hsi, though in fact probably a "barbarian" myth, is assigned a birthplace in the Wei valley,[21] in the loess region of Shensi. Perhaps this indicates a late fusion of Chinese and barbarian legend.

Shen Nung, though deriving from the legends of the Yangtze region, is described as born in the valley of the Han [22]—the natural corridor between the loess region of Shensi and the middle Yangtze. He is also described as having ruled first in the valley of the Wei, later in the Huai region intermediate between lower Yellow River and lower Yangtze, and still later in Shantung. Here again there may be a late confluence of legends.

For the interval—nominally very long—between Shen Nung and the Yellow Emperor there is an account of a time of troubles and rebellion.[23] The drive of the rebellion, supposedly, was from the great bend of the Yellow River eastward to Shantung, and from Shantung the ruler fled northward. Order was restored by the Yellow Emperor, Huang Ti, to whom a birthplace in Honan is attributed.[24] He was then active in the Huai basin, made his capital in the Great Plain, near the present Peiping, and finally was buried in Shensi. As in the other allegedly early but probably late and mixed legends, these indications give no clear

[21] Chavannes, Mémoires historiques, Vol. I, 1895, p. 5, n. 4 and 5; also p. 8. Compare Wieger, Textes historiques, Vol. I, 1929, p. 19. For this and the following references to Wieger, compare also his maps opp. pp. 18 and 30.
[22] Chavannes, op. cit., p. 14, n. 6; Wieger, op. cit., p. 21.
[23] Chavannes, op. cit., p. 29; Wieger, op. cit., pp. 22-23.
[24] Chavannes, op. cit., p. 26, n. 2, and p. 36, n. 3; Wieger, loc. cit.; Legge, Chinese Classics, Vol. III, Part I, p. 108 (Bamboo Books) of the Prolegomena.

idea either of an original focus or of a line or lines of expansion.

Next comes the still nebulous age into which recent Chinese workers have tried to trace the legendary genealogy of the Shang rulers. For Shao Hao and Chuan Hsü (whose mythical reigns are sometimes combined as one) there is mention of alternating "capitals" in Shantung and the plain of the Yellow River.[25] There is mention also of northern Honan and southern Hopei, nearer to the great bend of the Yellow River. Chuan Hsü, if regarded as a separate figure, is described as born in Ssuch'uan. This attribution has a relative kind of importance, because at a later time there was in fact an important line of passage from western Shensi and southern Kansu into Ssuch'uan. The mixture of the undoubtedly late with the possibly early continues, in other words, to be inextricable.

For K'u (Ti K'u) there is mention both of the Huai basin and of the valley of the Lo, in northern Honan, which opens into the Yellow River.[26] Then comes Yao, who is called a son of K'u.[27] Though brought up in the Huai basin, "in the country of his mother," he is later placed successively in the lower Yellow River plain, in the mountains that divide what are now the provinces of Hopei and Shansi, and in the south of Shansi. He is credited with subduing the "easternmost barbarians" and given a burial place in Shantung.

Shun, the "virtuous minister" who succeeded Yao, is assigned a birthplace in the southwest corner of Shansi, where the Fen enters the Yellow River.[28] He is credited with extending "China" into the plains of the lower Liao,

---

[25] Chavannes, op. cit., p. 78, n. 1; Wieger, op. cit., p. 25; Legge, op. cit., p. 109 of the Prolegomena.
[26] Chavannes, op. cit., p. 39, n. 4; Wieger, op. cit., p. 28; Legge, op. cit., p. 111.
[27] Chavannes, op. cit., pp. 40 et sqq.; Wieger, op. cit., p. 28; Legge, op. cit., p. 112.
[28] Chavannes, op. cit., p. 52, n. 3, etc.; Wieger, op. cit., p. 35; Legge, op. cit., p. 114.

in the south of Manchuria. He had a minister, according to the story, who invaded distant barbarian territory to the south of the Yangtze, and he himself, the story continues, died while on a kind of imperial progress to the south of the Yangtze and was buried there; but these references must be classed as improbable. Except for these adornments his career is made to center closely about the great bend of the Yellow River.

Shun also was followed by a "virtuous minister." This was Yü, supposedly founder of the Hsia "dynasty." [29] He is a culture hero of irrigation and reclamation works. The dating of the period thus described is disputed, but the account certainly reflects a genuine tradition of some kind.

So much for the geographical details. Obviously they are not enough in themselves to justify any elaborate structure of theory. Yet they compare well with the widely accepted idea that the origins of Chinese history are to be looked for in the region of the great bend of the Yellow River—the region where the loess highlands overlook the Great Plain. Nor do they contradict the idea that before a separate line of "Chinese" culture and history began to develop, a primitive population, or series of populations, may have been scattered all the way from south of the Yangtze up to the loess highlands and the steppe. Taken at their narrowest they may perhaps indicate a very early period of indecision or oscillation, in which it was uncertain whether the eastern margin of the loess highlands or the western margin of the Great Plain would become the historical center of gravity. It is possible that they may also indicate that even before the center of gravity became determined, the population which eventually gathered about the center of gravity was in touch along natural lines of geographical passage with populations that eventually were to become peripheral and "barbarian."

[29] Chavannes, *op. cit.*, pp. 81 *et sqq.*; Wieger, *op. cit.*, pp. 37 *et sqq.*; Legge, *op. cit.*, p. 117.

Sociological and Cultural Evidence in the Legends

On the whole, the sociological or cultural references are more important than the not very firm geographical details. First, it may be noted that the *eldest* son of K'u was borne, according to the account, by his *fourth* wife. This is hardly likely, but a simple emendation would make the passage read realistically. It may be conjectured that the tradition originally preserved an account of the "borough English" or "junior right" system of inheritance, under which the youngest son succeeds to the household property; and that in a later age, when this had become unintelligible, the tradition was changed enough to make the youngest son into an eldest son but not enough to hide the original form of the legend.

The principle of junior right is that each son, as he grows up, is given out of the family property enough to set himself up independently, while the youngest son remains with the parents and eventually inherits the nucleus of what the family owns. The principle is not exclusively associated with any one kind of environment or society. It can occur as an early stage of development in any society that is not yet sophisticated enough to group itself in large concentrations of people, that has room in which to expand, and that accordingly finds it convenient to split up and spread out in small family units. There are traces of the system among the Mongols of the steppe,[30] and among the "aboriginal" peoples in the jungle to the south of the Chinese,[31] among the early Chou,[32] and also among the early

[30] Vladimirtsov, Social Structure of the Mongols, 1931, pp. 49, 54-55, 98, 111 (in Russian). The Mongol term *ejen*, "owner," "lord," and in later use "emperor," derives from an older term for "younger son," which in turn has the root meaning "he who inherits the hearth-fire."

[31] Bishop, Beginnings of North and South, 1934, p. 319, citing the Tso Chuan and Ch. 40 of the Shih Chi. The Tso Chuan, covering the period 722-468 B.C., is "the main historical source from the momentous epoch when the classical Chinese culture attained its first ripeness" (Karlgren, On the Authenticity and Nature of the Tso Chuan, 1926).

[32] Bishop, *op. cit.*, p. 311, citing Shih Chi, Ch. 31.

Ch'in Chinese [33] in what is now Shensi and Kansu, before
they had moved inward on the center of China to set up
the first recognizable centralized Chinese Empire, in the
third century B.C. What is interesting here is that the system vanished so completely from the later society of China
that the conventional Chinese historian and scholar would
never have admitted it to be Chinese at all. This is an indication that these legends of a very ancient China, though
their present wording must be relatively late and must
represent a considerable variation from the remote orig-
inals, do nevertheless preserve some faint but genuine details of a primitive age that really existed.

Even more important is the suggestion of a change in
the organization of society that can be detected in the legend
that the succession from Yao to Shun and from Shun
to Yü did not pass from father to son but from ruler to
"virtuous minister." This may be a late "rationalizing,"
at a time when the facts were no longer familiar and understood, of an older account describing a society organized in
clans of matrilineal descent. The men might rule, in the
sense of having the real power, but inheritance was through
the women. Shun, for instance, is described as the "minister" of Yao; but it is also related that he married the
daughters of Yao. It may be, therefore, that he "inherited"
the position of Yao through marrying the daughters of
Yao's wife—a story that had to be altered and made cred-
ible at a later time, when male descent and inheritance had
become the norm. When Yü succeeded Shun the tale is
repeated with minor differences. It is not stated that Yü
married a daughter of Shun, but on the other hand it is
explicitly stated that he was more "worthy" to succeed than
the son of Shun. After Yü the succession of the supposed
rulers of the Hsia period goes either to a son or to a nephew
(in the male line), indicating a society organized in clans
of male descent, with inheritance passing from one male

[33] K. A. Wittfogel, personal letter of August 5, 1938.

generation to the next male generation, and with sons and nephews on the male side belonging to the same general classification of relationship—a classification that still holds in the contemporary Chinese society.

In primitive societies, descent and inheritance through the mother are widely though not exclusively associated with economic and social systems in which women cultivate the land (and, in Asia, tend chickens and pigs, which are adjuncts of the house), while men hunt, fish, or gather in war bands to make raids. In such communities the son may inherit the personal possessions of his father—nets and boats (unless the boats belong to groups of men), hunting gear and fighting weapons, and even some kinds of rank—while the inheritance of land goes with the woman and her daughters; that is to say, through the female side of the clan, regarded as a group and subdivided by generation levels.[34]

The "rule" of women, under such conditions, can easily be exaggerated. Underlying the "rights" of the women, which often include the right of selling the product of the land, there is the assumption that they represent a labor ad-

[34] For this subject in general, see Wittfogel, Wirtschaftsgeschichtliche Grundlagen der Entwicklung der Familienautorität, 1936. C. W. Bishop, in a personal letter of July 12, 1938, points out that among the American Indians the Algonquins and Iroquois were neighboring tribes. They were at the same level of culture. The men fought and hunted and the women planted. Yet in one tribe succession was patrilinear, in the other matrilinear. In a striking case like this it may be that one tribe was in a condition of static balance between society and environment while in the other the balance had recently shifted, or was beginning to shift, with resultant changes in the society. Legge (op. cit., Vol. II [Mencius], pp. 345-346) shows that there are hints of social change in the Shun story. Mencius, when asked why neither Yao nor Shun had consulted Shun's parents about the marriage of Yao's daughters to Shun, replied that this was because the parents, if they had known, would have forbidden the marriage; yet the marriage was justifiable, even without the consent of the parents, because of the human need for posterity (p. 313). Such argument, by the standards of male-line filial piety, is casuistry. What seems to me significant is not the explanation but the need for an explanation; it indicates a feeling of uneasiness about something that had come to seem socially anomalous to a later generation. This is only to be expected if we do in fact have here a story from the period when the man entered the woman's clan transmitted into a period in which the woman entered the man's clan.

junct without which the land does not have its full value. Therefore, although the woman "inherits" the land the truth is that she and the land together are delivered over to the man to whom she is given in marriage. The son of this man, when the time comes, acquires different land by marrying into another clan of matrilineal descent, while the land of this man and wife passes to the daughter generation and acquires its necessary male when a new man marries into the clan.

While some of the manifestations of a system like this may linger after the system itself has been outlived, they are likely to be of minor importance. What it is important to determine, for the purpose of dissecting the origins of Chinese culture and history, is the point at which the men of a society begin to find it to their interest to separate the apportioning of women from the owning of land. This change appears to come about when the men themselves begin to do more of the work of cultivation than the women. The change need not always originate in the same way. It may be prompted by the increasing profit of agriculture. It may occur when a people is conquered and forced to pay a heavier tribute than the work of the women can produce. It may be due to a technical advance in the methods of cultivation

In any case, the effect of the change is to make cultivation, which was formerly regarded as an auxiliary part of a mixed economy, into the major activity. The men, in consequence, replace the women in working the land, and the women thenceforth are sold or given or married or inherited separately from the land and assigned to still more conspicuously minor and auxiliary work about the house and in weaving and other home production. There is likely also to be a concomitant redivision of the work of men. When women constitute the labor adjunct of cultivated land all men tend to be more or less equal in all kinds of men's work —hunting, fishing, war. When men become the labor ad-

296 INNER ASIAN FRONTIERS OF CHINA

junct of the land some men tend to fall to what used to be
the women's position and to become exclusively peasants.
Other men retain for themselves the former kinds of men's
work, especially hunting and war, and these kinds of
"work" tend in consequence to become enhanced in prestige and to be regarded as aristocratic privileges and not
as work at all. At the same time this new, socially superior
class of men enjoys and elaborates new kinds of ownership—especially in land, with its labor adjunct of unprivileged men.[35]

On putting together the geographical and the social content of this mythical ancient China, there emerges a faint
but significant outline of something more than myth. Geographically, there are indications of rather uncertain foci
in the loess highlands, the lower Yellow River plain, and
the marshy Huai basin. Socially, there are indications of
a system based on the cultivation of land by women. With
Yü this period closes and there is a change, presumably
in the Hsia period, to a system of inheritance through clans
of male descent.

Slight as they are, these indications warrant, I think, the
general conclusion that before any specifically Chinese line
of evolution and development originated there was wide
primitive settlement in what is now China. The restricted
territory about the great bend of the Yellow River, in
which the earliest evolutionary development began, may not
have been peopled any earlier or more thickly than the
lower Yellow River plain, which we know must have been
subject to flood because of the silting up of the river, or
than the Huai basin which must certainly have been
marshy, or the Yangtze valley with its ancient jungle

[35] Compare Chapter V, above. It may be conjectured that the real status
of women, when women are the main labor adjunct to the cultivation of the
land, probably varies according to the skill and "lore" associated with planting. If the amount of real or apparent skill is enough to make cultivation
seem mysterious to the men the position and authority of the women may well
be relatively high.

growth. There was as yet no distinction between "Chinese" and "barbarians," though there may well have been ethnic differences between the peoples of this wide land, and there must have been cultural differences between groups living in different environments. These, however, can only have been differences on the same general plane, not differences between markedly "higher" and "lower" cultures.

An apparent contraction of the geographical field goes with the stirrings of change that led to the genesis of Chinese history. That this contraction did not really mean a severance of contact between the nuclear region at the great bend of the Yellow River and the territories peripheral to it is indicated by Eberhard's provisional classification of a series of primitive cultural groups contributing to the "Chinese" culture either at its beginning or not long after.[36] It is possible, then, that the actual phenomenon which determined the character of the time was an acceleration of change at about the line of geographical demarcation between the loess highlands of the middle Yellow River and the wide plain of the lower Yellow River—accompanied, perhaps, by a movement of people out of the lower, more flooded, and more marshy lands toward the relatively treeless and easily cleared loess. Adding to this the indications of a change from women's agriculture to men's agriculture, it is at least suggested, though not proved, that this time of change had something to do with a changing way of life which made the loess region more profitable and able to hold a more concentrated population than other parts of North China. The changes themselves may have been the result of the first primitive attempts at irrigation, through working the soft loess with stone and wooden tools,

[36] Eberhard, Early Chinese Cultures, 1938. Eberhard's classification of a number of culture complexes is of most interest from the aspect of geographical distribution, but suffers from lack of sufficient allowance for the different time levels of evolution within cultures, as he himself warns (p. 515). That a western culture area existed, for instance, is important; that it had always and from the beginning "a strong element of pastoral nomadism with a rigidly organized patriarchate" is more than doubtful.

or they may have been due simply to the greater ease of clearing the light natural growth that covered the loess soil in order to extend cultivation—a change that was followed only later by irrigation, undertaken as a means of compensating for the irregularity of the rainfall.

Certainly it is probable that up to this point the process of social differentiation was not one of conflict between "Chinese" and "barbarians," even though there was undoubtedly migration and contact between peoples. It is more probable that the main process was the gradual transformation of some barbarians into primitive Chinese, while other barbarians remained what they had always been.[37] Only after this was the initial contraction of the field of history converted into a phase of expansion, accompanied by conflict and the gradual invasion of barbarian territory by the proto-Chinese, which was accompanied, in turn, by development of the loess technique of agriculture to the point where it could be extended into other kinds of terrain.

The development of the argument thus far is, I think, strengthened by the fact that it rests on the grouping together of a number of general considerations. Any one of these considerations could be considerably modified without destroying the force of the argument as a whole. The reasoning adopted does not depend on the linking up of a single chain of evidence in which the impairment of one link would break the whole continuity.

THE HSIA AND SHANG PERIODS

Nevertheless, the welding of at least one link must be attempted. Chinese investigators have attempted to trace back the genealogy of the Shang rulers to figures that appear in the conventional account of the Hsia period. Does this mean that there really was a Hsia period and that the

---

[37] Maspero, La Chine antique, pp. 10-11.

Shang period derived from it, either directly or as an off-shoot? Is it perhaps possible that the Hsia period is to be identified with that hypothetical phase of economic change and social mutation in which, as I have just suggested, women's agriculture gave way to men's agriculture, while the wide focus of prehistoric China "contracted" and centered on the nuclear territory at the great bend of the Yellow River? Could it even be possible that the Hsia are to be identified either with the "painted pottery" or the "black pottery" sites of late neolithic China?

Creel, whose great caution makes him a valuable guide, does not go as far as this. Indeed, he specifically rejects an attempt by Hsü Chung-shu to identify the Hsia people with the painted pottery culture.[38] In this he is probably correct, for Hsü's argument rests too exclusively on etymological speculation, which for this remote horizon of history is necessarily of limited cogency. Creel himself, however, holds that a Hsia state "must have existed," though "its dates, its kings and its events appear to be wholly legendary." [39] Even the written name has not been satisfactorily identified on the oracle-bones,[40] but still "it is probable that there was a certain degree of linguistic significance to the term Hsia." [41] It was also a culture, ancestral to the true Chinese culture.[42] Its geographical focus was "in the general region of the lower Yellow River Valley," [43] a territory "roughly oval in shape, with its long axis running east and west and tilted slightly toward the northeast," [44] extending from the middle of the modern Honan into Hopei, and into Shantung on the east and Shansi on the northwest. Moreover, "the fact that the

[38] Creel, op. cit., p. 127, citing an article by Hsü in the "Reports on Excavations at Anyang," edit. Li Chi (in Chinese).
[39] Creel, op. cit., p. 131.
[40] Ibid., p. 130.
[41] Ibid., p. 118.
[42] Ibid., p. 117.
[43] Ibid., p. 131.
[44] Ibid., p. 116.

term Hsia was later used so persistently to mean 'Chinese' and 'the Chinese states' in a cultural sense leads us to infer that this state was the leading exponent of Chinese culture in its day." [45] Creel also emphasizes that mention of the Hsia is made both very early and very often.[46]

It seems as though there ought to be some reasonable explanation of the rather striking fact that from *relatively* early times the name Hsia has been used as a literary and "cultural" equivalent for "the Chinese," while in *very* early times the name cannot be proved to have existed at all. One possible explanation seems both reasonable and simple. Peoples very often have a name of their own by which they call themselves while they are known to other peoples by a quite different name. The people who called themselves Shang were also known as Yin. It is at least open to conjecture that the term Hsia was originally used by the Chou people; that the Chou, themselves a rather barbarous people on the edge of the nuclear territory of the "early Chinese," referred to the main body of this people by the ethnic or cultural term Hsia and used the term Yin as the political name of a more limited group, which had held a kind of hegemony for a considerable period of time at the heart of this "early Chinese" population, and which called itself neither Hsia nor Yin, but Shang.[47]

This is only a conjecture, not a theory of Chinese origins. I put it forward here for the sake of emphasizing a group of ideas about early Chinese evolution and differentiation which I think may prove to be sound. Particular aspects of these ideas may not be correct; it is with the general concept that I am concerned. This is the concept of multiple historical processes and different rates of historical change which I stated at the end of the previous chapter. If neolithic groups—not yet "Chinese" and not yet "barbarian"

[45] *Ibid.*, p. 130.
[46] *Ibid.*, p. 100.
[47] For the argument that Yin as a name for the Shang "dynasty" was originally a Chou usage, compare Creel, *op. cit.*, pp. 64-66.

—were scattered rather widely over China; if in North China some of these groups began to "become Chinese" rather rapidly, while others also began to "become Chinese" not so rapidly; if still other groups did not follow this trend at all but took one that led them eventually to "become barbarians": then the names of Hsia and Shang and Chou may be used in a diagram of the whole process, indicating both geographical distribution and the time-levels of history.

Hsia, to begin with, may be a general index to the later phases of the "painted pottery" and "black pottery" neolithic cultures of North China and, perhaps, an index to the "black pottery" and the development of a "progressive" late neolithic phase in particular. This is not the same thing as the attempted identification of the Hsia and the "painted pottery" by Hsü Chung-shu.[48] The argument as drawn by Hsü is too narrow: it aims at linking particular supposed Hsia characteristics with a particular "painted pottery" site. It is probably sounder to say that there are enough echoes of a Hsia period to warrant the working theory that the Hsia must have had a number of characteristics that distinguished them from the late neolithic culture and period as a whole, but to admit, at the same time, that these characteristics cannot, as yet, be certainly distinguished as a complete cultural organism.

Geographically, again, the Hsia area as plotted by Creel [49] shows a rough but significant distribution over a region in which the edges of the Great Plain of the lower Yellow River are overlooked by the lower loess highlands and other hilly formations that must have stood above the primeval marsh and flood levels. This encourages the assumption that the Hsia period may have had something to do with the beginnings of differentiation between neolithic groups in favored areas that encouraged agricultural evo-

[48] See the same, p. 127.
[49] Ibid., pp. 116, 131.

lution, and other groups, originally similar, which tended to fall behind because they occupied less favorable areas. If the "black pottery" can in fact be identified with a relatively rapidly evolving culture and the "painted pottery" with the less rapidly evolving fringe of the same culture, then there is ground for at least the preliminary assumption that the Hsia period is to be identified more with the "black pottery"—and especially with the "black pottery" as a component of the later Shang culture—than with the "painted pottery," as argued by Hsü Chung-shu.

Next, the Shang period and culture may be described in terms of a still more definite agricultural evolution: a firmer economic and social outline of walled towns, which must have been the political centers of agricultural districts; the rapid development of a high technique in the working of bronze; and a distinction, which must have been sharp and important, between bronze-using rulers and stone-using subject people. There is good reason also to believe that there was a transition from matrilineal clans with women's agriculture to patrilineal clans with men's agriculture. If so, there must also have been important new differentiations between the various activities proper for men. By taking over agriculture, which had been women's work, some of the men's clans "fell" to what had been the status of women. Other individual men or men's clans continued the traditional men's work of war and hunting. Thus in a sense they remained static, but at the same time they "rose," for to these old activities they also added the new function of protecting—and therefore governing and exploiting—the men who had "fallen" socially, as the society as a whole "rose" economically and the technical improvement and specialization of agriculture made it profitable and necessary for some of the men to give the whole of their time to work in the fields. In this way the traditional men's work of hunting and war became economically less necessary, but at the same time became symbols of luxury and high social status.

How far all these changes were contemporary and interacting, and how far they proceeded out of each other in historical succession, it is impossible to say. For one thing, the rich Bronze Age material from Anyang, worked over so much in recent years, does not go back to the early Shang period, so that the all-important initial modes of Shang development are as obscure as the whole Hsia period which preceded them. The least hazardous way of marking out the margins between which fell the probable line of Shang development seems to be as follows: Continuity of some kind between the Hsia and the Shang is probable. The Shang genealogies point far back toward the Hsia period, if they do not reach right into it. The Chou, successors of the Shang, assumed that the Shang had been successors of the Hsia.[50] The succession, however, need not have been direct. Shang history may not have been the product of the continuous and even development of the whole of the Hsia area, people, and culture.

On the contrary, it may have been the result of an accelerating development, either at the heart of the Hsia culture or perhaps on one of its margins, which affected only part of what had been Hsia. In other words, part of the old Hsia may have been intensified, so to speak, into a new and more political entity of Shang, while the rest remained Hsia in a rather vague ethnic and cultural way. The actual term Hsia, however, may not yet even have come into existence; it may have originated later as a term for people of the stock and culture out of which the Shang had arisen, who had lagged behind the Shang in evolution. Earlier conversion of the Shang group from matrilineal clans to patrilineal clans and a more advanced agriculture worked at by men who became a subject peas-

[50] For the "political propaganda" aspect of this, see the same, pp. 51-52.

ant class, may have been one of the differentiating processes. It is not essential, however, to this view of Chinese origins to attempt to define categorically whether this kind of social change marked the end of the Hsia phase in general or the beginning of the Shang phase in particular.

This prepares the way for a similar treatment of Chou origins. To hold that Shang history represents essentially a narrowing down of the focus of Chinese origins is not the same thing as to say that all the remainder of what had been Hsia was left behind in barbarism. Some of those who were left outside the new focus of more intense development may eventually have "become barbarians," but others may, in time, have "become Chinese," though more slowly than the Shang vanguard. With differentiation thus becoming more and more complicated, and with more than two cultural levels becoming distinguishable, processes of interaction in many degrees of intensity must have become important.

For one thing, it is obvious that in the Shang Bronze Age there was a great increase in wealth and in the concentration of wealth, as compared with anything that the late neolithic period had produced in North China. It is evident also that this wealth nourished a remarkable sophistication and subtlety of culture at the top of Shang society. The Shang people, or at least their noble class, were also great warriors. This, however, does not prove that the Shang wealth and culture produced the maximum military superiority or efficiency of the age. Or there may have been an initial military superiority which was converted into inferiority toward the end of the Shang age. By way of hypothesis the following stages may be suggested.

1. Accelerating development within a limited area led to the rise of the Shang out of the general body of Hsia culture. The mixed neolithic economy of hunting, food gathering, and weak agriculture gave way to a stronger and more specialized agriculture. Some of the men be-

came wholly identified with the fields, as peasants or subjects. Other men became the owners or rulers of both peasants and land. These men had the leisure to keep up hunting; and skill in hunting being allied to skill in war, the first step was taken toward a feudal class of nobles who were warriors, hunters, owners of slaves, and heads of landowning clans. This, and the rapid improvement of bronze weapons made for the ruling warriors by protected metal workers, contributed to a great superiority in war. The rapidly developing Shang people were able to raid the more backward groups to which they had once been kin, taking captives to use in human sacrifice [51] and also as slaves.

2. Other groups began to follow, though more slowly, the same line of evolution as the Shang, some of them becoming tributaries while others remained independent and hostile though imitating as far as they could the characteristics that had given strength to the Shang. Some of these groups, which had not been sufficiently advanced in general culture to develop for themselves the technique of working in bronze as the Shang had developed it, were able to take over this technique once it had been developed. This narrowed the gap in military efficiency between what had now become backward or "less-Chinese" groups and the progressive Shang or "more-Chinese" group. Advance by borrowing was as good as independent advance.

3. As the backward groups became more formidable in war the most advanced and cultured group became more vulnerable. War, for the Shang people, came to mean not only the raiding of others but the protection of their own slaves, granaries, wealth, and lands. The difference between slave cultivators and ruling warriors meant that interest in war was not equal throughout the society. More backward groups with fewer slaves and more free warriors, even though they were less "noble" than the

[51] *Ibid.*, pp. 214-218.

Shang aristocracy, became able to hold their own in war against the Shang.

4. When this equalizing process had gone far enough it was only a question of time until the Shang should be overthrown by a cruder people who were not necessarily invaders from beyond the horizon of what was now definitely the early Chinese culture but a people already belonging to the Chinese culture although not to its most refined and advanced form.

The Chou Period

The Chou Chinese were the people who initiated this new phase. The early Chou period is not much more historical than the late Shang period, just as the early Shang period is not much more historical than the Hsia period. Nevertheless, the Chou are of very great importance, for just before their second period (B.C. 771-222) begins the accurate dating of the long record of Chinese history.

Up to this point I have laid the main emphasis on the way in which Chinese culture was created by evolution, the evolutionary processes being stimulated by the differentiation of neolithic society in North China at a number of "advanced" and "backward" levels. In so doing I do not mean to ignore altogether the possibility that China was also influenced from very early times by invasions and migrations. The Chinese tradition that the Chou people had a smell of the barbarian about them is clear and persistent. Bishop holds that many prime elements of the later Chinese culture were brought into China from Central Asia and the Near East. This was accomplished by migration, invasion, and culture diffusion. He attributes a non-Chinese origin to wheat, millet, and the technique of irrigation; also to the ox-drawn plough, which did not reach China until the fourth century B.C.[52] In conformity

[52] Bishop, Origin and Early Diffusion of the Traction-Plow, 1936, p. 545; also, for irrigation (of rice), Beginnings of North and South, 1934, p. 299.

with this general view, he believes that the early Chou people were "in touch with regions far away in Central Asia." [53]

This may well be true. It is quite possible that non-Chinese cultural characteristics and techniques "filtered through" to the early Chou people, much as the knowledge of how to work with copper and bronze filtered through the western part of neolithic North China until it reached the area where conditions most favored its further development. It seems to me no longer disputable, however, that the Chou people belonged in the main to the same "Chinese" culture as the Shang [54] and that in the strict sense they had not "acquired" this culture from the Shang, although to a certain extent they had developed it by imitation of them. What I mean by this apparently contradictory statement is that the Shang and the Chou both derived their chief heritage from the same antecedent culture, although the Shang began their advance to a higher stage earlier and carried it further, whereas the Chou started to mature later, hastened their advance to some extent by imitation of the Shang, and were still at a comparatively crude level, taking their culture as a whole, at the time when they became politically ascendant over the Shang. It is in this sense that they must be spoken of as belonging to the culture rather than as acquiring it. Conversely, if any characteristics of the Chou must be described as "barbarian" in the sense of being definitely un-Chinese, not merely pre-Chinese, then it must be assumed that these were characteristics that the Chou had acquired by culture diffusion or contact with migrating peoples, not characteristics that belonged to the original matrix of Chou society and culture.

If I am correct, then it was natural for the Chou, when

[53] *Ibid.*, p. 312 and footnote.
[54] Bishop (*op. cit.*, p. 310) holds that on the contrary the Chou may have been distantly related to the Tibeto-Burman linguistic stock. For the question of linguistic groups and culture groups, see also Chapter XIV, below.

they moved in from the horizon of Shang history toward the Shang political center of gravity, to regard themselves not as conquering invaders but as legitimate heirs of the whole culture within which the Shang had held the political hegemony. They derived, that is, from the Hsia period of history, just as did the Shang themselves, though by a more "provincial" line of descent. In order to assert their leadership it would have been natural for them to depreciate the particular sanctions that had been gathered about the political and cultural primacy of the Shang and to emphasize instead their own legitimacy as the new leading group in a number of groups which were of common origin though not all of them stood at the same level of evolution. This, again, may well have led to an artificial glorification of the Hsia as the origin of everything Chinese, and to the political teaching that there had been a single Hsia empire in a golden age of the past, whereas in fact there had only been a Hsia area of comparatively rapid cultural and social innovation at the end of the neolithic period in North China. In its essentials this view agrees, I think, with Creel's theory that the Chou people built up a Hsia myth; [55] and Creel also believes apparently that the Chou were a provincial, marginal people who belonged nevertheless to the Chinese culture of the time, not an intruding, definitely un-Chinese people who "acquired" the culture that enabled them to overthrow the Shang.

EARLY DIFFERENTIATION BETWEEN THE PEOPLES OF THE LOESS HIGHLANDS AND OF THE GREAT PLAIN

Having stated in this way a method of approach to the problem of Chinese origins which assumes that Hsia, Shang, and Chou were all akin, I have in fact denied that what we think of as "China" was the result of the invasion and conquest of primitive agricultural peoples by primitive

[55] Creel, *op. cit.*, p. 51, etc.

steppe nomads. Only major invasions and the idea of large movements of people over great distances have been ruled out, not the idea of culture diffusion, which must have accompanied the infiltration of small bodies of people. These migratory movements may not have involved long journeys. More probably the migration of any one group was limited, but, as one group came into contact with another, culture diffusion was accomplished by a series of borrowings. Nevertheless, the society of steppe nomadism did have a great importance in later Chinese history. It is therefore necessary to deal with the problem of when and how steppe nomadism began to operate on the inland Frontier of China. This I shall do in the next chapter; but first it is necessary to recapitulate the problem of ancient Chinese geography as a whole and to examine the primary historical characteristics of agricultural societies and nomad societies.[56]

An article by Fu Ssu-nien offers a good approach.[57] He holds that the first differentiation between Chinese and barbarians involved a cleavage between east and west, entirely different from the north-south cleavage of later centuries. He distinguishes the people of the loess highlands from those of the Great Plain. The people of the loess congregated in the river valleys; the people of the plain built on high ground—presumably to avoid floods.

---

[56] The whole problem could be made clearer if a distinction were habitually made between *migration* and *nomadism*. So far as I know, this is not done by either Chinese or Western writers. Yet societies that migrate from place to place, practicing an agriculture that is permanent as a habit though temporary as to locality, are functionally different from nomads. This is true if they also practice hunting, fishing, and the gathering of uncultivated plants. Groups which also have some domesticated animals, used partly as a source of food and partly for transport, are marginal between the migratory classification and the nomadic classification. True nomadism, however, is unmistakable. It is the technique of interposing animals between the human society and the geographical environment: the people live either wholly or to a determining degree on the produce of their herds and must move in an orbit of seasonal migration (transhumance), accommodating themselves to the needs of the herds in the way of food, shelter, and change of pasture.
[57] Fu Ssu-nien, An East-West Theory of the I and Hsia, 1936 (in Chinese).

The loess terrain was easily defended and a good base from which to expand. The Great Plain was easily invaded and a weak base for expansion. The loess was relatively poor in productivity, but breeding of livestock could be combined with farming. The plains were much more productive, except for livestock, which must have been hard to breed before the swamps of the lower Yellow River were drained. There was a natural transition from the Great Plain to the lower part of Manchuria, and a corresponding transition from the loess highlands to the steppes of Mongolia.

The peoples of the plains and the highlands influenced each other alternatingly. There are two groups of loess peoples: first, the Hsia, centering on the valley of the Fen, in Shansi, and extending also into Honan; and later, the Chou, identified with the three great rivers of Shensi—the Wei, the Ching, and the Lo—all with headwaters reaching back into Kansu. There are also two peoples of the plains: the Shang, in the northern part of Honan and in Hopei; and the I, in Shantung, Eastern Honan, and the northern part of Kiangsu, and also in South Manchuria and Korea. Thus the Shang held the northern part of the lower Yellow River plain, while the I, later known conventionally as the Eastern Barbarians, extended from the southern part of the same plain into the Huai basin and were also in primitive communication by a short and easy sea passage with the south of Manchuria and the coast of Korea. The Shang and the I not only held contiguous territories but were contemporary, while in the loess country there was a time gap between the Hsia and the Chou.

The alternating ascendancy of these peoples created the Chinese nation. The sequence is: a first loess-highland phase under the Hsia, with warfare between the Hsia and the I; a Great Plains phase under the Shang, who strengthened themselves by drawing on the manpower and economic resources of the I; and a second loess-highland phase under the Chou.

In B.C. 770-769, the Chou capital was moved from Shensi into the Great Plain, and from this time the Chou political power declined. In the third century B.C. western ascendancy was reasserted under the Ch'in. The most stubborn opponent of the loess-highland state of Ch'in was the Yangtze valley state of Ch'u. Although Ch'in conquered Ch'u and founded the first unified Chinese Empire, the dynasty did not last. Resistance to it centered among the Huai and Yangtze peoples, and, drawing on the strength of this resistance, the Han dynasty was founded in B.C. 206. The dynasty at once established its capital in the loess country, and at the same time completed the conquest of the Yangtze valley, thus confirming both the unity of the empire and the ascendancy of the North.

This theory provides for the gradual conversion of an east-west cleavage into a north-south opposition, as barbarian resistance wheeled from the coastal regions of North China down to the Yangtze. The pivot of this change was the Yangtze state of Ch'u. Thus there was established the conventional scale running from steppe barbarians in the extreme north to northern or "true" Chinese; then to Yangtze valley Chinese (the ancient southerners) ; then south of the Yangtze, where the modern southern Chinese are descended from "southern barbarians" who were "converted" into Chinese at different periods ; then to the still surviving aborigines of the far south and southwest of China.

In one or another variation this theory is widely supported in China.[58] It is a good working theory,[59] for

[58] Compare Feng Chia-sheng, The Northeast in Extreme Antiquity, 1936 (in Chinese). This valuable survey lists not only leading Chinese theories but the most important work in Japanese and the European languages.

[59] Fu Ssu-nien tends to work largely by weaving the theories of others into

though any one detail may be restated as more evidence accrues, its emphasis is obviously on the main point that there was an early differentiation along the line of meeting between the loess highlands and the Great Plain. Here the true Chinese order, in which agriculture became increasingly the dominant interest, arose out of much more varied primitive activities—hunting, fishing, and food gathering, a scattered agriculture, the domestication first of dogs and pigs, which are easily fed on refuse, and then of sheep and cattle.

BEGINNINGS OF IRRIGATION IN RELATION TO CULTURAL DEVELOPMENT

What, then, are the forces that make for evolution and specialization in agriculturally based societies, and can they be accounted for in a way that fits this description of primitive China? There are a number of possibilities. An agricultural society may evolve toward something different, as in Western Europe, where industrialization originated; or it may evolve by specialization, as in China (and Egypt), where irrigation and drainage were so important that they shaped the whole economy by their insistence on immense reserves of human labor, which checked any tendency toward the evolution of industrialism; or it may remain for century after century at one level, as among the trans-Yangtze peoples whom the Chinese have not yet entirely displaced or "converted" into Chinese.

Irrigation lies at the core of the Chinese agriculture and the Chinese way of life, but not necessarily at the very roots. Wittfogel believes that the Chou people had an irrigated agriculture even before they defeated the Shang,

larger patterns of his own, a method which runs the risk of becoming over-speculative. It is also likely to be weakest where it is most philological or literary. He is capable, for instance, of arguing that peoples that have the same legends must be of common historical origin. (Li Chi, in his "Manchuria in History," 1932, makes the same slip in discussing the same cycle of legend.) This, however, does not diminish the value of Fu Ssu-nien's work as an index to trends in recent Chinese work on ancient origins.

and thinks it possible that the Shang themselves also practiced irrigation. This cannot be definitely proved, however,
and therefore the whole problem should be handled with
extreme caution.[60] In the same way it can be pointed out,
as I have pointed out earlier, that small irrigation ditches
could have been dug in the soft loess even with stone tools;
but this does not prove that even the most advanced neolithic people in North China did in fact irrigate their fields.
The whole problem has been moderately stated by Hsü
Chung-shu: irrigation in China is probably much older
than has hitherto been assumed. Such complicated enterprises as irrigation and embankment against floods could
not be rapidly brought to a high state of development. In
the period of the Warring States, in the fourth century
B.C., conservancy works of both kinds were of very great
importance in China. Their origin, accordingly, must lie
very far back.[61]

The technique of irrigation could not have established
itself in China at an early time except under very special
conditions. Whether the technique originated independently in China or whether it was transmitted to China
from the Middle East or Central Asia, as Bishop thinks
more probable, this would be equally true. The necessary
conditions include: 1) an environment offering both wild
game and wild plants, fruits, and berries; 2) a vegetation
suggesting or making easy the transition from collecting
wild plants to improvement of the supply by cultivation;
3) a climate of such a kind that either the scarcity or the
irregularity of rainfall, together with the presence of running water, would encourage the idea of bringing water
from a short distance to fields already planted but already

[60] Wittfogel, Economic and Social History (1940), with a survey of recent
Chinese opinion on the problem.
[61] Hsü Chung-shu, in an article in the *Bulletin of the Institute of History
and Philology of the Academia Sinica,* Vol. V, Part II, Peiping, 1935.
This reference, which I owe to K. A. Wittfogel, I have not been able to
check personally.

suffering from lack of rain; 4) a soil that was not encumbered with heavy forest growth requiring more than
the simplest tools for its clearing and that could be easily
worked with such tools, and which was also responsive to
the application of water alone without elaborate practices
of cultivation and manuring.

These conditions exactly describe the valleys of streams
running through the loess highlands. A further point is to
be noted, however. Most of these conditions would equally
favor a gradually increasing emphasis on cultivated crops,
even without irrigation, in what had originally been a
mixed economy of hunting and food gathering. For this
reason it is not necessary to assume that irrigation goes
all the way back to the origins of Chinese agriculture. On
the whole, it is more probable that the first development
was an increase in crops gathered from small and primitive fields without irrigation. If so, it may be that the
first effect of success in improving the permanent food
supply was to improve the cohesion and social strength
of those groups that were relatively large in number and
that cultivated comparatively large fields continuously, as
against the groups that moved in small numbers, migrating from one hunting ground to another and from one
catch crop to another.

Fishing does not require migration in the way that the
hunting of wild game does. It is possible, therefore, that
the very first tendency to shift from a desultory to a
slightly more regular agriculture was in the easily worked
loess country, but that this was followed by more rapid
success along the line of cleavage between the loess and
the Great Plain because of the advantage held by groups
that could fish in the marshes and streams, cultivate open
fields between the water and the higher land, and also continue to send hunting parties into the hills. Perhaps this
is, in fact, what accounts for the hints of a wavering emphasis between the loess highlands and the Great Plain

at the hazy beginning of Chinese history, for the cleavage between "painted pottery" and "black pottery" peoples, and for the Hsia period which presumably was transitional between the end of the neolithic period and the opening of the Shang Bronze Age.

With the beginnings of irrigation, however, even if those beginnings came a good deal later, there must have been a return to emphasis on the loess terrain. The smaller the valley in the loess, if only that valley had running water, the easier the first attempts at irrigation on a small scale. The larger the valley and the stream, however, the greater the return. Even with the more rapid rate of evolution shifting from the plains to the loess, therefore, the first successful irrigating society must have begun once more to move downstream. Thus it would again converge on the Yellow River, a little above and a little below the great bend, by the valleys of the Wei, Ching, and Lo in Shensi, the Fen in Shansi, and the Lo in Honan.[62] The focus of evolution would in this way be brought back within range of the Great Plain and open up still another phase of development.

Increase of irrigation must have encouraged living and working in larger and larger groups. At the same time, the expanding scale of production must have made for better working methods and tools. Logically, a spread out into the open plain would make possible production on an even larger scale, but improved social organization would have to come first. The plains required not only irrigation but drainage and embankments against flood.[63] The first attempts at irrigation could be made by a family, or a few families informally associated, but drainage and

[62] Note the difference between the Lo River in Shensi and the Lo River in Honan.

[63] For the differences (especially in scale of operation) between the technique of irrigation and that of drainage and embankment, compare Wittfogel's categories of "too little water" and "too much water" (Wirtschaft und Gesellschaft Chinas, 1931, pp. 189 et sqq.).

embankment in the wide plains of North China, dominated by the Father of Floods, the Yellow River, demanded a society under firm control.

In the early growth of the Chinese culture, therefore,
geographical spread and social evolution must have interacted closely. It did not need a great technical advance to
adapt the methods of irrigation to the methods of drainage and embankment. The development of these methods
must have been simple and natural; but they could not be
put into effect without social changes that made a difference in the personal and public life of all the people concerned—in the allotment of labor and its rewards, and of
duty and responsibility; in the nature of wealth, property,
and rank, and consequently in marriage, inheritance, and
the structure of the clan and the family.

Therefore, the process of change could not stop at the
point where primitive agriculture without irrigation had
been transformed into primitive irrigated agriculture. Momentum had been acquired: irrigated agriculture, though
still primitive, could not remain as nearly timeless and
balanced as the agriculture that had preceded it. The
process by which it had come into being was bound up with
other changes, both quantitative in the scale of enterprise
and qualitative in the ratio of return to labor expended.

The question of scale affected the individual, the family, the local community, and the state. Larger enterprises
—especially embankment and drainage in the open plain,
which differed in a significant way from the irrigation of
a self-contained valley—demanded a steady growth of authority. Evolution of this kind created new problems. In
time, the basic technique of what the Chinese call *shui i,*
water benefits, was further applied to work on great canals
that served simultaneously for irrigation, for flood prevention (by heightening of their banks), for drainage,
and for transport. This affected the way in which regions

were related to each other.[64] Irrigated agriculture in self-contained regions could be profitably administered by a feudal nobility. Communication between regions and enterprises great enough to affect more than one region made for the rise of a central power able to subordinate the feudal nobles.

Problems of efficiency must also have modified the social structure and the distribution of power, partly by interacting with the growth of the scale of enterprise but especially by accelerating the rate of development. In advancing from the use of stone to the use of metal, for instance, there is a critical difference between an advanced primitive society ready to take advantage of the superior efficiency of metal, and a backward primitive society which is not prepared to exploit the potentialities of metal. This can be stated in terms of equilibrium. The more backward a society the more likely it is to be at rest and in balance, with the result that it is either unreceptive to changes and innovations or accepts them in such a passive way as to cause the minimum change of balance. The more progressive a society the more likely it is that the very processes of change and evolution have upset the old balance—the balance within the society and the balance of adjustment between society and environment—with the result that innovations enhance the effect of the forces already at work, not only by increasing the proportion of change but by intensifying the rate of change.

Warfare, in particular, is an activity which is more likely to develop decisively in combination with other social activities than alone. In a stable primitive society warfare is normally one of the activities that maintain equilibrium: it bleeds the resources of the society but keeps it the same kind of society. For a society that is already in a state of change things are different: success in war

[64] Ch'ao-ting Chi, Key Economic Areas in Chinese History, 1936.

means increased territory, a greater subject population, and larger revenue to be acquired and enjoyed by combining military superiority with superiority in economic method and social organization. In this way rapid specialization and improvement is promoted not merely in weapons but in the whole concept and technique of war. Whatever the exact levels of history at which the technique of irrigation and the technique of working in metal began to operate, therefore, it can certainly be assumed that the one that came first prepared the way for ready acceptance and use of the other. From the time that both were in operation, moreover, each must have stimulated the other.

These considerations provide an entirely rational and realistic standard for assessing the quality of the Shang age and also that of the Chou culture, which arose partly out of it and partly to one side of it. Among the Shang people metal had not entirely displaced stone. The use of metal for weapons, chariots, and articles of luxury establishes the importance of a ruling class whose warriors, fighting from chariots, had a great advantage over the plebeian foot soldier. It can hardly be doubted that within their own society the Shang people were advancing rapidly in the technique of agriculture, the concentration of wealth, and the organization of a subject majority to suit the needs of a ruling minority. At the same time they were in an ascendant phase in their wars with other groups. As a result, some of their neighbors fell under their rule and were recruited to the number of their subjects, while others maintained independence only by converting themselves into groups imitative of the Shang society even though hostile to it or wary of it.

The multiplication of groups like the Shang people, and the degree of closeness with which each of them more or less reproduced the Shang comity, must have been governed largely by geographical factors like distance, climate, water supply, soil, and the existence of natural frontiers between some regions and not between others. This once more confirms the hypothesis of a double process—one of geographical spread, partly by conquest and partly by "conversion" and imitation, from the focal area in which the people of the loess and the people of the plain met and influenced each other; and one of retraction, as new focal areas tended to form wherever the environment favored them.

FIRST ENLARGEMENT OF CHINESE HORIZON TOWARD BOTH EAST AND WEST

Since the two largest homogeneous areas were the Great Plain on the east and the loess highlands on the west, it is likely that the first enlargement of the "Chinese" horizon was toward both east and west, with only minor trends toward the north and northwest in upper Shansi and upper Shensi, and toward the south and southeast in the Huai basin. In this first phase it does not greatly matter whether the I of the east and the Jung of the west be taken as Eastern and Western Barbarians,[65] or as tribes cognate with the Shang Chinese though less advanced in culture— "survivors," in a manner of speaking, of the brothers of the great-grandfathers of the Shang people. It may be conjectured, though, that historically the change from a standard of comparison between "more-Chinese" and "less-Chinese" to one of differentiation between "Chinese" and "un-Chinese" was rather gradual.

That change, I suggest, was brought about in the following way: In the first spread east and west the emphasis was on the *similarity* between the loess highlands and the Great Plain as environments in which the same

[65] Fu Ssu-nien, *op. cit.*, assumes a very wide distribution of the earliest I peoples; as do the writers (now not generally followed) who believe in a "proto-Tungus" migration from Shantung to Siberia (Feng Chia-sheng, *op. cit.*). C. W. Bishop, in a personal letter of July 27, 1938, points out that the wide and loose application of the term I is a later usage and that the I peoples properly so-called ranged from Shantung southward to the mouth of the Yangtze, but not northward into Manchuria.

kinds of economic practice and social form could flourish. Then, as the spread widened, the inherent *differences* between the two environments began to assert themselves. The topography of the loess favored political independence in each major valley. The topography of the Great Plain favored an inclusive state on a much larger scale; but the political creation of such a state demanded the evolution, necessarily slow, of long-range communications, a warfare of great numbers and long range, and political and administrative forms also capable of operating over great areas. The result—entirely congruent with the known facts— was that it was many centuries before any one state could effectively rule the whole of what was already China in a cultural and social sense. In the meantime, some of the factors pointed out by Fu Ssu-nien operated with maximum effect. The loess highlands, though economically poorer, were strong in offense and defense, while the Great Plain, though economically richer, lay open to attack and could not yet be effectively organized for offense.

Consequently, the small and poor states of the loess highlands were able to advance more rapidly in every kind of evolution—economic and political as well as military— than the richer states of the Great Plain. The scale of their geographical units permitted a better integration because it suited better the still immature level of evolution. The decisive steps initiating each new phase of political development therefore came from the west, from Shensi, first under the Chou about the opening of the last millennium B.C., and then under the Ch'in, in the third century B.C. Each of these advances was followed by a reaction as the improved methods developed on a small scale felt the strain of being applied on an immensely expanded scale. Both the Chou and the Ch'in first attained eminence because they were able to go ahead independently of the larger China to whose cultural orbit they belonged; but since the need for centralization of the Great Plain worked against the tradition of independence of the loess highlands, both the Chou and the Ch'in had to attempt to apply, under terms of responsibility for a greater China, institutions which they had improved while asserting their independence of the rest of China. The fluctuating action and reaction between West and East, spoken of by Fu-Ssu-nien, could not therefore strike an equilibrium prevailing over the whole of China until the time of the Han (last two centuries B.C. and first two centuries of the Christian Era) when institutions long known in theory had at last been adapted to practical working efficiency on the scale required.

RISE OF A SECOND FOCAL AREA IN SOUTH CHINA

Another aspect of the whole process must also be discussed. The early spread westward differed in an important respect from the spread eastward. There was no major difference of environment between the western edge and the eastern edge of the Great Plain. The methods developed at the western edge, near the great bend of the Yellow River, could spread eastward to the sea, any variation between different communities and early states being less the product of geographical contrasts than of the differing social intensity or integration as between groups transformed by conquest *from* the focal area and groups transformed by imitation *of* the focal area. This was true until the sea had been reached; then the spread could only be continued toward the north or the south.[66]

On the south, in the Huai basin, and still more in the Yangtze valley, a new terrain had to be penetrated, with progressively increasing changes in climate and crop con-

[66] The wheeling movements from eastward to southward and from westward to northward began to develop in middle and late Chou times (second half of the last millennium B.C.), and so are a good deal later than the early processes which are the main subject of this chapter; but they grew out of the earlier processes and are therefore mentioned here.

ditions. In this terrain the new "Chinese" methods, as originated at the edge of the loess and the plains, and as modified in the plains, could still be applied, but only with further modifications. Given the lag between cultural spread and political development and unification, this meant that to the difference between direct conquest and imitation there was added a further degree of difference.

South China's rice culture (taking the Yangtze valley as the South of ancient times) was based on irrigation. The technical methods that made it possible were probably not derived from North China or transmitted, through North China, from some more distant region. If they did not originate somewhere between the Yangtze and the deeper South they may have reached China by a southern route of culture diffusion from India through Assam and Burma.[67] The problem of origin is not so critical as another aspect of irrigated rice culture. Even without irrigation, rice can be harvested by primitive people if the rainfall is heavy enough and regular enough and there are bottom lands available to hold the water. The importance of irrigation is that it sophisticates rice culture; it makes double-cropping possible and also increases the yield per acre of each crop. Either without irrigation or with an irrigation of primitive character, if no other stimulus were at work, a primitive society based on rice culture could presumably remain "balanced" or stagnant for an indefinite time without generating an evolutionary trend of its own.

It may be suggested therefore that the early impact of North China on the Yangtze valley was not important because of the spread of irrigation—or because of the spread of irrigation alone—but because there had become active in North China a society that was "out of balance" and therefore adapting itself to new methods at a comparatively high rate of evolution. The potential millet and wheat productivity of the North was lower than the po-

[67] Bishop, Beginnings of North and South, 1934, p. 316.

tential rice productivity of the South; but actual productivity and social organization in the North, taken as a complex or complete way of life, were at this time more highly developed and mature than in the South.[68] Since the people of the North, in spite of this relative superiority, were not yet capable of a range of action enabling them to conquer the South, the main phenomenon of early impact was the penetration of the Yangtze and Huai areas by northern methods of social organization and control, enabling the South to improve its productive methods and the integration of society and economy. °

There thus arose in the South—the Huai and the Yangtze—a secondary focus of the Chinese culture as a whole.[69] The centuries that passed before the powers of government were strong enough to operate over the whole field of the Chinese culture, from north to south, gave time for a vigorous independent development within this secondary focal area. In fact, the growth of the Yangtze South, nourished by its rich rice harvests, made it so formidable that it expanded aggressively against the North, so that in the wars between Ch'in and Ch'u in the third century B.C., when Ch'in had become master of the North and Ch'u master of the South, the ancient antagonism between East and West was converted into a struggle between North and South, Yangtze and Yellow River, for the control of a unified China.[70]

[68] C. W. Bishop, personal letter of July 27, 1938: "What superiority there was—and I think there probably was some—was, I fancy, the result of better organization rather than of better technique."

[69] This of course does not exclude the possibility that even earlier, at the most primitive level, the Stone Age people of the South were recognizably different from the people of the North in a number of cultural characteristics. (See Eberhard's theory as stated in his Early Chinese Cultures, 1938.) This would represent a category of "static" differentiation, with each cultural group closely adapted to its environment and even subordinated to it. The later differentiation belongs to a different category, being more "dynamic" as the result of increasing control over the environment, beginning earlier and later in different groups, progressing at different rates, and further complicated by the interacting of the different lines of evolution.

[70] See Chapter XII, below.

OBSTACLES TO WESTWARD AND NORTHWESTWARD
SPREAD OF CHINESE CULTURE

In the westward and northwestward spread of the original Chinese culture, from the line of meeting of the loess and the plains back into the remoter loess highlands, there was also a change of terrain and a progressive change in climate. To the north and northwest the loess merges into the steppe of Inner Mongolia. Fu Ssu-nien, thinking undoubtedly in traditional, conventional terms of the military superiority of mounted steppe nomads (although mounted nomad warfare had not been evolved at this period), points out the military significance of this but does not follow up the other implications. Yet there was a difference of decisive historical importance between the northern "hinterland" of the loess and the southern "hinterland" of the North China plain. The economic and social line of evolution emerging from the Great Plain could accommodate itself to the needs of the Yangtze region. Certain changes were demanded, but they were changes of a kind that brought profitable results in the rich rice culture of the Yangtze. The line of evolution, accordingly, brought not only equal returns but increasing returns. In the poorer hinterland of the loess, on the contrary, the line of evolution that had been established as profitable in the greater valleys met with decreasing returns as the attempt to practice irrigated agriculture was pushed toward the margin of the steppe. The valleys that could be irrigated grew smaller and smaller, and finally the spread was checked by the steppe, where the lack of running water barred irrigation altogether.

Nor could irrigated, intensive agriculture be "shaded off" into an extensive agriculture without irrigation, which was dependent on rainfall. It is true that in wide marginal areas of the steppe an extensive agriculture is quite possible. The rainfall is irregular, but the yield in good years is enough to provide a reserve for bad years, especially if mixed farming is practiced, with enough grazing of live-stock to vary the economy and spread the risk. This was not possible for the new society of China, which, being committed to irrigation, could not flourish unless the population was concentrated—in order to furnish the maximum supply of labor for the necessary key enterprises, the canals, which had to be dug and kept up by the united resources of the whole community in order to provide water for the fields of each private holding.

Along with this there went the necessity for simple but still specialized activities engaged in strictly according to season, so that between seasons it would be possible to muster the labor that would otherwise be idle and employ it in maintaining, cleaning, deepening, and if possible extending the canal system. The greater the potentially idle labor supply the cheaper the cost of maintenance and new enterprises. Consequently, even the cattle kept for ploughing could not be increased in number and elaborated into a secondary economy for the supply of milk and meat in quantity because the people engaged in tending them would be withdrawn from the necessary labor reserve.

Political control of the society, therefore, had its own line of evolution. Its growth toward more elaborate forms demanded the fostering of the reserve of labor. For this reason it created, eventually, a large class of tenants and landless peasants whose economic need made labor docile as well as cheap. This could only mean that the political tradition had from the very beginning to be hostile to any diversification of the basic intensive agricultural economy, and to treat as recalcitrants any marginal communities whose local interest would otherwise have prompted them to farm extensively, to multiply their livestock, and to make themselves individually independent by eliminating idle time and engaging in the maximum number of different kinds of activity.

Origins of Pastoral Nomadism

All of this emphasizes the importance of the fact that there has never been along the steppe frontiers of China an important independent society based on extensive agriculture, or agriculture combined with livestock breeding, intermediate between the intensive economy of China and the pastoral economy of steppe nomadism. Marginal groups have been of the greatest significance along different sectors of the Frontier at various times; but these have been societies that were marginal in the sense of an uneasy compromise, more political than economic, between regional powers based partly on the resources of the steppe and partly on those of China. They have not been societies with an integral order of their own and a historical "style" independent of both China and the steppe.

Here the general character of steppe history and its relation to Chinese history must be considered. Granting a "primary" line of North China evolution and a somewhat later "secondary" line of South China evolution—which first ran parallel to each other, then clashed in the time of the Warring States in the fourth and third centuries B.C., and finally merged in a common style of history after the Ch'in and under the Han dynasty—what kind of evolution or historical mode of development marked the steppe society? The determining factor in Chinese history as a whole appears to have been the trend toward intensive agriculture nourished by irrigation. The technical practices of irrigation were stimulated in their development by the character of the environment; and they in turn, in proportion as they became more efficient, transformed both landscape and people, making them more and more typically Chinese. Was there any corresponding dynamic factor in steppe history?

Stone Age peoples, especially the more primitive societies, made as many different kinds of use of their environments as they could. Their economy was mixed and unspecialized. Agriculture was created by the evolution and specialization of some aspects of this original mixed economy, accompanied by the gradual withering of other aspects. Pastoral steppe nomadism is also obviously a product of high specialization, but does not appear to derive so directly from the original mixed level of economy. In all probability it is also a later form of specialization than is agriculture. The relative lateness can be accounted for by the fact that it was first necessary to domesticate animals. Before man could live in the open steppe by the control of herded animals he had to learn how to keep animals under control, and until he had learned to do this he had to live by some other means. Consequently, domestication was not a technique that originated in isolation but was gradually developed in the shelter of other ways of living.

It follows that while specialized hunting societies and agricultural societies could emerge directly out of mixed, unspecialized ways of living, pastoral nomadism was more likely to develop out of forest hunting societies and partly specialized but still marginal groups whose main resource was agriculture. Hunters in the northern forests of Manchuria and the southern forests of Siberia and Urianghai (Tannu-Tuva) could domesticate reindeer in small numbers.[71] From the forests they had access to two kinds of terrain: to the north they could take reindeer out of the forests and live in the open tundra by herding the reindeer in greater numbers; to the west of Manchuria and to the south of Siberia and Urianghai they could reach the edge of the Mongolian steppe and make a transition from the herding of reindeer to the herding of horses, cattle, and sheep.

[71] Wild reindeer can be more easily domesticated than wild horses, owing to their taste for human urine; this makes it possible to teach them to stay near the camp, even without tethering them or putting them in fenced enclosures (Hatt, Notes on Reindeer Nomadism, 1919, p. 108 and n. 5).

Undoubtedly the main source from which the nomadism of the steppe derived, however, was not hunting and the forest, but agriculture—and agriculture of a particular kind, at the edge of the steppe, practiced by societies that were unable to specialize their agriculture further by migrating toward better terrain, because the better terrain was already occupied by similar but more advanced societies. In fact, it must be assumed that marginal societies were actually being crowded toward the steppe by stronger, more flourishing agricultural groups. Otherwise, there is no impetus to account for the venture into the steppe; and an impetus there must have been, because without it the steppe would look like a poor and even a dangerous environment to a society that had any agriculture at all, even if it also had domesticated animals. Rather weak and small groups, whose independence was being threatened by people who were better, richer, and more strongly organized cultivators, were therefore the ones most likely to be forced into the steppe, where they learned to control animals in larger numbers and to convert the control of animals from an ancillary technique into a self-sufficient technique.[72]

RELATIONS OF NOMADIC TO SETTLED POPULATIONS

Pastoral nomadism, accordingly, can be described as a line of specialization and evolution deflected away from previous lines of specialization or partial specialization. Nevertheless it was evolution, and an evolution requiring a highly special skill, that created pastoral steppe nomadism. In spite of this it has been held that a true people of

[72] See also Chapter VI, above. At this point the danger of assuming that primitive migratory habits are the same thing as primitive pastoral nomadism may once more be mentioned. Creel (op. cit., pp. 183-189) makes it clear that the grazing of cattle was an important economic resource of the Shang Chinese, and cites Andersson (Children of the Yellow Earth, 1934, p. 242) for the existence of "hunters and cattle-raising nomads" on the Kansu-Tibetan border. The use of the word "nomads" is here the criterion. I think that Andersson and Creel use the word loosely, and that they are describing mixed societies, not true nomad societies. See note 56, above.

the steppe, once it has established its typical social forms in a suitable environment of pasture, semi-desert, and desert, no longer evolves at all but moves at most within a very narrow cycle of alternating tribal concentration and dispersal. Therefore, it is argued, when nomads irrupt into the history of settled peoples it is only because of the working of natural physical phenomena, like climatic change and the drying up of pastures, which force the nomads to migrate and conquer.[73]

Certain characteristics of pastoral nomadism appear at the first analysis to confirm this reasoning. Its economy is notably self-sufficient. Its herds provide the basic necessities of food, clothing, housing, fuel, and transport; whereas a settled society, and especially an agricultural society, may for reasons of climate or other environmental deficiency not be able to supply some of its own essential wants. Nomadic life by no means prevents the working of metal on a small scale by individual craftsmen. The necessary forges, tools, and supplies of raw material can be carried about. Indeed, the individuals of such a mobile society have more free access to necessities that are not everywhere available—like salt, metal, wood—than the people of a settled society.

Both economic power and political power, considered purely in themselves, might be supposed to operate somewhat differently in settled and nomadic societies. Stored up grain—the governing form of wealth in the agricultural state that evolved in China—had several kinds of capital value. It could be used to influence the market so as to buy in new harvests at cheaper prices. It could be used to provision armies or to feed laborers assembled in immense numbers to embank rivers or dig canals for drainage, irrigation, and transport—thus providing machinery

---

[73] Compare Toynbee, A Study of History, 1934, Vol. III, pp. 7-50, 395-454; also my criticism of this view in The Geographical Factor in Mongol History, 1938.

for the further accumulation and control of the grain supply. Since the areas of maximum production did not necessarily coincide with the points of maximum strategic advantage, the state in China, in its later, matured form, tended to commit itself to the maintenance of a capital chosen for strategic reasons and communicating by river and canal (for cheapness of transport) with "key economic areas" of grain production.[74] Grain, in short, both in the daily life of the people and in sophisticated terms of high policy, represented the prime form of accumulation: it had a higher symbolic value than even the land that produced it.

Cattle, on the other hand, had nothing like the same significance as the prime form of accumulation in a nomadic society. Stored grain does not depreciate, whereas cattle first decline in value and then perish. This even offsets the fact that cattle, in their years of maximum value, multiply themselves. Grain, once it has become the standard of a whole society, promotes political change and evolution. Usually those who control the grain must work to increase their profit from such control, since this is an effective way of weakening competitors who might otherwise try to take social control away from them. Nor can a state based on such an economy tolerate political independence in neighboring territories. It must spread into those territories if it can in order to keep up its control of both the absolute and the symbolic value of grain. Since the penetration of new territory entails further political adjustment the scope of evolution is extremely wide—though not, as the history of China proves, unlimited.

In a society of pastoral nomads it may be argued theoretically—but only theoretically—that the scope is much more limited. It may be argued that when a great nomad chief has accumulated herds up to a certain size the decrease in value from mortality so offsets the increase in

[74] Ch'ao-ting Chi, *op. cit.*

value from breeding that further accumulation causes more trouble than it is worth. Beyond a certain point the surplus value can neither be consumed nor "stored" nor "saved" within the economy. Such a chief, if he owns or controls most of the cattle within his reach and has no dangerous enemies in sight, no longer has an incentive to increase the kind of power on which his authority rests. Therefore his influence is thrown toward stabilization and against evolution. His cattle, and the people who herd his cattle for him, or herd their own cattle under his protection, represent a phase of maximum concentration. Since, however, the maximum rate of profit to be made out of this concentration has also been reached, the speculative profit to be made out of dispersal automatically begins to increase. The big concentration therefore tends to break up into smaller concentrations, and a new phase of the cycle begins in which each dispersed unit tries once more to realize the maximum concentration that can be made out of accumulation.

Such 'force as this reasoning has—and it has a certain theoretical value in tracing tendencies in nomad history—depends very largely on the assumption of a "closed world" of nomadism. No closed world of this kind ever existed, however.[75] In the particular case of the steppe Frontier of China, the spread of the Chinese economy must have affected naturally rich and naturally poor agricultural regions in different ways. The people of the Yangtze valley were able to take over the Chinese complex of economy and society for themselves, remaining for a long time politically independent in spite of their cultural indebtedness. In poorer environments the Chinese complex was more likely to be introduced by direct conquest. It is accordingly probable that the development of livestock breeding to the

[75] "It is possible that there may have existed nomads limiting themselves exclusively to meat, milk, and the wool of their herds; but no such nomads have ever been known in historical times" (Cahun, Introduction à l'histoire de l'Asie, 1896, pp. 49-50).

point that made true nomadism possible was partly stimulated, along the Inner Asian Frontier, by the effort of previously non-nomadic "barbarians" to escape being made into a subject agricultural population. Thus even for the origins of nomadism a "closed world" of the steppe cannot be posited.

Once pastoral nomadism had begun to develop, moreover, there must have been competition between cultivators and herdsmen for the use of marginal land along the Frontier, where the seaward-flowing rivers of China are replaced by the small streams and inland-drainage basins of the steppe. It is probably this that accounts for the lack of strong, independent economies of mixed farming and herding intermediate between the pastoral steppe and the intensive irrigated agriculture of China. Antagonism between the extremes of "extensive" and "intensive" economy forced any marginal, mixed-economy group into political dependence on either the steppe or China.[76]

Failing an absolute and closed Frontier, it must be conceded that the nomad way of life could not remain totally self-contained and independent. Any accumulated surplus of herds, wool, hides, and so on that could not be consumed profitably within the nomad society could be disposed of in trade with agricultural communities. From the extreme edge of agriculture, at the same time, grain could be transported more cheaply to the steppe than back to China, and sold more profitably. Competition for the control of this exchange of wealth between two kinds of society naturally took political forms. Were agricultural regions to exploit auxiliary grazing economies, or were nomad chiefs to patronize and at the same time to exploit auxiliary subject populations of cultivators?

Two things have aided nomad people in this kind of struggle: the mobility of the whole population and its property, making it possible to get away from expeditions

[76] See also Chapter XVI, below.

invading the steppe from the settled land, and the special mobility of nomad cavalry, which makes them formidable in raiding settled populations. Both aspects of the matter have an economic as well as a purely military significance. The cost of equipping mobile expeditions is much higher for settled peoples than for nomads; while the nomads can cause far more loss by destroying crops, plundering granaries, and carrying off prisoners than they suffer themselves when forced to escape a punitive expedition by moving their camps and driving away their cattle.

For these reasons it is easy to assume that nomads have an inherent superiority over settled peoples in striking power and conquering power.[77] The matter is not so simple, however. The nomad chief who marks out any settled region to provide him with tribute, whether he is conquering or merely raiding, sacrifices a part of his initial advantage. He may have to defend his asserted right of rule or plunder against rival nomads. He must therefore establish an advantage of position and in so doing sacrifice at least some of the advantages of mobility. A preoccupation of this kind has further consequences. A nomad society that adapts its economy to the acquisition of wealth and power from partly non-nomadic sources must alter its own social structure correspondingly. The nature of its new vested interests converts it into something that is no longer a pure nomad society.[78]

Consequently, the problem of the evolution or lack of evolution in pastoral nomadism cannot be considered apart, but must be studied in conjunction with the modes of development of any settled society that comes within its range of action. I do not mean by this that nomad societies can be strictly classed as either predatory or parasitic. What I do mean is that, in spite of recurrent antipathy,

---

[77] I have myself long tended to overemphasize this military and political advantage; compare, *e.g.*, China and the Barbarians, 1934.
[78] Lattimore, review of Grenard's Genghis-Khan, 1937.

there is a kind of symbiosis between every major group of pastoral nomads known in history and some settled society—perhaps more than one. The degree of symbiosis varies of course with distance and the difference between direct and indirect contact. Neither the general economic and social structure nor the particular political history of any pastoral nomads can be correctly gauged if this phenomenon is neglected.

These criteria must be borne in mind when examining the transformation of Shang China into Chou China, the appearance of a primary focus in the Yellow River valley and a secondary and somewhat later focus in the Yangtze valley, the conversion of east-west expansion and resistance into a north-south stratification, and the rise of the pastoral nomads on the steppe horizon of China's Inner Asian Frontiers.

PART III

THE AGE OF NATIONAL STATES

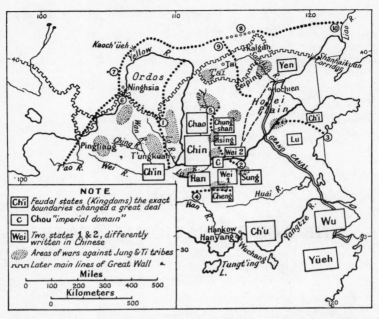

MAP 10—Feudal states in the Yellow River and Yangtze River valleys and walls constructed at different periods. Only those "feudal states" are indicated which are mentioned in text. No boundaries are given because they changed greatly. For instance, the states of Chao, Han, and Wei 1 were originally parts of China.

Numerals in circles refer to the walls.

1: First wall of the state of Wei 1. 2: Later wall of the state of Wei 1. 3: Wall of the state of Ch'i. 4: Wall of the state of Ch'u. 5: Wall of the state of Chungshan. 6: Pre-imperial wall of Ch'in. 7: Post-imperial wall of Ch'in (conjectural). 8: Uncertain continuity between Ch'in, Chao, and Yen walls. 9: Wall of the state of Chao. 10: Wall of the state of Yen.

The approximate Great Wall under Ch'in Shih-huang-ti was: 6-7-9-8-10. West of the Ordos the line of the later Great Wall indicated is in the main that of the Han dynasty, B.C. 206-A.D. 220; east of the Ordos it is in the main that of the Ming dynasty, 1368-1643. Under the Han, the actual line of the Chinese occupation varied between the Ch'in line (6-7-9-8-10) and the later line of the Great Wall.

CHAPTER XI

NORTHERN AND SOUTHERN CHINESE HISTORY

THE CHIEF KINGDOMS OF THE CHOU PERIOD

The Chou period may be divided into two parts. The first runs from B.C. 1050 to 771 (or, conventionally, from B.C. 1122 to 771); the second from B.C. 770 to 221.[1] The Chou are traditionally represented as a people of barbarian or semi-barbarian origin with an acquired Chinese culture.[2] Nevertheless the Chou, whatever their barbarian tinge, were not pastoral nomads and not horse-riding warriors. Their aristocracy fought from chariots. True pastoral nomadism enters the scope of Chinese history only well within Chou times. The explanation of this appearance of steppe nomadism is, from the point of view of the history of the Inner Asian Frontiers of China, the main phenomenon of the Chou age.

The Chou people arose on the western and northwestern

[1] For dating, see Bishop, Chronology of Ancient China, 1932; Creel, Studies in Early Chinese Culture, 1937, pp. xvi-xxii.

[2] Ting Shan (Cultural Relations of the Chou People with the Western Regions, 1937, in Chinese) holds that, while the Chou originated in, the west of China, their connection with Central Asia and the Near East is not definitely established. They had, however, a seven-day week while the Shang people had a ten-day cycle, and he compares this with the Semitic reckoning. The Chou also kept their chronology by reference to major events while the Shang kept their dates by reigns. Here he compares the Chou system with the Babylonian system. The Chou also set the date at the beginning of a document while the Shang set it at the end.

Creel (op. cit., p. 18, n. 2) states that a "conspicuous difference" between the Chou and the Shang was that the Chou tombs were marked by tumuli, while those of the Shang were not. He also states that the term T'ien, "heaven," derives from the Chou and was unknown to the Shang, whose deity was Ti (p. 56).

Bishop (Beginnings of North and South, 1934, p. 312 and footnote) believes that the early Chou were "in touch with regions far away in Central Asia," but that the contact was broken after the middle of the tenth century B.C.

horizon of the Shang or Shang-Yin Chinese, in Shensi, and when the Shang society was "in decay" they broke through from the outer edge to the heart of what was then China by following down the Wei River to the great bend of the Yellow River at the point where the provinces of Shensi, Shansi, and Honan now join. They took over the "empire" of China, but kept their capital in the Wei valley, thus for a number of centuries moving the center of gravity of the Chinese culture farther west, into the heart of the loess country. The "empire" thus acquired by the Chou is held to have been relatively powerful and well centralized; but it must be remembered that the records are still fragmentary and the dates uncertain.

Then, in B.C. 771, the Chou were disastrously defeated by "western barbarians"[3] who were still, presumably, what the Chou themselves had once been. After this defeat the Chou moved their capital to the east, thus making northern Honan, which had been the metropolitan area under the Shang-Yin, once more the cultural center of China. The loess valleys of Shensi became a border domain, ruled by a hereditary line of nobles who were, so to speak, "wardens of the Western Marches." This line was founded by the feudal noble who covered the retreat of the Chou from the western barbarians,[4] and from it developed the feudal state of Ch'in, which eventually overthrew the Chou line in the third century B.C. and created a new and much more centralized empire.

For this second part of the Chou period the records are increasingly complete and the dates more and more certain. According to the traditional reading the "imperial power" of the Chou declined; the "feudal states" became more and more independent and fought each other for the control of the weakling Chou emperors, who came to be con-

[3] Shih Chi, Ch. 28; Chavannes, Mémoires historiques, Vol. III, Part 2, p. 419. These barbarians were the Jung; and in Ch. 110 the Jung tribes are described as precursors of the Hsiung-nu.
[4] Shih Chi, Ch. 5; Chavannes, op. cit., Vol. II, p. 14.

fined to the north of Honan within a small domain that was politically and militarily much less important than the other, major states of China. Control of the Chou emperor, however, did not mean a change of sovereignty.

Parallel with the supposed decay of political unity, however, there was a steady increase in the geographical area occupied by the Chinese culture and filled with the events of Chinese history. This was particularly noticeable in the Yangtze valley, which was still "the South." In fact, the wars between the states of the South, in the Yangtze valley, formed for some centuries a series distinct from the similar wars of the North, in the Yellow River valley. They led to the rise of the great state of Ch'u, founded near the point where the Han River enters the Yangtze from the north. This is where Hankow now stands; it corresponds, in the Yangtze valley, to T'ungkuan at the great bend of the Yellow River. The rulers of Ch'u, it is related, derived from a follower of the second Chou king but the people were distinct from the Northern Chinese.[5] Expanding down the Yangtze to the coast, Ch'u eventually conquered several other states, like Wu and Yüeh, which were distinctly of a "Man" or "Southern Barbarian" character.[6] As a result of this expansion Ch'u came to dominate the South before any one state had secured the hegemony of the North. Consequently, the final devastating cycle of wars that closed the Chou period took on a double character: it was not only the hegemony of the North that had to be decided, but the question whether China was to center on the Yellow River or the Yangtze valley. Ch'in, the state that finally triumphed, was able to settle the issue partly by thrusting across from Shensi into the immensely rich basin of Ssuch'uan on the upper Yangtze, thus turning the flank of the direct approaches to the middle Yangtze from the north, which were held by Ch'u.

[5] Bishop, *op. cit.*, p. 318.
[6] *Ibid.*, pp. 322-324.

A Modification of the Traditional View of
Barbarian Invasion in the Chou Period

This is the briefest possible summary. It must be remembered that the documentary material is largely political and much of it fragmentary and obscure. Scholars, therefore, have naturally worked most on textual criticism and attempts to piece the political account together and make it coherent. Such work is necessary, but it cannot go beyond a certain point. Political events are only the surface phenomena of history. The forces that create them lie deeper, and these forces derive from the interaction of society and environment. The beginnings of history depend on the scope that the environment allows to a primitive and weak people. Further development works itself out as a complex product of the initial momentum, the degree in which the environment stimulates or retards the society, and the degree in which the society can free itself of control by the environment and establish instead control of the environment. For a period like that of the Chou, accordingly, of which the formal narrative account can never be fully reconstructed, a broad historical understanding—as distinguished from expert critical knowledge of the patchwork of details—demands a constant return to the consideration of the general character of the environment and the general character of the society.

When this method is applied certain standards of reference emerge at once. The Chou period, to begin with, exhibits unmistakably that interplay of contraction and expansion of the geographical field of history that was also characteristic, in a somewhat more vague way, of the Shang period, and still more vaguely of the Hsia period. At times the emphasis appears to be on the increasing area over which the events of Chinese history are distributed; but there is no corresponding political centralization, and so at other times the emphasis appears to be on the formation of separate states, none of them very large at first and all of them increasingly at war with each other. Certainly the total increase in area is not so great that it can be called the main phenomenon of the Chou period. Indeed, if the rise of the Chou be taken in the orthodox way as a "conquest" of China from the periphery, carried out by a people who were of "barbarian" origin although they had become partly Chinese in culture even before they began the conquest, an important question must be answered. Why were the geographical changes not more sweeping, and why, instead of taking new forms, as might be expected after a conquest directed from the periphery toward the center, did they so largely continue the old spasmodic process of alternating expansion and contraction, or retraction?

Study of the "barbarian" wars of the Chou period heightens the significance of this question. In the first place, these wars did not center on the northwestern periphery of China, from which the Chou themselves came. They ranged all over the eastern part of North China —the supposedly "Chinese China" which the Chou had conquered, according to the orthodox interpretation. In the second place, the Chou period does not open with a clear distinction between China as a whole and the steppe as a whole. It took many centuries to prepare that differentiation and it was not completed until the close of the period. Throughout the main course of the Chou period itself none of the "barbarian" enemies of the Chinese are recognizably described as pastoral nomads of the steppe. The unmistakable mounted warfare of true steppe nomadism does not appear before the end phase of the period, and when it does appear the whole character of the historical record begins to change very rapidly in China itself as well as along the Great Wall line of cleavage between China and the steppe. The question may therefore be put in a more precise form: Did the barbarian wars of the

Chou period result from a wide invasion of an already homogeneous agricultural China by peoples of the steppe?

Chinese historical writers, both the old and the modern, assume that of course the Chinese were defending themselves against invaders. The tribes against whom they fought are broadly classified as Jung on the western side of North China and Ti on the eastern side. There are many variations and sub-variations of the names applied to these tribes, both in forms that are differently written but have the same sound and in forms differently written and differently pronounced.

Wang Kuo-wei, examining the main groups of names, concludes that the Kueifang, Hun-i or K'un-i, Hsün-yü, Jung, and Ti were all connected with each other and that they spread from the east of Kansu and the north of Shensi to the range that divides Shansi and Hopei, and pressed inward on China. The names used for them varied both according to the periods at which the Chinese were in contact with them, according to locality, and according to whether the Chinese used their own names for the tribes (such as Jung and Ti) or transcribed the names that the tribes used themselves (such as Hun-i or Hsün-yü). Hsiungnu and Hu were later names for the same group of peoples.[7] This recalls Herrmann's attempt at etymological identification of the names Hun and Hsiungnu with the Hun-i and Hsün-yü group of names.[8] Fang T'ing, commenting in approval on Wang Kuo-wei's discussion of these names, adds that Chin (in Shansi) and Ch'in (in Shensi), important Chinese states of the Chou period, absorbed important groups of the Ti tribes; but in spite of

[7] From Ch. 13 of a work by Wang Kuo-wei called "Kuan T'ang Chi Lin." This I have not consulted myself; I cite from notes made for me several years ago by Mr. T'ung Kuei-t'ing (see Origins of the Great Wall, 1937, p. 529, n. 1). Compare Pelliot, L'Edition collective des oeuvres de Wang Kouo-wei, 1929, pp. 114 et sqq.

[8] Herrmann, Die Westländer, etc. (in Hedin, Southern Tibet, Vol. VIII, 1922), p. 134.

this phrasing he also takes it for granted that in the Chou period the Chinese were on the defensive against the barbarians.[9]

Basing his argument on an inclusive citation of the original sources, Meng Wen-t'ung undertakes in two articles to deal in detail and in historical sequence with both the Jung and the Ti as the main groups of "northern barbarians." He describes a whole cycle of wars against the Jung in Shensi, at the end of which they were pinched out of the northeastern part of Shensi by the eastward expansion of Ch'in and the westward expansion of Chin. Part of them escaped to the north of Honan, to the region where a minor range of hills forms the watershed between the Lo [10] and the Yellow River on the north and rivers flowing to the Huai and the Yangtze on the southeast and south. Here they formed a buffer between Chin, of the North China group of states, and Ch'u, of the Yangtze group. They also fought against states well to the east of them, such as Lu and Sung in Shantung on the northern side of the Huai. Eventually they were destroyed in the wars between Chin and Ch'u. Another group of Jung in the northwest of Shensi was driven into Inner Mongolia by the expansion of Ch'in and became, according to Meng Wen-t'ung, the Hsiungnu.[11]

Meng Wen-t'ung places the Ti originally in Shensi, like the Jung. Moving round by the north of Shansi, they came to the T'ai Hang Shan, the range that runs from north to south between the rich Fen valley in Shansi on the west and the Hopei plain on the east. From this base they fought against the Chinese "feudal states" of the

[9] Fang T'ing, On the Ti, 1934 (in Chinese).

[10] Note that this was a southward "escape" of the Ti, since the Lo River referred to is the Lo in Honan, not that in Shensi.

[11] Meng Wen-t'ung, Eastward Invasions of the Ch'uan Jung, 1936, p. 7, quoting the Tso Chuan, and p. 16, citing Shih Chi, Ch. 110, and Hou-Han Shu, Ch. 117, which links the Western Ch'iang of later times with the Jung and Ti.

lower Yellow River plain, sometimes by themselves and sometimes in alliance with other Chinese states. Some of the Jung people also became involved with the Ti.[12]

Similarly De Groot (who, like Herrmann, traces the Hsiungnu to the Hun-i, K'un-i, Hsün-yü, etc.) takes the T'ai Hang range between Shansi and Hopei as the base of operations of the Ti. This he deduces from the fact that wars against the Ti are recorded in the annals of the states of Chin (in Shansi), Yen (northern part of the Hopei plain), Ch'i (in Shantung), Wei (north of the Yellow River, in the south of the modern Hopei), Sung (in the Huai basin), Cheng (in Honan), the small state of Hsing (forming an enclave between Chin, Yen, and Ch'i), and the region of the Chou "imperial domain" after B.C. 771 (between Wei in Hopei and Cheng in Honan). Although he admits that there is no evidence that the Ti were in contact with steppe peoples in Mongolia, he suggests that they must have been and that together with the Jung they must have had a main homeland in the north. Otherwise they could hardly have fought the Chinese for several hundred years. These wars, he thinks, were more than the raids of scattered hordes; they must have been directed by a major tribal power which was attempting the conquest of the China of that day. He even discusses the possibility that, had it not been for the resistance of Ch'i, which in the seventh century B.C. was the most powerful of the Chinese states, there might have been established in China a barbarian overlord rule comparable to the later conquests of the Toba, Khitan, Juchen, Mongols, and Manchus.[13]

CHINESE EXPANSION MORE IMPORTANT THAN BARBARIAN INVASION

Thus modern Chinese and Western scholarship alike support the older Chinese tradition that the Jung and the

---

[12] Meng Wen-t'ung, Eastward Invasions of the Red Ti and White Ti, 1937.
[13] De Groot, Die Hunnen der vorchristlichen Zeit, 1921, especially pp. 13 and 28.

Ti penetrated into China as the advance guards of barbarian hordes attempting to conquer the Chinese from the steppes to the north and northwest of China. I suggest that this is entirely wrong and that these tribes, like the Man peoples of the southeast and south, were in fact rearguard detachments lingering in territory into which the Chinese culture was expanding. They may not have been ethnically distinct from the Chinese. Possibly, and even probably, they were backward, less developed groups of the same stock as that from which the Chinese had evolved —a stock anciently holding the whole of North China, both the loess highlands in the west and the Great Plain in the east, and very likely also the southern parts of Mongolia and Manchuria. Even the modern Chinese critical historians have been biased by the old tradition that the Chinese, as the bearers of "the" civilization of Eastern Asia, never fought except in defense of civilization, and that consequently all their wars against "barbarians" must have been precipitated by "barbarian attacks." In much the same way Western scholarship tends to be misled by its lingering obsession that the Chinese culture must have been largely developed by "penetration," "migration," and "culture diffusion," either from Central Asia or passing through Central Asia.

Support for the new interpretation here proposed can be drawn both from the annals of the wars themselves and from the general aspect of the times.

When all the references to the Jung and Ti are collated, as by Meng Wen-t'ung and De Groot, and then examined afresh with regard to both geography and the political sequence of events, two things become plain. In the first place, although the general purport of the wording gives the impression that the Chinese were defending themselves, the specific accounts of attacks, expeditions, invasions, and encroachments on territory reveal that the Chinese took the initiative of aggression more often than they were forced back on the defensive. In the second place, during the period as a whole the Chinese were indisputably increasing the total territory under their control; and this process was accompanied by a steady alteration in the balance of power between the Chinese "feudal states," the states that rose to major power being those that fought most continuously against the "barbarians" and won the most territory from them.

The trend was not altogether steady, it is true; but the indications are that when the Chinese were driven back it was because they had been too headlong and so had aroused a resistance which for the time being was more than they could overcome. This conclusion is reinforced by the fact that the earlier accounts, on the whole, deal with straightforward opposition between Chinese and "barbarians," while the later accounts deal more and more frequently with campaigns in which the "barbarian menace" took the form of wars between Chinese states using barbarian allies against states that either had weaker barbarian allies or no such auxiliaries at all. If these mixed wars had resulted in a growth of the power of the barbarians as a whole and the weakening of the Chinese as a whole, it could be argued that there was a real pressure of barbarian invasion; but since the result was exactly the opposite it can only be concluded that the Chinese were expanding and in the ascendant, so that they could safely enlist barbarians in regional wars against each other.

Geographically, again, when the wars are plotted on the map a significant distribution is revealed. The Chinese were based on the agriculturally richer valleys and plains, while the "barbarians" held the agriculturally poorer hills where irrigated farming was not possible at all or needed greater technical skill; and they held this kind of territory not as invaders but as defenders. The Chinese carried out their expansion in several ways. Along the main course of the lower Yellow River they moved downstream, spreading out over the Great Plain. In the valleys of the Lo in Honan and of the Fen in Shansi they moved upstream from the wider terrain that they had presumably first brought under irrigated cultivation toward the headwaters and into the side valleys, which presumably they found profitable as population increased and technique improved. In Shensi they moved from valley to valley, first occupying the valleys of the streams that flow into the Yellow River from the west and then successively the northwest of Shensi, the east of Kansu, and the south of Ninghsia, where a number of "sub-oases," [14] intermediate in geographical character between the typical loess valleys and the true oases of Chinese Turkistan, cluster along the loop of the Yellow River north of the Ordos.

Indications of the kind of society that the Chinese were displacing must also be taken into account. It is in this respect that the annals are least satisfactory—because, as the tenor of the wording indicates, the Chinese were so confident of the superiority of their culture that it was enough for them to classify their opponents as barbarians without going into the details of barbarism. This, it should be noted, is itself evidence that the "pressure" of the time was on the whole Chinese and not barbarian; for the characteristics of a people who are being conquered need not be given much attention, whereas a people who are feared as possible conquerors are likely to be described in some detail, however much they may be hated. The most valuable Chinese accounts of "barbarians" come from later periods, when China really was being attacked and invaded.

Still a number of details have been preserved, though apparently more or less casually. In the eighth century B.C. in a battle between the Jung and the state of Cheng (in

<hr />

[14] For the use of this term, see Chapter VI, above.

the north of Honan), the Chinese fought in chariots and the Jung on foot.[15] In the sixth century in a victory of the state of Chin over the Ti in Shansi the Ti had only foot soldiers.[16] Neither the Jung nor the Ti, therefore, can have been typical pastoral nomads, able to migrate rapidly and over great distances and fighting as a matter of course as mounted raiders. On the other hand, a Chou noble of the ninth century B.C. is credited with taking a thousand horses from the Jung;[17] and in the fifth century B.C. a Jung chieftain of Tai in the northern part of Shansi beyond the headwaters of the Fen, whose territory produced good horses, made a present of horses to the ruler of Chao, the state based on the upper Fen valley.[18]

Obviously, however, such mention of horses, even in large numbers, is not conclusive evidence of pastoral nomadism. Taken in conjunction with other evidence it points rather to a mixed economy. One of the early, more or less fabulous Chou rulers is described as bringing back four wolves and four white stags after a campaign against the Jung.[19] Regarded as tribute, this would indicate a hunting people rather than a pastoral people; regarded as the booty of a campaign, it gives even less ground for believing that the chief wealth of the Jung was in livestock. Moreover, a very interesting reference describes a group of Jung who, driven out of Shensi by the state of Ch'in, were granted lands in Shansi by the state of

[15] Neither Meng Wen-t'ung nor De Groot gives this interesting passage. Wieger (Textes historiques, 1929, Vol. I, p. 109) gives it as follows: the Count of Cheng was afraid that the Jung footmen would encircle the Cheng chariots, but his son showed him how to draw the Jung into an ambush. Wieger does not give the original source, which is in the Tso Chuan. Compare Legge, Chinese Classics, Vol. V, Part I, p. 28, of the Ch'un Ch'iu and Tso Chuan.

[16] De Groot, op. cit., pp. 30-31, citing the Tso Chuan.

[17] Wieger, op. cit., Vol. I, p. 95; source not cited.

[18] Meng Wen-t'ung, op. cit., p. 76, citing the Lü Shih Ch'un Ch'iu.

[19] Meng Wen-t'ung, Eastward Invasion of the Ch'uan Jung, p. 1, citing the Chou Yü, in the Kuo Yü. See Herrmann (op. cit., pp. 178-188) for the contention that this legend does not prove an early Chinese knowledge of Central Asia. Compare Chavannes, op. cit., Vol. I, p. 259.

Chin; these lands, previously uncultivated, they reclaimed and occupied as farmers.[20] The wording seems to take it as a matter of course that the Jung should be subordinate to a Chinese state, thus implying that they were weaker in organization than the Chinese, or in some other way inferior in status; but there is no hint of a "conversion" from pastoralism to agriculture.

Although these indications do not go very far they are congruent as far as they go with Herrmann's enquiries into early Chinese knowledge of the northwest and of Central Asia. Although the political power of the Chou originated in Shensi, Herrmann demonstrates that until the end of the Chou period the Chinese knew very little indeed about the northwest of Shensi, the eastern part of Kansu, and what is now Ninghsia, and still less about Turkistan.[21] If, however, the Jung and the Ti had really been "waves" rolling in on China from a developed pastoral nomadic society in Mongolia and Central Asia, it is hardly possible, considering the great number of references, that no mention of a recognizable steppe homeland and pastoral society, standing behind the many fronts on which the Chinese encountered the Jung and the Ti, should have been preserved. Yet the fact is that the whole literature of the subject gives a shallow, frontal impression; the Chinese encountered the Jung and the Ti at a great number of points but the accounts do not describe hordes issuing from a hostile hinterland. The whole idea of depth of hinterland and of a movement of people inward on China is a later creation built up by listing the regions in which the wars were fought, noting the chronological sequence of the "attacks," and disregarding the fact that the cumulative result of the "barbarian invasions" was the enlargement of Chinese territory.

[20] Meng Wen-t'ung, op. cit., p. 7, citing the Tso Chuan. The reference mentions clearing the land of wild animals but does not mention herding.
[21] This is the main contention of Herrmann's Die Westländer in der chinesischen Kartographie (in Hedin, op. cit.).

CHARACTER OF CHINESE EXPANSION IN
RELATION TO ENVIRONMENT

Why, then, the persistent tradition of oncoming barbarians? The explanation, I think, lies in the very nature of wars between peoples of advancing culture and peoples of backward culture, and in the fact that it is the developing, advancing peoples who leave behind them the written material of history. A people that considers itself civilized is never in its own opinion doing more than "consolidating its position," even when it is in fact encroaching on a more backward people. Moreover, the warfare of the backward people, even when it is really in self-defense, normally takes the form of raids, and these are normally chronicled as "attacks" which justify a further assertion of the authority of the superior people.

Taking the geographical evidence in combination with the political record of the various wars, I think that the following interpretation of the whole Chou period is justified. By about 1000 B.C. a definite "Chinese" form of agriculture had been established. It had evolved out of an antecedent mixed economy which included agriculture. What distinguished the new agriculture was the practice of irrigation, which made possible a more certain harvest year by year in spite of irregular rainfall. It also made possible a heavier crop per acre and a greater accumulation and concentration of wealth. This in turn made the population more dense in the irrigated areas than in the areas where the old mixed economy prevailed. The society of the old areas remained relatively stable, but in the new areas the denser population and greater concentration of wealth, working together, brought about social changes which, when they had gone far enough, established a differentiation between "Chinese" and "barbarians."

The rate of evolution was at first more important than the rate of geographical spread. The new kind of society had to rise to a certain level, both of technique and of organization, before it could establish itself outside of the most favorable and easily developed areas. The first spread was therefore to similar areas, leaving less tractable terrain untouched; the second spread was probably to areas in which the technique of irrigation could easily be applied to problems of drainage on a scale not too large for the still immature society.

In both late Shang and early Chou times, therefore, little concentrations of the new kind of society were islanded in larger expanses of territory occupied, but more thinly, by the old kind of society. Both the needs and the profits of the new kind of economy and society encouraged rapid progress, not only in the practice of irrigated agriculture itself but in every related technical and cultural activity, such as the use of metal, writing, and political organization.

Then there began a second spread, this time not so much by the establishment of new nuclei in similar areas as by the enlargement of the already existing areas, the people of which had reached a proficiency enabling them to irrigate or drain lands that had been too difficult for the original methods to penetrate. Antagonism between the old kind of society and the new must have existed already but probably did not go beyond occasional raids on the granaries and other accumulated wealth of the "Chinese" and occasional seizure from the "barbarians" of a stretch of land that could easily be irrigated. From this time on, however, the antagonism must necessarily have become more acute, as the widening of the areas controlled by the new kind of society left less and less room for the survival of the old.

Two kinds of conflict can, I think, be discerned. One was within the old society itself, from which groups began to detach themselves and go over to the new or Chinese way of life either as adherents of already formed Chinese communities or by setting up imitative but independent communities of the same kind. Such groups were "barbarian" only in the sense of being late converts to the already established Chinese culture; and this very likely explains the origin of the Chou people, rising on the periphery of China of the Shang age. From this mingled process of conquest and conversion the second kind of conflict then began to differentiate itself and to grow steadily more important—the resistance to the Chinese of those barbarians who remained obstinately barbarian.

The resistance of these groups focused probably on such of the chiefs of the old society as preferred to defend their old privileges, even in retreat, rather than to enter the new society as subordinate members.[22] Maintenance of their authority involved withdrawing from territory in which the Chinese held the advantage to territory not yet pressed on by the Chinese but rich enough for the old mixed economy. So great was the expanse of North China that it took centuries to push these recalcitrant barbarians back to the extreme natural confines of the Chinese geographical environment. In the meantime the bitterness of the struggle increased as the territory familiar to the old society was narrowed down. As they enlarged their control the Chinese also improved the quality of their technique; and, in addition, wherever intensive agriculture was established the increase of population created a fresh demand for land, including land that until then had not been considered "good." The rating of "good enough" land thus fell continuously as the necessity for occupying poorer land and the ability to exploit it in the Chinese manner developed together.

Ultimately this process brought both the retreating bar-

---

[22] See Chapter VII, above; also Stevenson, Notes on the Human Geography of the Chinese-Tibetan Borderland, 1932, for comment on the aloofness of certain kinds of marginal peoples.

barians and the advancing Chinese to the edge of the steppe, where they confronted an altogether new geographical environment. Over a great part of the loess and mountain territory of North China the spread of the Chinese had been slowed down by the lack of streams or by streams running in deep-cut valleys. This made it increasingly difficult to establish a closely settled society held together by an intensive agriculture based on irrigation. Such terrain, however, was marginal and could be mastered to a certain extent by increasing skill in technique. Even though irrigation was not possible everywhere, it could be applied to enough of the territory to determine the character of the society as a whole, subordinating the communities that could not intensify their agriculture to those which could practice irrigation.

The new environment, on the other hand, was determined by the rise to the edge of the steppe, beyond which the streams no longer flow inward to China and the great Yellow River basin, but are much rarer and smaller and flow outward to a vast region of inland drainage. A great deal of the southern fringe of the steppe could be cultivated by the methods of extensive agriculture and could therefore still be called marginal to the area of intensive Chinese agriculture. There was, however, a difference in the quality of the margin, for here a true pastoral nomadism could be practiced on the very largest scale. Historically, the difference can be stated thus : the social groups of the inner, Chinese marginal terrain were bound to gravitate toward China, toward agriculture, and toward a closeness of settlement and a degree of economic intensivity governed by the standards prevailing in China although inferior to them. The social groups of the outer, steppe marginal terrain were just as inevitably bound to gravitate away from China and toward the steppe, away from agriculture and toward pastoral nomadism, becoming a thinly dispersed population, with a degree of economic extensivity governed by the standards of the more arid part of the steppe, though not always to the degree typical of the arid steppe.[23]

Two Ages of Conflict Between the Chinese and the Barbarians

When this analysis is tested by reference to the fact that the line of cleavage between the two kinds of marginal terrain became in time the approximate main line of the Great Wall, and by reference also to the late historical period in which wars between the Chinese and true pastoral nomads begin to be chronicled, a carefully defined statement of two ages of conflict between the Chinese and the barbarians of the north is made necessary. In the first age a specialized culture based in part on irrigation and in part on drainage, but in both cases committed to an increasingly intensive agriculture, arose in the midst of a widely distributed, unspecialized, primitive culture of mixed food gathering, hunting, fishing, primitive agriculture and so forth, which undoubtedly varied somewhat in different regions. The social cohesion made possible by intensive agriculture led to a wide expansion of the groups that practiced it. These groups became "the Chinese" while groups that resisted or evaded the new way of life became "the barbarians."

In the course of time there was an increasing distinction between two main groups of the barbarians, in the north and in the south. The geographical environment of the south favored a long survival of barbarians who remained, generally speaking, simply "pre-Chinese." In the north the spread of the Chinese pushed the surviving barbarians toward a new environment in which they ceased

---

[23] For the transition from marginal terrain favoring China to marginal terrain favoring a steppe society, see Lattimore, Origins of the Great Wall of China, 1937.

to be "pre-Chinese" and became "non-Chinese." Thus there opened the second age of conflict between the agriculture of China and the nomadism of the steppe.

This interpretation does not mean that the pastoral nomadism of Central Asia and Mongolia originated entirely as the result of the retreat of primitive peoples from North China into the steppe. There are at least three main origins for the pastoral nomadism of Inner Asia: the edges of the Siberian forests,[24] the edges of the Central Asian oases,[25] and the steppe margins of North China.[26] It must be realized that the high culture of China did not have to fight in its early years against repeated waves of steppe nomads and was not fortuitously and senselessly plagued in its mature age by steppe nomads whose history had no organic connection with that of China. On the contrary, the "nomad curse" of the history of China's Great Wall Frontier was generated at least in part by the qualitative development of the special characteristics of Chinese civilization and its quantitative spread in area occupied.[27]

The details of the transition from the first age to the second are so important that they require separate discussion, which must be prepared by a review of the main outlines of the way in which the Chinese developed their economy, their society, and the political structure of their state.

CHANGING CENTERS OF POWER DURING THE CHOU PERIOD

If the genesis of Chinese history is not to be regarded as the result of a struggle between invading steppe nomads

[24] Vladimirtsov, Social Structure of the Mongols, 1934, pp. 33-46 (in Russian), where the overlapping of early steppe and forest life is well described.
[25] See Chapter VI, above.
[26] For the general question of the convergence of several different contributing origins of steppe nomadism, see Lattimore, The Geographical Factor in Mongol History, 1938.
[27] Wittfogel, commenting on some of my earlier speculations on this topic, has seen the meaning of them better than I did at the time and has partly anticipated me in this conclusion. See his Die Theorie der orientalischen Gesellschaft, 1938, p. 111 and n. 4.

and the nascent agriculture of China, then it is plain that the Chou conquerors of Shang China cannot be regarded as conquerors from the steppe. They were not invaders who won a. foothold on the fringe of China, were partly assimilated by their Chinese subjects, and eventually, by combining what remained of their barbarian vigor with what they had acquired of Chinese sophistication, were able to move inward and set up a dynasty ruling the whole of what was then China. They must, instead, have grown up between the Shang Chinese on the eastern side of the loess highlands and the barbarians or "old society" on the western, poorer, less watered side of the loess highlands. This would mean that they were "converts" to the spread of Chinese culture, not invaders who encroached on the Chinese. The restatement may appear to be slight but I believe it to be of exceptional importance, not because it greatly alters the generally accepted fact of the barbarian or semi-barbarian origin of the Chou people but because it implies a different understanding of the dynamics of this phase of history and the direction in which the processes of evolution were working.

In this connection it is well to emphasize the fact that even the most conventional accounts of the Chou "dynasty" represent it as developing out of frontier nobles who were "feudatories" of the Shang dynasty.[28] In the same way the house of Ch'in, which founded the Ch'in dynasty, has a history which runs at the side of the Chou history for centuries. It began with a line of "loyal feudal nobles," who developed into the rulers of a state that was more and more independent. When the house of Chou, after being "defeated by the barbarians," "retreated" from Shensi to the Great Plain and fixed its capital near the point where Shensi, Shansi, and Honan touch, it was the house of Ch'in that "covered the retreat" and kept up the war

[28] Shih Chi, Ch. 4; Chavannes, *op. cit.*, Vol. I, pp. 209 *et sqq.*

against the barbarians.[29] This great retreat of the house of Chou did not result in a permanent loss of territory to the barbarians. On the contrary, the Ch'in gradually increased their territory at the expense of the barbarians. It is therefore at least a reasonable conjecture that what really happened was that the formation of the Ch'in people at the side of the Chou, and between them and the "old society" barbarians, caused a pressure that resulted both in wars on the barbarians for the acquisition of wider territory and in the eastward withdrawal of the Chou. Such a phenomenon, it is obvious, would have every appearance of repeating the rise of the Chou themselves between the Shang Chinese and the "old society" barbarians, but in a somewhat more complicated form corresponding to the higher development reached by the "new society" in the course of a number of centuries.

This in turn directs attention to a number of shifts in the geographical center of gravity during the Chou period, from about 1100 or 1000 B.C. to the wars of ever-increasing intensity in the fifth, fourth, and third centuries B.C. in which the Chou society was melted down and recast in the transitional form of the Ch'in society, which in turn gave way to the society of the Han and a China of a new order.

The first emphasis is on the west, with the rise of the Chou themselves, who asserted their superiority over the Shang center of culture, lying nearer the line of cleavage between the loess highlands and the Great Plain, and established a new center of their own on the Wei River in the largest valley in Shensi. This emphasis continued until the "retreat" of the Chou eastward from Shensi into Honan, though even this did not mean a real shift in the

[29] Shih Chi., Ch. 5 (Annals of the Ch'in). For the degree to which the Ch'in were in this sense partly "Chinese" and partly "barbarian," or as I have described it "old society," see Meng Wen-t'ung, The Ch'in as a Jung Tribe, 1936 (in Chinese).

center of gravity, for the withdrawal of the Chou "dynasty" was paralleled by the rise of the house of Ch'in. This first stage as a whole was marked by wars against the Jung and Ti,[30] chiefly in the north of Shensi. Among the Chinese no political center developed that could rival the power of the Chou rulers, unless it be conceded that at the end of the stage the eastward move of the Chou was caused as much by the rise of the Ch'in as by the "pressure" of the barbarians.

A second stage follows, from 770 to 636 B.C. This was marked by a shift of emphasis to the state of Ch'i, the territory of which lay mainly in Shantung, reaching from north of the lower Yellow River to the Huai basin. In this stage wars against the Jung and Ti continued in Shensi and Shansi, but a new series of wars was also fought in Hopei, Shantung, and Honan, principally against the Ti.[31] There was also a clear increase in the importance of the different regional states, while the house of Chou was confined to a small "imperial domain," overlooked by the major states of Ch'i in the east, Chin in Shansi on the north, and Ch'in in Shensi on the west. By 636, moreover, war was no longer only a matter of opposition between Chinese and barbarians. Different groups of barbarians were already fighting as allies or auxiliaries of different Chinese states. In this year the Chou emperor was actually married to the daughter of a Ti chieftain, creating a state of confusion that was cleared up by an alliance between the states of Chin in Shansi and Ch'in in Shensi.[32]

A third shift of emphasis was thus effected, from Ch'i in the east to Chin in the north. This stage lasted until B.C. 453, and was marked by the continued decline of the

[30] Meng Wen-t'ung, Eastward Invasions of the Ch'uan Jung, 1936, and Eastward Invasions of the Red Ti and White Ti, 1937; also De Groot, op. cit.

[31] Meng Wen-t'ung, op. cit.; De Groot, op. cit.

[32] Meng Wen-t'ung, op. cit.; De Groot, op. cit., especially pp. 14-19, citing the Tso Chuan and the Shih Chi, Ch. 4 and 32, etc.

house of Chou. Wars between the regional states of China continued, but the important wars against the barbarians were chiefly in the north of Shensi and Shansi.[33] The Chinese of Ch'in and Chin advanced steadily northward until they had occupied the whole of the typically Chinese terrain and reached the edge of the steppe. This resulted in changes that altered the whole aspect of Chinese history. The state of Chin broke up into three new states —Chao in the north, Han in the southwest, and Wei in the southeast.[34]

The changes that took place in the state of Chao are the key to the significance of this partition. Here in the north of Shansi, although the Chinese had greatly increased their territory by defeating the barbarians, they were no longer able to "convert" the people they had conquered to the standards of Chinese agriculture and society; instead they themselves began to "turn barbarian." Considering both the character of the social change and the advance of the state of Chao right up to the edge of Inner Mongolia, it is evident that a critical new frontier had been established. Until this point the state of Chin had grown steadily greater, incorporating and assimilating each new conquest. Once this point had been reached and passed, the Chinese culture of the derivative state of Chao was found to have reached out too far beyond the terrain and environment that favored it. A terrain had been reached which the Chinese were no longer able to draw to themselves: instead, it drew them away from China in spite of the fact that the whole complex of agricultural practices, social organization, and political structure that together constituted the Chinese way of life must have been growing steadily more cohesive and pronounced in character as the major Chinese states developed and expanded. The state of Chao held the upper Fen valley in Shansi—an old

[33] Meng Wen-t'ung, *op. cit.*, De Groot, *op. cit.*
[34] De Groot, *op. cit.*, p. 32.

and typical Chinese environment—and also the mountainous region of Tai, north of the headwaters of the Fen and south of the Inner Mongolian steppe. In its geographical characteristics Tai or north Shansi is marginal both to the typical Chinese kind of terrain and to the steppe. The marked barbarization of Chao therefore means that for the first time a marginal territory was able to resist assimilation to Chinese territory and to draw a typical Chinese territory under its own influence.[35]

The situation was different in the state of Ch'in, which had also expanded up to a marginal steppe territory. Here the decisive geographical factor was the great northern loop of the Yellow River. This loop encloses the steppes of the Ordos, which Ch'in had conquered; but on the western and northwestern sides of the Ordos the river links together a number of oasis-like regions. These are more akin to the sub-oases of Kansu than to the pronounced oases of Chinese Turkistan. They are easily irrigated and extremely fertile, and I am convinced that this accounts for the fact that Ch'in was not pulled asunder by its marginal conquests as was Chin. Although it had also reached far out into marginal territory the balance of marginal characteristics continued as yet to favor gravitation toward China and to prevent too strong a pull away from China, in spite of the fact that Ch'in also was influenced and modified by its conquests.[36]

From 453 B.C. there begins another stage, which may be regarded either as the fourth in the series of shifts of emphasis that have just been reviewed, bringing the focus back to the west or northwest as at the rise of the Chou, or else as the beginning of an altogether new phase. Parallel with the rise of Ch'in, the Frontier barbarians against which it fought took on the unmistakable character of

[35] Lattimore, Origins of the Great Wall, 1937.
[36] Ibid.

steppe nomads as rapidly as Ch'in itself developed into a new kind of Chinese state. At the same time there began the internal wars of China in the Spring and Autumn Period and the Period of the Contending States, and the whole history of China matured into a new style.[37]

Pastoral Nomadism and the Rise of the Chinese Society and State

On each of the shifts of emphasis that have been noted there converge several lines of historical development. From the history of the barbarian wars alone it would be possible to argue that the era as a whole was one of a barbarian menace that first grew increasingly insistent and then gradually receded; that the waves of the barbarian attack first broke on the northwest, then swung round by the north to the northeast, and after penetrating far into the heart of China were only dammed back at last by the increasing power of resistance of the Chinese. This interpretation, however, cannot hold against an interpretation that takes into account the barbarian wars in combination with the growth of the separate states in China. The shift of emphasis of the barbarian wars corresponded with the growth in territory and alternating political preëminence of states in the west. east, north, and once more in the west of what was then North China. It therefore seems more likely that the real prime phenomenon was the maturing of the new Chinese order of society, based on an increasingly adept and increasingly specialized and exclusive practice of agriculture. Taking place in the midst of a wide terrain occupied by an older, unspecialized society, this led to pressure of the more closely organized new groups on the loosely distributed older groups, whose resistance, manifested in destructive raids and occasionally

[37] See Chapter XIII, below.

formidable thrusts from a great number of points on the edge of each area of Chinese expansion, gave the impression of "waves" of barbarian attack seeking to penetrate and overwhelm the orderly domains of the Chinese.

It is to be noted, further, that this interpretation allows for both the appearance and the fact of considerable barbarian migration, and also for the fact that the Chinese, who had evolved from the undifferentiated barbarians, eventually created for themselves a new kind of enemy. This was the society of the true pastoral nomads, which also evolved at least in part from the pre-Chinese barbarians of the "old society," though by a different line of derivation. The appearance of barbarian migration is accounted for by the fact that the political states organized by the Chinese probably did not originate simultaneously and certainly did not grow at the same rate of speed. Thus the phases of most rapid Chinese growth, occurring in different regions and at different times, and each in turn creating a new focus of maximum barbarian resistance, produced what looked like a wide movement of nomadic barbarians pressing inward on China. Nor was this apparent movement altogether illusory, for it is obvious that the expansion of the Chinese must have forced those barbarians who resisted "conversion" into considerable migratory movements.

Although these were migrations of retreat, not of attack, as generally supposed, any movement from north to south is likely to be misconstrued as an "invasion." Here the proper criterion is not simply the direction of movement but the kind of terrain. Meng Wen-t'ung, for instance, makes the point that before the famous eastward move of the Chou in B.C. 771 there were no Jung barbarians in the upper valley of the River I (a tributary of the Lo in the north of Honan) and a number of contiguous regions. By the Spring and Autumn Period, however, in the fifth and fourth centuries B.C., these regions were bar-

barian strongholds.[38] The inference is that, since the eastward movement of the Chou was followed by a southward
or southeastward movement of the Jung, the Chinese must
have been in retreat before the barbarians. Yet Meng
Wen-t'ung also clearly states that the Jung groups in
question lived originally in the northeast of Shensi and
were squeezed out of the valleys that they held by the
combined expansion of the states of Ch'in in Shensi and
Chin in Shansi.[39]

It is plain that a simple restatement of the whole matter
is required: the pressure of Ch'in and Chin on these Jung
communities was greater than the resistance that Chou
could offer to the Jung. Accordingly, the Jung invaded
Chou because they were retreating from Ch'in and Chin,
not because they were "invading nomads" pure and simple.
Through this invasion-by-retreat, moreover, the land in
which the Jung acquired a new foothold was not a terrain
of open valleys and broad plains, favoring the rapid development of the Chinese economy, but the most hilly
terrain in Honan and the most difficult to develop by irrigated agriculture on a large scale. The whole "invasion"
of these Jung, accordingly, comes down to the fact that
they were forced to abandon better land to some Chinese
but succeeded in taking poorer land from other Chinese.

The course of this particular migration is important in
two ways. In the first place, it confirms the suggestion
already made that the eastward move of the Chou in B.C.
771 was probably due more to the rise of new Chinese
states than to "barbarian pressure." In the second place,
it confirms the suggestion that the barbarians were being
driven into poorer and poorer terrain. This in turn establishes the probable line by which pastoral nomadism
evolved from the remains of the mixed economy out of

---

[38] Meng Wen-t'ung, op. cit., p. 7, citing the Cheng Yü, in the Kuo Yü,
and the Tso Chuan. See also note 40, below.
[39] Meng Wen-t'ung, op. cit., pp. 1-6.

which Chinese agriculture had already emerged by a different line of evolution. As the barbarians were driven from all the land in which intensive agriculture could be carried on profitably, they were forced to rely more and more on hunting and domestic livestock. As the further advance of the Chinese pushed them away also from the mountains and the headwaters of the streams that the Chinese wanted, they were deprived of forest game and forced to the edge of the steppe. Those who approached nearer to the true steppe were thus more and more obliged to develop the technique of controlling herds of livestock; and as this technique developed the line of evolution toward true pastoral nomadism became steadily more profitable.

So far as I know the literature, this is, I believe, a new combined interpretation of the rise of the Chinese society and state and the evolution of true pastoral nomadism on the Chinese edge of the steppe. There is evidence, however, in contemporary Chinese work of a tendency toward a similar line of thought. Thus Ch'ien Mu emphasizes the fact that the China of the Chou period was not a solid territory with an outer frontier against the Jung and Ti, because the Jung and Ti were also strongly established well within China. From this he goes on to the very interesting theory that the eastward "retreat" of the Chou in 771 B.C. was not due principally to barbarian attacks from the west but to the power of one of the feudal states on the east, which was able to draw the Chou sovereign under its influence and protection after taking part in the war in which his predecessor was killed, in B.C. 771. This feudal state had barbarian allies.[40] This theory, being

[40] Ch'ien Mu, The Jung Disasters of the Western Chou, 1934-35. The argument is here carried to an extreme; but its value, as a reaction against the conventional Chinese tradition, is that it brings forward the evidence for the existence of "pockets" of barbarian people well within the Chinese terrain. In fact, comparing Ch'ien Mu with Meng Wen-t'ung, it may be tentatively suggested that what was described above as "migration" from Shensi into Honan can be largely explained by the supposition that people who were already in the hill valleys became more evident and more troublesome as the Chinese filled up the better land.

based simply on the interpretation of texts without reference to the character of differing and developing social orders, approaches the interpretation that I have essayed without anticipating it. It is more than likely that a wider search of the work being done by Chinese critics of history would establish a fairly broad tendency toward similar interpretations linking up the early history of Chinese and barbarians instead of maintaining the old theories of abysmal cleavage between the two.

GROWTH OF INDEPENDENT STATES IN THE CHOU PERIOD

On turning now to the general development of the separate Chinese states that have so often been mentioned, it is to be noted first of all that the varying fortunes of the individual states may be described in terms of alternating emphasis on the loess highlands and the Great Plain. The Chou arose in Shensi in one of the greatest of the loess valleys, displacing the Shang in Honan, who were established near the line of cleavage between the loess and the plain. The ascendancy of the Chou lasted from about 1100 or 1000 B.C. to B.C. 771. They were not displaced abruptly, for during this period there arose beside them the house of Ch'in; so that although the eastward "retreat" of the Chou after 771 has the appearance of suddenness and disaster, it does not in fact mean that there was a general retreat of the Chinese from the west. On the contrary, the removal of the Chou simply left a wider field of action for the Ch'in. From 770 to 636 B.C. the political emphasis was on the state of Ch'i, which was conspicuously a state of the Great Plain. This also, however, does not mean a decline of the Chinese power in the west where, in fact, the state of Ch'in was continuing to grow; what it does mean is that the rate of growth had for a while become more rapid in the Great Plain than in the loess highlands. The later shift to Chin in Shansi and back finally to Ch'in in

Shensi can similarly be better stated in terms of the acceleration of the rate of growth in particular regions than in terms of rise in any one region compensated by a decline in other regions.

This view is corroborated by reference to the history of the Yangtze valley states. Here the state of Ch'u, centering originally on the middle Yangtze, grew to a political stature more impressive than that of any individual state in North China. It drew an immense wealth from the rich, watered lands of the Tungt'ing Lake, south of the Yangtze in the modern Hunan, and of the Han River, north of the Yangtze in the modern Hupei. In the fifth century B.C. it began to annex territory between the Han valley and the Huai basin, and in the Huai basin itself.[41] In the fourth century it expanded into the lower Yangtze valley, annexing the state of Yüeh, which had previously conquered the state of Wu.[42] From this time Ch'u controlled not only the Yangtze delta but the seacoast as well from a point well south of the Yangtze up to the Huai. The whole Yangtze or southern area of Chinese history forms a secondary region as compared with the primary Yellow River region. The Chinese culture developed here somewhat later than in the north and even more largely by the "conversion" of barbarians, but although the region as a whole was undoubtedly later than the primary northern region in coming to political importance, yet the state of Ch'u probably grew to an earlier political maturity than any northern state. Certainly it controlled a larger territory and maintained a longer and more continuous ascendancy in its own region.

Comparison of the Yangtze valley field of history as a whole with that of the Yellow River as a whole, and of the alternating ascendancies of different geographical re-

[41] For a short, clear account of Ch'u, see Bishop, Beginnings of North and South, 1934, pp. 318-322.
[42] Ibid., p. 324.

gions and political states within the Yellow River field of history, shows that the history of the last millennium B.C. cannot adequately be described by assuming a single line of development. There must have been a number of parallel lines of development. Some of these were of major and some of minor importance, and some were of later origin than others. No one line, however, abruptly destroyed or succeeded another. Although the Chou "dynasty" destroyed and succeeded the Shang "dynasty," the age of the Shang decline can also be described as the age in which the Chou were growing to strength. Even more clearly, the rise of Ch'i in the east and later of Chin in the north did not mean the decline of Ch'in in the west, but merely a transfer of emphasis that signified a temporary increase in the importance of one region and its rate of historical development without necessarily implying the supersession of other, parallel lines of development in other regions. Even less did the growing importance of the Yangtze region and the state of Ch'u signify weakness or decay among the Yellow River states.

The period as a whole, in other words, was one of the growth of independent states belonging to the same general culture but not always developing that culture and its political and other institutions at the same rate of growth. The varying rate of growth and the transfer of emphasis from region to region can be clearly referred to both geographical and social factors. The smaller scale of the loess valleys favored the maximum development of intensive cultivation, the maximum of social cohesion, and the relatively early appearance of institutions based on these factors. The larger geographical scale of the Great Plain, and the fact that drainage enterprises had to be carried out on a greater scale of economic and social organization than the irrigation works of the loess highlands, encouraged the further development of methods and institutions developed earlier on a smaller scale by the loess communities.

Water transport was much easier on the Yangtze than on the rivers of the north; and this, combined with the great richness of rice harvests as compared with the wheat and millet of the north, made the rate of growth extremely rapid, although the resulting political structure was not able in the end to survive in war against the north.

It is evident that the Chou "dynasty" cannot have ruled a centralized empire containing such diverse regions, inhabited by communities developing at different rates of growth. The "empire" must have been of a feudal kind, its emperors holding great power at first but later falling into pathetic insignificance, while the descendants of various powerful feudal nobles gradually developed into the royal sovereigns of independent states. For a time these states could tolerate each other within a feudal framework, the strongest of the states dominating the powerless imperial court. In the end, however, as political and military institutions developed by war against the barbarians and between the states, and as the homogeneity of the common culture more and more demanded integration of the economic life and political rule of all regions, it became necessary to create a new, centralized empire to supersede the nominal, feudal empire. This meant the forcible compression of the old, independent, parallel lines of history into one major line, which tolerated only regional variations of no commanding importance.

CHAPTER XII

KINGDOM AND EMPIRE IN ANCIENT CHINA

CHINESE AND EUROPEAN FEUDALISM

Society in the Chou era, it is generally agreed, was feudal;[1] but the feudalism of China, like every feudalism known in history, was not static. It varied considerably in different regions at different times and had specially developed features of its own. It is therefore possible to speak of a crude feudalism early in the last millennium B.C. and of a mature feudalism in the fourth and third centuries B.C., when the feudal order was about to be transformed into a more centralized imperial order; but it is not possible to select any interval in the whole span of time as the most typical or perfect phase of feudalism.

European feudalism was founded on two kinds of raw material, one provided by a degenerative process and the other by a process of evolution.[2] Although the collapse of the Roman Empire was so ruinous that it was followed by a "dark age" of barbarism, not all of the achievements of Roman civilization were destroyed utterly. There survived a partial framework of towns and trade routes, a landscape that was not virgin wilderness and in which the essential practices of several different kinds of agriculture remained, and a residuum of literacy. As the central imperial power degenerated, some of these focal points were seized by provincial magnates, or by the commanders of

[1] See the tabulation of theories of Chinese authorities in Wang Yü-ch'üan, Development of Modern Social Science in China, 1938.
[2] For the diversity of elements in European feudalism, see Bloch, Feudalism, 1931. The article by Franke on Chinese Feudalism in the same publication is rather conventional and does not take into account the fact that the subject has been vigorously discussed in China itself in recent years. The companion article by Asakawa on Japanese Feudalism is especially useful for comparative purposes.

armies and garrisons, which by then were extremely heterogeneous. Others became the spoil of Germanic, Celtic, and other chieftains who thus acquired a kind of power additional to their tribal power, instigating and hastening the evolution from tribalism to feudalism. The result was a feudalism which, though everywhere feudal, ranged over a wide scale of differing environments, climates, and periods of time, in which agriculture was not always uniform and town life not everywhere equally developed. The degree to which livestock economy was mixed with agriculture also varied widely, and so did the degree of reliance on predatory military expropriation. Within European feudalism, accordingly, there were any number of varieties, with the result that there was a great deal of difference·in the time level at which national states began to form out of feudalism, and a great deal of difference in the quality of the states themselves.

Chinese feudalism developed in a geographical setting that was much more uniform, though not entirely uniform, and out of a much more homogeneous antecedent society. There was no process of devolution from a higher but decayed society to combine with the process of evolution from primitive society. Everywhere within the field of Chinese feudal history, therefore, common characteristics were more strongly marked than in Europe and divergent characteristics less important, with the result that the rate of development and historical change was relatively even, though not monotonously even. This in turn makes it much more easy to distinguish the prime factors of evolution and growth, which have been authoritatively classified by Wittfogel.[3]

Irregular rainfall, streams from which water could easily be led, and a soil that responded unfailingly to the application of water even without the use of fertilizers, governed

[3] See especially his Foundations and Stages of Chinese Economic History, 1935.

the evolution of a notably intensive agriculture out of the primitive mixed economy of China. The environment first permitted irrigation on a small scale and then encouraged not only irrigation but works of drainage and flood prevention on an increasingly larger scale. In this way there was established a trend both toward more emphatic specialization and toward the exclusion of alternative systems of economy and social organization.

Except on the very smallest scale irrigation demands coöperative organization, not only for the digging of canals but in order to regulate the ownership of irrigable land and the right of access to water, and also to protect the vested interests which irrigated agriculture automatically creates. Since even in the most favorable terrain there must have been a limit to the number of sites with ready access to water that could easily be cultivated on a small scale by a single family and that could be easily defended against attack, collective and coöperative enterprise for the utilization of larger areas must have begun very early. It is therefore not difficult to see how feudalism arose in China and how it was forced at an early stage to develop tendencies leading to its own limitation and eventual supersession.

In valley after valley of the loess highlands of China there are areas admirably suited to a feudal society, being neither too large nor too small, and easily defended on a feudal scale of warfare. Granting that the emergent society of China—what I have here called the "new society"— must have been from the beginning in conflict with the "old society," a feudal phase of organization was inevitable. Irrigation made for greater crops to the acre and greater population to the square mile. The communities of the "new society" had also to organize themselves against raid and blackmail. Their granaries were worth plundering and their irrigation works not only immobile but vulnerable. The communities of the "old society," planting only catch crops here and there, were more mobile and less easily crippled by a single defeat or the loss of a particular fragment of territory. In the circumstances, the peaceful development of intensive agriculture had necessarily to be safeguarded by a warrior class; ánd as the allotment of war service under the military chiefs had to be coördinated with the division of collective labor in establishing and maintaining irrigation, the situation favored the development of a territorial nobility monopolizing both military and civil control.

While the interests of this kind of nobility favored the selection of secure loess valleys, the technical methods for the control of water and the development of intensive agriculture inseparably linked with it, which had created first the "new society" and then its ruling nobility, were capable also of promoting a still more broadly based society. The tools, working methods, and collective organization that could bring a fairly large valley area under irrigation could be simply and easily applied to the exploitation of the Great Plain of the lower Yellow River. Here ditches had to be dug to drain a large part of the land and embankments raised to prevent floods. The profits realized made this development inevitable, although it drew the nobility from the environment that favored them most into a terrain that favored a social development away from feudalism.

A petty baron could maintain himself in a quite small valley if it could be easily defended and if it could be irrigated so as to produce a heavy and regular crop, but the scale of enterprise in the Great Plain inevitably developed to such a point that no one feudal lord could mark off his domains with a secure and permanent frontier. The larger the undertaking—particularly in flood-prevention works—the greater the profit; but this meant that the feudal nobles had to act together, forming new and larger combinations which in time, because they centered on a common interest in public works, took the form of national states.

THE GROWTH OUT OF FEUDALISM

Since this immediately made possible even larger works, the states in turn were drawn together into more ambitious kingdoms. Feudalism was burst asunder by the force of this growth. The feudal noble was bound to a locality by his interest in his land, serfs, and local revenues, but warfare and the machinery for the maintenance of order grew beyond the scope of feudal organization. Under feudalism the number of permanent men-at-arms that could be maintained even by a great noble was necessarily small in relation to the total number of people under his control, for beyond a certain point the increase in expense, combined with the loss through men withdrawn from productive work, became disastrous. Feudal wars were fought between harvests with levies gathered around a nucleus of trained fighting men. Campaigns could not be planned to cover great distances or be kept up for an indefinite period. Neither in war nor in civil administration, therefore, could feudalism cope with the increasing scale of both economic and political enterprise.

The formation of a centralized empire was inevitable. In no other way was it possible to maintain a state apparatus capable of initiating, operating, and supervising immense public works which transcended regions and made profitable a uniform level of intensive cultivation. The culmination of this final phase was closely associated with the development of transport by water. Because the Yangtze is a better natural artery than the Yellow River, on which upstream navigation has always been difficult and unprofitable, and because the rice harvests of the south provided an even greater surplus of grain than the most intensive cultivation of wheat or millet in the north, the south was brought into special prominence. Natural waterways alone did not account for this. The decisive technical factor, requiring social coördination of a very high order, was the digging of canals long enough to link natural waterways and large enough to carry grain barges, while serving in addition as main channels either for irrigation or for the carrying away of flood water.

A single technique—the control of water by ditches and embankments—could be applied both to the stabilization of agriculture in the northwest where rainfall was irregular, to the prevention of flood in the lower Yellow River plain, and to the superlative intensification of agriculture in the south, where the monsoon rainfall made rice cultivation practicable and the additional use of irrigation made possible two and even four crops a year. The technique developed from simple. irrigation to irrigation combined with drainage and flood control, and finally to the complex form of combined irrigation, drainage, flood control, and transport.[4] It could not be profitably employed, however, much less developed from simple to complex forms, without a suitable organization of the people who employed it.

The essential requirements were: intensive cultivation in order to get back an adequate return on the cost of water conservancy works, subordination of private interest to public interest in order to mobilize labor for initial enterprise and subsequent maintenance, emphasis on human labor in order to cut down "visible" capital costs and distribute the "invisible" costs as widely as possible, emphasis on the maximum possible population to the square mile in order to be able to mobilize the largest possible number of workers in the shortest possible time.[5]

Each of these requirements involved a corresponding disability and the disabilities all interacted on each other, as did the positive requirements. Insistence on intensive cultivation involved the neglect of extensive agriculture

[4] Ch'ao-ting Chi, Key Economic Areas in Chinese History, 1936, passim.
[5] See also Chapter III, above.

and mixed agriculture. The demand for human labor at a low visible cost led to the institution of forced labor without pay, which acted as a check on the development of machines requiring capital investment. The need for a closely concentrated population, like the need for intensive cultivation, involved the neglect of mountain country and indeed of all land that could not be irrigated by ditches or wells. The demand for the largest possible number of people led to such institutions as early marriage and "filial piety," providing an ethical sanction for child labor. All such institutions, making for cheap replacement and increase of the labor supply, interacted again with the other factors maintaining the human-labor standard and inhibiting the development of labor-saving devices.

Feudalism, political states based on larger regions than a true feudalism could organize, and finally a bureaucratically administered empire presiding over partly integrated regions, marked the stages by which the society of China advanced toward the realization of its own requirements. It is not possible, however, to distinguish absolutely between any of these historical phases because the same prevailing economy nourished every one of them, and consequently the rate of elaboration of technical methods, social organization, and political institutions was not always equal though all of them affected each other.

Chinese feudalism must have begun very early to develop institutions that only attained their full importance under the imperial state that replaced feudalism. It was necessarily interested in public works of a kind that were not characteristic of European feudalism. The labor of serfs on the domain of the feudal lord did not meet all the requirements of an economy founded on irrigation. In addition, the labor of the whole community had to be regulated for the maintenance of public works—water rights had to be allotted and grain stored and issued for the labor gangs. Even under feudal conditions, accordingly, there was a more urgent need for clerkly functions than in Europe.

CLERKS, EUNUCHS, AND SCHOLAR-GENTRY

In European feudalism the clerk was for a long time roughly identified with the priest and especially with the monastic orders. Church endowments and monastic foundations were used by kings to offset the territorial power of great feudal families. As impersonal, self-perpetuating corporations they had stability and continuity without family succession. Their interest, accordingly, was to support the stability and continuity of the central power and their personnel could be drawn on for scribes and civil servants who would not identify themselves too closely with individual noble houses. This at least was the main tendency, although counter tendencies developed to complicate the play of politics; notably, the practice of dedicating junior sons of noble families to the church in order that the great families might acquire two kinds of power.

In Europe the central state power needed clerkly services more than the nobles did. In China, on the other hand, where intensive agriculture and irrigation demanded complicated accounts, lists, and computations, the feudal nobles needed clerkly services at least as much as the central state power. In attempting to meet this need and at the same time keep power in their own hands they necessarily developed a tradition of literacy and administrative competence that made them less crudely militaristic than the feudal nobles of Europe. The first professional civil servants in China, accordingly, were not from the beginning anti-feudal in function, as in Europe, but developed out of the feudal order itself. It is true that this development increasingly warped and weakened the structure of Chinese feudalism, but it also made less clear the contrast between centralized administration and regional administration, thus protracting the struggle to convert a group of kingdoms into a single empire.

Attempts at creating an administrative personnel free of the principle of inheritance were also made in China, it is true. The earliest device to become important was the employment of eunuchs. They were at first household attendants in the retinues of great lords and rulers. It was natural to place confidential negotiations in their hands because as a general rule they were slaves or captives of poor or unknown family, so that their own interests encouraged loyalty. It is significant that they seem to have developed as an important institution first in the northwestern state of Ch'in,[6] which took the lead in political, military, and economic innovations of all kinds in the trend hat first strengthened the quasi-national states of feudal China and then made inevitable the subordination of national independence to a centralized empire.

Eunuchs were used thereafter as a powerful weapon for checking the influence in politics of the tenacious Chinese family system. The weapon was two-edged, however. There were times when the corruption of eunuchs at court became as dangerous to the state as the corruption of great families arrogating power to themselves in the provinces. The truth seems to be that the Chinese family proved itself in the long run able to penetrate and control the eunuch system. Thus under the last dynasty—that of the Manchus—eunuchs were drawn almost entirely from the one district of Hochien in what is now Hopei province. This was because both rich and powerful eunuchs and poor eunuchs without other influence were able to have nephews

---

[6] They had been known from Chou times, however. See Bishop, Beginnings of North and South, 1934, p. 313. Wittfogel (*op. cit.*, p. 55 and n. 2) cites a number of sources and points out that eunuchs were at first harem and palace attendants and only later became "civil servants." To his references may be added the mention by Li Chi (Manchuria in History, 1932, p. 32) of the eunuch who in 1411 carried the power of the Ming Empire in Manchuria to its farthest north in Siberia.

or other near relatives made eunuchs and brought to court. In this way a family connection could be maintained and money saved and invested.

The impersonal corporation of celibate monks was also a device employed in China, as in Europe, but it did not become important until the end of the Han dynasty (last two centuries B.C. and first two centuries A.D.). The Buddhist church, and to a lesser extent the Taoist church, became great landholders. Their influence in the provinces offset that of the families of the great and powerful, whose natural inclination was to hang on to some of the surviving functions of feudalism even when feudalism as a whole had given way to a new order. Buddhism in particular, penetrating to China from India under the Han dynasty and under imperial patronage, was useful at first as an ally of the imperial interest in subordinating the still powerful remnants of feudalism.[7] As in Europe, however, this function generated a counter function and created a kind of ecclesiastical feudalism. While most priests and monks were drawn from the common people, the church itself became a great vested interest with an outlook sympathetic in some ways to that of the powerful families of which it was in other ways a rival.

Eventually the process that mastered all other processes was the evolution, from within the original feudal families themselves, of a new order—the scholar-gentry.[8] As this new order of society shaped itself it shaped also the character of the imperial state that superseded the feudal and national states. Imperial state and scholar-gentry thereafter interacted on each other, the mode of interaction accounting both for the strength of the state when the state was strong and the weakness of the state when

---

[7] Buddhism suffered several persecutions and ceased to be a serious rival to the triumphant bureaucracy after the Sung dynasty. For Buddhism in China generally see Franke, Geschichte des chinesischen Reiches, especially Vol. II, 1936 (references in his index, Vol. III, 1937).

[8] See also Chapter III, above.

it was undermined by the family interests of the scholar-gentry. These are later developments, but their roots go back to the late Chou feudalism.

STEPPE TRIBALISM IN RELATION TO FEUDALISM

Against this background must be considered the Inner Asian Frontier of China—the way in which it took shape and the way in which it drew from and contributed to the stream of history in China. The tribalism of this barbarian borderland differed from the tribalism that contributed to the creation and rise of European feudalism.

The barbarians who swarmed in to loot and occupy the ruins of the Roman Empire in Western Europe were chiefly barbarians of the forest. They had a mixed economy of herding and farming in addition to hunting. The herding of swine was of special importance because pigs could feed on the beechmast and acorns of the European beech and oak forests.[9] Because of this the forests, which were preserved for the royal and noble sport of hunting, were also able to produce an economic revenue. For the war chiefs of these tribes the transition to feudalism was easy. They had only to seize for themselves as much territory as their war following could hold. This kind of settling down and territorial identification could easily be imitated even beyond the lands that the Romans had once occupied and organized. The identification of land and nobility was a prime aspect of feudalism. The noble of Europe exercised a real sovereignty.[10] He fought or made peace according to his own judgment, held his own civil and criminal courts, and collected his own revenues. The freeman, originally a free warrior, held land from his noble chief in return for service in war. The serf was the labor adjunct of the land, was therefore attached to the

[9] For the difference between the herded swine of Europe and the house-yard, scavenging pigs of Asia, see also Chapter V, above.
[10] Bryce, Holy Roman Empire, pp. 122-124 (tenth century); p. 229 (thirteenth and fourteenth centuries).

land, and was "protected" only by the legal convention that he could not be sold away from one landholding to another landholding. The king was accurately described as *primus inter pares*. He was by origin only a greater war chief. He was properly a sovereign only in the royal domain. From his "peers" he drew levies in war and an income of personal dues, which did not eliminate the direct right of the nobles to tax their own domains and subjects. Royal sovereignty in civil and criminal law and in the collection of taxes was built up slowly by encroachment on the quasi-sovereign domains of the nobles. It was possible to make this encroachment cumulative and to create out of it something new because the central position of the king enabled him to play the nobles against each other in turn. For this reason civil war was a perennial and essential aspect of feudalism.

In China these aspects of feudalism belong to the period of emergence from "pre-Chinese" barbarism. Traces of them survive among the "not-yet-Chinese" barbarians of the far southwest and to a certain extent along the Yün-nan-Ssuch'uan-Tibetan borderland.[11] In proportion as the late neolithic and Bronze Age people of North China "became Chinese" by the uneven development of the agricultural side of their primitive mixed economy into a specialized economy, they also became feudal. The "tribal problem" of the steppe frontier was a by-product of this evolution. By spreading into all the territory that their new society could take over and exploit, the early feudal Chinese drove before them a fringe of people who, though akin by culture and probably by blood to the early Chinese, cut themselves off from evolution into feudalism by refusing to become feudal at the price of being conquered. They clung, instead, to the "old society" and the old mixed economy.

[11] For some of the "principalities" of this border, see Dr. Joseph Rock's forthcoming volume on the region.

Gradually those who were driven toward and into the steppe found themselves in a terrain and environment that would not tolerate either the old mixed economy as a whole or the special emphasis on agriculture that had become the mark of "being a Chinese." They were forced, instead, to work out for themselves a new line of specialization in the control of herded animals in the wide steppe. This emphasis on a single technique [12] produced in due course a society even more one-sided than that of China, but sharply different from it and in the main antagonistic to it. The forest tribalism of Europe may therefore be described as converging on the evolution of feudalism, while the steppe tribalism of Asia diverged from the evolution of feudalism.

Steppe tribalism—the society of pastoral nomadism—cannot properly be described as feudal even in its origins. Nevertheless, it had certain feudal aspects. Although it evolved out of a struggle against feudalism and reached a point where it became a separate order of society, pastoral nomadism did not sever itself entirely from feudal China. By the fact of becoming pastoral and nomadic this new tribalism acquired the ability to face about, cease retreating from the Chinese, and press inward on them. This reactive pressure from a new force that Chinese feudalism had created was a factor in forming the later and no longer feudal society of China. At the same time, however, steppe tribal society wavered in different periods of history between true pastoral nomadism and a degree of adaptation to feudalism,[13] according as the society of the steppe withdrew into the steppe or pressed inward on China from the steppe. It is doubtful, however, whether the steppe society, even when adapted to feudalism, was ever converted into true feudalism.

[12] Hunting was important and valuable in the steppe economy, but it merely supplemented the pastoral way of life and was not strong enough to convert it into a different kind of economy.

[13] Lattimore, review of Grenard's Genghis-Khan, 1938.

The Warring Kingdoms (453-361 B.C.)

In the previous chapter the summary record of barbarian wars in North China was brought down to the year 453 B.C., when the powerful state of Chin broke up into the three new states of Han, Wei, and Chao. These three states are also known collectively as the Three Chin. It was from this time on that the spread of the Chinese toward the steppe, subjugating barbarian tribes in each new territory taken over and making Chinese of them, began to be complicated by a new process—the creation of the steppe society.[14] This was a new kind of society. Whereas the "old society" barbarians with whom the "new society" Chinese had been dealing up to this point can be described in the main as backward groups of people who had not yet become Chinese, the new steppe society was both independent of the society of China and alternative to it. Interaction between the agriculture of China and the pastoral nomadism of the steppe created new kinds of historical phenomena. The Chinese, not having lost the momentum of their spread, attempted to dominate the new frontager groups; but these groups were no longer simply resistant. They were capable even of drawing some of the Chinese into the steppe and converting them into "barbarians."

In B.C. 461 the state of Ch'in had defeated a Jung tribe or tribal state in what is now northern Shensi and eastern Kansu.[15] Continuing this movement, Ch'in also defeated another group of the Jung in B.C. 444, in the valley of the Wan River in eastern Kansu.[16] This is part of the headwater system of the Wei River. In B.C. 430, however,[17]

[14] See also Chapter XIII, below.
[15] Meng Wen-t'ung, Eastward Invasions of the Ch'uan Jung, 1936, p. 12; De Groot, Die Hunnen der vorchristlichen Zeit, 1921, p. 33; both quoting the Shih Chi, Ch. 5, for which see Chavannes, Mémoires historiques, Vol. II, p. 55 and n. 1.
[16] Meng Wen-t'ung, op. cit., p. 13; De Groot, loc. cit.; Chavannes, op. cit., pp. 55 and 56, n. 1.
[17] Meng Wen-t'ung, loc. cit.; De Groot, loc. cit.; Chavannes, op. cit., p. 56.

this tribe was able to make a raid or counter invasion which penetrated the main territory of Ch'in south of the Wei.[18]

Evidently Ch'in, based on the Wei valley, was able to expand profitably both east and west, though not without reverses. Its expansion eastward to the Yellow River, which divides Shensi from Shansi, must have threatened the balance of power in North China, where the nominal Chou Empire was dominated at this time by the Shansi state of Chin. It was also bringing new territory under control to the west. On the whole, therefore, the growth of Ch'in was not of a kind that drew it out of the orbit of the internal affairs of China; on the contrary, the accretion of new Frontier power enabled Ch'in to press inward also on China. The terrain into which it was expanding was as yet well on the hither side of the steppe, so that the Chinese could use it better than the barbarians.

The Shansi state of Chin had in the same period passed the point of diminishing returns in taking over marginal territories. In B.C. 457 the feudal lord of Chao, in the northern part of Chin, had made an expedition over the mountains that divide central from northern Shansi. By doing this he extended his power all the way to the escarpment of the Inner Mongolian plateau, in the region of Tai (the modern Tat'ung), and came into touch with new and outlying tribes of the Ti people.[19]

There followed almost immediately the breakup of the state of Chin into the three states of Chao, Wei, and Han. Of these, Chao held the northern part of Shansi, a mountain country reaching as far as Inner Mongolia. It also held the mountains that divide Hopei from Shansi—the

---

[18] Thus, at the same time that Ch'in was advancing north and northwest into really new territory the barbarians were still able to raid into the territory which they had disputed with the Chinese several centuries before.

[19] Compare the discussion of the difference between this Chin expansion, which drew the Chinese away from the territory that best suited them, and the Ch'in expansion, which recruited new strength to the Chinese, in Lattimore, Origins of the Great Wall, 1937.

T'ai Hang Shan, once a stronghold of barbarian tribes [20] —but not the Peiping plain, which belonged to the state of Yen. Wei held the Fen valley, one of the oldest regions of irrigated, intensive agriculture, and also an appanage in Shensi, west of the Yellow River, though this was threatened and eventually occupied by the growth of Ch'in. Han fell heir to the most Chinese and least barbarian territories of Chin, in Honan, bordering on the south with the Yangtze valley state of Ch'u and reaching on the east to the headwaters of the Huai. It was therefore the key state in determining the balance of power between the feudal states of the Yellow River and those of the Yangtze.

In B.C. 444 Wei and Han, in alliance, "exterminated" the Jung tribes of the hilly Lo country in northern Honan.[21] These must have been isolated remnants of the Jung and Ti peoples against whom the Chinese had fought in this region in the seventh century B.C. Probably this campaign was only the political completion of an already advanced process of economic and cultural absorption. Although the people subjugated or destroyed are still described as barbarian, the war cannot be called a step in the enlargement of the Chinese frontier, for these Ti and Jung had been left behind and islanded as the true frontier between Chinese and barbarians moved to the north.

Even the northern wars became for a long time less important. Ch'in is described as adopting from the barbarians in B.C. 417 the custom of sacrificing girls to the Yellow River.[22] Probably this refers to the northern part of that stretch of the Yellow River that flows from north

[20] De Groot, op. cit., p. 28.

[21] Wieger, Textes historiques, Vol. I, 1929, p. 155 (no reference to source). Meng Wen-t'ung, op. cit., with a series of citations from the Tso Chuan, makes it clear that this was the end of a series of wars in which the remnants of the Honan Jung were squeezed between the northward expansion of the Yangtze state of Ch'u and the efforts first of the state of Chin and then of the states of Wei and Han to maintain a southern frontier against Ch'u.

[22] Wieger, loc. cit. (no reference to source). See the Shih Chi, Ch. 126.

to south between Shensi and Shansi. It indicates that the
people of Ch'in were penetrating into terrain that favored
the survival of the barbarian way of life against the Chinese trend of evolution to such an extent that the people of
Ch'in began to take on a number of barbarian characteristics, instead of wholly subordinating the barbarians to
the new Chinese way of life.[23] The barbarians also were
still able to strike back against the Chinese, for in B.C.
378 they defeated the state of Wei in the Fen valley in
Shansi.[24] Ch'in, meanwhile, continued its expansion into
Kansu with a victory over the Huan (a Jung tribe) in
B.C. 361.[25]

On the whole, however, from the end of the fifth century to the end of the fourth century B.C. there is a
decided shift in the main emphasis, from wars between
Chinese and barbarians to wars between the states of
China. There is in this a strong confirmation of the argument that the barbarian wars were not primarily the result
of a barbarian drive inward on China from the remote
steppe but the result of an outward spread of the Chinese,
extruding groups that were originally a kind of "backward

[23] In western Inner Mongolia I have heard several variants of a Mongol
folklore account of the death of Chingghis Khan in A.D. 1227. Chingghis
died just when he had conquered the Tangut-Tibetan (Tanggot) kingdom of
that time. Its capital was at Ninghsia. (The -hsia in this name is the
Chinese name of the Tangut kingdom.) According to the legend Chingghis
took the wife of the Tangut king, but with a knife she had hidden she
castrated him. Chingghis did not die of this wound; some day it would
heal and Chingghis would return to lead the Mongols. The princess then ran
to the Yellow River, jumped in, and was drowned. For this reason one of
the Mongol names for the Yellow River is Khatun Gol, "River of the
Princess." Above the point where she jumped in the water supposedly runs
clear, below that point it runs muddy. I am sure that this legend harks back
to the ancient custom of sacrificing women to the Yellow River. Compare
Sanang Setsen's version, Mongol text, pp. 100, 102; Schmidt's translation,
pp. 101, 103.

[24] Wieger, op. cit., p. 159 (no reference to source). Meng Wen-t'ung,
(Eastward Invasions of the Red Ti and White Ti, 1937, p. 85) cites a
number of sources, especially Shih Chi, Ch. 44, and links these barbarians,
who were Ti, with the small state of Chung Shan which had been destroyed
30 years before. Compare Chavannes, op. cit., Vol. V, p. 148.

[25] De Groot, op. cit., p. 33, citing Shih Chi, Ch. 5, for which see Chavannes, op. cit., Vol. II, p. 63.

Chinese" and forcing them gradually to convert themselves into a steppe society. If there had been at this time a real steppe society harbored in a Mongolian and Central Asian homeland, the increasingly savage wars between the states of China would have opened up wonderful opportunities for mounted warriors to raid into the settled lands. There is accordingly reason to suppose that what was happening in China was still the main determinant in creating a marginal, by-product society of the steppe.

Barbarian Wars and Wall Building
(End of Fourth Century b.c.)

Barbarian wars of a new kind, beginning at the end of the fourth century b.c., reinforce this line of reasoning once more. For a hundred years the states of North China had turned inward against each other; partly, it may be supposed, because the expansion of the northern states toward though not yet quite up to the steppe had been slowed down by terrain that it was less and less easy or profitable to exploit by irrigation and intensive agriculture. In this terrain and during this period the retreating "old society" groups were given time to begin the evolution of a "new society" of their own—the rudimentary steppe society, which was better able to resist the agricultural "new society" of China. As compared with China the steppe environment was poor and inhospitable as a setting for the primitive mixed economy, but in proportion as this mixed economy was converted into a new specialized economy of pastoral nomadism the steppe became relatively a rich environment. From this time on, the conversion of barbarians into Chinese alternated with the conversion of Chinese into barbarians—not by relapse into the old, primitive, mixed-economy barbarism, but by transition to a new, specialized, monocultural barbarism, invigorated by the pastoral economy of the steppe.

At the end of the fourth century b.c., accordingly, an

unmistakably nomadic warfare is vividly described. In the earlier barbarian wars, though horses are mentioned, there is no recognizable description of a specialized pastoral economy and the barbarians are specifically called foot-soldiers. The new period begins with Wu Ling, a sovereign of the state of Chao, the northern succession-state of Chin, who "changed the customs [of Chao], wore the costume of the Hu and trained mounted archers." On one campaign he "set out to the northwest, dressed as a Hu, at the head of his war councillors and won possession of the Hu territory in that region, with the intention of making an attack southward . . . to invade Ch'in." He even attempted to appear before the ruler of Ch'in disguised as a tribal envoy in order to spy out his rival, but was detected and had to ride for safety.[26]

Li Mu, a general of the same state, continued the development of the new methods during the first half of the third century B.C. He stationed officers to collect taxes, presumably in kind, which were brought to the camps for the maintenance of the army. Herds must have been as important as agriculture, for he slaughtered cattle daily for the feeding of his army. He also trained his troops in mounted archery and used signal towers to make mobilization rapid. In one campaign against the Hu he spread herds of cattle out over the country to make it look undefended. This was reported by small parties of nomads, who must have been riding in peacefully to trade along the border. Tempted by these reports the barbarians made a raid and were drawn into ambush and defeated, with heavy loss. The state of Chao then pushed its control farther toward the steppe, coming into contact with tribes that until then had been considered outlying.[27]

These accounts rather clearly indicate a border territory

[26] Shih Chi, Ch. 43, 110; compare De Groot, *op. cit.*, p. 34-36; also Lattimore, Origins of the Great Wall; Chavannes, *op. cit.*, Vol. V, pp. 70-88.
[27] Shih Chi, Ch. 81; De Groot, *op. cit.*, p. 37.

with a mixed economy of agriculture and herding—by no means a typical Chinese economy of intensive agriculture. The troops approximate to the standard of the mounted steppe warriors of later times: they were mounted archers, they were given a large meat ration, and they were so far habituated to a life much like steppe nomadism that it is recorded that they were eager to take the offensive. The border conditions were those of a nomad society—free passage for small parties of men but not for bodies large enough to be dangerous. The mixed, partly pastoral economy is further indicated by herds large enough to tempt the raids of nomads and to mask the front of an army. When the Chinese took the offensive they used the tactics of nomad warfare—swift movement in open country, maneuver, ambush, and sudden assault.[28]

Chao was not the only state to go through these changes. Ch'in, to the west of it, became increasingly known for its mounted archers—Chinese who were like barbarians in their way of fighting. The mounted archer, in fact, destroyed the old feudal nobility of China who traditionally fought from chariots, just as the Welsh and English longbow (used on foot) defeated the chivalry of France. Yen, to the east of Chao, based on the Peiping plain, also produced a great cavalry leader in the third century B.C. He had been a hostage among the Hu and seems to have learned to fight as they did, for he organized an army in Yen which drove through the mountainous country in what is now the southern part of Jehol.[29]

Mounted warfare was contemporary with another new development that might seem to be completely contradictory—the building of walled fortifications hundreds of miles long. It was in the fourth and third centuries B.C., when the Chinese were everywhere reaching territories marginal to the true steppe and so being slowed down in

[28] Lattimore, *op. cit.*
[29] Shih Chi, Ch. 110; De Groot, *op. cit.*, p. 37.

their advance, that the great age of wall building began.[30]

Under Chao, who ruled in Ch'in from B.C. 306 to 250, a wall was built from the valley of the T'ao River, in Kansu, northward to the Yellow River, thence along the Yellow River to the oases or semi-oases of the Ninghsia region, and from Ninghsia southeastward, skirting the southern edge of the Ordos steppe to the Yellow River again.[31] Under Wu Ling who ruled in Chao from B.C. 325 to 298 (the same who has just been described as adopting the costume and ways of the barbarians), there was built about the year 300 a wall running from the point called Kaoch'üeh, northeast of Ninghsia in Inner Mongolia, eastward to a point in the mountain country between Kalgan, at the edge of the Inner Mongolian plateau, and Peiping.[32] About the year 290 the state of Yen also built a wall, running from a point near the eastern end of the Chao wall to the lower valley of the Liao River, in Manchuria. This wall seems to have followed not the southern edge of the Jehol hills but the northern edge, in such a way that it divided the steppe of northern Jehol from the hills of southern Jehol, and guarded communication between the agricultural plain of the lower Liao, in Manchuria, and the Great Plain of North China.[33] The main line of the Great Wall of China as established only a few decades later did not wholly confirm this demarcation of the borders between Ch'in, Chao, Yen, and the steppe bar-

[30] Herrmann, Die Westländer, etc. (in Hedin, Southern Tibet, Vol. VIII, 1922), p. 268, n. 1, lists a kind of proto-Great Wall at the impossible date of 1169 B.C. There are several very early references to "building"—the one cited by Herrmann is also cited by Meng Wen-t'ung (Eastward Invasions of the Ch'uan Jung, p. 1), though not as an instance of frontier wall building. The commonsense way to approach the problem is to remember that long walls can only be built by societies that are organized in a rather special way to provide the necessary concentration of labor. Therefore all very early references must be taken to mean fortified settlements or outposts.

[31] Herrmann, loc. cit.; De Groot, op. cit., p. 34; Shih Chi, Ch. 110.

[32] Herrmann, De Groot, and Shih Chi, loc. cit. According to Shih Chi (Ch. 43; Chavannes, op. cit., Vol. V, p. 64) this wall was built by the father of Wu Ling—an interesting indication that this was an age of wall builders. See also Ch'ien-Han Shu, Ch. 64, first section.

[33] Herrmann, loc. cit.; De Groot, op. cit., p. 36; Shih Chi, Ch. 110.

barians, but obviously it did confirm the idea of a closed world of Chinese agriculture and an excluded world of nomad pastoral tribes.

Such amazing activity, concentrated within a very few years, predicates a long, slow gathering of momentum—the converging of a number of tendencies which, when they had reinforced each other sufficiently, discharged their combined energy in an apparently sudden burst of novel enterprise. It is not enough to say simply that the Chinese had expanded up to the margin of the steppe and that this resulted in a tendency for some of the border Chinese to take on barbarian ways and also in a tendency to fix permanent frontiers between Chinese and barbarians. Both of these tendencies can be recognized, but they were part of a much larger, more complex process of growth, differentiation, and re-combination that was going on in the heart of China as well as at the edges of expansion. For one thing, frontiers were fortified with walls not only between Chinese and barbarians but between different states in China, and also between the China of the lower Yellow River and the China of the Yangtze. Both the building of walls and the increasing cleavage between agricultural China and the pastoral steppe were part of a great general change—the amalgamation of separate states into a unified empire and the transition from a feudal order of society. What happened on the Inner Asian Frontier was part of this change but it was not the prime phenomenon.[34]

Chinese Feudalism and City-and-Country "Cells"

In feudal China, as in feudal Europe, the real unit of sovereignty was not the nation but the domain of the feudal lord.[35] The Chou "emperors" represented the center of

[34] Lattimore, *op. cit.* See also Chapter XIII, below.

[35] The authorities already cited on the subject of feudalism tend to emphasize the theory of the suzerainty of the overlord; but it can be argued that this was an ideal aimed at, while practical working sovereignty, including taxation and law as well as military service, was compartmented fief by fief.

gravity of a widely spread culture but they did not rule an integrated empire by direct administration of each territory that composed it. All that they could claim was the allegiance, within the limits of feudalism, of a number of great nobles each of whom claimed in a similar way the allegiance of minor nobles. Taxation, civil and criminal justice, and the levy of troops were autonomous in each feudal holding, not centralized under an imperial civil and military service. The Chou rulers also had their own personal domain which they administered not as emperors but as great feudal nobles. As an emperor, therefore, the Chou ruler had only the strictly feudal status of *primus inter pares*.

It is more than probable that the early Chou conquerors, who drove inward on China from the northwestern rim of the Shang cultural area, were unable to make their conquest equally definite all over North China. Although they carried the development of feudalism a long way forward from the rudimentary feudal or even pre-feudal level of Shang times, the area that they controlled was not nearly so large as the area that they overshadowed. It can be surmised, therefore, that the feudal states nearest to the Chou personal domain in the Wei valley were well under the "imperial" control of the Chou sovereigns (according to the feudal standard of control), while in the rest of North China this example promoted the development of states equally feudal but not nearly so well controlled by the Chou sovereigns. Once the feudal phase of history had really begun to unfold, in other words, the feudal phenomenon of war between feudal nobles and revolt against feudal superiors became as important as the feudal striving toward a schematic "pyramid" of emperor, kings, and nobles.

Moreover, the Chou conquest, by stimulating the growth of feudalism all over the eastern part of North China, created for itself the problem of dealing with a host of new feudal magnates, not all of them equally well under control. This preoccupation with the eastern area of expansion allowed the feudal house of Ch'in, in Shensi, to grow up right at the side of the Chou sovereigns, just as the Chou power had originally formed and gathered strength at the side of the Shang Chinese. When the House of Chou moved its capital from Shensi to Honan, in B.C. 771-770, it was, according to the chronicle account, because the Chinese were being pressed hard by barbarian invaders from the northwest. The loyal house of Ch'in remained behind in Shensi to cover the Chou withdrawal.[36]

Now it is perfectly clear from the later course of history that it was not "the Chou Chinese" who withdrew from Shensi but simply the Chou court. The Chinese of Shensi remained in Shensi. They became Ch'in Chinese rather than Chou Chinese, but instead of retreating before the barbarians or being conquered by them it was they who enlarged the area of Ch'in control—at the expense of the barbarians. It therefore seems highly probable that the main reason for the eastward move of the Chou court was the uncomfortable growth in power of its "loyal" feudatory, the House of Ch'in, which made it necessary for the Chou sovereign to look for the support of his eastern feudatories against the great western feudatory. The move was not successful and the power of the Chou sovereigns declined from this time on.

This indicates a difference between the histories of Chinese and European feudalism. In Europe steady encroachment of the royal authority on the "sovereignty" of the great nobles, until both the functions and the legal definitions of sovereignty really were identified for the most part with royal titles and functions, had a great deal to do with the conversion of feudalism into something else. Successful encroachment was made possible largely by alliance

[36] Shih Chi, Ch. 5; Chavannes, op. cit., Vol. II, p. 14.

with classes whose interests differed from those of the nobles—the religious orders and the burgesses—as well as by supporting nobles alternately in their wars against each other.

China followed another line of evolution. In the later centuries of the Chou period it was the nobles who cropped and trimmed the power of the court. National states arose not out of power accruing to the titular sovereign but out of the power consolidated by feudatories in a number of regions. In part, at least, this must have been because the power of the towns and that of a new class, the "professional" administrators, arose out of the interests of the nobles and was fostered to begin with by the nobles themselves instead of being manipulated by the imperial interest in order to hold the nobles in check. Thus it can be said that when feudalism in China was converted into a new and different order it was not because the nobles had been subordinated by the court and the allies of the court, but because the nobles themselves had transformed themselves into something else—the scholar-gentry.

Nor is it simply fortuitous that Europe changed in a way that led to a money economy and industrialism, while China changed in a way that created a centralized imperial bureaucracy, of which the personnel was recruited generation by generation from the landed gentry, whose combination of landed interest and administrative interest kept capitalism well in check and prevented industrial development almost entirely. In Europe a varying landscape encouraged a number of different kinds of extensive farming and mixed farming. Even under feudalism there was a considerable need for trade, and for trade in necessities as well as in luxuries. The products and by-products of agriculture were processed more and more in towns in different regions, which traded with each other. The towns, in fact, had a productive function besides being centers of distribution. In China, by comparison, the landscape was more uniform and the economy, even under feudalism, almost monocultural. Grain was by far the most important surplus product, and there was no need for towns to sell surplus grain to each other.

A cellular structure of economy and society was consequently established. Walled cities—which had existed since late neolithic times—were typical both under feudalism (as in Europe) and throughout later centuries. Although the economy of China was agricultural, the walled city was an essential characteristic of the rural landscape.[37] Both the maintenance of armies and the feeding of laborers conscripted for water-conservancy works depended on granaries established in the nuclear cities. As canals and irrigation projects became more complex, therefore, the walled city-in-the-country became even more fixed as the standard of government and administration.

Within the unitary city-and-country "cell" trade moved at short range. The village—normally without a wall— was the unit of agricultural production, but the surplus of grain produced by the village land was concentrated in the walled city for storage. It was the walled city that was garrisoned, and the walled city was the center of artisan crafts producing cloth, tools, utensils, and most other commodities of trade for the countryside. Only a few things—like salt, iron, tea,[38] silk—were produced in limited areas and traded in at long range. Except for these the cell structure could be indefinitely repeated all over China, and certain of its functions were the same both under feudalism and under the later imperial order.[39]

This was not the case with all of them, however. The

---

[37] Since nightsoil is the most important Chinese fertilizer and can be obtained in the largest quantities from cities, the most concentrated and highly developed agriculture is just outside the walls of cities. Thus "most rural" and "most urban" are closely linked. Compare Thorp, Geography of the Soils of China, 1938, pp. 430-432.

[38] Tea, however, was not generally used in China until the T'ang Empire (seventh and eighth centuries). Compare Encyclopaedia Sinica, 1917, article "Tea."

[39] See also Chapter III, above.

regional unit of controlling city and dependent country-side was admirably suited to the range of action of a feudal society, but only, it may be surmised, so long as the scale of irrigation enterprise remained within the radius of the walled-city cellular unit. Judging by the standard of economic range in the China of later times, this meant a maximum distance of thirty to sixty miles—a journey of one or two days by foot or by cart. Transport of grain and of low-priced goods for everyday use was uneconomic at greater distances because the cost of feeding cart animals tended to become greater than the margin of profit.

The scale of irrigation enterprise must have tended to exceed these distances at a rather early period, while the scale of other economic operations tended to remain constant. In the wider plains, especially, both the flow of water for irrigation and the building of embankments against flood could best be managed on a scale affecting more than one of what I have called the cellular units of walled cities and the districts tributary to them. Consequently, it seems probable that feudalism must have begun to modify itself by developing a tolerance for some kinds of activity ranging beyond the reach of a single noble, while tenaciously conserving other aspects of the limited, regional sovereignty characteristic of feudalism.

It was owing to this, I believe, that the class that eventually superseded the feudal nobles developed out of the ranks of the feudal nobility instead of in competition with it. I have mentioned already the reasons for believing that even under feudalism China had a special need for clerkly functions—a need that was common to China and the great civilizations of Mesopotamia and Egypt, but not to China and Europe.[40] Labor had to be collected and assigned to the digging of ditches and the raising of embankments: quantities of water had to be calculated,

[40] Wittfogel, Die Theorie der orientalischen Gesellschaft, 1938.

priority of access to water allotted, and volume of water distributed according to area of land. When society was organized in a feudal way there was no reason why the nobility itself should not assume these functions in order to benefit by them in taking a privileged share of the profits of irrigation. It was also natural for the nobility itself to continue these functions as long as it could, when the scale of enterprise had become large enough to link feudal holdings together. In this way the same people became concerned with the maintenance of feudal separatism, divided sovereignty, and the feudal resistance to centralization, while at the same time they became concerned with functions that tended to override these limitations. As this dualism became more pronounced the necessity for subordinating one aspect to the other became more urgent.

Confucianism in Relation to Feudalism

Successive political phases of Chou history confirm these assumptions. The original Chou conquest of Shang China, striking inward from the periphery, created an "imperial" unification; but this was of a limited, feudal kind. It was not an administrative centralization but an ascendancy in war strong enough to make the feudal rulers of the time acknowledge a Chou emperor—while continuing, nevertheless, to administer and rule their own territories. A typically feudal reaction toward separatism then followed, reaching its height in the eighth century B.C., when the Chou court was forced to move from Shensi to Honan. From this time on, feudal power encroached on imperial power until the "policy" of the court indicated merely which feudal kingdom was dominant.

As early as the seventh century, however, a new kind of centralization began to operate. The feudal kingdoms, while continuing to fight each other one by one, keeping up the permanent condition of war typical of all feudalism, also began to form "leagues" of several kingdoms. The main characteristic of these leagues was regional. One, in the Yangtze valley, was headed by the state of Ch'u.[41] The other, in the Yellow River valley, was headed first by Ch'i in the east [42] and then by Chin in the north.[43] Ch'in in the northwest began to develop the character of an outlaw state, fighting against both leagues and against individual kingdoms within the leagues. The fact that each league occupied a major geographical region while Ch'in, in the northwest loess highlands, also dominated a distinct region, strongly indicates that within the still feudal order of China a new order was taking shape. A new range of action was becoming operative. Political combinations evolved by the feudal kingdoms themselves— not combinations imposed on them by the encroachment of a central, imperial power—were destroying the old separatism. This new power of political combination must have been made possible by an ability to integrate economic enterprise and social cohesion on a wider scale. The range of action was not yet sufficient to work with equal effect all over China, but it was enough to make the major geographical regions dominant over the separate states within the regions.

At the end of the sixth century B.C. the career of Confucius [44] makes it possible to estimate some of the phenomena of change. The significance of Confucius is that he was both a product of feudalism and a prophet of the new order arising out of feudalism and superseding it. He was

[41] Franke, Geschichte des chinesischen Reiches, Vol. I, 1930, p. 159.

[42] Ibid., pp. 160-161. Franke emphasizes the importance of salt and iron in contributing to the wealth and power of Ch'i. Iron was apparently at this time rapidly coming into general use, but must have been known and worked before. See Karlgren, The Authenticity of Ancient Texts, 1929, p. 173.

[43] Franke, op. cit., p. 165. Franke considers that the main phenomenon of the time was the self-defense of Yellow River China against the rapid expansion of the still much less Chinese state of Ch'u, in the Yangtze region.

[44] Confucius was born in B.C. 551 and died in 479. See Franke, op. cit., pp. 203 et sqq., and many other references, especially in his Vol. I.

a great creative thinker, whose ideas about the family, the state, and the need for a professional class of non-hereditary administrators replacing the feudal nobility prepared the Chinese for the creation of a new kind of "universal" empire.[45]

What Confucius taught about the family, especially, was calculated to destroy feudalism. His concept of a "filial piety" governing the duties of sons toward fathers, and an equivalent quasi-filial piety governing the duty of subjects of the state to officials of the state and the duty of officials to the state itself, was in itself a system of ethics. The significance of this ethical system was that it discarded the feudal standard of regulating the duty of a man according to the class into which he was born and the land to which he was attached by birth and by which he was obligated to certain services and entitled to certain kinds of protection. For this feudal concept Confucius substituted obedience and the transmission of orders. Confucian ethics, in short, justify the direct assessment of taxes and the relaying of orders all the way from the supreme government to the taxpayer. The precept of filial piety also justifies large families, child labor (the children being responsible to the parents, not the parents to the children), and authority of the father even over adult sons.[46] It thus fits exactly the need of the intensive Chinese agriculture for a swarming population and human labor at low cost.[47]

Confucius looked into the society in which he lived for sanctions to uphold the nonfeudal order that he was trying to define. Rudiments of this order were already appearing

[45] For the documents of the Confucian cast of thought and the philosophy that grew out of it, see Legge, Chinese Classics.

[46] Under the Confucian system children are responsible both for their parents and to them, while parents are not responsible to their children but are responsible for their crimes or debts.

[47] See, in addition to Franke, op. cit., the interesting review of a number of the ideas of Confucius with reference to the social changes of his time in Wittfogel, Foundations and Stages of Chinese Economic History, 1935, pp. 48-50 and footnotes.

in the tendency to break down the feudal barriers of separatism. It may be that Confucius mistook these rudiments for vestiges of a better order that had once existed, for it is the way of a philosopher to identify the scheme of things as he thinks they ought to be with the inherent nature of mankind. At any rate, Confucius reinterpreted the remote history of China as a golden age in which virtuous rulers had followed the precepts that he laid down for the rulers of his own time and the future. He stood, that is, between an age in Chinese history that was only just being foreshadowed and an age that had never existed in the form in which he idealized it. To what were really prophetic speculations he added sonorous justifications claiming to be staunchly conservative.

In this way Confucius was a pioneer in the appeal to a sanctified but in many ways imaginary past and did much to create what was eventually the "upper-class" outlook of "the best people," the people of "culture" in China. The order that he foresaw and began to shape was destined to supersede feudalism, but only several centuries after his time. Moreover, the state of Ch'in, which finally assured the emergence of the imperial order from the feudal order, turned at the same time against the "scholasticism" of the Confucians, who by then had become so accustomed to the appeal to an imaginary ideal order that they did not recognize the real new order when they saw it. Probably his emphasis on a sober permanence was what finally established the social respectability of Confucius as a sound conservative when, after the Ch'in period of turbulence, the new order had shaken down and had become the accepted standard.

CH'IN AND THE BEGINNINGS OF AN IMPERIAL ORDER

In the meantime intermediate stages had still to be traversed. During the sixth and fifth centuries B.C. states of the lower Yangtze were already appealing to Yellow River states for alliances against the state of Ch'u, which was building up a dominant control of Yangtze China.[48] Ch'u itself also made alliances with marginal Yellow River states.[49] Not only were the feudal partitions of separatism between the states within the major Yellow River and Yangtze regions breaking down; the currents of history were also beginning to flow back and forth between these two great regions.

Then in the fourth century Ch'in, in the northwest, began the development of the final phase.[50] Ch'u, though it annexed the state of Yüeh, which had previously annexed the state of Wu,[51] was unable to achieve a decisive supremacy. It might have succeeded had not the stronghold of Ch'in in the northwestern loess region been so easy to defend against invasion from Ch'u. The north began to reassert supremacy—but through the lone state of Ch'in and not through the leagued states of the lower Yellow River.

Ch'in defeated the combined states of Chao, Wei, and Han (the succession states of Chin) in B.C. 364,[52] and the wars of imperial conquest and unification began. One indication of this is that the nature of war itself began to change. The interminable "permanent" state of war of feudalism developed a more dynamic character. In feudal war the defeated ruler or noble was "conquered" in only a limited way. He "acknowledged" the victor and paid over either a flat ransom or a periodical tribute, but he himself collected the tribute. His territory retained its identity and was "joined" to the victor's territory only as a

[48] See the well-documented account in Franke, *op. cit.*, pp. 167 *et sqq.*
[49] The struggle in this period turned largely on the control of the valley of the Huai River, intermediate between Yellow River China and Yangtze China.
[50] The beginning of the rise of Ch'in thus corresponds with the dismemberment of Chin, after B.C. 453. Compare Franke, *op. cit.*, pp. 180, 182.
[51] Yüeh took Wu in 473 (Franke, *op. cit.*, p. 177); Ch'u took Yüeh in 333 (pp. 188-189).
[52] Shih Chi, Ch. 5; Chavannes, *op. cit.*, Vol. II, p. 59.

satellite. Moreover, the joining—subordination—might be merely temporary. Even the feudatory of a state that was at the height of its power might go over to a rival state, thus altering the grouping but not the structure of power.

The new tendency, exploited most successfully by Ch'in, was to destroy the structure and identity of the conquered side. The tendency itself already existed and was not peculiar to Ch'in. From the fifth century[53] on it was increasingly common to massacre the whole ruling house of a defeated territory and to annex the territory itself—not merely to add it as an appanage but to incorporate it with the victor state. Ch'in converted this tendency into a policy. A mark of the new method was the Ch'in system of taking heads and paying for them.[54] By this the "polite" conventions of feudal war were shattered. All men in armed service on the losing side, and corpses too, were decapitated and a reward paid for the heads. Extermination of the army destroyed loyalties of the feudal kind and made it easier to merge the conquered population into the enlarged and directly administered state. One result of this cold-blooded policy was a horror of Ch'in which has never faded from Chinese history. The policy of slaughter was of course regarded as an attribute of the "half-barbarian" character of Ch'in.[55] The policy itself may very well have grown out of the wars between Ch'in and its fringe of barbarian tribes; but it must also be considered a part of the complex change, within China, in the nature of society, state, and the aims of war.

Contemporary changes of other kinds confirm this view.

[53] Compare the "unchivalrous" fighting between the nobles who destroyed and divided the state of Chin, and the usurpation of power in the state of Ch'i (Franke, *op. cit.,* pp. 180-182).

[54] In the victory of the year 364, mentioned above, Ch'in claimed 60,000 heads; in a victory of the year 318, 82,000 heads, and so forth. For premiums on the taking of heads, see Duyvendak, The Book of Lord Shang, 1928, pp. 297-302.

[55] For the traditional dislike of Ch'in among Chinese historians—and especially, of course, the dislike for Ch'in Shih-huang-ti—compare Franke, *op. cit.,* p. 225.

An important stage in the emergence of a new class out of the ranks of the feudal nobility was the appearance, in the fourth century B.C., of men who made a career of politics and war and who went from one state to another selling their services. They were men of minor noble origin, not great nobles who had a personal interest in the maintenance of feudalism, but men who knew the working processes of state affairs. They were not feudal; they did not bring with them the support of a territory and feudal retainers. What they did was to offer their knowledge of how to administer a state, collect its revenues, and make its army formidable. Confucius himself was an early exponent of this professionalism, but his ambition was to offer advice on the theory of doing things. The men of the fourth century were practical professionals. The greatest of them all, Kung-sun Yang, took service with the state of Ch'in, where he was made Lord of Shang.[56] The title does not mean that he acted as a feudal supporter, for he was a general administrator of the whole state.

Among the Ch'in policies was the promotion and improvement of irrigated agriculture, the necessary public works being a direct enterprise of the state.[57] Taxation, concurrently, was more and more definitely organized in such a manner as to make the head of a family the unit of social computation by treating him as the subject of the state, not as a man-with-land sub-unit which the state could approach only indirectly through the feudal lord.[58] The all-pervading sovereignty of the state was in this way fed

[56] Duyvendak, *op. cit.*

[57] A sage, in establishing laws, alters the customs, and causes the people to be engaged in agriculture, night and day (*ibid.*, p. 235); grain should be made dear and non-farmers taxed heavily (to increase the profit of agriculture) (p. 313); immigration should be encouraged, in order to develop more of the land of Ch'in (pp. 266 *et sqq.*). For the importance of irrigation in making Ch'in powerful, see Shih Chi, Ch. 29; Chavannes, Vol. III, Part II, pp. 524-525.

[58] Taxes should be according to the measure of grain (not land) Duyvendak, *op. cit.*, p. 176); there should be no rank without office (p. 185); rank should be in accordance with the production of grain (pp. 205, 253).

by making duties even more specific than they had been under feudalism, while destroying the protective sanctions and privileges of feudalism.

THE TRANSITION FROM FEUDALISM TO AN IMPERIAL ORDER

The transition from feudalism to the imperial order could not of course proceed with the smooth logic of a triumphant theory. The friction of advance crushed some of the manifestations of feudalism but hardened others into stubborn resistance. Encroachment of the national states on the "imperial" prerogatives of the Chou court had long ceased to be significant; the Chou sovereign was no longer anything but a feeble symbol. Now, by the rise of Ch'in, what did become significant was the reverse process of encroachment on the identity and integrity of the national states. For this reason there was, I believe, a reaction within the loose "leagues" toward defining firmly the exact and immutable boundaries of sovereignty, checking the long trend toward the coalescence of states that had common interests within major geographical regions. Wall building was the expression of this tendency. It was as if the "cellular" units of walled cities, each with its adherent rural population, were grouped in agglomerations of cells, each with a wall that identified it as a major unit compounded of minor units.

In addition to the northern walls of Ch'in, Chao, and Yen, facing the already emergent steppe Frontier, the state of Wei built a wall running roughly north and south, in Shensi, in the fourth century B.C.[59] This was not a wall against the barbarians but against the state of Ch'in. It protected a reach of territory (originally held by Jung barbarians) that belonged to the state of Wei but lay across the north-south stretch of the Yellow River from the main territory of Wei. In spite of the wall Ch'in

[59] Herrmann, *loc. cit.*; De Groot, *op. cit.*, p. 33.

very soon invaded and took over these lands.[60] Later the state of Wei built another wall, running north and south across the lower course of the Yellow River, to protect its much diminished territory.[61]

The state of Ch'i in the northern part of Shantung built a wall running from east to west across Shantung.[62] The northern face of this wall appears to have been regarded as an embankment against the flooding of the lower Yellow River; the southern face looked toward the Huai basin, where the great Yangtze state of Ch'u, having expanded all the way to the coast, was pushing its influence northward through the penetration or conquest of a number of minor states.

At the beginning of the third century, finally, the state of Ch'u also built a wall. Less is known about this than about any other wall, but it seems to have barred the line of passage from north to south between the headwaters of the Huai and the valley of the Han, a great north-bank tributary of the Yangtze.[63]

Wall building, it is apparent, cannot be called a phenomenon peculiar to the hardening of the Inner Asian Frontiers of China. It was a general phenomenon of the last phase of national, feudal separatism in China. Nevertheless, a more and more permanent Inner Asian Frontier along the edge of the steppe was in fact coming into being. The special significance of the preliminary "Great Walls" of the north was this: the unification of China as a whole obliterated regional walls within China, but simultaneously China as a whole was differentiated from Inner Asia

[60] Franke, *op. cit.*, pp. 181-182, 184.

[61] Another wall was that of Chung Shan, a small state on the mountain border between the modern provinces of Shansi and Hopei. See De Groot, *op. cit.*, p. 46; Franke, *op. cit.*, p. 188. Two studies in Chinese, formerly in my possession, I have unfortunately been unable to consult again: Hsü Chü-ch'ing, A Study of the Northern Frontier Great Walls, 1929, and Wang Kuo-lang, A Study of the Development of the Great Walls of China, 1928.

[62] De Groot, *op. cit.*, p. 45; Franke, *op. cit.*, pp. 187-188.

[63] De Groot, *op. cit.*, p. 46; Franke, *op. cit.*, p. 188. This may have been a series of fortified points, rather than a wall.

as a whole, and therefore the northern walls gave way only to a newer and greater fortified Frontier.

In the Chinese terminology this closing phase of national separatism is known as the Perpendicular and Horizontal [64] period, because the Yangtze state of Ch'u, by "perpendicular" alliances with the Yellow River states, was attempting to check the "horizontal" conquering advance of Ch'in from west to east. In the wars of this time each advance of Ch'in meant a wider and more thorough destruction of the feudal order and a clearer shaping of the new imperial order. The destruction of Ch'u by Ch'in, however, was more of a war of rival claims to imperialism protracted over several decades, because Ch'u was engaged in assembling and centralizing an empire of the Yangtze valley which matched and in some ways anticipated the Yellow River empire of Ch'in. The empire of Ch'u was water-linked. It grew by expansion from the middle Yangtze to the seacoast, and it is interesting to note that canals were an important part of the apparatus of centralization. As early as the fifth century B.C. the state of Wu, later conquered by Yüeh and finally absorbed by Ch'u, had dug a "grand canal" from the Yangtze to the Huai basin.[65]

Because of the importance of communication by water Ch'u made its conquests largely by the use of war boats.[66] Undoubtedly this was one factor in the final triumph of Ch'in, which could adapt its fighting methods to the water-logged south better than Ch'u could undertake the invasion of the dry northwest. A more important factor was the conquest by Ch'in of most of the modern province of Ssuch'uan, at the end of the fourth century B.C.[67] In this way Ch'in turned the flank of the defensive alliances of

[64] Franke, *op. cit.,* p. 193.
[65] Bishop, Beginnings of North and South in China, 1934, p. 325.
[66] *Ibid.,* p. 320; also p. 324 (for the state of Yüeh); also his Long-Houses and Dragon-Boats, 1938.
[67] Franke, *op. cit.,* pp. 186-187.

Ch'u, penetrating through the mountain country on the borders of Shensi, Kansu, and Ssuch'uan, and then from Ssuch'uan—a rich agricultural base—moving down the Yangtze against Ch'u, as well as down the valley of the Han and through the gap between the Han and the Huai.

In B.C. 223 Ch'u was destroyed [68]; in B.C. 221 the conquest of Shantung was completed,[69] and the ruler of Ch'in set himself up as Shih-huang-ti, the First Emperor of a new kind of China. It is the Inner Asian Frontier aspect of this new China that must next be considered.

[68] Franke, pp. 198-199.
[69] Ibid.

CHAPTER XIII

THE BEGINNINGS OF A "FRONTIER STYLE" IN CHINESE HISTORY

China was not "created" by the penetration of invading conquerors into the plains of its great rivers, nor yet by the "pressure" of barbarians on an autochthonous Chinese people of higher culture. The origins of both Chinese and barbarians go back to a remote age in which all culture was about equally primitive, though it must be supposed that regions varied somewhat in cultural aspect according to the differences in their natural resources. Nor can it be established that the terms "Chinese" and "barbarian" connote separate racial origins. Physical characteristics that are now considered typically Chinese can be traced a long way back,[1] but it is also probable that ethnic groups distinguishable from each other in stature and other respects moved about in China long before there was a Chinese culture.

What made for a differentiation of cultures in the first place, and thus for an increasingly sharp cleavage between the "progressive" and the "backward" and eventually between the Chinese and the barbarian, was no single attribute of race, or society, or geographical environment. It was rather the range of variety between groups of characteristics: what aspects of the environment made it easy or difficult for primitive people to live; whether in order to make use of the environment it was better to live in large or small groups, widely scattered or within close reach of each other; whether normal use of the environment at the most primitive level encouraged a stable society resistant

[1] Compare the discussion in Creel, Studies in Early Chinese Culture, 1937, pp. 153, etc.

to change, or a society prone to experiment and leading to change and evolution.

Once change had begun it was bound to proceed at different rates of development in different regions, being influenced by the total sum of environmental and social factors. Since, moreover, differences in the rate of change and development were bound to accentuate the measurable differences between any given groups at any given time, all kinds of differences must have had the general tendency to stimulate each other. Thus it can be said that although the creation of China cannot be attributed to any one invasion of people or migration of culture, the development of China, once the process of differentiation and change had begun, must have been stimulated and complicated by any and every movement of people and transmission of technique and culture that came within range of what was going on in China.

In the same way it cannot be said that the progress of agricultural China through its ancient feudalism toward a centralized imperialism was primarily the result of conquest or pressure by people of the steppe; but it can certainly be said that from the moment that a Chinese agricultural way of life and a steppe pastoral way of life became distinguishable from each other the things that happened within each kind of society affected the evolution of the other kind of society. On the whole, as I have argued above, it does not seem likely that the feudal age in China was the result of the conquest of an agricultural people by mounted nomad warriors of the steppe. It is more probable that China contributed to the creation of the steppe society by extruding fragments of "backward" groups, originally akin to the ancestors of the Chinese themselves, from the kind of environment that favored the increasingly intensive and specialized agriculture on which the evolving society of China was based.[2]

[2] See also Chapter XI, above.

Nevertheless, once these groups had ceased to be merely backward and marginal and began to evolve instead into an independent and alternative steppe society there arose a new question. Which was to be politically ascendant, the steppe and its mobile society or China and its landfast society? This question affected only the Inner Asian Frontier of China. To the south, beyond the Yangtze, there also lay vast "barbarian" lands which the Chinese were able to penetrate and make Chinese only in the course of many centuries—in fact, the process has never been completed. Beyond the Yangtze, however, there lay no steppe and consequently the southern barbarians never advanced out of the category of being merely backward and not-yet-Chinese. It was the north that became historically important. Here, along the line of transition from China, the land of rivers and canals, to the Inner Asian world of inland drainage, desert, oasis, and steppe, herding people and farming people had access to each other. Their effect on each other became so important that in later centuries it is impossible to judge the stability and soundness of a dynasty in China without reference to its control of the Great Wall Frontier. In fact, a distinct "Frontier style" in Chinese history became recognizable: either a dynasty was founded beyond the Frontier or on the Frontier, and moved inward to establish its control over China, or it was founded within China and moved outward to establish control over the Frontier and sometimes beyond the Frontier.

ASSOCIATION OF THE FRONTIER STYLE WITH THE MARGINAL TERRITORIES

In a way, the rise of the Chou Chinese on the rim of Shang China, and indeed the rise of Shang China at the edge of the loess highlands and the Great Plain, can be called foreshadowings of this "Frontier style." In these earlier ages, however, the main process was the stemming off of more progressive, rapidly evolving groups, and the interaction between these advanced groups and the more backward groups. The true Frontier style becomes recognizable only toward the end of the Chou age, when specialization and improvement of the Chinese agriculture, combined with the spread of that agriculture into regions where the older mixed economy still survived, converted some of the remnants of the old mixed society into genuine steppe nomads. The appearance of these nomads at the edge of China, the increasing specialization of their pastoral economy, and the impossibility of merging them permanently with the agriculturally based Chinese were phenomena contemporary with the political rise of the state of Ch'in. It was the simultaneous growth in power of the steppe nomads and the Ch'in Chinese that brought into operation the true Frontier style.

When, in the fourth and third centuries B.C., the state of Chao expanded northward through what is now Shansi up to the edge of the Inner Mongolian steppe, the Chao Chinese began to adopt the style of warfare of the mounted nomads.[3] This they could do successfully only by adopting also the economy of the nomads and other aspects of the nomad way of life, at least in part. In so doing they opened a new historical phase.

Up to this time the Chinese had been continuously evolving a more and more specialized society geared to a group of technical practices in agriculture and water conservancy. Sociologically, therefore, the term "barbarian" really meant people who had not yet begun to evolve in this Chinese way or were evolving more slowly than the main body of the Chinese. There was little difference in this between the barbarians of the north and those of the south, until some of the barbarians of the north began to develop a distinctive society and economy of pastoral nomadism. What they thus created was an alternative to the Chinese

[3] See also Chapter XII, above.

way of evolution. In the terminology of the Chinese, a barbarian of the steppe was just as barbarous as an "un-evolved" barbarian within China; but from the point of view of the steppe people themselves what had been accomplished was a great advance in evolution from the older mixed-economy barbarism—an evolution that depended just as much on a body of special technical practices as did the agriculture of the Chinese.

Consequently, what happened in the northern part of Shansi, causing the breakup of the state of Chin into the three states of Chao, Wei and Han, can be described in two ways. From the Chinese point of view, the Chinese of Chao halted their evolutionary advance and began to devolve back toward barbarism; and to the Chinese it did not seem significant that this was not in reality a return toward the old barbarism, with its unspecialized, mixed economy, but rather a shift over to a new kind of barbarism with a specialized economy. From the point of view of steppe history, on the other hand, the partial transformation of the state of Chao was highly significant. It meant that the steppe kind of specialization could, in its own terrain, withstand the Chinese kind of specialization, and that the steppe way of life could even, within a certain range of marginal terrain, prevail over that of the Chinese.

The Frontier style in history, in other words, is closely associated with territories marginal both to the steppe and to agricultural China. The Chinese had been spreading out for centuries because the steady improvement of their methods of controlling water and crops enabled each generation to take over lands that the previous generation had not yet been able to penetrate. "Marginal" territory, during this whole period, meant only territory still held by barbarians who had not begun to be transformed into Chinese. In the same way, the "history" of the barbarians can best be studied by attempting to discern which barbarian groups were able to maintain their old, pre-Chinese way of life, even though they had to retreat before the Chinese, and which gave up the struggle and began to be converted into Chinese.

When some of the remnants of these old barbarians were forced up to the edge of the steppe, where they could not preserve their old mixed economy and way of life, they could only keep up their resistance and refusal to become Chinese by becoming a new kind of barbarian. From the margin of the steppe they broke away into the open steppe and became true pastoral nomads. One result of this was a regrouping of historically significant kinds of geographical environment. Formerly there had been only one series: optimum terrain for the early development of Chinese agriculture, secondary terrain which could be made approximately as profitable as the optimum terrain when irrigation and other technical practices had been suitably developed, and "marginal" terrain into which the Chinese agriculture had not yet penetrated. Another series now became established: strict steppe which permitted only pastoral nomadism, steppe-like terrain in which pastoral nomadism was more profitable than "extensive" agriculture or mixed agriculture and herding, and marginal terrain in which it had to be proved whether agriculture or herding would prevail. Where the two series overlapped, accordingly, two kinds of marginal terrain were henceforth to be in dispute: one in which the balance of the factors favored the Chinese but in which, nevertheless, the Chinese tended in some ways to "devolve" toward a more extensive economy; and one in which the balance favored the nomads but in which the nomads nevertheless tended in some ways to be influenced by the Chinese and to evolve toward a more intensive economy.

Ch'in, Chao, and Yen

By taking into account this factor of terrain it is possible to distinguish differences between states like Ch'in,

Chao, and Yen, which held the line along which the Great Wall of China was eventually built.

Chao, before it became independent, was the northern territory of the state of Chin in Shansi. The core around which Chin had grown was the valley of the Fen River, one of the oldest centers of irrigated agriculture in China. Toward the northern part of Shansi there is a watershed. Here all the land is high, the highest part being the knot of mountains known as Wut'aishan, which reach about 10,000 feet. South of this watershed the headwaters of the Fen converge on the main Fen valley and wide areas can be irrigated. North of the watershed the main valley is that of the Sangkan River, which flows first to the north-east and then bends to the southeast and joins the Pei Ho system of the Peiping-Tientsin plain. In this and the other northern valleys, however, neither irrigation nor rainfall has ever supported an agriculture as rich as that of south Shansi.

This northern territory, once held by the state of Chao, is also known as the land of Tai. For century after century its uplands were fought for by herdsmen from Inner Asia and cultivators from China, though it was not the optimum environment for either way of life. For nomad herdsmen it was not open enough; whenever they entered it some groups would tend to break away from the main body and settle as cultivators at the most favored points. As these points were often strategically important, the herding society lost both social cohesion and military security. For Chinese cultivators, on the other hand, most of the land was a little too high and a little too poor. Agriculture could not here support so solid a state structure as it could farther to the south, and the even homogeneity of farming tended to be broken up by much more grazing—of sheep and goats especially—than is normal in the Chinese economy. Sheep and goats, it may be pointed out, though not popularly associated with the galloping mobility of the steppe nomad, are more fundamental to the steppe economy than are horses.

So doubtful was it whether the land of Tai belonged properly to China or to Inner Asia that across north Shansi the main line of Great Wall fortifications ran in two variants, occupied at different times according to the tide of history. One masked the plateau escarpment of Inner Mongolia, the other covered the watershed between north Shansi and south Shansi. Most of what had once been the strategic center of the state of Chao was thus in later centuries completely walled around.

This land of Tai was repeatedly entered and held, but never permanently, by Turkish and Mongol peoples. Here was bred the Li family[4] which founded the great T'ang dynasty of A.D. 618-907. Although they considered themselves Chinese they had Turkish blood. Their dynasty was founded on the use of Turkish and half-Turkish cavalry and upheld thereafter by a system of tribal alliances that spread all over Mongolia, Chinese Turkistan, and Manchuria, and into Tibet. It was the T'ang dynasty which, making use of canals already dug under the Sui dynasty which preceded it, set up in full working order the Grand Canal system of drawing surplus grain from the Yangtze to feed and garrison the strongholds of empire in the North.[5] It was the T'ang dynasty which finally established the examination system of the civil bureaucracy. In many ways it was the most Chinese dynasty China ever had, but it was founded and maintained by using the wealth of China to subsidize "barbarian" troops. A relic of this interpenetration of China and the Inner Asian Frontier is the cult of the five holy peaks of Wut'aishan, to which pilgrims continue to come from hundreds of miles away

---

[4] See Giles, Chinese Biographical Dictionary, Nos. 1239 and 1196, for short notices of Li Yüan, founder of the T'ang dynasty, and his son Li Shih-min. For the Turkish connection, see Parker, A Thousand Years of the Tartars, 1895, p. 194.

[5] Ch'ao-ting Chi, Key Economic Areas in Chinese History, 1936, pp. 112-121.

in Mongolia and Tibet, as their ancestors did, and where the lama dignitary who in recent years has managed the affairs of one of the most important monasteries is a "Kalmuk," a Torgot of the Volga in South Russia.

With all this in mind it seems reasonable to reconstruct the history of Chao as follows: The great age of the state of Chin was from the middle of the sixth to the middle of the fifth century B.C. Before this, in the eighth and seventh centuries, the Chin Chinese of the Fen valley had rather gradually won an ascendancy over the Ti and Mountain Jung tribes in the mountains east, north, and west of the Fen. By 541 the last of the Ti in the southern part of Shansi were "exterminated." [6] From then until B.C. 457 Chin was the greatest single state in China, but in that year the Chin noble who founded the state of Chao a few years later began the conquest of the northern part of Shansi.

This can only mean that the state of Chin was built up by a steady expansion of Chinese control on both sides of the Fen River. Much of the hill country thus taken over from the barbarians was not ideal for the Chinese type of agriculture, with its growing emphasis on irrigation; but unless they controlled the sides of the valley the Chinese could not exploit the main valley in peace. This, therefore, was all marginal territory the acquisition of which benefited the Chinese. It improved their military position, the rich Fen valley provided an economic focus for it, and, although within the enlarged state of Chin not all agriculture could be brought to the same high level of development, the intensive irrigated agriculture of the main Fen valley was able to set the standard for the whole state.

When military expansion passed beyond the northern watershed a new set of conditions was created. Here the land was higher, more broken, and not nearly so favorable to irrigation. It is probable that this was one of the territories in which the "old style" barbarians, pushed away

[6] See Chapter XI, above.

from the good river lands by the Chinese, began to convert themselves into "new style" barbarians—the true nomads of succeeding centuries. Moreover, the Chinese who pursued them into this terrain were affected by the same conditions: while the "old style" barbarians began to *evolve* toward steppe nomadism the Chinese who dealt with them began to *devolve* from the highest level attained by the Chinese way of life toward what was for them a lower level, because it was a return toward a mixed economy. In another sense this was not strictly devolution but rather a shift over to a different field of history altogether, within which "evolution" meant a further approach to the extreme of extensive, pastoral nomadic economy instead of toward the extreme of intensive, irrigated agriculture, whereas "devolution" still connoted a reversion toward the ancient, mixed, undifferentiated economy which lay in the background of both specialized pastoral nomadism and specialized irrigated agriculture.

Politically, at the same time, the process of accretion, by which the Chinese had been attaching to themselves new territory and those of its inhabitants whom they could subordinate or "convert," gave way to a pull which tended to detach the border Chinese from their river-valley center of gravity. The newly invaded territory north of the headwaters of the Fen was not drawn inward to the state of Chin but broke away from it, forming the new state of Chao. Nor did it break simply at the edge of what had until then belonged to Chin. On the contrary, Chao dragged away with it part of what had been the best and most profitable part of Chin. The border became dominant over the center. What was left of Chin then broke into two other new states, Wei and Han, which had a far less than proportionate share of the old power of Chin.

The Chin-Chao type of transition can accordingly be best described by saying that up to a certain point the Chinese of the Fen valley profited by increasing returns as they spread out from their agricultural base, but the accretion of political power in territory controlled was greater than the economic increment because the marginal terrain was not so well adapted to intensive agriculture as the nuclear terrain, which governed the norm of the society as a whole. Further expansion therefore brought diminishing returns. The political power of the margin became too unwieldy for the economic strength of the nucleus, and a new grouping of dominant territory and subordinate territory was the inevitable consequence.

Now China as a whole, during this period, was gravitating toward the center; the main historical trend favored the evolution of increasingly larger and more centralized states, grouped around the areas that provided the richest revenues from intensive irrigated agriculture. The Chin-Chao change of structure was an aberration from this tendency because it represented the ascendancy of border-ers, who were in the process of becoming less-Chinese, over a nuclear territory in which the natural tendency was to become more-Chinese. An internal conflict resulted, first in Chin and then in Chao, its main successor state, between the evolutionary trend of its agricultural economy and the devolutionary trend on which its border military power was based. This weakened the structure of the state in such a way that, although the armies of Chao won victories under leaders like Wu Ling and Li Mu,[7] the state in the end was overwhelmed by the imperial conquests of Ch'in.

Something of the same kind probably happened in Yen, though rather less is known of the border wars of Yen, which was not so closely involved in the development of the Yellow River basin as Chin and its three successor states of Chao, Wei, and Han. Geographically, the core of Yen was the Peiping-Tientsin plain. The narrow Shanhaikuan corridor, pinched between the mountains and the

---

[7] See Chapter XII, above; also Lattimore, Origins of the Great Wall, 1937.

sea, links this plain with the similar terrain of the lower Liao basin in South Manchuria. For this reason agriculturally-based states in North China and South Manchuria have always tended to affect each other closely and to merge politically whenever possible. For the same reason the highlands of Jehol, though never an ideal terrain for either agriculture or pastoral nomadism, have always been the political and military key to the control of this part of the world, because they overlook both the Peiping-Tientsin plain and the lower Liao together with the Shanhaikuan corridor which connects them.

What we now call the province of Jehol contains two major geographical provinces[8]—the mountains of the south and the steppe of the north. As a marginal terrain the hills of the south may be compared to the land of Tai in North Shansi. They favor agriculture a little more than they do pastoral nomadism, but they cover so large an area that the Chinese and Chinese agriculture, even when dominant, tend to devolve from the Chinese norm in answer to steppe influences penetrating from the north. Because the tendency to gravitate toward China is thus modified by a tendency to pull away from China, political ascendancy throughout history has been ultimately decided by a third factor—the range of action[9] and of control at a distance developed at any given period by the major societies of China and of the steppe. It may also be remarked, in passing, that as the hills of Jehol were at one time well forested, especially in the west, groups of forest hunters probably contributed to the original evolution of steppe nomadism in the eastern steppe of Inner Mongolia.[10]

[8] Fumio Tada (in Section III of the Report of the First Scientific Expedition to Manchukuo, 1937; in Japanese, abstract in German) distinguishes a third region, marginal to Manchuria.

[9] See Chapter XV, below.

[10] Compare the references, beginning with Ssu-Ma Ch'ien in the Han dynasty (Shih Chi, Ch. 110), to "Forest Hu" in this general region. Moreover, in this region, as again far away in the Tannu-Tuva region, the long-surviving tribal name Urianghai (Oriyangghan, Oriyangkit) indicates forest origin.

It is accordingly a reasonable conclusion that the history of Yen as a Chinese feudal kingdom was in a general way like the histories of Chin and Chao. Probably the range of action of Yen, at the feudal level of organization, was not great enough to enable it to hold the mountains of Jehol firmly enough, with the result that its border warriors tended to pull Yen out of what was then the chief orbit of history in China. Therefore, when Ch'in overwhelmed both the China of the Yellow River and the China of the Yangtze, Yen fell as the succession states of Chin had fallen.

The Rise of Ch'in

Appreciation of what happened in Chao and Yen opens the way to an understanding of the rise of Ch'in. Geographically, there was a difference between the Ch'in sector of the Inner Asian Frontier and the Chao and Yen sectors. The core of Ch'in was the Wei valley in Shensi, just as the core of Chin and later of Chao was the Fen valley. North of the Wei, and roughly parallel to it, are two more rivers—the Ching and the Lo. The Ching flows into the lower Wei, and the Wei and the Lo both discharge into the Yellow River at the great bend.

Because of this topography it was possible for Ch'in to expand without weakening its agricultural evolution and simultaneously to improve the political methods of linking agricultural territories together on the largest scale possible under feudalism. When the lower courses of the Wei, the Ching, and the Lo had been occupied, Ch'in controlled in Shensi an impressively large area which was homogenous with the agricultural China of the lower Yellow River but politically eccentric to it.

Moreover, while the Wei, the Ching, and the Lo all flow toward the north-south course of the Yellow River, the headwaters of all three reach back toward the upper Yellow River west of the Ordos Loop. Here the Yellow River flows between agricultural China on the south and the steppes of Inner Mongolia on the north, but the division between the two types of terrain is not abrupt. Between the cities of Lanchou and Ninghsia a number of streams enter the Yellow River from the south. The headwaters of these rivers reach back into the loess highlands of Liup'anshan, and it is from the same highlands that the Wei and the Ching flow to the southeast. Several of the streams that flow north actually overlap with streams that flow southeast in an interdigitated pattern. Both along the Yellow River from Lanchou to Ninghsia and along the streams that enter it from the south are scattered patches of territory suitable for irrigation. They cannot exactly be called oases because they are not surrounded by true steppe or desert and are not isolated enough, but they are so oasis-like that they can best be described as "semi-oases." [11]

Consequently, the Chinese of Ch'in, as they pushed up the headwater streams of the Wei, the Ching, and the Lo, subduing barbarians, converting some of them into Chinese and driving others on toward the steppe to become pastoral nomads, did not enter a terrain like the land of Tai or the mountains of Jehol, which threatened to pull them away from their base of expansion. Even as they approached the steppe they were able to occupy "semi-oases" in east Kansu and the Ninghsia region. Here the richness of irrigated agriculture, in patches not large enough to form separate states but large enough to affect the general balance of economy in a marginal region, emphasized and continued the process of accretion toward the center instead of setting up a counter process of drag away from the center

One result of this territorial accretion was a very rapid enlistment of new barbarian subjects. The traditional Chinese view is that the tribal, barbarian element in Ch'in was

[11] See also Chapter VI, above, and Chapter XV, below.

great enough to swamp the Chinese element. I do not think this is true. It seems more probable that two kinds of change were going on at the same time. In the first place Ch'in was ahead of the rest of China in developing the specifically Chinese enterprises of irrigation and intensive agriculture on a larger and larger scale. This in itself is an argument against the idea that the rise of Ch'in was the result of "waves" of non-Chinese barbarians pressing in from the northwest. In the second place, the increasing numbers of barbarians that Ch'in was drawing in from its expanding northwestern territories were entering a part of China in which evolutionary change was going on very rapidly. They therefore did not need to "settle down" to a period of being absorbed by the generation that represented the older, feudal China but could press ahead to take part in the creation of a newer, imperial China. Their very rawness contributed to the speed and decisiveness of innovation and helped to prevent vested interests from forming and settling into a too firm stratification.

In short, the truth appears to be that the "barbarism" of Ch'in, which the orthodox Chinese tradition so strongly emphasizes, was not the result of the barbarization of the Ch'in Chinese but the result of the rapid enlistment of tribal peoples who were in process of being converted into Chinese of a new sort at the same time that they were being used to destroy the old Chinese feudal order.[12] We know that the Ch'in cavalry had a good deal of the barbarian about them; this was one of the "un-Chinese" things that account for the Chinese dislike of Ch'in (a permanent

---

[12] Perhaps the introduction of the ox-drawn plough had a special importance in the territory of Ch'in. It may have made profitable the cultivation of a certain amount of land between the semi-oases that could not be agriculturally exploited before. This would have the result of spreading the population a little more evenly, in addition to increasing the crop area. The ox-drawn plough came into use very late in China. V. K. Ting (How China Acquired Her Civilisation, 1931), citing Hsü Chung-shu's article in Chinese "On the Lei and Ssu," dates it to the third century B.C. Bishop, (Origin and Early Diffusion of the Traction-Plow, 1936) gives "latter half of the fourth century."

historical tradition) as the destroyer of everything that was feudal, conservative, and "cultured." Yet there was a difference, apparently slight but of the most significant importance, between this cavalry, trained in Frontier warfare, whose rapid maneuver and striking power won an empire for Ch'in, and the similar Frontier cavalry of Chao.

The Ch'in cavalry served as an instrument for carrying to completion the processes of centralization and of advance from feudalism to unified empire—processes inherent in the course of development that China was already following. They could serve this use because they were a by-product of the adherence to the Chinese way of life of wide marginal territories. The Chao cavalry, on the contrary, originated in the partial adherence of border Chinese to the nomad way of life. The society of which these troops were the striking arm was unable to promote the evolution inherent in the Chinese forms of society and the state because it was based on a Frontier trend away from the norm of China. The function of the Frontier must therefore have been quite different in Ch'in and in Chao during the wars in which feudalism was destroyed and a new kind of empire created. In Chao the Frontier dragged away from China; the Chao borderers were centrifugal. In Ch'in the Frontier was part of a coördinated centripetal process; it contributed to the pressure of Ch'in on the rest of China.

The Frontier Territories Acquire a Political Importance of Their Own

The "Frontier style" in Chinese history, then, connotes two things: a change in the character of Chinese expansion and the working of a new political factor which could promote either centralization or decentralization. Until this time the Chinese had been expanding by the occupation of territorial units that could be organized on a feudal scale. The "cellular" unit of this kind of structure was the walled city with its tributary rural area. The largest feudal unit was a major valley or plain, watered by a river, and tending to be politically most stable when marked off from other similar regions by such natural frontiers as watersheds. From this time on the same kind of expansion could continue indefinitely toward the south, and the cellular city-rural unit persisted; but on the north the Chinese had encountered the edge of a different kind of terrain which resisted piecemeal conversion to the Chinese methods of land usage, demanding instead modifications of the Chinese way of life.

Between the full steppe, in which the Chinese agriculture could not prevail, and the well-watered landscape of China, in which pastoral nomadism was obviously inferior to agriculture, there lay a belt of marginal lands. Increasing Chinese occupation of these lands promoted the specialized pastoral nomadic society in the true steppe beyond; but in proportion as the nomads prospered in the terrain best suited to them they became able to dispute with the Chinese the control of the marginal territories between the steppe and China. It then became evident that some kinds of marginal terrain favored the Chinese, on the whole, more than the nomads, while other kinds favored the nomads more than the Chinese.

Politically, these disputed border territories began to acquire an importance of their own because they could influence the trend of history both in the major agricultural world and the major steppe world. For the very reason that they were not fully homogeneous with either China or the steppe they did not have to the full either the particularism of China (the walled city and its adjacent rural community) or the particularism of the steppe (the blood-related clan or group of families claiming rights of pasture in a limited region). When, therefore, they tended to adhere to China it was likely to be because the movement of history was against particularism and in favor of political unification. When, in the same way, they tended to adhere to the steppe it was likely to be because a movement of tribal unification was overriding the local freedom of migration of clan groups.

It is accordingly an axiom of the Frontier style that it can be described both positively and negatively in any selected historical period. When the Frontier or any part of the Frontier was dragging away from China it tended to draw China apart and to prevent unity, but it was likely to gravitate at the same time toward any movement of unification in the steppe. On the other hand, when the Frontier was gravitating toward China it was likely both to contribute to the unity of China and to draw steppe tribes, or parts of tribes, out of the orbit of the steppe and attach them to China.

A peculiarity of the Ch'in conquest was the fact that it raised problems which might have been solved singly but could not be solved simultaneously. A corollary of the idea of imperial unification was the idea of stabilization and permanence, but the forces that made unification possible were moving forces not under the control of any tradition of halting and stabilizing. A corollary, again, of the idea of an empire that included everything that was properly Chinese was the idea of an outer steppe world with which China need have nothing to do; but there was nothing to prevent the steppe world from attempting to break in on the world of China.

On such problems as these the Ch'in Empire foundered under the son of the man who had created it. Among the legacies it left behind were these: the concept of unified empire, not as something to be attained but as something to be recovered and restored; the idea of a unified Frontier as a corollary of unified empire; the practical problem of dealing with this Frontier not as a hard and fast line but as a zone of territory that was always an essential part of China yet never quite homogeneous with China; the Frontier style itself, which in the nature of things meant a not-entirely-Chinese method of dealing with problems essential to China. The attempt to deal with this legacy accounts to a large extent for the character of Chinese history under the Han dynasty, from B.C. 206 to A.D. 220.

THE IMPERIAL AGE

CHAPTER XIV

UNIFIED EMPIRE AND UNIFIED FRONTIER— THE GREAT WALL OF CHINA

PRE-IMPERIAL WALL BUILDING

Even though Ch'in drew strength from the Frontier to turn inward and overwhelm the kingdoms of China it also built an early "Great Wall" along the section of the Inner Asian Frontier that it held.[1] In this it was like the kingdoms of Chao and Yen, though in other aspects its Frontier expansion was different. It is important therefore to determine, if possible, whether there was any difference in function between the sector of the fortified Frontier held by Ch'in and the sectors held by Chao and Yen.

In the first place, as I have already pointed out, wall building was not a regional phenomenon but the characteristic of an age.[2] Probably both within China and on the Inner Asian Frontier the sudden and widely spread activity in building walls, in the last decade or two of the fourth century B.C. and the first decade of the third century B.C., was primarily a symptom that the limit of growth under feudalism had been reached. The rulers of each major region, when they had brought under control the maximum area of political agglomeration that could be conveniently ruled under feudal forms, felt the need to establish their boundaries "forever." Wall building was the natural method to adopt because Chinese feudalism was already based on an exclusively agricultural economy

---

[1] Ch'in, during this period of rapid growth, was not only attacking the states to the east of it, but through the penetration of what is now the province of Ssuch'uan was gaining control of the upper Yangtze; its walled Frontier was thus both a rear defense and a flank defense.

[2] See Chapter XIII, above.

and on "cellular" areas dominated by walled cities, with the result that slow campaigns and sieges were the norm of warfare.

The building of walls hundreds of miles long meant the assembling of laborers on a far greater scale than was necessary for the castle building of feudal Europe; it recalls the frontier walls or *limites* of the Roman Empire. This indicates that the mature feudalism of China had already developed to a high point the use of forced labor —an institution characteristic of the succeeding period of unified empire and an institution that, probably, had much to do with the transition from feudalism to empire because it could be handled better under a centralized administration than under decentralized feudal methods. Although already used on a large scale, forced labor could not yet be put to use on an unlimited scale, and consequently each wall-building state did not ring itself with a wall but fortified only that part of its frontier that was most threatened by invasion.

On the Inner Asian Frontier the general idea of what may be called "maximum convenient political agglomeration" was modified by local peculiarities of terrain and society. The building of a wall assumes that a society or state can cleanly mark off the territory that it occupies by a hard and fast line : but an essential characteristic of the Inner Asian Frontier is that it is not linear. North China merges into Inner Asia through a series of zones, the edges of which are not sharply defined. The fluctuations of history attest how difficult it has always been to decide where a marginal zone that favors the Chinese and their agriculture against the nomads and their herds begins to give way to a zone that favors the herdsman against the farmer, and the tent against the town.

Here once more it is the history of Chao—and of Yen also, though less clearly—that makes it possible to understand the history of Ch'in. When Chao began "to wear

the costumes of the barbarians" and to use their style of
fighting it was because the Chinese of north Shansi had
crossed a watershed. Behind them lay one of the most
prosperous and typical strongholds of Chinese agriculture,
a region where irrigation had begun early and flourished
strongly. After several centuries of war all barbarians had
either been cleared from the valley of the Fen or converted
into Chinese. In this process the Chinese themselves had
not become barbarized at all, because within this terrain the
overmastering trend of history had not only been toward
making the barbarians Chinese but toward making the Chinese more-Chinese. Before these very Chinese who had
been becoming more-Chinese there now lay a terrain which
did not wholly favor them but which in some ways favored
the barbarians whom until now they had always defeated
or absorbed.

In this terrain the Chinese could only advance if they
consented to become in some respects less-Chinese. Yet
even though they did in some ways become barbarized or
tribalized, in other and more important ways they remained
Chinese. Above all they continued to be Chinese, and
feudal Chinese at that, in their ideas of wealth, of power,
of the rewards of rule. It was the military aspect of their
partial barbarization that was most important—and for
this reason they continued to be feudal in outlook instead
of moving toward the evolution of some new order out of
their mixture of barbarian and Chinese characteristics.
The reward of their development as warlike borderers was
the ability to turn back and exact tribute—and tribute of
the Chinese kind, which was what they thought of as worth
having—from the land they had left behind.

In the structure of the state of Chao power derived from
control of the border levies, and therefore each noble of
the border with the levies that belonged to him was prepared to fight against the passing of feudalism. Given
this feudal cast of society, it was natural for the borderers

who ruled in Chao to build a northern wall that served a feudal use. Though they had been drawn somewhat away from China by the Frontier changes in their society, they did not want to continue to change or to be drawn farther away. It profited them to limit the marginal zone in which they lived, artificially if necessary, so that they could continue to draw tribute and revenue from those on the south, who were more Chinese than they, while preventing those on the north, who were more barbarian than they, from getting access to the same revenue-bearing lands.

THE FRONTIER CHARACTERISTICS OF CH'IN

In the border expansion of Ch'in the spread did not go so far beyond the headwaters of the streams that determined the character of the inner territory. Nor was the fringing territory into which the people of Ch'in penetrated "marginal" in the same way as the land of Tai. Instead of passing over gradually to an outer margin that favored nomadism more than agriculture, it offered the Chinese a relatively firm abutment in the semi-oases of the upper Yellow River. Intensive agriculture could flourish in these little areas. The scale of enterprise possible was not large enough to support an independent agricultural state but large enough to support the outposts of an agricultural state that was growing in strength. The possession of these oasis-like outposts gave the Frontier held by Ch'in a firm character; it gave an emphasis that approximated to the idea of a linear limit. Beyond lay the steppe; but instead of approaching the steppe through a vague intermediate land, which worked on them in such a way as to diminish their Chineseness, the borderers of Ch'in were able to station themselves along a line of positions which helped to accentuate the difference between their society and the society of the steppe. Probably the most uncertain part of the Ch'in Frontier was the reëntrant of the Ordos plateau, but even here the borderers of Ch'in had an edge to deal with rather than a margin. Beyond the watershed of the streams flowing down into Shensi lay, not a landscape of mixed character as in the north of Shansi, but an arid steppe: it did not tempt the borderers to advance farther but warned them to halt.

Outer edge and inner terrain thus worked together. Where the expansion of Ch'in halted the prospect beyond was foreign. The Chinese who here confronted barbarians were, by comparison with the borderers of Chao and Yen, full and unmodified Chinese. They were probably in some cultural ways cruder than the Chinese of the middle and lower Yellow River, but the trend of their evolution was firmly set toward becoming more Chinese. Their Frontier situation was of a kind to make them hold back against being drawn into the steppe, and at the same time the changes that were going on in the inner land of rivers and agriculture were of a kind to make soldiers and men of political career adhere to the main body of the state instead of attempting to dismember it and attach pieces of it to their own Frontier strongholds. By the binding together of the different river provinces of Ch'in under a strong royal state, feudalism here on the rim of China was being destroyed more rapidly than in the center of China. Border troops and even border barbarians could be enlisted and drafted toward the center of the land where, being in royal service, they helped to break down what was left of the feudal military system.

Because of all these converging changes the rate of Ch'in's advance beyond feudalism accelerated. It was more profitable for the whole state, growing more united, to press inward against the other states of China, which were attempting to fix and stabilize the late and cumbrous forms of feudalism, than it was for border captains to try to wrench away pieces of the state and set up for themselves Frontier kingdoms partly Chinese and partly barbarian in character. Consequently, the heavy enlistment of barbarians and semi-barbarians did not make less Chinese in character the changes that Ch'in effected. Indeed, it is very probable that such people were even more useful in breaking down the feudalism that stood in the way of Ch'in than were Chinese whose outlook was hampered by inherited ideas, and they could take over and work out as rapidly as true Chinese the new ideas that were necessary. For all these reasons Ch'in, up to the moment that the last feudal kingdom had fallen (in B.C. 221) and the unified empire had been proclaimed, did not have to "hold" the Inner Asian Frontier against Inner Asia but only as an accessory to power within China.

Social Importance of the Labor Employed in the Building of the Early Walls

Just as the gradual working out of a line of cleavage between the people of China and the people of the steppe was due primarily to the line of evolution followed within China, so the concept of a man-made Great Wall, so enormous in execution as to rival a work of nature, was more a product of the kind of state created within China than of the kind of pressure against China from the steppe. Naturally enough, it is the military aspect of the Great Wall that has commanded most attention, and this has distorted its true historical significance. Since it was a particular kind of society that attempted thus to insulate itself from a kind of contact that it wanted to exclude, it is pertinent to examine both the economy that supported this immense effort and the methods of organizing the labor that went into it.

When the states of Chao and Yen built Frontier fortifications, at the end of the fourth and the beginning of the third century B.C., how was the work done? In Chao certainly and in Yen probably, as the analogy suggests, the state was controlled by warriors who, themselves partly barbarized, fought against the barbarians to the north of them and drew tribute from the unbarbarized Chinese in the part of the state to the south of them. The military account of the way in which the northern armies of Chao were organized indicates clearly that the society of the region was rather thinly dispersed. Settlement was not close and agricultural; the economy by which the people lived included herding, and the country was open and empty enough to encourage the maneuvering warfare of mounted nomads as against the positional warfare and siege operations of Chinese feudalism. If this be true, the population must have been very small to have furnished the labor required to build fortifications that ran for several hundred miles. This points to the probability that conscript labor was part of the tribute that the northern and less-Chinese parts of these two states drew from the southern and more-Chinese parts.[3]

The Frontier wall of Ch'in, on the other hand, was built at a time when the whole feudal system of the state was being broken up. Taxation was being revised in a way that helped to convert the feudal serf, whose assessment of so many days of labor on the land of his lord represented both rent and taxes, into a peasant who owed rent to his landlord and taxes to the state.[4] Under feudalism there was conflict between the noble and the state, because if the state conscripted the serf he could not at the same time work out his labor-due to his lord. Under the new system the state increased its power at the expense of both lord and peasant. The noble could no longer claim personal service, which gave him the option of using the serf as a soldier, but rent only. The peasant, if his labor were conscripted by the state, was not thereby freed from the obligation of paying rent: his family had to redistribute their work in order to pay it for him. Undoubtedly this

[3] Compare the biography of Li Mu in the Shih Chi, Ch. 81.
[4] For the ruthless and even Fascist ideas that were guiding the centralization of power in Ch'in, see Duyvendak, The Book of Lord Shang, 1928.

change placed a greatly increased reserve of labor at the service of the state to be used in public works.[5] In the case of Ch'in, therefore, the probability is that wall building did not represent a tribute of a feudal kind paid by the inner territory to the lords of the Frontier, but was part of a general reorganization which gave the state authorities increased control both at the periphery and at the center of the state.

In the case of the walls built by states like Wei and Ch'i [6] the conditions were again different. Here it was not a question of setting Chinese agriculture apart from steppe nomadism but of attempting to define the maximum territories that could be ruled under feudal combinations. The conflict between state authority and feudal authority must accordingly have been important in the building of these walls, for in such a situation even the effort to stabilize feudalism must have made it necessary to weaken the feudal nobles and increase the power of the state—at least to the extent of giving the state prior claim in requisitioning labor on a great scale.

Finally, there is the Ch'u wall,[7] in the gap between the Yellow River plain and the Yangtze valley, somewhere near the headwaters of the Huai. Here again it may be supposed that wall building was in some ways like the other wall building of the time and in some ways different. The nuclear territory of the state of Ch'u was the region about the modern cities of Hankow, Wuch'ang, and Hanyang, where the Han River enters the Yangtze from the north. By a down-river expansion along the Yangtze Ch'u had created an empire of its own that might have become the first united empire of all China had it not been possible for Ch'in to strike effectively at Ch'u during the final cycle of wars in the third century B.C., while Ch'u

[5] Wittfogel, Foundations and Stages of Chinese Economic History, 1935, pp. 42-44.
[6] See Chapter XII, above.
[7] Or series of strongholds; see the references in Chapter XII.

could not campaign so effectively against Ch'in because the military side of its empire had largely been developed by the use of war boats along the Yangtze and in the Yangtze delta. Nevertheless, what Ch'u ruled was really an empire; in particular, its coastal subject peoples were less akin to the main body of the Chinese than the people of any of the other nations of the time.

Because the military organization of the Ch'u Empire could not easily be changed from the use of river flotillas to the training of great land armies, its "imperial" policy in the north had come to work more and more through the use of auxiliaries and allies. The final test of strength between Ch'in and Ch'u came in the "Perpendicular and Horizontal" period when Ch'u, by creating a "perpendicular" structure of alliances reaching up to the north, attempted to stop the "horizontal" eastward advance of Ch'in in the third century B.C. It seems therefore as though the Ch'u wall can best be described as marking the boundary between the area directly administered by Ch'u and the area that it attempted to control as a "sphere of influence." This would indicate that the wall building of Ch'u was also a phenomenon of a confused and hesitant period, in which feudalism was in some ways being defended while in other ways it was being destroyed by the only measures of defense that were possible.

EXCESSIVE MILITARY DEVELOPMENT OF THE KINGDOM OF CH'IN

Once the kingdom of Ch'in had completed its military conquests within China it became necessary to revise entirely the place and function of the soldier in society, but this raised problems that Ch'in was unable to solve. The new imperial state was encumbered with a huge army. It had been developed as the most massive striking force of the age, but it no longer had anything at which to strike. Nor was it easy to demobilize. Feudalism having been destroyed, the troops could not simply be dispersed under their feudal chiefs. The victorious army was a state army for which the state alone was responsible.

It is impossible to tell exactly how many hundred thousand men had now to be put to one use or another, but the number must have been very large. The annals list campaigns, battles, and even casualties in round figures of several hundred thousand men at a time.[8] Although it is not at all necessary to accept these figures, it is apparent that for several reasons the real numbers must have been large enough. Ch'in had developed a style of fighting in which both mass and maneuver were important. Under feudalism, although warfare was chronic, large armies could not keep the field for long. Each noble had only a rather small number of paid, "professional" retainers permanently under arms. Large armies could be called out for short campaigns, but if superiority was not clearly established in a short campaign the main army broke up and the war went on as a slow business of sieges and sorties. The large forces had to disperse because feudal economy was based on the serf, who worked part of the time on the field to which he was bound and part of the time on his lord's fields. When drafted for war service he could not do either properly. Even the free warrior, who held land in return for the duty of service in war, could not be called on for permanent service but only for stated terms. At the same time, war could go on even when the levies had fulfilled their obligations and gone home, because walled feudal strongholds could be both defended by small numbers and besieged by small numbers; and when a siege had become desperate it could often be

[8] Shih Chi, Ch. 5; Chavannes, Mémoires historiques, Vol. II: in a battle in B.C. 293, Ch'in claimed the taking of 240,000 heads (p. 82); in a campaign in B.C. 256, 40,000 heads in one battle, and 90,000 killed and taken prisoner in another. These figures may be exaggerated but they must have been meant to symbolize, at the time, extraordinarily large armies and operations.

raised by calling out levies again for a short campaign to drive away the besiegers.

The way to destroy feudalism, therefore, was to develop professional armies in the service of the state, which could hold the field at all times; to maneuver widely in order to outrange feudal armies, in which each group came from a different territory and disliked being drawn too far away from that territory; and to use weight and mass, in order always to have an advantage over the fluctuating numbers commanded by feudal nobles. These things Ch'in had learned and put into practice in the course of its wars of conquest; but when all the wars were over it was embarrassed in the possession of a large fighting force for which it must find use.

The number of troops that could be used for garrison duty was limited, because too heavy garrisons would have raised the danger of a recrudescence of feudalism. A long-continued war of conquest in the far south was out of the question. From this time on the slow spread of the Chinese through the wide country beyond the Yangtze was never a question of great military operations. The tribes of the south, though many of them were good warriors, were not people who fought in armies; and the more jungly or swampy or forested or mountainous the country the more this was true. They were dispersed peoples, who fought mile by mile before they surrendered each pocket of land, but that was all. The spread of the Chinese was therefore a problem of social cohesion and economic organization, of drainage and irrigation, roads and trade and administration; and this was a problem that each generation of the southward-advancing Chinese took up afresh and on the spot, as population grew and capital was accumulated in each area.

Nor was a great war of expansion on the steppe Frontier something that would bring relief. The excessive military development of Ch'in was conspicuous and difficult to deal with, and it largely explains why the dynasty fell so soon and with an uproar even more destructive than the noise and terror of its advance to imperial rule; but other aspects of the time were, in the long run, more important. Above all, the change from feudalism to empire had been attended by changes in the whole complex of society. The trend was toward increased centralization and efficiency in the control of a growing population, which was closely settled and dependent on an economy that was increasingly intensive and increasingly in need of great public works. It would have been impossible to complete these changes within China and at the same time to carry out a new expansion in steppe terrain that favored an extensive economy and decentralized methods of rule. Instead of expanding into the steppe Ch'in was constrained to make as permanent and absolute as possible the sundering of China from the steppe.

WHY THE CH'IN SUCCEEDED IN UNIFYING THE FRONTIER BUT FAILED IN ESTABLISHING A LASTING STATE

These are the main conditions to be kept in mind, and they explain both why the Ch'in dynasty succeeded within a few years on the Frontier in executing the enormous labor of the Great Wall and failed in China to tie its vast military conquests together into a lasting state.

The Great Wall of Ch'in Shih-huang-ti ran from a point in Kansu to a point on the seacoast in Manchuria. It masked the highlands of Tibet, which look down on Kansu, and the whole escarpment of the Inner Mongolian plateau, which looks down on North China. In part, it confirmed the lines of the old "little Great Walls" of Ch'in, Chao, and Yen; in part, the lines of these older walls either stood behind the new line or in advance of it. The labor expended on the task is legendary, and it must be remembered that this was not the only forced public labor of the time. The building of great strategic roads was part of the same activity as the linking up of the Great Wall.[9]

In spite of the military appearance of these enterprises, the military expansion of Ch'in beyond what had been the territories of the feudal kingdoms was not very great. The only important encroachment on the steppe was the annexation of the Ordos plateau,[10] which brought the whole of the northern loop of the Yellow River under control and made it possible to straighten the Inner Asian Frontier in such a manner as to include both the oases and semi-oases of the Kansu-Ninghsia area and the old marginal terrain of the land of Tai in north Shansi.

Considering the immense military strength that could have been turned toward external conquest at that time, this is not very much. Nor was there any real danger of attack from the steppe, for the only wars against barbarians of the Inner Asian Frontier were not wars of defense but clearing operations for the straightening of the new Ch'in Great Wall.[11] Formidable though the Great Wall was, therefore, it is to be inferred that there was no really desperate Frontier menace to be faced. The true purpose of both wall building and road building had to do with stabilizing the conquests that had been made in China itself, and with setting to rights a new order of society.

This is confirmed by the Ch'in policy of completing the destruction of serfdom. Ch'in Shih-huang-ti did not create a new feudal nobility from among his important followers and the members of his own clan. Instead, he divided the empire into administrative districts under appointed of-

[9] Shih Chi, Ch. 6; Chavannes, *op. cit.*, pp. 168, 174.

[10] Shih Chi, *loc. cit.*; Chavannes, *op. cit.*, p. 168.

[11] Shih Chi, Ch. 110. It is clear from Ssu-ma Ch'ien's account of the advance into the Ordos and beyond by Meng T'ien, Ch'in Shih-huang-ti's general, that the object was to annex territory but not to destroy the "barbarian" society. These operations were very different from the campaigns in China, which had not only won victories but effected a revolution.

ficials.[12] At the same time peasants were made owners of their land, so that they paid taxes to the state instead of being subject to stated demands for labor by the feudal nobles—a reform which completed the system of taxation and administration begun in the kingdom of Ch'in itself before the conquest of the rest of China.[13] One result of these measures was to set free from the land immense numbers of men who were not landowners and heads of families and therefore not fixed units of the taxation system.

Mobile surplus manpower of this kind, subject to the despotic orders of the sovereign and the state apparatus under his control, had probably been the most important single instrument in the Ch'in conquests. The same measures had now to be extended to the rest of China, both in order to break up the old structure of society and in order to make the new structure uniform; but with no more feudal kingdoms to conquer the use of the increased surplus of manpower created new problems. Undoubtedly this was the real driving force behind the fortifying of the Great Wall Frontier, the building of roads to link the empire together, and also the campaigns undertaken to the south of the Yangtze, which did not permanently open up the still barbarian wilderness of South China but did get rid of a lot of old troops and new landless peasants.[14]

Here, moreover, is the link between the successful— though probably, on the whole, needless—consolidation of the Great Wall Frontier and the failure of Ch'in in the heart of China. The striking power of Ch'in had grown to be enormous during its years of conquest, but there was not yet the custom and experience needed to convert strik-

---

[12] Franke, Geschichte des chinesischen Reiches, Vol. I, 1930, pp. 229-230, citing the Shih Chi, Ch. 6.

[13] Wittfogel, op. cit., pp. 50-51, with footnote references to a number of earlier and later sources.

[14] For the vagueness of the southern limits of the new empire, compare Franke, op. cit., p. 228.

ing power into a stable system of exploitation and rule. Destruction had still to go on, otherwise feudalism, which had been beaten down, might grow up again. The new system, though inherently superior to feudalism, could not at once provide food, work, and wealth to keep busy and under control the immense numbers of people it had set free from feudalism. Under the new system a few tax-paying families, working all of the time on their own land, could produce as much as a whole village of serfs whose time was inefficiently divided between the lord's land and the village fields; but under feudalism the work, though low in productivity, had been shared out to all and all were attached to the land in a way that prevented them from banding together for insurrection; they also had security of a kind at a primitive level of existence. Under the new system hundreds of thousands had been impressed into service under professional captains and made accustomed to violence, while at the same time they had been detached from the land and freed from the restraints that had until then been conventional.

In the circumstances it was inevitable that the new empire should break apart—not through risings of the feudal nobility attempting to restore the old order, for the old order had been too thoroughly destroyed even though elements of it survived, but because troops mutinied [15] and seized the power of which they had until then been the instruments, and were joined by swarms of landless peasants and other malcontents. It is also significant that the collapse did not begin along the Inner Asian Frontier. The empire broke apart in the region of the Huai River —the old debatable land between the Yellow River valley and the Yangtze valley. Dynastic wars and Frontier campaigns must have had more to do, therefore, with the pressures of change in the structure of society in China than with the pressure of barbarian attacks from the steppe.

[15] Dubs, History of the Former Han Dynasty, 1938, pp. 4, 37.

Fall of the Ch'in and Foundation of the Han Dynasty (b.c. 206)

The founder of the Ch'in dynasty came to the throne of the kingdom of Ch'in in b.c. 246, at the age of thirteen, and in b.c. 238 took over the rule from the minister who had been regent. In b.c. 221 he completed the conquest of the feudal states and assumed the title of Ch'in Shih-huang-ti, First Emperor of Ch'in. He died in b. c. 210, at the age of fifty, having ruled as king for twenty-five years and as emperor for twelve.[16] The succession passed to a son, whose reign is dated from b.c. 209 to 207.[17] Insurrection began in b.c. 209 and there followed a period of terrible wars, lasting until b.c. 202, when the founder of the Han dynasty, having defeated all the other ambitious generals of the time, assumed the style of emperor; but the Han dynasty is formally dated from b.c. 206, when the second emperor of Ch'in had committed suicide and the third had surrendered.

The founder of the Han dynasty won his power only step by step through a series of wars of a new kind.[18] The wars of the Ch'in conquest had been both destructive and creative. Feudalism, even in decay, remained a social order in which military power was disproportionately distributed: that part of the feudal society that it was most necessary to destroy was best able to defend itself. Consequently the state of Ch'in, though it led the rest of China in developing a new and more efficient economy, was even further ahead of the rest of China in militarization. Historically, Ch'in was the focus of the most creative development in China; but even so, its military development,

---

[16] The earliest account of his career is in the Shih Chi, Ch. 6, translated in Chavannes, *op. cit.,* Vol. II.

[17] Shih Chi, *loc. cit.,* and Chavannes, *loc. cit.,* at the end of account of Shih-huang-ti.

[18] Dubs, *op. cit.,* gives the record in detail as translated from the dynastic annals.

necessary for the creation of the empire, so far outran its economic and administrative development that when the wars were over it was impossible to convert to other uses the hardened armies that had won the conquest and in winning it had arrogated to themselves too much of the productive and distributive forces of society.

With this in mind as a standard of comparison, it can be said that the Han wars, though economically wasteful like all wars, were not destructive. It was not their historical function to obliterate the kind of empire that Ch'in Shih-huang-ti had created, but to reintegrate it and at the same time to confirm the kind of society and state administration necessary to maintain it.

Before Ch'in Shih-huang-ti there had been the possibility of a centralized empire based on the conquests of Ch'u, in the Yangtze valley, as well as the possibility of an empire based on Ch'in in the northwest. Ch'in was the more formidable in striking power, especially because of its mobile cavalry; but Ch'u was potentially richer as a source of revenue because of its rice harvests, and it was a more difficult state to destroy than the feudal Yellow River states because its conquests of minor states in the Yangtze valley had already given it an approximately imperial character. Ch'u was therefore much harder to take over than the Yellow River states. As a subordinate area it was too vast and too distant to be administered by Ch'in, which stood on the Inner Asian periphery of China.

In view of the kinds of strength and weakness inherent in both Ch'in and Ch'u, the critical area of the time was that in which the kind of power that could be based on Ch'u and the kind of power that could be based on Ch'in overlapped each other. This was in the low-lying Huai basin, between the Yellow River and the Yangtze. It was in this region, accordingly, that the Ch'in Empire broke down and it was only by standing astride this region, in order to influence both Yellow River China and Yangtze

China, that a new united empire, that of the Han, could be established.

It is not possible here to narrate the full history of the Han dynasty, but the analysis I have sketched is borne out by a number of facts. The wars of the time began with appeals to legitimism—that is, to the old order of things. A number of the feudal states were temporarily revived, but by far the most conspicuous leaders came from noble families of the state of Ch'u, which had been more imperial than feudal. Gradually, however, the noble contenders exhausted each other and themselves, and the way was left open for Liu Chi, or Liu Pang, the founder of the Han dynasty.[19]

Liu Pang was a native of the critical Huai area, so that as far as possible he was prepared to understand and deal with the overlapping influences of North and South. Moreover, he was neither a feudal noble, biased by too strong a desire for the restoration of feudalism, nor a professional captain, with a mind limited by military ambitions. He had been a minor official, and as a minor official of the region in which lay the balance of power he had insight both into the working of state affairs in the major regions of the Yellow River and the Yangtze and into the society of the common people below him and the privileged groups above him [20]—both the surviving hereditary nobles and the partially established professional administrators. It was by working with all these forces until he had found the degree of balance possible in his own age that he was able to found a stable dynasty.

Because it was based on a conjunction of forces that could be made to work, the Han period immediately flowered into a great civilization, in spite of the waste and slaughter of the wars that led up to it. There was a partial

[19] Dubs, *op. cit.*
[20] For the importance of such men of ambivalent social status, see Chapter XVII, below.

reversion toward feudalism, but the feudal order was by no means restored. This was already impossible. Those of the feudal nobles who survived were no longer competent to handle the affairs of the only kind of state that would work, as was proved in the course of the wars in which the feudal champions went down and Liu Pang, the founder of the Han, made good his mastery. As emperor he granted territories and titles to his followers, most of whom were eventually replaced by his own relatives;[21] but these were territories and honors that could no longer be maintained except by subservience to the state. In the same way the seat of the dynasty was established on the periphery of China, in the old Ch'in territory, instead of being kept in the central Huai area where the dynasty had been founded; but this was possible because a working balance between imperial power and regional power had been effected.

Ssu-ma Ch'ien's Account of the Frontier

Approaching the history of the Great Wall thus by way of the history of China, it can be seen that even the prodigious idea of a fortified zone from Tibet to the sea was a shadow cast by the shape that society took in China. Neither at the fall of the Ch'in nor during the wars out of which the Han arose was there any need for a desperate stand against "hordes" of nomad barbarians pouring in from the steppe. Nor was the use of walls the only or even the best way of holding steppe nomads away from China, as had already been proved by the end of the fourth century B.C., when the Chao frontiersmen of north Shansi had shown that border territories could best be entered and occupied by Chinese who made themselves partly like the nomads. The walls that such people built, in Chao and Yen and Ch'in, delimiting the territory that they had taken over, were more important in giving them power over the

[21] Dubs, *op. cit.*; Franke, *op. cit.*, pp. 269 *et sqq.*

"Chinese" territory behind them than as a sign of domination over the steppe. They marked out a land between the true China and the true steppe.

By the time of the transition from Ch'in to Han, however, there was also a transition to a new phase in steppe history. The main source for our knowledge of this period is the 110th chapter of the *Historical Memoirs* of Ssu-ma Ch'ien; and Ssu-ma Ch'ien himself, in turn, reviews in this chapter a great deal of what survives from the Chou material about the still earlier barbarians.

While it is fortunate that Ssu-ma Ch'ien recorded so much of what was known at the time he wrote (in the early Han period), it is unfortunate that so much of the material should thus have passed through the hands of a single writer, becoming in the process less amenable to comparative treatment. For it is evident both from the manner in which Ssu-ma Ch'ien links the remote past with the past that was nearer to his own time, and from his description of the customs and society of the steppe people, that the Chinese at the beginning of the Han dynasty had already developed a strongly conventional idea of the steppe nomads. It was already usual to describe in stock terms their virtues and vices and their habits in peace and war.

Nevertheless, this consecutive account provides a historical outline that is convincing as far as it is complete. The sequence from Jung and Ti tribes to Hu and Hsiung-nu peoples as related by Ssu-ma Ch'ien agrees at least in continuity with the reconstruction, as I have attempted it, of a history of scattered "old barbarians" being driven back by the evolving Chinese to the edge of the steppe, there to become "new barbarians," or true pastoral nomads. Naturally, he does not deal in terms of an evolution from a primitive, non-nomad economy to a highly specialized nomadism; but his change from the terms Jung and Ti to the terms Hu and Hsiung-nu, at the end of the Chou feudal period, tends to confirm the assumption that these new names do not denote new peoples but rather a new kind of people emerging out of the old stock.[22]

Ssu-ma Ch'ien's account also suggests, though unfortunately without specific details of the transition, that while the change from feudalism to empire was going on in China there was a simultaneous and parallel change going on among the "northern barbarians"—from a dispersed and local tribalism in valleys and hills at the edge of the steppe to a collective, general tribalism of the full expanse of the steppe.

When Ch'in Shih-huang-ti set up his empire in China he cleared the skirts of the land along the edge of the steppe, unifying the Great Wall system of fortifications. This was carried out by Meng T'ien, his greatest marshal, with tens of thousands of men.[23] The people of the steppe were driven back from certain debatable areas, but Shih-huang-ti did not invade the main steppe. It was not his purpose to make a dual empire linking together the agricultural Chinese and the nomad herdsmen. His Great Wall, like the earlier walls, confirmed his control over China but did not win control over the steppe.

During the bitter seven years of war in the time between Ch'in and Han the nomads came back into some of the marginal territory from which they had been driven, especially the Ordos loop of the Yellow River,[24] but they made no general attack on China. The Han dynasty made good its title as a dynasty that was the master of China. It did not come to power by defending China against invasion, yet it had barely been acknowledged as a dynasty when, in B.C. 201, it had to begin to fight against the nomads.[25] An understanding of the character of these wars must obviously be of the greatest value in determining

[22] Shih Chi, Ch. 110.
[23] Ibid.
[24] Ibid.
[25] Ibid.; also Dubs, op. cit., pp. 115-117.

what forces were really at work in differentiating the field of history in China as a whole from that of the steppe as a whole.

THE HSIUNGNU AND THE APPEARANCE OF A NEW TYPE OF RULER IN THE STEPPE

Only about a generation had passed since Ch'in, with its back to a firm Frontier, had sent its great armies to the conquest of China. In that short time men had seen the feudal age go down and had seen the Great Wall flung from the edge of Tibet to the edge of the ocean, replacing the lesser walls of the feudal states that until then had fronted toward Inner Asia. Men still alive and active in the new age could remember the age that had passed. This must be recalled when reading the Chinese historian's account of how the ruler of the nomads, "unable to prevail against Ch'in," migrated away.[26] After the death of Meng T'ien, Shih-huang-ti's great marshal, and the fall of the Ch'in Empire, the settlers brought to the Ordos began to disperse. The Hsiungnu, led by the son and successor of the chief who had left in the time of Shih-huang-ti, then had room to return and "again gradually crossed the Yellow River southward into China, and set the boundary of their nation at its old limit."[27]

The name of the first of these two great Hsiungnu chiefs is given as T'u-man, which almost certainly is the Turco-Mongol word *tumen,* meaning "ten thousand" also "an infinite number," and often used as a personal and tribal name. His title is recorded as *ch'eng-li* (or *t'ang-li*) *ku-t'u shan-yü,* and translated as "great son of heaven (*shan-yü*)"—a close approximation of the Chinese imperial title. The word *ch'eng-li* or *t'ang-li* must be the Turco-Mongol *tengri,* "heaven."[28] Here we have for the very first time

[26] Shih Chi, Ch. 110.
[27] *Ibid.*; this refers, of course, to the Ordos, not to other territory south of the Yellow River.
[28] Since writing this I find that De Groot, Die Hunnen der vorchristlichen

in a Chinese chronicle the name of a barbarian ruler given in what is beyond conjecture the barbarian and not the Chinese form. Also, we have for the first time a barbarian chief who is not simply called a "chief" (or some equivalent term) in Chinese but is listed both with his title in the non-Chinese language and with the Chinese translation of the title. Moreover, the language itself must be of the original stock from which both Turkish and Mongol derived in later centuries.

In leading up to his account of the relations between the Hsiungnu and the Han dynasty, Ssu-ma Ch'ien not only describes Tumen as "unable to prevail against Ch'in" but states that "at this time the Tunghu were expanding and the Yüehchih were flourishing." [29] The Tunghu or Eastern Hu can be identified from the time when the Chinese began dealing with "barbarians" who were clearly horse-riding nomads, at the turn of the fourth and third centuries B.C.[30] The term Hu is generic rather than tribal, denoting a barbarian of a certain kind; but the term Tunghu is tribal—the Tunghu lay to the north of the states of Yen and Chao (Peiping region and Shansi region). The term Hsiungnu is also tribal, denoting the tribes to the north of the Ordos, who apparently, judging from the sequence of the chronicles, developed at least in part out of the pre-nomad Jung and Ti of the northerly frontiers of Ch'in. The Yüehchih are here named suddenly for the

---

Zeit, 1921, p. 47, renders T'uman as T'oban. De Groot is no infallible guide in such matters, but neither am I. However, F. W. K. Müller, a very great scholar, in his Toxrī and Kuišan (Küšän), 1918, seems to have accepted the probability that the name which I have transcribed below as Modun was really Moduk, Mokduk, Makdur, or Bakdur, and hence equivalent to the more modern form Bagatur. It is better, therefore, not to claim correctness for my reading of these two names. There is no doubt, however, that the Hsiungnu spoke a Turkic language (the reading Bagatur would again confirm this). Nor is there any doubt about the reading tengri. Finally, Franke (op. cit., Vol. III, 1937, p. 180), citing another article by F. W. K. Müller, which I have not seen, reads ku-t'u as qut, "majesty," so that tengri qut becomes "heavenly majesty."

[29] Shih Chi, Ch. 110.
[30] Ibid.

first time; their territory overlapped the oasis, desert, and steppe regions of Chinese Turkistan, Western Kansu, and the edges of Tibet.

Politically, Ssu-ma Ch'ien's account suggests that the appearance of a nomad ruler who was a kind of crude equivalent in the steppe of the new Chinese kind of supreme emperor was not only contemporary with the Ch'in unification of China but in some way attendant on it. The account also clearly dates for us a new phase in Inner Asian history—the transition from a period of chronicles that deal with no more than the Chinese edges of the steppe to a period in which there was undoubtedly a history of the main steppe, always linked with the history of China but also independent of it. Two phenomena appear at the same time: a steppe ruler with some kind of claim to be supreme in the steppe, and constellations of steppe tribes intermittently at war both with each other and with the Chinese and claiming against each other the title of supremacy in the steppe. These two phenomena must be examined both from the side of the steppe and from the side of China.

THE CHANGE FROM MARGINAL NOMADISM TO FULL NOMADISM

In view of the probably diverse origins of steppe nomadism,[31] there seems very strong reason to believe that in this period many different groups of nomads, who had developed the technique of nomadism at different edges of the steppe, were spreading into the main steppe and thus creating a steppe society that was no longer marginal but competent to develop within a much larger geographical scope. Vladimirtsov has established a strain of forest-hunter derivation among the northern Mongols at the edge of Siberia, Urianghai, and the Altai.[32] The burial finds

[31] See also Chapters IV and VI, above.
[32] Vladimirtsov, Social Structure of the Mongols, 1934, pp. 33 et sqq. (in Russian).

at Pazyryk in the Siberian Altai have strongly confirmed the assumption that forest-hunters, using reindeer for transport, could at the edge of the steppe convert the herding of small numbers of reindeer into the pasturing of larger numbers of other animals, and thus transform themselves into true pastoral nomads.[33] Other nomads undoubtedly originated at the edges of oases in Chinese and Russian Turkistan.[34] The Tunghu may have become steppe nomads partly by evolution and adaptation at the edge of the Jehol forests and the Inner Mongolian steppe and partly by pressure from the expanding Chinese of the state of Yen. Other tribes may have formed similarly at the edges of the Manchurian forests and the steppe of Eastern Mongolia and Western Manchuria. Finally, there is the strong historical probability that a number of groups of Jung and Ti "old barbarians," extruded from the north of China by the expansion of the Chinese agricultural society, were transformed into "new barbarians" of the steppe.

It is impossible to say when the first vague and weak contacts between early nomads began, spreading around the Siberian, Manchurian, Chinese, and Turkistan margins of the main steppe, or even across rather wide expanses of steppe. It will probably never be possible to determine the exact point of change from marginal nomadism to full nomadism of the main steppe; indeed, it is likely that this change began at somewhat different times on different sides of the steppe. It is a clear and strong probability, however, that the change proceeded very rapidly, once it had begun, and that its consequences were sudden and far-reaching. From the moment that the first marginal groups of nomads, clinging to oases and the kinder stretches of pasture at the edge of the steppe, let go of the compromises and adaptations inherent in a border

[33] Griaznov and Golomshtok, The Pazirik Burial of Altai, 1933; Lattimore, The Geographical Factor in Mongol History, 1938.
[34] See Chapter VI, above.

life and ventured into the full steppe an immense discharge of new forces was precipitated.

Migration was at once transformed from a slow drift and seepage of men and cultures and social practices around the edge of the steppe into the more direct and rapid movement of larger bodies of people over very great distances. The relatively small groups that had hung about the edges of the world of planting and harvests could link up with a startling rapidity, working out a new kind of cohesion. The new society that resulted, though living by a more narrowly specialized technique, commanded a wider and more general domain. Although the total number of nomads did not necessarily increase greatly, the much wider scope of movement and the ability to disperse rapidly and concentrate suddenly made the pastoral society of the steppe nomads in its new form more elusive when defending itself and much more formidable in attack.

It is therefore not at all surprising or mysterious that the Chinese account records the results of this period of accelerated change without analyzing the character of the change. When the focus of pastoral nomadism shifted from the edge of China into the remoter steppe the workings of nomad society passed beyond the comprehension of the orthodox Chinese historian. Ssu-ma Ch'ien's narrative, accordingly, turns without explanation from the older fringing barbarism to the new barbarism of the open steppe. It preserves the continuity but takes for granted a conventional treatment even of the newer barbarism, as if it were something of which the barbarous origin need not be examined in detail.

A Tentative Linguistic Differentiation of the Frontier Peoples

Although Ssu-ma Ch'ien traces the continuity between the more ancient tribes and the Hsiungnu, there are other questions to which he gives no answer. While there was continuity between the Jung and the Ti and the Hsiungnu and Hu, there was also a sharp differ-

UNIFIED EMPIRE AND UNIFIED FRONTIER   455

entiation. Names like K'un-i and Hsien-yü[35] and their variants
hint that even the general tribal name of Hsiungnu may trace back
to some subtribal group of the Jung. The problem of differentiation, on the other hand, is hidden behind the fact that, while the
Chinese had been in contact with the Jung and Ti for centuries,
it is only suddenly at about the beginning of the second century
B.C. that some of the words of a "barbarian" language are recorded. This, the language of the Hsiungnu, belongs to a family
of languages not even remotely related to Chinese. The problem of
language is related to the problem of tribal names.[36]

Finally, by way of language and tribal names the aspect of differentiation may be linked up with the aspect of continuity. If the
society of the steppe was formed partly out of marginal remnants
of the "old society" from which the society of China had also
formed, why is it that the dominant languages of the steppe belong to the Ural-Altaic family, which is so different from Chinese
that it cannot be related even to proto-Chinese?

Nowhere, not even in the most ancient references, is there any
indication that the Chinese had a generic term for non-Chinese[37]
equivalent to the Greek *barbaroi*. There are a few names that are
in one sense classificatory. Chiang or Ch'iang indicates a shepherd
people; Ching a jungle people. Such names, however, do not in
themselves prove that the people referred to were non-Chinese.
Most other names can be fairly positively described as tribal,
and many if not most of them can be more or less clearly identified as Chinese phonetic transcriptions of non-Chinese names.
This holds even when the name has an allusive meaning as written in Chinese: Hsiungnu literally means "fierce slaves," but this
is merely because it was convenient or satisfactory to the Chinese
to transcribe in such a manner a non-Chinese name that sounded
something like Hsiungnu. The tribal name Man can be identified
in the language of the Yao tribes that still live in South China:
mun or *mién* is "man," "people." The P'an Ku Yao call themselves "Yu-mién" and call the Red-Headed Yao "Bu-lung-mién,"
and so forth.[38] Such tribal names can easily become regional: Min

[35] See the table of tribal names, based on Karlgren's restoration of ancient
pronunciations, in Herrmann, Die Westländer, etc. (in Hedin, Southern Tibet,
Vol. VIII, 1922), p. 134. De Groot's restorations and explanations of ancient
names in his work cited above must be taken cautiously.
[36] For an interesting, though in the present state of knowledge speculative,
discussion of proto-languages and proto-cultures, see Menghin, Weltgeschichte
der Steinzeit, 1931, pp. 541 *et sqq.*
[37] Maspero, La Chine antique, 1927, p. 5, n. 1.
[38] Yen and Shang, Yao People of Lingyün in Kuanghsi, 1929, pp. 22, 31
(in Chinese).

(Fukien) and Mien (Burma) are very likely related to Man. These southern names, however, belong in a different category from the steppe names since they come from languages more or less distantly related to Chinese. I suppose it is possible, though it may be only accidental, that the Man group of names is related to the Chinese word *min*, "people," "folk."

Four linguistic families are involved in this problem of tribal names.

1. *Sino-T'ai*. From this derive Chinese itself and the Indochinese (T'ai) languages and dialects.

2. *Tibeto-Burman*. To this group the Chiang or Ch'iang tribes probably belonged, either from the most ancient times or at least from the second century B.C., when they were distributed along the Kansu-Tibetan border. Bishop believes that the Chou Chinese may also have belonged to this linguistic group,[39] whereas the Shang Chinese belonged to the Sino-T'ai group. This is not impossible, especially in view of the fact that the Sino-T'ai and Tibeto-Burman language families are probably distantly related or else were influenced by each other at a very early period.[40]

3. *Indogermanic*. To this group belonged the Tokharoi (T'uhulo, Ta-hsi), whose antiquity and original geographical distribution have been much disputed, especially by German writers.[41] It can certainly be said that about the second century B.C. they were established in at least the western oases of Chinese Turkistan—near the edge, that is, of the Iranian world. The Yüehchih probably belonged to the same ethnic and linguistic group.[42] The Yüehchih, until driven away by the Hsiungnu, are generally agreed to have held the territory along the foot of the Nanshan, in Kansu. Here a number of streams flowing from the mountains to the steppe support fertile oases. In their later history also the Yüehchih were more an oasis people than a nomad people. All of this points to an ancient and wide oasis distribution of the Indogermanic language group.

4. *Ural-Altaic*. The Turkic, Mongol, and Tungus languages and dialects are all included in this family, which was very probably in remote origin a forest speech that spread later into the steppe and also into the sub-Arctic and the oasis world.[43]

[39] Bishop, Beginnings of North and South in China, 1934, p. 310.
[40] Maspero, *op. cit.*, p. 18.
[41] Herrmann, *op. cit.*, p. 169; Franke, *op. cit.*, Vol. III, 1937, p. 80; also his many references under Skythen, Ta-hia, Tocharer, Yüe-tschi, etc.
[42] Franke, *op. cit.*, p. 180; F. W. K. Müller, *op. cit.*, pp. 566 *et sqq.*
[43] Pelliot (Les Mots à H initiale, 1925), deprecates "en l'état actuel des études" an inclusive Ural-Altaic grouping of the Finno-Ugrian and Samoyed

If a language frontier between the society of the steppe and that of China had really formed as abruptly as might be inferred if there were no other evidence available than Ssu-ma Ch'ien's account of the Hsiungnu, the only possible explanation would be that the Chinese margin of the steppe had little or nothing to do with the origins of steppe society. It would have to be admitted that the Hsiungnu broke suddenly into the field of Chinese history as invaders from a distance. The problem is much easier to understand, in its broad outlines if not in detail, when it is realized that there must have been a very ancient multiple language frontier between the loess of northwestern China, the highlands of Tibet, the Central Asian oases, and the steppe.

It is dangerous to attempt too neat a hypothesis, but in very broad terms I think it is possible to state a working theory of combined cultural, linguistic, and geographical differentiation that is historically significant. There may have been at the neolithic level—and more probably the early neolithic than the late neolithic —four primitive language groups: those of the loess peoples, the peoples of the Chinese plains, the oasis peoples, and the Siberian, North Mongolian, and Manchurian forest peoples. Of the four groups the Chinese loess language and the plains language may have been differentiated from a still more primitive common speech.

Language, as the vehicle of thought, is intimately affected by the way in which people live and act. As Stefansson has pointed out in modern times, the real difficulty in learning the Eskimo language is not the difficult vocabulary and complicated structure but the need for a different way of thinking.[44] In discussing neolithic China I have argued that there was a backward neolithic society and a progressive neolithic society. It was where the loess habitat and the plains habitat met that the first relatively rapid progress was made. This led to a diffusion of higher cultural forms both into the major loess terrain and the major plains region. The result, I suggest, may have been eventually to create a common language of the loess people and the plains people, and this in turn

---

languages with the Turkish, Mongol, and Tungus family. I retain the old convention here, however, because the questions to be considered are not linguistic alone, but both linguistic and cultural.

[44] Stefansson, The Friendly Arctic, 1921, pp. 104-105: "The principles of the language are entirely different from those of European languages, and in order to talk Eskimo you have first to adopt in general a different mode of thought." It is obvious that this "different mode of thought" is not arbitrarily created by the language; it must be a property which the language acquired in the course of the evolution of a culture highly specialized to suit its environment.

pushed back the original loess language in one direction, where the Tibeto-Burman languages were gradually formed, and the original plains language in the other direction, where in the jungle habitat the Sino-T'ai languages were gradually differentiated.

The people of the loess, however, were interpenetrated by the people of the oases. The increasing ascendancy of the Chinese way of life in the semi-oases of Kansu was accompanied by a gradual displacement of the Indogermanic language group from its extreme eastern range of distribution.[45] Here the issue was complicated by the emergence of the steppe way of life, which was being formed not only on the margins of China and the oases but also on the forest margins of Siberia and Manchuria.

In the upshot Tibetan prevailed (with strongly marked dialects according to the degree of isolation of various groups) in Tibet; Chinese prevailed over almost the whole of Kansu and Ninghsia; and the Ural-Altaic languages first spread from the forests over the steppe, then into the steppe oases, and eventually, very much later, into the desert oases. The older Indogermanic oasis languages were forced back to Iran.

I think it is legitimate to suggest—though still speaking only in terms of a very flexible preliminary hypothesis—that these indications of a redistribution of language areas may be connected with evolving and spreading cultures. The rough order might be as follows:

1. *Ural-Altaic languages* (*early stage*). Forest hunters. Domestication of reindeer, which did not lead to the domestication of other animals because the technique of domesticating reindeer is different from that of other animals.[46] Nor did it lead to steppe pastoralism because reindeer could not graze on steppe pasture. The result was a genuine but limited nomadism.

2. *Indogermanic languages*. People of the Central Asian oases. Domestication of the horse, the sheep, and so forth, at the edges of oases. This did not lead to compulsory evolution into nomad-

---

[45] I do not mean to imply that when a language was displaced the people who spoke it were necessarily driven away. There may have been no migration, complete migration, or—most probably—partial migration.

[46] For references to Laufer and Hatt on reindeer nomadism, see the Bibliography. Among recent writers, Flor (Zur Frage des Renntiernomadismus, 1930), believes that the domestication of the reindeer probably preceded that of the horse. The problem is not limited to the priority of the domestication of one animal or another. At each historical level a culture must be considered, a way of living adapted to an environment. Therefore "borrowings" between cultures and transitions from one form to another must always concern complexes of associated techniques; and a complex borrowed in relatively simple form may later be borrowed back in a more developed form.

ism. Combination with some other factor was needed—cultural exchange or pressure driving people from the edges of oases out into the steppe.

3. *Ural-Altaic languages (later stage)*. Acquisition of sheep, horses, etc., by the forest people, who were already nomads but did not have the kinds of animals that could be herded in the steppe. By cross-stimulation this may have led simultaneously or almost simultaneously to the stemming off of nomad groups from oasis groups; but in all steppe groups, whatever their origin, the Ural-Altaic languages spread rapidly and became dominant because they had earliest been associated with the mentality of a nomad life.

4. *Sinic languages (possibly both Sino-T'ai and Tibeto-Burman)*. The Chinese margins of both the steppe and the oasis world. The retreat into the steppe of people who refused to follow the developing Chinese way of life. Most of these people were "backward" kin of the Chinese themselves, but those farthest to the northwest may have belonged to a different ethnic group and to the Indogermanic language group. These people were very rapidly converted to the Ural-Altaic languages that went with the steppe life, but they had a strong political influence quite different from that of the steppe nomads of either forest or oasis origin because they were the first to have felt the stimulating and maturing effects of contact with the major Chinese culture and resistance to it.

As has been stated, all of this is meant as the roughest sort of general theory. As set down it appears to be much more precise than is intended because of the difficulty of presenting the idea clearly without overstating it. Differences between primitive languages must have been rather haphazard; the association between language and culture cannot have been strong; it may well have been more or less accidental which language was first associated with which culture. But the more strongly a culture became differentiated, and the more it developed, the more it was bound to mold the usages of speech in which the people of the culture conveyed thought and emotion to each other."

THE CAREER OF TUMEN

Considering further the political aspect of Ssu-ma Ch'ien's account, it is clearly to be inferred that while

[47] From the citations in Menghin, *op. cit.*, and Griaznov and Golomshtok, *op. cit.*, it is evident that there is an important recent literature in Russian, especially in the "Japhetic" theory of language and culture of the late N. Y. Marr. This literature, unfortunately, I have been unable to consult.

the life and society of the steppe were henceforth more independent of China—and in a new way—the politics of
Inner Asia were still shaped largely by what happened in
China—though also in a new way. The spread from the
margins into the open steppe, especially the spread from
the borders of China, had created a new general society
of nomads. The Chinese in the course of a few decades had
to become accustomed to dealing with nomads whose main
focus could be transferred from one region to another
over an immense reach of territory, instead of with local
tribes or borderers. Conversely, the nomads, though they
could henceforth unite themselves with a new effectiveness,
had also to cope with the mass of the Chinese Empire as
a whole in addition to their dealings with the lords of different sectors of the Great Wall Frontier.

While the Chinese and nomad kinds of society were thus
diverging sharply from each other, they continued necessarily to interact on each other; and the acuteness of the
effect of interaction must have increased in proportion to
the divergence. Action and reaction, impact and recoil,
must have been so close that there is a danger of overem-
phasis in attempting to determine whether the prime cause
of the historical forces at work lay more in China, or in
the steppe, or on the margin of the steppe. Allowance
must be made for the immediacy and potency of steppe
influences along the Inner Asian Frontier and for the fact
that nomad history at once began to draw a fresh vigor
from totally un-Chinese reserves in Central Asia and Siberia as soon as its focus had shifted from the widely separated margins of the steppe to the main steppe itself; but
even so, the prime forces at work on the Chinese Frontier
of Inner Asia were undoubtedly Chinese forces.

As far as the origins of the Great Wall are concerned,
the shaping of the Inner Asian Frontier was less a product of "nomad pressure" than of Chinese growth, which
was antecedent to the rise of a major nomadism along

those edges of the steppe that the Great Wall confronts. Even when the people of the steppe had so enlarged their scope that it included territories far beyond the direct reach of Chinese influences, the political history of steppe nomadism in Manchuria, Mongolia, and the eastern stretches of Turkistan continued to follow a bias imparted by contact with China.

Certainly the careers of Tumen, the first great khan of the Hsiungnu—a kind of emperor in the steppe—and of Modun (Mao-tun), the son who murdered him and created a still greater power, were influenced by the consolidation of the Great Wall Frontier under Ch'in Shih-huang-ti. In spite of wide and free movement within the steppe, the growth of an imperial range of steppe history lagged until the consequences of empire in China had taken effect among the nomads beyond the Great Wall. "Nomad pressure," it appears, was not of acute importance either in the fall of the Ch'in dynasty or in the setting up of the Han dynasty.

Tumen, to begin with, was a contemporary of the great conqueror of China. There is nothing to show that he attacked the Frontier while Ch'in Shih-huang-ti was engaged in conquest within China. He is first mentioned as "migrating away" from the Ordos when Meng T'ien, linking up the old walls of Ch'in and Chao, drew the main line of the Great Wall to take in the whole of the Ordos.[48] It is quite possible that this did not mean a general departure of the border nomads beyond the Chinese horizon, but rather an affirmation of Chinese rule in such a manner as to include some marginal territories and their populations and also to initiate new political orientations among those nomad chiefs who recoiled from the limits of the Chinese Empire as thus arbitrarily determined. Tumen himself, therefore, may have been at first a border barbarian who lost some of his grazing lands and some of his

[48] Shih Chi, Ch. 110.

followers when Meng T'ien brought the Ordos under direct Chinese administration. By his departure into the farther steppe, accordingly, both Tumen and the followers that remained to him may have been constrained to start working out an accelerated political development of steppe nomadism.

The general character of the history of the time is here more important than the missing details of the personal career of Tumen. Up to this time the Ch'in armies which were conquering China had undoubtedly been recruiting numbers of barbarian cavalry, and it is likely that the barbarians whom it was easiest to use were border nomads who had been in contact with border Chinese. Service with Ch'in, under these conditions, must have offered the most attractive career open to a nomad chief of the border. Tumen was a chief of this kind, according to Ssu-ma Ch'ien's account. His tribal grazing lands were in the Ordos. It seems likely, therefore, that he "could not prevail" against Ch'in because, once the conquest in China had been rounded out, Ch'in had to determine how much was to be included in the empire and how much excluded. It was best to administer as "Chinese" only territory in which it was possible to promote the increasingly intensive agriculture on which the new standard of empire was based. The Ordos, a reëntrant of the steppe—a wedge pointing southward into China—was an exception; the Chinese needed to take it over for strategic reasons and in order to secure the Ninghsia oases.

This meant that border chiefs of the nomads were no longer needed in the service of China. In such marginal terrain as the Chinese felt it profitable to annex both the tribesmen and the chiefs, unless they withdrew into the steppe, would be subordinated to Chinese administration. Chiefs like Tumen were in this way rebuffed from China with the loss of part of their lands and following. "Careers" and the functions of chieftainship were thrown back on the steppe. The result must have been to hasten the growth among the nomads of a kind of power and organization adapted more to the open steppe and less to the border between steppe and agriculture.

Modun's Career as Illustrative of the Rise of a New Type of Steppe Society

Modun, son of Tumen, who about a decade later reappeared on the Chinese horizon, was a chief of a different kind. The account of Modun given by Ssu-ma Ch'ien is of extraordinary interest. The first descriptions of Chinese border kings and captains, like Wu Ling and Li Mu, of the kingdom of Chao, are several centuries earlier. Modun is the first non-Chinese of the Inner Asian Frontier to be noticed more than perfunctorily. Moreover, there is very good reason to believe that what Ssu-ma Ch'ien says of Modun is actually taken from an epic or heroic account current among the Hsiungnu themselves. It is therefore worth summarizing.

Modun was placed as a hostage among the Yüehchih by his father, Tumen, who wished to get rid of him in favor of another heir. Tumen then suddenly attacked the Yüehchih, expecting that they would kill Modun; but Modun took one of the best horses of the Yüehchih and escaped back to the Hsiungnu. Tumen then accepted him as a hero and gave him command of ten thousand horsemen. Modun trained these followers to obey the signal of a "whistling" arrow, putting to death those who failed to draw on any target at which he aimed a signal arrow. After exercising them in this way, when hunting, he shot at his own favorite horse, and put to death those who did not follow the signal. He then tested them again in the same way, but more severely, loosing an arrow against one of his favorite wives, and again killed those who did not obey the signal. Again, when hunting, he shot a "whistling" arrow at a fine horse of his father's. All of his followers answered the signal. Judging them now sufficiently disciplined, Modun at last went hunting together with his father. During the hunt, he drew his bow against Tumen: his followers did the same—so that all were guilty—and Modun was free to seize the tribal power.[49]

There followed a war of tribal supremacy. The Tunghu demanded of Modun a horse of the Hsiungnu that had been famous in Tumen's time. Against the advice of his lieutenants Modun surrendered the horse. Thinking he feared them, the Tunghu then demanded from Modun one of his wives. Modun surrendered her, still against the word of his lieutenants. Finally, the Tunghu claimed a stretch of land that lay between their borders and those of the Hsiungnu. Modun consulted his advisers, who said that it did not matter whether he gave up the land or not. This time Modun was angered. Saying "Land is the root of a nation; how can we cede it?" he put to death all those who had advised him to yield. Moreover, he followed this up by attacking the Tunghu before he could be attacked. The Tunghu, being unprepared, were defeated and conquered in this one campaign; then Modun, without a pause, turned back to the west and defeated and "drove away" the Yüehchih. This evidently left him unchallenged in the steppe and free to raid Yen, the land of Tai, and the Ordos—the whole Great Wall fringe of China—recovering all that had been taken from the Hsiungnu by Meng T'ien.[50]

All of this recital is notably different from the chronicles of Chinese history, not only in detail, which is to be expected, but in style. Though somewhat modified by translation and by the terse wording of Chinese literary composition, it echoes, I think, an original account current among the Hsiungnu themselves in epic or saga-like form. Even as it stands it is clearly more akin to such nomad

[49] Shih Chi, Ch. 110.
[50] Ibid.

history in legendary form as the older (pre-Chingghis) material in the *Secret History of the Mongols* than it is to the conventions of Chinese historical writing.[51]

Perhaps this means that the exact details of the career of Modun have here been distorted by being adapted to, or woven into, an already existing fabric—a convention already established among the nomads for reciting the great deeds of their chieftains. Even so, the loss of clarity in detail is probably less important than the fact that the preservation of such an epic fragment is extremely valuable in estimating the character of the Hsiungnu people as a whole two centuries before Christ: the kind of society they had and the way that tribes rose and fell and kings came to power—in short, the historical setting in which moved such figures as Tumen and Modun.

Indeed, if I am correct in my analysis this echo of Hsiungnu legend both confirms the creation of a new kind of society by contact across the steppe and between the distant margins of the steppe, and the suddenness with which the new society became an active historical force. Probably the horse was domesticated at the edges of the Central Asian oases before it was domesticated in China;[52] probably it was on the fringe of the steppe also that the superiority of light cavalry over chariots was proved. Yet the decisive advantage of the steppe horseman was the use on horseback of the compound reflex bow. This bow was known in China in Shang times, when the chariot had not yet been challenged by the mounted archer, and was known perhaps even in neolithic times, before the chariot was in use.[53]

[51] In addition to the Russian translation of the "Secret History" by Palladius, parts are available in German translation in Haenisch, Untersuchungen über das Yüan-Chao Pi-Shi, 1931; also Die letzten Feldzüge Cinggis Han's und sein Tod, 1932.
[52] See Chapter VI, above.
[53] Creel, Studies in Early Chinese Culture, 1937, pp. 195-196. The invention of the stirrup, which is known to be rather late, is of great functional importance in this connection. Accurate mounted archery is impossible with-

It was the combination of the Chinese bow and Central Asian mastery of the horse that made the men of the steppe formidable in war; but even this conjunction was not enough to create a people of the steppe. For the horse was not by any means the prime characteristic of the pastoral economy, the art of living in the steppe. The key to nomadic life was the herding of sheep and cattle, especially sheep, away from fixed habitations and without reliance on sheltered pens and stored forage.[54] Semi-nomadic herding certainly developed in the margin between China and the steppe four or five centuries before Christ, and it probably developed also, and much earlier, on the edges of the Central Asian oases along the skirts of the Tibetan plateau[55]; and in a different way on the edges of the Siberian and Manchurian forests as hunters and food gatherers, who had learned to domesticate reindeer, adapted themselves to the herding of sheep and goats in the open steppe. When all these practices of economy, travel, and war met and blended, the slow convergent evolution toward pastoral nomadism leaped forward suddenly into the full scope and range of the steppe society.

So far as the Inner Asian Frontier of China is concerned, it is all the more to be noted that this rapid maturing of steppe nomadism did not lead at once to attempts of the nomads to conquer China. Even Ssu-ma Ch'ien, who undoubtedly regarded the Hsiungnu as a plague, does not ascribe to them the fall of the Ch'in dynasty. He plainly says that it was when Ch'in had fallen and the Chinese

---

out it. See Arendt, Sur l'apparition de l'étrier chez les Scythes, 1939. According to Griaznov and Golomshtok (*op. cit.*, p. 37), the "reindeer type" saddles of Pazyryk, of about the first century B.C., did not have stirrups. The true Mongol saddle, so short between pommel and cantle that it forces the rider to sit askew, is an archer's saddle; it facilitates shooting to the side and rear.

[54] Hence the attempt to convert even a decadent steppe nomadism into modern "ranching" has a distorting social effect. See Lattimore, The Eclipse of Inner Mongolian Nationalism, 1936.

[55] Creel, *op. cit.*, p. 188, citing Andersson, Children of the Yellow Earth, 1934, p. 243.

fought among themselves that the Hsiungnu were able to encroach along the borders.[56] He describes Modun as a formidable conqueror in the steppe, but treats him only as a raider of the Chinese Frontier who did not invade deeply or even aim at conquest.

More than that, the importance of Modun was not that he was able to take and hold any important part of China but that Chinese generals on the Frontier, when pressed too hard by the central power that was essential in a solid empire, were able to go over to the Hsiungnu. This is why Ssu-ma Ch'ien introduces the Hsiungnu, with a sketch of their historical background. It was the point at issue when the founder of the Han dynasty, having already won control of the strategic regions in China, found himself constrained to begin fighting the Hsiungnu in B.C. 201,[57] as is convincingly apparent when these wars are listed all together—as by Ssu-ma Ch'ien in his chapter on the Hsiungnu, or in the similar chapter of the *Han History*—and not separated by other matter as they necessarily are in the annals of emperors in the *Han History*.[58]

Accordingly, it is not surprising to find that the great soldier and administrator who reunited China under the Han dynasty had no ambition to conquer the Hsiungnu. Instead, he made treaties with Modun,[59] even treaties of marriage, and granted a subsidy of silks, wine, grain and food—a subsidy which it would not be hard to describe as tribute, or a kind of danegeld. It was already apparent that the kind of state power most stable in China was bound to overreach itself if any attempt were made to expand into the terrain held by the nomads. The problem at issue was not, as yet, either one of Chinese empire over the steppe or steppe conquest and empire in China: it was one of controlling the relations between Hsiungnu and

[56] Shih Chi, Ch. 110.
[57] *Ibid.*
[58] Compare Dubs, *op. cit.*, especially pp. 115-117, 128-129.
[59] Shih Chi, Ch. 110; Ch'ien-Han Shu, Ch. 94; first section.

Chinese. To the extent that the central power of the Chinese Empire could hold its Frontier satraps under control, the unity of the nomads was conditioned by the necessity of dealing, whether in trade or in war, with Chinese officials who were agents obeying one command. To the extent that Chinese wardens of the marches when controlled too strictly by the central government were likely to go over to the Hsiungnu, trade and war were likely to be combined as raiding and blackmail.

Out of this never perfectly stabilized balance there was to grow, in time, an in-between, border world of the Inner Asian Frontier itself—a world permeated by the influences of both China and the steppe but never permanently mastered by either.[60] Because of this, in turn, the border became a factor both in the cycles of tribal agglomeration and dispersal in the steppe and in the cycles of dynastic rise and fall in China. The people of the steppe could never wholly master China, because those who entered China permanently became Chinese, while those who remained behind continued to adhere to the life of the steppe. Similarly, Chinese who ventured too far into the steppe were drawn away from China and went over to the society of the steppe, while those who remained in China continued to develop and accentuate the characteristics of Chinese life. Only between them, in the marginal terrain where both kinds of life could survive without wholly losing their integrity, did both influences overlap. Consequently, it was the mixed culture of the steppe margin that had the widest reach both back into China and back into the steppe.[61]

[60] Compare Lattimore, Mongols of the Chinese Border, 1938.
[61] See Chapter XVI, below.

CHAPTER XV

THE FACTOR OF RANGE: OASIS HISTORY AND GREAT WALL HISTORY

CONTRAST BETWEEN CHINESE EXPANSION TO THE SOUTH AND ON THE INNER ASIAN FRONTIERS

During the Han period [1] the full geographical scope of Chinese history was determined, though it was not until the T'ang [2] or even the Sung [3] period that the society and culture of the Chinese as a whole grew to final maturity. The character of this maturity was influenced in important ways by the earlier delimitation of the geographical field of Chinese history, but the geographical range within which the Chinese were able to operate had in a general way been predetermined at a still earlier date by the characteristics of Chinese agriculture. These characteristics had begun to form as early as the neolithic period and had formed as they did largely in adaptation to a relatively limited environment in the Yellow River valley.

Spreading from the Yellow River valley, the Chinese found that the conditions of the Yangtze valley enhanced a number of trends toward the intensification of agriculture and the specialization of society that were already inherent in the Yellow River culture. The scope of Chinese expansion toward the south was thus marked out, although the exact limits of growth were far from being

[1] Earlier or Western Han, B.C. 206 to A.D. 8; interregnum of Wang Mang, A.D. 9-22; Later or Eastern Han, 23-220.

[2] 618-906; second great period of Chinese expansion into Inner Asia.

[3] 960-1126; 1127-1278. The first period is that of the Northern Sung, during which North China was partly conquered first by the Khitans, who founded the Liao dynasty of 907-1119, and then by the Jurchids or Juchen, who founded the Chin dynasty of 1115-1234. The second period is that of the Southern Sung, during which the whole of China was gradually conquered by the Mongols, who founded the Yüan dynasty of 1260-1367.

exactly set; provinces like Kuangsi, Kueichou, and Yünnan have not even yet been fully occupied by the Chinese.
In their advance to the south, however, the Chinese had
only to master problems of magnitude—the scale of
transport, the reach of administration, the adjustment of
the imperial superstructure to the provincial and regional
substructure.

As they spread northward and began to approach the
steppe, on the other hand, they encountered problems of
a different order. Here successful adaptation to the environment required a reversal of tendencies that were already at work. Southward spread did not set up any conflict between the colonizing margin of advance and the
solid core of China. Expansion to the north did set up
a conflict because if carried too far it began to create at
the margin a different kind of society. The state itself,
being a product of those tendencies and processes of
growth that were most typically and essentially Chinese,
had therefore a constant—though not always dominant—
reason to restrain its borderers from venturing into the
steppe.[4]

Between the true steppe environment and the true Chinese environment there lay a debatable margin. The
hither side of this margin could be successfully occupied
and bound to China; here the advance of the Chinese resulted, other things being equal, in an accretion. The far
side, on the other hand, gravitated away from China and
toward the steppe. There was accordingly a border—a
Frontier—determined by a complex balance of cultural,
economic, social, and military factors which Chinese in-

[4] Thus in B.C. 68 the Shanyü or Khan of the Hsiungnu died. For several
years the Hsiungnu had been defeated in one campaign after another, not
only by the Chinese but by steppe tribes. The Tingling and Ch'engjo (or
Shengjo) harried them from the north, the Wuhuan from the east, and the
Wusun from the west. It is said that they lost 30 per cent of their population and 50 per cent of their livestock. Yet the Chinese did not take advantage of this to extend their imperial control. Instead, they "abandoned
the outer walls [north of the main Great Wall], in order to relieve the
people [of taxes and forced services]" (Ch'ien-Han Shu, Ch. 94, first section).

dividuals and communities could not cross without passing beyond the influence of China and becoming influenced by the steppe.[5] The Great Wall may therefore be described as an effort on the part of the state to fix this Frontier and to limit the proper field of Chinese activity as well as to exclude the peoples of the steppe.

Along the Great Wall the Chinese had to deal with conditions that retarded the kind of evolution inherent in their already well-defined culture and society and in this way limited the extent of territory that they could occupy. The powers of growth generated out of their "cellular" structure of rural communities grouped about walled cities worked slowly and cast forward on the front of advance only a weak fringe of adventurers, traders, and pioneers. Between the relatively impenetrable steppe on the north and the "colonizable" reaches of the south, which could be penetrated but not very rapidly, the outward spread of the Chinese was less important than the phenomena of proliferation and elaboration within the older terrain that most favored their ways of life. Here the roots of the Chinese culture struck deeper and deeper and its upper foliage grew more dense and intricate.

A distinction must be made between the spread of a society into new territory and the outward reach of its

[5] In b.c. 33, at a time when the Hsiungnu were divided, the Khan of their southern tribes offered to make himself responsible for the western sector of the Great Wall. A counsellor of the Chinese emperor gave a number of reasons for not allowing this: the marginal territory just north of the Great Wall contained wood from which the nomads made bows and arrows, while the northern steppe had less grass and wood and more sand; many of the people along the border, under Chinese rule, were of Hsiungnu origin and might return to their old allegiance; the Chinese had encroached on and abused the Tibetan border nomads (in the course of the Han expansion into Central Asia), and a Chinese withdrawal would lead to fighting; the descendants of those who had accompanied the Chinese troops in occupying the Frontier were poor and destitute and might go over to the nomads; the slaves of the border population were discontented, and having heard of the happier life of the nomads might run away to join them; escaping criminals would also have a refuge. This one passage reveals a number of gradations between the kind of territory and population that represented an accretion to China and the kind that tended to gravitate toward the steppe (Ch'ien-Han Shu, Ch. 94, second section).

political power into territory that it does not actually occupy. To the south, as the Chinese expanded, the wilderness of mountains and subtropical jungle was converted
into a Chinese landscape of closely settled valleys, terraced and irrigated ricefields, and walled cities. The Chinese themselves multiplied, and the conversion into Chinese
of some of the barbarians they encountered was historically much more significant than the killing off of those
barbarians who resisted or the successful retreat of those
barbarians who withdrew into more inaccessible terrain.
For the very reason that the land became Chinese and the
society continued to be Chinese the political recoil along
this front of advance was never of great importance.

On the steppe Frontier there was an entirely different
equation of advance and recoil. Here the main body of
the Chinese could not advance intact. The land and the
climate constrained those who moved out too far in advance of the main body to become more and more a different kind of people. A political conflict resulted between society and geography. Of itself the environment
encouraged a fusion between the typical Chinese way of
life and the typical steppe way of life, but in proportion
as the main body of steppe society and the main body of
society in China developed their own characteristic and
specialized political structures they became antagonistic to
each other. Each kind of political power demanded uniformity and homogeneity in the society on which it was
based, and therefore both the main society of the steppe
and the main society of China resisted and attempted to
subordinate the aberrent, compromise forms of society
that tended to arise in the margin between them.

IMPOSSIBILITY OF A RIGID FRONTIER

Out of this there grew an unending struggle. The interest of the state in China favored a rigid Frontier, to include all that was truly and properly Chinese and exclude

whatever could not be fitted to the Chinese norm. The Great Wall itself was the grand expression of this idea. Yet the fact that the marginal Frontier terrain and the main steppe beyond it were of little interest to China as a whole, and certainly not essential to growth and evolution within China, could not override the inherent tendency of the marginal terrain to create a marginal society. Moreover, the outlying Chinese had an interest in trading and dealing with the marginal society, and the marginal society projected this interest by further trade and contact with the main steppe. Then again, the fact that the steppe was not suitable for occupation by unmodified Chinese communities did not prevent a part at least of the surplus population from attempting to adapt itself to steppe life, whatever the policy of the state might be.

For all these reasons the Great Wall idea of a rigid, absolute Frontier could never be more than approximately carried out in practice. Since the formation of marginal groups could not be entirely prevented, the groups themselves had at least to be brought under control; and since intercourse could not be cut off altogether it had to be made as far as possible tributary to China, instead of being allowed to drain wealth and strength away from China. In this way the forces of expansion, which in the south satisfied themselves by a gradual enlargement of territory, became translated in the north into forces of imperial conquest, control, and manipulation. In the steppe the influence of China became a matter of range—the amount and kind of surplus power that China could mobilize, the depth to which it could penetrate an un-Chinese terrain, and the extent to which it could conquer, or administer, or indirectly control societies that could not be converted to the Chinese norm.[6]

However powerful the Chinese might be at any given time, they could not, in dealing with the steppe people,

[6] Lattimore, Origins of the Great Wall, 1937.

use their power in a normal Chinese way. The result was that state policy worked changes both among those to whom it was applied and among those who applied it. A corollary, in other words, of the power that China was able to radiate outward was the reflection of this power back on to China. In the first place, those Chinese who acted as agents of empire along the Frontier acquired, by the use of the power vested in them, stature and influence within China itself. In the second place, the tribes of the steppe margin, acting sometimes as political and military auxiliaries of China and sometimes as auxiliaries of the main steppe tribes, alternated between radiating Chinese pressure outward and transmitting steppe pressure inward. In the third place, the outer steppe tribes, defeated by the Chinese in some campaigns but victorious in other campaigns, were themselves able to generate a surplus of "imperial" power which could at times drive far into China.

Such was the frame within which worked the processes of history on the steppe Frontier, once the expanding Chinese had deployed fully along the edge of the steppe and once the Great Wall had been linked together as a single system. While this phase of the Chinese advance was being completed the main steppe itself had been entered by groups of people who had originally kept close to one or another of the margins of the steppe. They had now become true nomads, able to move freely in any direction and for great distances and so to establish a steppe world as large in geographical sweep, though not so thickly inhabited, as the world of China. While the technique, the economy, and the social structure of the true or main steppe life derived from diverse origins in marginal oasis and forest zones on other sides of the steppe, as well as from the tribes that had been barbarians on the fringe of the early Chinese culture, the attainment of a certain level of maturity by the Chinese culture had been a necessary antecedent to the creation of a political life embracing the whole steppe. It was when the Chinese occupied the Great Wall Frontier solidly enough to jolt loose tribes that had been clinging to the marginal terrain that mere wandering in the farther steppe was given a political orientation. From this time on the Great Wall, which for the Chinese was a periphery, became for all Inner Asia a focus.

From this time on, accordingly, the Inner Asian Frontier of China must be looked at as closely from the side of Inner Asia as from the side of China. Two kinds of primary force acted upon this Frontier. The economic, social, and cultural power of the Chinese themselves, as well as their political energy, radiated beyond their own containing Great Wall into the steppe. From the other side the steppe society, having now developed independent potentialities of its own, began also to exercise an imperial range of power, asserting itself against that of the Chinese. From the friction of these primary forces, furthermore, were generated secondary forces that modified and made more complicated the interaction of the primary forces.

China and the Steppe Reach Political Maturity

The Han dynasty, founded in B.C. 202, lasted until A.D. 220, with an interregnum from A.D. 9 to 22 under the usurper Wang Mang. The period before Wang Mang is known as the Western or Earlier Han, the period after the usurpation as the Eastern or Later Han. Under the Earlier Han the main characteristics of "Great Wall" history were worked out to such an extent that they furnish guiding principles for the study of the whole subsequent history of China and Inner Asia down to the nineteenth century, when the rise of industrialism in Europe and America attained such a vigor that a new kind of imperialism spread all over the world and gave a new bias to the affairs of the Far East. It is therefore especially important to analyze the kind of change that took effect under the Earlier Han. The scope of Chinese history was now so wide that it ranged over the whole of China, or almost the whole of it; even beyond the Yangtze the future was already, so to speak, mortgaged to the Chinese.

A corollary of this change from the history of separate Chinese kingdoms to the history of the Chinese Empire was the maturing of steppe history to a point where it was no longer concerned simply with the fortunes of small tribes hanging at the fringe of Chinese expansion but spread out to fill the steppe environment as a whole. The Chinese may from this time be called a separate order of mankind, and so may the people of the steppe. There was a norm, so to speak, of Chinese history to which all parts of China corresponded more or less closely, so that every important change or evolution spread out over the whole of China. There was a corresponding norm of steppe history affecting all the peoples of the steppe, even when they were not politically united in major confederations of tribes. From this there arises a further corollary: although China was, up to a point, a separate world, what affected China as a whole governed the relation of the Chinese world to the steppe world. In the same way, what affected the steppe world of Inner Asia as a whole governed the relation of the world beyond the Great Wall to the world within the Great Wall.

Liu Pang, founder of the Han Empire, died in B.C. 195.[7] Modun, lord of the steppe empire of the Hsiungnu, died in B.C. 174.[8] In this period the Hsiungnu were pressing inward on China. In B.C. 140 began the reign of the greatest of the early Han emperors, known under the dynastic style of Wu Ti, the Martial Emperor. He died

[7] For the annals of his reign, see Dubs, History of the Former Han Dynasty, 1938.
[8] The accounts of his career are in Shih Chi, Ch. 110; Ch'ien-Han Shu, Ch. 94, first section.

in B.C. 87. Under Wu Ti the political power of China was expanded enormously: a Central Asian colonial empire was created, some of the Hsiungnu tribes became Chinese allies and auxiliaries, and the main body of the Hsiungnu were held back at a distance in Outer Mongolia. At about the same time the tribes of the western steppe, in Central Asia west of Outer Mongolia, and the tribes of the eastern steppe, partly in Outer Mongolia and partly in Manchuria, rose in importance.[9] They dealt independently both with the Hsiungnu and with the Chinese, but this did not result in permanent stabilization or a secure Chinese "outer empire" over the steppe. Sometimes these tribes fought against the Hsiungnu, either in purely tribal wars or in alliance with the Chinese; but they also fought against the Chinese. Even the fact that under Wu Ti the Chinese built up a relatively strong "colonial-imperial" position in South Manchuria and Korea,[10] corresponding to their hold over Central Asia, did not enable them to project a strong control into the main steppe.

EARLY HAN POLICY AIMED TO PREVENT DEFECTION OF CHINESE LEADERS ALONG THE BORDER

Superficially, it appears as though the depth of Chinese penetration into Central Asia and the degree of nomad pressure on the Great Wall Frontier depended on nothing more than the alternating appearance of "strong" emperors, generals, and khans among the Chinese and among the nomads. This is misleading, because there is enough material in the Chinese records to show that in both China and Inner Asia important changes were going on. New kinds of power were being discovered and tested, and the shape of empire was not governed entirely by the separate evolution of the Chinese and Inner Asian so-

[9] Shih Chi, Ch. 123; Ch'ien-Han Shu, Ch. 96, first and second sections.
[10] Shih Chi, Ch. 115; Ch'ien-Han Shu, Ch. 95.

cieties but by interaction between the two. Only after examining both the separate orders of Inner Asian and Chinese life and their effect on each other is it possible to discern what the courses of evolution were and why they never resulted in a firm weaving together of Chinese and Inner Asian history as one fabric.

Under Modun the Hsiungnu attacked different parts of the Great Wall Frontier and recovered the Ordos,[11] which Ch'in Shih-huang-ti had attempted to bring under permanent Chinese administration.[12] Obviously these were successes that must have reinforced the centralized military control of the great Hsiungnu khan. Less obvious, but equally important, is the fact that these encroachments had a more than local effect. Although the Han Empire was only just being consolidated, the question of the total balance of power between China and the steppe was already at issue. What mattered was no longer whether tribesmen or Chinese occupied a particular sector of marginal terrain adjacent to the Great Wall, but whether the local "important people" and other "important people" near them, with whom they were in touch, were to look toward the steppe or toward China for command and confirmation of their status and rule. There was already a norm of characteristic steppe life and a norm of characteristic Chinese life, but neither steppe pastoralism nor Chinese agriculture could entirely prevent devolution away from the norm in the marginal terrain at the edge of the steppe, where neither pastoralism nor agriculture was imperative but both were optional.

When the conflict between Hsiungnu Empire and Chinese Empire in the time of Modun is examined from this point of view, it becomes apparent that the early Han wars along the Frontier were fought not so much against the Hsiungnu as against the "Wardens of the Marches"

[11] Shih Chi, Ch. 110; Ch'ien-Han Shu, Ch. 94, first section.
[12] Shih Chi, Ch. 88 (biography of Meng T'ien), in addition to Ch. 110.

—the Frontier commanders who were historical descendants of the border campaigners of the old northern Chinese feudal states. Whether the Hsiungnu themselves occupied a little more territory or a little less meant neither disaster nor success for the Han Empire; but since the Han Empire stood for centralization and integration within China, the ability of a border commander to refuse imperial orders and to go over to the Hsiungnu, if pressed too hard, raised issues that were dangerous in the extreme. Such defections might spread and result in a general disintegration of the empire. The urgent preoccupation of Liu Pang was the establishment of his imperial and supreme authority within China. There was no pressing need to enlarge the territory of China, or even to defend such a marginal, outlying territory as the Ordos. Liu Pang could easily have let the Hsiungnu take even more, had that been all.

The whole aspect of China at this time shows that this must have been true; and if it was true, then the reason that compelled Liu Pang to turn aside from the interior of China and engage in major Frontier campaigns, when the empire had not yet been set in order, must have been the imperative necessity for preventing Chinese generals from defying the imperial power and setting up border states capable of resisting imperial control by appealing to the Hsiungnu. This reasoning is conclusively proved by the facts of Liu Pang's Frontier campaigns. In B.C. 201 the Hsiungnu "besieged" the Chinese general who held the northwestern part of what is now Shansi. This general had been a companion of Liu Pang in the wars leading to the creation of the new Chinese Empire. Yet he "surrendered" to the Hsiungnu. Liu Pang immediately and in person took the field and attacked this general, who "fled to the Hsiungnu." [13]

[13] Dubs, *op. cit.*, p. 116; Ch'ien-Han Shu, Ch. 1, second section; Shih Chi, biography of Han Wang Hsin in Ch. 93, see also Ch. 110; Ch'ien-Han Shu,

From this it is clear that the Hsiungnu had not themselves occupied the territory. What made the territory important was the defection of a Chinese general. Furthermore, this general and his friends did not act as if they were being rescued from temporary submission to the Hsiungnu; they collected troops, set up under a puppet king a "kingdom" that suited their purpose of the moment, and leagued themselves with the Hsiungnu to resist the emperor and his army.

That resistance to the emperor and the empire was the real political issue of the time, and not the invasion of the Hsiungnu as such, is confirmed by an incident of the following year, B.C. 200. The Hsiungnu attacked the ancient land of Tai in North Shansi; the ruler of this territory abandoned it and fled back to the emperor, in China. He was forgiven and made a marquis.[14] It could hardly be clearer that for the interest of the state in China it was more important that wardens of the northern marches should look to the emperor, be personally loyal to him, help him to keep unshaken control within the main territory of China and not depart from his orbit to become satellites of the Hsiungnu, than that they should successfully prevent the Hsiungnu from entering this or that sector of the Great Wall Frontier.

PURPOSE OF FRONTIER STATECRAFT TO HOLD FRONTIER POPULATIONS WITHIN THE CHINESE ORBIT

By working forward from this clarification of the kind of policy that was vital on the Frontier when the Han Empire was being set up and organized it is possible to follow up the trends created by such a policy. For the

biography of Han Wang Hsin in Ch. 33, see also Ch. 94, first section. Another companion of the founder of the Han dynasty who went over to the Hsiungnu was Lu Wan, whom he had made ruler of the border territory of Yen. His biography is in Ch. 34 of the Ch'ien-Han Shu. The descendants of both Han Wang Hsin and Lu Wan returned to their Chinese allegiance.
[14] Dubs, *op. cit.*, p. 117.

Han dynasty and every succeeding dynasty it was imperative that the working machinery of the empire should be centripetally balanced. The loss of a little territory near the steppe did not in itself throw the machinery of empire out of gear; neither did the winning of a little territory add to the vigor and soundness of the state. The governing consideration was that satraps of the Frontier should not initiate centrifugal processes, either by going over to the Hsiungnu or by setting up little border kingdoms. Escape from dynastic control meant that they could shake the principle of dynastic authority by negotiating with the Hsiungnu when it did not suit them to submit to the emperor.

Had the edge of the steppe been either a real desert or a "frontier of indefinite expansion," like the lands beyond the Yangtze, it would have been possible to order in a much more rigid way the principles of state inherent in the agricultural economy and society of China, which were already well on the way to becoming mature and decided in their characteristics. The trouble was that it was impossible either to cut off contact with an un-Chinese way of life beyond the Great Wall or to assimilate the people of the steppe to the steadily developing Chinese norm, as the trans-Yangtze barbarians could be assimilated. The edge of the steppe was not abrupt but shaded by an indefinite margin of debatable terrain, in which there worked spontaneously and in varying degrees both the tendency for some of the steppe tribes to evolve toward the Chinese norm and for some of the Chinese borderers to devolve away from the norm.

The people of the margin were governed by their own interests, which constantly suggested to them that they make use both of the Chinese technique of agriculture and the steppe technique of herding as far as each was profitable. In order to do so, however, they had to modify both the agriculture, making it less intensive and less Chinese, and the pastoralism, making it less extensive or mobile and therefore less nomadic. Now a semi-nomadic fringe was just as anomalous for the major nomadic society of the open steppe, just as much a departure from the norm, and just as disturbing to good order, as a semi-agricultural fringe was for the major society of Yellow River China. So far as trade and cultural exchange were concerned the people of the margin could deal profitably with both China and the steppe; but they could never attain to the stature of a separate people with an independent order of life, partly because the territory they occupied was not large enough and partly because the Chinese order and the steppe order were both already so well advanced that they cramped the marginal people between them. Consequently no truly integrated mixed culture of the margin ever matured, and the interests of the marginal people wavered century after century between gravitation toward the steppe and toward China.

This being so, it became the concern of Chinese Frontier statecraft to see that the population of the steppe Frontier, when it could not be fully assimilated to the Chinese norm, should at least be held within the Chinese orbit. The kind of society, the kind of wealth, the kind of power that recurrently tended to form along the line of the Great Wall were not essential to the well-being of China, but it was necessary to keep them oriented toward the Chinese center of gravity—if only to keep them from coalescing into centrifugal bodies. This could only be ensured by making it economically more profitable for the wealth of the Frontier to flow toward China than toward the steppe, and politically more profitable for those who controlled the power of the Frontier to look toward China than toward steppe chieftains and coalitions of steppe tribes.

From this a number of important conclusions are to be drawn. The idea of a stable and exact Frontier—a Great

Wall Frontier—was inherent in the structure of China as a whole. What could not be included must be excluded. In practice this idea could never be executed, and even the Great Wall could never be maintained as a more than approximate Frontier. In proportion as a mixed way of life had to be tolerated in any sector of the Frontier it created local standards of wealth and power which inevitably grew in potency and demanded more scope. In order to prevent the exponents and agents of the Frontier kind of power from either turning against China and encroaching on the major Chinese domain or turning away from China and toward the steppe—which came to much the same thing—thus reversing the centripetal flow of wealth and power, it was necessary to make local Frontier growth appear to be the instrument of an expansion generated within China. In point of fact, the expansion of the Chinese up to the steppe Frontier had of course grown outward from the heart of China, but attempts at penetrating the steppe itself were certainly stimulated more by new and partly anomalous developments at the periphery than by the normal growth of the main body of China. Naturally, the continued development of China as a whole did produce a surplus of power making for expansion; but the channels through which this power flowed, when it turned toward Inner Asia, were chiefly opened up by the forces that were at work along the Frontier itself, and this is one very important reason why Chinese "colonial" activity in Inner Asia has always been so different from the "colonizing" expansion beyond the Yangtze.

THE HAN AND THE HSIUNGNU

The ideas that have here been presented must be compared with the actual record of history. As the Han dynasty became secure within China the "pressure" of the Hsiungnu—that is to say, the defection to the Hsiungnu of Chinese border generals—became less immediately dangerous, but it did not cease. There is perhaps nothing more curious in the whole of Frontier history, both in Han and later times, than the "chronic" phenomenon of change of allegiance. Chinese generals went over to the barbarians even at times when the Chinese were winning victories, and nomads came over to the Chinese even when the forces of the steppe were on the whole ascendant.

In B.C. 140 there began the great period of Wu Ti, who reigned until B.C. 87. In this period the Chinese carried out an astonishingly deep and rapid penetration of the oasis world of Central Asia; and at the same time a number of Chinese generals campaigned successfully against the Hsiungnu, far out in the open steppe, with troops that matched the nomads in mobility and striking power. It is not at all surprising that many of these generals were bred in regions on or near the border.[15] It can be taken for granted that along the border a certain number of Chinese had acquired a tinge of the steppe way of life. Men who had herded sheep [16] and tended horses from boyhood, had grown up skilled in archery from horseback, and perhaps knew the Hsiungnu language, had a natural advantage. They knew how to fight the Hsiungnu and were familiar with the technique of leading troops out into the steppe, away from fixed bases, which favored their

[15] Li Kuang, the Chinese who more than any other could handle troops in the nomad manner, came from the Shensi-Kansu border and was famous for his use of the bow. His grandson, Li Ling, when in command of 5,000 foot archers from the Yangtze region, fought a skillful action in retreat but was captured by the Hsiungnu, who treated him with honor. (Biographies in Shih Chi, Ch. 109, and Ch'ien-Han Shu, Ch. 54.) (It was for defending the conduct of Li Ling that Ssu-ma Ch'ien, the great historian who compiled the Shih Chi, was castrated. See Ch'ien-Han Shu, loc. cit.; biography in Ch. 62.) Of other commanders, Kung-sun Ao came from the Shensi-Ninghsia border; Chao Shih-ch'i from Kansu, then a border territory; Kuo Ch'ang from North Shansi; Lu Po-te from Kansu; Li Hsi from North Shensi; Li Tsu from North Shansi. (Biographies in Shih Chi, Ch. 111, and Ch'ien-Han Shu, Ch. 55.)

[16] Wei Ch'ing, the greatest commander of "heavy" columns, had been a shepherd as a boy. His nephew, Huo Ch'ü-ping, was one of the most distinguished cavalry commanders. (Biographies in Shih Chi, loc. cit., and Ch'ien-Han Shu, loc. cit.)

success and promotion during a generation of warfare. It is not surprising that some of these generals were of partly barbarian origin, or were even barbarians who had taken service with the Chinese.[17] Whether such men enlisted with the Chinese or took the nomad side depended on the tide of the time.[18]

Much more important is the fact that there were so many of these campaigners. Evidently the sending of an expedition against the Hsiungnu did not depend on whether there happened to be a competent general in the imperial service. There was a whole class of such men. This can only mean that border and steppe warfare were characteristic manifestations of the time. The drive outward against the Hsiungnu cannot have been the product simply of forces of expansion generated in the heart of China. Forces inherent in the nature of the Frontier itself were drawing the periphery of China toward the steppe and compelling the main body of China to support the periphery.

[17] Kung-sun Ho was descended from the I-ch'ü, a tribe first mentioned on the steppe border of the kingdom of Ch'in at the time when true steppe nomadism was just beginning. Chao Hsin was a Hsiungnu who "surrendered" to the Chinese, or rather entered their service. Later he was defeated and captured by the Hsiungnu, and thenceforward served them. (Biographies in Shih Chi, loc. cit., and Ch'ien-Han Shu, loc. cit.)

[18] Chao P'o-nu (his personal name means "vanquisher of the Hsiungnu") was a man of Shansi who had once "deserted" to the Hsiungnu. Later he came back to serve with the Chinese armies. He commanded expeditions both to the oases and in the steppe. Eventually he was defeated and captured by the Hsiungnu. After living among them ten years, he "came over" to the Han once more. (Biography in Shih Chi, loc. cit., and Ch'ien-Han Shu, loc. cit.) Li Kuang-li, an even greater Chinese general, traversed the whole oasis region as far as Ta Wan (Ferghana region of Russian Turkistan). On his last campaign, in the open steppe, he was captured by the Hsiungnu, who were at first delighted and gave him high rank. This angered Wei Lü, an adviser who had long been influential among the Hsiung-nu. He started an intrigue which led to the butchering of Li Kuang-li as a human sacrifice. (Biography in Ch'ien-Han Shu, Ch. 61.) Wei Lü himself was a man of nomad extraction who served first with the Chinese and then with the Hsiungnu. (Biography in Ch'ien-Han Shu, Ch. 54, at end of biography of Li Kuang.) The names in this and the preceding list are only a selection. See also the chapters on the Hsiungnu wars, Shih Chi, Ch. 110, and Ch'ien-Han Shu, Ch. 94. There are also additional biographies of individuals in both the Shih Chi and the Ch'ien-Han Shu which I have not cited here.

Moreover, while barbarians and half-barbarians entered the service of the Chinese,[19] there were also Chinese who went over to the Hsiungnu; [20] and among them were some of the most brilliant commanders of imperial armies.[21] Whenever such a desertion is recorded in the Chinese annals it is attributed to fear of reprimand and disgrace after a defeat, fear of being accused by a rival at court, or some such thing. Jealousy at court and professional rivalry, however, could have had other results if the general conditions prevailing had not made it relatively easy for a proved commander to behave like a soldier of fortune, taking service according to the promise of reward—not for bribery but rather for a career.

These indications do not suggest that the Han Empire was "imperialistic." On the contrary, they agree with the trend of development in China as a whole during the Western Han period: in land tenure, the family system, taxation, and the way in which the state was administered, the changes attendant on the passing of feudalism were continuing to progress.[22] Undoubtedly these changes created in China a surplus of energy, and probably also a surplus of population; but there was enough new activity possible within the terrain congenial to the norm of Chinese

[19] Chin Mi-ti was the son of a prince or chief of a tribe on the Kansu border of the steppe that had wavered between allegiance to the Chinese and to the Hsiungnu. He rose high in the service of the Chinese, eventually becoming a regent of the empire. (Biography in Ch'ien-Han Shu, Ch. 68.) For other Hsiungnu, including men of the most noble blood, who intrigued with the Chinese or actually went over to them, see Shih Chi, Ch. 110, and Ch'ien-Han Shu, Ch. 94.

[20] Compare the preceding footnotes.

[21] For campaigns and embassies in general, see De Groot's posthumous Die Westlände Chinas in der vorchristlichen Zeit, ed. O. Franke, 1926. For cursive accounts, compare Wieger, Textes historiques, Vol. I, 1929, especially pp. 390-417, 487-490, 510-526, and Parker, A Thousand Years of the Tartars, 1895, 2nd edit., 1926; unfortunately, neither of these authors has any idea of history as a process of growth and transformation, and they rival each other in their purely anecdotal treatment of the succession of events.

[22] Franke, Geschichte des chinesischen Reiches, Vol. I, 1930, pp. 269 et sqq. A recent major work in Chinese is Wan Kuo-ting, Agrarian History of China, Vol. I, 1933; see review by C. M. Chang, 1935.

development to make it unnecessary to attempt a deliberate expansion into steppe territory uncongenial to the Chinese norm. Indeed, so far as the main body of China is concerned the trend of development must have favored the idea of a set and absolute Great Wall Frontier. In short, a comparison of China proper with the Frontier confirms the assumption that although the assertion of imperial power beyond the Frontier was able to draw on the growing strength of the main body of China, it was not the internal growth of China that prompted expansion but the nature of the local forces at work on the Frontier.

Furthermore—and I do not think that the significance of this has ever been pointed out before though the facts are well known—there was also a "norm" of steppe development. In the reign of Hsiao Wen (also known as Wen Ti, B.C. 179-157), a Chinese princess had been given in propitiatory marriage to the ruler of the Hsiungnu. With her, as escort, went a eunuch, a man born in the territory of the old border kingdom of Yen.[23] Because he had been sent against his will this eunuch declared that "he would yet become a calamity to Han"; he devoted himself to the interests of the Hsiungnu as against those of the Han dynasty. What the Chinese records describe as advice offered by him to the Hsiungnu, or as debates between him and envoys from the Han court, may of course be merely part of the conventional knowledge and views of the time. Nevertheless, this material makes it clear that there was a difference between life in the outer steppe, where tribal characteristics were normally dominant, and life along the Frontier, where the choice of ambitious and powerful men hesitated between alliance with the Hsiungnu and allegiance to China.

This eunuch rebuked the Hsiungnu ruler for coveting the silks of China and its foods. The Hsiungnu, he said, did not equal in numbers the population of one Chinese

[23] Shih Chi, Ch. 110; Ch'ien Han Shu, Ch. 94, first section.

prefecture, yet they were strong because they did not depend on China for clothing or food or other things. Now if the Khan were to change the customs of the Hsiungnu by creating a demand for Chinese products it would need only a fifth of the production of China to turn all of the Hsiungnu toward China—that is to say, to turn them away from their own ruler. Moreover, the silks obtained from China made clothes that were destroyed by galloping through the thorns of the steppe and were not equal to felts and skin clothing; and all the foods of China were not as convenient and satisfactory as milk and milk products. Similarly, in argument with envoys from China the eunuch maintained that the "barbarous" customs and social organization of the Hsiungnu were excellent for the purposes of the nomadic life and that this kind of life had its own validity and therefore could not simply be condemned as inferior to the life of China and savage by the standards of China.

It is not only the character of the steppe "norm" that is delineated in this account. Within its norm the steppe life produced the essentials of clothing and food—and, of course, housing; [24] and the combination of mobility and economic independence made the steppe society so formidable in war that the Hsiungnu could defy China and take the offensive against China whenever they wished, in spite of their conspicuously small numbers. (Incidentally, this disposes in an emphatic way of the common assumption that a nomad "horde" is a swarm of irresistible numbers.) The account also makes it clear that there was a danger to the form of authority based on the steppe norm, just as there was to Chinese authority, in compromise forms of society, economy, trade, and tribute, along the margin of the steppe and on the fringe of the steppe order.

Like the society of China, therefore, the society of the

[24] Lattimore, The Eclipse of Inner Mongolian Nationalism, 1936.

steppe engendered certain typical processes that made for
self-sufficiency and for complete severance between China
and the steppe. As from the society of China, however,
there sprang from it also peripheral activities and interests
that tended to confuse the less typical margin of the steppe
with the less typical margin of China. This created a zone
of uncertainty in which men could never see clearly
whether their interest lay with the steppe or with China.
Uncertainty at the margin, again, was affected by the relative stability and soundness, at the moment, of the steppe
order in the heart of the steppe and the Chinese order in
the heart of China.

Beginnings of Chinese Penetration of Central Asia

Comparison of the steppe norm, the Chinese norm, and
the Great Wall Frontier, along which each norm tended to
break down, provides a series of values by which it is possible to gauge the astonishing penetration of the Chinese
into Central Asia at this time. According to the Chinese
records this penetration began with the great journey of
Chang Ch'ien, an emissary of the Han emperor Wu Ti.
The journey began not long after B.C. 140, and is described as a calculated effort to get in touch with the Yüehchih.[25] This tribe, or people, to the west of the Hsiungnu,
had been defeated by the great Hsiungnu warrior Modun,
as already described. Part of the Yüehchih had migrated
farther to the west. The mission of Chang Ch'ien was to
persuade them to an alliance that would turn the flank of
the Hsiungnu and relieve pressure on China.

[25] Chang Ch'ien's biography is in Shih Chi, Ch. 111; Ch'ien-Han Shu, Ch.
61. See also the chapters on the Western Regions, Shih Chi, Ch. 123,
Ch'ien-Han Shu, Ch. 96; also De Groot, *op. cit.*, pp. 9 *et sqq.* There is a
strong tendency to treat Chang Ch'ien himself as a great romantic figure;
partly because of this, probably, his barbarian companion has been neglected,
but judging from the little recorded of him he seems to have been a striking
figure.

Since this is commonly treated as the beginning of a Chinese "conquest" in Central Asia it should be made quite clear that there was no conquest. Chang Ch'ien was almost certainly not venturing into an unknown world. He was accompanied by a man of nomad-barbarian extraction. The Chinese knew from the Hsiungnu that the Yüehchih were one of the most important of the Central Asian peoples; but they must have known also that there were other tribes, peoples, and regions that were within reach of China and not under Hsiungnu rule. In short, it is hard to suppose that the sending of Chang Ch'ien was just a sudden idea; it is far more likely that there was already a tendency for Chinese influence, especially in the form of trade, to spread out into the oases of what is now Chinese Turkistan, and that an effort was now made to see whether these vague connections could be profitably used against the Hsiungnu.

At the very beginning of his journey Chang Ch'ien was captured by the Hsiungnu. He lived among them for ten years or so, was given a wife, and must have become thoroughly acquainted with the affairs of the steppe. The light condition of his captivity eventually made it possible for him to escape and travel farther. He visited peoples and kingdoms in Russian and Chinese Turkistan but failed to conclude any alliances. On his way back to China he was again captured by the Hsiungnu but got away after a shorter captivity. In all his journey had lasted thirteen years. Only his wife and his original nomad companion got back to China with him, although he had set out with a train of more than one hundred people. He brought back information that indicated that there must be a trade route from Ssuch'uan into India and thence back into Central Asia, but the Chinese were not as yet able to open up direct communication by this route. His later service included campaigning in the eastern part of Inner Mongolia and another mission to Central Asia—this time to the

Wusun, in the northern part of what is now Chinese Turkistan.

UNDERLYING MOTIVES OF CHINESE PENETRATION OF CENTRAL ASIA

After the discoveries of Chang Ch'ien the Chinese began to spread their political influence through the oases of what is now Chinese Turkistan. It is easy to assume that the expansion was a result of the new knowledge acquired; that Chinese trade sought expanding markets to be reached by the "Silk Road" through Central Asia; that the vigor of the state demanded an external, "colonial" empire; that armies were sent out to conquer the new territories needed. The assumption is not warrantable.

In the first place, although Chinese forces did penetrate Central Asia to a remarkable depth, these exploits did not equal the impressive campaigns during the same period in the open steppe.[26] Chinese troops maneuvering in the steppe had to detach themselves from their bases in China and to match the nomads in mobility. Columns that marched through Central Asia had to negotiate stretches of poor and sometimes desert territory in which they could not secure provisions, and had therefore to make themselves competent in matters of transport; but nevertheless they campaigned from oasis to oasis, and as they found in each oasis agriculture and a settled population that could not well escape them they could reprovision themselves much as if they had been campaigning in China. War in the steppe required real technical virtuosity; war among the oases of Central Asia demanded only that the field

[26] An adequate military study of these wars has yet to be written. It is evident from the accounts of campaigns in the Shih Chi and Ch'ien-Han Shu, and also from the terminology (military ranks and kinds of troops), that the Chinese used heavy columns with cumbrous transport, light columns which were more mobile but worked usually in conjunction with the heavy columns, and also troops which we may call auxiliaries (probably mixed Chinese and nomad mercenaries), fighting in very much the nomad style. In addition there were border garrisons of regular troops, and border militia.

force be not too cumbrous to make long marches yet strong enough to overawe each oasis that it entered.[27]

In the second place, there can have been no trade expansion that was of major importance to the economy of China as a whole. There is probably not an oasis in Chinese Turkistan that ever had a population of more than about a million. In structure each oasis was a miniature China.[28] The basis of life was agriculture—an irrigated and therefore an intensive agriculture. While archeological discoveries have revealed that both at this time and later there were wealthy, luxurious, and sophisticated people in these oases, it is also clear beyond a doubt that the majority of the people were poor peasants whose purchasing power must have been very low, although the economy of which they were a part yielded rich taxes to the local rulers.

The basic products and commodities of these agricultural oases were like those of China; consequently there was no demand for exchange with China except in luxury goods that could stand a high cost of transport. For such goods there can have been no quantity demand in the sense of popular demand, although the trade may have been considerable at times when transport was relatively safe and the number of wealthy consumers relatively large. Trade in a commodity like silk, therefore, must not be estimated in terms of the possible percentage of China's annual silk production that could be "unloaded" on the Central Asian market or disposed of, through Central Asia, in the Near East and the Roman Empire, but only in terms of the value of silk as gifts or disguised subsidy to petty Central Asian kings and nobles; or in terms of the high profit to a few middlemen of dealing in such a luxury. This in turn means that the economic factor in

[27] Criminal exiles were conscripted for oasis campaigns and garrison duty but not for fighting in the steppe, or at least very rarely—a tacit comment on the quality of the men needed.

[28] See Chapter VI, above.

the relations between China and Central Asia must have worked chiefly through the "pull" of trans-Frontier caravan merchants and middlemen rather than through the "push" of an expanding silk production in the silk-growing regions of China.

It is true that there is an almost universal assumption among Western writers that the Chinese were interested in "keeping open the Silk Road"; that although the Chinese had only a vague knowledge of the remoter part of Central Asia it must have been important for them to maintain the export of silk. There is an old belief, which I have not been able to trace back to the Chinese records, that the knowledge of how to rear silkworms and make silk was kept secret so as to protect the Chinese monopoly. Probably this belief arose out of the very fact that it was not the Chinese themselves who promoted and handled the trade in silk. There was a demand from beyond China for the acquisition of silk but no pressure within China to increase the export. Consequently the traffic was mostly in the hands of Central Asian caravan traders and middlemen. It may even be that the primary export of silk arose out of gifts and subsidies, that bolts of silk thus became a standard of luxury value, that the rulers of little states who received silk as gifts and subsidy acquired an actual surplus, and that trade thus arose at a secondary level in order to dispose of the silk in more distant markets. Reaching eventually the hands of middlemen who did not know what its raw material was or how it was made, it created its own legend of a secret Chinese monopoly.

As a matter of fact it would have been impossible to guard such a secret, and probably the knowledge of how to breed silkworms actually spread into Central Asia very early though rather slowly. Stein found at Tunhuang silk damask woven with "Sassanian" patterns. He suggests three possible explanations: either silk was carried all the long way from China to Persia, woven there into fabric, and carried as far back as the borders of China; or the Chinese actually made up silks with "foreign" designs (as porcelain was later made for the European market); or else Khotan, "an early home of transplanted sericulture," was "the industrial center which, being in close touch with the Oxus regions and Iran, was able to turn out fine silk fabrics in a style closely approaching the 'Sassanian' patterns." [29] The last explanation is by far the most probable; the first two depend on the assumption, probably to a large degree unconscious, that the structure of Chinese economy in Han times, or at least in T'ang times, was of a kind that created within China itself a demand for the discovery of foreign trade outlets, and this is most improbable. Even as late as the nineteenth century the Chinese demand for foreign trade was inconsiderable and was either not encouraged or actively discouraged by the policy of the state.

In the third place, neither the state nor the dynasty needed a "colonial" empire. The court, it is true, was interested in luxuries like jade or horses of celebrated breed,[30] just as rulers and traders in Central Asia and even far beyond were interested in the silk of China. Nevertheless, the economic difficulties just mentioned made it impossible to wring "colonial" profit out of Central Asia on a national or even a dynastic scale. Although the figures given in the Chinese records are insufficient for computing the expense of the Central Asian campaigns, and although "visible" military expenditure must have been cut down by the commandeering of supplies and by the use of criminals as troops, the inability to trade in necessities and goods consumed in quantity must have

[29] Stein, Ruins of Desert Cathay, Vol. II, 1912, pp. 208-210.
[30] Such as the "blood-sweating" horses of Ta-Wan (the Ferghana region), (Ch'ien-Han Shu, Ch. 61). Compare Warner, The Long Old Road in China, 1926, for the explanation of this blood-sweating, which is caused by a parasite.

made the expense of "conquest" much greater than the profits.

Finally, there is direct evidence to show that the Chinese were not attempting conquest for the sake of conquest. Whenever the purposes of an expedition are stated in the chronicles, trade and the acquisition of luxuries appear to be of subordinate importance; and I do not believe that revenue is mentioned at all. Only two questions of policy are constant, and these are essentially aspects of the same policy—either the control of Central Asian oases and tribes in order to build up alliances against the nomads of the steppe, or the defensive occupation of oases that otherwise would be laid under tribute by the nomads and used by them as bases. Neither aspect of policy was best served by "conquest" as the term is commonly understood. The real need—and undoubtedly the real aim—of Chinese statecraft was to shape a situation in which the petty oasis rulers would find it more profitable to look to China for support than to submit as vassals to the nomads.

DIFFICULTIES OF CHINESE POSITION IN THE STEPPE MARGINS

All things considered, it seems that the Chinese did not launch themselves into Central Asia but were drawn into the land of the oases, just as they were drawn into distant steppe campaigns during the same period. Among the oases, as in the steppe, marginal terrains and populations upset the balance toward which trended the major characteristics of China. The Chinese campaigned in Central Asia at the same time that they struck most deeply into the steppe, and for the same reasons: the major and nuclear interests of China demanded a closed economy, a self-sufficient world and an absolute Frontier, but minor and peripheral interests raveled the edges of this ideal pattern and made it impossible ever to cut cleanly asunder the world of China and the world of Inner Asia.

By the same token, the Inner Asia of Chinese history can be divided into a land of oases and a land of pastoral nomadism. The differences between the two are significant.

Along that part of the Frontier that faced the main steppe of Mongolia there was a gradual and in many places uncertain transition from a first marginal zone which favored a mixed economy but permitted a relatively high proportion of "Chinese" factors. Here the population gravitated, on the whole, toward China, though at times when political disintegration in China coincided with po- litical integration in the steppe Chinese borderers might be drawn out of the orbit of China and into the orbit of nomad power. Beyond this lay a second marginal zone which also favored a mixed economy but permitted a higher proportion of "nomad" factors. Here the popula- tion gravitated normally toward the steppe; but again it might be detached from the steppe and drawn back toward China when the strength of the local factors was over- ridden during periods in which China as a whole was ascendant over the steppe as a whole. The two zones, each of which can be further subdivided, can to a large extent be distinguished by varying soil characteristics; the nature of the soil, in turn, being to some extent determined by rainfall, vegetation, and other factors of climate. North of the main line of the Great Wall a number of outlying walls and Frontier fortifications can be traced, and these coincide in a remarkable way with the edges of soil zones.[31]

Within these transitional zones the Chinese attempted by a number of methods to draw up a firm political front that would satisfactorily separate the agriculture of China from the nomadism of the steppe. Every method known from the later history of the Great Wall Frontier appears to have been tried in Han times.

Direct colonization by the settlement of Chinese farmers

[31] Thorp, Colonization Possibilities of Northwest China and Inner Mon- golia, 1935, p. 452; also Geography of the Soils of China, 1938, p. 118.

was pushed to an uneconomic extreme.[32] The costliness of
this method and its lack of success indicate that the
intention was to establish farming populations in territory
that would not in the ordinary way have been reached and
settled by Chinese, because poor environment and difficulties of transport did not suggest that normal Chinese communities could there survive or keep up a contact with the
main body of China close enough to ensure homogeneity.
The standard of colonization must therefore have been
political—the preventive occupation of territory that would
otherwise have been entered by the nomads and the maintenance there of communities fully Chinese in character—
because a mixed way of life, without state intervention and
support from China, was bound to become tributary to the
nomads and to strengthen them in further encroachment
on the fringe of China. This method failed as often as it
was tried, and was bound to fail, because the idea of an
agricultural economy costing the state more in investment

[32] Chu-Fu Yen, a counsellor of the great Wu Ti, criticized the settling of
Chinese in the Ordos. He said that Ch'in Shih-huang-ti himself had been
advised against sending Meng T'ien to occupy the Ordos. The Hsiungnu had
no cities to conquer; they were impossible to rule [in the Chinese manner].
The provisioning even of light troops to penetrate their territory deeply was
difficult; their land was unprofitable. When Meng T'ien nevertheless was
despatched to the Ordos the land proved to be marshy and salt, unfit for
cultivation. The Chinese losses were immense. Grain had to be transported
all the way up the Yellow River from Shantung at such cost that very little
of it arrived. The colonists could not grow enough to clothe or feed themselves. The resulting discontent was the beginning of the downfall of the
Ch'in dynasty. Now, under the Han, the Hsiungnu campaigns were ex-
hausting the treasury. Defection of border settlers and troops to the enemy
was easy. Yet the same counsellor later completely reversed his position,
recommending occupation of the "fertile" Ordos as the solution of the Hsiungnu problem, though he was opposed by other ministers. Wieger (*op. cit.*,
p. 393) therefore treats him contemptuously as a shallow politician. He misses
the point that these policies also concerned internal problems of the size of
the landholdings of great lords and the limitation of their power. The true
explanation seems to be that the remnants of Chinese feudalism were considerable, that the continuing destruction of these remnants was producing a surplus of manpower, and that steppe campaigns and colonization,
though expensive, helped to get rid of the surplus and were less expensive
than the defection of Chinese border generals when Chinese policy was not
"strong." See the biographies of Kung-sun Hung and Chu-fu Yen, in Shih
Chi, Ch. 112, and Ch'ien-Han Shu, Ch. 58 and Ch. 64, first section.

and maintenance than it could possibly return in revenue was a perversion of the whole order of the state and society in China.

Chinese policy therefore was driven to compromise, although it was admitted, or virtually admitted, even by those who recommended compromise, that the real problems were being evaded and that no permanent solution was possible.[33] Either border Chinese were allowed to fend for themselves and given only such government support as was absolutely necessary, or barbarians were taken under Chinese "protection" and encouraged to make themselves as Chinese as they could. Each of these methods defeated itself. In proportion as the support of the state was withdrawn the Chinese of the border could only survive by adapting themselves to local conditions in such a way that they became partly barbarian in character and interest. When this adaptation had gone far enough it became doubtful whether a man were more barbarian or more Chinese; it became as easy for him to enter the nomad orbit as to stay in the Chinese orbit, and his allegiance might shift under the influence of a comparatively slight change in the total balance between China and the steppe. As for the barbarian who abandoned part of his nomad heritage in order to adhere to the Chinese edge of the marginal terrain, he might easily revert to the steppe unless his allegiance were made profitable. The change from receipt of subsidy to demand for blackmail was dangerously easy.

Given a series of zones and populations, all of them transitional between the full Chinese order and the full steppe order but transitional in varying degrees of admixture, it is obvious that there was no form of conquest that could settle the matter. Neither in the marginal terrain

---

[33] Compare the recurrent debate—whether to fight the Hsiungnu or negotiate with them (chiefly by marriage alliances, in which the valuable "gifts" were those given by the Chinese). A good example is in the biography of Han An-kuo, Shih Chi, Ch. 108; Ch'ien-Han Shu, Ch. 52.

nor in the steppe itself, nor yet beyond the steppe, was there anything upon which the edge of Chinese expansion could rest with certainty. More than that, the greater the depth to which Chinese forces advanced the less those very forces could be depended on to uphold the interests of China. In order to campaign at long range and to fight the people of the steppe successfully Chinese troops had to learn how to live and survive in the steppe. They themselves thus acquired some of the techniques and characteristics essential to the life of pastoral nomadism, while their commanders learned how to use a kind of power that was like that of steppe chieftains. This was true not only in the actual conduct of campaigns but in the administration of border territories between campaigns—the replenishment of supplies and the supervising of relations between Chinese troops and the tribal auxiliaries who served with them.

In the Chinese armies prolonged warfare developed both troops and commanders whose very success made their position equivocal: they came to realize that it was their own power that held the balance between China and the steppe and that they could, if they chose and if it suited their interest, change the balance by electing to identify themselves with the steppe edge of the marginal terrain instead of with the Chinese or Great Wall edge. Conversely, the appearance of peace could only be preserved between wars by accommodating a fringe of nomad auxiliaries and their chiefs on the far side of the territory held and directly administered by the Chinese. Unless they were accommodated by trade as well as by subsidies and titles it was more profitable for these chiefs and their warriors to relapse into raiding. If they were accommodated, then the chiefs of farther outlying tribes would adhere to and deepen the fringe, requesting similar treatment, and in this way the buffer of Chinese garrisons and nomad auxiliaries would again weld itself into a powerful mixed society, demanding ever more lavish privileges and subsidies under the threat of allying itself with the independent tribes of the steppe.

THE CHINESE POSITION IN THE OASES

Where the oases differed from the steppe was more in the firmness of the positions that could be won and held than in the depth to which a single campaign could penetrate. The oases of Chinese Turkistan were already at this time what they have ever since remained—centers of a prosperous, intensive, irrigated agriculture. For this reason, the fact that their populations differed from the Chinese in physical appearance and language was not so important as the fact that their economy and social structure were essentially "Chinese" in structure. In order to reach the distant oases a Chinese army had to be more mobile and self-contained than an army operating in China, but once it had reached an oasis it found ready prepared a base that was like a fragment of familiar China set down in an alien wilderness. The advance of the Chinese into Central Asia, therefore, did not "fray out" like the repeated but inconclusive advances into the steppe; it fetched up against a number of relatively firm points. Although they were outposts at a great distance from the main body of China, the garrisons could remain Chinese in character; they did not have to alter both their way of fighting and their way of living, as did troops campaigning in the steppe. Thus a stable occupation could be based on the oases if other conditions were favorable.

These "other conditions" must be examined. To begin with, there is the difference between the marginal terrain along that part of the Great Wall that faces the Mongolian steppe and along that part that faces toward the Central Asian oases. Where it divides China from Mongolia the Great Wall allots to China most of the terrain in which the old Chinese way of life has always had the advantage over steppe nomadism. Some of the terrain included requires a thinning out and weakening of the characteristic Chinese agriculture, but it is north of the Wall that most of the debatable terrain lies. Toward Central Asia, on the other hand, the Great Wall actually encloses great stretches of marginal or debatable terrain. Here, in the modern provinces of Ninghsia and Kansu, the landscape is one of "semi-oases" [34]—patches of land that can be irrigated for intensive agriculture separated by stretches of land that permit extensive agriculture but encourage herding and therefore a considerable devolution from the Chinese norm Inner Mongolia—the approach to the main steppe of Outer Mongolia—lies beyond the Wall, but "Inner Central Asia" is on the hither side.[35] Immediately beyond the Wall begin the most pronounced deserts, and in them lie the most sharply isolated oases.

Presumably the irrigable, oasis-like patches in Kansu and Ninghsia account for this difference. These areas were naturally homogeneous with China, and consequently their attachment to China depended less on the raising of the quality of China's economy and culture than it did on the growth of China in mass and scale. Once China had become a sufficiently large, cohesive body these peripheral areas naturally gravitated toward it. Difficulties of transport, exchange, and trade, it is true, because of the poor and "un-Chinese" land separating the semi-oases, made the separatism of this northwestern territory even more pronounced than the regionalism of the main body of China; but never quite to the point of destroying cohesion with China. Hence the curious aspect of Kansu and Ninghsia in later centuries, with their contrasts of incongruity and congruity.[36] There the defiant separatism of Islam, which has never become Chinese as Indian Bud-

[34] Compare Chapter VI, above.
[35] Lattimore, Chinese Turkistan, 1933.
[36] Lattimore, Kimono and Turban, 1938.

dhism did, and which repeatedly turns to political organization and military action, is offset by the stubborn persistence of a way of life that is more Chinese than Moslem. Perhaps most important of all is the ascendancy of the Chinese language. Only a few of the more remote Moslem communities continue to speak Turkish, and this probably means that the majority, who speak Chinese, also in many ways think like Chinese in spite of their tenacious Moslem separatism.

CHINESE VERSUS NOMADIC INFLUENCE IN THE OASES

The difference between Kansu and Ninghsia within the Great Wall and Chinese Turkistan beyond the Wall can be stated in terms of distance and mass. In the nearer territory the mass of China is close enough to dominate each oasis-like area separately, in spite of the way in which these areas are more or less isolated from one other. In Chinese Turkistan the potency of China is diminished by the greater distance, with the result that the influence of China over any one oasis has historically tended to be less important than the separateness of each oasis from other similar oases. Consequently, the tone or norm of history in the oasis world has always been set by the degree of development within each oasis and the degree of separation between oases.

A further distinction must be made between oases divided from each other by deserts and oases divided—or perhaps it would be better to say connected—by steppe.[37] Between steppe-connected oases grazing—and consequently the migration of pastoral nomads—is possible, and such oases can therefore be not only penetrated but permeated by the influence of nomad tribes. Between desert-divided oases travel is possible but not migration, and therefore the nomads, whenever they conquered such oases, con-

[37] Compare Chapter VI, above.

quered them much as the Chinese did—by sending expeditions. Neither nomads nor Chinese could surround such oases with their own life.

The steppe-connected oases lie in Jungaria, the northern part of Chinese Turkistan, easily entered from the main steppes of Mongolia, Russian Turkistan, and Siberia. They were thus affected by the proximity and mass of the steppe and steppe society, much as the region of Kansu and Ninghsia was affected by its proximity to the Chinese orbit. The desert-divided oases, distributed in an oval around the Taklamakan in the southern part of Chinese Turkistan, can accordingly be best described in terms of their relative inaccessibility both from the steppe and from China. They could only be reached by expeditions and held by garrisons; they could not be occupied by a spreading out of the edge of either the steppe society or the society of China.

In one respect, however, Chinese forces that penetrated to these desert-divided oases had the advantage over nomad forces. They had necessarily to act as detached outposts at a precarious distance from the main body. Yet they could at least remain garrisons of a Chinese kind. Except in scale of area and size of population, and except for its isolation, each oasis was like an administrative unit or garrison post in China. The occupations of the people were familiar to the garrison troops, and so was the relation of the walled city of the oasis to the circumjacent rural area. This familiarity of life and habit was more important than the unfamiliarity of speech or costume. Even if the local garrison and its commander became integrated with the local population and its rulers in such a manner as to form a little satrapy no longer entirely subservient to the imperial policy of the distant Chinese court but able to assert its local interest and to establish some degree of autonomy, the result was no more than an extreme example of the kind of regionalism typical of China itself. The nature of the local economy remained what it had always been, and the values and sanctions of the local society, though changed in political orientation, were changed without strain or distortion.

On the other hand, nomads who first spread to the steppe-connected oases and then penetrated to the desert-divided oases underwent a progressive "denomadizing" transformation. In the northern oases, at the edge of the steppe, nomad migrations and conquests undoubtedly flooded over the oasis agriculture and society from time to time, perhaps even obliterating them for longer or shorter intervals.[38] Nevertheless, the tendency to revive agriculture in the areas that favored it could not be destroyed.[39] The rulers of the nomads derived their power from certain aspects of the nomad society—above all, from its mobility. Yet they were tempted to use this power to make themselves overlords of oases that yielded them a rich and easy revenue, in spite of the fact that they thus limited their mobility and damaged the structure of their own power. In this way there was perpetuated a conflict within the nomad society itself.[40]

Whenever nomads pushed on from the steppe oases to the desert oases this kind of distortion became more acute. By thus going beyond the environment that favored their kind of society the nomads created for themselves exactly the kind of problem that the Chinese encountered whenever they ventured too far into the steppe. Those of the

[38] Lattimore, Chinese Turkistan, 1933.
[39] This was true under the Mongol Empire of the thirteenth century. Ch'ang Ch'un, in the year 1221, mentions agriculture near Dalai Nor in Inner Mongolia (Bretschneider, Mediaeval Researches, Vol. I, 1888, p. 48, n. 114); Ch'ang Te, in 1259, mentions Chinese engaged in agriculture in the Altai region (ibid., p. 124, n. 311). Marco Polo describes the mixed herding and agriculture of the Kueihua-Inner Mongolia region (Yule, Marco Polo, Vol. I, 1921). Probably "patronized" agriculture here and there in the steppe region reached its maximum in the 'fourteenth century.
[40] That the old Central Asian oases, under the Mongol conquest, everywhere remained agricultural and were not converted to a pastoral economy is evident from the narratives of all the travelers of the time.

nomads who held the advanced positions were forced by the way they lived—by such elementary things as the kind of food they ate and the way they got it—to devolve away from the norm of pastoral nomadism. The chiefs especially were affected. Those who attached themselves to steppe oases began to exercise in a novel way the power based originally on unhampered mobility, but those who went on as far as the desert oases found themselves before long more or less completely detached from the steppe and forced to rely on a new kind of power.

For the steppe nomad society as a whole this meant that somewhere between the steppe oases and the desert oases there was a line, or perhaps rather a zone, of diminishing returns. At the near edge of the zone there was distortion of the steppe way of life; at the far edge, distortion passed over into transformation and diminishing returns into severance from the nomadic way of life, determining a range beyond which the power of a nomad society could not be permanently maintained.

Now the society of the oases themselves was an atomic society. The nature of the oasis environment is that it creates a relatively dense population in a relatively small area, surrounded either by a desert in which there are almost no people or by a steppe in which there are only thinly scattered nomads. The populations of oases within the same general area tend to be homogeneous with each other, but not amalgamated. Partly because they tend in the nature of things to be self-sufficient and partly because the scale on·which they can develop does not permit them a wide outward reach, it is difficult to erect a pyramid of political unity on the basis of their homogeneity.[41]

The collective history of the oases of Chinese Turkistan has therefore tended always to be governed by the depth to which one major society or another could penetrate the oasis area as a whole and the range at which an overlord

[41] Lattimore, Chinese Turkistan, 1933; see also Chapter VI, above.

power could operate successfully in linking the oases, one by one, to itself and to each other. Given the difference in degree of isolation between steppe oasis and desert oasis, this has meant that as units the oases have had a local history of their own but that collectively they have wavered between the orbit of the steppe and the orbit of China, with minor influences penetrating to them also through the difficult mountain approaches from India, Iran, and Tibet.[42]

FLUCTUATIONS IN THE BALANCE OF POWER ON THE FRONTIER

Politically, the Chinese of Han times described their first great advance into Central Asia—an advance renewed with especial vigor in later Han times, in the period of the T'ang dynasty (from 618 to 906), and under the Manchu dynasty of 1644-1911—as an effort to "cut off the right arm of the nomads." [43] The reference is partly to the danger that the nomads of the open steppe might reach across Ninghsia and Kansu to link up with the nomads of the Tibetan plateau, partly to the hope of turning the nomads who were associated with the steppe oases against the nomads of the main steppe.

To this contemporary explanation there must be added other reasons, drawn from a study of the societies of China, the steppe, and the oases themselves. To a certain extent peripheral groups of both Chinese and nomads were drawn toward and into both the oasis region and the steppe region.

---

[42] Duman, in his Agrarian Policy of the Ch'ing Government in Sinkiang, 1936 (in Russian), carefully documents the way in which landownership and political control changed hands during one protracted period of three-cornered rivalry between the local oasis rulers, the outgoing "steppe" overlordship of the Western Mongols, and the incoming "agricultural" (and bureaucratic) overlordship of the Manchus and Chinese. Compare review by Lattimore, 1939.

[43] This expression is used in the account of the second mission of Chang Ch'ien to the Wusun tribe (approximately in the Ili region, on the north side of the T'ien Shan), Ch'ien-Han Shu, Ch. 61. Since the nomads faced south to the Great Wall, their "right arm" was on the west.

To a certain extent vigorous growth at one period or another impelled the main body of either China or the steppe society to attempt the penetration of the oasis region adjacent to one sector of the Frontier or the marginal zones lying between the main steppe and the rest of the Frontier. In such periods the drive outward from the center reinforced the more or less permanent attraction from the periphery, but in other periods the interests of the periphery and the main body worked against each other.

Depth of penetration varied according to whether the periphery and the major part of the society were working together or against each other, but in either case the mere fact of expansion or penetration created its own consequences. The major consequence was a devolution away from the norm of the expanding society, and this was equally true for the Chinese and for the peoples of the steppe. Either society encountered, sooner or later, a zone of diminishing returns. Had the mean line of diminishing returns been the same for both societies the result might have been stabilization, with some peripheral areas or zones remaining permanently within the orbit of the steppe and others within the sphere of influence of China. The line varied, however, in terms of both time and space, and consequently it is clearer and historically more significant to speak of zones than of a mean line. Even within a zone that predominantly favored either the nomads or the Chinese the front of occupation and the phase of advance or retreat varied. A period of vigor and ascendancy might carry the outposts of one society into terrain that ordinarily did not favor it. A period of weakness might constrain the outposts to withdraw from territory that had long been held with comparative ease. Moreover, these fluctuations were accompanied by changes in the composition and aspect of the Frontier society, in the degree to which nomads adhered to the Chinese or Chinese went over to the nomads. Changes of this kind, again, might precede and partly cause the variation in depth of territory occupied, or follow as a consequence of retreat or advance. Finally, the shifting of the perpetually sensitive balance might begin either with a change along the periphery, which drew to itself the strength of the main body, or with an accretion of strength in the main body, enabling it to reinforce and push forward its outposts.

For the study of any period of Great Wall or Inner Asian Frontier history it is therefore necessary to examine the proportions and significance of each one of a number of varying elements of pattern or composition. First, there is the norm and stage of development of society in China and in the steppe. Second, there is the tension, the degree of balance or unbalance, between the periphery and the center of gravity in each major society. Third, there is the compound structure of the mixed societies ancillary to the normal societies of China and of the steppe—the difference of proportion from zone to zone and the degree of poise or of inclination to gravitate in one direction or the other. The distribution of emphasis as between front and flank must be included in this third aspect, taking as front the debatable terrain of Inner Mongolia lying between the main steppe and the main bulk of agricultural China, and as flank the steppe oases and desert oases of Chinese Turkistan. The range at which China could operate effectively against the nomads—or the nomads against China —in any selected period of history was a resultant or function of the balance between all these factors.

In the Han period the Hsiungnu nomads raided far into China while the Chinese, in turn, campaigned at even greater distances in the steppe. These may be described as frontal or Great Wall wars. Sometimes coinciding with these frontal wars and sometimes alternating with them were campaigns and expeditions on the flank, among the oases of Chinese Turkistan. Here the advantage wavered as between the steppe oases, to which the nomads had the best approach, and the desert oases, to which the Chinese had a better approach. When the Chinese had the upper hand their influence among the tribes that adhered partly to the steppe oases and partly to the unbroken steppe resulted in a wide unsettling of tribal allegiances and in wars between different groups of the nomads. During one of these periods, in the first century after Christ, some of the Hsiungnu tribes left the main body and migrated westward, and it is an old belief that this may indicate a link between the Hsiungnu of Chinese history and the Huns of late Roman history. While this cannot be proved one way or the other, there is another inference that is quite clear and more important: migration and conquest in the open steppe could be set in motion by disturbing the poise of tribes which did not themselves belong to the norm of steppe life but to its periphery.

Conversely, the Chinese created for themselves the problem of a Tibetan Frontier when they advanced into Central Asia, cutting or impeding communication between the tribes of the steppe-like Tibetan highlands and the typical Mongolian steppe. It seems probable that this promoted the formation of border Tibetan groups, because in the Tsaidam and Kokonor highlands there was not a rich enough range of pasture to support a major, independent nomad society. Having access both to the oasis-like areas on the fringe of Kansu and to the southern desert oases of Chinese Turkistan, these border Tibetans were especially difficult to control. They could be enlisted as auxiliaries but they could also raid the Chinese corridor of communication with Central Asia, or threaten to ally themselves with Hsiungnu raiders from Mongolia. To conquer them was both difficult, because of the mountainous approach to the Tibetan plateau, and expensive, because the territory to be reached was not worth occupation by the Chinese.

Conquest and expansion, in short, were illusory. There was no kind of success to be attained by either nomads or Chinese that did not create its own reaction. When too wide a margin of mixed societies was brought under Chinese control the "absoluteness" of the Great Wall Frontier was not made sharper. On the contrary, the deep fringe of partly un-Chinese people thus acquired set up a kind of infection among the border Chinese. At the same time the "nomad problem" was not settled, for the most characteristic nomads living in the most typical steppe were driven back on the essentials of the pastoral nomadic life and compressed into a smaller but more resistant nucleus holding exactly the kind of territory in which it was most easy for them to defy the Chinese. Analagous problems were created for the nomads by the "denomadizing" of their society when they pressed too far inward into China or the oases of Central Asia. The eternal fluctuation thus engendered suggests that somewhere between the most characteristic landscape of the steppe and the walled towns and watered fields of the typical or normal Chinese agriculture lie the secrets of migration and conquest along the Inner Asian Frontier.

CHAPTER XVI

MARGINAL SOCIETIES: CONQUEST AND MIGRATION

FAILURE OF SOCIETIES OF CHINA AND OF THE STEPPE TO FUSE

Once the Inner Asian Frontier had been demarcated, in the course of the Ch'in and Han wars, it became a constant factor in the history not only of China but of the deep steppe, with its fringes of arable terrain, desert, rich oases, and forest, stretching away from the comparatively clear horizon of the Great Wall into the vague hinterlands of Tibet, Central Asia, and Siberia. The societies of China and the steppe each attained a norm that was well understood by the people adhering to it; but the value and authority of each norm was weakened by a periphery of compromise and devolution away from the nuclear, characteristic order of society. Even the Great Wall itself, the symbol of the cleavage between the two norms, to the maintenance of which blood and wealth were sacrificed for century after century, was therefore only a standard of reference. No linear Frontier between China and Inner Asia could be permanently held and kept clean and clear by either the pastoral society of the steppe or the agricultural society of China. In practice, the front on which met the two major orders of society, and the numerous minor, satellite societies that oscillated between them, always broadened into a series of zones of impact and recoil, conquest and counter conquest, assertion and compromise.

Something inherent in the society of China and something cardinal to the nature of steppe society prevented the fusion of the two in a compound, integrated order of extensive and intensive economy, dispersed and concentrated society. Neither could hold away from the other, and yet neither could absorb or even permanently subdue the other. Hence for about two thousand years, from the time of the Earlier Han to the middle of the nineteenth century, the combined history of Inner Asia and China can be described in terms of two cycles, distinct from each other as patterns but always interacting on each other as historical processes—the cycle of tribal dispersion and unification in the steppe and the cycle of dynastic integration and collapse in China.

It is the penetration of all Asia by the European and American industrialized order of society that is putting an end to the secular ebb and flow by making possible—indeed, imperative—a new general integration. This consummation is being deferred, partly by inertia and partly by active resistance within the old orders, and again partly by conflict between the collectivized industrialism of the Soviet Union penetrating Inner Asia from the hinterland and the industrialism of private initiative and profit deriving from the capitalist world and penetrating China from the seacoast. It is being deferred, but it is inevitable.

The failure to evolve industrialism, then, is the key to the ebb-and-flow history of the Inner Asian Frontier of China. Was this failure separately inherent in the Chinese order of life and the steppe order, or did it have something to do with their interaction on each other? The more accurately this question is answered the better it will be possible to understand not only the history of the past but the problems of the present in China and Inner Asia. This is a negative statement of the problem, but it can be made positive by reviewing the discussion of the way in which the societies of China and the steppe became differentiated from each other, and linking it up with the earlier discussion of the historical characteristics of the main regions of

China itself, and of Manchuria, Mongolia, Chinese Turkistan, and Tibet.[1]

VARIATIONS OF NOMAD SOCIETY:
MOBILITY AND WAR

It is easy to assume that in the history of steppe nomadism there was a single dominant factor—the "real"
nomads, living an unmodified pastoral life, affected very
little or not at all by trade, and not ruling over settled
subject peoples. It is easy to suppose that migration and
conquest were supplementary aspects of this way of life—
that leaders of bands of such nomads fought each other
over pasture rights; that out of such fighting there arose
intermittently a supreme warrior who united all the nomads. This is as much as to state that unity, among the
nomads, depended only on leadership, and that attacks of
the nomads on settled peoples depended only on the ambition of such leaders—except when "changes of climate"
forced "hordes" of savages to erupt from the steppe. A
part of this view of nomadic history is the assumption that
each period of unity was followed either by the "absorption" of the nomads among the settled people whom they
conquered or the dispersal of the tribes when a supreme
leader divided among a number of sons the tribes and
territories he had ruled.

These are oversimplifications. The truth is, as I believe
has been adequately made clear in the preceding discussion, that the relatively "pure" forms of nomadic society
are not the point of departure of nomadic activity but that
on the contrary they represent an extreme phase, an extreme point attained in a process that fluctuated over a
wide range of variation. The "original" nomads were
people of mixed economy and culture. They were not even

---

[1] See the earlier chapters dealing with these regions, especially that on
Mongolia.

a single people. Some of them entered the steppe from the edge of agricultural China, others from the edges of the Central Asian oases and the fringes of the Siberian and Manchurian forests.

The solidity, the mass and homogeneity of China, spreading up to and creating the Great Wall Frontier, imparted a special and very strong bias to the political history of Inner Asia as a whole. Nevertheless, there was also a far side of Inner Asia opening into Siberia, Russia, and the Middle East, and although I have not been able to treat this far side in detail I must not ignore its importance. The persistence among the Inner Asian peoples of the Turco-Mongol-Tungusic languages is one very significant indication that the groups that entered the steppe after being "shaken loose" from the Great Wall Frontier were by the conditions of the steppe life severed completely from China—in everything except politics. Any "old-Chinese" or "proto-Chinese" dialects that may have been brought into the steppe from China failed to survive among the non-Chinese Ural-Altaic languages that spread into the land of the nomads from the far side.

Since the nomadism of nomads was not the point of departure of their evolution but an extreme form attained in the course of their history, and since the real points of departure were in a number of mixed groups at different sides of the steppe, it seems necessary first of all to deal with the mobility of the nomad society. To do so raises at once the problem of the difference between migration as a technique of using the resources of the steppe in order to keep alive, and conquest as a particular application of mobility not to the routine of keeping alive but to the political uses of exacting service and tribute both from peoples of the steppe and from peoples outside the steppe. The problem can also be posed in another way: which generated more ferment and impulse toward change, the steppe life itself as practiced in the typical steppe environment, or friction at the edge of the steppe, where mobile people encountered landfast people?

A rational consideration of the characteristics of nomad pastoralism should make it apparent at once that war is no more and no less a "necessary" concomitant of nomadism than it is of settled agriculture. Each kind of society keeps the peace, when it is living at peace, because it recognizes a code. Each code, when it breaks down in war, breaks down because growth and change—which may have been slow or sudden in coming to a head—have so strained the old sanctions that they no longer work, and because within the society different groups have different ideas about the new sanctions that ought to be accepted and codified. This reasoning leads to the corollary that war is likely to break out first at the margins of a society and to begin with those classes that are least "typical" or "normal." What is accepted as normal and typical is likely to be a vested interest of that part of the society that grew up with and is identified with "the old order." Extreme disturbances of the social order, such as war, are therefore still more likely to begin where the fringes of different kinds of society overlap each other.

When this logic is applied to the history of nomads it becomes evident that there is also a time factor to be considered. If true steppe nomadism evolved out of non-typical, semi-nomadic societies at the edges of the steppe, then the first groups that moved out to follow a strictly steppe manner of life must have represented a new order, not an old one, and must have been in more or less violent reaction against the original mixed culture which for them represented "the old order." Only after their pastoral way of life had made itself entirely independent of agriculture and had become securely established in the kind of geographical environment that best suited it, did it in turn become "an old order." This represented attainment of what I have called the extreme phase. Thereafter, any reverse movement of groups around the margin of the steppe toward either oasis agriculture or Chinese agriculture meant a devolution from the extreme phase and a challenge to what had now become "the old order" in the main expanse of the steppe.

The inference is clear: migrations of the kind that led to war over wide areas, and to invasions and conquests, probably did not begin normally with well-established nomad groups that had been practicing the strict pastoral mode of life—especially if they had been practicing it for some time—in regions that did not encourage experiments with agriculture. They were much more likely to begin either with groups that broke away from mixed cultures in order to create a true nomadism, or with groups that broke away from strict nomadism in order to revert toward a mixed way of life.

Given a code or norm of steppe society, the appropriation of pastures by a mobile people was not necessarily any more a "cause" of war than the exercise and transfer of landownership in settled societies. Nevertheless, war was a concomitant of the nomad way of life. It was an intermittent phenomenon of the process by which a strong chief gathered clans and tribes under his personal rule and protection, dividing them again later between a number of his heirs. In the course of such wars there must necessarily have been much changing of pastures occupied, as well as of political allegiance; but something more than this is needed to account for the way in which the social mobility of migration interacted with the political mobility of war and conquest.

The truth is that even such terms as "true," or "strict," or "normal" nomadism are too broad. Pastoral nomadism as a whole, being based on the principle of extensive economy with a thin dispersion of the pastoral people, does constitute an extreme departure from the intensive economy and close concentration of an agricultural people, especially a people whose agriculture is further intensified by irrigation. Within the "extreme" of nomadism, however, there are differences of extremity. In a herding economy cut off entirely from agriculture and with trade reduced to a minimum—especially trade between nomads and non-nomads—there are still relative differences of extensivity.

Camels, cattle, horses, goats, and sheep require different degrees of dispersal. They flourish on different kinds of pasture. There is an infinite range of relative advantage in combining the ownership of different kinds of herds and the use of their products. Each possible combination requires a corresponding adjustment of the pastures and orbit of annual migration claimed by a tribe. The degree to which hunting is practiced as an auxiliary economy introduces another variable, and this again requires differentiation between steppe hunting and forest hunting, and between hunting for food and "useful" clothing and hunting for "luxury" products used mostly for tribute or trade. (The high-priced furs come mostly from the forest, not the steppe, while forest tribes are naturally poor in the ownership of horses, which give power in war, and are also dispersed in even smaller groups than the steppe nomads because of their manner of living; hence the recurrent subjection of forest tribes to steppe tribes.) [2]

Finally, for the ruler of a steppe people there is the delicate problem of balance between wealth in revenue and advantage in war. The sheep is the most useful provider

[2] For the fur tribute exacted from hunting nomads, compare the earlier references to Koz'min, Kabo, and Baddeley (see Bibliography). As the fur tribute became commercialized it led to a curious phenomenon: each pelt became a token, often costing the hunter more than its "market" value, because it was the symbol of a certain amount of effort demanded from him. The good pelts were privately appropriated by the officials in charge of the fur tribute and poor pelts were substituted for delivery to the court. Thus the good pelts cost the appropriator nothing, while an unnatural demand for poor pelts was created. The cost fell on the hunters, who were forced to slaughter immature animals, thus diminishing the permanent supply, so that each year they had to wander farther and work harder.

of food, clothing, housing (felts), and fuel (dung).[3] The camel provides transport, especially for long journeys across poor country. The horse is formidable in war but economically of minor importance. To control firmly and profitably the rule of both sheep herders and horse herders —let alone wider combinations of camel herders, forest hunters, cattle herders, yak herders (in the Altai), and so on—has always meant for steppe chieftains a fluid adjustment of method, year by year and occasion by occasion, in a manner that could not possibly become stable or permanent.

For these reasons it is not too much to say that a "pure" or "strict" steppe nomadism at any period of which we have any knowledge must have been more theoretical than actual; that the attainment of the "extreme" of nomadism must always have been only approximate. Only when broadly regarded as a technique of living in the steppe, capable potentially of doing without either agriculture or trade, can nomadism be considered homogeneous and consistent. On more narrow examination and by the test of practice it becomes evident that steppe nomadism is really compounded of a number of related and more or less consistent, but by no means identical, techniques. There was inherent within steppe nomadism as a whole a variability and instability that recurrently led it back from the more extreme phases that it attained—back toward the edge of the steppe and the mixed cultures in which it had originated.

Geographically, the steppe was not divided into obvious compartments of which each favored one of the kinds of nomadism—that of the horse, that of the sheep, and so on. To a very large extent the different kinds of environment interpenetrated each other. Consequently, no major political power could be founded in the steppe without linking together several kinds of pastoral nomadism. Once com-

[3] Lattimore, The Eclipse of Inner Mongolian Nationalism, 1936.

promise had been admitted to this extent it was impossible not to go further. The power of a tribe or group of tribes, if it grew at all, was bound sooner or later to acquire a fringe that was not wholly nomadic but only semi-nomadic. Nor was this fringe acquired only by conquest on the margins of the steppe. It has regularly been the practice of steppe rulers also to draw foreign trade [4] into the steppe itself, and even to build in the steppe permanent cities, and to import farmers and settle them in oasis-like tracts that permitted or favored agriculture.[5] This was only a logical extension of the practice of combined control over different kinds of nomads.

THE CYCLE OF NOMAD RULE

Certain characteristics of the structure of nomad political power can therefore be readily discerned. In the first place, rule over nomads alone produced a surplus of sheep, horses, wool, and so forth that could readily be used in trade—although trade was not imperatively necessary. Similarly, the command of a large number of mounted warriors did not make war inevitable but might well suggest, from time to time, that war could be made profitable. In the second place, trade between different kinds of nomads could easily be regulated, but trade between the nomads as a whole and non-nomad communities of a differ-

---

[4] See the Bibliography for such travelers as Rubruck, Carpine, and Marco Polo, all of whom take the activity of traders as a matter of course. Bret-schneider (Mediaeval Researches, Vol. I, 1910, p. 269), Barthold (Turkestan, 1928, p. 414), and Vladimirtsov (Social Structure of the Mongols, 1934, p. 35), all mention the Moslem trader, Hasan, who travelled to the far northeast of Mongolia with 1,000 sheep and a white camel to trade for sables and squirrel skins. He there encountered Chingghis, whose service he then or later entered; this was in 1203, before the greatest conquests of Chingghis. The ultimate source of this reference is the "Secret History" (see Palladius, p. 46 of the reprint edition of 1910, in Russian).

[5] Koz'min, On the Question of Turco-Mongol Feudalism, 1934, pp. 38-44 (in Russian), with specially interesting references to the Minusinsk region of Siberia and to Urianghai (Tannu-Tuva); also Lattimore, Caravan Routes of Inner Asia, 1928; A Ruined Nestorian City in Inner Mongolia, 1934; and Mongols of the Chinese Border, 1938.

ent order in the oases of Turkistan or in China raised at
once the question of who should control the trade and
appropriate the major profits.[6] This must repeatedly have
suggested the use of nomad military power first to govern
the profits of trade with non-nomads and then to exact
tribute.

Out of these processes there arose a second stage of
nomad rule—the use of nomad warriors to maintain a
mixed state, drawing tribute and revenue from non-nomad
subjects engaged in agriculture, trade, and handicrafts.
The subject people were normally of two kinds : those who
lived in non-nomad regions conquered by the nomads and
those who had been imported into the steppe to serve the
nomads. To these two categories there corresponded two
categories of the nomads themselves: those who garrisoned subject territory beyond the true steppe and those
who remained in the steppe but were entitled to a share of
subsidy and privilege.

By such an extension of the compromises that were
inherent even within groupings of simple nomads the factors of instability were gravely accentuated. A third stage
followed, of which the characteristic phenomenon was the
conflict between the different interests of the ruler.[7] With
what was his power chiefly concerned—revenue or war?
And again, which of his nomad subjects were the more
important—those who garrisoned possessions beyond the
steppe or those who remained within the steppe? Those
of the nomads who continued to live the steppe life were
important as a military reserve; but they themselves produced little revenue, and any revenue diverted to them in
subsidy reduced the amount that could be used for the

---

[6] Goods that had been acquired in the first place as tribute from the subjects of a nomad ruler had a special importance in trade. See Koz'min, The
Khakas, 1925, p. 6 (in Russian); cited in Kabo, Studies in the History and
Economy of Tuva, 1934, p. 52 (in Russian).
[7] Compare Chapter IV, above.

luxury of the court and granted in rewards to the ministers who "produced" revenue by governing dependencies. On the other hand, those of the nomads who were allotted to garrison duty became "denomadized" by the third or even the second generation. They lost the mobility and the other usages of nomad life that had made them effective as warriors in the first place. Yet it was they who occupied the richest sources of revenue. Consequently, they were able to divert and consume more of the revenue than those who remained in the steppe, even though, as soldiers, they rapidly became worthless as compared with the unmodified steppe people.

Such conditions brought on a fourth and final stage. The ruler whose grandfather or great-grandfather had commanded troops in person now appealed to a tradition or sanction of command but was no longer capable of exercising it. Of the nobles under him some were still chiefs of tribes but had little influence at court, others held tribal titles but had really become townsmen or landlords. In other words, those on whom conquest had originally been founded had become victims of their own empire, while those who had become most like the conquered people had most of the privileges of empire. When this difference between real wealth and nominal power on the one side and real or potential power and relative poverty on the other side had become intolerable, there began a breakup of the composite state and a "return to nomadism"—politically—among the outlying nomads.

Generally speaking, such periods appear to begin with trouble at the top of the social structure rather than at its base, although the real cause is usually the exhaustion of the sources of revenue at the base. Quarrels—which may arise out of disputes over the division of the declining revenue—break out between factions. This leads to appeals for support and consequently to a sharp emphasis on the differences between the groups that compose the state. The social structure then begins to split at its base and to break up into its component parts.

Here the special characteristics of nomadism once more become evident. As war continues, and especially if it is prolonged, the nomads begin to make use of their mobility —some of them at least can get away. Migration in the sense of movement within an orbit of summer and winter pastures can be converted into migration to entirely new pastures. By sloughing off trade and other nonessentials a part at least of the nomad society can seek the least accessible part of the steppe and there escape wars that concern the political fusion of different orders of society. In so doing those who escape make it clear that nomad mobility has two aspects—the limited range of normal movement and the unlimited range of potential movement.[8] They also make it clear that it is the poor nomad who is the pure nomad: [9] by stripping themselves of the accessories and luxuries that a prosperous nomadism acquires they establish afresh the possibility of survival under strictly steppe conditions, and even in the harshest parts of the steppe, and thus attain once more the extreme phase of departure from the edge of the steppe. It is obvious that this means also a return to the starting point of a new cycle of the variations of steppe history.

Among the people at the edge of the steppe, in such periods, there are other important phenomena. Those who are most purely agricultural, most landfast, are least able to escape the border warfare between different orders of economy and society. Those who are already of mixed culture—who have a partly pastoral economy but one which is not nomadic—can actually convert themselves into nomads. They are most likely to do so if the warfare

---

[8] "The essential thing [about nomads] is not that they *do* move, but that they *can* move" (Lattimore, Caravan Routes of Inner Asia, 1928, p. 519).
[9] Lattimore, The Geographical Factor in Mongol History, 1938, p. 15.

is long continued. If they do so, and depart into the steppe, they can actually repeat the history of the creation or evolution of steppe nomadism, and thereby reinforce the stock of the steppe nomad society.

THE HSIUNGNU HISTORY AS AN EXAMPLE OF A COMPLETE NOMAD CYCLE

Consequently, it can be said that while the strict or extreme phases of steppe nomadism are, so to speak, the determinant of steppe history, life at the edge of the steppe is probably a more dynamic factor in migration and conquest. Major groupings of different kinds of nomads, even if all of them are "true" nomads, require compromise and an unstable adjustment. It is when compromise and adjustment are extended to the margins of the steppe, however, to include semi-nomadic and even non-nomadic peoples, that instability is likely to lead to catastrophe and to the most urgent migration. It is what happens at the edge of the steppe, in fact, that is likely to produce the widest movement within the steppe and the strictest forms of steppe nomadism; but at the same time the extreme phases of steppe life are in themselves a determinant because they provide an escape from fusion at the edge of the steppe and an alternative to permanent integration of the mixed way of life.

Naturally I have here been speaking in the most general terms. Reference to the whole historical scope of the Inner Asian Frontier of China would show the extraordinary range of particular variation within these general characteristics. Here I shall cite only Ssu-ma Ch'ien's account of the Hsiungnu in the second century B.C., the *locus classicus* for early Chinese knowledge of the details that distinguish true nomads from semi-nomads.[10] Ssu-ma Ch'ien says quite definitely that the Hsiungnu "have each their own territory, [within which] they move and migrate,

[10] Shih Chi, Ch. 110; compare also Ch'ien-Han Shu, Ch. 94.

following water and grass." Modun, their *shanyü* or supreme khan, established a "court" which was probably in the northern part of Shansi. The commentaries point out that the word used does not necessarily mean a city; but nevertheless it is clear that the result of unifying the nomads was a tendency to set up a permanent capital. Certainly the later Hsiungnu khans had a capital that was undoubtedly a city, though built far out in the steppe and probably a poor city as compared with the great towns of China.

Furthermore, in describing the tribal wars that led to the unification of the steppe tribes Ssu-ma Ch'ien attributes to Modun the statement that "land is the root of a nation," although the land in question—for the title to which Modun fought the Tunghu or eastern steppe tribes— is described as uninhabited. This part of Ssu-ma Ch'ien's account was very probably taken direct from the tradition current among the Hsiungnu, and it states that the Hsiungnu and the Tunghu "each dwelt on their own side" of the disputed territory "as an *ou-t'ou.*" The word *ou-t'ou* is plainly a Chinese transcription of a Hsiungnu word, and it seems almost certain that this is the word that survives in the Mongol language as *otog.*

Vladimirtsov [11] relates this term to the ancient Sogdian *otak,* meaning "country, territory." Sogdian was an Iranian language not related to the Ural-Altaic languages, but various forms of the word *otog* are met with in Turkish, Mongol, and Tungus dialects with the meaning of "place, territory," and so forth, including the meanings of "hut" and "station." This wide distribution confirms the ancientness of the word. Now the Chinese commentaries on the *Shih Chi* also interpret the *ou-t'o* not only as "a place name," but as "earthen buildings for spying on the Chinese," "caves in the earth," and "signal mounds." [12]   It

[11] Vladimirtsov, *op. cit.,* p. 133 and notes 2 and 3.
[12] Shih Chi, Ch. 110.

would be rash to build too much on the interpretation of a single word, but it seems at least open to conjecture that this nomad war may have been fought not merely for a tract of pasture (which in any case is described in the text as "abandoned" or unoccupied) but also for the control of a garrisoned frontier.

At any rate, the victory of the Hsiungnu over the Tunghu on the east was immediately followed by a successful attack on the Yüehchih to the west, and also by the subjection of nomad tribes far out in the steppe (the Tingling, for instance, were even then probably on the boundary of Chinese and Russian Turkistan), and by encroachment on the Inner Asian Frontier of China. The control of a congeries of "true" nomad tribes, and probably also of semi-nomads, was followed by the setting up of a state ruled by nomads but including subject peoples of mixed culture and even of non-nomad culture.

Almost at the same moment that they appear in history as the major nomad power, therefore, the Hsiungnu are described as drawing in on China. This must be compared with the apparent suddenness of their rise, which I attributed in an earlier chapter to the fact that "true" steppe nomadism originated in the departure of semi-nomads from the edge of the steppe into the full steppe, whence they appeared again with the effect of suddenness and surprise. If this hypothesis is correct—and it has the support of the ancient and continuous Chinese tradition linking the Hsiungnu with the earlier Ti and other tribes, who certainly were not true steppe nomads—then the Hsiungnu history presents, in the second century B.C., the complete nomad sequence or cycle. This hypothetical sequence begins with the departure of semi-nomads into the open steppe—very likely to escape the "time of troubles" at the end of the Chou period, and the border wars of Yen, Chao, and Ch'in. There a "true" nomadism was created, which drew not only from the Chinese edge of the steppe but from the Central Asian, Siberian, and Manchurian edges. Even in this "primitive" nomadism, to continue the hypothesis, there must have been differences between various groups of the nomads, probably connected with differences in the kinds of animals they herded and the "extensivity" of their economy. Although all nomads were homogeneous with each other as nomads, they were differentiated from each other by particular kinds of nomadism, and this diversity made it easier to add a fringe of semi-nomad and non-nomad subject peoples.

LATER CYCLES

The cycle of the Hsiungnu was completed and another nomad cycle begun in the "time of troubles" that came with the fall of the Han dynasty at the beginning of the third century A.D. Some of the border Hsiungnu then moved farther into China and even set up minor "Chinese" dynasties, including a pseudo-Han dynasty. Other borderers departed into the steppe, there to renew their nomadism and, so to speak, their "nomadicness." This accounts for the fact that when the next "true" nomads gathered on the Inner Asian horizon of China—the Hsienpei in the east of Mongolia and the Juan-juan and Turks in Outer Mongolia and Central Asia—they were no longer Hsiungnu, but were as nomad as ever.

The Hsiungnu pseudo-Han dynasty was founded by Liu Yuan-hai, a descendant of the "southern *shanyü*" of the Hsiungnu who became a vassal of the first emperor of the Later or Eastern Han (A.D. 25-55).[13] Under the House of Wei (220-264) of the Three Kingdoms period which followed the Han, these Hsiungnu were divided into five tribes and settled as far south as T'aiyuan in Shansi (so that they must have become assimilated to the Chinese). Liu Yuan-hai, in the time of the Western Chin dynasty

[13] Hou-Han Shu, Ch. 119.

(265-316), bore the name of Liu because it was the clan name of the Han house from which he descended through the Han princess given to Modun, the Hsiungnu. He claimed that by virtue of the ancient treaties the Han and Hsiungnu imperial houses had been like elder and younger brothers, and that "when the elder brother dies, the younger succeeds." In 304 he took the style of Han, but his line was later known as Chao, the name being taken from the ancient Chao state in Shansi. Although another clan soon displaced his successors, Hsiungnu chiefs continued to rule this part of North China until the founding of the Northern Wei or Toba Wei dynasty—also of "barbarian" origin—in 386.[14]

The Hsienpei, like the Wuhuan, are linked with the Tunghu of Hsiungnu times. They are mentioned under the Later Han of 25-220,[15] and under the kingdom of Wei (220-264) in the time of the Three Kingdoms,[16] when one of their leaders had such prestige that "many Chinese went over to him." Probably this marked a period of instability and differentiation, with some nomads going back to the steppe and others gravitating toward China. At any rate, under the Chin dynasty [17] a Hsienpei chief set up a quasi-Chinese kingdom of Yen—named after the ancient kingdom in the Peking region.[18] While some of the Hsienpei were thus turning from the steppe others were turning back to it—like the Tukuhun (or T'u-yü-hun, or To-yü-hun),[19] the legend of whose eponymous chief is one of those that read as though the Chinese chronicler had followed the nomad version very closely.[20] The

---

[14] Chin Shu, Ch. 101-107.
[15] Hou-Han Shu, Ch. 120.
[16] San-Kuo Chih, Ch. 30.
[17] Western Chin, 265-316; Eastern Chin, 317-419; named after the ancient state of Chin in Shansi.
[18] Chin Shu, Ch. 107-111.
[19] Giles, Chinese Dictionary, No. 12,100.
[20] Chin Shu, Ch. 97; Wei Shu, Ch. 101.

Northern Wei, or Toba Wei dynasty, of 386-534, was also of Hsienpei derivation.[21]

The Juan-juan tribe was "founded" by a nomad captive slave who was made a free warrior; he can be dated by a reference to an emperor of the Eastern Chin who reigned from 345 to 361. Later, under penalty of death (apparently for being late when summoned for military service), he fled to the steppe. There he gathered other fugitives; the nucleus of the "tribe," therefore, probably consisted of men from the margin of the steppe taking refuge in the open steppe. Attacked by the founder of the Toba Wei (beginning of the fifth century), the tribe began a series of migrations and became powerful in the north and west of Mongolia.[22]

The myth that the Turks were descended from a wolf, recorded in the Chinese chronicles, is widely spread in Central Asia; but it is also said more specifically that they were "mixed barbarians" of the P'ingliang region in Kansu, who fled from the Wei dynasty to the Juan-juan—another instance of the "creating" of nomads by migration into the steppe. They were referred to by the Juan-juan as "smith-slaves"—possibly another sign of non-nomad origin, since nomad smiths are of honorable status. In the sixth century the Turks revolted against the Juan-juan and allied themselves with the Wei dynasty; they then replaced the Juan-juan as the masters of the northern steppe.[23] Later, under the Sui dynasty (605-618), again in a "time of trouble," the old process was repeated—Chinese fled to them. They were so many that the Turkish tribe "became strong and dominant; from the Khitan and Shihwei in the east, all the way west to the Tukuhun and Turfan all the nations submitted to them in allegiance." [24]

[21] Pei Shih, Ch. 1; Wei Shu, Ch. 1 and 2.
[22] Pei Shih, Ch. 98; Wei Shu, Ch. 91.
[23] Pei Shih, Ch. 99; Sui Shu, Ch. 84.
[24] T'ang Shu, Ch. 194, first section; see also Hsin T'ang Shu, Ch. 215.

Thus they became a mixed state; the Khitan (at this time) were more nomadic than they, while Turfan was one of the most important oases of Central Asia.

There was, then, a recognizable periodicity in the fluctuations of steppe history. There was also a pronounced cyclical alternation in the history of China. If it can be shown that these two kinds of ebb and flow interacted on each other in a significant manner, and not merely by accident, then it will be possible to round out an understanding of the way in which the historical "laws" of the Inner Asian Frontier of China worked as a whole.

Additional note to pp. 491-495, above: For a theory of the silk trade and Chinese penetration into Central Asia which differs considerably from my own estimate of the trade factor, see Frederick J. Teggart, China and Rome, Berkeley, 1939.

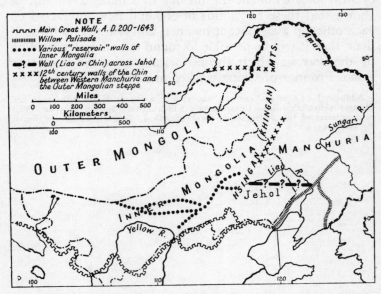

MAP 11—The Great Wall and other walls to the north.

CHAPTER XVII

THE CYCLES OF DYNASTIC AND TRIBAL HISTORY

THE PERIODICITY OF CHINESE HISTORY

Many writers have commented on the periodicity of Chinese history, the rhythm of which appears to follow a marked pattern. Although the social outlook of the Chinese is notable for the small honor it pays to war, and although their social system does not give the soldier a high position, every Chinese dynasty has risen out of a period of war, and usually a long period. Peasant rebellions have been as recurrent as barbarian invasions. Frequently the two kinds of war have been simultaneous; both have usually been accompanied by famine and devastation, and peace has never been restored without savage repression. The brief chronicle of a Chinese dynasty is very simple: a Chinese general or a barbarian conqueror establishes a peace which is usually a peace of exhaustion. There follows a period of gradually increasing prosperity, as land is brought back under cultivation, and this passes into a period of apparently unchanging stability. Gradually, however, weak administration and corrupt government choke the flow of trade and taxes. Discontent and poverty spread. The last emperor of the dynasty is often vicious and always weak—as weak as the founder of the dynasty was ruthless. The great fight each other for power, and the poor turn against all government. The dynasty ends, and after an interval another begins, exactly as the last began, and runs the same course.

The question is whether this is the whole phenomenon of Chinese history or only a striking symptom of something much wider, deeper, and more complicated. Have we here nothing but a simple alternation of increasing returns and diminishing returns—a Chinese history that can be explained by a very crude economic interpretation? Or should we look for a social explanation equally crude and simple—the average number of generations needed for the descendants of a great man to degenerate to the point of feeble-mindedness?

Given the obvious presence of a strong rhythm and given the fact that in so many centuries, during which events have been recorded in copious detail, even the strongest rhythm must show many variations, the play of interpretation becomes very wide. It is, in fact, possible to plot the cycles of Chinese history in many ways.

J. S. Lee has divided the whole history of China into cycles of 800 years. First there is a rather tentative cycle covering the Chou period; then follow three cycles, from the final unification of the Ch'in Empire in B.C. 221 to the present day—the last cycle being, of course, incomplete. This extreme rigidity of pattern Dr. Lee achieves by dealing with groups of dynasties rather than the succession of individual dynasties. In this way he provides for a sort of clearing of the ground by a dynasty that is powerful in war but does not last very long. The short dynasty is followed by two longer dynasties. The break between these two provides, as it were, an intercycle; but on the whole the two dynasties represent a relatively well-sustained "plateau" of peace and prosperity. The end of the 800-year cycle, however, breaks down into a welter of short cycles of war and minor dynasties, with an increasing antagonism between North China and South China. At last there comes another ground-clearing dynasty to prepare the opening of another cycle of 800 years.[1]

[1] J. S. Lee, The Periodic Recurrence of Internecine Wars in China, 1931; quoted at length in Lin Yutang, My Country and My People, 1935.

CH'AO-TING CHI'S THEORY OF DYNASTIC CYCLES

The chief weakness of this rigid classification is that it allows an arbitrary distinction between the short and violent dynasties that end a cycle and the short, violent dynasty chosen to begin a cycle. Ch'ao-ting Chi, though also dealing with phases that repeat each other, shows that it is possible to penetrate deeply into the causes that underlie the events of Chinese history. He recognizes a "first period of unity and peace" under the imperial system as created by Ch'in Shih-huang-ti and reaffirmed under the Han, from B.C. 221 to A.D. 220. This was followed by a "first period of division and struggle" under the Three Kingdoms—the Chin and the Southern and Northern dynasties—from 221 to 589. Then there was a return to a "second period of unity and peace" under the Sui and T'ang dynasties (589-907) followed again by a "second period of division and struggle" under the Five Dynasties—the Sung and the Khitan-Liao and Juchen-Chin. A "third period of unity and peace" under the Mongol-Yuan, the Ming, and the Manchu-Ch'ing brings the sequence up to modern times (1280-1912).[2]

There is nothing arbitrary about Chi's classification. It is true that bloody intervals like that between Ch'in and Han, or that between the Yuan dynasty of the Mongols and the restoration of Chinese rule under the Ming, are included by him in periods of "unity and peace," not in periods of "division and struggle." He is entitled to do this because he is not working simply with the patterns that can be made by arranging the dates but is estimating the growth of China by a standard independent of the figures themselves. The standard he takes is the practice of conservancy works, including not only flood-control and irrigation but canal transport. This is not a "dead" standard,

[2] Ch'ao-ting Chi, Key Economic Areas in Chinese History, 1936, pp. 9-10.

so to speak, but a "live" one, because it is cardinal to the Chinese technical mastery of agriculture, the essential stuff of the whole fabric of Chinese culture.

In Chi's "first period of unity and peace" the standard of reference is the agricultural area of the Ching and Wei Rivers in Shensi, the Fen River in Shansi, and the lower Yellow River as a whole. This was the core of China— what Chi calls the "key economic area." Within it the formative processes of Chinese history were so over- whelmingly concentrated that everything else was marginal and secondary. The "first period of division and struggle" is calculated in a similar way. The events of the time turned on the fact that there was doubt as to the real cen- ter of gravity of the most advanced, efficient, and profitable agriculture. The old nuclear area had not declined in abso- lute importance, but in relative importance other areas were rising both in the mountain-enclosed but immensely rich territory of Ssuch'uan and in the lower Yangtze valley.

In the "second period of unity and peace" the stability of the main structure was restored because the new center of gravity had been fixed. This was in the Yangtze valley, but a further technical advance had made it possible to link the Yangtze valley as a whole with the Yellow River val- ley as a whole by means of the Grand Canal. "China" therefore now meant something so much greater in scale that it was almost something new : it was possible to main- tain a political center of gravity in the North—in the old "key economic area"—and from it to exploit at a consid- erable distance the new area of rich agricultural concentra- tion that had become the major source of revenue. In time, however, the new structure again broke down into a "sec- ond period of division and struggle," partly because the new area of agricultural concentration, though already the richest area on which a dynasty could be based, was not yet well enough consolidated to be exploited as a unit. "Hills and mountains cut the regions into six distinct subregions which made unity difficult under the level of economic development at that time." [3] Finally, although a "third period of unity and peace" was reached another kind of diminishing returns was encountered: while the key economic area of the South fed the political center of gravity in the North, it did so at such a cost in transport that a given quantity of grain cost several times its own value in transit.[4] The shakiness of the Manchu-Ch'ing dynasty after the T'ai-p'ing rebellion of the middle of the nineteenth century was due largely to the fact that the system had become economically so unsound that it had little resilience to absorb political shock.

Although he limits himself in the main to his chosen scale of economic and technical reference, Chi also points out that a dynasty, even when apparently in full vigor, really began to weaken when the servants of the state were in a position to abuse the public service for their own private interest. "The reason for the impotence of the government . . . lay in the fact that the offenders were actually the most powerful personages in the government." [5]

Wang Yü-ch'üan has gone over this aspect of the problem in detail. Taking the Ch'ing dynasty as an example, he describes the typical cycle:

The record of the Manchu dynasty, beginning with the redistribution of land and the lightening of taxes and ending with the degeneration of the ruling class, the swollen accumulation of estates in the hands of private, privileged, tax-evading landholders, extortionate taxation of the poor peasantry, and helplessness in the face of foreign invasion, is an epitome of Chinese economic and social history. . . . The process of corruption may be described briefly as one in which the central government was robbed of real wealth and power, which were transferred to the very individuals who, as members of the ruling class, controlled the government. They could not possibly be restrained because, while responsible as officials and as a class for protecting the interests of the nation,

---

[3] *Ibid.*, p. 131.
[4] *Ibid.*, p. 145.
[5] *Ibid.*, p. 137.

they were as private individuals the sole beneficiaries of corruption. While some of them, as officials, understood what was wrong, the most they could accomplish as a class was to try to protect both the government interest and their class interest by trying to make up for the taxes which they themselves evaded by increased taxation of the poor and unprivileged classes.[6]

It was this that eventually "exhausted the peasantry and drove it to revolt." The conflict between private interest and state interest described by Wang was rooted in the fact that the imperial administration had necessarily to be recruited almost entirely from the landed gentry. The scale of public works in flood control and irrigation enterprises necessary to keep up a rich, concentrated agriculture as a source of revenue demanded a large educated personnel. The necessary education was expensive and required years of work. It could only be afforded by well-to-do families. Candidates at the "open" and apparently democratic imperial examinations were therefore drawn chiefly from prosperous families—which, in China, meant landholding families. Now the main source of state revenue was the land tax, and the main income of the scholar-gentry was land rent. The family from which an official came and the state which he served were therefore competitors for the same ultimate source of wealth. This made absolutely unavoidable an alternation between periods of "strong" government when the state was able to force the scholar-gentry to collect more in taxes than in rent, and periods of "weak" government when the officials were unable to force their own families and social equals to deliver as much in taxes as they collected in rent.[7]

REPETITION OF DYNASTIC CYCLES

So much for a normal cycle; but why were the cycles repetitive? Wang describes how a typical dynasty foun-

[6] Wang Yü-ch'üan, The Rise of Land Tax and the Fall of Dynasties in Chinese History, 1937, p. 202.
[7] See Chapter III, above.

dered in peasant revolts. Chi points out that such rebellions usually began in a number of scattered localities. "Owing to the locally self-sufficient economy" of China— what I have described as the "cellular" structure of city-and-country units—"consolidation of the scattered forces of the peasants was difficult." [8] The struggle therefore tended to last a long time, and it tended to be of a double character, for it involved both a general revolt against the old dynasty and a struggle between regional groups for the claim to establish a new dynasty. In the long run the group that won control of the "key economic area" of the time was the most likely to gain a permanent advantage.

The fact that in such a "time of trouble" China tended to fall apart into its constituent regions offers an approach to the problem of repetitiveness. It is true that unity might be restored by invaders from the steppe, but this may be left out of consideration for the moment. What was the aspect of China likely to be at such a time? In the first place, the sovereign power of the state could not be asserted. It had already decayed because the great families from which came its most important officials had themselves diverted from it the main sources of wealth. In the second place, these families were paralyzed by fear of the catastrophe that they had brought about. Many of them were of kingly private wealth, but for the protection of this wealth they had relied on the use of the public apparatus of government, and it had become bloated out of all proportion to their actual power. With the collapse of government their instinct was to buy over some of the rebels if they could, in order to protect as much of their wealth as possible and not jeopardize the whole of it in the desperate attempt to set up a new dynasty. Indeed, no such family was in a position to expose itself, because once the dynasty had fallen the clans and estates of those who had been prominent under the dynasty were the most

[8] Chi, *op. cit.*, p. xiv.

tempting objects of attack. While the great families as a class might stand together on the defensive in a rather loose and unorganized way, no one of them was likely to come forward as the representative of the class.

In the third place, the peasants who were the active rebels were only able to organize region by region and not on a national scale. Even if, in any one region, the revolt against imperial authority were followed by extermination of the scholar-gentry, the peasants still were helpless. It was impossible for them to create a new kind of China by preventing the restoration of the imperial order and substituting some other kind of China. If the region was below the average level in the development of irrigated agriculture it was more likely to revert to a "pre-Chinese" level of barbarism than to create a new and superior culture. If it was one of the regions in which irrigation had been highly developed and the population was closely concentrated then the neglect and destruction of canals and embankments during the revolt was likely to bring famine and a desperate need for repair of the public works—and this meant "restoration of order" on a scale that permitted public enterprise.

Such conditions overwhelmingly favored one kind of man—a man who was a hanger-on of the old order. He had to be low enough in either social origin or status to be able to voice the grievances of the peasants even if he did not "represent" them. He had also to know enough of the ways, the outlook, and the organization of the great families to be able to make more use of them than they could make of him; he had to know how to threaten them and frighten them into tolerating or even supporting him, though he might afterwards betray them. Above all, he had to have enough experience and knowledge to be able to take hold of the remnants of public enterprise and public administration in order to restore agriculture. Once he had done this he could mollify the peasants by giving them grants of land that had been abandoned, water to grow their crops, and a reduction in taxes. At the same time he could bully those of the rich who remained—prevent them from taking in rent the revenue which the state needed in taxes and force them to serve in organizing, supervising, and administering, in surveying for the repair or construction of public works, and computing and collecting the returns—under fear of being thrown back again into the horror of a peasant revolt. Such a man could found a new great family which, being new, was not vulnerable as were the old families; at the same time, because his army still remained a peasant army he could make the survivors of the great serve him before their own interests.

Naturally in any time of wide turmoil a number of men like this would appear, tempted by the possibility of immense rewards and having little to lose. Hence the importance of Chi's "key economic region." Among a number of contestants of the same caliber, the man who was working under conditions that allowed him to organize relative wealth and prosperity sooner than his rivals and thus to control a large and concentrated population could set up a dynasty that controlled either the whole of China or some well defined region, according to the resources of his base of operations. Liu Pang, who founded the Han dynasty, was a man of this class—not quite of the gentry but a hanger-on of the gentry.[9] So also was Chu Yuanchang, the founder the Ming dynasty;[10] and so were the founders of a number of minor dynasties. Liu Hsiu, who founded or restored the Han power as the Eastern Han,

[9] "He was a former village official who had become a bandit as the result of official oppression and bad luck" (Dubs, History of the Former Han Dynasty, 1938, p. 5).
[10] Ming Shih, Ch. 1. He was for a time a priest, then a rebel against the Mongol (Yüan) dynasty; he was a favorite and bodyguard of the rebel chief under whom he first served.

was of the imperial blood.[11] In his case, however, there had been a usurpation (under Wang Mang) which threatened all members of the imperial clan with the danger of being put to death,[12] and this made Liu desperate enough to strike out boldly. Other dynasties, again, were set up on foundations prepared by a brief preceding dynasty: thus the Sung followed the Later Chao. In such cases it was not a question of peasant revolt but of political war, and if there was "revolution" it was likely to be palace revolution.

DYNASTIES ORIGINATING BEYOND THE GREAT WALL

There is a striking resemblance between the origins of Chinese dynasties and of dynasties beyond the Great Wall. Modun, the great Hsiungnu, can be compared with Liu Hsiu who restored the Han dynasty. He was of the imperial blood, but he knew that his father was plotting to kill him, and became desperate enough to take risks.[13] The "founder" of the Juan-juan tribe was an escaped slave-soldier.[14] From the way the account of him is worded it seems likely that he had once been a favorite at court, so that he both knew the kind of people he led and how to lead them. The great Chingghis himself was of a clan that had been noble, but in his boyhood he was poor and hunted.[15] Nurhachi, again, the founder of the Manchu line, was a noble but of a clan that had fallen to the hanger-on aristocracy.[16]

The modern Chinese writers, as far as I know, have treated the dynasties of steppe origin ruling in China only

[11] Hou-Han Shu, Ch. 1, first section. His relatives were frightened by his venture into the struggle for power and feared they would all be killed.

[12] Liu Hsiu was for a time an official under Wang Mang—a position that must have been extremely insecure.

[13] Shih Chi, Ch. 110.

[14] Pei Shih, Ch. 98; Wei Shu, Ch. 91.

[15] Palladius, trans. of the "Secret History," edit. 1910, pp. 18 *et sqq.* (in Russian); Sanang Setsen, Mongol text, pp. 66-68; Schmidt's trans., pp. 67, 69.

[16] See Chapter V, above.

rather casually. Contemporary interest in problems of the nature of Chinese economy and society and the working of Chinese history has been so overwhelming that similar problems beyond the Great Wall Frontier have as yet not been taken up in detail. Wittfogel, however, has taken the position that nomad invasions of China cannot have been matters of accident or fate. Athough war was frequent in China, he points out, the economy and society of China were not organized for war. On the contrary, they were both extremely vulnerable in war, especially on account of the irrigation works that could be destroyed or ruined simply through neglect. As against this the nomad society could turn easily from peace to war. Moreover, the plunder of China was of a kind to tempt nomads, whereas a conquest of the steppe offered no kind of temptation to a Chinese emperor. Consequently, the nomads must have been disposed to look for every opportunity to invade China—and naturally the best opportunities were likely to appear when China was in turmoil.[17] Wittfogel carries this analysis further by pointing out that the cycle, though political in its manifestations, was forced to its recurrent crises by the nature of the struggle between private interest in land rent and the state interest in the land tax.[18]

The depth to which any barbarian invasion penetrated China did not depend simply on an accidental equation at the time between the relative weakness of China and the relative strength of the tribal invaders. I do not think it has ever before been pointed out that the great "nomad conquests" of China did not come from the open steppe at all, but from the border of the steppe. In other words, they were not the work of unmodified, typical nomads but

[17] Wittfogel, Probleme der chinesischen Wirtschaftsgeschichte, 1927, p. 325; also Foundations and Stages of Chinese Economic History, 1935, p. 53. The work of both Chi and Wang, cited above, has also been influenced by Wittfogel's ideas.
[18] Wittfogel, Die Theorie der orientalischen Gesellschaft, 1938, pp. 109-114.

of peoples of mixed culture adjacent to the Inner Asian Frontier. The Hsiungnu, at the height of their power in the open steppe, did not conquer China. The Liao-Khitan did not appear suddenly out of the steppe but rose gradually just beyond the Great Wall. The Juchen-Chin, again, rose gradually at the edge of the Liao-Khitan territory. Even the great Chingghis did not emerge from the wildest part of the Mongolian steppe. His clan had been hangers-on of the Juchen-Chin at the edge of their Manchurian territory, and held a title from them. Nurhachi, finally, did not first organize and lead those of the Manchu-Tungus tribes that lived in the far depths of Manchuria but those that clustered along the Chinese-held border of South Manchuria.

FUNCTION OF THE MARGINAL ZONE OF THE STEPPE IN THE DYNASTIC CHANGES

The reasoning that applies separately to the steppe and to China also applies to both of them in combination. The typical steppe society and the typical Chinese society represented extremes. Those who held the central power in China were best pleased when they had least to do with the steppe. Those whose power was based beyond the Frontier were greedy for the luxuries they could get from China and the power they could assert in China, but they were equally anxious to keep their "tribal" subjects—who had a special military value—from being "contaminated" by Chinese ways.[19]

Nevertheless, the two societies could not be sharply sundered. The line of contact inevitably deepened into a margin which was occupied by steppe tribes that showed different degrees of Chinese admixture and influence and by Chinese who showed steppe influence and admixture in corresponding gradations. At times of sharp disturbance this margin tended to become narrower, as some of the

[19] Lattimore, review of Grenard's Genghis-Khan, 1937.

border steppe people drew back into the steppe and some of the Frontier Chinese retreated toward China. During long periods of stability, on the other hand, the margin tended to become wider, and the wider it became the more it approached the status and importance of a separate order of society. It never became fully differentiated because there always remained parts of the steppe in which it was impossible to compromise with the settled life, and areas of concentrated agriculture in China in which the dominant characteristics of China could not be affected by distant influences from the steppe. However, it probably did radiate an influence, both into the steppe and into China, that weakened the structure and solidity of the typical societies.

When a long period of stability began to break down—not in sudden, widespread wars but in gradually increasing wars—it was impossible for the mixed societies of the border to revert hastily to the alternatives of "strict" steppe society and "strict" Chinese society. These were the very times in which men who stood not merely between two classes but between two kinds of society could come to power. Men of the border, who knew the structure of power both in the steppe and in China, could at such times make skillful use of their knowledge. They were not likely to make bold enough use of it, however, if they were great chiefs of the border. In such times the great were shaken and afraid, anxious to hold on to as much as they could and not to take risks. The men who were bold were those whose family connections gave them a knowledge of power and a hunger for it, but who had fallen so far in status that they could not arrive at power unless they took risks.[20]

Men of this kind, and probably of this kind only, were able to found "nomad" dynasties whose power overlapped both into the steppe and into China. The true Chinese might try to spread their power up to the Inner Asian

[20] Compare Chapters IV and V, above.

Frontier, but not beyond it. The true nomads might raid and plunder China, but they did not know how to occupy and rule it. Whether these border conquerors based the power that they had won primarily on the border itself, or in the steppe, or in China, depended on the depth of the border and the numbers of its mixed population at the time, and on the state of poise and solidity of the true China and the true steppe.

The final shape taken by a dynasty growing from such origins and the extent to which it remained attached to the border, or partly detached itself and shifted either toward the steppe or toward China, or spread into both of them, was determined by a number of forces. The T'ang dynasty, for instance, was the creation of a swashbuckling Chinese father and son of partly Turkish blood.[21] Turkish cavalry gave it the striking power to deal quickly with the preceding Sui dynasty and thus to take over the great Sui irrigation and canal works without the deterioration that they would have suffered in a long war. Thereafter the T'ang influence was projected far into the steppe and into Central Asia, but the dynastic center of gravity remained definitely on the agricultural, Chinese side of the Inner Asian Frontier.

Whereas the T'ang dynasty moved quickly inward on China from the edge of the Frontier, Chingghis Khan moved first away from the Frontier into the steppe and then back toward China. The conquest of China by the Mongol Yüan dynasty was far from sudden. Chingghis was not a man of the deep steppe but of the steppe margin. He united the tribes of the steppe but he was not so much a steppe emperor as was Modun of the Hsiungnu. In his time the world was loose : two centuries of war and partial

[21] Although its power was based on North Shansi, the clan traced back to an ephemeral Hsiungnu "dynasty" in the Ti Tao region of Kansu. See T'ang Shu, Ch. 1 ; Hsin T'ang Shu, Ch. 1.

conquests had torn the edges of China; the oasis world of
Chinese and Russian Central Asia lay open; Persia was as
weak as China. Because of this looseness Chingghis, driven
into the steppe in boyhood, had a more rigorous training
in the hard techniques of mobility and war than most of
his peers. The "steppe" tribes that he mastered were permeated with oasis influences, and by the time that he came
back toward the edge of the steppe he had at his command
men of the mixed cultures who could introduce him to
each new sphere of conquest and organize it as fast as he
conquered it—Uighur Turks, and above all the great Yehlü Ch'u-ts'ai [22] of the once imperial Khitan house, a man
versed in the knowledge both of the Chinese border and
of China itself. It must be remembered, moreover, that
it was only under Khobilai Sechin (Kublai Khan), the
grandson of Chingghis, that the Mongols really conquered
China. And by that time it was not a tribe that conquered
the Chinese but a dynasty already formed and immensely
powerful. The Liao-Khitan and Juchen-Chin dynasties
grew more slowly and out of even longer wars. In them
another principle was dominant: a long war deep in China
was likely to cause terrible destruction and almost complete
exhaustion before one man of the sword had dealt with
all his rivals, but a long war on the edge of the steppe,
while it destroyed that part of the mixed society that was
more dependent on agriculture, also had the effect of welding together that part which inclined to be more pastoral
and migratory. This was because, although at first the
settled people might hold their own in a long war, gradually agriculture itself was bankrupted and land went out
of cultivation. On the other hand, among those who already depended more on their livestock than on farming,
war fostered those aspects of nomadism that are most military: the technique of the mobile life, the ability to as-

[22] Biography in Yüan Shih, Ch. 146; Hsin Yüan Shih, Ch. 127.

semble quickly for attack or defense, the ability to withdraw all encampments and herds from the country
through which an enemy threatens to pass.

Consequently a long war not only increased the relative
strength of the nomads, but it also increased the ability of
nomads to administer and exploit a settled economy instead
of merely raiding the settled people. Where a "true"
nomad from the far steppe might have understood only
plunder and tribute, a border nomad knew how to handle
different kinds of men. The border dynasties that came
to power after a long war had accordingly a double character. They knew how to use the Chinese economy and
even how to revive it when it had been largely destroyed.
At the same time, the more nomad part of their following
was likely to have increased during the years of war.
Moreover, these nomads were not mere auxiliaries, like
the Turkish cavalry of the T'ang, suddenly drafted into
China and quickly returned to the Frontier. By long
service they had become an integral part of the strength of
the dynasty.

Such forces had to be handled skillfully. They could not
be simply paid off and sent away while the dynasty itself
settled down in China, because they might turn against
a leader who neglected them. Nor could they be moved
bodily into China, where they would consume too much of
the revenue that needed to be carefully managed and increased. It was in such periods, accordingly, that the
phenomenon of the "reservoir" [23] was most important.
The dynasty had to establish a gradation between the territory it controlled and the peoples it ruled.

Within the Frontier it was the Chinese economy that was
most profitable, and therefore the administration, even
under nomad conquerors, had to be Chinese in character.
This meant that Chinese who entered the service of such
conquerors remained Chinese, while those of the conquer-

[23] See Chapter VIII, above.

ors who engaged in the administration of China did not remain nomads or even borderers but also became Chinese. Garrisons of nomad troops might also be stationed in China, especially at first, and these, too, rapidly became Chinese.

Adjacent to the Frontier, in what I have called the "reservoir," there was a garrison of another kind, not stationed at fixed points but consisting of pastoral nomads whose duty it was to be ready for immediate military service, and whose privilege, in return, was the receipt of special subsidies. The "reservoir" garrison and the subsidies were needed for two purposes. The tribes of the "reservoir," under chiefs to whom all kinds of hereditary titles were granted, might be drafted into China at need; they also served to keep away from the Frontier any outlying steppe tribes that had not taken part in the conquest but which might nonetheless demand a share of the spoils. Subsidies had therefore to be heavy since otherwise the "reservoir" tribes might join the tribes of the outer steppe instead of holding them off.

Consequently under dynasties of border origin even more than under strictly Chinese dynasties, outlying Frontier walls beyond the main Great Wall were repeatedly built; these may be called the "reservoir walls." Running roughly east and west, they can be traced almost throughout Inner Mongolia. Perhaps the most remarkable outwork system of all is that of the Hsingan (Khingan) wall which runs from south to north along the face of the Hsingan range, masking the western or steppe frontier of Manchuria. This was almost certainly built by the Juchen-Chin dynasty though it may have been begun by the Khitan-Liao dynasty before it. The outwork in the northeast of Outer Mongolia known as the "Chingghis Khan wall" was probably part of the same system.

For although the "reservoir" was by origin and intention a reservoir of nomads, the tribes that held it could not remain true pastoral nomads in character. Since its warriors had to be at the service of a dynasty with a fixed capital in China it was necessary to have known points of assembly, each with its quota of troops. Even in peace, therefore, pastures could not be allotted simply according to the needs and uses of a pastoral economy but had to subserve the need of grouping the defense of the fixed Frontier of an agricultural country.

Even more important in distorting the "nomad" character of the "reservoir," undoubtedly, was the interest of the chiefs. They were the peers of the chiefs who entered China with the dynasty and they coveted not only the same titles and honors but the same luxuries.[24] It was impossible to prevent them from drawing into their "tribal" pasturages Chinese traders, artisans, and even cultivators, from building for themselves rather outlandish imitations of Chinese palaces and "cities," and from diversifying their revenue as far as they could. In this way the mixed culture of the border, while it tended to become more nomad during long wars, tended to become more settled during long years of peace, and in this way the margin of the steppe was again differentiated from the outlying main steppe. Probably it is this also that accounts for the very important fact, noted by Thorp, that the Inner Mongolian "reservoir walls" coincide roughly with soil frontiers:[25]

[24] Novitskii (Journey Through Mongolia, 1911; in Russian) notes the "greater independence and pride of bearing" of Inner Mongolian princes as compared with those of Outer Mongolia. One reason, he thought, was their more frequent personal contact with the court at Peking. This was in 1906, not long before the Mongol and Chinese revolutions of 1911. At that time the difference between "inner" and "outer" princes—deriving originally from the distinction between allies of the Manchus and tribes living beyond the "reservoir"—had long been stratified. The same author comments on the more "Chinese" costumes of Inner Mongolian princes.

[25] Thorp, Geography of the Soils of China, 1936, p. 118. The walls beyond the Great Wall have been only partly mapped. For the eastern outer walls, see map of Leagues, Banners, and other tribal territories (mainly based on a South Manchuria Railway edition of a Japanese Staff map) in Lattimore, Mongols of Manchuria, 1934. For the western outer walls the best map is that attached to Hedin, De vetenskapliga resultaten av våra expeditioner i Centralasien och Tibet 1927-1935, 1935; also the section of this report by

the culture of the "reservoir," as it became a mixed culture, settled down within the limits of the environment that would tolerate a mixed culture and did not venture farther into the steppe.

PERSISTENT LACK OF INTEGRATION BETWEEN CHINA AND THE STEPPE

Even this mixed culture, it will be noted, was not an integrated new way of life. On the one side it depended too much on the tastes and privileges of princes whose functions were artificial and political and not organic to the steppe way of life. On the other side, instead of projecting itself in forms that could also survive in the more pronounced steppe, it cut itself off from the steppe, thereby leaving the "determinant" part of the steppe to foster and perpetuate the old steppe technique of living. In fact, the steppe itself remained a "reservoir" of nomadism. The mixed culture was a bridge between the steppe and China, and over it passed influences in both directions; but it was only from halfway across the bridge that the two worlds appeared as if linked. At each head of the bridge it could be seen that they were still two different worlds.

The only bridge that can really integrate a society that is essentially agricultural with one that is essentially pastoral —the intensive and the extensive economies—is the bridge of industrialism. The cycles of history in China and in the steppe that I have here discussed do not fully explain why industrialism was never evolved on either side of the Inner Asian Frontier, but I think they go part way toward an explanation. In the irrigated agriculture of China the heavy emphasis on human labor, and on an over-abundant supply of it to keep it cheap enough, created a vested social interest that resisted the machine. (This, of course, is by

---

Bergman, Arkeologiska undersökningar; also Bergman's earlier article, Något om Mongoliet i forntid och nutid, pp. 110-113. Note especially his reference there to a northern frontier wall of the Tangut (Hsi Hsia) kingdom.

no means the full explanation but merely one aspect of a complex problem.) [26] In the society of the steppe the deterrent vested interest was mobility.[27] Yet in either world, if it had been a closed world, the recurrent cycles of history might in certain circumstances have broken down the old order so completely that it could not be restored and yet left enough of it to be incorporated into a new and different order.

It seems very probable that the reason this never happened was that neither cycle operated only in its own society but that each interacted on the other. Because of this interaction the breakdown was never complete. There was always left in China a "determinant" part of the environment that favored the old intensive irrigated agriculture, and here the old order was nursed back to vigor. There was always left in the steppe a "determinant" area in which mixed nomadism was forced to return to and preserve the strictest techniques of nomadism.

There remains a further point to be considered: whether the two interacting cycles, each of which had its independent phases, were independent in origin. Probably not. Inasmuch as the evolution of the Chinese agriculture and society, by the pressure it put on the people of the steppe margin, helped to create the true steppe society,[28] the nomad cycle was at least in part a product of the Chinese cycle.[29]

[26] Compare Wittfogel, Die Theorie der orientalischen Gesellschaft, 1938.

[27] Hence the inhibitions among the Mongols—probably originating in social prohibitions—against laying up supplies of hay for the winter, against digging too many wells, against fishing, and so forth. All of these would have increased general prosperity; but they would have meant a greater degree of attachment to locality. Anciently this would have impaired the power which the chiefs had over a nomad people. The prejudice lingered even after nomadic habits had been modified by the vassal relationships of the princes to the Manchu emperors, who required strict observance of territorial frontiers. Compare Chapter IV, above.

[28] See Chapter XII, above.

[29] Wittfogel (op. cit., p. 111, n. 4), commenting on some earlier contributions of mine to the problems of nomad history, has already stated the derivation of the nomad cycle from the Chinese cycle more clearly than I had then seen it.

Once established, of course, the nomad cycle acquired a vigor that enabled it to interact on the cyclical history of China with independent force. Further studies of war between nomads and invasions of China by nomads, and above all, a wider documentation of the ambivalent societies whose fortunes rose and fell between China and the steppe, will undoubtedly improve our knowledge of the character of steppe nomadism and the style in action of steppe history. Such research will probably make clearer, also, the degree to which the nomadism of the Inner Asian Frontiers of China derived from other ways of life, and the difference between what China contributed to the creation of steppe nomadism and the later influence of China on steppe nomadism when it had become independent.

Already this much appears to be clear: In prehistoric Asia primitive man did not differ greatly in China and in Central Asia. The early beginnings of the great cultures—in China, India, Mesopotamia, and so forth—created more than the great cultures themselves. Each great culture developed first in the environment that offered it the most shelter and encouragement in its weak and tentative stage, then gravitated toward the environment that had most to offer when it had become vigorous and mature. As it grew, a culture like that of China not only developed and improved those practices that it found most profitable but also discarded or neglected other practices and thrust aside those who would not conform to the standard.

Among the marginal groups thus formed in marginal environments there were some who found it possible not merely to conserve what did not conform to the standard, but to develop out of it a new, alternative standard. In this way the Chinese, as they evolved into Chinese, helped to create the steppe way of life as well as the Chinese way of life. Thus the steppe life may be said to belong to a secondary order, although it was not a dependent or a parasitic order but one capable of independent development from secondary origins to primary importance.

What is true of origins is also true of developments that lie ahead in the future. China today is the major field of historical action in the Far East. What is happening in China in our time is being reflected beyond the Inner Asian Frontier. More important than Japan's aggression are the changes that are taking place in Chinese life as a necessary part of the resistance to Japan. Ripples from the changes that are going on in China are spreading beyond the Inner Asian Frontier. This does not necessarily mean that there will be a new standard in Inner Asia marginal to the new standard in China, or subordinate to it. The new standard will be capable of integrating China and its Inner Asian hinterland; but because of the historical differences between the various peoples the kinds of change are not the same, and because the impact of industrialization and other new factors is not evenly distributed the rates of change are not the same. Historical study of the Inner Asian Frontier and of the relation of different kinds of society to different kinds of environment offers the possibility of appreciating each new phase as it takes form and of participating in and helping to shape the events of our time instead of submitting passively to them.

BIBLIOGRAPHY

ADAMS, HENRY. The Education of Henry Adams. Boston and New York, 1918.

ANDERSSON, J. G. The Cave Deposit at Sha Kuo T'un in Fengtien. *Palaeontologia Sinica,* Geol. Surv. of China, Peking, Ser. D, Vol. I, No. 1, 1923.

————. Children of the Yellow Earth: Studies in Prehistoric China. London, 1934.

————. Der Weg über die Steppen. *Bull. Mus. Far Eastern Antiquities,* Stockholm, No. 1, 1929.

————. Preliminary Report on Archaeological Research in Kansu. *Memoirs Geol. Surv. China,* Peking, Ser. A, No. 5, 1925. [Includes "A Note on the Physical Characters of the Prehistoric Kansu Race" by Davidson Black.]

ANDREW, G. FINDLAY. The Crescent in North-West China. London, 1921.

ANONYMOUS. Article on Mongol population in Manchuria, in *The People's Tribune,* Shanghai, August 1, 1935.

ANONYMOUS. Tribal Problems of Today. *Journ. Central Asian Soc.,* London, Vol. XVII, April, 1930.

ARENDT, W. W. Sur l'apparition de l'étrier chez les Scythes. *Eurasia Septentrionalis Antiqua,* Helsinki, Vol. IX (Minns Volume), 1934.

ARENS, M. Yaponskaya agressiya vo Vnutrennei Mongolii (Japanese Aggression in Inner Mongolia). *Tikhii Okean (Pacific Ocean),* Moscow, No. 4(10), 1936.

ASAKAWA, K. Article on "Feudalism, Japanese," in *Encyclopaedia of the Social Sciences,* Vol. VI. New York, 1931.

BADDELEY, J. F. Russia, Mongolia, China: Being Some Record of the Relations Between Them From the Beginning of the XVIIth Century to the Death of Tsar Alexei Mikhailovich A.D. 1602-1676 . . . 2 vols. London, 1919.

BALES, W. L. Tso Tsungt'ang: Soldier and Statesman of Old China. Shanghai, 1937.

BARBOUR, G. B. Recent Observations on the Loess of North China. *Geogr. Journ.,* London, Vol. LXXXVI, January, 1935.

BARTHOLD, W. Turkestan Down to the Mongol Invasion. Translated by H. A. R. Gibb. 2nd edit. London, 1928.

BARTON, SIR WILLIAM. The Problems of Law and Order under a Responsible Government in the North-West Frontier Province. *Journ. Royal Central Asian Soc.,* London, Vol. XIX, January, 1932.

BELL, SIR CHARLES. The North-Eastern Frontier of India. *Journ. Central Asian Soc.,* London, Vol. XVII, April, 1930.

BERGMAN, FOLKE. Archaeological Researches in Sinkiang, *constituting* Reports from the Scientific Expedition to the North-Western Provinces of China under the Leadership of Dr. Sven Hedin, Vol. VII. Stockholm, 1939.

————. Något om Mongoliet i forntid och nutid. *Ymer,* Stockholm, Vol. LV, No. 2, 1935.

————. Newly Discovered Graves in the Lop-Nor Desert. *Geografiska Annaler,* Stockholm, Vol. XVII, 1935 (Hedin Seventieth Birthday Volume).

————. *See also* HEDIN, SVEN. De vetenskapliga resultaten . . .

BERTHELOT, ANDRÉ. L'Asie ancienne centrale et sud-orientale d'après Ptolémée. Paris, 1930.

BERTRAM, JAMES. First Act in China: The Story of the Sian Mutiny. New York, 1938.

————. Unconquered: Journal of a Year's Adventures among the Fighting Peasants of North China. New York, 1939.

BISHOP, CARL WHITING. The Beginnings of North and South in China. *Pacific Affairs,* New York, Vol. VII, September, 1934.

————. The Chronology of Ancient China. *Journ. American Oriental Soc.,* Baltimore, Vol. LII, 1932.

————. Long-Houses and Dragon-Boats. *Antiquity,* Gloucester, Vol. XII, December, 1938.

————. The Neolithic Age in Northern China. *Antiquity,* Gloucester, Vol. VII, December, 1933.

————. Origin and Early Diffusion of the Traction-Plow. *Antiquity,* Gloucester, Vol. X, September, 1936.

————. The Rise of Civilization in China with Reference to Its Geographical Aspects. *Geogr. Rev.,* New York, Vol. XXII, October, 1932.

BLACK, DAVIDSON, and others. Fossil Man in China: The Choukoutien Cave Deposits with a Synopsis of Our Present Knowledge of the Late Cenozoic in China. *Geological Memoirs,* Geol. Surv. of China, Peiping, Ser. A, No. 11, 1933.

————. The Human Skeletal Remains from the Sha Kuo T'un Cave Deposit, in Comparison with Those from Yang Shao Tsun and with Recent North China Skeletal Material. *Palaeontologia*

Sinica, Geol. Surv. of China, Peking. Ser. D, Vol. I, No. 3, 1925.

————. *See also* ANDERSSON, J. G. Preliminary Report . . .

BLOCH, MARC. Article on "Feudalism, European," *in* Encyclopaedia of the Social Sciences, Vol. VI, New York, 1931.

BOEKE, J. H. The Recoil of Westernization in the East. *Pacific Affairs,* New York, Vol. IX, September, 1936.

BONVALOT, GABRIEL. Across Tibet. New York, 1892. [Chapter IV, "An Excursion to Lob Nor," by Prince Henry of Orleans.]

BREASTED, JAMES H. A History of Egypt. 2nd edit. New York, 1912.

BRETSCHNEIDER, E. Mediaeval Researches from Eastern Asiatic Sources: Fragments Towards the Knowledge of the Geography and History of Central and Western Asia from the 13th to the 17th Century. 2 vols. London, 1888 (reprinted 1910).

BROCK, H. LE M. Air Operations on the N.W.F. [North-West Frontier], 1930. *Journ. Royal Central Asian Soc.,* London, Vol. XIX, January, 1932.

BROOMHALL, MARSHALL. Islam in China. London, 1910.

BRUCE, C. E. The Sandeman Policy as Applied to the Tribal Problems of Today. *Journ. Royal Central Asian Soc.,* London, Vol. XIX, January, 1932.

BRYCE, JAMES. The Holy Roman Empire. New York-London, 1904.

CABLE, MILDRED. The New "New Dominion." *Journ. Royal Central Asian Soc.,* London, Vol. XXV, January, 1938.

CAHUN, LÉON. Introduction à l'histoire de l'Asie: Turcs et Mongols, des origines à 1405. Paris, 1896.

CARPINI, PIAN DE. *See* ROCKHILL, W. W. The Journey of William of Rubruck.

CARRUTHERS, DOUGLAS. Unknown Mongolia. 2 vols. London, 1913.

CHANG, C. M. Review of Wan Kuo-ting, "Agrarian History of China." *Nankai Social and Economic Quarterly,* Tientsin, Vol. VIII, July, 1935. *See also* WAN, KUO-TING.

CH'ANG CH'UN. *See* PALLADIUS.

CH'AO-TING CHI. *See* CHI, CH'AO-TING.

CHAVANNES, E. Les deux plus anciens spécimens de la cartographie chinoise. *Bull. de l'École française d'Extrême-Orient,* Hanoi, Vol. III, 1903.

————. Inscriptions et pièces de chancellerie chinoises de l'époque mongole. *T'oung Pao,* Leyden, Ser. II, Vol. V, 1904, and Vol. VI, 1905.

————. Mémoires historiques de Se-Ma Ts'ien. 5 vols. Paris, 1895-1905. [A translation of the first 47 *chuan* of the Shih Chi, or "Historical Memoirs," of Ssu-ma Ch'ien.]

CHEN, HAN-SENG. A Critical Survey of Chinese Policy in Inner Mongolia. *Pacific Affairs,* New York, Vol. IX, December, 1936. *See also* LATTIMORE, O.

————. The Good Earth of China's Model Province. *Pacific Affairs,* New York, Vol. IX, September, 1936.

————. Landlord and Peasant in China: Agrarian Problems in Southernmost China. New York, 1937.

————. The Present Agrarian Problem in China. Shanghai, 1933.

CHEN, PARKER T. *See* HÖRNER, NILS G.

CHEN, WARREN H. An Estimate of the Population of China. *XIX* Session de l'Institut international de Statistique, Tokio, 1930. Shanghai, 1930.

CHI, CH'AO-TING. The Economic Basis of Unity and Division in Chinese History. *Pacific Affairs,* New York, Vol. VII, December, 1934.

————. Key Economic Areas in Chinese History, as Revealed in the Development of Public Works for Water-Control. London, 1936.

CHI LI. *See* LI, CHI.

Ch'ien-Han Shu. [The history of the earlier or Western Han dynasty, B.C. 206 to A.D. 24. The chief compiler was Pan Ku.] *See also* K'ai Ming.

CH'IEN, MU. Hsi Chou Jung Huo K'ao (The Jung Disasters of the Western Chou). *Yü Kung* (Tribute of Yü), *The Chinese Historical Geography Semi-Monthly Magazine,* Peiping, Vol. II, Nos. 4 and 12, 1934 and 1935.

Chilin T'ungchih. In 6 vols. (*t'ao*). Preface dated 1891. [Gazetteer of Kirin Province.]

Chin Shu. [The history of the Chin dynasty, 265-419. The chief compiler was Fang Chiao.] *See also* K'ai Ming.

China Year Book. H. G. W. Woodhead, ed. Shanghai. 1934 and 1935.

Chinese Eastern Railway. North Manchuria and the Chinese Eastern Railway. I. A. Mihailoff, ed. Harbin, 1924.

Chinese Year Book. Council of International Affairs, Chungking, 1938-39. [Shanghai?], 1939. [The large folded map attached to this Year Book has also been used for reference.]

CHU, COCHING. The Aridity of North China. *Pacific Affairs,* New York, Vol. VIII, June, 1935.

COATMAN, J. The North-West Frontier Province and Trans-Border Country under the New Constitution. *Journ. Royal Central Asian Soc.*, London, Vol. XVIII, July, 1931.

Commercial Press. Ta-Ch'ing Tikuo Ch'uant'u (Atlas of the Ta-Ch'ing [Manchu] Empire). Shanghai, 1905.

CONRADY, A. Article on "China" in *Weltgeschichte*, J. von Pflugk-Harttung, ed. Vol. "Orient." Berlin, 1910.

COULING, S. *See* Encyclopaedia Sinica.

COURANT, M. L'Asie centrale aux XVII° et XVIII° siècles : Empire kalmouk ou Empire mantchou? Lyon-Paris, 1912.

CREEL, HERRLEE GLESSNER. The Birth of China. London, 1936.

————. On the Origins of the Manufacture and Decoration of Bronze in the Shang Period. *Monumenta Serica,* Peiping, Vol. I, No. 1, 1935.

————. Studies in Early Chinese Culture. First Ser., Baltimore, 1937.

CRESSEY, GEORGE B. China's Geographic Foundations. New York, 1934.

CUNNINGHAM, SIR GEORGE. Reforms in the North-West Frontier Province of India. *Journ. Royal Central Asian Soc.,* London, Vol. XXIV, January, 1937.

DE GROOT, J. J. M. Die Hunnen der vorchristlichen Zeit. Berlin-Leipzig, 1921. [Part I *of* Chinesische Urkunden zur Geschichte Asiens.]

————. Die Westlände Chinas in der vorchristlichen Zeit. O. Franke, ed. Berlin-Leipzig, 1926. [Part II *of* Chinesische Urkunden zur Geschichte Asiens.]

DE HARLEZ, CH. La Religion nationale des Tartares Orientaux : Mandchous et Mongols . . . Paris, 1887.

DE MAILLA, JOSEPH. Histoire générale de la China. 13 vols. Paris, 1779. [Translated from the T'ung-chien Kang-mu, and other sources.]

DIXON, ROLAND B. The Racial History of Man. New York-London, 1923.

DMITRENKO, V. V. When Horns Were in the Velvet. *Asia,* New York, Vol. XXXIII, December, 1933.

DOKSOM. Istoricheskie uroki 15 let revolyutsii (Historical Lessons of 15 Years of Revolution). *Tikhii Okean* (Pacific Ocean), Moscow, No. 3(9), 1936. [Report by Doksom, President of the Little Khural, to the Jubilee 21st Session of the Mongol People's Republic, together with résumé of the Report of Amor.]

DUBS, HOMER H. ed. and transl. The History of the Former Han Dynasty by Pan Ku. Vol. I. Baltimore, 1938.

DUERST, J. U. Animal Remains from the Excavations at Anau . . .
in PUMPELLY, Explorations in Turkestan, Vol. II, Part VI.
For complete reference see PUMPELLY.

DUMAN, L. I. Agrarnaya politika tsinskogo pravitel'stva v Sin'tszy-
ane v kontse XVIII veka (Agrarian Policy of the Ch'ing
[Manchu] Government in Sinkiang at the End of the XVIII
Century). Moscow-Leningrad, 1936. *See also* LATTIMORE, O.

DUYVENDAK, J. J. L. The Book of Lord Shang. London, 1928.

EBERHARD, WOLFRAM. Early Chinese Cultures and Their Development: A New Working Hypothesis. *Smithsonian Report for
1937*, Washington, D. C., 1937. [Translated by C. W. Bishop
from *Tagungsbericht der Gesellschaft für Völkerkunde*, 2nd
session, Leipzig, 1936.]

ELIAS, NEY. Narrative of a Journey through Western Mongolia.
Journ. Royal Geogr. Soc., London, Vol. XLIII, 1873.

Encyclopaedia Sinica. S. Couling, ed. Shanghai, 1917.

FANG, T'ING. Lun Ti (On the Ti. *Yü Kung* [Tribute of Yü],
The Chinese Historical Geography Semi-Monthly Magazine,
Peiping, Vol. II, No. 6, 1934.

FENG, CHIA-SHENG. Yüanshih Shihtai chih Tungpei (The Northeast in Extreme Antiquity). *Yü Kung* [Tribute of Yü], *The
Chinese Historical Geography Semi-Monthly Magazine*, Peiping, Vol. VI, Nos. 3 and 4, 1936.

Fifth Report on Progress in Manchuria. *See* South Manchuria
Railway.

FLOR, FRITZ. Zur Frage des Renntiernomadismus. *Mitt. Anthrop-
ologischen Gesellsch. in Wien*, Vienna, Vol. LX, 1930. (Fest-
gabe dem sechsten Deutschen Orientalistentag.)

Fourth Report on Progress in Manchuria. *See* South Manchuria
Railway.

FOX, RALPH. Genghis Khan. New York, 1936.

FRANCKE, A. H. The Kingdom of gNya khri btsanpo, the First
King of Tibet. *Journ. and Proc. Asiatic Soc. Bengal*, Vol. VI,
1910.

FRANKE, OTTO. Beschreibung des Jehol-Gebietes in der Provinz
Chihli. Leipzig, 1902.

————. Article on "Feudalism, Chinese," *in* Encyclopaedia of
the Social Sciences, Vol. VI, New York, 1931.

————. Geschichte des chinesischen Reiches. Berlin-Leipzig,
Vol. I, 1930; Vol. II, 1936; Vol. III, 1937.

————. *See also* DE GROOT.

FRITERS, GERARD M. The Development of Inner Mongolian Independence. *Pacific Affairs,* New York, Vol. X, September, 1937.
————. The Prelude to Outer Mongolian Independence. *Pacific Affairs,* New York, Vol. X, June, 1937.
FU, SSU-NIEN. I-Hsia Tung-Hsi Shuo (East-West Theory of the I and Hsia). Ch'ing chu Ts'ai Yüan-p'ei Liushihwu Sui Lünwen Chi (Studies Presented to Ts'ai Yüan-p'ei in Honor of His Sixty-fifth Year). Academia Sinica, Peiping, Vol. II, 1936.
FUCHS, WALTER. Beiträge zur mandjurischen Bibliographie und Literatur. Tokyo, 1936.
————. The Personal Chronicle of the First Manchu Emperor. *Pacific Affairs,* New York, Vol. IX, March, 1936.
————. Das Turfangebiet, seine äusseren Geschicke bis in die T'angzeit. *Ostasiatische Zeitschrift,* Berlin, N.S. III, 3/4, 1926.

GIBERT, LUCIEN. Dictionnaire historique et géographique de la Mandchourie. Hongkong, 1934. *See also* LATTIMORE, O.
GILES, HERBERT A. China and the Manchus. Cambridge, 1912.
————. A Chinese Biographical Dictionary. London-Shanghai, 1898.
————. A Chinese-English Dictionary. 2nd edit. Shanghai, 1912.
GILMOUR, JAMES. Among the Mongols. New York, [1884]?
GOLDMAN, BOSWORTH. Red Road Through Asia. London, 1934.
GRAHAM, STEPHEN. Through Russian Central Asia. London-New York, 1916.
GORSKI, V. O proiskhozhdenii rodonachalnika nyne tsarstvuyushchei v Kitae dinastii Tsin i imeni naroda Man'chzhu (On the Origin of the Founder of the Present Ruling Dynasty of Ch'ing in China, and the Name of the Manchu Tribe), *in* Trudy Chlenov Rosiiskoi Dukhovnoi Missii (Works of the Members of the Russian Religious Mission), Vol. I. Peking, 1852; reprinted 1909.
GREGORY, J. W. and C. J. To the Alps of Chinese Tibet. London, 1923.
GRENARD, FERNAND. Haute Asie. *Géographie universelle,* Vol. VIII. Paris, 1929.
————. Genghis-Khan. Paris, 1935. *See also* LATTIMORE, O.
GRIAZNOV, M. P., and E. A. GOLOMSHTOK, ed. The Pazirik Burial of Altai. *Amer. Journ. of Archaeology,* Vol. XXXVII, January-March, 1933.
GROUSSET, RENÉ. L'Empire des Steppes: Attila, Gengis-Khan, Tamerlan. Paris, 1938.

HAENISCH, E. Die letzten Feldzüge Cinggis Han's und sein Tod nach der ostasiatischen Ueberlieferung. *Asia Major,* Leipzig, Vol. IX, 1932.

————. Untersuchungen über das Yüan-Ch'ao Pi-Shi, die geheime Geschichte der Mongolen. *Abhandl. der philologisch-historischen Klasse der Sächsischen Akad. der Wissensch.,* Leipzig, Vol. XLI, No. 4, 1931.

HAHN, E. Die Haustiere und ihre Beziehungen zur Wirtschaft des Menschen. Leipzig, 1896.

HANWELL, NORMAN D. The Dragnet of Local Government in China. *Pacific Affairs,* New York, Vol. X, March, 1937.

HASLUND, HENNING. Men and Gods in Mongolia. New York, 1935.

HATT, GUDMUND. Notes on Reindeer Nomadism. *Memoirs Amer. Anthropological Assn.,* Washington, D. C., Vol. VI, 1919.

HAUER, ERICH. General Wu San-kuei. *Asia Major,* Leipzig, Vol. IV, October, 1927.

————. Huang-Ts'ing K'ai-kuo Fang-lüeh, die Gründung des mandschurischen Kaiserreiches. Berlin-Leipzig, 1926.

HEDIN, SVEN, and others. De vetenskapliga resultaten av våra expeditioner i Centralasien och Tibet 1927-1935. *Ymer,* Stockholm, Vol. LV, No. 4, 1935. [Includes report by Folke Bergman, "Arkeologiska undersökningar. . . ."]

HEDIN, SVEN. The Flight of "Big Horse." New York, 1936.

————. Southern Tibet. 9 vols. and atlas. Stockholm, 1922. [Vol. VIII, Part II, "Die Westländer in der chinesischen Kartographie," by Albert Herrmann.]

————. Trans-Himalaya: Discoveries and Adventures in Tibet. 3 vols. New York, 1909.

HERRMANN, ALBERT. Die Gobi im Zeitalter der Hunnenherrschaft. *Geografiska Annaler,* Stockholm, Vol. XVII, 1935 (Hedin Seventieth Birthday Volume).

————. Historical and Commercial Atlas of China. Cambridge, Mass., 1935.

————. *See also* HEDIN, SVEN. Southern Tibet.

HILARION, O. Ocherk istorii snoshenii Kitaya s Tibetom (A Sketch of the History of the Relations of China with Tibet), *in* Trudy Chlenov Rossiiskoi Dukhovnoi Missii (Works of the Members of the Russian Religious Mission), Vol. II, Peking, 2nd edit. 1910.

HÖRNER, NILS G. and PARKER T. CHEN. Alternating Lakes: Some River Changes and Lake Displacements in Central Asia. *Geo-*

grafiska Annaler, Stockholm, Vol. XVII, 1935 (Hedin Seventieth Birthday Volume).

Hou-Han Shu. [The history of the later or Eastern Han Dynasty, A.D. 25 to 220. Compiled by Fan Yeh.] *See also* K'ai Ming.

HOWORTH, H. H. History of the Mongols. 4 vols. London, 1876-1888.

HROZNY, FRIEDERICH. Article on "Hittites" *in* Encyclopaedia Britannica, 14th edit. New York-London, 1930.

Hsin T'ang Shu. [The history of the T'ang dynasty of 618-906. The chief compilers were Ou-yang Hsiu and Sung Chi.] *See also* T'ang Shu, another compilation for the same period; *and* K'ai Ming.

Hsin Yüan Shih. [The "new" history of the Mongol dynasty in China, 1280-1367. Compiled by K'o Shao-ming.] *See also* Yüan Shih, a similar compilation but containing also earlier material; *also* K'ai Ming.

HSÜ, CHÜ-CH'ING. Pei Pien Ch'angch'eng K'ao (A Study of the Northern Frontier Great Walls). *Shih-hsüeh Nienpao* (Historical Annual) of the Historical Society of Yenching University, Peiping, No. 1, 1929.

HSÜ, CHUNG-SHU. Lei Ssu K'ao (On the Lei and Ssu): On some Agricultural Implements of the Ancient Chinese. *Bull. National Research Inst. of History and Philology,* Academia Sinica, Peiping, Vol. II, Part I, 1930.

————. *See also under* LI CHI, ed., Anyang Fachüeh Paokao.

HUC, R.-E., and J. GABET. Travels in Tartary, Thibet and China. edit. Paul Pelliot, London, 1928.

HUMMEL, A. W., transl. Ku Chieh-kang: The Autobiography of a Chinese Historian. Leyden, 1931.

HUNTINGTON, ELLSWORTH. The Pulse of Asia. Boston-New York, 1907.

KABO, R. Ocherki istorii i ekonomiki Tuvy: Chast' pervaya, dorevolyutsionnaya Tuva (Studies in the History and Economy of Tuva: Part I, Pre-revolutionary Tuva). Moscow-Leningrad, 1934. *See also* LATTIMORE, O.

K'ai Ming. The K'ai Ming edition, Shanghai, of the "Twenty-five Dynastic Histories." [The separate histories referred to in the footnotes have all been consulted in this edition.]

KARLGREN, BERNHARD. The Authenticity of Ancient Chinese Texts. *Bull. Mus. of Far Eastern Antiquities,* Stockholm, No. 1, 1929.

————. On the Authenticity and Nature of the Tso Chuan.

Göteborgs Högskolas Årsskrift, Göteborg, Vol. XXXII, No. 3, 1926

KOZ'MIN, N. N. K. voprosu o turetsko-mongol'skom feodalizme (On the Question of Turco-Mongol Feudalism). Moscow-Irkutsk, 1934.

————. Khakasi: Istoricheskii, etnograficheskii i khozyaist-vennyi ocherk Minusinskogo kraya (The Khakas: Historical, Ethnographical and Economic Sketch of the Minusinsk Region). Irkutsk, 1925.

KU, CHIEH-KANG. Ku Shih Pien (Notes on Ancient History). Vol. I, Peiping, 1926.

LATTIMORE, OWEN. Articles on Mongolia and Chinese Turkistan (Sinkiang) in *China Year Book,* 1935.

————. Caravan Routes of Inner Asia. *Geogr. Journ.,* London, Vol. LXXII, December, 1928.

————. China and the Barbarians, *in* Empire in the East, Joseph Barnes, ed. New York, 1934.

————. Chinese Colonization in Inner Mongolia: Its History and Present Development, *in* Pioneer Settlement, *Amer. Geogr. Soc. Spec. Publ. No. 14.* New York, 1932.

————. Chinese Turkistan. *The Open Court,* Chicago, Vol. XLVII, March, 1933.

————. The Desert Road to Turkestan. London, 1928.

————. The Eclipse of Inner Mongolian Nationalism. *Journ. Royal Central Asian Soc.,* London, Vol. XXIII, July, 1936.

————. The Geographical Factor in Mongol History. *Geogr. Journ.,* London, Vol. XCI, January, 1938.

————. The Gold Tribe, "Fishskin Tatars" of the Sungari. *Memoirs Amer. Anthropological Soc.,* No. 40, 1933.

————. High Tartary. Boston, 1930.

————. The Historical Setting of Inner Mongolian Nationalism. *Pacific Affairs,* New York, Vol. IX, September, 1936.

————. Inner Mongolia—Chinese, Japanese, or Mongol? *Pacific Affairs,* New York, Vol. X, March, 1937. *See also* CHEN, HAN-SENG.

————. The Kimono and the Turban. *Asia,* New York, Vol. XXXVIII, May, 1938.

————. Land and Sea in the Destiny of Japan. *Pacific Affairs,* New York, Vol. IX, December, 1936.

————. The Land Power of the Japanese Navy. *Pacific Affairs,* New York, Vol. VII, December, 1934.

————. The Lines of Cleavage in Inner Mongolia. *Pacific Affairs,* New York, Vol. X, June, 1937. *See also* ARENS, M.

————. Manchuria: Cradle of Conflict. New York, 1932. 2nd edit., revised, 1935.

————. Mongols of the Chinese Border. *Geogr. Mag.*, London, Vol. VI, March, 1938.

————. The Mongols of Manchuria. New York, 1934.

————. On the Wickedness of Being Nomads. *T'ien Hsia*, Shanghai, Vol. I, August, 1935.

————. Open Door or Great Wall? *Atlantic Monthly*, Boston, July, 1934.

————. Origins of the Great Wall of China: A Frontier Concept in Theory and Practice. *Geogr. Rev.*, New York, Vol. XXVII, October, 1937.

————. Prince, Priest and Herdsman in Mongolia. *Pacific Affairs*, New York, Vol. VIII, March, 1935.

————. Review of L. I. Duman, "Agrarian Policy of the Manchu Government in Sinkiang . . ." *Pacific Affairs*, New York, Vol. XII, September, 1939. *See also* DUMAN, L. I.

————. Review of L. Gibert, "Dictionnaire historique et géographique de la Mandchourie." *Pacific Affairs*, New York, Vol. VIII, December, 1935. *See also* GIBERT, L.

————. Review of Fernand Grenard, "Genghis-Khan." *Pacific Affairs*, New York, Vol. X, December, 1937. *See also* GRENARD, F

————. Review of R. Kabo, "Studies in the History and Economy of Tuva." *Ibid. See also* KABO, R.

————. Review of F. Tada, "Geography of Jehol." *Pacific Affairs*, New York, Vol. XII, September, 1939. *See also* TADA, F.

————. Rising Sun—Falling Profits. *Atlantic Monthly*, Boston, July, 1938.

————. A Ruined Nestorian City in Inner Mongolia. *Geogr. Journ.*, London, Vol. LXXXV, December, 1934.

————. Russo-Japanese Relations. *International Affairs*, London, Vol. XV, July-August, 1936.

————. Where Outer and Inner Mongolia Meet. *Amerasia*, New York, Vol. II, March, 1938.

LAUFER, B. Ocherk Mongol'skoi literatury (A Sketch of Mongol Literature). Leningrad, 1927. [Translation by V. A. Kazakevich of "Skizze der Mongolischen Literatur," *Revue Orientale*, 1907, with an introduction and additional material by B. Ya. Vladimirtsov.]

————. The Reindeer and Its Domestication. *Memoirs Amer. Anthropological Assn.*, Vol. IV, 1917.

LAWRENCE, T. E. Seven Pillars of Wisdom. London, 1935.

LECOQ, ALBERT VON. Auf Hellas Spuren in Ostturkistan. Leipzig, 1926.

LEE, J. S. The Periodic Recurrence of Internecine Wars in China. *China Journ. of Science and Art*, Shanghai, March and April, 1931.

LEGGE, JAMES. The Chinese Classics. 5 vols. in 8. Hongkong-London, 1861-72.

LI, CHI. ed. Anyang Fachüeh Paokao (Reports on Excavations at Anyang). Academia Sinica, Peiping, Vols. I-II, 1929; Vol. III, 1931; Shanghai, Vol. IV, 1931. [Contains an article by Hsü Chung-shu on the Hsia, cited by Creel as being on pp. 533 *et sqq.*]

LI, CHI. Manchuria in History. *Chinese Social and Polit. Sci. Rev.*, Peiping, Vol. XVI, 1932-33.

LIN, T. C. Manchuria in the Ming Empire. *Nankai Social and Econ. Quart.*, Tientsin, Vol. VIII, No. 1, 1935.

————. Manchurian Trade and Tribute in the Ming Dynasty. *Nankai Social and Econ. Quart.*, Tientsin, Vol. IX, No. 4, 1937.

LIN, YUTANG. My Country and My People. New York, 1935.

LINDGREN, E. J. North-Western Manchuria and the Reindeer-Tungus. *Geogr. Journ.*, London, Vol. LXXV, June, 1930.

LOWDERMILK, W. C. Man-Made Deserts. *Pacific Affairs*, New York, Vol. VIII, December, 1935.

Manchou Shihlu (Manchu Chronicles). Northeastern University, Liaoning (Mukden), 1930. *See also* FUCHS.

MASPERO, H. Chine et Asie centrale, *in* Histoire et historiens depuis cinquante ans. 2 vols. Paris, 1927.

————. La Chine antique. Paris, 1927.

————. Les Origines de la civilisation chinoise. *Annales de géographie*, Paris, Vol. XXXV, March, 1926.

MENG, WEN-T'UNG. Ch'ih Ti Po Ti Tung Ch'in K'ao (Eastward Invasions of the Red Ti and White Ti). *Yü Kung* [Tribute of Yü], *The Chinese Historical Geography Semi-Monthly Magazine*, Peiping, Vol. VII, Nos. 1-3, 1937.

————. Ch'in wei Jung Tsu K'ao (The Ch'in as a Jung Tribe). *Ibid.*, Vol. VI, No. 7, 1936.

————. Ch'uan Jung Tung Ch'in K'ao (Eastward Invasions of the Ch'uan-jung). *Ibid.*

MENGHIN, OSWALD. Weltgeschichte der Steinzeit. Vienna, 1931.

Mengku Yumu Chi (Records of the Mongol Pastures). Preface dated 1859.

MERZBACHER, G. The Central Tian-Shan Mountains. London, 1905.

Ming Shih. [The history of the Ming dynasty of 1368-1643. The chief compiler was Chang Ting-yü.] *See also* K'ai Ming.

MONTECORVINO, JOHN OF. *See* YULE, Cathay and the Way Thither.

MOORE, HARRIET. Review of Vladimirtsov, "Social Structure of the Mongols," *Pacific Affairs*, New York, Vol. IX, March, 1936.

MUCKE, J. R. Urgeschichte des Ackerbaues und der Viehzucht. Greifswald, 1898.

MORSE, H. B., and H. F. MCNAIR. Far Eastern International Relations. Boston and New York, 1931.

MÜLLER, F. W. K. To*x*rī und Kuišan (Küšän). *Sitzungsber. K. Preuss. Akad. der Wiss.*, Berlin, 1918 (pp. 566-586).

North Manchuria and the Chinese Eastern Railway. *See* Chinese Eastern Railway.

NOVITSKII, V. F. Puteshestvie po Mongolii v predelakh Tushetu-khanskago i Tsetsen-khanskago aimakov Khalkhy, Shilin-gol'skago chigulgana i zemel' Chakharov Vnutrennei Mongolii, sovershennoe v 1906 gody (Journey through Mongolia, in the Territories of the Tushetu Khan and Tsetsen Khan Aimaks of Khalkha, the Silingol Chigulgan and the Lands of the Chahars of Inner Mongolia, Accomplished in 1906). St. Petersburg, 1911.

ORLEANS, PRINCE HENRY OF. *See* BONVALOT, GABRIEL.

OU-YANG, YING. Chungkuo Litai Chiangyü Chancheng Hot'u (Chinese Historical Atlas of Regions and Wars). Wuchang, 1933.

PALLADIUS, ARCHIMANDRITE. Hsi-yü Chi, ili opisanie puteshestviya na Zapad, *in* Trudy Chlenov Rosiiskoi Dukhovnoi Missii (Works of the Members of the Russian Religious Mission), Vol. IV. Peking, 1866; reprinted 1910. [Translation from the account of the journey of the Taoist priest Ch'ang Ch'un to visit Chingghis Khan.]

————. Starinoe Mongol'skoe skazanie o Chingiskhane (An Ancient Mongol Chronicle of Chingghis Khan). *Ibid.* [Translation of the Yüan Ch'ao Mi Shih, the "Secret History" of the Yuan (Mongol) dynasty.]

PARKER, E. H. A Thousand Years of the Tartars. London, 1895; 2nd edit., New York, 1926.

PEGOLOTTI. *See* YULE, Cathay and the Way Thither.

Pei Shih. [The history of the northern kingdoms of 386-581. Compiled by Li Yen-shou.] *See also* K'ai Ming.

PELLIOT, PAUL. L'Edition collective des oeuvres de Wang Kouo-wei. *T'oung Pao*, Paris, Vol. XXVI, 1929.

————. Les Mots à *H* initiale, aujourd'hui amuie, dans le mongole des XIII° et XIV° siècles. *Journal Asiatique,* Paris, April-June, 1925.

People's Tribune, The. Shanghai. See anonymous article in No. 24, August 1, 1935.

PIAN DE CARPINE. *See* ROCKHILL, Journey of William of Rubruck.

Polo, Marco. *See* YULE, Marco Polo.

POMUS, M. I. Buryat Mongol'skaya ASSR (The Buriat-Mongol Autonomous Soviet Socialist Republic), Moscow, 1937.

PRINCE HENRY OF ORLEANS. *See* BONVALOT.

PUMPELLY, RAPHAEL, ed. Explorations in Turkestan. Expedition of 1904. Prehistoric Civilizations of Anau. *Carnegie Inst. of Washington Publ. No. 73.* 2 vols. Washington, D. C., 1908.

RASHIDEDDIN. *See* YULE, Cathay and the Way Thither.

RADLOV, V. V. Die alttürkischen Inschriften der Mongolei. Die Denkmäler von Koscho-Zaidam. Part I, Text, Transscription und Uebersetzung. Part II, Glossar, Index und die chinesischen Inschriften, übersetzt von V. P. Vassilev. St. Petersburg, 1894.

Report on Progress in Manchuria to 1932. *See* South Manchuria Railway.

RIASANOVSKY, V. A. Fundamental Principles of Mongol Law. Tientsin, 1937.

RICHTHOFEN, FERDINAND FREIHERR VON. China: Ergebnisse eigener Reisen und darauf gegründeter Studien. Vol. I. Berlin, 1877.

RISH, A. Mongoliya na strazhe svoei nezavisimosti (Mongolia Guards Its Independence). *Tikhii Okean* (Pacific Ocean), Moscow, No. 4(6), 1934.

ROCKHILL, W. W. The Journey of William of Rubruck . . . With Two Acounts of the Earlier Journey of John of Pian de Carpine. London, 1900.

————. The Land of the Lamas. London, 1891.

ROERICH, GEORGE N. Trails to Inmost Asia. New Haven, 1931.

RUBRUCK, WILLIAM OF. *See* ROCKHILL.

SANANG SETSEN. *See* SCHMIDT, I. J.

San-Kuo Chih. [Records of the Three Kingdoms, third century A. D. Compiled by Chen Shou.] *See also* K'ai Ming.

SAUER, CARL O. American Agricultural Origins: A Consideration of Nature and Culture, *in* Essays in Anthropology Presented to A. L. Kroeber in Celebration of His Sixtieth Birthday. Berkeley, 1936.

SCHLAGINTWEIT, EMIL. Die Lebensbeschreibung von Padma Sambhava, dem Begründer des Lamaismus. Part I in *Abhandl. des königlich-bayerischen Akad. der Wissensch.*, Munich, Vol. XXI, No. 2, 1899; Part II, *ibid.*, Vol. XXII, No. 3, 1903.

SCHMIDT, HUBERT. The Archeological Excavations in Anau and Old Merv, *in* PUMPELLY, Explorations in Turkestan, Vol. I, Part II. *See* PUMPELLY.

SCHMIDT, I. J. Geschichte der Ost-Mongolen und ihres Fürsten-hauses verfasst von Ssanang Ssetsen Chungtaidschi der Ordus. St. Petersburg, 1829. [German translation with notes, and Mongol text.]

SCHRAM, L. Le Mariage chez les T'ou-jen du Kan-sou (Chine). *Variétés Sinologiques*, No. 58, Shanghai, 1932.

SCHUYLER, EUGENE. Turkistan: Notes of a Journey in Russian Turkistan, Khokand, Bukhara and Kuldja. 2 vols. New York, 1877.

"Secret History." *See* PALLADIUS.

SHAKHMATOV, V. Ocherki po istorii Uiguro-Dunganskogo nat-sional'no-osvoboditel'nogo dvizheniya v XIX veke (Studies in the History of the Uighur-T'ungkan National-Liberation Move-ment in the XIX century). *Transactions Kazak Sci. Research Inst. of National Culture*, Alma Ata-Moscow, Vol. I, 1935.

SHANG, CH'ENG-TSU. *See* YEN, FU-LI.

SHAW, ROBERT. Visits to High Tartary, Yârkand, and Kâshghar. London, 1871.

Shih Chi. *See* SSU-MA CH'IEN; *also* CHAVANNES, Mémoires his-toriques.

SHIROKOGOROV, S. M. Social Organization of the Manchus. Shang-hai, 1924.

SIMUKOV, A. Mongol Migrations. *Sovremennaya Mongoliya* (Con-temporary Mongolia), Ulan Bator, No. 4(7), 1934. [Cited in Ralph Fox, "Genghis Khan."]

SKRINE, C. P. Chinese Central Asia. Boston, 1926.

SNOW, EDGAR. Red Star Over China. New York, 1938.

South Manchuria Railway. Fifth Report on Progress in Man-churia. Dairen, 1936.

————. Fourth Report on Progress in Manchuria. Dairen, 1934.

————. Third Report on Progress in Manchuria to 1932. Dairen, 1932.

SSU-MA CH'IEN. Shih Chi (Historical Memoirs) [A compendious history of China from the most ancient times to the second century B. C.]

STANFORD, EDWARD. Atlas of the Chinese Empire . . . Specially Prepared for the China Inland Mission. London, 1908.

STEFANSSON, VILHJALMUR. The Friendly Arctic. New York, 1921.

STEIN, SIR AUREL. Innermost Asia: Its Geography as a Factor in History. *Geogr. Journ.,* London, Vol. LXV, May and June, 1925.
————. Ruins of Desert Cathay. 2 vols. London, 1912.
————. Serindia: Detailed Report of Explorations in Central Asia and Westernmost China . . . 5 vols. Oxford, 1921.
STEVENSON, PAUL H. Notes on the Human Geography of the Chinese-Tibetan Borderland. *Geogr. Rev.,* New York, Vol. XXII, October, 1932.
————. The Chinese-Tibetan Borderland and Its Peoples. *Bull. Peking Soc. of Nat. Hist.,* Peiping, Vol. II, Part II, 1927-28.
Sui Shu. [History of the Sui dynasty of 581-617. The chief compiler was Wei Cheng.]
SUN, YAT SEN. San Min Chu I. F. W. Price, transl. Shanghai, 1929.
SYKES, ELLA, and SIR PERCY. Through Deserts and Oases of Central Asia. London, 1920.

Ta Ch'ing Huitien. 60 vols. (*t'ao*). Peking, 1818 edit. ["Institutions" of the Manchu Empire.]
TADA, FUMIO. Geography of Jehol. Section III, Report of the First Scientific Expedition to Manchoukuo under the Leadership of Shigeyasu Tokunaga, Tokyo, 1937. [In Japanese; title in English; abstracts in German.] *See* LATTIMORE, O.
T'ANG SHU. [The history of the T'ang dynasty of 618-906. The chief compiler was Liu Hsü.] *See also* Hsin T'ang Shu, another compilation for the same period, *and* K'ai Ming.
THOMSEN, VILHELM. Inscriptions de l'Orkhon déchiffrés. *Mémoires de la Société Finno-Ougrienne,* Vol. V, Helsingfors, 1896.
THORP, JAMES. Colonization Possibilities of Northwest China and Inner Mongolia. *Pacific Affairs,* New York, Vol. VIII, December, 1935.
————. Geography of the Soils of China. Nanking, 1936.
TING, SHAN. K'ai-Kuo Ch'ien Chou jen Wen-hua yü Hsi-yü Kuan-hsi (Cultural Relations of the Chou People With the Western Regions, Before Their Establishment of Empire). *Yü Kung* [Tribute of Yü], *The Chinese Historical Geography Semi-Monthly Magazine,* Peiping, Vol. VI, No. 10, 1937.
TING, V. K. How China Acquired Her Civilisation, *in* Symposium on Chinese Culture, Sophia H. Chen Zen, ed. Shanghai, 1931.
————. Professor Granet's "La Civilisation chinoise," *Chinese Social and Political Science Review,* Peiping, Vol. XV, No. 2, 1931.

TOYNBEE, ARNOLD J. A Study of History. 6 vols. London, 1934-1939.

TSEN, SHIH-YING. [Contributor to the section on geography in *China Year Book,* Shanghai, 1935.]

T'UNG SHIH-HENG. Chunghua Minkuo Hsin Ch'üyü T'u (New Regional Atlas of the Chinese Republic). Shanghai, Commercial Press, 1915; 4th edit., 1917.

UTLEY, FREDA. Japan's Feet of Clay. London, 1936.

VIKTOROV, S., and I. KHALKHIN. Mongol'skaya Narodnaya Respublika (The Mongol People's Republic). Moscow, 1936.

VLADIMIRTSOV, B. YA. Obshchestvennyi Stroi Mongolov: Mongol'skii kochevoi Feodalizm (Social Structure of the Mongols: Mongol Nomadic Feudalism). Leningrad, 1934. *See also* MOORE, H.

WADDELL, L. A. The Buddhism of Tibet. 2nd edit. London, 1934.

WANG, KUO-LANG. Chungkuo Ch'angch'eng Yenko K'ao (A Study of the Development of the Great Walls of China). Shanghai, n.d. [about 1928].

WAN, KUO-TING. Chungkuo T'ienchih Shih (Agrarian History of China). Vol. I. 1933. *See also* CHANG, C. M.

WANG, KUO-WEI. Kyan T'ang Chi Lin. *See* PELLIOT, L'Edition collective des oeuvres de Wang Kouo-wei.

WANG, YÜ-CH'ÜAN. Development of Modern Social Science in China. *Pacific Affairs,* New York, Vol. XI, September, 1938.

————. The Rise of Land Tax and the Fall of Dynasties in Chinese History. *Pacific Affairs,* New York, Vol. IX, June, 1936.

WARNER, LANGDON. The Long Old Road in China. New York, 1926.

Wei Shu. [The history of the Wei dynasty of 386-556. Compiled by Wei Shou.] *See also* K'ai Ming.

Weitsang T'ungchih. Edit. 1896, 1 vol. (*t'ao*). [Gazetteer of Central Tibet.]

WIEGER, LÉON. Textes historiques: Histoire politique de la Chine depuis l'origine jusqu'en 1912. 2 vols., reissued, Hien-hien, 1929.

WIGRAM, SIR KENNETH. Defence in the North-West Frontier Province. *Journ. Royal Central Asian Soc.,* London, Vol. XXIV, January, 1937.

WITTFOGEL, K. A. Economic and Social History of China. [To be published in 1940.]

————. The Foundations and Stages of Chinese Economic History. *Zeits. für Sozialforschung,* Paris, Vol. IV, No. 1, 1935.

————. A Large-Scale Investigation of China's Socio-Economic Structure. *Pacific Affairs,* New York, Vol. XI, March, 1938.

————. Probleme der chinesischen Wirtschaftsgeschichte. *Archiv für Sozialwissenschaft und Sozialpolitik,* Tübingen, Vol. 57, 1927.

————. Die Theorie der orientalischen Gesellschaft. *Zeits. für Sozialforschung,* Paris, Vol. VII, No. 1/2, 1938.

————. Wirtschaft und Gesellschaft Chinas, Erster Teil, Produktivkräfte, Produktions- und Zirkulationsprozess. Leipzig, 1931.

————. Wirtschaftsgeschichtliche Grundlagen der Entwicklung der Familienautorität, *in* Studien über Autorität und Familie. Paris, 1936.

WU, G. D. Prehistoric Pottery in China. London, 1938.

YEN, FU-LI, and CH'ENG-TSU SHANG. Kuanghsi Lingyün Yao-jen Tiaoch'a Paokao (Report on an Investigation of the Yao People of Lingyün in Kuanghsi). Academia Sinica, Division of Sociology, 1929.

YOUNGHUSBAND, SIR FRANCIS. The Heart of a Continent. London, 1896.

Yüan Ch'ao Mi Shih. *See* PALLADIUS.

Yüan Shih. [The history of the Mongol dynasty in China, going back to the time of Chingghis, before the actual establishment of the dynasty in China. The chief compiler was Sung Lien.] *See also* Hsin Yüan Shih, a similar but modern compilation, without the earlier material; *also* K'ai Ming.

YULE, SIR HENRY. The Book of Ser Marco Polo. Henri Cordier edit. 2 vols. 3rd edit., reprinted London, 1921.

————. Cathay and the Way Thither. Henri Cordier edit., revised. 4 vols. London, 1914.

ZAKHAROV, IVAN. Polnyi Man'chursko-Russkii Slovar' (Complete Manchu-Russian Dictionary). St. Petersburg, 1875.

INDEX

The subject references are suggestive rather than exhaustive. The reader is also referred to the analytical table of contents (pp. vii-xiv).

Proper names not followed by an explanation (such as "city," "region," "a history,") refer to persons, except in such obvious cases as "Japan," "Korea," etc.

References in the footnotes to authors (except the author of the present volume) and to certain titles have been entered in the index, but no references in the Bibliography (pp. 553-570) have been so entered.